# *Of Mice and Women*

# Of Mice and Women

## *Aspects of Female Aggression*

Edited by

KAJ BJÖRKQVIST
*Department of Psychology*
*Åbo Akademi University*
*Turku, Finland*

PIRKKO NIEMELÄ
*Department of Psychology*
*Turku University*
*Turku, Finland*

ACADEMIC PRESS, INC.
*Harcourt Brace Jovanovich, Publishers*
San Diego New York Boston
London Sydney Tokyo Toronto

This book is printed on acid-free paper. ♾



Academic Press, Inc.
1250 Sixth Avenue, San Diego, California 92101-4311

*United Kingdom Edition published by*
Academic Press Limited
24–28 Oval Road, London NW1 7DX

Library of Congress Cataloging-in-Publication Data

Of mice and women : aspects of female aggression / Kaj Björkqvist and Pirkko Niemelä, editors.
p. cm.
Includes bibliographical references and index.
ISBN 0-12-102590-X
1. Women--Psychology. 2. Aggressiveness (Psychology)
3. Aggressive behavior in animals. I. Björkqvist, Kaj.
II. Niemelä, Pirkko.
HQ1206.03 1992
155.2'32--dc20 92-8880
CIP

PRINTED IN THE UNITED STATES OF AMERICA
92 93 94 95 96 97 MM 9 8 7 6 5 4 3 2 1

*To*

*Kirsti Lagerspetz,*

*pioneer in the study of female aggression,*

*colleague, and friend.*

# Contents

*Contributors* xix

*Preface* xxiii

THE MYTH OF THE NONAGGRESSIVE FEMALE

*1. New Trends in the Study of Female Aggression*
Kaj Björkqvist and Pirkko Niemelä
I. INTRODUCTION: THE PHENOMENA OF "FEMALE AGGRESSION" 3
II. FEMALE AGGRESSION: DEFINITION AND FORMS 4
III. THE "MALE" PERSPECTIVE 5
IV. THE DANGER OF ETHNOCENTRISM 6
V. THE PROBLEM OF METHODOLOGY 6
VI. RECENT STUDIES: METHODOLOGICAL AND CULTURAL CHANGE 7
VII. AN EMERGING PERSPECTIVE 8
VIII. ARE MALES MORE AGGRESSIVE THAN FEMALES? 8
IX. CONCLUSIONS 13
REFERENCES 15

**2. *Biology Does Not Make Men More Aggressive Than Women***
David Adams
I. INTRODUCTION 17
II. A POLITICALLY USEFUL MYTH 18
III. INSTITUTIONAL IS DIFFERENT FROM INDIVIDUAL BEHAVIOR 19
IV. MALE ANIMALS ARE NOT CONSISTENTLY MORE AGGRESSIVE THAN FEMALES 21
V. THE COMPLEX RELATION OF HUMAN AGGRESSION TO ANIMAL AGGRESSION 23
VI. CONCLUSION 24
REFERENCES 25

**3. *The Aggressive Female Rodent: Redressing a "Scientific" Bias***
Paul F. Brain, Marc Haug, and Stefano Parmigiani
I. INTRODUCTION 27
II. SPECIES 28
III. CONCLUDING COMMENTS 33
REFERENCES 34

**4. *Hormones and Human Aggression***
David Benton
I. INTRODUCTION 37
II. ORGANIZING INFLUENCES OF TESTOSTERONE 38
III. PUBERTY 40
IV. TESTOSTERONE AND ADULT AGGRESSION 41
V. DISCUSSION 43
VI. CONCLUSION 45
REFERENCES 46

**II**

**THE DEVELOPMENT OF FEMALE AGGRESSIVE PATTERNS**

**5. *The Development of Direct and Indirect Aggressive Strategies in Males and Females***
Kaj Björkqvist, Karin Österman, and Ari Kaukiainen
I. INDIRECT AGGRESSION: CONCEPTIONS AND MISCONCEPTIONS 51

II. WHY HAS INDIRECT AGGRESSION NOT BEEN INVESTIGATED? 53
III. THE RESEARCH TOOL 54
IV. SEX DIFFERENCES IN AGGRESSIVE STYLES DURING ADOLESCENCE 55
V. A DEVELOPMENTAL THEORY OF AGGRESSIVE STRATEGIES 58
VI. TWO KINDS OF COVERED AGGRESSION DURING ADULTHOOD 61
VII. CONCLUSIONS 62
REFERENCES 63

**6. *Sex Differences in Aggressive Play and Toy Preference***
Jeffrey H. Goldstein
I. INTRODUCTION 65
II. CONSEQUENCES OF SEX-DIFFERENTIATED PLAY 69
III. ORIGINS OF SEX DIFFERENCES IN PLAY 71
IV. SUMMARY 74
REFERENCES 74

**7. *Differing Normative Beliefs about Aggression for Boys and Girls***
L. Rowell Huesmann, Nancy G. Guerra, Arnaldo Zelli, and Laurie Miller
I. INTRODUCTION 77
II. METHOD 79
III. RESULTS 80
IV. DISCUSSION 84
V. SUMMARY 86
REFERENCES 86

**8. *Gender Differences in Violence: Biology and/or Socialization?***
Leonard D. Eron
I. INTRODUCTION 89
II. THE TWO STUDIES 90
III. FINDINGS 91
IV. CONCLUSION 96
REFERENCES 96

9. *Changes in Patterns of Aggressiveness among Finnish Girls over a Decade*
Vappu Viemerö
I. INTRODUCTION 99
II. QUANTITATIVE DIFFERENCES IN AGGRESSIVENESS BETWEEN GIRLS AND BOYS 100
III. CHANGES IN GIRLS' AGGRESSIVENESS IN THE EARLY 1990S 102
IV. DISCUSSION 104
REFERENCES 105

10. *Patterns of Aggressive-Hostile Behavior Orientation among Adolescent Boys and Girls*
Adam Frączek
I. CONTEXT AND QUESTIONS 107
II. MAIN RESULTS 108
III. FINAL REMARKS 111
REFERENCES 112

11. *The Path to Adulthood for Aggressively Inclined Girls*
Lea Pulkkinen
I. INTRODUCTION 113
II. ARE THERE GENDER DIFFERENCES IN THE STABILITY OF AGGRESSION? 115
III. ARE THERE GENDER DIFFERENCES IN THE PATTERNS OF ADJUSTMENT? 116
IV. DISCONTINUITY IN FEMALE AGGRESSIVE BEHAVIOR 119
V. CONCLUSIONS 119
REFERENCES 120

12. *Gender Differences in Coronary-Prone Aggression*
Liisa Keltikangas-Järvinen
I. INTRODUCTION 123
II. COLLECTION OF THE PRESENT DATA 124
III. EVIDENCE SUPPORTING THE HARMLESS EFFECT OF AGGRESSION IN BOYS AND THE RISK EFFECT IN GIRLS 125
IV. CONCLUSIONS 127
REFERENCES 129

*13. Expressions of Aggression in the Life Stories of Aged Women*
Jan-Erik Ruth and Peter Öberg
I. WAY OF LIFE AND LIFE HISTORY RESEARCH 133
II. THE COLLECTION AND ANALYSIS OF LIFE STORIES 134
III. SOCIETY AND FAMILY AS THE SOURCES OF AGGRESSION 136
IV. A LIFE WITHOUT AGGRESSION 140
V. DISCUSSION 143
REFERENCES 145

**III**

**CULTURAL DIFFERENCES IN REGARD TO FEMALE AGGRESSION**

*14. Matrifocality and Female Aggression in Margariteño Society*
H. B. Kimberley Cook
I. INTRODUCTION 149
II. ETHNOGRAPHIC BACKGROUND 150
III. THE FORMS AND CONTEXTS OF FEMALE AGGRESSION 151
IV. FEMALE SEX-ROLE BEHAVIOR AND AGGRESSION 156
V. MATRIFOCALITY AND FEMALE AGGRESSION 156
VI. CONCLUSIONS 160
REFERENCES 161

*15. Interfemale Aggression and Resource Scarcity in a Cross-Cultural Perspective*
Ilsa M. Glazer
I. INTRODUCTION 163
II. SOCIAL FORMATIONS, RESOURCE CONTROL, AND GENDER 164
III. AGGRESSION AND GENDER 164
IV. AIM OF THE STUDY 165
V. ONE-ON-ONE AGGRESSION IN PREMODERN AND MODERN ZAMBIA 165
VI. INTERGROUP AGGRESSION BETWEEN SOCIAL CLASSES IN MODERN ZAMBIA 167

VII. ONE-ON-ONE AGGRESSION IN TRADITIONAL CHINA 167
VIII. INTERGROUP AGGRESSION IN REVOLUTIONARY CHINA 168
IX. ZAMBIA AND CHINA COMPARED 170
X. CONCLUSION: CROSS-CULTURAL PERSPECTIVES 170
REFERENCES 171

16. *"Women Are Women and Men Are Men": How Bellonese Women Get Even*
Rolf Kuschel
I. INTRODUCTION 173
II. A BRIEF HISTORY OF BELLONA 174
III. THE SOCIAL POSITION OF WOMEN ON BELLONA 175
IV. BELLONESE WOMEN'S ACTION POTENTIALS 178
V. CONCLUSION 184
REFERENCES 184

17. *Female Aggression among the Zapotec of Oaxaca, Mexico*
Douglas P. Fry
I. INTRODUCTION 187
II. DEFENSE OF THE COMMUNITY 188
III. POLITICAL VIOLENCE 188
IV. AGGRESSION DURING THE REVOLUTION 189
V. INTERPERSONAL HOMICIDES 189
VI. PHYSICAL AGGRESSION 190
VII. APPEAL TO AUTHORITIES 193
VIII. PHYSICAL PUNISHMENT OF CHILDREN 193
IX. VERBAL AGGRESSION 193
X. INDIRECT AGGRESSION: GOSSIP AND WITCHCRAFT 194
XI. CHILDREN'S AGGRESSION 195
XII. DISCUSSION 196
REFERENCES 198

18. *Lady Macbeth as a Problem for Shakespeare*
Pekka Niemelä
I. MACBETH WAS A VIKING 201
II. THE WITCHES WERE NORDIC NORNS 202
III. A GUESS THAT LADY MACBETH IS A VIKING WOMAN 204
IV. IS THE GUESS FOUL OR FAIR? 204
REFERENCES 205

## FEMALE AGGRESSION AND ITS SOCIAL SETTINGS

*19. Sex and Violence on Acali: Six Females and Five Males Isolated on a Raft on the Atlantic and the Caribbean for 101 Days*
Santiago Genovés
I. INTRODUCTION: DISSATISFACTION AND AGGRESSION, SEX AND VIOLENCE 209
II. THE RAFT LABORATORY 211
III. SEX 211
IV. SEX AND FRICTION, CONFLICT AND VIOLENCE 212
V. SEX AND VIOLENCE ON ACALI: THE HYPOTHESIS 213
VI. SEX AND VIOLENCE ON ACALI: THE EVIDENCE 213
VII. DISCUSSION AND DISCUSSIONS OF SEX AND VIOLENCE ON ACALI 213
REFERENCES 214

*20. Sex Differences in Conflict and Aggression in Individual and Group Settings*
Jacob M. Rabbie, Charles Goldenbeld, and Hein F. M. Lodewijkx
I. INTRODUCTION 217
II. EXPERIMENTAL PROCEDURE 220
III. SEX DIFFERENCES IN CONFLICT AND AGGRESSION 221
IV. CONCLUSION 225
REFERENCES 226

*21. The Other Sex: How Are Women Different? Gender, Dominance, and Intimate Relations in Social Interaction*
Bodil Lindfors
I. THE INVISIBLE SEX 230
II. THE PASSIVE SEX 230
III. THREE STUDIES ON SOCIAL INTERACTION 231
IV. DOMINANCE AS AN INTERVENING VARIABLE IN SEX-TYPED BEHAVIOR 233
V. THE NONVERBAL RESIDUAL 234
VI. SOCIAL CONTEXT: THE INHERENT LOGIC OF THE RELATIONSHIP 235

VII. CONCLUSIONS: HOW ARE WOMEN DIFFERENT? 236
REFERENCES 237

22. *Alcohol and Female Disinhibition*
Ralf Lindman
I. INTRODUCTION 241
II. ANXIETY 241
III. SEXUALITY 243
IV. AGGRESSION 245
V. GENERAL PERSPECTIVE 246
REFERENCES 248

23. *Battling Amazons: Responses to Female Fighters*
Gordon W. Russell
I. INTRODUCTION 251
II. METHOD 253
III. RESULTS AND DISCUSSION 255
REFERENCES 259

THE AMBIVALENCE OF MOTHERHOOD

24. *The Great Mother*
Johannes Myyrä
I. INTRODUCTION 263
II. MOTHERHOOD AND FEMININITY 264
III. THE PRIMORDIAL UNITY 264
IV. THE GREAT MOTHER 265
V. THE SLAYING OF THE MOTHER 267
VI. THE SPLITTING OF THE MOTHER ARCHETYPE: CONTEMPORARY CULTURE AND THE PSYCHOANALYSIS OF PATRIARCHY 268
VII. CONCLUDING COMMENTS: ACCEPTING AND REJECTING THE SPLITTING OF THE ARCHETYPE 271
REFERENCES 271

*25. Vicissitudes of Mother's Hate*

Pirkko Niemelä

I. PROCESSING AMBIVALENCE 273

II. OBSTACLES TO PROCESSING 275

III. EXPRESSIONS OF MOTHER'S HATE 276

IV. EFFECTS OF MOTHER'S DENIAL OF HATE ON HER CHILD 280

V. DEFENSIVE HINDERING VERSUS EMOTIONAL PROCESSING 281

REFERENCES 282

*26. Vampire and Child Savior Motifs in the Tales of Isak Dinesen*

Adma d'Heurle

I. INTRODUCTION 283

II. THE VAMPIRE IN HISTORY, MYTHOLOGY, AND LITERATURE 284

III. PALLEGRINA LEONI, THE EMBODIMENT OF THE ARCHETYPE 286

IV. IMAGES OF THE CHILD SAVIOR 289

REFERENCES 292

**FEMALE AGGRESSION IN SUBHUMAN SPECIES**

*27. Female Aggression among the Great Apes: A Psychoanalytic Perspective*

Reijo Holmström

I. INTRODUCTION 295

II. THE OBJECTS OF THE STUDY 295

III. RESEARCH APPROACH AND METHODOLOGY 297

IV. THE NATURE OF AGGRESSION IN THE GREAT APES 297

V. ORALITY IN THE FEMALE 303

VI. FROM POLYGAMY TO MONOGAMY 303

VII. SUMMARY 304

REFERENCES 305

*28. Aggression in Canine Females*
John Paul Scott
I. INTRODUCTION 307
II. AGGRESSION IN CANINE FEMALES 309
III. THE EXPRESSION OF AGONISTIC BEHAVIOR IN RELATIONSHIPS BETWEEN PUPPIES AND HUMANS 312
IV. APPLICATIONS TO HUMAN AFFAIRS 314
REFERENCES 315

*29. Sex, Drugs, and Defensive Behavior: Implications for Animal Models of Defense*
D. Caroline Blanchard and Robert J. Blanchard
I. SEX DIFFERENCES IN ANTIPREDATOR DEFENSIVE BEHAVIORS 318
II. SEX DIFFERENCES: IMPLICATIONS FOR THE BIOLOGICAL BASES OF DEFENSE 323
III. IMPLICATIONS OF SEX DIFFERENCES FOR ANIMAL MODELS OF DEFENSIVE BEHAVIOR 324
REFERENCES 326

*30. Aggression and Aggressiveness in Female Golden Hamsters: The Attack Priming Effect as Tour Guide to the Central Mechanisms of Aggression*
Michael Potegal
I. FIRST STEPS 330
II. PHENOMENA THAT MAY BE EXPLICABLE IN TERMS OF AGGRESSIVE AROUSAL: THE PROMISED LAND 332
III. IN SEARCH OF THE NEURAL FLYWHEEL 334
IV. YOU CAN'T GET THERE FROM HERE: CIRCUMPERAMBULATIONS, DIGRESSIONS, AND DEAD ENDS 334
V. STUDIES OF AGGRESSIVE AROUSAL IN HAMSTERS AND RATS: ON THE YELLOW BRICK ROAD 335
VI. NOTES TOWARD A THEORETICAL MODEL OF AGGRESSIVE AROUSAL: TRAVELERS' TALES 336
VII. GENERAL APPROACH TO INVESTIGATING THE NEURAL MECHANISMS OF AGGRESSION USING THE PRIMING EFFECT: ROYAL ROAD OR PRIMROSE PATH? 338

VIII. THE EVIDENCE FOR NEUROANATOMICAL LOCALIZATION AND, MAYBE, MECHANISM OF AGGRESSIVE AROUSAL: THE FIRST MILESTONES 339
IX. THE FUNCTIONAL SIGNIFICANCE OF THE CMA LOCALIZATION: THE NEXT LANDMARK 340
X. ANNOTATING THE ITINERARY 341
XI. THE ROAD AHEAD 342
XII. THE HUMAN CONDITION: ANGER (CONSCIOUS AND UNCONSCIOUS), AGGRESSIVE AROUSAL, AND VIOLENT BEHAVIOR 343
XIII. THE MEDIAL AMYGDALA, TEMPORAL LOBE EPILEPSY, AND ANGER 344
XIV. FIGURE AND GROUND REVERSAL IN THE ANALYSIS OF AGGRESSION: LOOKING AHEAD TO LOOKING BACK 345
XV. A CONFLUENCE OF PILGRIMS 346
REFERENCES 347

*31. Aggressive Female Mice and Learning-Sensitive Open-Field Parameters*
Béatrice Kvist
I. INTRODUCTION 351
II. GENERAL METHODS 353
III. EXPERIMENT I 355
IV. EXPERIMENT II 357
V. DISCUSSION 360
REFERENCES 365

*32. Aggressive Behavior in Female Mice as a Correlated Characteristic in Selection for Aggressiveness in Male Mice*
N. Kenneth Sandnabba
I. INTRODUCTION 367
II. SELECTION FOR AGGRESSION IN MICE 368
III. MATERNAL AGGRESSION 369
IV. PREDATORY AGGRESSION 371
V. THE EFFECT OF ANDROGENS AND LEARNING ON AGGRESSION IN FEMALES 373
VI. PREFERENCES OF FEMALE MICE FOR MALE ODORS 375
VII. CONCLUSION 376
REFERENCES 377

**33. *Biological Correlates of Attack on Lactating Intruders by Female Mice: A Topical Review***

Marc Haug, Frank J. Johnson, and Paul F. Brain

I. STIMULUS CONDITION FOR AGGRESSION 382

II. ROLE OF GENOTYPE 382

III. ROLE OF HORMONES 385

IV. ROLE OF CENTRAL NEUROTRANSMITTER 387

V. BIOLOGICAL FUNCTIONS OF AGGRESSION 389

VI. FINAL COMMENTS 389

REFERENCES 389

**34. *Female Aggression in Mice: Developmental, Genetic, and Contextual Factors***

Kathryn E. Hood

I. INTRODUCTION 395

II. GENETIC AND SEX-RELATED DIFFERENCES IN CONTEXTS FOR AGGRESSIVE BEHAVIOR 396

III. DEVELOPMENTAL AND SEX-RELATED DIFFERENCES IN AGGRESSIVE BEHAVIOR 397

IV. CONTEXTUAL FACTORS IN THE STUDY OF FEMALE AGGRESSION 401

V. CONCLUSION 401

REFERENCES 402

***Index*** 403

# *Contributors*

Numbers in parentheses indicate the pages on which the authors' contributions begin.

***David Adams*** **(17)**, Psychology Department, Weslyan University, Middletown, Connecticut 06457

***David Benton*** **(37)**, Department of Psychology, University College of Swansea, Swansea SA2 8PP, Wales

***Kaj Björkqvist*** **(3, 51)**, Department of Psychology, Åbo Akademi University, SF-20500 Turku, Finland

***D. Caroline Blanchard*** **(317)**, Pacific Biomedical Research Center, Department of Anatomy and Reproductive Biology, John A. Burns School of Medicine, University of Hawaii, Honolulu, Hawaii 96822

***Robert J. Blanchard*** **(317)**, Department of Psychology, University of Hawaii, Honolulu, Hawaii 96822

***Paul F. Brain*** **(27, 381)**, School of Biological Sciences, University College of Swansea, Swansea SA2 8PP, Wales

***H. B. Kimberley Cook*** **(149)**, Fundacíon La Salle de Ciencias Naturales, Instituto Caribe de Antropología y Sociología, Caracas, Venezuela

***Adma d'Heurle*** **(283)**, Mercy College, Dobbs Ferry, New York 10522

***Leonard D. Eron*** **(89)**, Department of Psychology, University of Illinois at Chicago, Chicago, Illinois 60680

***Adam Frączek*** **(107)**, The Maria Grzegorzewska College for Special Education, 02-352 Warsaw, Poland

***Douglas P. Fry*** **(187)**, Anthropology Department, Eckerd College, St. Petersburg, Florida 33711

***Santiago Genovés*** **(209)**, Instituto de Investigaciones Antropologicas, Universidad Nacional Autonoma de Mexico, Ciudad Universitaria, 04510 Mexico, D. F., Mexico

***Ilsa M. Glazer*** **(163)**, Barnard College, Columbia University, New York, New York 10027

***Charles Goldenbeld*** **(217)**, Department of Social and Organizational Psychology, University of Utrecht, 3508 TC Utrecht, The Netherlands

***Jeffrey H. Goldstein*** **(65)**, Department of Social and Organizational Psychology, University of Utrecht, 3508TC Utrecht, Netherlands

***Nancy G. Guerra*** (77), Department of Psychology, University of Illinois at Chicago, Chicago, Illinois 60680

***Marc Haug*** **(27, 381)**, Laboratoire de Psychophysiologie, Université Louis Pasteur, 67000 Strasbourg, France

***Reijo Holmström*** **(295)**, Department of Psychiatry, University of Turku, 20840 Turku, Finland

***Kathryn E. Hood*** **(395)**, College of Health and Human Development, The Pennsylvania State University, University Park, Pennsylvania 16802

***L. Rowell Huesmann*** (77), Department of Psychology, University of Illinois at Chicago, Chicago, Illinois 60680

***Frank J. Johnson*** **(381)**, Department of Biological Sciences, University of Southern California, Section of Neurobiology, Los Angeles, California 90089

***Ari Kaukiainen*** **(51)**, Department of Psychology, Turku University, SF-20500 Turku, Finland

***Liisa Keltikangas-Järvinen*** **(123)**, Department of Psychology, University of Helsinki, 00100 Helsinki, Finland

***Rolf Kuschel*** **(173)**, Psychological Laboratory, University of Copenhagen, 2300 Copenhagen S., Denmark

***Béatrice Kvist*** **(351)**, Department of Psychology, Åbo Akademi University, SF-20500 Turku, Finland

***Bodil Lindfors*** **(229)**, Department of Psychology, Åbo Akademi University, SF-20500 Turku, Finland

***Ralf Lindman*** **(241)**, Department of Psychology, Åbo Akademi University, SF-20500 Turku, Finland

***Hein F. M. Lodewijkx*** **(217)**, Department of Social and Organizational Psychology, University of Utrecht, 3508 TC Utrecht, The Netherlands

***Laurie Miller*** (77), Developmental Pediatrics, Columbia University, New York, New York 10027

***Johannes Myyrä*** **(263)**, Department of Psychology, Åbo Akademi University, SF-20500, Turku, Finland

***Pekka Niemelä*** **(201)**, Kukolainen, 21160 Merimasku, Finland

***Pirkko Niemelä*** **(3, 273)**, Department of Psychology, Turku University, SF-20500 Turku, Finland

***Peter Öberg*** **(133)**, Kuntokallio Center for Gerontological Training and Research, 01100 Östersundom, Finland

***Karin Österman*** **(51)**, Department of Psychology, Åbo Akademi University, SF-20500 Turku, Finland

***Stefano Parmigiani*** **(27)**, Institute of Zoology, University of Parma, 43100 Parma, Italy

***Michael Potegal*** **(329)**, National Research Council, Walter Reed Army Institute of Research, Washington, D.C. 20307

***Lea Pulkkinen*** **(113)**, Department of Psychology, University of Jyväskylä, 40351 Jyväskylä, Finland

***Jacob M. Rabbie*** **(217)**, Department of Social and Organizational Psychology, University of Utrecht, 3508 TC Utrecht, The Netherlands

***Gordon W. Russell*** **(251)**, Department of Psychology, University of Lethbridge, Lethbridge, Alberta, Canada TIK 3M4

***Jan-Erik Ruth*** **(133)**, Kuntokallio Center for Gerontological Training and Research, 01100 Östersundom, Finland

***N. Kenneth Sandnabba*** **(367)**, Department of Psychology, Åbo Akademi University, SF-20500 Turku, Finland

***John Paul Scott*** **(307)**, Department of Psychology, Bowling Green State University, Bowling Green, Ohio

***Vappu Viemerö*** **(99)**, Department of Psychology, Åbo Akademi University, SF-20500 Turku, Finland

***Arnaldo Zelli*** **(77)**, Department of Psychology, University of Illinois at Chicago, Chicago, Illinois 60680

# Preface

Male aggressiveness has been thoroughly studied; however, little has been written on female aggressiveness. We felt a need existed for a compilation of research on this topic from the diverse disciplines that treat it: anthropology, social psychology, animal research, psychoanalysis, and literature. *Of Mice and Women: Aspects of Female Aggression* is such a compilation, and we hope that it will be a source for researchers in the field. As an interdisciplinary study, it may also serve teaching purposes in distinct disciplines.

Several basic questions are considered in this book. Is the belief that females of all species are less aggressive than males a myth? Is female aggressive behavior perhaps only *qualitatively*, and not necessarily *quantitatively*, different from its male counterpart? Does female aggression within the human species differ from that within the animal species? Are gender differences in aggressive patterns caused by hormones and neurobiology, or can they be explained by reference to learning mechanisms? What are typical patterns of female aggression, and how do they develop? Are there perhaps cultures in which the patterns of female aggression differ drastically from those seen in the West, and are women in some cultures more aggressive than women in others? How have the different forms of female aggression been portrayed in literature?

Addressing these questions and others of their kind necessitated a multidisciplinary approach. We asked several distinguished scientists from different disciplines—many of whom belong to the *International Society for Research on Aggression*, and all have conducted research on female aggression—to write a chapter about their research.

This book is dedicated to and many of its chapters directly inspired by the work of Kirsti Lagerspetz, a pioneering investigator of the antecedents of both human and subhuman female aggression. Her discovery of the genetic component of aggression in mice and its interaction with learning mechanisms has proved to be of extreme importance in the field of animal aggression. During recent years, her interest has turned to human female aggression and its various forms, specifically indirect aggression. Her research has always been exactly on the pulse of time, describing new, relevant topics. A book about the current state of knowledge on female aggression could hardly be dedicated to a more deserving person.

The editing process of this book has been a valuable experience for both of us. We now certainly know more about female aggression than we did before, and by reading all the chapters we have had many inspiring insights and ideas. At the same time, we have come to realize how much research is still needed in the field.

A book of this kind can naturally not be accomplished without help and support from a variety of sources. Financial support has been given by the Research Council for the Social Sciences, the Academy of Finland, The Research Foundation of Åbo Akademi University, and the Turku University Foundation. We greatly appreciate their aid.

In addition to the contributors of this volume, whom we thank wholeheartedly, there are several people whose help we would like to acknowledge. We would like to thank Nikki Fine at Academic Press for her kind encouragement at all stages of the editing process. Her letters were always a source of inspiration to us. Several people have aided us with the proofreading and typing, and we would like to thank Lindsey Hair, Anthony Johnson, Outi Nieminen, and Jacqueline Välimäki for their assistance.

Two persons have given us invaluable help in the editing process, and we want to express our very special gratitude to them. One is David Morton, who is responsible for the style of much of this work. He has spent many long hours proofreading and revising manuscripts under great time pressure. His linguistic skills and ability to phrase complicated terminology into readable English has certainly made the book more accessible to the reader. His work has been extremely valuable to us.

The other person is Karin Österman, who has facilitated our work in many respects. As a researcher in this field, she has also given professional suggestions. Her skill with computers and sense of organization have been indispensable to us; she has typed, taken care of files, and dealt with much of our correspondence. She is an invisible "third editor" without whose assistance this work would have been difficult to accomplish.

*Kaj Björkqvist*
*Pirkko Niemelä*

# I

# THE MYTH OF THE NONAGGRESSIVE FEMALE

# 1

# *New Trends in the Study of Female Aggression*

Kaj Björkqvist and Pirkko Niemelä

I. INTRODUCTION: THE PHENOMENON OF "FEMALE AGGRESSION"
II. FEMALE AGGRESSION: DEFINITION AND FORMS
III. THE "MALE" PERSPECTIVE
IV. THE DANGER OF ETHNOCENTRISM
V. THE PROBLEM OF METHODOLOGY
VI. RECENT STUDIES: METHODOLOGICAL AND CULTURAL CHANGE
VII. AN EMERGING PERSPECTIVE
VIII. ARE MALES MORE AGGRESSIVE THAN FEMALES?
A. Is Physical Aggression the "True" Form of Aggression?
B. Female–Male Encounters
C. Female–Female Encounters
IX. CONCLUSIONS
REFERENCES

## I. Introduction: The Phenomenon of "Female Aggression"

The study of female aggression as a phenomenon in itself has only recently begun to receive due attention. This chapter is an examination of developmental trends in the new research on human female aggression, considering the present stage of knowledge about, and discussing the reasons for, its various forms in different cultures as well as its occurrence during diverse life stages and situations. Since much of this research has been an attempt to describe in what way such aggression varies from its male counterpart, attention is necessarily drawn here to the question of differences between the sexes; again, of the many reviews of sex differences in regard to aggression, it is only one written in the last few years that has focused specifically on female forms of aggressive behavior (Burbank, 1987).

In consequence, we will question whether the statements "males are in general more aggressive than females" or "males are in general *not* more aggressive than females" are meaningful at all.

## II. Female Aggression: Definition and Forms

Aggression (unspecified by gender) may be defined as an act done with the intention to harm another person, oneself, or an object. Aggression and aggressiveness are considered to be two separate, but related, concepts, one an act, the other a personality trait. It may be useful to identify also the *motivational state* of having the intention to hurt, harm, or cause pain, in the definition of aggression. Zillmann (1979), for example, differentiates between the *attitude* hostility and the *behavior* aggression. This is not always done (Dollard *et al.*, 1939; Buss, 1961; Baron, 1977), perhaps because of the long tradition of behaviorism which states that motivational states may not be directly observed. We suggest though, that if not only acts, but also the motivational states, the intentions to hurt are considered as aggression, concepts like "repressed" and "displaced" aggression become meaningful.

Since Buss (1961), aggression has been categorized into dichotomies, such as *physical* versus *verbal*, and *direct* versus *indirect*. Feshbach (1964) coined the dichotomy *instrumental* versus *hostile* (*emotional*) aggression. A more common, but equally important dichotomy is *attack* (generally considered unjustified) versus *defense* (justified). Receptively, the harm or pain induced by aggressive acts may be either *physical* or *psychological* by its nature. We think that these categories may still be useful when we try to map sex differences with respect to aggression in various cultures, life situations, and life stages.

Aggression may occur at the *interpersonal* (between individuals), *group* (between groups), or *institutional* (institutionalized by society, one group suppressing another) level. Females may be involved at all these levels, indeed at each we may distinguish between *male–female*, *female–male*, and *female–female* (inter-female) aggression. The oppression of women, still a fact in a majority of cultures in the world today, is a vivid example of institutional aggression, which has been analyzed as the ultimate male–female aggression (see Myyrä, Chapter 24, this volume).

During the various stages of life, females are members of different groups, and may accordingly get into a variety of conflict situations. We may differentiate between aggression within the *primary group* (the family), and aggression within *secondary groups* (school, work, etc.).

During childhood, female aggression within the family is likely to appear in the form of *sibling rivalry*, although young girls may also feel hostility toward their parents, which becomes manifest as aggression elsewhere (see Eron, Chapter 8, this volume).

Among adolescents, aggressive acts occur mostly within the same gender, although some aggression is directed toward individuals of the other sex (Lagerspetz & Björkqvist, 1992). Status, dominance, and competition seem to be important mediators of aggression.

During adult life, we again have to distinguish between aggression within the primary group and within secondary groups. At home, we talk about *domestic violence* (fights between partners and child abuse). *Maternal aggression*, mothers defending their offspring, has been studied primarily among subhuman species, and hardly at all among humans. This has been the only acceptable type of aggression for mothers described so far in the literature; mothers' ambivalent feelings for their children, not to speak of hate and anger, has remained taboo outside psychoanalytic discourse.

## III. The "Male" Perspective

Female aggression is much less investigated than its male counterpart. Two possible reasons for this situation are: (1) the phenomenon itself [male aggression, being typically (or stereotypically) physical, is easier to discern and therefore a more obvious object of study]; and (2) factors concerning the researchers [the majority being males, they may, for personal reasons, find male aggression easier to understand and a more appealing object of study]. Frodi, Macaulay, and Thome (1977), in their careful review of gender differences in regard to aggression, commented that of 314 experimental studies conducted in the period 1967–1974, 54% concerned men only, while, in comparison, they could find only 8% describing aggression experiments in which only females took part. This fact is certainly revealing.

Simone de Beauvoir (1957) refers to woman as the "second sex." The first sex, man, defining everything from his point of view, from his interests and wishes, finds it favorable to conceive of women as friendly, virtuous and giving, and caring for man's needs, while he himself is brave and aggressive. The male prototype is thus the warrior, while the prototype of the female is the self-sacrificing mother, and scientists maintain, like everybody else, the favorite myths of their culture, seeing females, whether mice, primates, or humans, in accordance with their own cultural stereotypes. Major reviews of psychological studies of gender differences of human aggression have all been written by women (Maccoby & Jacklin, 1974; Frodi, Macaulay, & Thome, 1977; White, 1983; Hyde, 1984; Eagly & Steffen, 1986).

We suggest that the characteristic "male" perspective has greatly biased aggression research. Male investigators have not only usually chosen male subjects, but their *operationalizations* of aggression have favored typically "male" forms, even when the research *object* has been female aggression. Accordingly, the myth about the "nonaggressive female" has been difficult to avoid.

The review by Terman and Tyler (1954) stated categorically that males are more aggressive than females, and explained this difference, at least in part, by biology. Even Maccoby and Jacklin (1974), in their classic review, favor the same opinion.

Later reviews (such as Frodi, Macaulay, & Thome, 1977; White, 1983; Hyde, 1984; and Eagly & Steffen, 1986), are much more cautious. Even when they acknowledge sex differences (in quality, if not so much in quantity), they avoid offering opinions about the biology versus socialization controversy. Physical aggression is less and less considered to be the "true" form of aggression.

## IV. The Danger of Ethnocentrism

Aggression research has, with few exceptions [notably Burbank's (1987) cross-cultural review of female aggression], been ethnocentric. The best-known reviews of sex differences of aggression (mentioned above) base their analyses largely on North American studies (Hyde, 1984, and Eagly & Steffen, 1986, exclusively so). We do not wish to question the value of these two extremely thorough meta-analyses. It should be obvious, however, that inferences in such cases can be made only for the culture in which studies have been conducted.

Rohner (1976), examining a world sample of 101 societies and reviewing 130 studies done in the United States, found culture to be more predictive of aggression than gender. With Burbank's (1987) study, this review makes it obvious that female aggression may appear in a remarkable variety of forms in different cultures. In the present volume, Chapters 17, 14, 15, 16, and 18 by Fry, Cook, Glazer, Kuschel, and Niemelä, respectively, demonstrate this fact.

## V. The Problem of Methodology

The operationalizations of aggressive behavior mostly favored in research, of children as well as of adults, are likely to exaggerate sex differences. Child subjects have often been observed in school yards or in day-care centers (cf. the majority of studies reviewed by Maccoby & Jacklin, 1974, and Hyde, 1984). Observational studies inevitably favor physical (typically "male") aggression, since indirect aggression (more typical of females, according to Lagerspetz, Björkqvist, & Peltonen, 1988) or any means intended to cause psychological harm (also more typical of females, according to Eagly & Steffen, 1986) are almost impossible to observe. Indeed, when actual aggression has not been observed to a sufficient degree to facilitate analyses of data, aggression has been operationalized as "rough-and-tumble play" in order to get more data (e.g., Whiting & Edwards, 1973), an inclusion likely to magnify gender differences. We think this observational one-sidedness may explain Hyde's (1984) finding that sex differences are greater in naturalistic than in experimental studies.

Observational studies of adults, on the other hand, have preferably been conducted in the laboratory, utilizing the Buss (1961) "teacher–learner" paradigm, in which "victims" are delivered electric shocks; in other experiments, the "aggressive" stimuli has been a loud noise (e.g., Shortell & Biller, 1970).

Miller, Gillen, Schenkler, and Radlove (1974) found females have different attitudes toward electric shock than males, expressing more doubts about shocks' efficacy in controlling the behavior of another person. One should accordingly, in the Buss paradigm, expect less *a priori* willingness among females to induce electric shocks.

It is, in the opinion of the present authors, not correct to make inferences about "physical aggression" or "psychological harm" from such experiments, however valuable the information they may give in other respects. In actual life, adult female aggression is something which takes place mainly at home, at work, or in other social contexts. It is hard to see the similarity between an electric shock and a blow or a punch, or how a disturbing noise is comparable with mental cruelty.

## VI. Recent Studies: Methodological and Cultural Change

Recent reviews find fewer sex differences with respect to aggression. In 1974, Maccoby and Jacklin held the opinion that aggression was the area in which perhaps the most clear sex difference could be found, but more recent studies do not agree. Frodi, Macaulay, and Thome (1977) give a detailed description of how male and female aggression varies *situationally*. Although Eagly and Steffen (1986) conclude, as a result of their meta-analysis of North American experimental studies of adult (over 14 years of age) aggression, that men were somewhat more aggressive than females, results were inconsistent across studies, and while men were more inclined than women to instigate physical harm, women were more ready than men to induce psychological harm.

Hyde (1984) concludes that only 5% of the variation in aggression scores is explained by sex differences, with 95% explained by within-gender variation or by chance. Hyde finds gender differences in general to be smaller in more recent studies than in previous ones, and suggests three possible explanations for this:

1. Null findings may have become more likely to be published;
2. Experimenters and observers may have changed their perception of what aggression is;
3. Socialization practices and cultural norms may have changed.

Minturn and Guthrie (1978) demonstrate the truth of the first of these, and due to the work of Lagerspetz, Björkqvist, and Peltonen (1988) the second is accepted. In this volume at least two chapters (Chapters 8 and 9 by Eron and Viemerö, respectively) suggest that changes in socialization practices have made females appear to behave more "aggressively" than they had formerly seemed to.

## VII. An Emerging Perspective

Typical of recent studies of female aggression is a decreased interest in the question of whether females are less aggressive than males or not, in favor of a closer focus on female aggression as a phenomenon in itself. In which situations are females likely to get into aggressive encounters, and what techniques are they likely to use?

*Female–male* encounters are frequent, especially within the domestic sphere, but also at work. These will be covered later in this chapter.

*Interfemale* aggression has become a more popular research object; the review by Burbank (1987) is a good example of this trend. It is an important focus of study; the most frequent aggressive conflicts (outside of the family) are, as previously mentioned, within-sex. Dominance hierarchies exist between females, and competition with other females takes place more often than with males (Burbank, 1987).

Another trend is the new interest in *indirect aggression.* This form, in which the instigator manipulates others to attack the victim, or, by other means, makes use of the social structure in order to harm the target person, was suggested by Lagerspetz, Björkqvist, and Peltonen (1988) and by Björkqvist, Lagerspetz, and Kaukiainen (1992) to be a form of aggression more typical of females than of males. It is a kind of aggression which may not be observed in laboratory studies, nor in school yards; self-estimated aggression scales will not measure it, since few would admit to being manipulative even to themselves, much less to others. However, by the use of peer estimation, indirect aggression can be measured. The concept of indirect aggression has been utilized in studies of female aggressive strategies such as those by Holmström and Fry (Chapters 27 and 17, respectively, this volume).

## VIII. Are Males More Aggressive Than Females?

This question is, in our opinion, meaningless if put without specification. What is "more" aggression?

1. Should we measure the number of aggressive acts?
2. How do we compare male–male aggressive acts with female–female aggression?
3. Should we consider only female–male encounters? If so, should we consider who starts the attack, who wins, or the pain induced?
4. How do we measure intensity of pain?
5. Which is worse, physical or psychological pain?
6. Is the motivation to hurt as important an indicator as the act itself?
7. Is direct aggression worse than indirect aggression?
8. Is attack worse than defense? Attack and defense against what?

The list of problems we encounter in the attempt to determine which sex is the more aggressive could easily be made longer. These examples should, however, make it obvious how problematic it is to claim that individuals of one sex are more aggressive than those of the other.

In the following, we will discuss a few of these problems, starting with the question of physical aggression, which appears to have been of crucial importance in the description of gender differences.

## A. IS PHYSICAL AGGRESSION THE "TRUE" FORM OF AGGRESSION?

Many studies and reviews (e.g., Terman & Tyler, 1954; Omark, Omark, & Edelman, 1975; Whiting & Edwards, 1973; Maccoby & Jacklin, 1974; Hyde, 1984; Eagly & Steffen, 1986) conclude that males are more aggressive than females. As mentioned, older reviews state this claim with more certainty. When we take a closer look at the evidence, we find a remarkable emphasis on physical aggression among children and adolescents as the indicator of greater aggressiveness among males. The study by Eagly and Steffen is an exception; their review consists essentially of laboratory studies with adults. Two of the studies mentioned (Omark, Omark, & Edelman, 1975; Whiting & Edwards, 1973) are crosscultural comparisons. However, both base their claim on observations of frequencies of rough-and-tumble play, pushing, and hitting in young children, a basis, as we suggest above, with an inbuilt gender bias. Maccoby and Jacklin (1974) and Hyde (1984) base their evidence largely on studies of children and adolescents in the United States and Canada. Hyde (1984) concludes correctly that sex differences are clearest in naturalistic (observational) studies.

There has been a debate over the opinion of Patterson, Littman, and Bricker (1967) that greater frequency of physical aggression among boys actually is an artifice due to their higher level of activity. This debate seems unresolved; although Barrett (1979) found more physical aggression among 5- to 9-year-old boys than among girls, when White (1983) corrected Barrett's data for social activity level, the difference no longer emerged.

Observational studies of children give poor information of aggressive strategies used later on in life, and generalizations should be made with caution. In this volume, Chapter 5 by Björkqvist, Österman, and Kaukiainen presents a developmental theory of *styles* of aggressive behavior. Based primarily on peer nomination techniques among adolescents, but also on studies of adult conflicts at work, it is suggested that direct physical aggression, direct verbal aggression, and indirect aggression (social manipulation) may be seen as developmental stages of aggressive behavior dependent on verbal and cognitive development. Aggression in animals and young children is mostly physical. When verbal skills develop, direct verbal aggression (yelling, abusing, threatening, etc.) is brought into the aggressive repertoire, replacing to a great extent physical means of aggression. Further on, when social intelligence and skills are refined, they make possible the utilization of indirect methods; the instigator of aggression manipulates others, or the social situation, in order to obtain goals and/or induce pain in the target person, while remaining unidentified.

A consequence of this developmental sequence of aggressive strategies in humans is that naturalistic studies of children will favor the observation of "male" aggression, while indirect aggression will go unnoticed. Naturalistic observational studies of adult aggression have not been conducted to the same extent as those of child subjects, with the consequence that the investigation of adult forms of aggression in everyday life has been neglected.

Inferences of the greater physical aggressiveness of males are also made from animal studies. Evidence from subhuman species, we think, may in fact be a significant reason why authors tend to be biased in favor of considering physical aggression to be the "true" form of aggression. The fact that human beings are much more complicated creatures than other species is too easily forgotten. The development of language gives humans the capability of behaving aggressively without having to resort to physical force. By social manipulation, a man or woman may inflict tremendous pain upon an antagonist (see, e.g., Chapter 16, this volume: Kuschel's report on this "hostile action potential" as a form of female aggression on Bellona). Among adult humans, physical violence is in fact the most infrequent form of aggression.

When used, however, human physical aggression may result in direct injury and death, and perhaps this seriousness explains in part its prioritization in the research. If we look at criminal records, then certainly we find, at least in western society, that males do commit more physically violent crimes than females do (Bowker, 1978).

There is, then, evidence that males are, during both childhood and adult life, physically more aggressive than females, in western and most other cultures (although here the opposite may be found; cf. Cook, Chapter 14, this volume). This is not surprising, given the fact that males are, in general, bigger and stronger, physically more active, and have more opportunities for the reinforcement of physical aggression (cf. Patterson, Littman, & Bricker, 1967). The role of androgens is an open debate; Benton (Chapter 4, this volume) suggests their role is overestimated.

The question remains, however: Is, at the interpersonal level (and, especially among adults), physical violence the most important form of human aggression, the one that causes the greatest amount of suffering? Is it a criterion important enough to justify the claim that males are more aggressive than females?

### B. FEMALE–MALE ENCOUNTERS

All major reviews of laboratory studies (Maccoby & Jacklin, 1974; Frodi, Macaulay, & Thome, 1977; Eagly & Steffen, 1986) conducted in western countries consistently reveal the social norm of *chivalry*: males being less aggressive toward females than toward other males. This finding is made in Buss machine experiments (e.g., Buss, 1961; Taylor & Epstein, 1967; Yousef, 1968), but also in experiments with noise as the "aggressive" stimulus (Shortell & Biller, 1970) utilizing 11-year-old subjects, revealing the existence of the rule of chivalry already at that age.

We may, however, question the ecological validity of these studies. In a laboratory situation, males are not likely to feel seriously threatened, so they can afford to be chivalrous. Eagly and Steffen (1986) point out that there are situations (when males are angered, or feel unjustly attacked) in which the rule of chivalry may be violated. In those cases, such as real-life domestic violence, women are more easily victimized, due to the greater physical strength of the males. Chivalry is reserved more for situations with unfamiliar females.

Female–male encounters take different forms during the various life stages. Among siblings, variation in physical strength may be a factor leading to the development of different strategies among males and females. The latter may more easily turn to parents or others for help (a kind of indirect aggression), or withdraw from the situation. This may partly explain why a gender difference with respect to both indirect aggression and withdrawal from conflicts is found among adolescents (Lagerspetz, Björkqvist, & Peltonen, 1988; Björkqvist, Lagerspetz, & Kaukiainen, 1992). In these studies, females revealed more of both kinds of behavior.

During adolescence, female–male encounters are more rare than within-sex aggression. Competition between individuals of the same sex and fighting for status in the same-sex dominance hierarchy appear more frequently. The rule of chivalry normally but not necessarily tempers boys' physical aggression toward girls. Attacks of males on females are slightly more frequent than the other way around, at least in western cultures (e.g., Lagerspetz & Björkqvist, 1992).

Among adults, male–female encounters are likely to become more common due to the fact the two sexes interact more than during adolescence. Encounters are likely to appear within the family, but also at work (or in other groups of importance where males and females compete for dominance or favors), with corresponding situational variation in forms of aggressive strategy. Domestic cruelty and violence may cause considerably more pain than conflicts within secondary groups, largely because male–female conflicts at work (in western society) seldom become physical, remaining verbal or indirect.

Aggressive strategies in fights between couples are likely to reveal more direct features, especially verbal, but also physical. The male has a physical edge, due to his greater strength; females, accordingly, may again have to resort to verbal as well as more indirect techniques, or withdraw. While there is evidence (from North American studies) that females at home may be as aggressive as their men, serious physical injury is reported more often as a result of male violence (e.g., Straus, Gelles, & Steinmetz, 1980). Burbank, in her 1987 review of female aggression in 137 societies, found adultery on the side of the husband to be the most frequent reason for women's physical aggression against male partners.

To our knowledge, there has been no systematic study of indirect strategies in conflicts between partners, although such means must be utilized frequently. However, great cultural variation is likely to exist; in Chapter 16, this volume, Kuschel describes how Bellonese women, living in a highly patrilocal society, may sing mocking songs as an effective form of covered aggression. Indeed, Burbank (1987) reveals a great variety of acts of aggression displayed by women against their husbands in different cultures; besides fighting him with weapons (more likely than using them against other women), they may destroy his property, shut him out of the house for the night, or refuse to cook or speak.

Kimberley Cook suggests (Chapter 14, this volume) that many culture-specific forms of aggression have hitherto gone unnoticed due to the general misperception of female aggression, and gives vivid descriptions of female–male encounters on Margarita Island in which the females have the edge, despite the greater physical strength of the men. In most societies, females resort (or, they are at least described to do so) to verbal and indirect aggression in their encounters with men. In Margariteño society, they use direct physical violence.

## C. FEMALE–FEMALE ENCOUNTERS

Interfemale aggression may, during childhood, appear among siblings as well as within the peer group. Since these types of conflicts are partly covered above, adult female–female encounters will mainly be examined here.

Burbank (1987) suggests several possible reasons for interfemale aggression: responses to frustration; expressions of anger; means of competing or defending; and attempts to dominate, or to resist domination. In her cross-cultural comparison, she found other women to be by far the most common targets of female aggression. Women were mentioned as targets in 91% of the 137 societies, while men were targets in only 54%. She contrasts this finding with the conclusion by Maccoby and Jacklin (1974) that females received less aggression than males from both male and female aggressors. The finding by Maccoby and Jacklin may be explained by the fact that the studies they reviewed consisted mostly of either observational studies of children or of laboratory studies having North American adults as subjects. The problems with these paradigms, as far as the investigation of female aggression is concerned, have already been mentioned. Burbank (1987) points out that the aggressive encounters of her reviewed samples are real-life conflicts, the subjects adults, in a large variety of cultures.

With what other women do females fight? Burbank (1987) finds aggression among adult sisters to be rare. She provides little data on aggression between female in-laws, but suggests it to be an important focus of study. In agreement with Collier (1974), she expects female aggression among in-laws to appear frequently in patrilocal societies, in which females are dependent upon males.

Competition between females both within and outside the family is highly dependent on the structure of the society. Glazer (Chapter 15, this volume; see also Schuster, 1983) suggests interfemale aggression to be frequent in patrilocal, but scarce in matrilocal societies, and she exemplifies this with a comparison between prerevolutionary China and premodern Zambia. This notion is of theoretical importance. While Collier (1974) claims the greater interfemale aggression in patrilocal societies to be a consequence of power struggles, Glazer is of the opinion that it may instead be explained by competition for scarce resources.

## IX. Conclusions

Research on human female aggression has to a great extent been restricted by a skewed perspective and serious methodological problems. Research strategies have favored male forms of aggression, leading to the myth of the "nonaggressive female." Buss (1961) regarded aggression mainly as a "male problem." A consequence of one-sided operationalizations of aggression has been the focus on the question of whether males are more aggressive than females, and if so, whether this is due to biology or socialization. The question itself seems, to us, meaningless without several specifications.

A more sensitive perception of what constitutes female aggression has recently started to emerge. Real-life data, particularly from anthropological sources, suggest hypotheses about when and how females are aggressive. Naturalistic studies of female aggression at work or in other secondary groups, are still, to a great extent, lacking. Domestic violence, in western societies, has been an important object of study.

In order to understand female aggression, we need a theory about the origins of aggressive behavior. We do not think that males are "by nature" more aggressive than females; we agree with Feshbach (1970), who suggests that the sexes may differ with respect to the mode of aggression, but not in regard to the motivation to instigate pain or to obtain favors by aggressive means. There is no reason to believe that women overall should be less motivated to be aggressive than men.

Laboratory studies reveal that females behave as aggressively as males when they are not in danger of being recognized, hence of being retaliated against (Grusec, 1972; Mallick & McCandless, 1966; see also Rabbie, Goldenbeld, & Lodewijkx, Chapter 20, this volume). This fact gives support for the view that women are as aggressive as men, as far as the motivation to hurt is concerned.

With respect to *styles* of aggressive behavior, variation depending on culture, situation, sex, and age may be discerned. This variation should be accounted for by comprehensive theoretical considerations. Aggressive behavior may be explained by (1) frustration, and (2) learning mechanisms. Although we do not agree with the frustration–aggression hypothesis in its most orthodox form ("aggression is always caused by frustration," Dollard *et al.*, 1939), we do think that most aggressive acts, at least at the phenomenological level, are experienced as having good reasons. The frustration experienced may have a variety of sources (competition about physical resources, emotional frustration, matters of status and dominance, etc.) as in the theories of Collier (1974) and Glazer (Chapter 15, this volume; see also Schuster, 1983). Female aggression is not only a matter of learned role behavior, but it is instigated by real-life frustration.

A careful analysis of cultural and situational variation is therefore needed. This should benefit not only the study of female aggression, but the study of human aggression in general. Degree of aggressiveness, as well as strategies utilized, are likely to be largely dependent on situation, revealing acceptance of serious aggression when the level of frustration is great. When aggression cannot, for one reason or another, be directed (physically or verbally) at its target, the perpetrator has to find other channels. Therefore, in societies where males dominate, *indirect* methods are likely to appear among females; the aggression may have to be *displaced* (cf. Dollard *et al.*, 1939) and may even have to be *repressed*, with resultant psychological problems.

*Modes* of female aggression are dependent on social norms and learning. Female aggression has often been explained as role behavior (e.g., Eagly & Steffen, 1986), and there is certainly a great degree of truth in this. Explanations in these terms are especially frequent in psychological research; several chapters of this volume describe socialization practices in western society and their relation to female expressions of aggression.

Roles are learned when one identifies with models. Björkqvist and Österman (1992) suggest that modeling may not be explained only in terms of the success of the model [Miller & Dollard's (1941) *vicarious conditioning*; see also Bandura's (1973) social learning theory], as unsuccessful aggressive models may be imitated as well as successful ones. A more important factor is the degree of identification with the model in question. Björkqvist and Österman (1992) therefore suggest *cognitive modeling*, emphasizing identification with the model, rather than vicarious conditioning as the key in the modeling process.

This thinking is in line with the *cognitive script* theory of Huesmann and Eron (1986). They found identification with aggressive models to be perhaps the most important factor explaining the effect of television violence (see also Eron, Chapter 8, this volume). To emphasize identification in the process of learning aggressive strategies fits also the "learning-of-roles" theory suggested by Eagly and Steffen (1986). Roles are learned, then, when an individual imitates cognitive scripts displayed by models with whom he or she identifies. Many of these scripts are expressions of social norms, varying from time to time and culture to culture. Others are individual scripts, specific only to the model in question. The first type of scripts explains between-culture variation with respect to modes of female aggression; the other type accounts for within-culture variation.

Female aggressive behavior may accordingly be described as resulting from a complex combination of cultural, situational, and individual-specific factors. The cognition of frustration, as well as its emotional experience, function as triggers of aggression, while learned scripts determine the mode, or pattern, of behavior.

## References

Bandura, A. (1973). *Aggression. A Social Learning Analysis.* Englewood Cliffs, New Jersey: Prentice-Hall.

Baron, R. A. (1977). *Human Aggression.* New York: Plenum Press.

Barrett, D. E. (1979). A naturalistic study of sex differences in children's aggression. *Merrill-Palmer Quarterly, 25,* 193–207.

Beauvoir, S. de (1957). *The Second Sex.* New York: Alfred A. Knopf.

Björkqvist, K., Lagerspetz, K. M. J., & Kaukiainen, A. (1992). Do girls manipulate and boys fight? Developmental trends regarding direct and indirect aggression. *Aggressive Behavior, 18,* 117–127.

Björkqvist, K., & Österman, K. (1992). Parental influence on children's self-estimated aggressiveness. *Aggressive Behavior* (submitted).

Bowker, L. H. (1978). *Women, Crime, and the Criminal Justice System.* Lexington, Massachusetts: Lexington Books.

Burbank, V. K. (1987). Female aggression in cross-cultural perspective. *Behavior Science Research, 21,* 70–100.

Buss, A. H. (1961). *The Psychology of Aggression.* New York: Wiley.

Collier, J. (1974). Women in politics. *In* M. Rosaldo & L. Lamphere (Eds.), *Women, Culture and Society.* Stanford: Stanford University Press.

Dollard, J., Doob, L. W., Miller, N. E., Mowrer, O. H., & Sears, R. R. (1939). *Frustration and Aggression.* New Haven, Connecticut: Yale University Press.

Eagly, A. H., & Steffen, V. J. (1986). Gender and aggressive behavior: A meta-analytic review of the social psychological literature. *Psychological Bulletin, 100,* 309–330.

Feshbach, S. (1964). The function of aggression and the regulation of aggressive drive. *Psychological Review, 71,* 257–272.

Feshbach, S. (1970). Aggression. *In* P. H. Mussen (Ed.), *Carmichael's Manual of Child Psychology.* New York: Wiley.

Frodi, A., Macaulay, J., & Thome, P. R. (1977). Are women always less aggressive than men? *Psychological Bulletin, 84,* 634–660.

Grusec, J. E. (1972). Demand characteristics of the modeling experiment: Altruism as a function of sex and aggression. *Journal of Personality and Social Psychology, 22,* 139–148.

Huesmann, L. R., & Eron, L. D. (Eds.) (1986). *Television and the Aggressive Child: A Cross-National Comparison.* Hillsdale, New Jersey: Lawrence Erlbaum Associates.

Hyde, J. S. (1984). How large are gender differences in aggression? A developmental meta-analysis. *Developmental Psychology, 20,* 722–736.

Lagerspetz, K. M. J., & Björkqvist, K. (1992). Indirect aggression in girls and boys. *In* L. R. Huesmann (Ed.), *Aggressive Behavior: Current Perspectives.* New York: Plenum.

Lagerspetz, K. M. J., Björkqvist, K., & Peltonen, T. (1988). Is indirect aggression typical of females? Gender differences in aggressiveness in 11- to 12-year old children. *Aggressive Behavior, 14,* 403–414.

Maccoby, E. E., & Jacklin, C. N. (1974). *The Psychology of Sex Differences.* Stanford: Stanford University Press.

Mallick, S. K., & McCandless, B. R. (1966). A study of catharsis of aggression. *Journal of Personality and Social Psychology, 4,* 591–596.

Miller, A. G., Gillen, B., Schenkler, C., & Radlove, S. (1974). The prediction and perception of obedience to authority. *Journal of Personality, 42,* 23–42.

Miller, N. E., & Dollard, J. (1941). *Social Learning and Imitation.* New Haven, Connecticut: Yale University Press.

Minturn, L., & Guthrie, P. (1978). Ethnographer oversight in reporting sex differences in aggression training. *Behavior Science Research, 13,* 282–293.

Omark, D. R., Omark, M., & Edelman, M. (1975). Dominance hierarchies in young children. *In* T. R. Williams (Ed.), *Psychological Anthropology.* The Hague, Netherlands: Mouton.

Patterson, G. R., Littman, R. A., & Bricker, W. (1967). Assertive behavior in children: A step toward a theory of aggression. *Monographs of the Society for Research in Child Development, 32,* Serial No. 113.

Rohner, R. P. (1976). Sex differences in aggression: Phylogenetic and enculturation perspectives. *Ethos, 4,* 57–72.

Schuster, I. (1983). Women's aggression: An African case study. *Aggressive Behavior, 9,* 319–331.

Shortell, J. R., & Biller, H. B. (1970). Aggression in children as a function of sex of subject and sex of opponent. *Developmental Psychology, 3,* 143–144.

Straus, M. A., Gelles, R. J., & Steinmetz, S. K. (1980). *Behind Closed Doors: Violence in the American Family.* Garden City, New York: Anchor Books.

Taylor, S. P., & Epstein, S. (1967). Aggression as a function of the interaction of the sex of the aggressor and the sex of the victim. *Journal of Personality, 35,* 474–496.

Terman, L. M., & Tyler, L. E. (1954). Psychological sex differences. *In* L. Carmichael (Ed.), *Manual of Child Psychology.* New York: Wiley.

White, J. W. (1983). Sex and gender issues in aggression research. *In* R. G. Geen & E. I. Donnerstein (Eds.), *Aggression: Theoretical and Empirical Reviews (Vol. 2).* New York: Academic Press.

Whiting, B., & Edwards, C. P. (1973). Cross-cultural analysis of sex differences in the behavior of children aged three to eleven. *Journal of Social Psychology, 91,* 171–188.

Youssef, Z. I. (1968). The role of race, sex, hostility, and verbal stimulus in inflicting punishment. *Psychonomic Science, 12,* 285–286.

Zillmann, D. (1979). *Hostility and Aggression.* Hillsdale, New Jersey: Lawrence Erlbaum.

2

# Biology Does Not Make Men More Aggressive Than Women

David Adams

I. INTRODUCTION
II. A POLITICALLY USEFUL MYTH
A. The Myth
B. Refuting the Myth
III. INSTITUTIONAL IS DIFFERENT FROM INDIVIDUAL BEHAVIOR
IV. MALE ANIMALS ARE NOT CONSISTENTLY MORE AGGRESSIVE THAN FEMALES
V. THE COMPLEX RELATION OF HUMAN AGGRESSION TO ANIMAL AGGRESSION
VI. CONCLUSION
REFERENCES

## I. Introduction

In 1988, the International Society for Research on Aggression formally endorsed the Seville Statement on Violence, four years after the workshops hosted by Dr. Kirsti Lagerspetz and her colleagues in Turku devoted to its planning. In a brief but important paper circulated at Seville, entitled "Are Wars Caused by Aggression?" she presented the following conclusion:

> In sum, to account for war on the collective level by psychological motives and characteristics on the individual level, it is not sufficient or pertinent to mention only aggression as an explanation. . . . we have mentioned fear, suggestibility, obedience, sociability, altruism, dutifulness, ambition, self-assertiveness, intelligence, language, fear of disapproval, desire for gain, search for security (fear of unemployment) and some other characteristics. Collective behavior never results from one type of motive only on the individual level.[1]

[1]The Lagerspetz paper circulated to the Seville signatories in preparation for their work was a draft provided at the Acapulco meetings of the International Congress of Psychological Sciences in 1984. Lagerspetz later expanded it into the paper cited in the references.

One will find almost this exact language in Proposition Five of the Seville Statement, since the Lagerspetz paper was specifically used in drafting it.

The results of the work at Seville are well known. The Statement on Violence has been endorsed and disseminated by scientific and cultural organizations around the world (including UNESCO), and used effectively to counteract the myth that warfare is an inevitable result of human biology (Adams, 1989). It can be said that it prepares the ground for the construction of a vision of world peace.

In this article, I shall address an issue discussed at Seville, but not incorporated into the final Statement, by my recollection, because there was considerable controversy about it; there seemed to be no way to reach a rapid consensus, and we only had a few days to do all the necessary work. The issue concerns the obvious fact that men, not women, fight wars, and whether this fact reflects biological or cultural causes.

## II. A Politically Useful Myth

### A. THE MYTH

It is politically useful for some to argue that male monopolization of warfare is evidence that war is a product of biology. For example, in a recent review criticizing the Seville Statement on Violence (Somit, 1990), the reviewer says that,

> Practically everyone who has studied this problem argues that, among mammals, the males are far more prone to aggressive behavior than females.

The author footnotes his remark by referencing two well-known scientific experts on aggressive behavior who have, indeed, made this claim. The claim is then used to argue against the Seville Statement by saying that Statement ignores what "practically everyone" knows.

No one disputes the fact that warfare is usually planned and carried out by men rather than by women, and that this is a very old tradition. According to Murdock's cross-cultural work, warfare is one of the few occupations which is almost exclusively done by one gender and not the other (Murdock, 1937). The only other occupations which are so gender specific are metalworking, hunting, and manufacture of weapons (all by men). I argue that hunting and metalworking are monopolized by men as adjuncts to their monopolization of war, because they also involve the use and making of weapons.

What is disputed, and what I will try to show is a myth, is the proposition that male mammals are more aggressive than females and that such a "fact" is relevant to the monopolization of warfare by human males.

### B. REFUTING THE MYTH

To refute the myth, it is necessary to refute the assumptions on which it is based: (1) that the gender differences in human institutional aggression (i.e., war) are causally related to gender differences in individual human aggressiveness; (2) that human individual aggressive behavior is homologous to that of other animals; and (3) that among other animals, males are generally more aggressive than females. In this article, I present evidence to show that both the first and third assumptions are false. The second assumption is probably true, but without the others cannot support the myth.

## III. Institutional Is Different from Individual Behavior

Underlying the Seville Statement on Violence is the assumption that institutional behavior is quite different from individual behavior. This assumption is contained in the Lagerspetz conclusion; "Collective behavior never results from one type of motive only on the individual level." The confusing of institutional and individual behavior is a common error among people who argue that human behavior is biologically determined. A particularly good treatment of this problem may be found in the recent book by Seville signatories Jo Groebel and Robert Hinde concerning the issues raised at Seville (Groebel & Hinde, 1989).

I have presented evidence elsewhere to show that the remarkable gender specificity of warfare is due to institutional considerations that are only remotely related to biology (Adams, 1983a). To put the argument most simply, male monopolization of warfare arose to resolve a contradiction between the institution of marriage and the institution of warfare. In cultures with patrilocal marital residency and internal warfare, such as probably prevailed in prehistoric times, there is a potential conflict of interest for a woman warrior: should she take sides with her husband and his relatives on one side of the war, or support her fathers and brothers on the other? Under such conditions, every married woman becomes a potential traitor to her husband's side. Male monopolization of warfare was probably instituted in order to protect male warriors against betrayal by their wives and to resolve the conflict of interest of the women themselves.

Evidence supports this hypothesis. Cultures in which no conflict of interest would be expected to arise, those with matrilocal marital residency or exclusively external warfare, have permitted women warriors in a number of cases. On the other hand, in none of the cultures surveyed have women warriors been permitted in societies where such a conflict of interest could arise.

One must assume that in the earliest societies, when war and marriage first arose, there would have been a tendency (*not* a monopolization) for more male than female warriors. Such a tendency can be easily explained by the obvious fact that a woman who is several months pregnant or nursing a baby cannot go on the long marches which war often requires.

The male monopolization of warfare had enormous consequences for all subsequent human history. First, it extended from warfare itself into the monopolization of the tools of war which meant a monopolization of big-game hunting and metalworking. Second, it extended from the act into the planning of warfare; with the development of the state, it extended into other aspects of state power as well. Since war required the organization of armies and economic support, these came under male monopolization; since war was used to acquire slaves, male power extended into the control of slaves, and, hence into economic and political power throughout the state.

In today's world, male power is signaled not only by the formal organization of power, but also by an intense complex of nonverbal behaviors that boys and girls learn to imitate in the course of childhood. These nonverbal behaviors are brilliantly reviewed and documented in the book *Body Politics: Power, Sex and Nonverbal Communication* (Henley, 1977). Male power has developed to such an extent, both extensively and intensively, that many people take it for granted as a "biological fact of life," rather than searching for its probable cultural origins.

In addition to an historical analysis, one can use purely behavioral analyses of contemporary warfare to show that institutional behavior is not a direct reflection of individual behavior. As Lagerspetz pointed out in the essay quoted above, the modern warrior need not be angry or otherwise aggressive in order to be effective. In fact, a great deal of the training of the modern soldier is designed to enforce obedience without regard to emotion, whether it is fear or anger. In this respect the modern warrior is not unique; I have pointed out elsewhere that fear and anger do not appear to be necessary for the warfare of New Guinean warriors whose methods are similar to those which prevailed in prehistory (Adams, 1984).

There is yet another contradictory fact: it turns out that there is little gender difference in the aggressive behavior of individual humans when that behavior is carefully analyzed. The most careful analysis I know is that of Averill who required subjects to keep daily questionnaires on when, why, and how they became angry or were the target of another's anger (Averill, 1982, 1983). Contrary to popular belief, he found practically no difference between men and women. The only difference he found, that women tend to cry more often than men, is one that can be explained quite simply by strong child-rearing pressures in our culture against crying by little boys.

## IV. Male Animals Are Not Consistently More Aggressive Than Females

The fact that men are not more aggressive than women when individual behavior is carefully analyzed, as cited above, should stimulate a fresh look at the sex differences in animals. Indeed there are indications in the literature that females may be as aggressive as males even in those animal species whose behaviors are usually cited as proving the opposite. For example, a recent paper by two top experimenters in the field (DeBold & Miczek, 1984) begins the discussion as follows:

> The present experiments illustrate the complexity of the sexual dimorphism in the aggressive behavior of rats. Females are not, as is commonly stated much less aggressive than males . . . In fact, they are more aggressive than males toward unfamiliar females. More correctly, male and female rats are sexually dimorphic in terms of the stimuli which elicit aggression and not in terms of males being aggressive and females nonaggressive.

In order to analyze the question in detail, it is necessary to consider the various types of aggressive behavior in animals. Five types will be distinguished here: offense against strange conspecifics; competitive fighting; maternal aggression; defense; and predation. Offense against strange conspecifics and competitive fighting are both under the control of an offense-motivational system, and maternal behavior may well be under its control as well. Defense is controlled by another system, a distinction which is agreed upon by a wide range of investigators (Adams, 1979). Predation is not a social behavior at all, but a behavioral system used to obtain food.

Since we know the brain mechanisms of aggression best from research on the rat, I will begin this discussion with a review of the hormonal factors in the control of rat aggressive behavior (Adams, 1983b).

In the rat there is a special androgen effect which enhances male aggression (offense) against other unfamiliar male rats. I have proposed that the effect is due to a sensory analyzer which is tuned to androgen-dependent pheromones and which facilitates an offense-motivational mechanism. This is responsible for the tendency of certain dominant males to establish and defend territories.

In many other mammals there appears to be a similar brain mechanism that enhances intermale fighting. It may be associated with male territoriality in some species and with intermale displays and fighting in the presence of females during the breeding season in other species. This fighting can be quite spectacular in species with sexual dimorphism in which the males have developed special tusks or antlers which are used in the fighting. It is this phenomenon, well publicized by mass media, which makes many people think that animal aggression is primarily by males.

There are many mammalian species which contradict the popular image because females are as territorial (and in some cases more so) as males against unfamiliar members of their species. I have reviewed this among muroid rodents and found that it is the case in the following genera and species: *Rattus rattus; Mesocricetus; Sigmodon; Notomys alexis; Otomys;* and *Microtus*. Also, under wild conditions, laboratory species such as rats and mice are more aggressive in general against unfamiliar intruders, and females in particular are more aggressive than in the laboratory. As a result, laboratory studies systematically underestimate female aggression. I have suggested that the decreased offense of laboratory animals may be due to a tendency for colony odors of laboratory animals to be more homogeneous, thus reducing the activation of the sensory analyzer for unfamiliar pheromones in the laboratory (Adams, 1980).

Pregnant and lactating females are especially aggressive in most mammalian species—a type of aggression which is obviously missing from males. In the laboratory rat, this maternal aggression is apparently due to activation of the offense-motivational system, according to recent data in our laboratory being prepared for publication.

There is no reason to think that the intermale aggression cited above is any more "important" or pervasive in mammals than is maternal aggression. In fact, one of the classic studies of wild rats found the most important determinant of a male's territoriality was the extent to which the male's mother had shown maternal aggression and protected her territory against the intrusion of other rats (Calhoun, 1962). A similar situation seems to hold in primates where the phenomenon has been studied; among Japanese macaques, dominant males are the sons of dominant females (Eaton, 1976).

Competitive fighting, which consists of fighting over food under conditions of starvation, is an important type of aggression which may be more pronounced in females than in males. It is apparently a special case of offense. Although the earliest study we published showed no sex differences, more recent data from our laboratory indicates that females have higher levels of competitive fighting than males in the laboratory rat. Our preliminary data indicate that this is due to a specific effect of estrogen on the offense-motivational mechanism. In any case, there is certainly no reason to say that males are more aggressive than females under these conditions.

As a general rule there is no sex difference in predation in those species in which this nonsocial form of aggression is found. This is the case not only in carnivores, but in other mammals. There is, for example, no sex difference in the mouse-killing behavior of rats.

Defense, as opposed to offense, is a type of aggression used against predators and other threatening species as well as against threatening animals of the same species. As a rule there is no sex difference in defense among most mammalian species. This is especially true for the biting defensive attack. Some might claim an exception in the greater tendency for male rats to show boxing in response to footshock, but I believe that this reflects the size differential of males and females, and is easily controlled by testing males and females in differing cages of a size proportional to body size.

In sum, we may conclude that female mammals are as aggressive as males, unless one narrows the focus to only one particular type of aggression or only one type of laboratory condition. In the broad view, it turns out that certain types of aggression are more pronounced in males, other types more pronounced or exclusive to females, and other types common to both sexes. In any case there is no support here for the myth that humans have inherited a general mammalian tendency for males to be more aggressive than females.

## V. The Complex Relation of Human Aggression to Animal Aggression

Since the first and third assumptions are contradicted, the second assumption is no longer so critical for our examination of the myth that male monopolization of warfare is biologically determined. That is, since male animals are not generally more aggressive than females, and since human institutional behavior is not necessarily a reflection of individual behavior, it does not seem so important if human individual aggression is homologous to that of other animals. However, the question deserves to be addressed.

One must begin with a careful distinction between institutional behavior and individual behavior. We have already seen that institutional behavior includes male monopolization of war and war-related activities, while individual behavior, outside of an institutional context, does not show such a gender difference. In general we may say that the institutionalized behavior of humans has no homologue in animals. By this I mean not only war, but also the complex hierarchical structures, as well as the informal, largely nonverbal systems of communication which, as mentioned earlier, have been described by Henley and many others.

Individual human behavior, on the other hand, may be compared to that of other animals. To make such comparisons, one may extend the type of analysis that I have done on the homologies between the motivational systems of the laboratory rat and the macaque monkey (Adams, 1981); I found a number of motivational systems appeared to be homologous in the two species. By extension, they may be present in humans as well. Two of them involve what is commonly called aggression: offense and defense. It seems likely that offense may be represented in humans by what is commonly called "anger" and "annoyance," while defense may be represented by fear and fear-driven attack.

Basing the analysis on the data of Averill (1982, 1983), I have suggested that most human anger is the expression of an offense-motivational system homologous to that found in the rat and monkey (Adams, 1986). Although the inner part of the system, the offense-motivational mechanism, has remained similar, the outer parts have been transformed in humans. On the sensory side, the analysis of motivation stimuli is now tuned to the actions of the other person rather than to their attributes. In particular, an analysis is made as to whether these actions are "just" or "fair." This obviates the importance of hormonal effects which are prevalent in other animal species and which affect the analysis of the attributes of the opponent, in particular the attribute of androgen- or estrogen-dependent pheromones. On the motor side, motor patterning mechanisms in humans are dominated by verbal behavior rather than action patterns that include physical assault.

Ironically, the evidence indicates that anger against injustice, which I have suggested is a human homologue of animal offense, is a critical component to the consciousness development of peace activists (Adams, 1986). Since anger against injustice, as shown in the data of Averill (1982, 1983), is as pronounced in women as in men, there is no reason to suggest that it underlies the gender difference in human warfare and its related social institutions.

## VI. Conclusion

In conclusion, I think we can categorically reject the myth that gender differences in human warfare reflect a biological basis. Two of the three logical assumptions necessary to support the myth are not supported by the evidence. Male animals are not generally more aggressive than females, and human institutional behavior is not a direct reflection of human individual behavior.

Unfortunately, the myth persists and has political effects. The most systematic study indicates that about half of the college students around the world believe the myth, and our evidence indicates that people who believe the myth are less likely to work for peace (Eckhardt, 1972; Adams & Bosch, 1987).

If the evidence does not support it, what then is the origin of this myth? I submit, as a working hypothesis, that the myth is a projection of our human institutional situation onto our models of animal behavior. To quote a favorite animal behavior study, "Most studies of physiology and behavior, in which the wild Norway rat or its various domesticated breeds have been used as subjects . . . have been based upon hypotheses primarily formulated on the basis of clinical studies on man" (Calhoun, 1962). Perhaps there has been some improvement, but these words seem as valid today as when they were written thirty years ago. Most investigators still establish situations in which males are the subjects and other males are their targets, intruders, or cage-mates. Experiments which use pregnant or lactating females, competitive fighting, or female subjects are becoming more frequent, but are still the exception rather than the rule.

It is my hope that the bias toward use of male subjects is beginning to change. At the 1984 meetings of the International Society for Research on Aggression, hosted by Lagerspetz and her colleagues, almost half of the papers on animal aggression used female subjects. It is important that the textbooks change as well. Finally, we can look forward to the day when the myth that male animals are more aggressive than females can no longer be used by those who would argue that war is the product of biology rather than culture.

## References

Adams, D. B. (1979). Brain mechanisms for offense, defense, and submission. *The Behavioral and Brain Sciences, 2*, 200–241.

Adams, D. B. (1980). Motivational systems of agonistic behavior in muroid rodents: a comparative review and neural model. *Aggressive Behavior, 7*, 5–18.

Adams, D. B. (1981). Motivational systems of social behavior in male rats and stumptail macaques: Are they homologous? *Aggressive Behavior, 7*, 5–18.

Adams, D. B. (1983a). Why there are so few women warriors. *Behavior Science Research, 18*, 196–212.

Adams, D. B. (1983b). Hormone-brain interactions and their influence on agonistic behavior. *In* B. B. Svare (Ed.), *Hormones and Aggressive Behavior*. New York: Plenum.

Adams, D. B. (1984). There is no instinct for war. *Psychological Journal (Moscow), 5*, 140–144.

Adams, D. B. (1986). The role of anger in the consciousness development of peace activists: Where physiology and history intersect. *International Journal of Psychophysiology, 4*, 157–164.

Adams, D. B. (1989). The Seville Statement on Violence: A progress report. *Journal of Peace Research, 26*, 113–121.

Adams, D. B., & Bosch, S. (1987). The myth that war is intrinsic to human nature discourages action for peace by young people. *In* J. M. Ramirez, R. Hinde, and J. Groebel, (Eds.), *Essays in Violence*. Seville, Spain: University of Seville.

Averill, J. R. (1982). *Anger and Aggression: An essay on emotion*. New York: Springer-Verlag.

Averill, J. R. (1983). Studies on anger and aggression: Implications for theories of emotion. *American Psychologist, 38*, 1145–1160.

Calhoun, J. B. (1962). *The Ecology and Sociology of the Norway Rat*. Public Health Service Publication 1008.

DeBold, J. F., & Miczek, K. A. (1984). Aggression persists after ovariectomy in female rats. *Hormones and Behavior, 18*, 177–190.

Eaton, G. G. (1976). The social order of Japanese macaques. *Scientific American, 235*, 96–106.

Eckhardt, W. (1972). Crosscultural theories of war and aggression. *International Journal of Group Tensions, 2*, 36–50.

Groebel, J., & Hinde, R. A. (1989). *Aggression and war: Their biological and social bases*. Cambridge: Cambridge University Press.

Henley, N. M. (1977). *Body politics: Power, sex, and nonverbal communication*. Englewood Cliffs, New Jersey: Prentice-Hall.

Lagerspetz, K. (1985). Are wars caused by aggression. *In* F. L. Denmark (Ed.), *Social/Ecological Psychology and the Psychology of Women*. Elsevier (North-Holland).

Murdock, G. (1937). Comparative data on the division of labor by sex. *Social Forces, 15*, 551–553.

Somit, A. (1990). Review essay: Humans, chimps, and Bonobos: The biological bases of aggression, war, and peacemaking. *Journal of Conflict Resolution, 34*, 553–582.

3

# *The Aggressive Female Rodent: Redressing a "Scientific" Bias*

Paul F. Brain, Marc Haug, and Stefano Parmigiani

I. INTRODUCTION
II. SPECIES
A. Mouse (*Mus domesticus*)
B. Rat (*Rattus norvegicus*)
C. Golden Hamster (*Mesocricetus auratus*)
D. Mongolian Gerbil (*Meriones unguiculatus*)
E. European Rabbit (*Oryctolagus cuniculus*)
III. CONCLUDING COMMENTS
REFERENCES

## I. Introduction

This paper takes as its starting point the diverse work of Kirsti Lagerspetz, in researching both the psychogenetics of mouse aggression and differences in aggression in the human species. When Lagerspetz, Björkqvist, and Peltonen (1988) studied Finnish school children, they found girls tended to make greater use of indirect forms of aggression and peaceful means of problem solving whereas males tended to resort to direct physical aggression. This suggests that viewing females as nonaggressive is a gross simplification. Could we then combine a re-evaluation of gender differences in aggression with Lagerspetz's initial animals, rodents?

In 1983, Brain, Haug, and vom Saal reviewed the evidence that, even within "lowly" rodents, the situation was biased with a majority of aggression studies being exclusively carried out on males and many examples of female aggression being largely ignored. This view, at that time, seemed very contentious, problems with publishers were rife, and the review was not published until 1991. Between 1983 and the present, many individuals (e.g., Brain, 1989; Svare, 1989; Parmigiani, 1989; vom Saal, 1989; Haug & Brain, 1989) studied aggression in female mice, while other authorities extended our knowledge of aggression in female rats, gerbils, rabbits, and other mammals.

Other workers also recognized the biased nature of the presumed relationship between sex and aggression. For example Hrdy and Williams (1983), discussing the "myth of the passive female" in an account largely based on primates, convincingly challenged the view that once one recognizes that the male's best reproductive strategy is to fertilize as many females as possible, one adequately explains the reproductive strategy of the species. Such a narrow view ignores the roles of female choice, female elicitation of male support and protection, mothering styles and skills, competition with other females, and cooperation between females. In the same volume, Wasser and Waterhouse (1983) attacked the obsession with the male dominance syndrome (the view that the male's large size and superior fighting ability enables it to dominate females) as ignoring the fact that males and females coevolve. Both sets of authors maintained the female has been short-sightedly ignored in most sociobiological accounts.

It is intended, here, to bring the state of knowledge concerning female aggression up to date by briefly reviewing new material; a format similar to that used in Brain, Haug, and vom Saal (1991) will serve as the basis, but the data will be arranged by species.

## II. Species

### A. MOUSE (*MUS DOMESTICUS*)

#### *1. Prenatal Hormones and Interfemale Aggression*

It is well established that exposure to sex steroids in perinatal life profoundly influences subsequent fighting behavior. For example, genetic females treated postnatally with either testosterone or estradiol have a greater propensity for showing "male" type aggressiveness in adulthood after steroid application. Of even greater interest is the finding that intrauterine location has an important impact on the female aggressiveness. Vom Saal (1991) has recently reviewed this area confirming that 0M females (developing between two "sisters") show a reproductive advantage when the population density is low, essentially being rapidly breeding, rather nonaggressive individuals. 2M females (developing between two "brothers") are more aggressive than 0M counterparts and may be at a reproductive advantage when population density is higher. 0M females are exposed to more estradiol and less testosterone (from their neighbors and the placenta) than their 2M counterparts. Vom Saal essentially regards the intrauterine phenomenon as a device for throwing up different behavioral phenotypes which thrive under different portions of the population density cycle (see Van Oortmerssen & Busser, 1989). Brain and Parmigiani (1990) also emphasize that intrauterine location influences "aggression" (and territoriality?) in female mice. Yousif *et al.* (1989) record that intrauterine location modifies infanticide by primiparous females, with 2M females showing the highest level of this form of attack.

### 2. *Spontaneous Interfemale Aggression*

Female mice of some inbred strains and from some wild-trapped selected lines show high incidences of interfemale aggression. This propensity covaries with maternal but not male aggression or cricket killing (Ebert & Green, 1984). Scott, Bradt, and Collins (1986) showed that the nonreproductive female mice of a strain selected for high laterality (the Collins HI strain) showed greater attack on a C57BL/6J female intruder than counterparts selected for low laterality (the Collins LO strain), suggesting a relationship between laterality and this form of attack.

Yasukawa *et al.* (1985) suggested that interfemale aggression has a powerful impact on population dynamics in wild-strain mice. Populations consisting of all females plus one male stopped growing at the same densities as colonies with a normal sex ratio. As the former populations approached their maximal size, females began to show wounding patterns and produce social hierarchies. Males in such populations were often badly wounded (including losing their tail!). Females formed social hierarchies only after reproduction and population growth, seeming to compete with each other for the establishment of territories. Chovick *et al.* (1987) examined these phenomena in further detail, noting that certain females patrolled and guarded territories, fighting and chasing intruders of either sex. However, nonaggressive females seemed to be more successful as breeders. Brain and Parmigiani (1990) have also suggested that female territorial aggression has an important role in population dynamics.

### 3. *Aggression Associated with Nonreceptivity*

Brain, Haug, and vom Saal (1991) reviewed the evidence of female mice showing increased aggression at pro- and metestrus but reduced levels of such behavior at estrus and diestrus. It has been suggested that reduced aggressiveness at estrus facilitates mating and that the probability of successful mating is enhanced by dispersing female rivals in proestrus. There are seemingly no new studies on this.

### 4. *Aggression Associated with Pregnancy*

Brain, Haug, and vom Saal (1991) reviewed a substantial body of evidence suggesting that pregnant mice attack both male intruders and juvenile conspecifics. Buhot-Averseng (1983) confirmed that cohabitation with a pregnant cage-mate stimulates attack by both pregnant and nonpregnant (but mated) female residents on male intruders.

### *5. Aggression Associated with the Postpartum Period*

So-called "maternal aggression" is a reliable form of defensive attack shown by female mice. Recent studies have shown that this form of attack covaries across different lines and strains with the levels of intersexual aggression and infanticide in males, suggesting both forms of attack are controlled by the same autosomal genes (Brain & Parmigiani, 1990). Haney, DeBold, and Miczek (1989) found lactating CFW mice attacked male intruders more quickly and more frequently than female intruders (cf. rats) and, although the behavior declined shortly after parturition, it was still evident in the third week of lactation. In contrast, Parmigiani (1986) and Parmigiani *et al.* (1988a) found that lactating mice attacked both male and female intruders but with different patterns of attack (attack on the former involved more biting of vulnerable regions and seemed accompanied by greater "fear"). Unfamiliar pairs of lactating females fight but they direct few bites to their opponent's vulnerable areas. Drugs also differentiate attacks on males and females by lactating residents as both the opiate antagonist naloxone (Parmigiani *et al.* 1988b) and the antihostility drug Fluprazine (Duphar bv) (Parmigiani *et al.* 1989a) inhibit attack on the latter type of intruder to a greater extent. These findings suggest attack on male intruders is defensive and on females is a form of competition. In contrast, Racine and Flannelly (1986) found that Fluprazine reduced attack by lactating female Swiss Webster mice on anosmic male intruders, and speculated that maternal aggression was an offensive form of attack rather than a mixture of offense and defense. They did not, however, use female intruders.

Pairs of lactating females show most attack behaviors shortly after parturition and the encounters generally lead to formation of a dominance/subordination polarity and creation of a communal nest (Parmigiani, 1986). The dominant lactating female generally determines where the communal nest is located, retrieving pups into it. Maestripieri and Rossi-Arnaud (1991) contrasted maternal aggression in sister and nonsister pairs of Swiss mice with communal nests. They produced no evidence that kinship influenced attack on intruder males but the cumulative litter size positively influenced the combined aggression scores of the pair. Litter size thus appears to be used by paired females as a major indicator of parental investment allocation. Paul (1986) found that lactating females did not show differential attack on males likely (strangers) or unlikely (sires) to attack their pups. One should note, however, that periods of separation in excess of 12 hours, as used in Paul's study, abolish familiarity in mice. Paul and Parmigiani, Palanza, and Brain (1989) suggest maternal aggression is a counterstrategy to male infanticide. As such behavior delays rather than thwarts the killing of pups by determined males, Parmigiani *et al.* (1988b) speculate that the behavior is a form of female sexual selection precluding breeding by males of poor fighting ability.

#### 6. *Aggression Directed to Lactating Females*

This is dealt with in Haug and Brain (1989), who basically showed that odor cues emanating from strange lactating females stimulate attack by isolated or grouped females or castrated males. Androgens and estrogens *inhibit* such attack in castrated males.

#### 7. *Other Forms of Attack in Females*

Brain, Haug, and vom Saal (1991) reviewed other situations of dubious "aggression" where males and females seem to have varied or similar potentials. These include pup-killing behavior (more likely in males than in females), predatory aggression (similar in both sexes), and tube-restraint induced attack on a metal target (generally equally seen in males and females).

### B. RAT (*RATTUS NORVEGICUS*)

#### 1. *Prenatal Hormones and Interfemale Aggression*

Although very few studies have been conducted on the impact of intrauterine location on this species (cf. the mouse), they demonstrate that location influences the degree of exposure of females to male sex hormones (Brain, Haug, & vom Saal, 1991).

Takahashi and Lore (1983) recorded that play fighting was less evident in juvenile female Long-Evans rats than in males. Piloerection was less frequent in social encounters involving females, and animals of this sex were less likely to retreat (when offered an opportunity to escape) from play activity if the partner was another female.

#### 2. *Spontaneous Female Aggression*

Blanchard *et al.* (1984) identified alpha females in small, mixed-sex (3 males and 3 females) groups of Wistar rats, which directed a majority of attacks to male intruders when the colony males were absent. In intact colonies, however, most aggression is directed at like-sex opponents. Female attack appeared defensive with many male intruders retaliating after attack. They suggest that cost-benefit considerations dictate that the female rat's optimal strategy is to always attack strange females but to only attack strange males when their own male is absent and when actually pregnant or lactating (see later). Lore, Nikoletseas, and Takahashi (1984) found females in all-female colonies attack male intruders but the presence of males in mixed-sex colonies inhibits such behavior.

Scholtens, van Haaren, and van de Poll (1988) and Swanson (1990) found that female rats (unlike males) do not become relatively "permanently" submissive after losing an aggressive encounter. When given a choice, female losers prefer a naive opponent to an aggressive winning opponent. This sexual dimorphism does not appear dependent upon the presence of testosterone during the period of postnatal sexual differentiation but is dependent on testosterone in the mature organism.

#### *3. Aggression Associated with Pregnancy*

Mayer *et al.* (1987) found that aggressiveness by female Sprague-Dawley rats toward unfamiliar males was increased in the later stages of gestation. Females were not, however, aggressive shortly before parturition.

#### *4. Aggression Associated with the Postpartum Period*

Lots of new evidence is accumulating about aggressive behavior shown by lactating rats. Lore, Nikoletseas, and Takahashi (1984) commented that such females were very aggressive and stimulated attack by colony-dominant males on male intruders; Mayer *et al.* (1987) found maternal aggression was highest in Sprague-Dawley rats on the first nine days of lactation but that such behavior sharply declined 14–24 days after parturition; Flannelly, Flannelly, and Lore (1986) essentially confirmed this finding, showing also that the shortest latencies to attack male intruders and the greatest number of bites delivered were seen near the day of parturition. These authors found, however, a second peak of aggression nine days after parturition, and speculated that this form of attack (as in the mouse) is a counter to the intruding male's infanticidal tendencies. As in mice, attacked males often retaliated after initial defense. Haney, DeBold, and Miczek (1989) found that lactating Long-Evans rats direct more attack to female than male intruders. As in the Sprague-Dawleys, the frequency of attack and threat declined with each passing week of lactation.

Mos, Olivier, and van Oorsocht (1990) pointed out that drugs (e.g., alcohol, *d*-amphetamine, haloperidol, naloxone, scopolamine, mianserine, imipramine, flesinoxan, methysergide, odansetron, and MDL 72222) produce remarkably similar actions on maternal attack by female rats and on intermale aggression. They suggest the neural substrates underlying these forms of aggressive behavior are similar.

### C. GOLDEN HAMSTER (*MESOCRICETUS AURATUS*)

As noted in Brain, Haug, and vom Saal (1991), the female golden hamster is notorious for her increased aggressiveness and relatively greater size than the male. It seems likely that female hamsters are intensely territorial because of a sparsely supplied environment and only tolerate males when they are sexually receptive.

Giordano *et al.* (1986) found aggressiveness toward cycling female intruders was low in early pregnancy, increased mid-gestation, and then declined to baseline. Animals tested on the day of parturition were more aggressive than subjects tested 24 hours prepartum. The characteristically high level of postpartum aggression was decreased when pups were removed 6–8 hours earlier. There was a nonsignificant tendency for cycling hamsters to show most attack on diestrus days 1 and 2 and lower levels of such behavior during proestrus and estrus.

Potegal (1984) studied the satiation shown by aggressive female hamsters if given the opportunity to attack a series of target hamsters, producing evidence of an habituation-like process. Potegal and Popken (1985) found retired female breeders show a "priming" response following exposure to an anesthetized female, which returns to baseline over 24 hours. They suggest the escalation of aggression observed in field encounters may be due to one or both hamsters engaging in relatively persistent motivational mechanisms rather than it being a "trial and error" appraisal of relative strengths.

### D. MONGOLIAN GERBIL (*MERIONES UNGUICULATUS*)

Brain, Haug, and vom Saal (1991) noted that female gerbils can and do show aggressive behavior. Le Guelte *et al.* (1987), indeed, found that adult females develop agonistic acts against short-term separated offspring earlier than do males, and attack and threaten juveniles but show almost no agonistic response to unrelated adults. This behavior could be part of a spacing mechanism.

### E. EUROPEAN RABBIT (*ORYCTOLAGUS CUNICULUS*)

This species has recently received more female-directed attention. Albonetti, Dessi-Fulgheri, and Farabollini (1990) found aggression was much more evident in unfamiliar females in groups of four in the initial stages of grouping, declining with the development of social structure. The behavior seemed clearly concerned with the establishment of social dominance, as submissive behavior became a feature of subordinates. Albonetti, Dessi-Fulgheri, and Farabollini (1991) confirmed these results and noted high-ranking females were more active and interactive than low-ranking counterparts.

## III. Concluding Comments

The data accumulated since the last review on this topic has confirmed that females of many rodent and lagomorph species are perfectly capable of showing threat and attack behavior under a diverse range of circumstances. The behaviors are now being studied in some detail and it appears certain that females have their own agendas, with attack and threatening serving valuable functions. Although females develop such behaviors under circumstances rather different to males, there is nothing to support the stereotypes of the vigorous aggressive male rodent and the passive, reproducing female. There are indications, in some species, that female agonistic behavior has a much more impressive effect on social structure than that of the male organism.

## References

Albonetti, M. E., Dessi-Fulgheri, F., & Farabollini, F. (1990). Intrafemale agonistic interactions in the domestic rabbit (*Oryctolagus cuniculus L.*). *Aggressive Behavior, 16*, 77–86.

Albonetti, M. E., Dessi-Fulgheri, F., & Farabollini, F. (1991). Organization of behavior in unfamiliar female rabbits. *Aggressive Behavior, 17*, 171–178.

Blanchard, D. C., Fukunaga-Stinson, C., Takahashi, L. K., Flannelly, K. J., & Blanchard, R. J. (1984). Dominance and aggression in social groups of male and female rats. *Behavioural Processes, 9*, 31–48.

Brain, P. F. (1989). The adaptiveness of House mouse aggression. *In* P. F. Brain, D. Mainardi, & S. Parmigiani (Eds.), *House mouse aggression*. Chur: Harwood Academic Publishers.

Brain, P. F., & Parmigiani, S. (1990). Variation in aggressiveness in house mouse populations. *Biological Journal of the Linnean Society, 41*, 257–269.

Brain, P. F., Haug, M., & vom Saal, F. S. (1991). Are female mice the docile sex? *In* M. Haug, D. Benton, P. F. Brain, J. Mos, & B. Olivier (Eds.), *The aggressive female*. Weesp: Duphar Publications.

Buhot-Averseng, M-C. (1983). A graphic representation of the effects of cohabitation upon aggression in pregnant mice. *Aggressive Behavior, 9*, 253–258.

Chovick, A., Yasukawa, N. J., Monder, H., & Christian, J. J. (1987). Female behavior in populations of mice in the presence and absence of male hierarchy. *Aggressive Behavior, 13*, 367–375.

Ebert, P. D., & Green, V. V. (1984). Predatory aggression in lines of wild mice selected for interfemale aggression. *Aggressive Behavior, 10*, 21–26.

Flannelly, K. J., Flannelly, L., & Lore, R. (1986). Post partum aggression against intruding male conspecifics in Sprague-Dawley rats. *Behavioural Processes, 13*, 279–286.

Giordano, A. L., Siegel, H. I., & Rosenblatt, J. S. (1986). Intrasexual aggression during pregnancy and the estrous cycle in Golden Hamsters (*Mesocricetus auratus*). *Aggressive Behavior, 12*, 213–222.

Haney, M., DeBold, J. F., & Miczek, K. A. (1989). Maternal aggression in mice and rats towards male and female conspecifics. *Aggressive Behavior, 15*, 443–453.

Haug, M., & Brain, P. F. (1989). Psychobiological influences of attack on lactating females: a variant on "typical" House mouse aggression. *In* P. F. Brain, D. Mainardi, & S. Parmigiani (Eds.), *House Mouse Aggression*. Chur: Harwood Academic Publishers.

Hrdy, S. B., & Williams, G. C. (1983). Behavioral biology and the double standard. *In* S. B. Hrdy & G. C. Williams (Eds.), *Social Behavior of Female Vertebrates*. New York: Academic Press.

Lagerspetz, K. M. J., Björkquist, K., & Peltonen, T. (1988). Is indirect aggression typical of females? Gender differences in aggressiveness in 11- to 12-year-old children. *Aggressive Behavior, 14*, 403–414.

Le Guelte, L., Le Berre, M., Coulon, J., & Amagat, C. (1987). Effects of the sex of the resident adult and of the sex of the opponent on interactions in Mongolian gerbils (*Meriones unguiculatus*). *Behavioural Processes, 15*, 27–36.

Lore, R., Nikoletseas, M., & Takahashi, L. (1984). Colony aggression in laboratory rats: A review and some recommendations. *Aggressive Behavior, 10*, 59–71.

Maestripieri, D., & Rossi-Arnaud, C. (1991). Kinship does not affect litter defence in pairs of communally nesting female House mice. *Aggressive Behavior, 17*, 223–228.

Mayer, A. D., Riesbick, S., Siegel, H. I., & Rosenblatt, J. S. (1987). Maternal aggression in rats: Changes over pregnancy and lactation in a Sprague-Dawley strain. *Aggressive Behavior, 13*, 29–43.

Mos, J., Olivier, B., & van Oorsocht, R. (1990). Behavioral and neuropharmacological aspects of maternal aggression in rodents. *Aggressive Behavior, 16*, 145–163.

Parmigiani, S. (1986). Rank order in pairs of communally nursing female mice (*Mus musculus domesticus*) and maternal aggression towards conspecific intruders of differing sex. *Aggressive Behavior, 12*, 377–386.

Parmigiani, S. (1989). Maternal aggression and infanticide in the House mouse: consequences on the social dynamics. *In* P. F. Brain, D. Mainardi, & S. Parmigiani (Eds.), *House Mouse Aggression*. Chur: Harwood Academic Publishers.

Parmigiani, S., Brain, P. F., Mainardi, D., & Brunoni, V. (1988a). Different patterns of biting attack employed by lactating female mice (*Mus domesticus*) in encounters with male and female conspecific intruders. *Journal of Comparative Psychology, 102*, 287–293.

Parmigiani, S., Rodgers, R. J., Palanza, P., & Mainardi, M. (1988b). Naloxone differentially alters parental aggression by female mice towards conspecific intruders of differing sex. *Aggressive Behavior, 14*, 213–224.

Parmigiani, S., Palanza, P., & Brain, P. F. (1989). Intraspecific maternal aggression in the house mouse (*Mus domesticus*): a counterstrategy to infanticide by male? *Ethology, Ecology and Evolution, 1*, 341–352.

Paul, L. (1986). Infanticide and maternal aggression: synchrony of male and female reproductive strategies in mice. *Aggressive Behavior, 12*, 1–11.

Potegal, M. (1984). The persistence of attack satiation in female Golden hamsters. *Aggressive Behavior, 10*, 303–307.

Potegal, M., & Popken, J. (1985). The time course of attack priming effects in female golden hamsters. *Behavioural Processes, 11*, 199–208.

Racine, M. A., & Flannelly, K. J. (1986). The offensive nature of maternal aggression in mice: Effects of Fluprazine hydrochloride. *Aggressive Behavior, 12*, 417–424.

Scholtens, J., van Haaren, F., & van de Poll, N. E. (1988). Effects of losing and testosterone upon subsequent behavior in male and female S3 (Tryon Maze Dull) rats. *Aggressive Behavior, 14*, 371–387.

Scott, J. P., Bradt, D., & Collins, R. L. (1986). Fighting in female mice in lines selected for laterality. *Aggressive Behavior, 12*, 41–44.

Swanson, H. H. (1990). Sex differences in behavioral consequences of defeat in the rat are not organized by testosterone during early development. *Aggressive Behavior, 16*, 341–344.

Svare, B. (1989). Recent advances in the study of female aggressive behaviour in mice. *In* P. F. Brain, D. Mainardi, & S. Parmigiani (Eds.) *House Mouse Aggression*. Chur: Harwood Academic Publishers.

Takahashi, L. K., & Lore, R. K. (1983). Play fighting and the development of agonistic behavior in male and female rats. *Aggressive Behavior, 9*, 217–227.

Van Oortmerssen, G. A., & Busser, J. (1989). Studies in wild house mice. 3. Disruptive selection of aggression as a possible force in evolution. *In* P. F. Brain, D. Mainardi, & S. Parmigiani (Eds.), *House Mouse Aggression*. Chur: Harwood Academic Publishers.

vom Saal, F. S. (1989). Perinatal testosterone exposure has opposite effects on adult intermale aggression and infanticide in mice. *In* P. F. Brain, D. Mainardi, & S. Parmigiani (Eds.), *House Mouse Aggression*. Chur: Harwood Academic Publishers.

vom Saal, F. S. (1991). Prenatal gonadal influence on mouse sociosexual behaviours. *In* M. Haug, P. F. Brain, & C. Aron (Eds.), *Heterotypical Behavior in Man and Animals*. London: Chapman and Hall.

Wasser, S. K., & Waterhouse, M. L. (1983). The establishment and maintenance of sex biases. *In* S. B. Hrdy and G. C. Williams (Eds.), *Social Behavior of Female Vertebrates*. New York: Academic Press.

Yasukawa, N. J., Mander, H., Leff, F. R., & Christian, J. J. (1985). Role of female behavior in controlling population growth in mice. *Aggressive Behavior, 11*, 49–64.

Yousif, Y. Y., Brain, P. F., Parmigiani, S., & Mainardi, M. (1989). Effects of genotype and intrauterine location on the propensity for infanticide by primiparous female mice. *Ethology, Ecology and Evolution, 1*, 283–290.

4

# *Hormones and Human Aggression*

David Benton

I. INTRODUCTION
II. ORGANIZING INFLUENCES OF TESTOSTERONE
III. PUBERTY
IV. TESTOSTERONE AND ADULT AGGRESSION
A. Questionnaire Measures
B. Aggressive Behavior
C. Changing Status
V. DISCUSSION
VI. CONCLUSION
REFERENCES

## I. Introduction

It has been repeatedly reported that human males are physically more aggressive than human females (Maccoby & Jacklin, 1974, 1980). A similar statement could be made for many mammalian species; males display more physical aggression than females and male aggression declines following castration. For example, this is true for rats, mice (Brain, 1977), and nonhuman primates (Bernstein, Gordon, & Rose, 1983). Given that in nonhuman species the role of testosterone in male aggression is a robust phenomenon (Brain, 1977), the possible role of hormones in the generation of gender differences in humans must be considered. Although few doubt the importance of psychosocial factors in determining gender differences in human behavior, some suggest that hormonal factors play a part (Donovan, 1985). The present chapter explores the evidence that the relative aggressiveness of the human male, and the relative lack of aggression of the human female, reflects, in part at least, the role of testosterone.

The distinction between *organizational* and *activational* influences of testosterone is frequently made. The exposure to testosterone during critical periods of development, either before or shortly after birth, results in anatomical changes.

These changes may be overt, for example, the development of male genitalia, or less obviously changes in the structure of the brain (Gorski *et al.*, 1980). A hormonally induced change in body structure is described as an organizational influence. The surge of testosterone in the human male at puberty is similarly associated with restructuring of the body. In contrast, an activational influence of a hormone is reversible; for example, testosterone modulates sexual and aggressive interactions in the adult male mouse (Brain, 1977). In practice the modulation of aggressive responses by testosterone usually requires exposure to the hormone both during maturation (organizational) and in adulthood (activational). The perinatal organizational influence of testosterone sensitizes the brain so that it responds to testosterone in the adult (Brain, 1977).

## II. Organizing Influences of Testosterone

Although obvious ethical considerations preclude the hormonal manipulation of the developing human fetus, a number of clinical syndromes give us relevant information. The congenital adrenogenital syndrome (AGS) results from a recessive gene that induces the adrenal gland to produce abnormally high levels of androgens (hormones that develop male characteristics, for example, testosterone) rather than cortisone. Progestin-induced hermaphroditism resulted from the prescription of progestins to prevent miscarriage. Another unfortunate side effect of this no longer offered treatment is masculinization. In both these conditions the female fetus is exposed to androgens with the consequent masculinization of the genitalia; this can result in anything from a mildly enlarged clitoris to a normal-appearing penis and empty scrotum. Treatment involves the surgical removal of the male genitalia; in addition, those suffering with AGS will have cortisol administered for the rest of their life. The question is whether the brain has been restructured with behavioral consequences.

Money and Ehrhardt (1968) studied 15 girls with AGS who were diagnosed and treated early in life and compared them with matched controls. Another set of 17 AGS girls were studied in Buffalo and compared with unaffected siblings (Ehrhardt & Baker, 1974). Fifty-nine percent of the Buffalo sample were identified as "tomboys" throughout their childhood, something true of none of the unaffected siblings. Those suffering with AGS liked active, outdoor sports and wore boys' clothes. So-called boys' toys rather than dolls were preferred and they displayed little interest in infants, something not typical of the controls; motherhood and marriage were less frequently seen as important whereas a career was often stressed.

Sexual identity was not, however, a particular problem, none wanted to change gender. When followed up in later life the AGS patients did not display higher levels of aggression and were not more likely to be dominant or leaders

(Money & Schwartz, 1976). These long-term programs have concluded that although fetal hormones may well influence subsequent psychosexual differentiation, such influences are limited, and do not induce anything approaching a complete psychosocial reversal of the genetic female.

Reinisch (1981) followed up children who had been exposed to synthetic progestogens (which are androgenic) during the first third of gestation. When hypothetical conflict situations were discussed, the members of the progesten-exposed group were significantly more likely to mention physical aggression as a response than the controls. Ehrhardt *et al.*, (1989) traced 30 women prenatally exposed to synthetic progestogens. Using interviews and questionnaires to collect information, they could find no evidence of an increased verbal or physical aggression in childhood or in the frequency of temper outbursts during either childhood or adolescence.

Another approach to the role of early circulating hormones on later behavior is the measurement of gonadal hormones in the blood of the umbilical cord. Jacklin, Maccoby, and Doering (1983) found that the level of testosterone in the cord blood correlated negatively with timidity in boys, but not girls, at six to eighteen months; however, the relationship was higher with progesterone levels. It is unclear whether the hormones measured in the umbilical cord originated from the mother or child. The significance of this finding is unclear as birth, unlike the months following birth, is a time when the two sexes do not differ in androgen levels.

The possibility must be considered that the behavior of AGS patients are mediated by mechanisms other than hormones. For those wanting to find them there are clear parallels between the perinatal androgenization studies in rodents, humans, and nonhuman primates. In all these species the fetal differentiation of genitalia is androgen dependent. The removal of androgens from genetic males at critical periods of development produces a female structure; the addition of androgens to genetic females masculinizes the genitalia. Parallels can also be seen in the resulting behavior. Female rhesus monkeys treated with androgens in the perinatal period display the rough and tumble play more typical of the male; the human female subjected to prenatal androgens is tomboyish.

Although simple analogies can be drawn, the complexities that characterize humans should not be ignored. It is difficult to exclude the possibility that nonhormonal factors influence the behaior of AGS girls. Will parents treat a daughter born with a rudimentary penis in a similar manner to somebody not so afflicted? May not a masculine appearance encourage the expectation that the daughter will become a tomboy? Can a child's self-image fail to be altered by her abnormal anatomy? Ehrhardt and Baker (1974) examined 17 AGS females, of whom six received surgery in the first year of life, seven between one and three years of age, and four later in life. The possibility of significant psychological reactions to the anatomy must be considered, particularly in those treated in later life.

Parental attitudes are difficult to discount in this area, particularly as interview data are frequently reported. Rarely has the behavior of AGS patients been recorded, rather the views of the child and the parent are examined. The data are essentially that AGS patients are perceived as more tomboyish. The question remains as to the origin of the perception of these children. Are they displaying altered behavior, or is it the parents' perception that is altered? If the behavior is different, is this a reflection of the style of upbringing or hormonally mediated changes in the brain?

Does the consistency of cross-species data demand that a simple biological explanation be accepted? The human data, reflecting as it does genetic and other accidents rather than well-designed experimentation, make it impossible to distinguish between biological and psychological explanations. The general impression that social and cultural experiences greatly influence human behavior makes it unlikely that a hormonal influence is the only mechanism at work. The possibility that subtle interactions between hormonal, psychological, and social factors determine behavior cannot be discounted, but many would see psychosocial mechanisms as overwhelmingly important.

## III. Puberty

In a wide range of species the male displays increased levels of aggression at puberty, a change in behavior that correlates with sexual maturation and the release of testosterone by the testes (Archer, 1988). Puberty is often associated with hormone-induced increases in body size and structure, some of which act as intraspecies signals important in aggressive behavior.

In contrast to animal studies there have been relatively few studies that have measured hormone levels and aggressiveness at puberty in human males. Olweus *et al.* (1980), as part of a longitudinal study of the development of aggression in boys, found substantial correlations between plasma testosterone levels and scores on an aggression inventory. The same group replicated the finding with a group of adolescent offenders (Mattsson *et al.*, 1980). Olweus (1986) noted that the items that showed the highest correlations with testosterone were those that involved a response to provocation, for example, "When a boy is nasty with me, I try to get even with him." Susman *et al.* (1987) found a positive relationship between mothers' ratings of delinquency and rebelliousness and the androgens androstenedione and dehydroepiandrosterone, the secretions of which increase rapidly at puberty.

In an early review Benson and Migeon (1975) noted the marked changes in the levels of luteinizing hormone and follicle-stimulating hormone, as well as sex steroids, at puberty in the human male, and tentatively implicated these in the development of a rebellious attitude during this time. In fact, the data concerning the behavior of boys at puberty is very limited, but the comparative literature, that describes a close correlation between the increased secretion of testosterone and aggressive behavior in many species, supports the suggestion that hormonal factors have a role in the aggressive responding of the human male. Hayes (1978) concluded that mood changes at puberty may reflect the lack of socially acceptable outlets for hormonally induced drives.

## IV. Testosterone and Adult Aggression

### A. QUESTIONNAIRE MEASURES

There have been several attempts to relate self-report ratings to circulating testosterone. After the initial report by Persky, Smith, and Basu (1971) that ratings on the Buss-Durkee Hostility Inventory significantly correlated with circulating testosterone in younger, but not older men, there were several attempts to replicate the finding. Kreuz and Rose (1972) took six plasma samples over a two-week period from prisoners chosen as representing the extremes of aggressive behavior, but found no significant relationship between self-ratings and hormonal values. Meyer-Bahlburg *et al.* (1974) failed to replicate the original finding when using a similar procedure.

Doering *et al.* (1974) took plasma samples every two days for two months. The most striking observation was the inconsistency of the relationship; in some individuals there was a positive relationship between testosterone levels and ratings of hostility, whereas some had a negative relationship, and some none at all. When individuals were compared there was a significant correlation between self-rated depression and plasma testosterone. Similarly, Monti, Brown, and Corriveau (1977), based on two blood samples a week apart, found no significant correlation between testosterone levels and hostility ratings, although there was a significant relationship with anxiety and suspicion.

Although individual studies have tended to produce findings that fail to reach statistical significance, Archer (1990) found that a meta-analysis of studies that related testosterone to the Buss-Durkee Hostility Inventory resulted in a low but positive relationship. In fact, the social environment was more highly correlated with testosterone than the hostility measure, although there was a closer association between the hormone and external assessments of aggression.

### B. AGGRESSIVE BEHAVIOR

A second approach is to compare the hormone levels of groups that have been distinguished in terms of the degree of aggression that they display. Kreuz and Rose (1972) related plasma testosterone to behavior in prison and criminal records. Although hormone levels did not relate to the level of aggression displayed in prison, those with high levels tended to have committed violent crimes during adolescence. Ehrenkrantz, Bliss, and Sheard (1974) found that aggressive and dominant prisoners had higher levels of testosterone than nonaggressive and nondominant prisoners.

Similar results have been obtained using psychiatric patients; Persky, Zuckerman, and Curtis (1978) found a positive relationship between urinary androgens and aggression as estimated by medical staff. Kendenburg, Kendenburg, and Kling (1973) also found a positive relationship between the level of testosterone and observed aggression in psychiatric patients. Rada, Laws, and Kellner (1976) reported that rapists who used physical violence had significantly higher levels of circulating testosterone than those using only threats, causing no injury other than that implied by the term rape. However, in a follow-up study, Rada *et al.* (1983) failed to find significant differences in the testosterone levels of child molesters and rapists distinguished in terms of their violence, although the rapists tended to have higher levels than other groups. Lindman, Jarvinen, and Vidjeskog (1987) classified young males into groups depending on whether they behaved aggressively when intoxicated with alcohol: those reacting aggressively when drunk had higher levels of testosterone in their saliva.

Dabbs *et al.* (1987) distinguished prisoners who did or did not have a record of violent crime and found that those with a history of violence had higher levels of saliva testosterone. Within the group without a history of violence there was a correlation between testosterone levels and the number of days that they had been punished for breaking the rules. Bain *et al.* (1987) found the testosterone levels of those charged with murder did not differ from those charged with property offences. Similarly, Bain *et al.* (1988) found that the testosterone levels of those charged with sexual assault were not different from prisoners charged with crimes unrelated to sex or violence.

Although testosterone is often described as a male hormone, androgens are also present in the blood stream of females, having been released by the adrenal cortex and the ovaries. Two studies have explored the relationship between female aggression and testosterone. Ehlers, Rickler, and Hovey (1980) distinguished young women with a history of violence from a nonviolent group who attended the same clinic; the violent group had significantly higher plasma testosterone levels. A similar study found that female prisoners convicted of unprovoked violence had higher levels of saliva testosterone (Dabbs *et al.*, 1988).

## C. CHANGING STATUS

A major concern when trying to interpret the finding that two groups differing in aggressiveness have different levels of circulating testosterone is to try to establish causality. Does the hormone modulate the behavior or does fighting and winning increase the release of hormone? Animal studies have repeatedly found that changes in the release of testosterone result from winning or losing an aggressive encounter (Leshner, 1983; Schuurman, 1980; Rose, Bernstein, & Gordon, 1975). Testosterone levels tend to be similar before an aggressive encounter yet afterwards the winners' levels are greater than those in the loser.

There is increasing evidence that, in part, human testosterone levels similarly reflect social status. An interesting pilot study was reported by Jeffcoate *et al.* (1986). Prior to a holiday the testosterone levels of four males confined on a boat were similar. After fourteen days on the the boat the women present rated the amount of dominance behavior that had been displayed by the men. Although a sample of four prevented a significant correlation, there was a positive relationship between the hormone levels and the ratings of dominance.

Mazur and Lamb (1980) found that the winning of a cash prize in a tennis competition was associated with increases in testosterone levels—something not true if the same sum was won in a lottery. The receiving of a medical degree was also found to be associated with an increase in blood testosterone. It was concluded that an increase in status, due to one's own efforts, was associated with the release of testosterone. In a similar study a university tennis team was followed throughout the season. Although there was a suggestion that the testosterone levels of the winners increased, and the losers decreased, the comparisons were nonsignificant (Booth *et al.*, 1989).

Elias (1981) monitored testosterone levels during wrestling bouts and found that both testosterone and cortisol levels increased as the bout progressed, although the level of binding globulin fell. The winners of competitions showed greater increases in hormones than losers. Salvador *et al.* (1985) found that a person's history of success in judo competitions correlated positively with changes in testosterone levels during a bout. It may be that previous competitive success influenced patterns of response when fighting, or alternatively, a greater release of testosterone while fighting is associated with physiological or psychological benefits that enhance performance.

## V. Discussion

To study the relationship between testosterone and aggression is to attempt, usually unsucessfully, to solve a series of methodological problems. Most studies have taken only one blood sample, when it is known that testosterone is released in bursts and varies throughout the day. In addition, its release is known to reflect longer rhythms. Only a small percentage of circulating testosterone is free; the majority is bound to protein, making an estimate of total plasma testosterone a gross overestimate of active hormone.

The measurement of behavior is equally associated with problems. What should you measure? Lagerspetz (1981) discussed difficulties with the concept of aggression and in particular the extrapolation from animal to human data. Although the classification of aggression is associated with many problems, she notes "an intriguing similarity in the aggressive behavior of man and other animals." Although a male rodent may display characteristic behavior that appears to be hard wired, can this be expected in the human situation? Is it reasonable to describe any human behavior as characteristically male? Cultural factors are vital in determining the form of particular aggressive acts; human behavior is not stereotyped. The display of aggression has been associated with the invention of tools such as guns, swords, and missiles; language allows the conveying of an infinite range of wishes and intentions to others; symbolic goals such as democracy, freedom, and religion may be the source of conflict; an aggressive act may be revenge taken a long time after the original event rather than an immediate reaction to provocation. The cultural, cognitive, linguistic, and experiential aspects of human nature suggest that any predominantly biological explanation of gender differences is likely to be wrong. Such considerations have lead some to conclude that no direct analogies from nonhuman to human species are justified (Scott, 1970). Others have concluded that an understanding of human aggression is a task for the social rather than the biological scientist (Tedeschi, Smith, & Brown, 1974).

The study of individual differences in aggression is made more difficult by the likelihood that aggression should not be viewed as a unitary concept. When Kreuz and Rose (1972) studied the aggressive behavior of prisoners, they found little relationship between past criminal behavior, aggressive behavior in prison, and psychological tests—experimental evidence, if this was needed, that the term aggression covers a wide range of behavior. Similar points have been made concerning animal aggression, in which it is known that different types of aggression have different anatomical and hormonal bases (Brain, 1981). These types of physiological considerations suggest that in nonhuman animals there is no single biological basis to all the behaviors we label as aggression; in particular, androgens influence some but not all such behaviors. If this is true in animals, how much more likely is it to be true when examining human gender differences? Although some have attempted to distinguish the nature of the human aggression influenced by testosterone (Olweus *et al.*, 1980; Mattsson *et al.*, 1980), most have not.

In rats, mice, monkeys, and other species the early exposure to androgens organizes the structure of both the brain and genitalia; particularly in the presence of the activating effect of androgens this predisposes toward sexual and aggressive behaviors that have been described as characteristically male. Should we therefore think of hormonal factors differentially predisposing human males and females to display aggressive behavior? Benton (1983a,b) argued that it was unwise to draw analogies between human and nonhuman animals. An argument in favor of a hormonal explanation of the human behavioral changes that follow androgenization is Lloyd Morgan's Canon of Parsimony; we should not evoke a higher level of explanation if the data can be interpreted in terms of an explanation lower in the psychological scale. Should complex cognitive explanations be avoided if biological explanations are available? The Canon of Parsimony, although often evoked, may prove to be misleading; if human behavior is by nature the product of many and varied factors, its nature is not changed by quoting an inappropriate principle.

Even in mice hormonal status interacts with previous history. Castration carried out after puberty is initially associated with a display of aggression similar to an intact animal, although it falls gradually. In contrast prepubertal castration results in a marked decline in aggression (Beeman, 1947). In mice, the experience of fighting modifies the impact of testosterone. Guhl (1964) reviewed the evidence that in hens previous experience of aggressive encounters greatly influenced the impact of testosterone. In rhesus monkeys the administration of testosterone has no effect on dominance relationships (Gordon *et al.*, 1979) and dominance does not correlate with testosterone levels (Bernstein, Gordon, & Rose, 1983). Although Lagerspetz (1964) was able to breed aggressive and nonaggressive mice, it was possible to train the nonaggressive mice to be aggressive, and the aggressive mice to be nonaggressive; a genetic predisposition is modified by experience (Lagerspetz, 1981). If biological factors are modified by previous aggressive experience in birds, rodents, and nonhuman primates, it is extremely probable that in humans the effect of testosterone is even more modified by lifetime's experience. Any behavioral differences between the human male and female are unlikely to reflect simply the level of a single hormone.

## VI. Conclusion

What then do we conclude? The animal data are very clear: in mammalian species testosterone at critical periods during development restructures the brain. A brain so restructured responds to testosterone in the adult by displaying aggressive behavior. The existence of such a consistent cross-species phenomenon suggests that we should take seriously the possibility of a human parallel. Although some studies are negative, the above review reports a substantial number of positive findings. The conclusion that testosterone has a role in the expression of human male aggression seems reasonable. The question is the nature and extent of that role. Although it is easy to point to positive findings, these have usually been achieved by examining a group displaying extremes of aggression. Even then the role of testosterone has been consistently found to be small, although statistically significant. The evidence is very limited that the display of aggression in the normal range of the population reflects the level of testosterone.

It may well be that the repeated study of highly aggressive individuals has systematically examined those with characteristics, other than testosterone levels, in common. For example, if groups of aggressive individuals tend to be young, lacking in social skills, and relatively unintelligent, you have a population that is not representative. A reexamination of the above literature gives some support for such a suggestion. It is easy to suggest that those lacking the cognitive and social skills to deal with a novel and powerful biological drive may be more likely to display aggressive behavior. Although such a suggestion would be important, should it be true, it would say nothing about the majority of the population. Although the weight of evidence supports the idea that testosterone plays a limited role in inducing aggression in small sections of the male population, there is little reason to believe it has even this limited importance in the majority.

It is easy to suggest why a biological variable such as testosterone appears to be a relatively unimportant factor in the human condition. Even in animal studies previous experience is found to modify the impact of testosterone. If this is true in birds and rodents it is certain to be more influential in humans. The general impression that human behavior is a reflection of psychosocial history leads to the expectation that the impact of a biological factor would be greatly modified by the environment. The majority of evidence indicates that in the general population differences in aggressiveness reflect the level of testosterone only to a limited extent, if at all. There is no reason to suggest that testosterone causes the behavior of males and females to differ markedly.

## References

Archer, J. (1988). *The Behavioural Biology of Aggression.* Cambridge: Cambridge University Press.

Archer, J. (1990). The influence of testosterone on human aggression. *British Journal of Psychology, 82*, 1–28.

Bain, J., Langevin, R., Dickey, R., & Ben-Aron, M. (1987). Sex hormones in murderers and assaulters. *Behavioral Science and the Law, 5*, 95–101.

Bain, J., Langevin, R., Dickey, R., Hucker, S., & Wright, P. (1988). Hormones in sexually aggressive men. I. Baseline values for eight sex hormones. II. The ACTH test. *Annals of Sex Research, 1*, 63–78.

Beeman, E. A. (1947). The relation of the interval between castration and first encounter to the aggressive behavior of mice. *Anatomical Record, 99*, 570–571.

Benson, R. M., & Migeon, C. J. (1975). Physiological and pathological puberty and human behavior. *In* B. E. Eleftheriou and R. L. Sprott (Eds.), *Hormonal Correlates of Behavior* (pp. 155–184). New York: Plenum.

Benton, D. (1983a). The extrapolation from animals to man: The example of testosterone and aggression. *In* P. F. Brain and D. Benton (Eds.), *Multidisciplinary Approaches to Aggression Research* (pp. 402–418). Amsterdam: Elsevier.

Benton, D. (1983b). Do animal studies tell us anything about the relationship between testosterone and human aggression? *In* G. C. L. Davey (Ed.), *Animal Models of Human Behavior* (pp. 281–298). Chicester: Wiley.

Bernstein, I., Gordon, T. P., & Rose, R. M. (1983). The interaction of hormones, behavior and social context in non-human primates. *In* B. B. Svare (Ed.), *Hormones and Aggressive Behavior* (pp. 535–561). New York: Plenum.

Booth, A., Shelley, G., Mazur, A., Tharp, G., & Kittok, R. (1989). Testosterone and winning and losing in human competition. *Hormones and Behavior, 23*, 556–571.

Brain, P. F. (1977). *Hormones and Aggression. Volume 1*. Montreal: Eden Press.

Brain, P. F. (1981). Differentiating types of attack and defense in rodents. *In* P. F. Brain & D. Benton (Eds.), *Multidisciplinary Approach to Aggression Research* (pp. 53–78). Amsterdam: Elsevier.

Dabbs, J. M., Frady, R. L., Carr, T. S., & Besch, N. F. (1987). Saliva testosterone and criminal violence in young adult prison inmates. *Psychosomatic Medicine, 49*, 269–275.

Dabbs, J. M., Ruback, R. B., Frady, R. L., Hopper, C. H., & Sgoutas, D. S. (1988). Saliva testosterone and criminal violence amongst women. *Personality and Individual Differences, 9*, 269–275.

Doering, C. H., Brodie, H. K. H., Kraemer, H. C., Becker, H., & Hamburg, D. A. (1974). Plasma testosterone levels and psychologic measures in men over a 2-month period. *In* R. C. Friedman, R. M. Riechart, & R. L. Vande Wiele (Eds.), *Sex Differences in Behavior* (pp. 413–431). New York: Wiley.

Donovan, B. T. (1985). *Hormones and Human Behaviour*. Cambridge: Cambridge University Press.

Ehlers, C. L., Rickler, K. C., & Hovey, J. E. (1980). A possible relationship between plasma testosterone and aggressive behavior in a female outpatient population. *In* M. Girgis & L. G. Kiloh (Eds.), *Limbic Epilepsy and the Dyscontrol Syndrome* (pp. 183–194). New York: Elsevier.

Ehrenkranz, J., Bliss, E., & Sheard, M. H. (1974). Plasma testosterone correlation with aggressive behavior and social dominance in man. *Psychosomatic Medicine, 36*, 469–475.

Ehrhardt, A. A., & Baker, S. W. (1974). Fetal androgens, human central nervous system differentiation and behavior sex differences. *In* R. C. Friedman, R. M. Richart, & R. L. Vande Wiele (Eds.), *Sex Differences in Behavior* (pp. 33–51). New York: Wiley.

Ehrhardt, A. A., Meyer-Bahlburg, H. F. L., Rosen, L. R., Feldman, J. F., Veridiano, N. P., Elkin, E. J., & McEwan, B. S. (1989). The development of gender-related behavior in females following exposure to diethylstilbestrol (DES). *Hormones and Behavior, 23*, 526–541.

Elias, M. (1981). Serum cortisol, testosterone and testosterone-binding globulin responses in competitive fighting in human males. *Aggressive Behavior, 7*, 215–224.

Gordon, T. P., Rose, R. M., Grady, C. L., & Bernstein, I. (1979). Effects of increased testosterone secretion on the behavior of adult male rhesus monkeys. *Folia Primatologica, 32*, 149–160.

Gorski, R., Harlan, R., Jacobson, C., Shryne, J., & Southam, A. (1980). Evidence for the existence of a sexually dimorphic nucleus in the preoptic area of the rat. *Journal of Comparative Neurology, 193*, 529–539.

Guhl, A. M. (1964). Psychophysiological interrelations in the social behavior of chickens. *Psychological Bulletin, 61*, 277–285.

Hayes, S. E. (1978). Strategies for psychoendocrine studies of puberty. *Psychoneuroendocrinology, 10*, 77–81.

Jacklin, C. N., Maccoby, E. E., & Doering, C. H. (1983). Neonatal sex-steroid hormones and timidity in 6–18 month old boys and girls. *Developmental Psychobiology, 16*, 163–168.

Jeffcoate, W. J., Lincoln, N. B., Selby, C., & Herbert, M. (1986). Correlation between anxiety and serum prolactin in humans. *Journal of Psychosomatic Research, 30*, 217–222.

Kendenburg, D., Kendenburg, N., & Kling, A. (1973). An ethological study in a patient group (unpublished manuscript).

Kling, A. (1975). Testosterone and aggressive behavior in man and non-human primates. *In* B. E. Eleftheriou & R. L. Sprott (Eds.), *Hormonal Correlates of Behavior* (pp. 305–323). New York: Plenum.

Kreuz, L. E., & Rose, R. M. (1972). Assessment of aggressive behavior and plasma testosterone in a young criminal population. *Psychosomatic Medicine, 34*, 321–332.

Lagerspetz, K. M. J. (1964). Studies on the aggressive behaviour of mice. *Annales de Academie Sciences Fennicae, Series B, 131/3, 1*, 1–131.

Lagerspetz, K. (1981). Combining aggression studies in intra-humans and man. *In* P. F. Brain & D. Benton (Eds.), *Multidisciplinary Approaches to Aggression Research* (pp. 390–400). Amsterdam: Elsevier.

Leshner, A. I. (1983). The hormonal responses to competition and their behavioral significance. *In* B. B. Svare (Ed.), *Hormones and Aggressive Behavior* (pp. 393–404). New York: Plenum.

Lindman, R., Jarvinen, P., & Vidjeskog, J. (1987). Verbal interactions of aggressively and nonaggressively predisposed males in a drinking situation. *Aggressive Behavior, 13*, 187–196.

Maccoby, E. E., & Jacklin, C. N. (1974). *The Psychology of Sex Differences*. Stanford, California: Stanford University Press.

Maccoby, E. E., & Jacklin, C. N. (1980). Sex differences in aggression: A rejoiner and reprise. *Child Development, 51*, 964–980.

Mattsson, A., Schalling, D., Olweus, D., Low, H., & Svensson, J. (1980). Plasma testosterone aggressive behavior and personality dimensions in young male delinquents. *Journal of the American Academy of Child Psychiatry, 19*, 476–490.

Mazur, A., & Lamb, T. A. (1980). Testosterone, status and mood in human males. *Hormones and Behavior, 14*, 236–246.

Meyer-Bahlberg, H. F. L., Boon, D. A., Sharma, M., & Edwards, J. A. (1974). Aggressiveness and testosterone measures in man. *Psychosomatic Medicine, 36*, 269–274.

Money, J., & Ehrhardt, A. A. (1968). Prenatal hormonal exposure: Possible effects on behaviour in man. *In* R. P. Michael (Ed.), *Endocrinology and Human Behaviour* (pp. 32–48). London: Oxford University Press.

Money, J., & Schwartz, M. (1976). Fetal androgens in the early treated adrenogenital syndrome of 46, XX hermaphroditism: Influence on assertive and aggressive types of behavior. *Aggressive Behavior, 2*, 19–30.

Monti, P. M., Brown, W. A., & Corriveau, D. P. (1977). Testosterone and components of aggression and sexual behavior in man. *American Journal of Psychiatry, 134*, 692–694.

Olweus, D. (1986). Aggression and hormones: Behavioral relationship with testosterone and adrenaline. *In* D. Olweus, J. Block, & M. Radke-Yarrow (Eds.), *Development of Antisocial and Prosocial Behavior: Research Theories and Issues* (pp. 51–72). New York: Academic Press.

Olweus, D., Mattsson, A., Schalling, D., & Low, H. (1980). Testosterone aggression physical and personality dimensions in normal adolescent males. *Psychosomatic Medicine, 42*, 253–269.

Persky, H., Smith, K. D., & Basa, G. K. (1971). Relation of psychologic measures of aggression and hostility to testosterone production in man. *Psychosomatic Medicine, 33*, 265–277.

Persky, H., Zuckerman, M., & Curtis, G. C. (1978). Endocrine function in emotionally disturbed and normal men. *Journal of Nervous and Mental Disease, 146*, 488–497.

Rada, R. T., Laws, D. R., & Kellner, R. (1976). Plasma testosterone levels in the rapist. *Psychosomatic Medicine, 38*, 257–268.

Rada, R. T., Laws, D. R., Kellner, R., Stivastava, L., & Peake, G. (1983). Plasma androgens in violent and nonviolent sex offenders. *Bulletin of the American Academy of Psychiatry and the Law, 11*, 149–158.

Reinisch, J. M. (1981). Prenatal exposure to synthetic progestins increases potential for aggression in humans. *Science, 211*, 1171–1173.

Rose, R. M., Bernstein, I. S., & Gordon, T. P. (1975). Consequences of social conflict on plasma testosterone levels in rhesus monkeys. *Psychosomatic Medicine, 37*, 50–62.

Salvador, A., Simon, V., Suay, F., & Llorens, L. (1985). Testosterone and cortisol responses to competitive fighting in human males: a pilot study. *Aggressive Behavior, 13*, 9–13.

Schuurman, T. (1980). Hormonal correlates of agonistic behavior in adult male rats. *Progress in Brain Research, 53*, 415–420.

Scott, J. P. (1970). Biology and human aggression. *American Journal of Orthopsychiatry, 40*, 568–576.

Susman, E. J., Inoff-Germain, G., Nottlemann, E. D., Loriaus, D. L., Cutler, G. B., & Chrousos, G. P. (1987). Hormones, emotional disposition and aggressive attributes in young adolescents. *Child Development, 58*, 114–1134.

Tedeschi, J. T., Smith, R. B., & Brown, (1974). A reinterpretation of research on aggression. *Psychological Bulletin, 81*, 540–562.

# II

# THE DEVELOPMENT OF FEMALE AGGRESSIVE PATTERNS

5

# The Development of Direct and Indirect Aggressive Strategies in Males and Females

Kaj Björkqvist, Karin Österman, and Ari Kaukiainen

I. INDIRECT AGGRESSION: CONCEPTIONS AND MISCONCEPTIONS
II. WHY HAS INDIRECT AGGRESSION NOT BEEN INVESTIGATED?
III. THE RESEARCH TOOL
IV. SEX DIFFERENCES IN AGGRESSIVE STYLES DURING ADOLESCENCE
V. A DEVELOPMENTAL THEORY OF AGGRESSIVE STRATEGIES
VI. TWO KINDS OF COVERED AGGRESSION DURING ADULTHOOD
VII. CONCLUSIONS
REFERENCES

## I. Indirect Aggression: Conceptions and Misconceptions

Buss (1961) suggested that aggressive behavior may appear in a variety of modes. He coined the categories of *physical* versus *verbal*, and *direct* versus *indirect* aggression. These two dichotomies have, on a theoretical level, been widely accepted; however, until recently, only the first one has been utilized to any great extent in actual operationalizations and measurements of aggression. This may have resulted in a one-sided view of aggressive behavior.

Reviews of gender differences with respect to aggression (Maccoby & Jacklin, 1974; Frodi, Macaulay, & Thome, 1977; White, 1983; Hyde, 1984; Eagly & Steffen, 1986) all agree that males are in general physically more aggressive than females. However, when it comes to verbal aggression, the situation is different. Although women often are thought to be verbally more aggressive than men, research has not been able to establish this notion as fact. Bandura (1973) did not in his studies find gender differences in regard to verbal aggression, while Sears, Rau, and Alpert (1965) actually found boys to be verbally *more* aggressive than girls.

We suggest that the reason for this discrepancy between everyday observation and research findings lies in the fact that there are actually several different *types* of verbal aggression which have not been distinguished by existing measurement techniques. On the contrary, these different types have so far been confounded, so the results obtained have been confusing.

Lagerspetz, Björkqvist, and Peltonen (1988) suggested indirect aggression to be more typical of females than of males. Two types of aggression, direct and indirect, were measured by means of peer estimation techniques in a sample of 11- to 12-year-old school children. Indirect aggression was conceptualized as a kind of social manipulation: the aggressor manipulates others to attack the victim, or, by other means, makes use of the social structure in order to harm the target person, without being personally involved in attack. Thereby, the aggressor stands a greater chance of going unnoticed and avoiding retaliation. Girls in the sample were found to use indirect means of aggression to a significantly greater degree than boys, at least at this age.

In the literature, there has been considerable confusion about the concept of indirect aggression. When Frodi, Macaulay, and Thome (1977) wrote their well-known review, they confessed that the notion of indirect aggression posed a problem for them. While some authors used the dichotomy of direct versus indirect aggression to distinguish between physical and verbal aggression (!), others used it to distinguish between aggression with and without a *target*. A third category of authors used it to distinguish between harm delivered in a face-to-face situation and harm delivered circuitously. The definition of indirect aggression in Lagerspetz, Björkqvist, and Peltonen (1988) is similar to that of this third category.

It is interesting to note that Frodi, Macaulay, and Thome (1977) themselves decided to define indirect aggression as aggression with a *substitute* target, either a substitute target person, or no concrete target at all. To us, neither of these two substituted forms of aggression are indirect aggression at all. We would conceive of aggression against a substitute target as *displaced* aggression (cf. Dollard *et al.*, 1939); aggression without a target would be either *free-floating* or *repressed* aggression, depending on the circumstances. In neither case does it come close to indirect aggression the way our research group has conceptualized it.

When the items of the subscale *indirect aggression* in the Buss-Durkee Hostility and Guilt Inventory (Buss & Durkee, 1957) are examined in detail, it becomes obvious that Buss himself conceived of this kind of behavior very differently than Lagerspetz, Björkqvist, and Peltonen (1988). His scale consists of items like: *"slamming doors"; "sulking"; "pouting"; "banging on tables"; "throwing things"; "breaking things"; "having temper tantrums"; "playing practical jokes"; "gossiping."*

Only the last two of these would fit our conceptualization of indirect aggression (the first one somewhat ambiguously). The rest, we would define in other terms. When we factor analyzed the Buss-Durkee Inventory, most of the items belonging to the subscale of *indirect aggression* in fact group together with another of the test's subscales, *irritability*. Indeed, Buss (1990) reported that factor analyses of the scales in the Buss-Durkee Inventory revealed a completely different dimensionality than the original subscales.

Feshbach (1969) conducted an observational study of girls' and boys' behavior toward newcomers. She found that during the first four minutes of social interaction, girls acted with more indirect aggression than did boys; later, there was no gender difference. Indirect aggression was coded as *"ignoring"; "avoidance"; "refusal"; "excluding."* This list of items comes much closer to the definition used by our research group (but does not include "*gossiping*"), although in Feshbach's study the items refer particularly to exclusion of a newcomer from the peer group. While some versions of our peer nomination scales of indirect aggression have also included items measuring deliberate exclusion from groups, subjects have been asked to estimate specifically what other individuals do when angry or in conflict with another person. In the Feshbach study, the reaction of girls may have been of shyness and fear (although these are also, in a sense, signs of conflict) rather than anger.

## II. Why Has Indirect Aggression Not Been Investigated?

One reason why indirect aggression has not been to a great extent investigated is certainly perspective: the focus has been more upon physical and direct verbal aggression. Another reason may have been a need for suitable research tools. In observational studies (the favorite technique when school children are investigated), indirect aggression is extremely difficult to recognize. Laboratory studies of adult aggression behavior have mostly utilized the "teacher–learner" paradigm (Buss, 1961) or similar techniques, where again it is hard to observe indirect aggression.

Self-ratings will not measure indirect aggression, due to the fact that, for example, gossiping and spreading false rumors are considered socially undesirable, and will accordingly not be admitted by the aggressors themselves. Also, indirect aggression can be unconscious; the perpetrator does not always acknowledge to him/herself that the behavior in question is aggressive. In our studies, as these facts suggest, we never found significant correlations between self-rated and peer-estimated indirect aggression: while with respect to physical and verbal aggression, the correlations were significant (Lagerspetz, Björkqvist, & Peltonen, 1988; Björkqvist, Lagerspetz, & Kaukiainen, 1992). These latter types of behavior seem to be socially acceptable among children.

*Peer nomination* as a technique for the measurement of aggressive behavior in a school setting was first developed by Eron, Lefkowitz, Walder, and Huesmann in Chicago. Numerous reports have been written by them and their colleagues, utilizing this research paradigm (e.g., Eron *et al.*, 1972; Lefkowitz *et al.*, 1977; Huesmann *et al.*, 1984; Huesmann, Lagerspetz, & Eron, 1984; Huesmann & Eron, 1986). They have, indeed, consistently used the same scale of ten items, so facilitating longitudinal research. Viemerö (Chapter 9, this volume) has also made use of their scale. These items measure a conglomeration of aggressive and antisocial behavior, and subscales are not identified. The only item which clearly measures indirect aggression is "*Who makes up stories and lies to get other children in trouble?*".

The peer nomination technique was quickly picked up by others doing research on aggressive behavior among school children: for example, Olweus (1977, 1978, 1980), Lagerspetz *et al.* (1982), and Björkqvist, Ekman, and Lagerspetz (1982). Although in these studies a variant other than the one developed by the Chicago group was utilized, it too did not allow for differentiation between various *kinds* of aggressive behavior by subscales.

The instrument invented by the Chicago group was an extremely important step in the development of research tools of aggressive behavior. Aggressiveness, in contrast with many other personality traits, is usually conceived of as socially undesirable, and will accordingly not so readily be measured by means of self estimation. Natural observation in school yards is an objective technique, but much will go unnoticed by the observer. The individuals who best know whether a pupil behaves aggressively or not are other pupils. They are the experts: they experience the behavior, including the indirect aggression, of the subject every day in a number of different situations.

## III. The Research Tool

Our research group has investigated three types of aggression: *direct physical, direct verbal*, and *indirect*. The scales have slowly been developed into their present form over a number of studies with subjects of different age groups (see below). There is an *aggressor* and a *victim* version of the test, allowing the investigation of both aggressive behavior and victimization.

The pupils estimate, on a five-point scale ranging from zero to four, to what extent *every other pupil of the class* behaves in a particular way when they are angry with, or get into conflict with, another pupil. The pupils also estimate their own behavior in such situations, which makes comparisons between peer-nominated and self-estimated behavior possible. Estimations made by boys and by girls can be compared: usually, the within-sex estimations are considered the most reliable, since the majority of aggressive acts take place between pupils of the same sex (Lagerspetz & Björkqvist, 1992).

In the latest version of the scales, developed by Björkqvist, Österman, & Lagerspetz, and so far unpublished, its items are the following:

1. *Physical Aggression.* This scale consists of seven items:
   *"hits," "kicks," "trips," "shoves," "takes things," "pushes," "pulls"*
   Cronbach's α of this scale = .93.
2. *Direct Verbal Aggression.* The scale consists of five items:
   *"yells," "insults," "says (s)he is going to hurt the other," "calls the other names," "teases"*
   Cronbach's α = .92.
3. *Indirect Aggression.* The scale consists of nine items:
   *"gossips," "tells bad or false stories," "becomes friend with another as revenge," "plans secretly to bother the other," "says bad things behind the other's back," "says to others: let's not be with him/her," "tells the other one's secrets to a third person," "writes nasty notes about the other," "tries to get others to dislike the person"*
   Cronbach's α = .93.

# IV. Sex Differences in Aggressive Styles during Adolescence

So far, we have gathered data from four different age groups of Finnish pupils: 8-, 11-, 15-, and 18-year-old children and adolescents. The results below are partly presented in Lagerspetz, Björkqvist, and Peltonen (1988), Björkqvist, Lagerspetz, and Kaukiainen (1992), and Lagerspetz and Björkqvist (1992).

The results reveal that boys are consistently *physically* more aggressive than girls; the two sexes usually do not differ significantly from each other with respect to direct *verbal* aggression (although considerable variation may be revealed on single items); girls are estimated by their peers to use *indirect* means of aggression significantly more than boys in all age groups except for the youngest (8-year-olds—at that age, it appears indirect means of aggression are not yet fully developed).

Figure 1 reveals gender differences with respect to these three scales at the age of fifteen. As may be noticed, verbal aggression is the most used by members of both sexes. Boys display more physical aggression, while girls utilize more indirect means of aggression.

Figures 2–4 present developmental trends for three individual items, *kicking, verbal abuse,* and *gossip.* These are presented in order to exemplify the

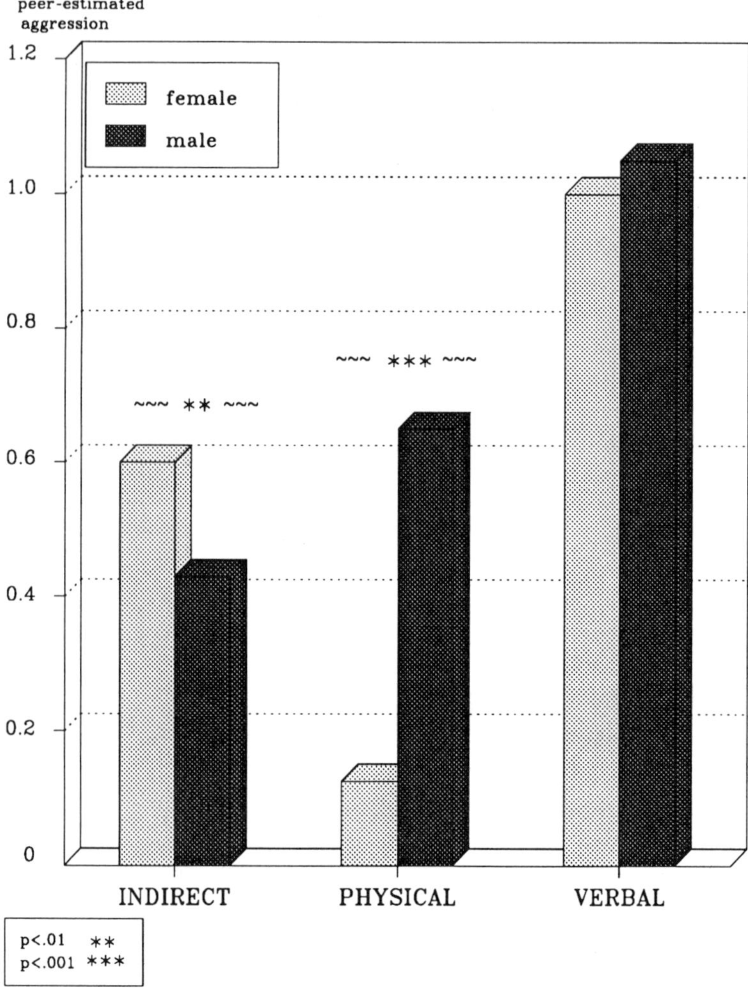


**Figure 1** Sex differences in aggressive strategies at age 15.

development of the three different strategies of physical, verbal, and indirect aggression. Other items of these subscales show similar developmental trends.

Notice the trends: *kicking*, high scores for the younger cohorts of boys, but diminishing scores for this sex by age, with girls not demonstrating much of this behavior; *verbal abuse* for both sexes reveals a sharp increase during the age of eleven, and scores stay high among older adolescents; *gossip* hardly occurs at all during the age of eight, but girls show high values for this among all other age groups.

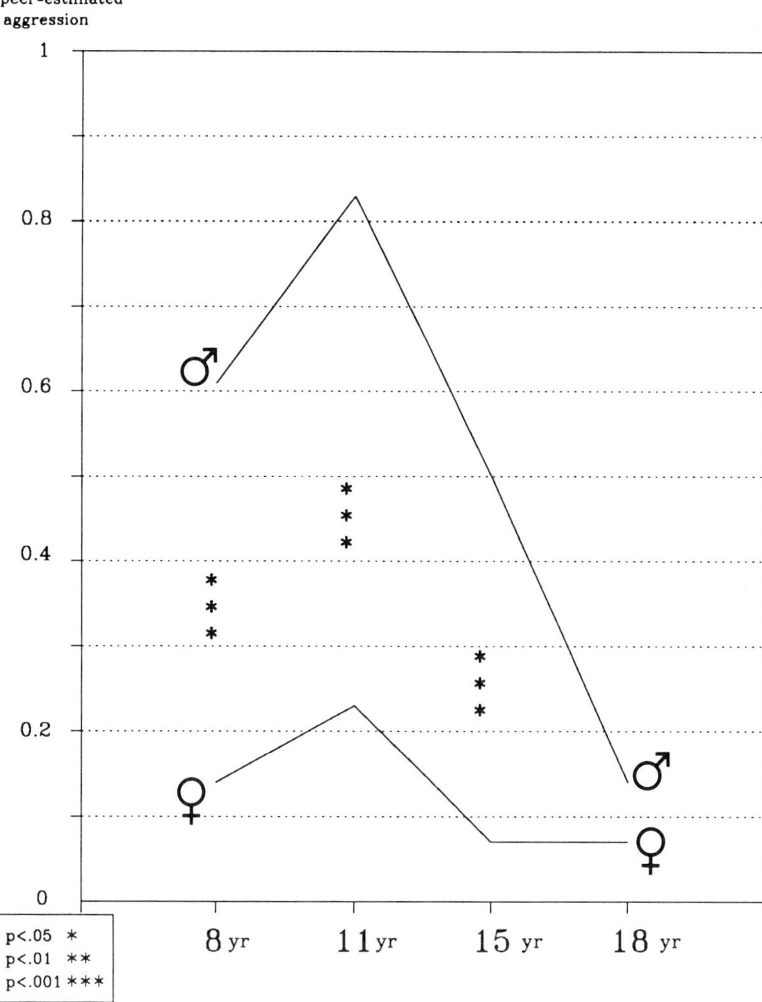


**Figure 2** Kicking (physical aggression).

Aggression has, in our research, been estimated to have a peak at the age of eleven. Why is this so? Our interpretation, based on sociometric measures which will not be described in detail here, is that peer relations in the class may be especially important during this period. With the onset of puberty, social relations, hence behavior, outside of the class may become as important as, or even more important than, the relations within one's class. It does not necessarily indicate a peak in aggressiveness at this age.

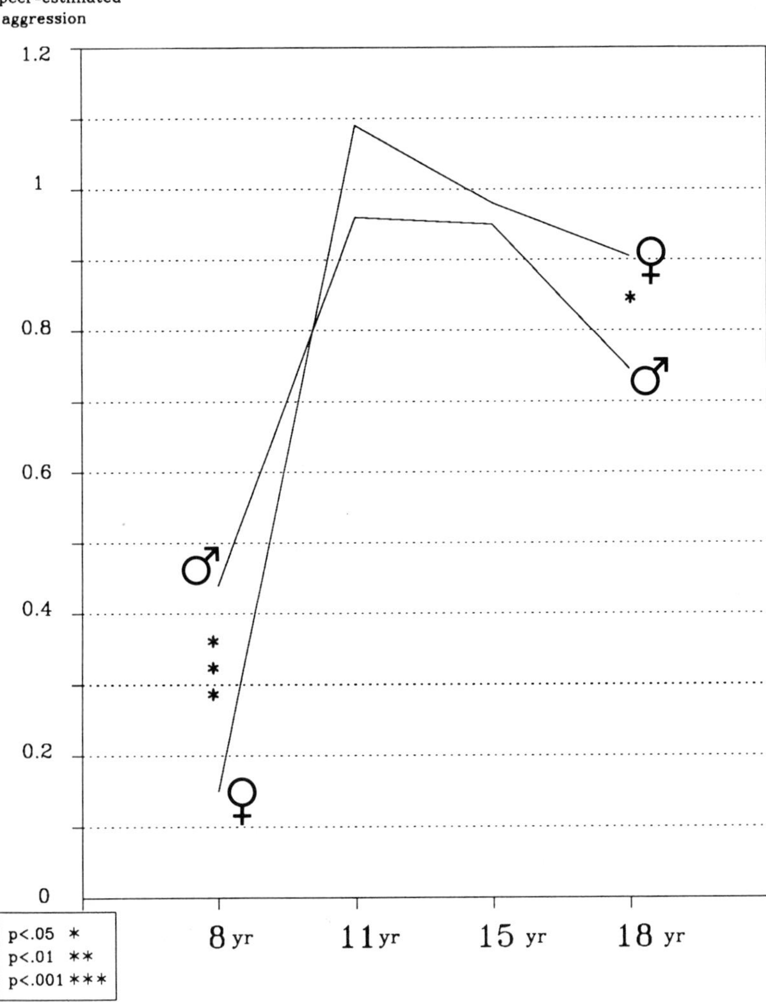


**Figure 3** Verbal abuse (direct verbal aggression).

## V. A Developmental Theory of Aggressive Strategies

We conceive of physical, direct verbal, and indirect aggression not only as three different strategies of aggression, but also as three developmental phases, partly following, partly overlapping each other.

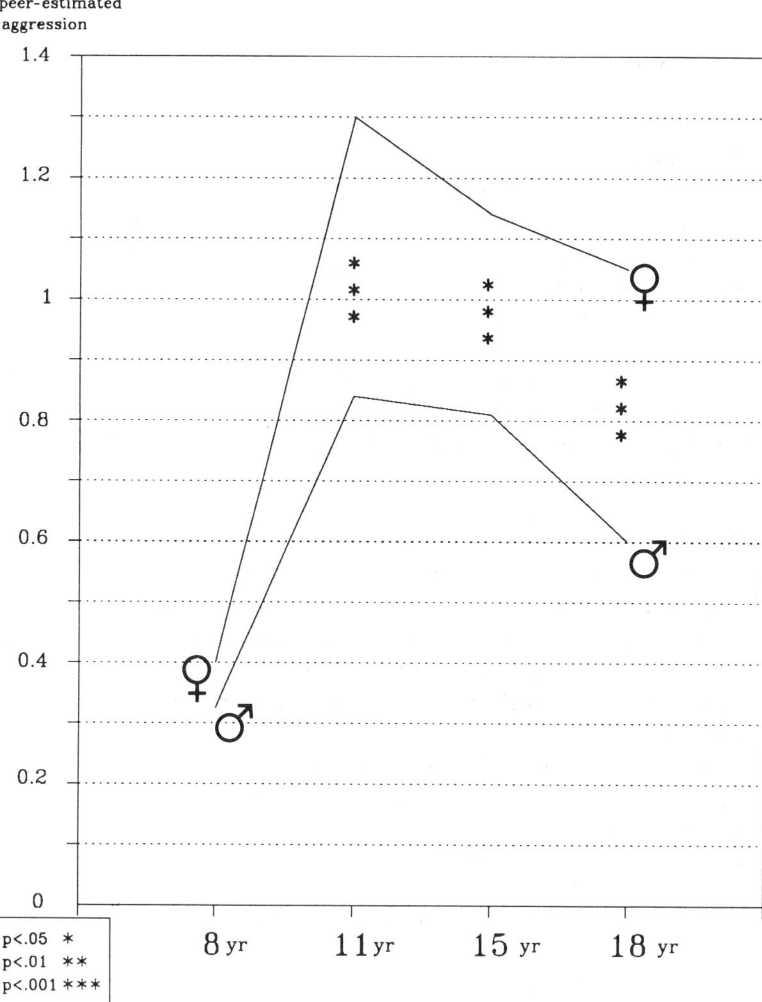


**Figure 4** Gossip (indirect aggression).

Aggressive behavior is considered undesirable in our society; accordingly, one should expect that the learning of this fact will lead to the transformation and change of aggressive strategies to less recognizable forms. Small children, who have not yet developed verbal and social skills to any considerable degree, will have to resort to physical means of aggression. In this respect, they recall members of subhuman species, who do not have a language. However, as among other mammals, there may be a lot of vocalization and display of threat, which may be compared to the direct verbal aggression of humans.

Boys, who are more active, and also often physically stronger than girls, are likely to develop physical means of aggression to a greater degree. Girls are likely to develop more withdrawal types of behavior (cf. Björkqvist, Lagerspetz, & Kaukiainen, 1992), as well as direct verbal and indirect means of aggression. Obviously, a lot of within-subject variation is likely to occur.

When verbal skills develop, they facilitate a rich amount of possibilities for the expression of aggression without one having to resort to physical force. Verbal aggressive strategies develop, and males and females seem to be, at least in our society, equally skillful at these. Due to their effectiveness, and also to the fact of physical aggression being socially unacceptable, these strategies soon replace physical aggressiveness. However, among certain individuals, whom society will refer to as "antisocial," physical aggression will still appear. A small amount of physical aggression will also appear among "normal" people under situations of stress. The amount of adult physical aggression accepted by norms may vary considerably from one society to another (cf. Chapters 15, 18, and 17 by Cook, Fry, and Kuschel, respectively, this volume).

When social intelligence develops, the individual also learns means of being indirectly aggressive. Thus, the perpetrator succeeds in inducing psychological, sometimes even physical, harm to a target person without putting him/herself at direct risk of retaliation. It is easy to claim that one has not been aggressive, one has only "told the truth," though the harm inflicted may be experienced as worse than physical injury.

Indirect means of aggression are expected to coexist with direct verbal means during later adolescence and adulthood. Direct verbal means are more suitable in certain situations, especially as expressions of anger (emotional aggression), or whenever direct strategies are called for. Indirect strategies fit better in other situations, especially when it is considered important not to be identified. Again, substantial within-subject variation in regard to chosen styles should be expected.

The fact that the females of our samples revealed higher levels of indirect aggression at all age levels during adolescence is intriguing. Is there something in the socialization of females which facilitates the learning of such strategies? In Lagerspetz, Björkqvist, and Peltonen (1988), it is suggested that the social structure of the peer groups during adolescence may be such a factor. Girls typically form small, intimate groups, often "pairs," while boys form bigger, less defined groups. Indirect aggression may be more effective in the girls' typical social setting.

Another factor may be the relative strengths of the two sexes. Girls may, at an early age, realize that indirect strategies (e.g., getting parents or older peers to help) may produce results more effectively than direct personal attack.

## VI. Two Kinds of Covered Aggression during Adulthood

One should expect indirect means to increase also among males during adulthood. In order to investigate whether this is the case, our research group has started a project in which aggressive strategies at workplaces are being studied. Places with mostly female employees are compared with places with mostly male employees, as well as those with employees of both sexes.

In our first study, *Aggression among university employees* (Björkqvist, Österman, & Hjelt-Bäck, in preparation), we found sex differences with respect to covered aggression, but in a new fashion. Future studies may hopefully shed light upon whether these patterns are typical only of universities.

After factor analyses of items describing aggressive behavior, two subscales were developed. After considerable discussion about how they should be interpreted, we decided to refer to the first one as *rational aggression*, aggression disguised by rational arguments, appearing and presented in rational form as "no aggression at all," but experienced by the victim as injurious and unjust behavior. The second subscale consists of items recalling the indirect scale in our studies of adolescents, and has been referred to as *social manipulation*. The items of these scales are presented below:

1. *Rational Aggression.* This scale consists of five items:
   *"reduced opportunities to express oneself," "being interrupted," "having one's work judged in an unjust manner," "being criticized," "one's sense of judgment being questioned"*
   Cronbach's $\alpha$ of this scale = .70.
2. *Social Manipulation.* This scale consists of seven items:
   *"insulting comments about one's private life," "insinuative negative glances," "backbiting," "the spreading of false rumors," "insinuations without direct accusation," "not being spoken to," "'do-not-speak-to-me' behavior"*
   Cronbach's $\alpha$ = .82.

As Figure 5 reveals, the rational form of aggression was the more popular among university employees in our sample ($t(170) = 8.19, p < .001$). A MANOVA multivariate analysis indicated a significant sex difference with respect to preferred choice of aggressive strategies ($F(2,166) = 8.250, p < .001$).

Males utilized rational-appearing aggressive strategies significantly more than did females ($F(1,167) = 6.250, p < 0.02$), while there was a trend for females to utilize social manipulation more than males ($F(1,167) = 3.584, p = .06$).

Is the rational-appearing aggression another development toward further "masking" of one's aggression? There are still many mysteries to be solved in regard to adult forms of aggression.

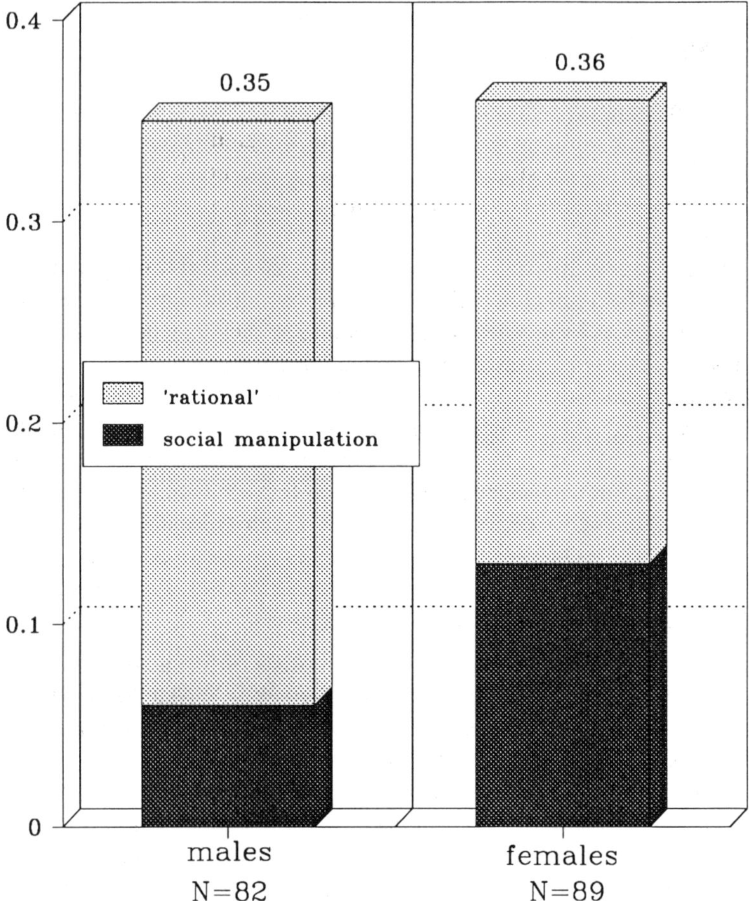


**Figure 5** Two types of covered aggression in adults.

## VII. Conclusions

There are reasons to believe that gender differences with respect to choice of aggressive strategies indeed exist, clearly so during childhood and adolescence, and likely so also during adult life. Developmental trends may also be identified: physical aggression appears at the earliest stages of life, then direct verbal means appear, and later on indirect ones. This sequence may be related to the developmental order of skills (physical-verbal-social).

The reason for the development of more refined strategies may also be pressure of social norms; aggressive behavior being socially undesirable, there is always the need to "mask" one's aggression, to make it appear as something else. Accordingly, more refined, sophisticated strategies are invented. There is a need to cover one's intentions; gossiping and other types of indirectly aggressive acts may be seen as a kind of *covered* aggression. The "rational" aggression found among adults is perhaps a further development of covered techniques, more sophisticated than usual indirect aggression, and even harder to counter. In the light of this work, it becomes increasingly evident that if adult human aggression is perceived only as physical and direct verbal aggression, one does not recognize more than the tip of the iceberg.

The results presented above have been obtained with samples of Finnish citizens as subjects. We are at present involved in cross-cultural comparative research, in order to find out whether similar gender differences and developmental trends may be found in other cultures.

## References


Bandura, A. (1973). *Aggression. A Social Learning Analysis.* Englewood Cliffs, New Jersey: Prentice-Hall.

Björkqvist, K., & Österman, K. (1992). Parental influence on children's self-estimated aggressiveness. *Aggressive Behavior* (submitted).

Björkqvist, K., Ekman, K., & Lagerspetz, K. M. J. (1982). Bullies and victims: Their ego picture, ideal ego picture and normative ego picture. *Scandinavian Journal of Psychology, 23,* 307–313.

Björkqvist, K., Lagerspetz, K. M. J., & Kaukiainen, A. (1992). Do girls manipulate and boys fight? Developmental trends regarding direct and indirect aggression. *Aggressive Behavior, 18.*

Björkqvist, K., Österman, K., & Hjelt-Bäck, M. (1992). Aggression among university employees (in preparation).

Buss, A. H. (1961). *The Psychology of Aggression.* New York: Wiley.

Buss, A. H. (1990). Components of Aggression. Paper presented at the IX Biennial ISRA meeting, Banff, Alberta, June 12–17.

Buss, A. H., & Durkee, A. (1957). An inventory for assessing different kinds of hostility. *Journal of Consulting Psychology, 21,* 343–349.

Dollard, J., Doob, L. W., Miller, N. E., Mowrer, O. H., & Sears, R. R. (1939). *Frustration and Aggression.* New Haven: Yale University Press.

Eagly, A. H., & Steffen, V. J. (1986). Gender and aggressive behavior: A meta-analytic review of the social psychological literature. *Psychological Bulletin, 100,* 309–330.

Eron, L. D., Huesmann, L. R., Lefkowitz, M. M., & Walder, L. O. (1972). Does television violence cause aggression? *American Psychologist, 27,* 253–263.

Feshbach, N. D. (1969). Sex differences in children's modes of aggressive responses towards outsiders. *Merrill-Palmer Quarterly, 15,* 249–258.

Frodi, A., Macaulay, J., & Thome, P. R. (1977). Are women always less aggressive than men? *Psychological Bulletin, 84,* 634–660.

Huesmann, L. R., & Eron, L. D. (Eds.) (1986). *Television and the Aggressive Child: A Cross-National Comparison.* Hillsdale, New Jersey: Lawrence Erlbaum Associates.

Huesmann, L. R., Eron, L. D., Lefkowitz, M. M., & Walder, L. O. (1984). The stability of aggression over time and generations. *Developmental Psychology, 20,* 1120–1134.

Huesmann, L. R., Lagerspetz, K. M. J., & Eron, L. D. (1984). Intervening variables in the television violence-aggression relation: A binational study. *Developmental Psychology, 20,* 746–775.

Hyde, J. S. (1984). How large are gender differences in aggression? A developmental meta-analysis. *Developmental Psychology, 20,* 722–736.

Lagerspetz, K. M. J., & Björkqvist, K. (1992). Indirect aggression in girls and boys. *In* L. R. Huesmann (Ed.), *Aggressive Behavior: Current Perspectives.* New York: Plenum.

Lagerspetz, K. M. J., Björkqvist, K., Berts, M., & King, E. (1982). Group aggression among children in three schools. *Scandinavian Journal of Psychology, 23,* 45–52.

Lagerspetz, K. M. J., Björkqvist, K., & Peltonen, T. (1988). Is indirect aggression typical of females? Gender differences in aggressiveness in 11- to 12-year-old children. *Aggressive Behavior, 14,* 403–414.

Lefkowitz, M. M., Eron, L. D., Walder, L. O. & Huesmann, L. R. (1977). *Growing up to be violent.* New York: Pergamon Press.

Maccoby, E. E., & Jacklin, C. N. (1974). *The Psychology of Sex Differences.* Stanford, California: Stanford University Press.

Olweus, D. (1977). Aggression and peer acceptance in adolescent boys: Two short-term longitudinal studies of ratings. *Child Development, 48,* 1301–1313.

Olweus, D. (1978). *Aggression in the Schools: Bullies and Whipping Boys.* Washington, D.C.: Hemisphere (Wiley).

Olweus, D. (1980). Familial and temperamental determinants of aggressive behavior in adolescent boys: A causal analysis. *Developmental Psychology, 16,* 644–660.

Sears, R. R., Rau, L., & Alpert, R. (1965). *Identification and Child Rearing.* Stanford, California: Stanford University Press.

White, J. W. (1983). Sex and gender issues in aggression research. *In* R. G. Geen & E. I. Donnerstein (Eds.), *Aggression: Theoretical and Empirical Reviews (Vol. 2).* New York: Academic Press.

6

# *Sex Differences in Aggressive Play and Toy Preference*

Jeffrey H. Goldstein

I. INTRODUCTION
A. Perception of Aggression in Children's Play
B. Toy Preference
II. CONSEQUENCES OF SEX-DIFFERENTIATED PLAY
A. Rough-and-Tumble Play
B. Boys' Preference for "War Toys"
C. A Methodological Note
III. ORIGINS OF SEX DIFFERENCES IN PLAY
A. Biological Bases
B. Sociocultural Factors
IV. SUMMARY
REFERENCES

## I. Introduction

This chapter focuses on differences, perceived and actual, in the play of girls and boys. The chapter first considers the perception of sex differences in play. For instance, boys' play is perceived as "aggressive" and girls' play is not. Boys' play is often regarded as a form of violence, or is seen to border on physical aggression. Studies of sex differences in toy preference are then reviewed. Biological and social origins of these differences are discussed. Among social origins of sex differences in toy preference and play are sex stereotyping in toy packaging and marketing, studies of which are reviewed.

### A. PERCEPTION OF AGGRESSION IN CHILDREN'S PLAY

Every social scientist learns that perception is a function of both the perceived and the perceiver. Yet some write of rough play and "war toys" as though it is possible to describe them objectively. Boys' play, far more often than girls' play, is viewed as a form of, or bordering upon, real violence (Carlsson-Paige & Levin, 1987, 1990; Miedzian, 1991; National Coalition on Television Violence, 1989). Is it? Many observers have commented upon how rarely fighting actually takes place among boys engaged in rough play (Fry, 1990; Pellegrini, 1988; Sutton-Smith, Gerstmyer, & Meckley, 1988; Wegener-Spohring, 1989). The most aggressive children appear least likely to engage in play fighting (Willner, 1991).

### *1. Observer Characteristics That Influence Perceptions of Toys and Play*

At least three characteristics of the observer play a role in the perception of children's play and toys as "aggressive": the age and sex of observers and their prior attitudes toward the objects and activities involved. There are probably many additional characteristics of observers that would influence these judgements (for example, their chronic level of aggression), but these have not been studied systematically.

*a. Age* Children and adults tend to view rough play differently. Children are aware of the differences between aggressive play and real violence. Studies of children in England (Smith & Boulton, 1990), Germany (Wegener-Spohring, 1989), Mexico (Fry, 1990), and the United States (Pellegrini, 1988; Sutton-Smith, Gerstmyer, & Meckley, 1988) found in each case that children reliably distinguish real fighting from play fighting. Employing interviews and videotapes, Smith and Boulton (1990) found that English children as young as 4 years of age differentiate between real fighting and play fighting. There was over 80% agreement among 8- to 11-year-olds as to when an episode was aggression or play. Fry reports similar observations of Zapotec children in rural Mexico.

Fry (1990) writes that play fighting evolved because it encouraged hunting and other survival skills, the "practice hypothesis." As a result, there are inevitable similarities between play fighting and real fighting, such as chasing, fleeing, grappling, and wrestling, that occur during both. The majority of children agree that play fighting can become real aggression, particularly when accidental injury occurs. This happens only occasionally, according to studies by Humphreys and Smith (1987), Pellegrini (1988), and Sutton-Smith, Gerstmyer, and Meckley (1988).[1] In Wegener-Spohring's observations, play fighting erupted into aggression when adults broke the "play frame" by interfering. From these observational studies, it appears that children are adept at assessing the playful or aggressive intentions of their playmates.

Why do adults sometimes confuse play fighting with real aggression? Perhaps because they focus on the similarities, rather than the differences, between

[1]Among university-age males, play fighting is correlated with actual fighting, according to Mary Gergen (1990).

them. Children differentiate play from real fighting by focusing on their distinctive features: (1) *facial expressions* and *vocalizations*: grimacing, clenched teeth, fixed gazes in real aggression; smiling and laughing in play aggression; (2) *outcomes*: children are less apt to suffer injuries and are more likely to remain together following aggressive play than actual aggression; (3) *frequency*: aggressive play occurs more often than real aggression, about 9 times more often in Fry's study. (4) *duration*: aggressive play lasts longer than real fighting. Fry concludes that, "Play aggression would seem to be a relatively safe, friendly, and enjoyable way for children to practice skills that sometimes prove useful later in life."

The difference in children's and adults' perceptions of aggressive play is consistent with the familiar distinction between actors and observers, or etic and emic perspectives. Play fighting appears different from the "inside" than from the "outside," probably because participants have access to greater and more varied information than do observers. Players experience the feeling tone and emotional accompaniments, while observers of play do not, or do so only to a minor degree.

*b. Sex* Among adults, the perception of aggression in children's play is a function of the sex of the observer. Connor (1989) videotaped 4- and 5-year-olds playing with neutral toys (trucks, dolls, crayons) or with "war toys" (G. I. Joe™, Rambo™ set with guns and grenade). Fourteen of these play episodes were shown to male and female university students, who rated each as "play" or "aggression." Males and females viewed 10 of the 14 episodes differently. For example, in one incident, two boys and a girl playing with toy guns agree that shooting a "dead" person with his own weapon restores him to life. In the incident, a "dead" boy is shot and revived in this way. Seventy-five percent of the males viewed this as playful while only 38% of the females viewed it this way. Aggression is in the eye of the beholder; females in comparison to males are more likely to label an aggressive play episode as "aggression."

*c. Prior Attitudes and the Perception of Aggression* It is nearly a universal belief that one's attitudes color judgments of social events (Sherif & Cantril, 1947). With regard specifically to the perception of aggression in play, Hastorf and Cantril (1954) conducted the classic study at an American college football game. In 1951, Dartmouth lost an important football game to Princeton. It was a particularly rough game, in which Princeton's All-American quarterback received a broken nose and a Dartmouth player suffered a broken leg. A week after the game, the researchers showed a film of the game to students at each university. The students were to note any rule violations they observed. When Dartmouth students viewed the game, they noted an average of 4.3 violations against the Dartmouth team. When Princeton students viewed the same film they noted 9.8 infractions against the Dartmouth team. Hastorf and Cantril conclude that "there is no such thing as a 'game' existing 'out there' in its own right which people merely 'observe.' "

Whether an observer will respond with increased hostility to observed aggressive play depends also on attitudes toward aggression. In one study, fans with favorable attitudes toward fighting in ice hockey became increasingly hostile as they viewed an aggressive hockey game. There was no increase in hostility among observers who disapproved of fighting (Harrell, 1981).

Prior experience also influences judgments of children's play. Females who had engaged in aggressive play or played with aggressive toys as children were less likely than other females to judge children's play episodes as "aggression" (Connor, 1989).

*d. Video Games* A growing body of research examines the uses and effects of computer and video games. Among the issues studied are sex differences and the effects of video/computer game thematic content.

Malone (1981) created two versions of a video game, one with and one without aggressive fantasy. Adding the aggressive theme increased the game's popularity among boys, but decreased it among girls. In other domains also, boys often prefer aggressive forms of play and entertainment (e.g., Ross & Taylor, 1989).

Computer educators have expressed concern over the diminishing number of girls acquiring computer skills. Until about 10 years of age, girls seem to have as much fascination as boys with computers. Yet in the crowds around video game machines, boys far outnumber girls. If video games are the entry point into the world of computers, as Greenfield (1984) maintains, then the fact that so many of these games involve aggressive fantasy themes may have the effect of turning many girls away from computers in general.

A study by Cooper, Hall, and Huff (1990) found that girls experience increased stress when using computer software that appeals to boys. Boys reported more stress than girls when working with female-oriented programs. In their study, 52 boys and girls in 6th through 8th Grade (age 11 to 14 years) used mathematics programs with themes that appeal mainly to boys (shooting or propelling objects through fantasy space, graphic feedback, action, aggression) or appeal mainly to girls (absence of aggression/shooting, verbal feedback, cooperative). These programs were used either in isolation or in a computer room with other students nearby. In the latter social setting, girls experienced greater stress using "masculine programs" and boys felt greater stress using "feminine programs." The authors express concern that basing educational materials on video arcade games may have the effect of increasing stress in girls and of contributing to their avoidance of computers. The main influence, however, appears to be peer disapproval, hence the effects are reported only when children were in the presence of schoolmates.

Girls become more interested in computers connected to programmable "digital trains" (Catherall, 1989). These are controlled by a computer chip in each locomotive, and 80 locomotives on the same track can be controlled by different "engineers" simultaneously. The ability to control over 250 accessory devices, such as switches and signals, places demands on players to cooperate in a play atmosphere.

### B. TOY PREFERENCE

In situations of free choice, children prefer toys that are not associated with either sex (Almqvist, 1989; Downs, 1983). When sex-typed toys are requested, boys prefer "boys' toys," and, to a lesser extent, girls prefer "girls' toys" (Almqvist, 1989; Eisenberg *et al.*, 1985). Among children in the United States, such preferences first appear at about 2 years of age (Caldera, Huston, & O'Brien, 1989; Fein *et al.*, 1985; Weinraub *et al.*, 1984).

How does a toy become sex-typed? According to a study by Shell and Eisenberg (1990), same-sex peer modeling determines the perception of the sex-appropriateness of a toy. The researchers found that 4- and 5-year-olds viewed a toy as a "boys' toy" if they previously observed mainly boys playing with the toy, and as a "girls' toy" if girls were shown playing with the toy.

## II. Consequences of Sex-Differentiated Play

### A. ROUGH-AND-TUMBLE PLAY

Rough-and-tumble play is primarily the prerogative of boys (DiPietro, 1981; Fry, 1990; Gergen, 1990; Pellegrini, 1988). As with war play, some psychologists argue that rough-and-tumble play leads to subsequent real aggression (e.g., Carlsson-Paige & Levin, 1987, 1990; Miedzian, 1991). Others state that it contributes to social and emotional development (e.g, Bettelheim, 1987; Sutton-Smith & Kelly-Byrne, 1984; Sutton-Smith, Gerstmyer, & Meckley, 1988). According to Pellegrini (1988), part of the reason for this confusion is the result of "definitional problems." Some researchers define rough-and-tumble play as including both fighting and mock fighting. Others count both verbal and physical attack as "aggression."

In her interviews with German children, Wegener-Spöhring (1989) found that 76% of the boys owned toy guns, as did 29% of the girls. During play, she observed 62 aggressive incidents by girls and 335 by an equal number of boys. "Are boys therefore 5 times as bad as girls? Certainly not." Boys are allowed and expected to display more aggressive behavior than girls. Girls are still supposed to be obedient and nice, and ashamed of being aggressive and quarrelsome, she notes. Björkqvist, Lagerspetz, and Kaukiainen (1991) found that girls are "aggressive" in ways that do not include the masculine forms of overt violence.

In some studies, overtly aggressive children were less likely than other children to engage in rough play (Willner, 1991). Rough-and-tumble play helps children realize the value of compromise, equality, and reciprocity, according to Willner's review, and serves an affiliative function. "By participating in comparatively fewer playful interchanges, aggressive boys are deprived of crucial experience. . . . Real aggression arising from play, besides being construed as a lack of self-control, could result from a failure to understand motivational signals and so misinterpret play invitations" (p. 145). She cites evidence by Dodge, Murphy, and Buchsbaum (1984) that aggressive children are less adept at interpreting the motivation of others.

## B. BOYS' PREFERENCE FOR "WAR TOYS"

Children play with toy weapons for many reasons, most of them having nothing to do with aggression and war. Play with any toy serves a multitude of purposes, from mastery of the environment to the development of physical coordination and social skills. Play with toy weapons is also motivated by attempts to understand mortality, stimulate fantasy, increase arousal, and imitate the behavior of adults.

There is a correlation between preference for toy weapons and behavioral aggression, though it is by no means clear what, if any, is the causal meaning of this relationship. Jacqueline Jukes in her doctoral dissertation (1991) reports that aggressive boys prefer aggressive toys. In her research, trait aggression is associated with a preference for "fighting toys." If children are first "primed" with aggressive stories, they are more likely to choose toy weapons for play (Lovaas, 1961; cf. Jukes, 1991). This is consistent with research on cognitive priming or salience and preference for violent entertainment (Boyanowsky, Newtson, & Walster, 1974; Goldstein, 1972). Some parents provide toy guns to already aggressive children in the hope of channeling their aggression into the more acceptable realm of fantasy play.

### *1. Toy Gun Play*

There are so few well-designed studies of the effects of toy gun play as to render any generalization questionable. If we take at face value the results of the dozen or so studies on toy weapons, it appears that toy gun play increases aggressive play, and perhaps also interpersonal aggression *while engaged in play or immediately following play*. Once the toys are put aside or withdrawn, antisocial behavior returns to its preplay level. The effects of toy gun play do not appear to be enduring, nor do they generalize from one setting to another (Turner & Goldsmith, 1976; Wolff, 1976). Given the amount of controversy that toy weapons provoke, it is curious that they are so seldom studied. Perhaps it is because issues such as media violence, toy weapons, and other forms of young people's entertainment provide a convenient arena for adults to profess ethical, political, and other personal views (see Goldstein, 1989).

## C. A METHODOLOGICAL NOTE

If studies of aggressive play and toys use only physical aggression, such as pushing and hitting, as the dependent variable, they are unable to detect other forms of aggression, such as those discussed by Björkqvist, Lagerspetz, and Kaukiainen (1991), or to notice other effects of these toys on social behavior. Play with any toy serves a multitude of functions and may have more pronounced effects on self-confidence, self-esteem, coordination, social organization, and emotional control than on the single (measured) variable of aggression. As researchers, we include control groups in order to ensure that our independent variable is what we intend it to be, while at the same time ignoring the possibility that our dependent variables in play research also require controls to ensure that what we are measuring is not merely a reflection of heightened arousal or activity level on the part of the players (Goldstein *et al.*, 1975), or of our own expectations.

The outcome of "war play" research is to some extent dependent upon its methodology. When the method involves *observation* of children at play, researchers are more apt to interpret play fighting as real aggression, and to conclude that such play contributes to, or is, aggression (e.g., Mendoza, 1972; Turner & Goldsmith, 1976). On the other hand, when children are *interviewed*, researchers, like the children themselves, are more apt to distinguish play fighting from actual fighting (e.g., Bonte & Musgrove, 1943; Sutton-Smith, Gerstmyer, & Meckley, 1988; Wegener-Spohring, 1989).

## III. Origins of Sex Differences in Play

As with other complex forms of social behavior, there exist data to support both biological as well as sociocultural foundations of sex differences in play.

### A. BIOLOGICAL BASES

Erik Erikson (1977) asserts that differences in children's play are an outgrowth of the biological, or more precisely morphological, differences between the sexes. He found that young boys built vertical constructions that involved active themes, whereas girls constructed enclosures with static themes. Girls' creations are said to mirror the passive, enclosed nature of female genitalia, whereas boys' constructions reflect the intrusive erect nature of the penis, with its active sperm cells. Needless to say, such an argument is controversial (Rubin, Fein, & Vandenberg, 1983).

Meyer-Bahlburg *et al.* (1988) have documented a relationship between prenatal exposure to a synthetic female hormone, progestogen, and a reduction in rough-and-tumble play in both sexes. This suggests that some of the difference between the play of boys and girls may be due to biological factors. Toy preference may be influenced, too, in that "war toys" may permit active play, which itself is hormonally influenced.

B. SOCIOCULTURAL FACTORS

Adults pass their own sex-role attitudes on to children along with the toys they purchase for them. Many studies find that parents are likely to purchase sex-stereotyped toys for their children, particularly if they themselves hold traditional sex-role attitudes (Eckerman & Stein, 1990; O'Brien & Huston, 1985; Rheingold & Cook, 1975). That is one reason that so many more boys than girls have toy guns.

Parents tend to play differently with sons and daughters. They respond differentially to the gaze and touch of sons and daughters. Fathers' play with infants tends to be more tactile, and mothers' more visual (Roggman & Peery, 1989). In such ways, parents contribute to their children's play and play styles.

Although boys and girls tend to play differently and to prefer different toys, the structure of the toy and the setting in which play occurs also elicit certain behaviors from players (Karpoe & Olney, 1983; Ross & Taylor, 1989). A Bobo doll, often used in aggression and toy research, invites punching, as teddy bears invite cuddling. It is true that "boys will be boys," but it is also true that "footballs will be footballs" and "dolls will be dolls."

### *Sex Roles in Advertising and Packaging*

Social learning of play styles is not restricted to personal influence, but also involves mass media effects, such as the portrayal of the sexes in toy packaging and advertising.

As early as age 3, heavy television viewers in the United States have more stereotyped views of sex roles than do light viewers. "Commercials are outstanding culprits in the presentation of sex role stereotypes," according to Greenfield (1984, p. 33).

Commercials for girls' toys contain more fades, dissolves, and background music; those for boys' toys contain more toy action, frequent cuts, sound effects, and loud music. Greer *et al.* (1982), created "pseudo-commercials" consisting of abstract shapes rather than real toys. Two types of commercial for abstract shapes were produced, one containing clusters of features that appeared mainly in advertisements for boys, and one with features appearing in advertisements for girls. These pseudo-commercials were shown to children. Children of all ages tended to identify the advertisements with girls' features as female and those with features from commercials for boys as male.

Schwartz and Markham (1985) obtained 392 pictures of children with toys from 12 toy catalogues and 538 pictures of children with toys from toy packages. Results show that the rated sex stereotype of the toy was strongly related to the sex or sexes of the children shown with the toy in catalogues (r = .89) and on toy packages (r = .87). Toys rated as moderately sex-typed were just as strongly stereotyped in toy ads as those rated strongly sex-typed. These findings suggest that toy ads follow conventional sex-role definitions.

Kline and Pentecost (1990) examined 150 toy advertisements randomly selected from children's television in North America. Their analysis of toy advertising "reveals that profound genderization persists." The types of toys that children are shown playing with are highly gender-differentiated. Doll play predominates among toy ads aimed exclusively at girls, accounting for 84% of these ads. By way of contrast, only 45% of the boys' ads feature doll play. These consist of ads for action-figure dolls. Boys are shown at play with a wider range of toys, including toy cars, guns, construction sets, and electronic video games. Despite the large number of doll ads in the sample, hardly any doll ads depict boys and girls playing together. Only a few ads (for stuffed animals) showed boys and girls playing together. Of the ads for dolls, 91% featured single-sex play groups whereas 66% of nondoll play (e.g., games, cars, guns) showed single-sex groups. Games, on the other hand, which were about 10% of the sample, always showed children playing in mixed-sex groups.

Kline and Pentecost believe that there is a difference in the way boys and girls are portrayed in relation to their toys. Although girls are often shown *interacting* with their toys, that is, adopting a separate identity that interacts with that of the toy, boys are most often shown *identifying* with toys, that is, taking on the character of the toy as their own. For example, in advertisements for My Little Pony(TM), girls do not become ponies but rather assume identities or roles in relation to the ponies. When boys play Batman, they *become* Batman.

Seventy-five toy commercials shown on British television prior to Christmas 1988 were analyzed by Smith and Bennett (1990). The commercials were coded for sex-role stereotypes and aggression. There was exactly equal representation of males and females. Aside from dolls and toy cars, there were no gender differences for other products. Boys were more often shown engaging in competitive play while girls were shown in cooperative play. Boys were more active compared to girls. The most dramatic finding of the British study was the overwhelming majority of male voice-overs: 74%.

What about aggression in toy advertising? Smith and Bennett (1990) found a low level of aggressive content. Sixty-seven percent of the observed commercials had no aggressive content at all, and no commercials contained overtly aggressive behavior, such as one child hitting another. The aggression that was observed was connected with the toy itself, for example, bombs destroying an enemy in a war-based board game. "This aggression is part of the inherent nature of the toy, for example, spaceships firing at each other, and thus removed from the real world. Generally, children from 3 years and upwards can clearly separate reality from fantasy, so it is not clear that these kinds of fantasy aggression would have any harmful effects."

## IV. Summary

Play researchers sometimes write as though aggressive play and aggressive toys are indistinguishable from actual violence and real weapons. But the evidence is abundant that the perception of aggression in children's play depends upon characteristics of the observer, including the observer's age, sex, attitudes, and experiences with the objects and actions observed. Children appear to distinguish more reliably than adults between real and play aggression. Among adults, men and women differ in their perceptions of children's interactions as "play" or "aggression." Women interpret more episodes of children's behavior as aggression than do men. These differences may result from differential childhood experiences with rough play and "war toys."

Although rough play is often perceived as a form of violence, it does not often become real aggression. Yet, adults sometimes confuse play fighting with real aggression, perhaps because they focus on the similarities, rather than the differences between the two.

Rough-and-tumble play and preference for "war toys" are greater among boys than among girls. Both biological and sociocultural factors, especially social learning, appear to be involved in these differences. Sex-stereotyped play is frequently portrayed on toy packaging and often in television commercials.

In situations of free choice, children prefer toys that are not associated with either sex. When sex-typed toys are requested, boys prefer "boys' toys," and, to a lesser extent, girls prefer "girls' toys." A toy becomes sex-linked as the result of peer modeling.

Children may play with toy weapons for many reasons: mastery of the environment, to develop and practice physical coordination and social skills, in an attempt to understand mortality, to stimulate fantasy, increase arousal, and in imitation of the behavior of adults.

In part because of the simulated war themes of video and computer games, they are more appealing to boys than to girls. One consequence of this may be to diminish the appeal and familiarity of computers to girls over the age of 10.

If researchers measure only physical aggression in studies of toy play, they will be unable to detect other forms of aggression, and other effects of toys, particularly those that may outweigh their contribution to aggression.

## References

Almqvist, B. (1989). Age and gender differences in children's Christmas requests. *Play & Culture, 2*, 2–19.

Bettelheim, B. (1987). The importance of play. *The Atlantic*, March.

Björkqvist, K., Lagerspetz, K. M. J., & Kaukiainen, K. (1991). The development of direct and indirect strategies: Gender differences during ages 8, 11, 15, and 18. *Aggressive Behavior, 17*, 60.

Bonte, E. P., & Musgrove, M. (1943). Influences of war as evidenced in children's play. *Child Development, 14*, 179–200.

Boyanowsky, E. O., Newtson, D., & Walster, E. (1974). Film preferences following a murder. *Communication Research, 1*, 32–43.

Caldera, Y., Huston, A., & O'Brien, M. (1989). Social interactions and actions and play patterns of parents and toddlers with feminine, masculine and neutral toys. *Child Development, 60*, 70–76.

Carlsson-Paige, N., & Levin, D. E. (1987). *The War Play Dilemma.* New York: Teachers College Press.

Carlsson-Paige, N., & Levin, D. E. (1990). *Who's Calling the Shots?* Philadelphia: New Society.

Catherall, T. S. (1989). Playing with electric trains in school classrooms. *Play & Culture, 2*, 137–141.

Connor, K. (1989). Aggression: Is it in the eye of the beholder? *Play & Culture, 2*, 213–217.

Cooper, J., Hall, J., & Huff, C. (1990). Situational stress as a consequence of sex-stereotyped software. *Personality and Social Psychology Bulletin, 16*, 419–429.

DiPietro, J. A. (1981). Rough and tumble play: A function of gender. *Developmental Psychology, 17*, 50–58.

Dodge, K. A., Murphy, R. R., & Buchsbaum, K. (1984). The assessment of intention-cue detection skills in children. *Child Development, 55*, 163–173.

Downs, A. C. (1983). Letters to Santa Claus: Elementary school age children's sex-typed toy preferences in a natural setting. *Sex Roles, 9*, 159–164.

Eckerman, C. O., & Stein, M. R. (1990). How imitation begets imitation and toddlers' generation of games. *Developmental Psychology, 26*, 370–378.

Eisenberg, N., Wolchik, S. A., Hernandez, R., & Pasternack, J. F. (1985). Parental socialization of young children's play. *Child Development, 56*, 1506–1513.

Erikson, E. H. (1977). *Toys and Reasons.* New York: Norton.

Fein, G., Johnson, D., Kosson, N., Stork, L., & Wasserman, L. (1985). Sex stereotypes and preferences in the toy choices of 20-month-old boys and girls. *Developmental Psychology, 11*, 527–528.

Fry, D. P. (1990). Play aggression among Zapotec children: Implications for the practice hypothesis. *Aggressive Behavior, 16*, 321–340.

Gergen, M. (1990). Beyond the evil empire: Horseplay and aggression. *Aggressive Behavior, 16*, 381–398.

Goldstein, J. H. (1972). Preference for aggressive movie content: Effects of cognitive salience. Unpublished manuscript, Temple University. (Summary in J. H. Goldstein, *Aggression and Crimes of Violence, 2nd Edition*, 1986, p. 48).

Goldstein, J. H. (1989). Violence in sports. *In* J. H. Goldstein (Ed.), *Sports, Games, and Play, 2nd Edition.* Hillsdale, New Jersey: Lawrence Erlbaum Associates.

Goldstein, J. H., Rosnow, R. L., Raday, T., Silverman, I. W., & Gaskell, G. D. (1975). Punitiveness in response to films varying in content: A cross-national field study of aggression. *European Journal of Social Psychology, 5*, 149–165.

Greenfield, P. M. (1984). *Mind and Media: The Effects of Television, Video Games and Computers.* Cambridge, Massachusetts: Harvard University Press.

Greer, D., Potts, P., Wright, J. C., & Huston, A. C. (1982). The effects of television commercial form and commercial placement on children's social behavior and attention. *Child Development, 53*, 611–619.

Harrell, W. A. (1981). Verbal aggressiveness in spectators at professional hockey games: The effects of tolerance of violence and amount of exposure to hockey. *Human Relations, 34*, 643–655.

Hastorf, A. H., & Cantril, H. (1954). They saw a game: A case study. *Journal of Abnormal & Social Psychology, 47*, 574–576.

Humphreys, A., & Smith, P. K. (1987). Rough-and-tumble in preschool and playground. *In* P. K. Smith (Ed.), *Play in Animals and Humans.* London: Basil Blackwell.

Jukes, J. (1991). Children and aggressive toys: Empirical studies of toy preference. Unpublished Doctoral dissertation. University College, London.

Karpoe, K., & Olney, R. (1983). The effect of boys' or girls' toys on sex-typed play in preadolescents. *Sex Roles, 9*, 507–518.

Kline, S., & Pentecost, D. (1990). The characterization of Play: Marketing Children's Toys. *Play & Culture, 3*, 235–255.

Lovaas, O. I. (1961). Effect of exposure to symbolic aggression on aggressive behavior. *Child Development, 32*, 37–44.

Malone, T. W. (1981). Toward a theory of intrinsically motivating instruction. *Cognitive Science, 5*, 333–370.

Mendoza, A. (1972). Effects of exposure to toys conducive to violence. *Dissertation Abstracts International, 33* (6-A), 2769–2770.

Meyer-Bahlburg, H. F. L., Feldman, J. F., Cohen, P., & Ehrhardt, A. A. (1988). Perinatal factors in the development of gender-related play behavior: Sex hormones versus pregnancy complications. *Psychiatry, 51*, 260–271.

Miedzian, M. (1991). *Boys will be Boys: Breaking the Link Between Masculinity and Violence*. New York: Doubleday.

National Coalition on Television Violence. (1989). *NCTV News, 10* (3/4).

O'Brien, M., & Huston, A. (1985). Development of sex-typed behavior in toddlers. *Developmental Psychology, 21*, 866–871.

Pellegrini, A. D. (1988). Elementary-school children's rough-and-tumble play and social competence. *Developmental Psychology, 24*, 802–806.

Rheingold, H., & Cook, K. V. (1975). The contents of boys' and girls' rooms as an index of parents' behavior. *Child Development, 46*, 459–463.

Roggmann, L. A., & Peery, J. C. (1989). Parent-infant social play in brief encounters: Early gender differences. *Child Study Journal, 19*, 65–79.

Ross, H., & Taylor, H. (1989). Do boys prefer daddy or his physical style of play? *Sex Roles, 20*, 23–33.

Rubin, K. H., Fein, G. G., & Vandenberg, B. (1983). Play. *In* P. H. Mussen (Ed.), *Manual of Child Psychology*. Vol. 4. New York: Wiley.

Schwartz, L. A., & Markham, W. T. (1985). Sex stereotyping in children's toy advertisements. *Sex Roles, 12*, 157–170.

Shell, R., & Eisenberg, N. (1990). The role of peers' gender in children's naturally occurring interest in toys. *International Journal of Behavioral Development, 13*, 373–388.

Sherif, M., & Cantril, H. (1947). *The Psychology of Ego-Involvements*. New York: Wiley.

Smith, P. K., & Bennett, S. (1990). Here come the steel monsters! *Changes, 8(2)*, 97–105.

Smith, P. K., & Boulton, M. (1990). Rough-and-tumble play, aggression and dominance: Perception and behavior in children's encounters. *Human Development, 33*, 271–282.

Sutton-Smith, B., & Kelly-Byrne, D. (1984). The idealization of play. *In* P. K. Smith (Ed.), *Play in Animals and Humans*. London: Basil Blackwell.

Sutton-Smith, B., Gerstmyer, J., & Meckley, A. (1988). Play-fighting as folkplay amongst preschool children. *Western Folklore, 47*, 161–176.

Turner, C. W., & Goldsmith, D. (1976). Effects of toy guns and airplanes on children's antisocial free play behavior. *Journal of Experimental Child Psychology, 21*, 303–315.

Wegener-Spöhring, G. (1989). War toys and aggressive games. *Play & Culture, 2*, 35–47.

Weinraub, M., Clemens, L. P., Sockloff, A., Ethridge, T., Gracely, E., & Myers, B. (1984). The development of sex role stereotypes in the third year: Relationships to gender labeling, gender identity, sex-typed toy preference, and family characteristics. *Child Development, 55*, 1493–1503.

Willner, A. H. (1991). Behavioral deficiencies of aggressive 8-9-year old boys: An observational study. *Aggressive Behavior, 17*, 135–154.

Wolff, C. M. (1976). The effects of aggressive toys on aggressive behavior in children. *Dissertation Abstracts International*. Order No. 76–25, 706.

7

# *Differing Normative Beliefs about Aggression for Boys and Girls*

L. Rowell Huesmann, Nancy G. Guerra, Arnaldo Zelli, and Laurie Miller

I. INTRODUCTION
II. METHOD
A. Subjects
B. Measures
C. Procedure
III. RESULTS
IV. DISCUSSION
V. SUMMARY
REFERENCES

## I. Introduction

Children are not born with preformed knowledge of standards for acceptable behavior. Through both observational and enactive learning, they gradually learn a complex set of self-regulating rules, or normative beliefs, about the appropriateness of an array of social behaviors (Bandura, 1986, 1989). By "normative belief" we mean a belief about what is considered acceptable social behavior—what an individual should do. However, a person's normative beliefs may deviate substantially from what most people believe is acceptable behavior.

The specific types of normative beliefs which children learn during a particular developmental period depend on a variety of factors, including cognitive abilities, age-typical behaviors, and the salient characteristics of the child's environment. For example, normative beliefs about dating behavior should emerge during adolescence. One function of normative beliefs is to serve as guides for action, thereby reducing the information-processing workload by providing shortcuts for deciding how to behave in a given situation. Therefore, once normative beliefs are well developed, one's behavior generally should be consistent with the norms one endorses.

It has been hypothesized by a number of theorists that normative beliefs play an important role in regulating aggressive behavior and that differences in normative beliefs are related to individual differences in the propensity of humans to respond aggressively (Bandura, 1986; Guerra & Slaby, 1990; Huesmann, 1988; Huesmann & Eron, 1989; Zumkley, 1984). Huesmann (1988) has conceptualized the role of normative beliefs within the framework of an information-processing theory for the development and maintenance of aggressive habits. He proposed that a person's social behavior is controlled to a great extent by internalized scripts for behavior that are learned at a young age, and which are influenced by concurrently developing normative beliefs. This early learning produces cognitive structures that are resistant to change and which promote the continuity of aggressive or nonaggressive behavior into later life.

Certainly there can be little doubt about the early emergence of aggressive behavior and its relative stability as the child develops. By age 8, children have adopted characteristic patterns of aggressive behavior (Eron, Walder, & Lefkowitz, 1971; Parke & Slaby, 1983), and these early aggressive behaviors are predictive of later aggression (Olweus, 1979). The more aggressive child is likely to become the more aggressive adult.

Equally clear is the early emergence of gender differences in physical aggression and the continuity of such differences over time (Eron & Huesmann, 1989). To the extent that these gender differences are the product of differential socialization, it has been hypothesized that gender typing of acceptable behaviors acts to bias behavioral choices in both boys and girls (Perry & Bussey, 1979; Tieger, 1980). That is, girls typically display less physical aggression than boys because they learn that they are not supposed to be aggressive, while boys learn that male aggressiveness is appropriate and even desirable (Bandura, 1965). Therefore, normative beliefs about gender-appropriate aggression are relevant to our understanding of gender differences in aggressive behavior.

Numerous studies have examined factors believed to influence gender typing of aggression in children, including differential treatment of boys and girls by parents from infancy (Condry & Condry, 1976; Rubin, Provenzano, & Luria, 1974), observation of differences in aggression by male and female television characters (Huesmann & Eron, 1986), and exposure to commonly held cultural stereotypes of gender-appropriate aggressive behavior (Mischel, 1970). However, very few studies have directly examined differences between boys' and girls' normative beliefs about gender-appropriate aggression.

One reason why such data has not been readily available has been that there was no generally accepted valid and reliable measure of children's normative beliefs about aggression. Recently, however, we have developed such a measure, and applied it to a substantial sample of elementary-age school children (Huesmann *et al.*, 1991). The data derived on this aggression approval scale for children have enabled us to examine more carefully the role that normative beliefs about aggression might play in the observed gender differences in aggressive behavior.

## II. Method

In the current study we compare boys' and girls' beliefs on the appropriateness of aggression and how these beliefs relate to boys' and girls' aggressive behavior.

### A. SUBJECTS

The subjects for the study were 293 elementary school children in four inner city Chicago schools. The schools had volunteered to participate in a study of aggressive behavior in children, and aggressive behavior was a major problem in the neighborhoods these schools served. All of the children in the 2nd, 3rd, and 4th Grade of these schools for whom parental permission could be obtained (88% of all students) participated. The sample was 85% African-American and contained 155 males and 138 females approximately equally distributed across the three grades and four schools.

### B. MEASURES

The *Aggression Approval Scale* (AGGAPS) is a 35-item scale derived to assess children's beliefs about the appropriateness of aggression. The development of the full scale and its psychometric characteristics have been described elsewhere in detail (Huesmann *et al.*, 1991). The questions on the scale are of the form, "It's O.K. (or it's wrong) for a boy (or girl) to hit (or scream at) another boy (or girl) if that boy (or girl) hits (or says something bad to) him first." The response options for each question are "NEVER," "SOMETIMES," "OFTEN," or "ALWAYS."[1] The full scale has 12 overlapping subscales which all have internal consistencies of .70 or higher for children age 7 to 10. The coefficient alpha for the full scale was .90 though the three-month stability was only about .50. Huesmann *et al.* (1991) concluded that normative beliefs can be measured reliably, but may not be very stable during this developmental period.

[1]In a more recent version of the AGGAPS, the form of the question has been changed to "Do you think it is O.K. (wrong) . . ." with the response options changed to "Yes, it's perfectly O.K; Yes, it's sort of O.K.; No, it's sort of wrong; No, it's really wrong." This new version seems to produce somewhat more reliable and valid data. However, the older version was employed in the current study.

The children's aggressive behavior was assessed from three sources: peers, teacher, and self. The *Peer-nominated Index of Aggression* scores were derived according to the procedure developed by Eron and his colleagues (Eron, Walder, & Lefkowitz, 1971; Huesmann, Lagerspetz, & Eron, 1984). Each child in a classroom nominates the other children who fit any of ten questions about aggressive behavior, e.g. "Who pushes and shoves other children?" A child's aggression score is the percentage of times the child is nominated on the key questions. This measure has been widely used in many countries and has internal consistencies of about .95 and one-month test–retest reliabilities of about .91. The teachers rated the children's aggression on the *Behavior Rating Scale* (Behar & Stringfield, 1974), and the children rated their own serious aggressive behavior on a 10-item scale of *Physical Aggression* developed by Huesmann *et al.* (1984). This scale assesses hostile feelings such as "I feel like picking a fight," more common aggressive behaviors such as slapping or kicking, and very serious interpersonal acts such as choking or beating another person. Both scales have demonstrated reliability.

### C. PROCEDURE

The children were interviewed and assessed in their classrooms during three one-hour sessions conducted by trained graduate research assistants. In addition, 99 mothers of these children responded to mail interviews, so their scores on the AGGAPS and the Physical Aggression scale were available.

## III. Results

The mean scores on the major subscales of the AGGAPS are presented for boys and girls in Table 1. A multivariate analysis of variance enabled us to reject the null hypothesis of no difference in means between boys and girls ($F(11,263) = 3.27$, $p < .001$). However, there was no gender-by-grade interaction, indicating that the differences between boys and girls do not change much between the 2nd and 4th Grade.

The significance levels for *post hoc* univariate *t*-tests for each subscale are shown in Table 1. One can see that on most of the subscales the boys' mean was significantly higher than the girls' mean, indicating greater approval of aggression. These means must be evaluated with reference to the response scale for the questions. A score of "1" corresponds to the response, "It's never O.K. (or it's always wrong)." A score of "2" corresponds to the response, "It's sometimes O.K. (or it's often wrong)." A score of "3" corresponds to the response, "It's often O.K. (or it's sometimes wrong)," and a score of "4" corresponds to the response, "It's always O.K. (or it's never wrong)." Therefore, on the average, the children rated all the aggressive behaviors as only "sometimes O.K."

**Table 1**
**A Comparison of the Mean Approval of Aggression Scores of Boys and Girls on the AGGAPS Scales and Their Mean Aggression Scores[a]**

| Scale | Boys mean (*N* = 148) | Girls mean (*N* = 127) | *p* < |
|---|---|---|---|
| Approval of: | | | |
| Aggression at children | 2.26 | 2.08 | .02 |
| Aggression at adults | 1.87 | 1.64 | .03 |
| Aggression when out of control | 2.06 | 1.83 | .05 |
| Aggression with weak provocation | 2.16 | 2.04 | ns[b] |
| Aggression with strong provocation | 2.55 | 2.36 | .05 |
| Boy's aggression | 2.30 | 2.00 | .001 |
| Girl's aggression | 2.21 | 2.16 | ns |
| Aggression at boy | 2.25 | 2.16 | ns |
| Aggression at girl | 2.27 | 2.00 | .001 |
| Boy's aggression at girl | 2.31 | 1.92 | .0001 |
| Girl's aggression at boy | 2.21 | 2.22 | ns |
| Believe adults approve of child agg. | 1.87 | 1.64 | .03 |
| Aggression: | | | |
| Peer nominations | 0.25 | 0.20 | .01 |
| Self-reports | 2.36 | 2.37 | ns |
| Teacher ratings | 0.67 | 0.43 | .0001 |

[a]All "OK" items are scored NEVER = 1, SOMETIMES = 2, OFTEN = 3 and ALWAYS = 4. All "WRONG" items are scored NEVER = 4, SOMETIMES = 3, OFTEN = 2 and ALWAYS = 1. Scale scores are the mean of the scores on the items on the scale that were answered by the child. Thus, each score represents the child's belief in the *appropriateness of aggression.*

[b]ns, Nonsignificant.

It is interesting to examine the scales on which boys did not score significantly higher than girls. On "aggression by girls against boys," "girl's aggression" overall, and general "aggression against boys," the mean approval scores for girls were almost exactly the same as for boys. Boys and girls also did not differ significantly in their approval of aggression following weak provocation, for example, "saying something bad to the person." However, boys and girls differed greatly in their willingness to approve of "boys aggressing against girls" and "boy's aggression" in general. Boys approved much more of both of these.

One can also see from Table 1 that boys scored significantly higher on aggression than girls on the three scales used (MANOVA $F(3,248) = 6.00$, $p < .001$). However, *post hoc* tests revealed that the differences obtained only on

**Table 2**
**The Mean Approval of Aggression Scores for the Mothers and Their Daughters and Sons on Four Major AGGAPS Scales[a]**

| Scale | Mothers mean | Mothers SD | Daughters (N = 42) mean | Daughters (N = 42) SD | Significance of difference |
|---|---|---|---|---|---|
| Total aggression (at children) | 1.58 | 0.39 | 2.04 | 0.54 | .0001 |
| Child agg. when out of control | 1.48 | 0.51 | 1.83 | 0.62 | .02 |
| Child agg. with weak provocation | 1.45 | 0.43 | 2.04 | 0.63 | .0001 |
| Child agg. with strong provocation | 2.02 | 0.67 | 2.25 | 0.70 | ns[b] |
| | **Mothers mean** | **Mothers SD** | **Sons (N = 47) mean** | **Sons (N = 47) SD** | **Significance of difference** |
| Total aggression (at children) | 1.57 | 0.38 | 2.31 | 0.75 | .0001 |
| Child agg. when out of control | 1.42 | 0.46 | 2.15 | 0.82 | .0001 |
| Child agg. with weak provocation | 1.50 | 0.40 | 2.29 | 0.86 | .0001 |
| Child agg. with strong provocation | 2.03 | 0.67 | 2.49 | 0.86 | .0001 |

[a]The response 1 corresponds to "NEVER" approving of the type of aggression, while 2 corresponds to approving of the type of aggression "SOMETIMES."

[b]ns, Nonsignificant.

peer-nominated and teacher-rated aggression. There were no significant differences on self-ratings.

In Table 2 the girls' and boys' mean scores are compared with their mothers' scores. On all the major scales the mothers scored substantially lower than their daughters and sons. The standard deviations of most of the mothers' responses was also low, indicating substantial consensus among the mothers that aggression should not be approved. The standard deviation was the highest for "aggression with strong provocation" indicating that the mothers disagreed with each other the most on approval of this kind of aggression. This was the one scale on which they did not differ significantly in approval rating from their daughters.

Both boys' and girls' approval of aggression ratings correlated substantially with their ratings of their own physical aggression, as Table 3 reveals. The correlations for boys were substantially higher, but the higher correlations for boys may reflect the higher means and greater standard deviations on both the AGGAPS and the Physical Aggression scale for boys. The girls' scores were more tightly packed close to zero on both scales. It is interesting to note that the highest correlation with girls' self-reported aggression is for the girls' "approval of aggressing at boys." On the other hand, "approval of aggressing at girls" which correlates highly with boys' self-reported aggression does not correlate at all with girls' self-reported aggression.

The correlations between the AGGAPS scores and peer-nominated aggression were not significant for girls. However, at least some were significant for boys, as Table 3 shows. In particular, "approval of a boy aggressing at a girl" correlated the highest with boys' peer-nominated aggression. A multiple regression analysis revealed that no scale added significantly to predicting a boy's aggression beyond boys' approval of aggression toward girls. The teacher ratings of aggression are excluded from the table because the teacher ratings of children's aggression did not correlate at all with the children's scores on the approval of aggression scale.

Finally, let us examine the age trends for approval of aggression in boys and girls. As Table 4 shows, for both boys and girls, approval of aggression did not decrease consistently on any of the scales from Grades 2 to 3 to 4. In fact, the tendency was for approval of aggression to increase among the older children. The increases for aggression in response to strong provocation were significant for boys and marginally significant for girls. The other increases did not reach statistical significance.

**Table 3**
**Correlations between Approval of Aggression Scores on AGGAPS and Actual Aggressive Behavior for Boys and Girls**

| | Boys ($N$ = 132) | | Girls ($N$ = 119) | | Total | |
|---|---|---|---|---|---|---|
| AGGAPS Scales | Peer-nom. Agg. | Self-rep. Agg. | Peer-nom. Agg. | Self-rep. Agg. | Peer-nom. Agg. | Self-rep. Agg. |
| Approval of: | | | | | | |
| Aggression at children | 0.15[+a] | 0.41*** | ns[b] | 0.23* | ns | 0.33*** |
| Aggression at adults | ns | 0.35*** | ns | ns | ns | 0.27*** |
| Agg. when out of control | ns | 0.44*** | ns | 0.22* | 0.11[+] | 0.35*** |
| Agg. with weak provocation | 0.16[+] | 0.35*** | ns | 0.18* | 0.11[+] | 0.27*** |
| Agg. with strong provocation | ns | 0.26** | ns | 0.18* | ns | 0.23*** |
| Boy's aggression | 0.17* | 0.42*** | ns | 0.17[+] | 0.12[+] | 0.30*** |
| Girl's aggression | ns | 0.36*** | ns | 0.26** | ns | 0.32*** |
| Aggression at boy | ns | 0.41*** | ns | 0.31*** | ns | 0.36*** |
| Aggression at girl | 0.17* | 0.39*** | ns | ns | 0.11[+] | 0.27*** |
| Boy's agg. at girl | 0.19* | 0.40*** | ns | ns | 0.12[+] | 0.25*** |
| Girl's agg. at boy | ns | 0.38*** | ns | 0.30*** | ns | 0.34*** |

[+a]$p < .10$, *$p < .05$, **$p < .01$, ***$p < .001$.
[b]ns, Nonsignificant.

**Table 4**
**Means on Approval of Aggression by Grade and Gender**

| | Girls | | | | Boys | | | |
|---|---|---|---|---|---|---|---|---|
| AGGAPS Scales | Grade 2 | Grade 3 | Grade 4 | $p <$ | Grade 2 | Grade 3 | Grade 4 | $p <$ |
| Aggression at children | 2.00 | 2.10 | 2.12 | ns[a] | 2.16 | 2.35 | 2.30 | ns |
| Agg. when out of control | 1.80 | 2.04 | 1.66 | .02 | 2.11 | 2.08 | 1.98 | ns |
| Agg. with weak provocation | 2.02 | 1.95 | 2.15 | ns | 2.03 | 2.32 | 2.19 | ns |
| Agg. with strong provocation | 2.20 | 2.31 | 2.56 | .10 | 2.34 | 2.65 | 2.72 | .03 |
| Boy's aggression | 1.93 | 2.05 | 2.02 | ns | 2.18 | 2.45 | 2.31 | .15 |
| Girl's aggression | 2.08 | 2.15 | 2.23 | ns | 2.13 | 2.25 | 2.28 | ns |
| Boy's agg. at girls | 1.81 | 1.97 | 1.96 | ns | 2.19 | 2.46 | 2.33 | ns |
| Girl's agg. at boys | 2.15 | 2.22 | 2.28 | ns | 2.08 | 2.26 | 2.33 | ns |

[a]ns, Nonsignificant.

# IV. Discussion

The results of this study indicate that boys and girls hold differing standards regarding the appropriateness of aggressive behavior. Boys' approval of aggression ratings were significantly higher than girls' ratings on eight of the twelve subscales of the Aggression Approval Scale. This finding supports the idea that gender typing of aggression is evident during the early elementary school years, and is reflected in differences in normative beliefs about aggression held by boys and girls. Thus, not only are boys more physically aggressive than girls from this early age, they are also more likely to believe that aggression is an acceptable behavior across a range of circumstances (i.e., out of control and strong provocation) and targets (i.e., girls and adults).

The observed gender difference in the subscale, "boy's aggression at girl," is of particular interest. The greatest difference in scores between boys' and girls' approval of aggression was revealed for this subscale. Furthermore, in comparing approval of aggression scores by differing targets of aggression (children, boys, and girls), boys' *highest* approval ratings and girls' *lowest* approval ratings of aggression were found for this subscale. It is unclear why boys as early as Grade 2 indicate greater approval for aggression against girls. Given that our sample is comprised of children living in inner city neighborhoods, we can only speculate that children may witness considerable amounts of violence directed at both males and females, and that in this environment violence against females may be considered acceptable masculine behavior.

Mothers of both boys and girls were also significantly less likely to approve of aggression across a range of situations. However, since the mean approval ratings of mothers of sons and mothers of daughters were almost identical, mothers' normative beliefs do not appear to be significant in the observed gender differences of their sons and daughters on these normative beliefs. Assuming that these gender differences in normative beliefs continue into adulthood, we would expect children's fathers (or important male role models) to be more likely to approve of aggression and perhaps to be more influential in the development of these early gender differences in aggression approval, particularly in terms of boys' higher approval scores.

It is an interesting point that children's aggression approval scores did not relate consistently to their actual aggressive behavior. While the highest correlations obtained were between aggression approval scores and self-report of aggression scores (particularly for boys), much of this relation may be attributed to the common method variance of self-reports. Teacher ratings of children's aggressive behavior did not relate at all to their approval scores. Peer nomination of aggression scores related to aggression approval scores for boys but not for girls. However, these relations were obtained for less than half of the subscales and were quite modest in size.

These findings suggest that gender differences in normative beliefs about aggression emerge during the elementary school years. At the same age, significant differences in aggressive behavior are very apparent between boys and girls, at least on physical aggression as measured by teachers' and peers' reports. However, these differences in approval of aggression seem to be of little value in understanding the observed differences in physical aggression between boys and girls as they only correlate slightly with aggression in the overall sample. They appear to be of more value in understanding differences in boys' aggressive behavior where some correlations are obtained.

There are several reasons why this may be the case. Children's beliefs appear to be only moderately stable at this age, and most children respond with ratings of "sometimes." As children get older, however, their normative beliefs may become more firmly established, with approval of aggression increasing in some (e.g., strong provocation) but not all situations. Furthermore, the lack of relations obtained between girls' aggression approval scores and aggressive behavior may be due, in part, to a floor effect stemming from the girls' low scores on both measures. Our findings suggest that while gender differences in normative beliefs about aggression emerge at an early age, they are of limited value in explaining early gender differences in aggressive behavior.

## V. Summary

The Aggression Approval Scale (AGGAPS) was administered to 293 2nd, 3rd, and 4th Grade predominantly African-American boys and girls from four inner city elementary schools and 99 of their mothers. In addition, children's physically aggressive behavior was measured by self-report, teacher ratings, and peer nominations. On 8 of the 12 AGGAPS subscales, boys were found to approve more of aggression than girls, and these differences did not vary by grade. However, older children approved of aggression slightly more than younger children. Mothers approved of aggression significantly less than both their sons and daughters. Overall, individual differences in children's aggressive behavior were not highly correlated with individual differences in AGGAPS scores, although some relations were obtained for boys. Our findings suggest that normative beliefs about aggression may be only moderately stable during the early elementary years and are of limited utility in understanding early gender differences in aggression.

## Acknowledgments

The authors gratefully acknowledge the assistance of Leonard Eron in this research. Portions of the text have appeared previously in Huesmann *et al.* (1991). This research was supported in part by Grants MH47474 and MH44768 from the National Institute of Mental Health to Huesmann and Guerra, and by a James McKeen Cattell Foundation fellowship to Huesmann. Requests for reprints should be sent to L. Rowell Huesmann, Department of Psychology, M/C 285, University of Illinois at Chicago, Box 4348, Chicago, Illinois 60680.

## References

Bandura, A. (1965). Influence of models' reinforcement contingencies on the acquisition of imitative responses. *Journal of Personality and Social Psychology, 1*, 589–595.

Bandura, A. (1986). *Social Foundations of Thought and Action: A Social Cognitive Theory*. Englewood Cliffs, New Jersey: Prentice-Hall.

Bandura, A. (1989). Self-regulation of motivation and action through internal standards and goal systems. *In* L. A. Pervin (Ed.), *Goals Concepts in Personality and Social Psychology* (pp. 19–85). Hillsdale, New Jersey: Erlbaum.

Behar, L., & Stringfield, S. (1974). A behavior rating scale for the preschool child. *Developmental Psychology, 10*, 601–610.

Condry, J., & Condry, S. (1976). Sex differences: A study of the eye of the beholder. *Child Development, 47*, 812–819.

Eron, L. D., & Huesmann, L. R. (1989). The genesis of gender differences in aggression. *In* M. A. Luszcz & T. Nettlebeck (Eds.), *Psychological Development: Perspectives across the Life Span* (pp. 55–67). Amsterdam: Elsevier.

Eron, L. D., Walder, L. O., & Lefkowitz, M. M. (1971). *The Learning of Aggression in Children.* Boston: Little Brown.

Guerra, N. G., & Slaby, R. G. (1990). Cognitive mediators of aggression in adolescent offenders: II. Intervention. *Developmental Psychology, 26*, 269–277.

Huesmann, L. R. (1988). An information processing model for the development of aggression. *Aggressive Behavior, 14*, 13–24.

Huesmann, L. R., & Eron, L. D. (1986). *Television and the Aggressive Child: A Cross-National Comparison.* Hillsdale, New Jersey: Erlbaum.

Huesmann, L. R., & Eron, L. D. (1989). Individual differences and the trait of aggression. *European Journal of Personality, 3*, 95–106.

Huesmann, L. R., Lagerspetz, K., & Eron, L. D. (1984). Intervening variables in the TV violence-aggression relation: Evidence from two countries. *Developmental Psychology, 20*, 746–775.

Huesmann, L. R., Eron, L. D., Lefkowitz, M. M., & Walder, L. O. (1984). The stability of aggression over time and generations. *Developmental Psychology, 20*, 1120–1134.

Huesmann, L. R., Guerra, N. G., Miller, L. S., & Zelli, A. (1991). The role of social norms in the development of aggressive behavior. *In* A. Fraczek & H. Zumkley (Eds.), *Socialization and Aggression.* New York/Heidelberg: Springer-Verlag.

Mischel, W. (1970). Sex-typing and socialization. *In* P. H. Mussen (Ed.), *Carmichael's Manual of Child Psychology (3rd Ed.).* New York: Wiley.

Olweus, D. (1979). The stability of aggressive reaction patterns in human males: A review. *Psychological Bulletin, 85*, 852–875.

Parke, R. D., & Slaby, R. G. (1983). The development of aggression. *In* P. Mussen (Ed.), *Handbook of Child Psychology* (pp. 547–642). New York: Wiley.

Perry, D. G., & Bussey, K. (1979). The social learning theory of sex differences: imitation is alive and well. *Journal of Personality and Social Psychology, 37*, 1699–1712.

Rubin, J. Z., Provenzano, F. J., & Luria, Z. (1974). The eye of the beholder: parents' view on sex of newborns. *American Journal of Orthopsychiatry, 44*, 512–519.

Tieger, T. (1980). On the biological basis of sex differences in aggression. *Child Development, 51*, 943–963.

Zumkley, H. (1984). Individual differences and aggressive interactions. *In* A. Mummendey (Ed.), *Social Psychology of Aggression: From Individual Behavior to Social Interaction.* Berlin: Springer-Verlag.

8

# *Gender Differences in Violence: Biology and/or Socialization?*

Leonard D. Eron

I. INTRODUCTION
II. THE TWO STUDIES
A. Measures
III. FINDINGS
A. Parental Behaviors
B. Games and Activities
C. Television Watching
D. The Stability of Aggression
IV. CONCLUSION
REFERENCES

## I. Introduction

The preponderance of evidence indicates that aggression, defined as "behavior intended to injure other persons" (Eron, 1987), is more characteristic of males than of females. This is apparent from popular lore (Klama, 1988) and anecdotal evidence (Miedzian, 1991), from crime and delinquency statistics (U.S. Department of Justice, 1989), and from studies conducted both in psychological laboratories (Bandura, Ross, & Ross, 1961) and under more natural conditions (Eron *et al.*, 1987). Such consistently one-sided findings would seem to indicate some underlying biological, perhaps hormonal, basis for the difference.

*Author's note*: "Gender Differences in Violence" is adapted from "The Genesis of Gender Differences in Aggression," an invited address to the XXIVth International Congress of Psychology, Sydney, Australia, August 1988. It reports on the author's experiences of two longitudinal studies of children's aggression, the first with regard to parental influence and the second to the influence of television. The author wishes to acknowledge the important contribution to this research of L. Rowell Huesmann.

There are many instances, however, of some females responding as aggressively as the most aggressive males. We have only to recall Ilse Koch, the so-called "bitch of Buchenwald," who personally whipped camp inmates with the riding crop she carried and made lampshades out of their skin. On the basis of their extensive review of literature regarding the respective aggressiveness of males and females, Maccoby and Jacklin (1974) conclude that although "relevant experiences can alter an individual's characteristic way of responding aggressively or unaggressively . . . there is a sex-linked differential readiness to respond in aggressive ways to the relevant experiences" (p. 247). Subsequent narrative reviews of the literature (Frodi, MacCauley, and Thome, 1977; White, 1983) and two meta-analyses (Hyde, 1984; Eagly & Steffen, 1986) substantiate stereotypical gender differences in aggressiveness, although the size—and even the direction—of differences are shown to be tempered by a number of social variables; Lagerspetz, Björkqvist, and Peltonen (1988) found that girls are more aggressive when the type of aggression is indirect, opposed to physical and/or verbal direct aggression.

## II. The Two Studies

For several years, my colleagues and I have been engaged in two large-scale longitudinal studies that document the differences between girls' and boys' expression of aggression and violence which then carry over into adulthood. Although producing results not inconsistent with a biological interpretation, these studies' associated findings compel the serious consideration of a social learning basis for the difference in aggression between males and females.

The first of these studies followed 632 children, from a 3rd Grade total of 875, in a semirural county of New York State in 1960 to age 30 in the summer of 1981 (Huesmann *et al.*, 1984). The most notable result of this study was the finding that early childhood aggression, as observed in school, is correlated with adult antisocial and criminal behavior.

The second study consisted of three-year longitudinal investigations conducted between 1977 and 1983 in five countries, the United States, Australia, Finland, Poland, and Israel (Huesmann & Eron, 1986). The focus of this study was the relation between television habits and the development of aggressive behavior; in all five countries such a relation was found.

Both studies, however, also revealed significant differences between male and female subjects' response to various parental child-rearing practices. These differences were, in turn, related to differences in aggression levels and were differentially predictive of aggression over time.

### A. MEASURES

#### *1. The 22-year Study*

As would be expected, male subjects scored higher than females on almost every measure of aggressive behavior considered in both studies. In the 22-year study there were 29 different measures of aggressive behavior over three waves, including peer nominations, self-ratings, ratings by the spouse, and criminal justice data. Male subjects obtained significantly higher scores than did female subjects in all but four of the measures, and in the remaining four the trend was in the expected direction in three of the four measures; thus of 29 measures, males scored higher on all but one. It is an interesting point that the one measure on which females obtained higher (if not significantly higher) scores was a self-rating measure of aggressive drive taken at age 30, indicating that although females often harbor the impulse to act in an aggressive manner, they successfully inhibit such impulses.

#### *2. The 3-year Study*

The 3-year study had only four measures which could be said to assess aggression, peer nominations of aggressive behavior, self-ratings on extent of aggressive fantasy, self-ratings of subject identification with aggressive TV characters, and self-ratings of similarity to hypothetical aggressive children. In each of the five countries, boys obtained significantly higher scores than girls on all but one measure. This exception was identification with aggressive TV characters in the United States and Australia, where girls received higher scores than boys, though not significantly so. One explanation for this apparent anomaly is that in both these countries boys rarely considered themselves to be like female aggressive characters, while girls were not reluctant to admit they were like male characters.

## III. Findings

### A. PARENTAL BEHAVIORS

#### *1. Punishment*

In terms of parental behaviors presumed to be precursors of aggressive behavior in youngsters, there was no difference in mean score on rejection by parents between boys and girls in the 22-year study. Nor was there a difference in nurturance. However, in the 3-year study, boys in the United States and Australia had higher rejection scores than girls, while again there were no differences between genders in scores on nurturance in any country.

The one parental behavior in the 22-year study which discriminated significantly between boys and girls was punishment for aggressive behavior. Overall, boys were punished more harshly than girls, although girls were more likely to receive psychological punishment, that is, love withdrawal, and boys to receive physical punishment. A comparison was made, in that study, of parents' judgments regarding how harsh a standard set of punishments would be for girls and for boys. Girls whose parents judged this set to be harsh for them were less aggressive in school than girls whose parents judged such punishments to be not harsh. This was not so for boys. Thus, not only is there differential punishment for boys and girls, but also, judged sensitivity of girls relates to school aggression, whereas that of boys does not. The 3-year study showed boys were punished more harshly in each country, although only in Finland was the difference statistically significant.

These findings of differential punishment for girls and boys predict not only that boys would be more aggressive than girls, but also that girls should be more closely identified with parents in terms of internalization of standards. This prediction is borne out by higher mean scores of females in the 22-year study on measures of confessing and guilt. Although these measures were not obtained in the cross-national study, Miller's (1988) *post hoc* analysis of that study derived a measure of identification based, as in the earlier study, on extent of discrepancy between parent and child self-ratings on items which were similar in the parent and child interviews. She found the same negative relation between (peer-nominated) aggression and identification with parent; the less identified the child was with the mother, the more aggressive he or she was in school.

It is interesting to note that Miller's analysis suggests a different causal effect for boys than girls. Whereas for boys aggression seems to precede low identification with mother, for girls this low identification itself leads to aggression. What seems to be happening is that aggressive boys are developing in other ways that are also out of keeping with their mothers' standards and values. Conversely, girls who do not subscribe to their mothers' traditional values and standards in other areas also become more aggressive; having thrown over mothers' norms from frustration or lack of personal satisfaction, they adopt a pattern more characteristic of boys.

This finding, of a causal effect of low identification on school aggression for girls, supports a conclusion drawn from the first phase of the 22-year study (Eron, Walder, & Lefkowitz, 1971). One consistent pattern to emerge from the welter of findings at that stage was that of a difference between the ways boys and girls respond to what goes on inside and outside the home; while girls' school aggression was related highly to punishment for home aggression, that of boys seemed to be more affected by fathers' occupational status, mobility orientation, and ethnicity. Boys' behavior was affected by the family's position in society, girls' by what went on in the home.

### *2. Socialization*

A further finding from the same phase points to the significance of parents' ambivalence in socializing children of different sexes. Girls' aggression at home, as rated by their parents, was highly correlated with (peers' ratings of) aggression at school, while for boys there was a zero-order correlation of the two measures. This seems to reflect conflicting tendencies in parents when describing sons' aggression. Although a generally undesirable behavior, aggression is a desirable *masculine* behavior, and this ambiguity may show as confusion in parents' ratings. Parents describing daughters' aggression had no such conflict, as the undesirability of aggressive behavior in general applies to girls in particular. Such differential expectations for boys' and girls' behaviors have been highlighted in a recent questionnaire study of 120 children, age 9 to 12 (Perry, Perry, & Weiss, 1989), which found boys expected less negative self-evaluation, as well as less parental disapproval, for aggression than did girls.

Additionally, differential socialization by parents is involved with their expectations and ambivalence, as is shown by correlations in the 22-year study between parents' church attendance and children's low aggression. The finding of such a correlation among females, age 18, whose parents had attended church when their daughters were age 8 is not reflected among males, possibly because Christian teachings of tolerance and passivity are consonant with "ladylike" behavior and dissonant with the "manly" expectations of boys who, certainly in the early 1950s, learned counteraggression instead of "turning the other cheek." This principle reflects, after all, the close association in western Christian societies of soldiering and masculinity; the opprobrium with which one such society views the suggestion that women "man" weapons of destruction is the basis of opposition to the United States Equal Rights Amendment.

## B. GAMES AND ACTIVITIES

In the first study a preference for girls' or boys' games was used as a measure of preferred gender role identification at an early age, although preferences for boys' and girls' games were never taken to be antipodal, that is high masculine sex-role preference does not imply low feminine sex-role preference for the same individual, and vice versa. It was found that boys who liked girls' games tended to be less aggressive in school than boys who did not, a correlation still present 10 years later. For girls, although the results were in the predicted direction, they were not statistically significant. However, lack of preference for girls' games was one of the most important predictors for high psychopathology scores in young adulthood. What seems to happen is that, while for boys the choice of feminine games acts in itself as a suppressor for both present and later aggression, girls' engagement in role-inappropriate behavior at an early age is more an *indication* of deviance which is revealed at a later stage. The reason for the significant relation between parents' reports of how harshly they punish their daughters' aggression and those daughters' psychopathology results may lie here also. Aggression is an inappropriate behavior for girls. Parents who say they punish their daughters severely for aggression are perhaps responding to that expectation and are already taking note of this deviance and labeling it for us.

Data obtained in the two follow-up periods in the 22-year study indicate that when adult females prefer stereotyped masculine activities, such behavior is positively related to aggression. For example, young women who prefer to watch contact sports on television are more aggressive than women who do not. Also, the more aggressive they are, the higher are these women's scores on the masculinity scale of the MMPI. Both of these scores reflect attitudes and behaviors which are normative for boys. For boys, however, there was no relation between aggression score and either viewing contact sports on television or masculinity on the M-F score. It is very probable that these lacks of relation lie in the minimal variability for boys on these variables; most boys watch contact sports and endorse the attitudes and interests comprising the M-F scale's masculinity items. Overall, these results indicate that the interests and activities of aggressive females tend to be deviant from gender norms and similar to the behavior of the male gender group.

## C. TELEVISION WATCHING

The later study, of television habits and aggression, shows that girls in general are less aggressive, watch violent television less, and do not believe so strongly that television is realistic. Although there is no significant difference in the frequency with which girls and boys watch television in general in any of the countries, boys in each country watch significantly more television violence than girls. Developmental trends, however, for the two genders are identical from ages 6 to 10, and the shapes of the growth curves are identical (Eron *et al.*, 1983). Indeed, not only was there a positive relation for both boys and girls in each of the five countries between the amount of television violence observed and aggression in school, but longitudinal effects over 3 years were demonstrated in all countries (in Finland for boys only) except Australia.

Contrary to the expectations from the earlier study, the United States sample produced a positive correlation between television violence viewing and aggression in girls, even stronger than the one for boys. Before this second study, it had been our hypothesis that the lack of relation between television violence and aggression for girls in the late 1950s and early 1960s was a result of the lack of violent female characters at that time. However, as indicated earlier, in this study girls did not identify more closely with female than with male characters, despite the many aggressive female models on television in the late 1970s; in fact, boys' and girls' aggressiveness related equally strongly to male and female actor violence. Necessarily looking elsewhere for reasons why girls are only now affected in their behavior by television violence, we hypothesize that the reason has to do with aggression now becoming a more acceptable and normative behavior for women; recent emphasis on the desirability for women to be more assertive, as well as more athletic, has probably caused girls to have fewer inhibitions about performing the aggressive behaviors they see on television, whether performed by male or female characters. Girls' own attitudes about what it is appropriate for them to do, and how they may or must act, have changed. And while this may be good for society, it has some negative effects.

## D. THE STABILITY OF AGGRESSION

The stability of aggressive behavior is an important respect in which males and females differ, as has been pointed out by Olweus (1981) and Roff & Wirt (1984). Aggressiveness stability coefficients in our 22-year study, .50 for males and .34 for females, compare favorably with other personality and intellect variables, compelling evidence that aggressive behavior remains stable after a child is 8 years old.

Depending on the manifestation of aggressiveness one chooses to analyze, it may appear stable more for male than for female subjects. Male aggression as rated by peers at age 8 was related to all the following age 30 measures: MMPI, spouse's rating of the subject's aggression, severity with which subjects punished their own children, number of criminal justice convictions and seriousness of offenses, number of moving-traffic violations and driving-while-intoxicated arrests. Conversely, from female aggression at age 8 there was significant prediction at age 30 on only two measures: MMPI and punishment of the subject's own children. Child punishment, though, may be the *only* area in which an adult female can express aggression without fear of observation by others and resulting social censure. When this does receive outside attention we call it child abuse and, as has been shown by a number of studies, most child abuse is indeed carried out by the mother in the privacy of the home.

On all other measures and in other arenas there is actually such a low frequency of aggressive behavior in females that successful prediction from earlier indications of aggression is very unlikely. Robins's (1986) large-scale retrospective study found conduct disorder in girls to be a relatively rare diagnosis as compared to boys and that its "low frequency . . . can best be described as a general depression of conduct problems, rather than as girls eschewing certain behavior that might be perceived as specifically masculine" (p. 392). However, female subjects who *had* conduct disorders as youngsters tended to have an *increased* rate of psychiatric disorders as adults, which was not true for males. Further, while for men conduct problems before age 15 predicted only externalizing diagnoses, such as antisocial personality and substance abuse, in women they also predicted an increased rate of internalizing symptoms, such as affective, somatization, and anxiety disorders. This is a further indication that girls engaging in masculine-type behaviors as youngsters are probably already singled out as deviant, and thus tend, as adults, to have an increased rate of psychiatric disorders.

## IV. Conclusion

All these results seem to point in one direction. Over and above any genetic, constitutional, or biological predisposition that may underlie the observed differences between males and females in aggressive behavior, there is something about the way we socialize boys and girls and the different expectations we have for males and females in our society that contributes in an important way to the differential incidence of antisocial aggression in these two groups of human beings.

## References


Bandura, A., Ross, D., & Ross, S. A. (1961). Transmission of aggression through imitation of aggressive models. *Journal of Abnormal and Social Psycholgy, 63*, 575–582.

Eagly, A. H., & Steffen, V. J. (1986). Gender and aggressive behavior: a metaanalytic review of the social psychological literature. *Psychological Bulletin, 100*, 309–330.

Eron, L. D. (1987). The development of aggressive behavior from the perspective of a developing behaviorism. *American Psychologist, 42*, 435–442.

Eron, L. D., Walder, L. O., & Lefkowitz, M. M. (1971). *The Learning of Aggression in Children.* Boston: Little-Brown.

Eron, L. D., Huesmann, L. R., Brice, P., Fischer, P., & Mermelstein, R. (1983). Age trends in the development of aggression, sextyping, and related television habits. *Developmental Psychology, 19*, 71–77.

Eron, L. D., Huesmann L. R., Dubow, E., Romanoff, R., & Yarmel, P. (1987). Aggression used as correlates over 22 years. In D. Crowell, I. Evans, & C. O'Donnell (Eds.), *Childhood Aggression and Violence. Sources of Influence, Prevention and Control* (pp. 249–262). New York: Plenum.

Frodi, A., Macaulay, J., & Thome, P. R. (1977). Are women always less aggressive than men? A review of the experimental literature. *Psychological Bulletin, 84*, 634–660.

Huesmann, L. R., & Eron, L. D. (1986). *Television and the Aggressive Child: a Cross National Comparison.* Hillsdale, New Jersey: Erlbaum.

Huesmann, L. R., Eron, L. D., Lefkowitz, M. N., & Walder, L. O. (1984). The stability of aggression over time and generations. *Developmental Psychology, 20*, 1120–1134.

Hyde, J. S. (1984). How large are gender differences in aggression? A developmental meta-analysis. *Developmental Psychology, 20*, 722–736.

Klama, J. (1988). *Aggression: the Myth of the Beast Within.* New York: John Wiley.

Lagerspetz, K., Björkqvist, K., & Peltonen, T. (1988). Is indirect aggression typical of females? Gender differences in aggressiveness in 11- to 12-year-old children. *Aggressive Behavior, 14*, 403–404.

Maccoby, E. E., & Jacklin, C. N. (1974). *The Psychology of Sex Differences*. Stanford, California: Stanford University Press.

Miedzian, M. (1991). *Boys Will Be Boys*. New York: Doubleday.

Miller, L. (1988). The relations among child identification with mother, television viewing habits and child aggression. Unpublished Master's thesis. University of Illinois at Chicago.

Olweus, D. (1981). Continuity in aggressive and withdrawn inhibited behavior patterns. *Psychiatry and Social Science, 1*, 141–159.

Perry, D. G., Perry, L. C., & Weiss, R. J. (1989). Sex differences in the consequences children anticipate for aggression. *Developmental Psychology, 25*, 312–319.

Robins, L. N. (1986). The consequences of conduct disorder in girls. *In* D. Olweus, J. Black, & M. Radke-Jarrow (Eds.), *Development of Antisocial and Prosocial Behavior*. New York: Academic Press.

Roff, J. D., & Wirt, R. D. (1984). Childhood aggression and social adjustment as antecedents of delinquency. *Journal of Abnormal and Child Psychology, 12*, 111–126.

U.S. Department of Justice, Bureau of Justice Statistics (1989). *Uniform Crime Reports for the United States, 1988*. Washington, D.C.; U.S. Government Printing Office.

White, J. W. (1983). Sex and gender issues in aggression research. *In* R. G. Geen and E. I. Donnerstein (Eds.), *Aggression: Theoretical and Empirical Reviews, Vol. II. Issues in Research*. New York: Academic Press.

9

# Changes in Patterns of Aggressiveness among Finnish Girls over a Decade

Vappu Viemerö

I. INTRODUCTION
II. QUANTITATIVE DIFFERENCES IN AGGRESSIVENESS BETWEEN GIRLS AND BOYS
III. CHANGES IN GIRLS' AGGRESSIVENESS IN THE EARLY 1990S
IV. DISCUSSION
REFERENCES

## I. Introduction

In the research of aggressive behavior, most studies have reported significant differences between girls and boys; girls have been found to be less aggressive than boys (Eron, 1980; Lagerspetz & Viemerö, 1986; Maccoby & Jacklin, 1974, 1980; Sinkkonen, 1990; Viemerö, 1986). The gender differences in aggressive behavior have been suggested to be due, for example, to parental attitudes toward upbringing (Eron, 1980; Eron & Huesmann, 1984). In Finland, these differences have also been explained to originate from the attitudes regarding the social roles of men and women (Haavio-Mannila, Jallinoja, & Strandell, 1984). More recently, researchers have begun to consider the question in a qualitative rather than a quantitative matter; that is, it has been shown that gender differences reflect different forms of aggression (Huesmann & Eron, 1986; Lagerspetz, Björkqvist, & Peltonen, 1988).

In this chapter, Finnish girls' aggressiveness is discussed against the background of gender differences. Several Finnish studies over the last decade serve as a starting point (Lagerspetz & Viemerö, 1986; Viemerö, 1986, 1990a). The main source of data originates out of the Finnish contribution to a 3-year international study on the effects of television viewing on viewers' aggression (Lagerspetz &

Viemerö, 1986) and a follow-up study of the same subjects (originally $N = 220$), which was performed over an 8-year period (Viemerö, 1986, 1989a). Aggression was measured in the study by the peer-nomination method and by the method of self-rating. Each child named all the children in his/her class who had displayed ten specific aggressive behaviors during the school year. Self-rating of aggression included items in which subjects rated their own similarity to children engaging in specific aggressive behavior.

## II. Quantitative Differences in Aggressiveness between Girls and Boys

In the first three stages out of six of the follow-up study, significant differences were shown to exist between the girls and boys with regard to peer-nominated aggression (1978–1980, when the subjects were 7- to 9- and 9- to 11-years old, respectively); in the years 1978 [$F(1,219) = 17.66$, $p < .001$] and 1980 [$F(1,174) = 8.43$, $p < .005$] (Viemerö, 1986) the figures indicate that the girls were perceived as being less aggressive than the boys. The gender difference was still significant in the fifth stage of the study, in 1983, when the subjects were 13 and 15 years old [$t(134) = 2.81$, $p < .005$] (Viemerö, 1989b).

With regard to self-rated aggression, an analysis of variance showed significant gender differences in the first three stages of the study [e.g., year 1978, $F(1,217) = 15.53$, $p < .004$]. Girls were less aggressive than boys also in the case of self-rated aggression, which form of aggression was not measured in the fifth stage.

In accordance with findings in other countries (Huesmann & Eron, 1986), concurrent correlations between peer nominations and self-ratings were significant for the Finnish boys (at the age of 7 and 9, $r = .25$, $p < .01$; 8 and 10, $r = .25$, $p < .05$; and 9 and 11, $r = .39$, $p < .001$), but significant for the girls only at the age of 11 and 13 years ($r = .33$, $p < .001$). It has been suggested that the lower correlations for the girls between peer-nominated aggression and self-rated aggression are a consequence of the girls' inability to admit that they are aggressive as well as of the girls' difficulty to understand and analyze their own aggression, although they are considered by peers to be aggressive (Huesmann & Eron, 1986). The lower correlations for the girls between peer-nominated and self-rated aggression have also been explained by the failure of aggression measures to differentiate between the separate forms of aggressive behavior employed by girls and boys. Girls use more indirect forms of aggression whereas boys employ direct means (Lagesrpetz *et al.*, 1988).

In 1988, ten years after the first measures of 7- and 9-year-old children's peer-nominated and self-rated aggression were made, another identical study was conducted in order to find out whether there had been changes in aggressive

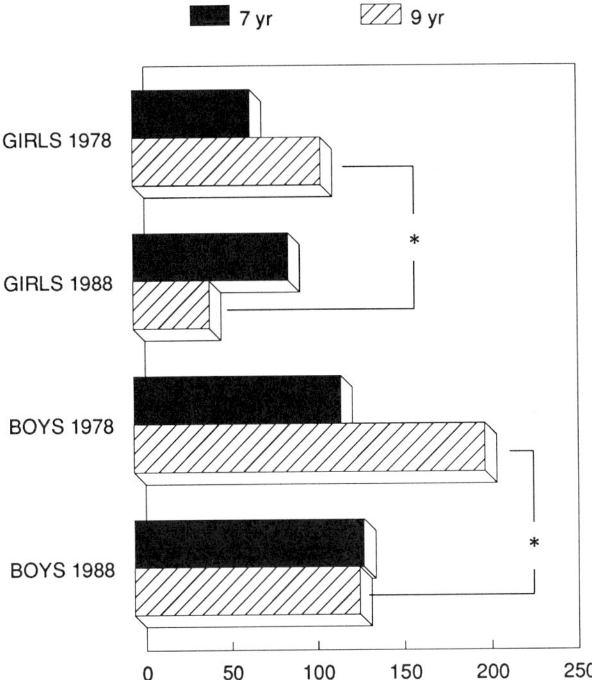


**Figure 1.** Mean peer-nominated aggression for 7- and 9-year-old subjects in 1978 and 1988. Asterisk (*), $p < .05$.

behavior over the elapsed time (Viemerö, 1989c). The same age groups of children ($N = 398$) from the same schools used in the former study served as subjects in the second study where the methods were also identical to those used ten years earlier.

Girls ($n = 204$) were once again found to be less aggressive than boys ($n = 194$), both with regard to peer-nominated aggression [$t(396) = 6.76, p < .001$] as well as self-rated aggression [$t(395) = 5.37, p < .001$]. In addition to gender differences, differences over time were found. Peer-nominated aggression was found in 1988 to be significantly lower for the 9-year-old subjects in comparison to that found in 1978 (Figure 1). This finding was considered to be unbelievable at a time of homogenization of cultures by the mass media, when aggression was perceived as being more acceptable, and when the number of aggressive models was more numerous (Groebel, 1986) than ten years earlier. A possible interpretation for this outcome is that the peer-nomination method for the young subjects in 1988 meant something else than it did for the same age group in 1978. The items were of the type: *"Who does not obey the teacher?"*, *"Who says unkind things?"*,

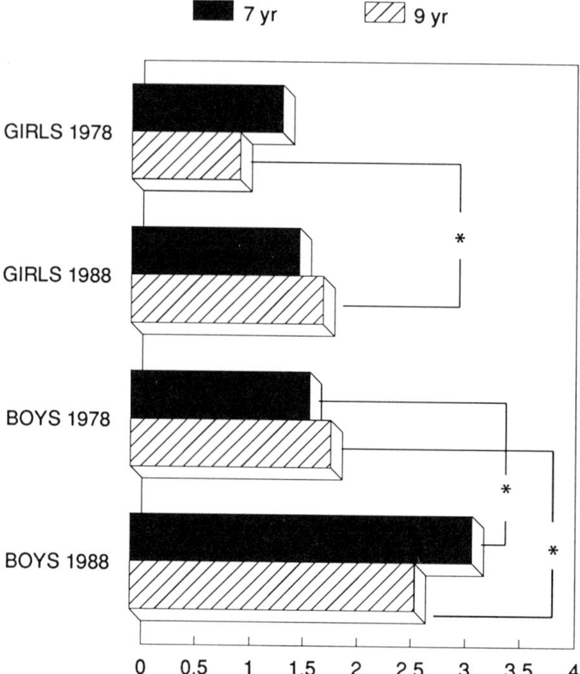


**Figure 2.** Mean self-rated aggression for 7- and 9-year-old subjects in 1978 and 1988. Asterisk (*), $p < .05$.

and *"Who pushes and shoves other children?"*. At the end of the 1980s, it was not particularly noteworthy if a pupil did not obey, pushed and shoved, or said unkind things to other people, when compared with the situation at the end of the 1970s. In other words, the meaning of the peer-nomination items had suffered an inflation. Self-rated aggression, on the other hand, was significantly higher for almost all subject groups in 1988 when compared with that in 1978 (Figure 2). Self-rated aggression was measured by identification with aggressive and nonaggressive models (Viemerö, 1989c).

## III. Changes in Girls' Aggressiveness in the Early 1990s

There have been changes in child/adolescent aggression in Finland as a consequence of changes in attitudes toward aggressive behavior. Attitudes, especially about girls' aggressiveness, have undergone change as a result of an increase in pressure toward competitiveness for social success and achievement (Haavio-Mannila, Jallinoja, & Strandell, 1984). This became apparent already during the above-mentioned follow-up study. The relationship between aggression and popularity were in the most recent measurements, significantly positive for girls, but not for boys (Viemerö, 1989b). This means that nowadays a girl must behave aggressively in order to be popular. A study conducted in 1990 (Viemerö, Hansen, & Norrgård, 1990b) with 143 9-, 11-, 13-, and 15-year-old subjects indicated only one significant gender difference in aggressiveness in the different age groups. Both self-rated aggression and the CATS (Children's Action Tendency Scale) aggression scale (Deluty, 1981) were used to measure aggressive behavior. On CATS, the subjects select between different alternatives in frustrating, provoking, or conflict-filled situations. The correlation between these measurements was .40 ($p < .001$) for all subjects. Thirteen-year-old girls scored highest with regard to self-rated aggression. Only at the age of 15 did the boys have significantly higher means than the girls on the CATS aggression scale. At the age of 9 and 13 years the girls had higher means (nonsignificant) than the boys.

The changes in the relationships between aggression and popularity as well as the lack of differences in aggression between girls and boys led the author to plan a study in which the target of aggression, the target's status, as well as the subjects' self-image were in the focus of interest when measuring aggressiveness (Viemerö *et al.*, 1990c). The meaning of the target of aggressive behavior has been almost totally neglected in recent research about gender differences in aggression, even if its importance has been indicated in earlier studies on aggression (e.g., Bandura, 1973). It has, for example, been taken for granted that the targets of child/adolescent aggression are in the peer group. Negative self-image has also been found to be a correlate of aggressive behavior (Schaughency, Frame, & Strauss, 1987).

Altogether 172 pupils were interviewed. They were from three different public schools. The subjects were 9, 11, 13, and 15 years old. Aggression toward adults and peers, aggression as defense in general, as well as aggression as defense against members of the same and the opposite sex were measured. In addition, self-rated aggression was measured. Rosenzweig's picture frustration test (The Children's Form of Picture-Frustration Study) (Rosenzweig, Fleming, & Rosenzweig, 1948) completed the aggression measures. The picture texts in Rosenzweig's test were coded in terms of successful coping (problem solving) and unsuccessful coping (introverted or extroverted aggression). Self-image was measured with questions like "I am satisfied with myself" (Viemerö, *et al.*, 1990c). The results showed that girls had a significantly higher tendency than boys [$t(170) = 3.44$, $p < .001$] to solve frustrating situations constructively, especially at the ages of 9 and 12. As far as aggressive behavior was concerned, there were only minor differences between the genders. Girls were significantly less aggressive than boys when aggressive behavior was used as defense [$t(170) = 4.4$, $p < .001$], both toward members of the same sex [$t(170) = 2.61$, $p < .01$] as well as

**Table 1**
**Correlations between Self-Image and Different Aggression Measures**

| | Self-image | |
|---|---|---|
| | Boys ($n = 65$) | Girls ($n = 77$) |
| Aggression toward adults | – | .35** |
| Aggression toward peers | .19* | .35** |
| Aggression as defense | – | .34** |
| Self-rated aggression | – | .43*** |
| Dominance | −.18* | .32** |
| Submission | – | −.32** |

* $p < .05$, ** $p < .01$, *** $p < .001$.

those of the opposite sex [$t(170) = 4.65$, $p < .001$]. A plausible interpretation is that defensive aggression is more typical for males than for females. When the target of aggressive behavior was an adult, girls used more (nonsignificant) forms of aggression, including physical ones, than boys. The same was found for 13- to 15-year-old girls when the target of aggression was in their own peer group. In contrast to the results of Schaughency, Frame, and Strauss (1987) girls with a positive self-image were the most aggressive. The girls had positive significant correlations between self-image and most aggression measures as well as with dominance measured by peer nomination (Table 1). It seems that bossy and dominant, aggressively behaving girls have a positive self-image.

The female subjects were divided into groups according to high and low self-image so that one third of the total number of girls formed the high group and one third the low group. The rest of the girls were left outside this analysis. A significant difference in aggression between 9- to 15-year-old girls who were high or low in terms of self-image (Table 2) was found (Viemerö *et al.*, 1990c).

## IV. Discussion

On the basis of the reviewed studies it can be claimed that there have been changes in the patterns of aggressiveness among Finnish girls over the last decade. Girls were less aggressive than boys in the 1980s according to both self- and peer estimations of aggressiveness. In the beginning of the 1990s, such obvious differences between the genders no longer exist. In some of the aggression measures, the girls score even higher than the boys. The findings point out that the aggressive behavior of girls is associated with popularity among peers, dominating behavior, and high self-image. Aggressive behavior seems to be something positive in girls'

**Table 2**
**Differences between Girls High or Low in Terms of Self-Image**

| | High self-image ($n$ = 22) | | Low self-image ($n$ = 22) | | | |
|---|---|---|---|---|---|---|
| | $X$ | SD | $X$ | SD | $t$ | $p$ |
| Aggression against adults | 1.75 | .62 | 1.31 | .45 | 2.76 | .009 |
| Aggression against peers | 2.18 | .93 | 1.48 | .73 | 2.71 | .010 |
| Aggression as defense | 3.09 | 1.31 | 2.28 | 1.01 | 2.43 | .020 |
| Self-rated aggression | 8.91 | 3.98 | 4.95 | 3.09 | 3.68 | .001 |
| Dominance | 28.64 | 26.39 | 11.14 | 13.26 | 2.78 | .008 |
| Submission | 9.82 | 12.28 | 25.73 | 21.67 | 3.00 | .005 |

social setting, something that makes the girl feel powerful, strong, and makes her popular.

The difference between self- and peer-estimated data (*in*crease according to self-estimation, *de*crease according to peer estimation), reveals a societal change with respect to attitudes toward aggression, especially among girls. The decrease revealed by peer-estimated data indicates that behavioral patterns that were once considered aggressive may not be regarded the same way at present. On the other hand, the increase in aggressiveness according to self-ratings, especially among girls, indicates a greater acceptance of aggressiveness during the 1990s in comparison with previous data. Girls like to conceive of themselves as aggressive. It may also reflect a change in actual behavior. The reasons for this kind of development among school-aged girls in Finland are important to find out. Our school system and our society may be putting too much presure on young girls in the form of competition for social success and achievement (cf. Haavio-Mannila, Jallinoja, & Strandell, 1984). This suggestion is supported by the finding that more highly educated mothers have more aggressive daughters as opposed to those less educated (Viemerö, 1986). At present, girls are more numerous than boys in higher education in Finland. It may be that mothers with a higher education are providing more aggressive and competitive female role models for their daughters in a society where men continue to hold the highest positions.

## Acknowledgments

I would like to express my thanks to the students of psychology at Åbo Akademi University for the time and effort they have contributed testing patterns of aggressive behavior with me, and to Christina Krause for her assistance with statistics and graphs.

# References


Bandura, A. (1973). *Aggression: A Social Learning Analysis*. Englewood Cliffs, N.J.: Prentice-Hall.

Deluty, R. H. (1981). Adaptiveness of aggressive, assertive, and submissive behavior for children. *Journal of Clinical Child Psychology*, Fall 1981, 155–158.

Eron, L. D. (1980). Prescription for reduction of aggression. *American Psychologist, 35*, 244–252.

Eron, L. D., & Huesmann, L. R. (1984). The relation of prosocial behavior to the development of aggression and psychopathology. *Aggressive Behavior, 10*, 201–211.

Groebel, J. (1986). International research on television violence: synopsis and critique. *In* L. R. Huesmann & L. D. Eron (Eds.), *Television and the Aggressive Child: A Cross-National Comparison*. Hillsdale, New Jersey: Lawrence Erlbaum.

Haavio-Mannila, E., Jallinoja, R., & Strandell, H. (1984). *Perhe, työ ja tunteet. Ristiriitoja ja ratkaisuja (Family, Work and Emotions. Conflicts and Solutions)*. Juva: Werner Söderström Oy.

Huesmann, L. R., & Eron, L. D. (1986). *Television and the Aggressive Child: A Cross-National Comparison*. Hillsdale, New Jersey: Lawrence Erlbaum.

Lagerspetz, K., Björkqvist, K., & Peltonen, T. (1988). Is Indirect Aggression Typical for Females? Gender Differences in Aggressiveness in 11- to 12-Year-Old Children. *Aggressive Behavior, 14*, 403–414.

Lagerspetz, K., & Viemerö, V. (1986). Television and aggressive behavior among Finnish children. *In* L. R. Huesmann & L. D. Eron (Eds.), *Television and the Aggressive Child: A Cross-National Comparison*. Hillsdale, New Jersey: Lawrence Erlbaum.

Maccoby, E. E., & Jacklin, C. N. (1974). *The Psychology of Sex Differences*. Stanford, California: Stanford University Press.

Maccoby, E. E., & Jacklin, C. N. (1980). Sex differences in aggression. A rejoinder and reprise. *Child Development, 51*, 964–980.

Rosenzweig, S., Fleming, E. E., & Rosenzweig, L. (1948). *The Children's Form of the Rosenzweig Picture-Frustration Study*. Provincetown: The Journal Press.

Schaughency, E., Frame, C. L., & Strauss, C. C. (1987). Self-concept and aggression in elementary school students. *Journal of Clinical Child Psychology, 16*, 116–121.

Sinkkonen, J. (1990). *Pienistä pojista kunnon miehiä (Little Boys Will Become Real Men)*. Porvoo: Werner Söderström Oy.

Viemerö, V. (1986). *Relationships Between Filmed Violence and Aggression*. Report from the Department of Psychology at Åbo Akademi University. Monograph Supplement 4.

Viemerö, V. (1989a). Viestinnän etiikka (The ethics of the mass media). *In Ihmisenkokoinen koulu. Eettinen kasvatus koulun uskontokasvatuksessa*. Uskontopedagogisen instituutin vuosikirja. Helsinki: Lasten keskus.

Viemerö, V. (1989b). Relationships between peer-nominated aggression, popularity and aggression anxiety at school age. *In* L. Pulkkinen & J. M. Ramiretz (Eds.), *Aggression in Children*. Sevilla: Publicaciones de la Universidad de Sevilla.

Viemerö, V. (1989c). *Developmental Trends in Violence Viewing Aggression Relationships Over Ten Years*. Paper presented at the 5th European Conference of ISRA, Zombathely, Hungary.

Viemerö, V. (1990a). Results of Finnish studies of the effects of watching TV on the viewer. *In* U. Carlsson (Ed.), *Medier människor samhälle*. Göteborg: Nordicom-Sverige.

Viemerö, V., Hansen, K., & Norrgård, P. (1990b). Children's Action Tendency Scale test i finska förhållanden. Unpublished manuscript.

Viemerö, V., Fredriksson, K., Krause, T., Peijari, J., Prytz, H., & von Weissenberg, J. (1990c). Aggressive Behavior Related to Self-Confidence. Paper presented at IX Biennial World Meetings of ISRA, Banff, Canada.

**10**

# Patterns of Aggressive-Hostile Behavior Orientation among Adolescent Boys and Girls

Adam Frączek

I. CONTEXT AND QUESTIONS
II. MAIN RESULTS
III. FINAL REMARKS
REFERENCES

## I. Context and Questions

The opinion that girls differ from boys with respect to aggressive behavior is based on common observation as well as on sophisticated studies. The differences concern various aspects of aggression, and today the old, general question whether girls/women are less aggressive than boys/men assumes much more analytical forms.

It has been shown, for instance, that among 3-year-olds differences in aggression are clearly pronounced, with "boys against boys" type being the most frequent, and "girls against girls" least frequent (Szegal, 1992). Aggressive behavioral patterns show stability from an early age (Olweus, 1979); there are stable differences in aggression by at least 3 years of age in boys, but Cummings *et al.* (1986) described short-term stability for some characteristics of aggression in children as young as 1–2 years. A less strong (but still significant) level of stability has been found for girls than for boys (Park & Slaby, 1983). For girls, a shift over time is also reported, with aggressive girls being at risk of internalizing problems as they grow older (McCord, 1986; Pulkkinen, Chapter 11, this volume).

The so-called *object-related aggression* (e.g., taking away and destroying toys) as well as *gross-motor aggression* (hitting, pushing, kicking, and chasing) are typically considered masculine, while verbal and symbolic aggression (e.g., yelling, gossiping) have been considered feminine, even at an early age (Szegal, 1992). Generally speaking, with age there occurs a transition from physical to verbal attack, but also growing children understand hostile *intent* differently (Ferguson & Rule, 1983). It has been well established that with age, boys and girls differ more and more as regards their manifestations of aggression and hostility (Lagerspetz, Björkqvist, & Peltonen, 1988; Björkqvist, Österman, & Kaukiainen, Chapter 5, 1992, this volume); direct interpersonal aggression in boys consists mainly in picking fights, whereas girls, from puberty on, manipulate social relationships as a means of aggression. Indirect manifestations of aggression among girls are somehow related to closer social relations within their peer group, while more direct forms of aggression among boys correlate with the looser relationships observed in boys' groups (Lagerspetz, Björkqvist, & Peltonen, 1988). This sex-related specificity in aggression manifestations is usually interpreted in terms of interactions between biological (mainly genetic, physiological) and sociocultural (mainly sex-related roles, stereotypes) codeterminants of the development of human aggression.

In this chapter, we present some fragments of research in which we did not aim at diagnosing *symptoms* or *forms* of aggressive behavior per se, but focused on identifying those *intrapsychic* elements of an individual which constitute his/her life orientations, including aggressive/hostile ones. The aim of the study was to identify characteristics of adolescent boys' and girls' aggressive/hostile life orientations and so to identify differences in this respect between the sexes. We also intended to establish relationships between aggressive/hostile life orientations of adolescents (as well as some other life orientations) on the one hand, and degree of aggression as based on self-report, on the other.

Aggressive/hostile life orientations can be described as constellations of certain psychological features of an individual, such as approval of one's own propensity to aggression toward other people; positive evaluation of accomplishments and goals somehow related to aggression/hostility in interpersonal contacts; perceiving other people as enemies or as sources of violence; and acceptance of norms or standards that permit aggressive/hostile interactions. One can say that this kind of life orientation consists not only of very specific striving and behavior patterns, but also of such psychological elements involved in personality as generalized life goals and values; expectations and evaluations concerning self and others; consistent interpretations of events (Kornadt, 1987); and is distinctive in all these respects from other life orientations (e.g., altruistic-friendly, anxious-withdrawing, etc.).

## II. Main Results

In order to collect appropriate material for the characteristics of aggressive/hostile life orientations, as well as alternative orientations among adolescents, we have used the "Questionnaire for the Description of Social Relations of Adolescents," developed originally by Kornadt (1986). This questionnaire contains such categories of statements as: attitude toward self (e.g., "once I release my anger I immediately feel better"); beliefs related to social and moral issues concerning interpersonal aggression (e.g., "we should avoid quarrels whenever we can"); general opinion of people and distrust in others (e.g. "it is good to be careful and suspicious of other people"); interpretation of adverse conditions (e.g., "when somebody has hurt me, I ask myself whether he/she really meant it"). The subjects express their approval/disapproval of each of 52 statements using a scale from "I completely disagree" to "I fully agree." According to the assumptions developed by Kornadt (1986), the statements may be grouped into several *a priori* categories. However, for the purposes of this study, we simply performed separate factor analyses of boys' and girls' responses in order to establish which specific groupings are considered expressions of various life orientations.

To measure various indices of aggressiveness, based on the self report data, we used "Choynowski's Comprehensive Inventory of Aggressiveness" (1982). This inventory includes such aspects of aggressiveness as physical aggression, verbal aggression, maliciousness, irritability, negativism, revengefulness, resentment, suspiciousness, vicarious aggression, assertiveness, lack of restraint, and nonconformity.

The subjects in this study were Warsaw primary school 8th Graders: 113 adolescents—57 boys, mean age 14.1 (range 13–16), and 56 girls, mean age 14.1 (range 13–16). Subjects were tested in groups, during school hours, in the absence of a teacher, by a trained experimenter.

Factor analyses of questionnaire items were administered separately for boys and girls, previous experience clearly showing differences in groupings of boys and girls. After several steps (Varimax procedure was used to rotate the factors), it was documented that a reduction of up to 5 factors, in both subsamples, resulted in maximal differentiation and, at the same time, in the strongest arrangements of groupings. The following important patterns were identified in the data, as well as similarities and differences between boys and girls in these respects.

First, it appeared that some of the same items grouped in the first, second, and third factors obtained very high loadings in both the subsamples of boys and girls. Furthermore, although the remaining items included in those factors, as we will show in detail later on, varied for boys and girls, it was not difficult to reach a consensus as to the general psychological meaning of these orientations and to identify them by using specific concepts.

The first factor consisted of approval of such norms, beliefs, felt emotions, and behavior as reflect and/or promote task-oriented but moral approaches in interpersonal or more general social relations. We propose that the items identified in this category be called *impunitive-normative* life orientaions in social relations. This category, common for boys and girls, included such statements as "those who cannot hold back their feelings of annoyance will no longer be respected by others." The noticeable difference between boys and girls as regards impunitive-normative life orientations is that boys referred here mainly to general rules or values (e.g. "we should avoid quarrels no matter what happens"), while girls introduce more personal feelings, mainly guilt, as an aspect of such orientations (e.g., such statements as "it does not matter whether it is justified or not, I feel guilty whenever I express my anger").

The second factor identified in our data consisted of approval of attitudes, norms, and beliefs related to negative, aggressive, and hostile aspects of contacts among people, as well as approval of personal anger-related emotions. We propose that this arrangement of items be named *aggressive-hostile* life orientation in social relations. This category includes statements, common to boys and girls, which indicate propensity to respond with anger (e.g. "there are a lot of things that make me angry"). At the same time, boys emphasized the normative aspect of aggression (e.g., the statement "if somebody has done me wrong, I want him/her to really be punished for it"), while girls mentioned more personal commitment to aggressive/hostile reactions (e.g., the statement "if somebody persists in his/her opinion, I feel invited to contradict").

The third factor common to boys and girls consists of items related to positive valuation of self-reliance in social relations, and the self-control that underlies independence and personal achievements. We propose that this grouping of items be defined as an expression of the *assertive-independent* life orientation of adolescents. Both boys and girls emphasize the value of strong self-control and strive for achievement (e.g., such items as "it is easy for me to suspend my views and my desire" or "those who demand a lot in life will get a lot"). In this orientation boys tend to ignore other people (e.g., such a statement as "those who show too much consideration for others will not advance in life"); girls present a more negativistic attitude and persistence within this orientation (e.g., such statements as "I will not be told how I am to behave" or "once I have planned something, nobody can make me change my plans easily").

Another factor was clearly noticeable only in the girls' subgroup. It comprises the items which referred to the fear of falling victim to aggression or attack (e.g., such items as "I often feel other people want to do me harm"), and to the need for self-confidence (e.g., a statement such as "I am afraid to oppose others"), but also the items which expressed approval for retaliation (e.g., the statement "if somebody does me wrong, he/she will regret it"). In this case we observe a specific combination of anxiety and tendency to aggressive counterattack; such a combination has been called an *anxious-retaliatory* life orientation in social relations.

Let us also look at some relationships between identified life orientations and self-rated characteristics of aggressiveness among adolescents. Without going into detail, one can notice in our data that in the cases of both boys and girls, the so-called aggressive/hostile life orientations are positively significantly correlated with such categories of aggressiveness (based on Choynowski's Comprehensive Inventory of Aggressiveness) as physical aggression, verbal aggression, irritability, negativism, and revengefulness. In boys, but not in girls, aggressive/hostile life orientations also correlated with maliciousness and nonconformity. Also exclusive to boys were statistically significant negative correlations between the so-called impunitive-normative life orientations and different indices of aggressiveness (physical aggression, revengefulness, and vicarious aggression). Therefore, the pattern of these relationships includes additional information on the structure and concomitants of aggressive/hostile life orientations of boys and girls.

Generally speaking, the aggressive/hostile life orientations of boys, as compared with those of girls, are more instrumental or task-oriented, much less implemented into anxious-retaliatory orientations, and clearly contradicted by impunitive-normative life orientations. On the other hand, girls' aggressive/hostile life orientations seem to be more emotogenically codetermined, and factors concerned with self-involvement may play a more important role in the development of, as well as in regulating, such interpersonal life orientations in girls.

## III. Final Remarks

One of the problems in the psychology of interpersonal aggression is the identification and description of the specificity of various forms of aggression, their conditions, and their functions in interpersonal contacts (Frączek, 1986, 1992; Frączek & Kirwil, 1992). For instance, Pulkkinen (1987) described differences between the so-called offensive and defensive aggression in interpersonal relations; this differentiation was based mainly on the recognition of associated events (i.e., provoked vs unprovoked act), but it was also shown that offensive aggression is positively correlated with strong self-control, while defensive aggression is related to weak self-control. The studies carried out and initiated by Lagerspetz (Lagerspetz, Björkqvist, & Peltonen, 1988; Björkvist, Lagerspetz, & Kaukiainen, 1990; Björkvist, Österman, & Kaukiainen, Chapter 5, this volume) present elaborate methods for diagnosing so-called *direct* versus *indirect* aggression, as well as the concomitants of these forms of aggression and their functions in regulating social relations.

The question that still remains is to what extent different forms of aggressive behavior are equivalent functionally, and whether these various forms are regulated by one specific intrapsychic mechanism or by several mechanisms that have been developed through transformations of quite different intrapsychic processes and structures (Frączek 1992). In the light of prevailing opinion on the development, conditions, and regulatory mechanisms of human interpersonal aggression, it seems more reasonable to assume that the phenomenon called aggressive behavior has many facets, and has to be related to various factors rather than one universal mechanism.

## References


Björkqvist, K., Lagerspetz, K., & Kaukiainen, A. (1992). Do girls manipulate and boys fight? Developmental trends in regard to direct and indirect aggression. *Aggressive Behavior, 18.*

Choynowski, M. (1982). Comprehensive inventory of aggression—modified and shortened: the Polish version by Frączek, A., Szustrowa, T., & Zakrzewski, J. (1986). Manuscript.

Cummings, E. M., Hollenbeck, B., Iannotti, R., Radke-Yarrow, M., & Zahn-Waxler, C. (1986). Early organization of altruism and aggression: Developmental patterns and individual differences. *In* C. Zahn-Waxler, M. Cummings, & R. Iannotti (Eds.), *Altruism and Aggression.* New York: Cambridge University Press.

Ferguson, T. J., & Rule, B. G. (1983). An attributional perspective on anger and aggression. *In* R. G. Geen & E. I. Donnerstein (Eds.), *Aggression, Vol. I.* New York: Academic Press.

Frączek, A. (1986). Socio-cultural environment, television viewing and the development of aggression among children in Poland. *In* L. R. Huesmann & L. D. Eron (Eds.), *Television and the Aggressive Child: Across-National Comparison.* Hillsdale, New Jersey: LEA Publishers.

Frączek, A. (1992). Socialization and intrapsychic regulation of interpersonal aggression. *In* A. Frączek & H. Zumkley (Eds.), *Socialization and Aggression.* Berlin: Springer-Verlag (in print).

Frączek, A., & Kirwil, L. (1992). Family life orientations and child aggression: Studies on some socialization conditions of development of aggression. *In* A. Frączek & H. Zumkley (Eds.), *Socialization and Aggression.* Berlin: Springer-Verlag (in print).

Kornadt, H.-J. (1986). Questionnaire for the description of social relations of adolescents-Ein Fragebogen zur Erfasung von Socialbezeitungen bei Jugendlichen-"SAS"; the Polish version by Jakubowska, W., & Frączek, A. (1988). Manuscript.

Kornadt, H.-J. (1987). The aggression motive and personality development: Japan and Germany. *In* F. Halish & J. Kuhl (Eds.), *Motivation, Intention, and Volition.* Berlin: Springer-Verlag.

Lagerspetz, K., Björkqvist, K., & Peltonen, T. (1988). Is indirect aggression typical of females? Gender differences in aggressiveness in 11-12 year-old children. *Aggressive Behavior, 14*, 303–315.

McCord, J. (1986). Instigation and insulation: How families affect antisocial aggression. *In* D. Olweus, J. Block, & M. Radke-Yarrow (Eds.), *Development of Antisocial and Prosocial Behavior: Research, Theory, and Issues.* San Diego, California: Academic Press.

Olweus, D. (1979). Stability and aggressive reaction patterns in males: A review. *Psychological Bulletin, 86*, 852–875.

Park, R. D., & Slaby, R. G. (1983). The development of aggression. *In* P. Mussen (Ed.), *Handbook of Child Psychology, Vol. IV.* New York:Wiley.

Pulkkinen, L. (1987). Offensive and defensive aggression in humans: A longitudinal perspective. *Aggressive Behavior, 13*, 197–213.

Szegal, B. (1992). Sex-related differences in aggression in early childhood. Paper prepared for XXV International Congress of Psychology, Brussels.

# The Path to Adulthood for Aggressively Inclined Girls

Lea Pulkkinen

I. INTRODUCTION
II. ARE THERE GENDER DIFFERENCES IN THE STABILITY OF AGGRESSION?
III. ARE THERE GENDER DIFFERENCES IN THE PATTERNS OF ADJUSTMENT?
IV. DISCONTINUITY IN FEMALE AGGRESSIVE BEHAVIOR
V. CONCLUSIONS
REFERENCES

## I. Introduction

There are generally held conceptions of gender differences in aggression. They concern, for instance, differences in the magnitude of aggressive behavior. Empirical studies do not, however, lend support to many of these conceptions, or gender differences are at least smaller than expected. As regards gender differences in the magnitude of aggressive behavior, a meta-analysis of 143 studies by Hyde (1984) indicated that although gender differences "appear fairly reliable, they are not large" and that there is "a modest negative association between magnitude of gender differences and age" (p. 722). It means that gender differences in aggression tend to be smaller at a later age than at a younger age. Gender differences in recent studies also tend to be smaller than in older studies, and they are smaller in self-reports or parent or teacher reports than when direct observation or peer report is used as the method of measurement. Only about 5% of the variance in aggression is explained by gender differences. An average difference between the genders in the means of aggression variables is half a standard deviation.

In addition to quantitative differences between the sexes in a certain type of aggression, there may be qualitative differences in girls' and boys' aggressive behavior as shown by Lagerspetz, Björkqvist, and Peltonen (1988); indirect aggression was more common among girls than among boys, whereas direct aggression was more common among boys, especially at the age of 11 to 12. At this point, too little attention has been paid to possible qualitative differences in male and female aggression. Therefore, the study by Lagerspetz, Björkqvist, and Peltonen (1988) is very interesting.

There are also generally held conceptions of gender differences in the quality of life paths to adulthood for aggressively inclined children. It is believed that aggressive behavior is more stable in boys than in girls, and that aggressive behavior is more predictive of boys' than girls' antisocial behavior. In the present paper, these conceptions are analyzed from three points of view: (1) Normative stability. The problem is whether girls' aggressive behavior is as stable over time as boys' aggressive behavior; (2) Types of adjustment patterns and their predictive power. The problem is whether similar adjustment patterns can be obtained for boys and girls and whether they predict adult outcomes, especially antisocial behavior, in a similar way for both sexes. (3) Discontinuity of aggressive behavior from childhood to adult outcomes. The problem is whether individual life paths show that girls' aggressive behavior may lead to some qualitatively differing life courses.

Data obtained in relevant longitudinal studies were considered in the analysis of the first question. The analysis of the second question was based on the comparison of two longitudinal data collected by Magnusson (1988) in Sweden and the present author in Finland, the Jyväskylä Longitudinal Study (JLS). The latter data were also used for the analysis of the third question.

The original sample of the JLS consisted of 173 girls and 196 boys, born in 1959. It was drawn in 1968 from 2nd-Grade pupils (average age 8 years) in the town of Jyväskylä. Six years later, when the subjects were 14 years old, 96.5% of the original sample was reached for a follow-up study. At the age of 26, 156 women (90.2%) and 171 men (87.2%) were reexamined.

The principal methods of data collection were peer nomination and teacher rating at the ages of 8 and 14. At the age of 8, 12 items for aggression were included in peer nomination and teacher rating for a total of 33 items. The aggression items included direct and indirect, defensive and offensive, and physical, verbal, and facial aggression (Pulkkinen, 1987). At the age of 14, peer nominations and teacher ratings of aggression were made on an item: "Who attacks without reason, teases others, says nasty things?" Other variables considered in the present analysis of life paths included school success (general point average) and teacher ratings on school adjustment. At the age of 26, the methods were a mailed questionnaire and a semistructured interview. Self-ratings on aggression were made on an item: "I get angry often and am easily involved in a quarrel or a fight." The criminal records were also examined in two registers: the government register, including information on offences, the sentence for which was imprisonment, and the local more informal register for arrests, held by the police. For adult outcomes, the following variables were also considered: length of education, career development (classified according to Sinisalo, 1986), and the age of entering parenthood.

## II. Are There Gender Differences in the Stability of Aggression?

In recent studies of aggression much attention has been paid to the stability, continuity, and predictability of aggression. In the 1970s Olweus (1979) published his often-cited review of studies on the normative stability of aggression as a reaction to the attack by Mischel (1968) and others against the concept of personality trait. Olweus (1979) claimed that individual differences in aggressiveness over age were virtually as stable as intelligence. Also Eron and Huesmann have in their articles (e.g., Huesmann *et al.*, 1984; Huesmann & Eron, 1989) strongly advocated the concept of the trait of aggression and its stability, based on their longitudinal study over twenty-two years. Their findings have shown (Huesmann *et al.*, 1984) that aggressiveness at the age of 8 was predictive of aggressiveness at the age of 30 (although not as strongly as intelligence was predictive of intellectual functioning) and of later serious antisocial behavior. Many other studies (Farrington, 1989; Loeber, 1990; Magnusson & Bergman, 1988; Pulkkinen, 1983, 1987) show that early aggressiveness is a significant antecedent of later frequency of criminal offenses.

The review by Olweus (1979) concerned the stability of male aggressive behavior. The stability of girls' aggressive behavior has been less known particularly from later childhood onward. Cairns and Cairns (1984) demonstrated that high-aggressive girls showed as much stability as high-aggressive boys from the 4th to the 5th Grade. Also, self-ratings of aggression and teacher ratings correlated as highly for boys and girls (0.38 at the 4th Grade). Based on the same sample, it was demonstrated later by Cairns *et al.* (1989) that the stability of teacher-rated aggressiveness was higher the shorter the time interval; the correlation coefficients were 0.40 to 0.56 for girls and 0.48 to 0.72 for boys between the successive years from Grade 4 to 9. The results also showed that the stability of aggression from the 4th to the 8th Grade was as high in girls as in boys (correlation coefficients 0.51 and 0.49, respectively), but girls' aggressiveness in the 9th Grade correlated with early aggressiveness less highly than boys' aggressiveness (0.13 and 0.36, respectively). The same was found for self-ratings.

The JLS (Pitkänen-Pulkkinen, 1981; Pulkkinen, 1987) showed, correspondingly, that peer-nominated aggressiveness was as stable for girls as for boys from the age of 8 (equivalent to the 3rd Grade) to the age of 14 (equivalent to the 8th Grade). The correlation coefficient was 0.37 for both sexes. The stability correlation of teacher ratings was of the same size (0.37) for boys but only 0.13 for girls.

In the study by Huesmann *et al.* (1984), the correlation coefficient between peer-nominated aggression at the age of 8 and aggression at the age of 30 (MMPI Scales F + 4 + 9) was 0.30 for males and 0.16 (0.20 after a skew-correcting transformation) for females. In the JLS, peer nominations on aggression at the age of 8 correlated with self-ratings on aggression at the age of 26 by 0.11 (nonsignificant) for males and by 0.20 ($p = .008$) for females. Thus, the stability of aggression over 18 years was even higher for females than for males when a self-rating of aggression was used as a criterion.

Regarding antisocial behavior, the correlation between peer-nominated aggression and criminal justice convictions was 0.24 ($p < .001$) for males and 0.10 (nonsignificant) for females in the study by Huesmann *et al.* (1984), and in the JLS (between peer-nominated aggression and the number of arrests), 0.29 ($p < .001$) for males and 0.11 (nonsignificant) for females. Thus, correlation coefficients which showed higher predictability of male than female antisocial behavior validated each other in two different cultures, although, due to a skewed distribution of antisocial behavior, correlation coefficients may not be reliable. A group comparison has revealed that not only high-aggressive males but also high-aggressive females differed from the respective middle- and low-aggressive groups in antisocial behavior twenty years later; these findings by Huesmann *et al.* (1984) were replicated in the JLS.

## III. Are There Gender Differences in the Patterns of Adjustment?

The early aggressive boys often are socially maladjusted at an early age in several respects as noted by Stattin and Magnusson (1989). They are restless, exhibit concentration difficulties, show low school motivation, and have poor relations. It is, however, to be noted that early aggressiveness may also appear outside a multiproblem pattern (Magnusson & Bergman, 1990). Only when aggression is a part of a multiproblem pattern does it predict antisocial behavior.

The patterns extracted by Magnusson and Bergman (1990) were replicated with the Jyväskylä longitudinal data (Pulkkinen, 1992) for boys. In the present paper, it was focused on the repeatability of the patterns in girls' behavior. The question was analyzed by using a clustering technique based on squared Euclidian distances (WARD; SPSS-x package) with six corresponding variables for boys and girls. The clustering variables were recoded on a semiabsolute scale from 3 (a pronounced characteristic) through 0 (no characteristic in question). The variables and their sources were as follows: aggressiveness (peer-nominations and teacher ratings at age 8); restlessness (Restlessness scale of a personality inventory and teacher rating on disobedience at age 8); lack of concentration (peer nominations and teacher ratings at age 14); low school motivation (teacher

**Table 1**
**Cluster Means in Clustering Variables Based on Data Collected at Ages 8 and 14**

| Cluster | Girls Boys | *N* | Aggres-siveness | Restlessness | Lack of concen-tration | Low school motivation | Low school achieve-ment | Poor peer relations |
|---|---|---|---|---|---|---|---|---|
| No problems | Girls | 81 | –[a] | – | – | – | – | – |
| | Boys | 51 | – | – | – | – | – | – |
| Poor peer relations | Girls | 20 | – | – | – | – | – | 2.1 |
| | Boys | 29 | – | – | – | – | – | 1.6 |
| Restlessness and aggressiveness | Girls | 17 | – | 1.0 | – | – | – | – |
| | Boys | 21 | 1.4 | 2.3 | – | – | – | – |
| Problems at school | Girls | 20 | – | – | 1.9 | 2.2 | 1.6 | – |
| | Boys | 24 | – | – | 1.4 | 2.2 | 2.0 | 1.0 |
| Agg. and lack of concentration | Girls | 31 | 1.1 | – | – | – | – | – |
| | Boys | 26 | 1.0 | – | 1.3 | – | – | – |
| Mild multi-problems | Boys | 17 | 1.9 | 1.9 | 1.5 | 1.9 | 1.6 | – |
| Severe multi-problems | Boys | 20 | 1.8 | 1.2 | 2.2 | 2.2 | 1.5 | 2.4 |

[a]Cluster mean of variable is less than one in the 4-point scale coded 0, 1, 2, 3.

ratings on interest in school work and truancy at age 14); low school achievements (grade point average at age 14); and poor peer relations (teacher ratings on popularity and leadership behavior at age 14). In the recoding of the variables, the same cut-off points were used for boys and girls.

Seven clusters were found for boys, five for girls, because the clusters for mild and severe multiproblems did not appear in girls (Table 1). The pattern of girls' adjustment problems was widest in scope in the cluster for Problems at school: low school motivation, lack of concentration, low school achievement, and a moderate aggressiveness (the cluster mean of aggressiveness was 0.8). Girls' aggressive behavior was most characteristic of a specific cluster for Aggressiveness where other problems were negligible. For boys, aggressiveness was characteristic of four patterns.

The analysis of data at the age of 26 revealed that arrest rate was highest in girls who had problems at school (Table 2). Most frequently they also had an unstable working career (many changes of the type of work and workplace as well as long and recurring periods of unemployment). An educational career (at least half of the last seven-year period was spent for education) was most common in the cluster for Aggressiveness. The arrest rate was low in the latter. For males, the arrest rate was highest and the unstable working career most frequently found

**Table 2**
**Clusters of Adjustment and Their Predictive Value over 12 Years (%)**

| | | | Age 26 | | | | |
|---|---|---|---|---|---|---|---|
| | | | Career lines | | | Antisocial behavior | |
| Data collected at ages 8 and 14 | | (*N*) | Unstable working career | Stable working career | Educational career | (*N*) | Arrested |
| No problems | F[a] | (74) | 25.6 | 48.6 | 25.7 | (81) | 11.1 |
| | M | (48) | 18.2 | 45.5 | 36.4 | (51) | 5.9 |
| Poor peer relations | F | (16) | 37.9 | 43.8 | 18.8 | (20) | 10.0 |
| | M | (25) | 20.8 | 45.8 | 33.3 | (29) | 17.2 |
| Restlessness and aggressiveness | F | (15) | 46.7 | 26.7 | 26.7 | (17) | 18.7 |
| | M | (20) | 21.1 | 31.6 | 47.4 | (21) | 23.8 |
| Problems at school | F | (18) | 66.6 | 22.2 | 11.1 | (20) | 40.0 |
| | M | (24) | 52.1 | 39.1 | 8.7 | (24) | 33.0 |
| Aggressiveness and lack of concentration | F | (28) | 21.5 | 39.3 | 39.3 | (31) | 12.9 |
| | M | (21) | 28.6 | 57.1 | 14.3 | (26) | 30.8 |
| Mild multi-problems | M | (16) | 31.3 | 50.0 | 18.8 | (17) | 29.4 |
| Severe multiproblems | M | (19) | 71.1 | 27.8 | 11.8 | (20) | 45.0 |
| Total | F | (151) | 33.1 | 41.1 | 25.8 | (169) | 15.5 |
| | M | (173) | 30.9 | 43.0 | 26.1 | (188) | 47.9 |

[a]F, Females; M, males.

in the severely multiproblem boys. Problems at school formed the second risk category.

The results were contrary to expectations concerning the high frequency of educational career and low number of arrests in the female cluster for Aggressiveness. Correspondingly for males, high frequency of educational career and a relatively low arrest rate was found in the cluster for Restlessness and Aggressiveness. For males, aggressiveness had a different predictive value depending on the pattern of behavior it included. When aggressiveness was only combined with restlessness, it did not predict antisocial behavior. It was confirmed that boys in the cluster for Restlessness and Aggressiveness had good school reports at the age of 14. A closer analysis of aggressive girls' life paths will be presented in the next section.

# IV. Discontinuity in Female Aggressive Behavior

The higher career orientation of aggressive girls was confirmed by comparing the high- and low-aggressive girls. The groups were formed by cross-tabulating peer nominations and teacher ratings by using the 30th and 70th percentiles as cut-off points. Thirty-nine percent of the high-aggressive girls and 25% of the low-aggressive girls had an educational career. The distribution of career lines was U-shaped for the high-aggressive girls, that is, both the educational and unstable careers were more common compared to the stable career in the high-aggressive girl, whereas the distribution was normal in the low-aggressive girls.

To find an explanation for the results, the homogeneity of aggression was analyzed by means of a factor analysis. It was found that aggressive behavior in 8-year-old girls was not unidimensional. Two factors were extracted from 12 aggression items by using a principal factor analysis and a Varimax rotation: verbally and facially aggressive girls and physically aggressive girls (Nenonen, 1991).

A short education was more typical of physically aggressive girls than of girls who express their aggression verbally or facially. Physically aggressive girls were less motivated toward school attendance and their school success was weaker compared to the verbally and facially aggressive girls. The youngest mothers were found among the physically aggressive girls. Low school motivation, early heterosexual activity, and young motherhood interrupted their education. Economic necessities forced some of them, however, to attend occupational training at a later age. They were thus categorized as having an educational career.

Most of the girls, especially verbally and facially aggressive girls, who had an educational career, had a GPA higher than the average at the age of 14. In addition, most of the aggressive girls who had an educational career were rated by their teachers as socially more active and energetic at the age of 14 than the girls who were less career oriented.

# V. Conclusions

Conceptions of a lesser magnitude, consistency, and stability of aggression in girls than in boys are often presented in scientific papers (e.g., Lagerspetz, 1990, pp. 111–112). Nevertheless, several studies show that in school age, gender differences (1) in magnitude of aggression are negligible (Hyde, 1984); are more qualitative than quantitative (Lagerspetz, Björkqvist, & Peltonen, 1988); (2) in consistency of findings with different methods of measurement are nonexistent (Cairns & Cairns, 1984); and (3) in stability of aggression before puberty are nonexistent (Cairns *et al.*, 1989; Pitkänen-Pulkkinen, 1981). In addition, high childhood aggression is predictive of female aggressive behavior even twenty years later in both sexes (Huesmann *et al.*, 1984).

It was found that women who were categorized as aggressive in childhood had an educational career more often than expected. A closer analysis revealed that social activity and intellectual functioning explained a U-shaped curve between early aggressiveness and the choice of career lines. Active, intelligent girls might have been found to be verbally aggressive in childhood possibly because of their strong temperament compared to other girls, and possibly because of current pressures in their life. In adolescence, their school success was, however, good and they oriented toward continuing their education. As shown by the cluster analysis, girls' aggressiveness may have combined with school problems or it could have been apart from them. Only in the former case was girls' aggressive behavior predictive of negative outcomes.

None of the aggressive girls who had an educational career existed in criminal registers. Social activity, intellectual functioning, and the length of education were factors which intervened in the development from aggressive to antisocial behavior. The latter path was more likely found in less active girls, whose school success was weaker, and who finished their schooling after comprehensive school.

## References

Cairns, R. B., & Cairns, B. D. (1984). Predicting aggressive patterns in girls and boys: A developmental study. *Aggressive Behavior, 10*, 227–242.

Cairns, R. B., Cairns, B. D., Neckerman, H. J., Ferguson, L. L., & Gariépy, L.-L. (1989). Growth and aggression: 1. Childhood to early adolescence. *Developmental Psychology, 25*, 320–330.

Farrington, D. (1989). Early predictors of adolescent aggression and adult violence. *Violence and Victims, 4*, 79–100.

Huesmann, L. R., & Eron, L. D. (1989). Individual differences and the trait of aggression. *European Journal of Personality, 3*, 95–106.

Huesmann, L. R., Eron, L. D., Lefkowitz, M. M., & Walder, L. O. (1984). Stability of aggression over time and generations. *Developmental Psychology, 20*, 1120–1134.

Hyde, J. S. (1984). How large are gender differences in aggression? A developmental meta-analysis. *Developmental Psychology, 20*, 722–736.

Lagerspetz, K. (1990). *Psykologia - järjen ja tunteen tiede*. Helsinki: Tammi.

Lagerspetz, K., Björkqvist, K., & Peltonen, T. (1988). Is indirect aggression typical of females? Gender differences in aggressiveness in 11- to 12-year-old children. *Aggressive Behavior, 14*, 403–414.

Loeber, R. (1990). Disruptive behavior in childhood and adolescence: Development and risk factors. *In* K. Hurrelmann & F. Lösel (Eds.), *Health Hazards in Adolescence*. Berlin: de Gruyter.

Magnusson, D. (1988). *Individual Development from an Interactional Perspective: A Longitudinal Study*. Hillsdale, NJ: Lawrence Erlbaum Associates.

Magnusson, D., & Bergman, L. R. (1988). Individual and variable-based approaches to longitudinal research on early risk factors. *In* M. Rutter (Ed.), *Studies of Psychosocial Risk: The Power of Longitudinal Data*. Cambridge: Cambridge University Press.

Magnusson, D., & Bergman, L. R. (1990). A pattern approach to the study of pathways from childhood to adulthood. *In* L. Robins & M. Rutter (Eds.), *Straight and Devious Pathways from Childhood to Adulthood.* Cambridge: Cambridge University Press.

Mischel, W. (1968). *Personality and Assessment.* New York: Wiley.

Nenonen, E. (1991). Aggressiivisuus tyttöjen sosiaalisen käyttäytymisen ennustajana. Master's thesis. University of Jyväskylä.

Olweus, D. (1979). Stability of aggressive reaction patterns in males: A review. *Psychological Bulletin, 86*, 852–875.

Pitkänen-Pulkkinen, L. (1981). Long-term studies on the characteristics of aggressive and non-aggressive juveniles. *In* P. F. Brain & D. Benton (Eds.), *Multidisciplinary Approaches to Aggression Research.* Amsterdam: Elsevier/North-Holland Biomedical Press.

Pulkkinen, L. (1983). Finland: Search for alternatives to aggression. *In* A. P. Goldstein & M. Segall (Eds.), *Aggression in Global Perspective.* New York: Pergamon Press.

Pulkkinen, L. (1987). Offensive and defensive aggression in humans: A longitudinal perspective. *Aggressive Behavior, 13*, 197–212.

Pulkkinen, L. (1992). Life-styles in personality development. *European Journal of Personality* (in press).

Sinisalo, P. (1986). Työvoimaura ja yksilön kehitys. Manpower Research Series nr. 63. Helsinki: Ministry of Labour, Planning Department.

Stattin, H., & Magnusson, D. (1989). The role of early aggressive behavior in the frequency, seriousness and types of later crime. *Journal of Consulting and Clinical Psychology, 57*, 710–718.

12

# Gender Differences in Coronary-Prone Aggression

Liisa Keltikangas-Järvinen

I. INTRODUCTION
II. COLLECTION OF THE PRESENT DATA
III. EVIDENCE SUPPORTING THE HARMLESS EFFECT OF AGGRESSION IN BOYS AND THE RISK EFFECT IN GIRLS
A. Aggression as a Subcomponent of Type A Behavior
B. Aggression as a Concomitant of Type A Behavior
C. Aggression as an Antecedent of Type A Behavior
IV. CONCLUSIONS
REFERENCES

## I. Introduction

Despite a slight decline in mortality in recent years, coronary heart disease (CHD) is still the leading cause of premature death among the middle-aged population in western societies. CHD has a long, multifactorial etiology. Atherosclerosis, a process underlying CHD, has been shown to begin as early as in childhood (Strong & McGill, 1969), and numerous biological, environmental, and behavioral factors interact in the development of CHD (Kannel, 1979).

Among the behavioral and psychosocial risk indicators of this disease, the most intensively studied factor has been the so-called Type A behavior pattern, originally found and described by the cardiologists Friedman and Rosenman in the 1950s (see Friedman and Rosenman, 1974). Type A refers to an action–emotion complex characterized by aggression, competitiveness, impatience, and a chronic sense of hurry. For twenty years, from about 1960, research strongly and consistently showed a positive correlation between Type A behavior and CHD. In the 1980s, however, the majority of studies have shown no significant relationship (Jenkins, 1988).

Several reasons for these negative findings can be suggested. One is that Type A behavior is a vague empirical notion characterized by a lack of clear psychological conceptualization. It is not known which are the most important psychological elements of Type A behavior. Nor is it known which are the most essential mechanisms for explaining how Type A behavior becomes somatic risk. Research focusing on elements of secondary importance may result in false negative findings regarding the association between Type A behavior and CHD.

Aggression was the first factor which was assumed to be a transmitting link between psychological and somatic functions. This was based on the observation that a tendency toward aggression was seen as an important, perhaps a defining, dimension of Type A behavior (e.g., Van Egeren, Abelson, & Sniderman, 1983). In another vein, it was noted that behavioral aggression was associated with cardiovascular and metabolic reactions which are important in the etiology of CHD: elevated blood pressure and increased pulse frequency are cardiovascular correlates of behavioral aggression (Lagerspetz, 1970); metabolic correlates are increased adrenalin secretion and decreased insulin secretion, which in turn lead to increased cholesterol risk (Nanjee & Miller, 1989). Thus the conclusion was made that aggressiveness explained the connection between Type A personality and somatic risk. This explanation is still very popular among researchers. There is, however, little research focusing on the particular problem of whether Type A persons exhibit a high level of aggression and whether this aggression is related to an increased coronary heart risk.

This chapter presents a series of empirical findings to suggest that aggression is a component of Type A behavior but not the crucial risk factor of CHD. Aggression may be related to coronary heart risk, but the associations are complicated. In addition, our findings show important gender-related differences. CHD is a disease of middle-aged men; a small minority of patients are women. Consequently, research on its etiology has focused on men, and there are important findings which have not been sufficiently tested on women.

## II. Collection of the Present Data

The present data have been collected in a randomly selected representative sample of 3596 healthy Finnish children, adolescents, and young adults who participated in the Finnish Multicenter Study on Atherosclerosis Precursors (later known as the Cardiovascular Risk in Young Finns study; Åkerblom, Viikari, & Uhari, 1985).

The sample was selected in the following way: Finland was divided into the five areas of the University medical schools. In each area, the subjects in the age cohorts of 3, 6, 9, 12, 15, and 18, were separately placed in random order on the basis of their social security number. Subsequently, a random sample of 60 boys and 60 girls was selected in each age cohort in four areas and, in order to ensure a geographic representation, 120 boys and 120 girls in the most eastern University city (Kuopio). This population was invited to a baseline study in 1980, and 3596 participated. These subjects have now been followed for 11 years; 72% of the subjects are still available for participation. Drop-out has not produced any systematic variance in the somatic risk factors or Type A behavior, and in the last follow-up the sample was still representative of the original one.

Behavioral variables in the present chapter refer to the following measures. Type A behavior of the subjects was both self-assessed (in the age groups of 12 years and older) and evaluated by subjects' mothers (in all age groups) with the AFMS (Type A behavior questionnaire for the Finnish Multicenter Study). General rationale for developing this test and its detailed construction have been given in Keltikangas-Järvinen and Jokinen (1989), and its reliability, construction, and concurrent validity in Keltikangas-Järvinen and Räikkönen (1990a). Childhood aggressiveness and hyperactivity were assessed by the mothers of 3-, 6-, and 9-year-old children, according to the Health Examination Survey (Wells, 1980). This was designed to screen children with behavioral problems and to be completed by nonprofessional persons.

The following variables were used as criterion variables for somatic risk. First, traditional somatic risk factors for CHD: serum total cholesterol, serum LDL cholesterol, serum triglycerides, body mass index, systolic blood pressure, and diastolic blood pressure. Second, apolipoprotein levels: increased levels of serum apolipoprotein B (apoB) and decreased levels of serum apolipoprotein A-I (apoA-I). The rationale for using both the serum apolipoproteins and serum lipids here were the observations that apolipoproteins rather than lipids regulate lipoprotein metabolism, and increased serum concentrations of apoB correlate better with CHD than serum low-density lipoprotein cholesterol levels. All details concerning the somatic measures are in Åkerblom, Viikari, and Uhari (1985).

## III. Evidence Supporting the Harmless Effect of Aggression in Boys and the Risk Effect in Girls

### A. AGGRESSION AS A SUBCOMPONENT OF TYPE A BEHAVIOR

Aggression was indeed an important subcomponent of Type A behavior in each group. It did not, however, exist independently, but was associated with other elements of Type A behavior. In adolescence it was associated with impatience (Keltikangas-Järvinen & Räikkönen, 1990a); in young adulthood and adulthood with competition (Keltikangas-Järvinen & Räikkönen, 1991). Both "aggression-impatience" and "aggression-competitiveness" had the same psychological concomitants. They correlated with low self-esteem, with an external locus of control (i.e., with a feeling that a person does not have control over his or her life), and with a low level of self-set goals. So, aggression manifested itself in different forms at different age levels, but kept its psychological correlates (Keltikangas-Järvinen & Räikkönen, 1990a; Keltikangas-Järvinen & Räikkönen, 1991).

This corresponds with Friedman and Rosenman's (1974) description of Type A personality. According to them, competitiveness and high achievement striving are defining dimensions of this behavior. Type A persons feel deeply threatened when they are not able to control an environment. Their way to reassert control is to work more and more. Because of low self-esteem they have no internalized standards for achievement but are dependent on external feedback. Independent of the results of their exertions they usually feel dissatisfied with themselves. As a result they have a deep sense of insecurity. Based on this knowledge it might be expected that persons who score high on the aggression factor of Type A behavior also exhibit a high level of somatic CHD risk. We studied relationships between aggression and traditional somatic risk factors. In addition to cross-sectional correlations, longitudinal associations were assessed. Thus, subjects who during the 6-year follow-up period continuously exhibited very high scores on somatic risk variables were compared with subjects having continuously low scores on those variables.

We found that aggression as a subcomponent of Type A behavior was not related to nor predicted a later somatic risk (Keltikangas-Järvinen & Räikkönen, 1989; Keltikangas-Järvinen & Räikkönen, 1990b). Some remote nonsystematic associations were found, but can be found at random in such a large sample. Thus, the present data did not support the assumption of the crucial role of aggression in the etiology of CHD. Where serum cholesterols were used as criterion variables there were no statistically significant gender differences.

## B. AGGRESSION AS A CONCOMITANT OF TYPE A BEHAVIOR

The most widely studied concomitants of Type A behavior have been coping strategies and emotions. There is disagreement whether problem-focused coping (see Hart, 1988) or a passive withdrawal and avoidance of the problems (see Pittner & Houston, 1980) is typical of Type A persons. These opposite strategies are the ways of coping most frequently associated with Type A behavior, and there is an equal amount of evidence for both strategies.

Although aggression has been associated with the Type A pattern, the likelihood of Type A persons behaving aggressively when frustrated has not been studied frequently. Our data showed that aggression as a coping mechanism was indeed related to Type A behavior in girls, while in boys the correlation was negative. In neither group was there a relationship between aggressive coping and somatic risk indicators of CHD (Keltikangas-Järvinen & Jokinen, 1989).

Though Type A behavior was originally seen as an action–emotion complex, research on the emotions of Type A persons is scanty. Because they are shown to easily express anger (e.g., Dembroski *et al.*, 1985), aggression (e.g., Diamond, 1982), and hostility (e.g., Manuck, Kaplan, & Matthews, 1986) in their behavior, aggression has also been assumed to be very central to their emotional life.

Our findings did not support this assumption. Type A persons did not report a higher frequency of aggressive feelings than did Type B counterparts. In addition, aggression as an emotion was not related to somatic risk. Instead, a tendency toward depression was the more elementary characteristic underlying Type A behavior, being related also to somatic risk (Keltikangas-Järvinen, unpublished manuscript).

### C. AGGRESSION AS AN ANTECEDENT OF TYPE A BEHAVIOR

Type A behavior has been identified in very young children (e.g., Lundberg, 1983). Yet, more important than Type A behavior as such, are some behavioral childhood characteristics. We do not know whether Type A children grow up to be Type A adolescents, but there is evidence that childhood hyperactivity and easily aroused aggressiveness significantly predict later Type A behavior (e.g., Bergman & Magnusson, 1986). This was supported by our data. Childhood aggression and hyperactivity correlated with adolescent Type A behavior over the 6-year follow-up period. The relationship between aggression and Type A behavior was evident among boys, while in girls childhood hyperactivity was a stronger predictor of a later likelihood to behave in a Type A manner (Räikkönen & Keltikangas-Järvinen, in press).

In girls, childhood aggression and hyperactivity correlated also with a higher risk level of apoB and apoA-I, but this was not so with boys, in whom the emotional distance from the mother as well as the mother's dissatisfaction with her role were the most significant psychological factors related to a high risk level of serum apolipoproteins (Räikkönen, Keltikangas-Järvinen, & Solakivi, 1990). So, aggression was an antecedent of Type A behavior both in boys and in girls, although the relationship was stronger in boys. Aggression was related to somatic risk only in girls.

## IV. Conclusions

In agreement with previous literature, aggression was shown here to be an important factor in Type A behavior. It was, however, not of primary importance, as had been previously suggested. In this context it also had a limited content. It pointed to an impatience, irritability and readiness to compete, and not to a high prevalence of aggressive *feelings* or an increased use of aggression as a coping mechanism.

Aggression was not related to a high level of somatic risk of CHD. This conflicts with previous literature. In order to explain our findings, cultural differences must be taken into consideration. Attitudes toward aggression are ambivalent in Finland. In general discussion, aggression is disapproved of, but among boys and young men it is likely to be highly admired (see Keltikangas-Järvinen & Jokinen, 1989). Therefore, self-reports are perhaps not a valid method here, but may reflect cultural values rather than the actual situation. It may also be that previous assumptions concerning the important role of aggression have been based on the general belief of the harmful effects of aggression rather than on empirical evidence of the relationship specifically between aggression and CHD risk.

The hypothesis regarding the pathogenic role of aggression was, however, likely to be true with girls. As could be expected, healthy girls and young women scored lower than healthy boys and young men on aggression factors. In addition, aggression was not a very apparent dimension of Type A behavior among girls and women. However, when aggression was present, it also predicted an increased somatic risk. The gender difference was especially apparent during childhood, the children being 3, 6, and 9 years old. This does not mean that the difference is likely to disappear when the children grow up, but probably indicates that the measures used to assess aggression in our study were more appropriate for younger children.

As mentioned before, research on CHD risk factors has focused on men. It has not been previously suggested that the behavioral etiology of CHD might be different in women and men. The present findings give reason to continue studying the gender differences here. When the development of morbid aggression has been studied, the importance of genetically determined factors has often been emphasized. A good example here is the suggestion that when inherited temperamental characteristics, such as a person's inherited activity, and environmental demands are incongruent, aggression is likely to be manifested (Eliasz & Wrzesniewski, in press).

Instead of inherited factors, a sociocultural explanation has been suggested here, based on two findings reported earlier from the present subjects. First, it has been suggested that aggressiveness of Type A children correlated with particular child-rearing practices of mothers. The mother who predisposed her child to aggressive Type A behavior was characterized by three dimensions. She could not tolerate her child's normal daily activity but required overcontrolled behavior from her child. She was very sensitive to her child's "aggressiveness," had very strict educational attitudes, and very easily punished her child. She easily became nervous in the company of her child and felt that the child was not emotionally significant but a burden who prevented her self-fulfillment (Räikkönen &

Keltikangas-Järvinen, in press). This educational model has been previously identified by Schafer (1959) as a "hostile child-rearing practice."

Second, it was found in the present sample that the Type A behavior of the 12-, 15-, and 18-year-old girls correlated with the Type A behavior of their fathers, while the Type A behavior of the same cohorts of boys and their mothers were related (Keltikangas-Järvinen, 1988).

Model learning has been perhaps the most popular frame of reference to explain the development of Type A behavior. There is indeed a lot of evidence showing that identification with Type A parents seems to be a way of becoming Type A persons (Bortner, Rosenman, & Friedman, 1979). Identification with the same-sex model has been reported in other papers. Strong correlation with the opposite-sex parent has been found only in the present sample.

These two findings may lead to the following suggestion: a mother who rejects her child emotionally and is likely to use hostile child-rearing practices encourages her child to behave aggressively. The mother does not give an identifying model to her daughter, so pushes her to identify with the father. The daughter becomes an aggressive, competitive, Type A person, whose masculine behavior is likely to conflict with the gender-role expectations of the society.

In another study we have found that behavior which is against the expected gender roles of the society may constitute a risk for illness. For instance, among the older age groups of the present sample it was found that the same characteristics can be risk and nonrisk behavior, depending on whether this behavior aligns with or goes against the gender roles of the society. A high level of social support, a large social network, a low level of hostility, and readiness to openly express emotions are expected to be "feminine" characteristics in our society, while the opposite is true for the "masculine" way of life. Our findings showed that hostility, a lack of social network, and an inability to express emotions were a higher risk for women than for men (Räikkönen, Keskivaara, & Keltikangas-Järvinen, in press).

Thus, in addition to other approaches, this sociocultural explanation might increase our understanding of the role of aggression as a behavioral component of CHD risk. If the "wrong" role identification happens, not based on "free choice" but as a result of inappropriate child-rearing practices, this may lead to an emotional distress which in turn creates a somatic risk.

## References

Åkerblom, H. K., Viikari, J., & Uhari, M. (1985). Atherosclerosis precursors in Finnish children and adolescents. General description of the cross-sectional study of 1980. *Acta Paediatria Scandinavica, 318 (Suppl)*, 49–63.

Bergman, L. R., & Magnusson, D. (1986). Type A behavior: A longitudinal study from childhood to adulthood. *Psychosomatic Medicine, 48*, 134–142.

Bortner, R. W., Rosenman, R. H., & Friedman, M. (1979). Familial similarity in pattern A behavior. *Journal of Chronic Diseases, 23*, 39–43.

Dembroski, T. M., MacDougall, J. M., Williams, R. B., Haney, T., & Blumenthal, J. A. (1985). Components of Type A, hostility and anger-in: Relationship to angiographic findings. *Psychosomatic Medicine, 447*, 219–233.

Diamond, E. L. (1982). The role of anger and hostility in essential hypertension and coronary heart disease. *Psychological Bulletin, 92*, 410–433.

Eliasz, A., & Wrzesniewski, K. (In press). Two kinds of Type A behavior pattern. *In* C. Spielberger, I. Sarason, & J. Strelau (Eds.), *Stress and Anxiety*, Vol. XIII. Plenum.

Friedman, M. C., & Rosenman, R. H. (1974). *Type A Behavior and Your Heart*. New York: Knopf.

Hart, K. E. (1988). Association of Type A behavior and its components to ways of coping with stress. *Journal of Psychosomatic Research, 32*, 213–219.

Jenkins, C. D. (1988). Epidemiology of cardiovascular disease. *Journal of Consulting and Clinical Psychology, 56*, 324–332.

Kannel, W. B. (1979). Cardiovascular disease: A multifactorial problem (insights from the Framingham study). *In* M. L. Pollack & D. H. Schmidt (Eds.), *Heart Disease and Rehabilitation* (pp. 15–31). New York: Wiley.

Keltikangas-Järvinen, L. (1988). Similarity of Type A behavior in adolescents and their parents. *The Journal of Social Psychology, 128*, 97–104.

Keltikangas-Järvinen, L. Emotional expressions and somatic risk factors of CHD. Unpublished manuscript.

Keltikangas-Järvinen, L., & Jokinen, J. (1989). Type A behavior, coping mechanisms and emotions related to somatic risk factors of coronary heart disease in adolescents. *Journal of Psychosomatic Research, 33*, 17–27.

Keltikangas-Järvinen, L., & Räikkönen, K. (1989). Pathogenic and protective factors of Type A behavior in adolescents. *Journal of Psychosomatic Research, 33*, 591–602.

Keltikangas-Järvinen, L., & Räikkönen, K. (1990a). Healthy and maladjusted Type A behavior in adolescents. *Journal of Youth and Adolescence, 19*, 1–18.

Keltikangas-Järvinen, L., & Räikkönen, K. (1990b). Type A factors as predictors of somatic risk factors of coronary heart disease in young Finns—a six-year follow-up study. *Journal of Psychosomatic Research, 34*, 89–97.

Keltikangas-Järvinen, L, & Räikkönen, K. (1991). Type A behavior and types of competitor in young adults. *European Journal of Personality, 5*, 61–69.

Lagerspetz, K. M. (1970). Research of human aggression from the perspective of animal research. *International Journal of Psychology, 5*, 285–292.

Lundberg, U. (1983). Note on Type A behavior and cardiovascular responses to challenge in 3–6-yr old children. *Journal of Psychosomatic Research, 27*, 39–42.

Manuck, S. B., Kaplan, J. R., & Matthews, K. A. (1986). Behavioral antecedents of coronary heart disease and atherosclerosis. *Atherosclerosis, 6*, 2–14.

Nanjee, M. N., & Miller, N. E. (1989). Plasma lipoproteins and adrenocortical hormones in men—positive association of low density lipoprotein cholesterol with plasma cortisol concentration. *Clinical Chemistry Acta, 180*, 113–119.

Pittner, M. S., & Houston, B. K. (1980). Response to stress, cognitive coping strategies and the Type A behavior pattern. *Journal of Personality and Social Psychology, 39*, 145–157.

Räikkönen, K., & Keltikangas Järvinen, L. (In press). Childhood hyperactivity and the mother-child relationship as predictors of risk Type A behavior in adolescence; a six year follow-up. *Personality and Individual Differences*.

Räikkönen, K., Keltikangas-Järvinen, L., & Solakivi, T. (1990). Behavioral coronary risk indicators and apolipoproteins A-I and B in young Finnish children: cross-sectional and predictive associations. *Preventive Medicine, 19*, 656–666.

Räikkönen, K., Keskivaara, P., & Keltikangas-Järvinen, L. (In press). Hostility and social support among Type A individuals. *Psychology & Health.*

Schafer, E. S. (1959). A circumplex model for maternal behavior. *Journal of Abnormal and Social Psychology, 59*, 226–335.

Strong, J., & McGill, H. (1969). The pediatric aspects of atherosclerosis. *Journal of Atherosclerosis Research, 9*, 251–265.

Van Egeren, L. F., Abelson, J. L., & Sniderman, L. D. (1983). Interpersonal and electrocardiographic responses of Type A's and Type B's in competitive socioeconomic games. *Journal of Psychosomatic Research, 27*, 53–59.

Wells, E. (1980). Behavioral patterns of children in school. *Vital and Health Statistics*, Series 11, No. 113.

13

# Expressions of Aggression in the Life Stories of Aged Women

Jan-Erik Ruth and Peter Öberg

I. WAY OF LIFE AND LIFE HISTORY RESEARCH
II. THE COLLECTION AND ANALYSIS OF LIFE STORIES
III. SOCIETY AND FAMILY AS THE SOURCES OF AGGRESSION
A. The Bitter Life
B. Life as a Trapping Pit
C. Life as a Hurdle Race
IV. A LIFE WITHOUT AGGRESSION
A. The Sweet Life
B. The Arduous Working Life
C. The Devoted Silenced Life
V. DISCUSSION
REFERENCES

## I. Way of Life and Life History Research

During the last decade, discussion on way of life research has grown at an accelerating rate within social sciences. The concept of *way of life* has been used with varied meanings. Roos (1988) describes it as the reflection of cultural undercurrents in people's lives, whereas Björnberg *et al.* (1982) define it as a regular pattern of action among groups with mutual material conditions in society. In this study we have taken Max Weber as a starting point and defined way of life as "the strategy which an individual uses in order to utilize those resources which his social background, education, tradition and the market economy have created" (Ruth *et al.*, 1989).

Life history as a method of data collection has experienced a renaissance in social studies, and has gained a foothold in gerontology. Life histories give an overall picture of the lives of the elderly, they tell about people in a certain social and historic situation, and they enable a way of life analysis without defined descriptions of reality being made in advance. Instead, we start from the elderly people's own concepts and definitions of their lives (Ruth *et al.*, 1989), so we can show how people interpret and handle situations, and how they understand themselves and their lives (cf. Gergen, 1988).

Life histories are identity constructions; people tell us who they are and how they have developed (Rubinstein, 1988). Here "I" can be seen as a storyteller who tries to integrate various life events into a coherent story. Life histories are constructions because people are not passive "containers" of their life experiences. They remodel their lives when they tell their stories (Saarenheimo, 1989). Starting from "the reconstruction theory," we assume that an objective memory is an unnecessary fiction, that it is just those subjective interpretations we actually understand with biographical memory (Saarenheimo, 1991).

Kvale suggests that the past cannot be recalled "as it happened" because it depends on subsequent events. Any event whatsoever is recalled by what it led to (Kvale, 1977); life histories reconstruct meaning into the past from the perspective of the present, thus describe the present projected on the past (Bertaux-Wiame, 1981; Kohli, 1981, 1986). Citing Erikson (1982), reminiscence in old age can either create despair or be psychologically integrating.

Epistemologically we start from a social science where humans are characterized by a *narrating form of reasoning*. These stories, or thought fragments, are culturally created, and they affect our understanding of ourselves and our social environment (cf. Bruner, 1990). Biographical material can be collected as stories structured by the researcher or as free autobiographies (Vilkko, 1987). In this study we have chosen a mixture of both methods. First, as freely as possible, the informants have been able to tell their life stories; second, we have completed data with thematic interviews about life in retrospect and life at present.

## II. The Collection and Analysis of Life Stories

On the basis of a biography study, Roos (1985a, 1985b, 1987) has divided the Finnish people of today into four generations. The first generation, people born between 1900 and 1920, he calls "the generation of the wars and the Depression," a generation characterized by the experiences of the Depression and the wars (the Civil War, 1917–1918, the Winter War, 1939–1940, and the Continuation War, 1941–1944). Typical experiences of this generation are: poverty; separation from family in childhood; parent's death; orphanage; illness; short or interrupted time at school; constant work and struggle; and a shortage of goods. Not everybody in this generation had all of these experiences, but still one can talk about a common world of experience that has affected this cohort (Roos, 1985a, 1985b, 1987).

The women of this generation were adult and middle-aged during a period known as "the prime of familism and the housewives," and they have experienced major changes in sex roles. In Finland, Haavio-Mannila, Jallinoja, & Strandell (1984) have described the familistic model of family life thus: people fall in love only once, and that is with the future spouse; the marriage takes a stable course of family life with an adequate number of children; sex life is channeled to the marriage but it is kept under control even there; the marriage is thought to last the whole lifetime. If possible, the mother in this model of family life stays at home when the children are small.

In this chapter we report expressions of aggression of single elderly women from the generation of the wars and the Depression, born between 1905 and 1915, and living in Helsinki (data are from the study "Way of life, aging and well-being," Ruth *et al.*, 1989). Respondents were chosen through a strategic sampling technique and participation was voluntary. People replied to an advertisement, "Tell about your life." The sampling was supplemented in order to reach people from different social strata. The occupational groups represented were careerists, entrepreneurs, employees, housewives, and daughters at home. In this type of study, it is not meaningful to discuss the representativity on an individual level. The question of representativity should be lifted to another level: how representative is the picture given of the described phenomenon (cf. Roos, 1988)?

In this study we interviewed 37 persons (23 women, 14 men) in their homes, two interviews per case. The average length of interview was 7 hours and 40 minutes per case, varying from 4 hours and 15 minutes to 16 hours and 25 minutes. Interviews were then written *in extenso*. The interviewees first told their life stories that were followed by theme interviews.

The data were analyzed using the "Grounded theory" method, that is, groups of qualitatively similar life histories were brought together into one category and labeled after the dominating qualities in the category (Glaser & Strauss, 1967; Strauss & Corbin, 1990). We found six different categories of way of life among the elderly which were named "the bitter life," "the sweet life," "life as a hurdle race," "life as a trapping pit," "the arduous working life," and "the devoted silenced life." All 23 women interviewed could be found represented in the above-mentioned ways of life. The basis of this typification was the way the interviewees started and ended their stories, what turning points their stories included, how they overcame major changes in their lives, and how they interpreted and evaluated these changes.

Reflections of class differences were noticeable in the life stories. A middle-class biography model was characterized by the separation of "the inner" and "the outer" worlds. Working-class biographies were not characterized by a focus on the problematical nature of the self, but rather dealt with how to cope with those conditions and values that social background offered. Working-class biographies reveal a totally different idea of the self from those of the middle-class individual (Vilkko, 1987).

The conditions for growing up in an agrarian or working-class environment could be seen in the forms of life called "the bitter life," "life as a hurdle race," and "the devoted silenced life." The childhood home was often a small cottage shared with the parents and a number of children. Affection or love was seldom shown and the parents were clear authorities. Physical punishment occurred occasionally and a whip was hanging over the doorpost as a warning. At the dinner table everybody sat quietly, with girls and boys on different sides. Gender roles were strongly differentiated and socialization to womanhood was strict; women were brought up by women. In early adolescence, after elementary school, one had to move to the city because there was no source of livelihood in the rural areas. But the rural childhood environment formed the life structure and attitudes. Entry into working life often happened as a maid in a middle-class family. The family gave the maid room and board but she lived and ate separately from them.

The conditions for growing up in a middle-class family were seen in the way of life categories "the sweet life," "the arduous working life," and, to a certain extent, "life as a trapping pit." The childhood home was often a large city apartment shared with relatively few siblings and a maid. The parents were often in active cooperation with the children; they played the piano, went to the movies, and read stories. Affection and love were important; the possible lack of these aspects was pointed out in these stories. Physical punishment did not occur.

Gender differences were also evident. The feminine is a social reality and culturally defined position that marks women's life histories. The women consider themselves as different and suppressed, and they consistently compare themselves to other people (Vilkko, 1987). It is common for female biographers at the beginning of the story to state their secondary position.

## III. Society and Family as the Sources of Aggression

In this study we examined how expressions of aggression emerged freely from the life stories in different life contexts. To start with, we can state that expressions of aggression and hate were rather rare in these life-history interviews.

### A. THE BITTER LIFE

When these expressions of aggression could be found, it was in the case of the disintegrated way of life we called "the bitter life." This category was dominated by single women. Also here the suppressed ego of these women led to a situation where they described themselves as objects and victims of other people's aggression and neglect.

Bertta is a 79-year-old unmarried ex-office employee from a rural family where she grew up as one of eight children. The aggressions she feels herself to be an object of come from a collective representation—society, authorities, married women—not from one single person. Her bitterness derives from the feeling of being an outsider in society:

> We who moved into cities from the country, the victims of rural depopulation and change, we were put down. We were exploited . . . we were crushed."

When Bertta expresses her aggressions through contempt she often changes her speech from past tense into present tense. She has not been able to work upon and integrate the contempt she feels. Rather, the contempt for everything she does not have in life is her coping strategy. In her aggression toward the surrounding world there can be seen a certain form of aggressive self-stimulation (cf. Lagerspetz, 1977).

But Bertta turns the bitterness inward, also. She says she looks terrible now that she is old and she despises her own reflection in a mirror. This self-contempt is often directed toward her own sex and the feminine in her, as in many other cases in this category of way of life. Another person in this category whose life has been one long case history expressed her inward aggression in two suicide attempts earlier in life and suicidal thoughts in later life.

Life histories include sometimes contradictory stories, where the interviewees give information that seems to be in total conflict with the dominating impression of the history. These contradictions have been considered typical of women's autobiographies (Fahlgren, 1987) but should be seen as an effort to cope. They can also reflect an ideal ego that the interviewee has never been able to reach. For example, in Bertta's case, she says she has been able to carry on because she has not been "bitter or sad." An existence without conflicts was a common ideal for the women in all of these ways of life. A good childhood family was described as "there were never any conflicts between the parents," no matter how life turned out to be.

The case of Brita, who grew up in an upper middle-class family as one of two children, deals with aggression from the family. Her story is about illness as a social heritage, and problematical human relations are a consistent theme. Brita was hated by her schizophrenic mother (she is always the object of her mother's aggressions in her story) because she was the reason for the misalliance between her parents.

> "She [the mother] tolerated me as a little girl but not anymore when I grew up, then it was difficult. She hated me from the bottom of her heart . . . And she told me how I ruined her life . . . and how I was ugly and stupid."

Brita has not been able to work upon these feelings. She has seen a psychiatrist, but the childhood traumas are still there, and recur in dreams in which she is threatened by her mother. She was exposed to psychological violence. Physical punishment was not involved. Brita made some efforts of reconciliation but was always rejected. She does not direct her aggression toward her mother but more to herself.

> "I tried to get her sympathy in every way . . . night after night I was knitting and saving money, trying to be as nice as I could, but it was no good. I thought that it was because I was so ugly and dumb . . . you have to be pretty and clever before people accept you."

Brita dislikes her reflection in a mirror and she can spend weeks without looking into one because she thinks that during the years she has started to look like her mother. Once she tried to talk about her problems with her mother but it ended up with the mother throwing a dishcloth in her face. This theme prevails all through her life history, which ends in panic and isolation in old age.

## B. LIFE AS A TRAPPING PIT

This way of life showed considerably fewer expressions of aggression. Faina is 74 years old, divorced, and with a rural background. She grew up as one of twelve children. She lost her mother when she was eight and was taken care of by her elder sister who thought that she could not grow up with men, her father and brothers. When she was a teenager the sister died and another sister took care of her. This sister married a rich man but there was no love between them. Faina was ill treated by the man. She got married but the husband was unfaithful and they divorced. After the war she started her own business with her sister and some influential businessmen. There was declining social mobility, first in her marriage and then in her work; she was moved from management to office employee and later on was fired. As an entrepreneur she experienced a lot of envy, first from her associates, then from the landlord of their business premises, and then from the authorities:

> "They started to envy us, that we [Faina and her sister] got rich, so they dumped us . . . Then the landlord started to envy us and he gave us a notice to move. There were a lot of envious people around and we got a one million Mark additional tax. The spirit was to destroy private entrepreneurs . . . they made us look like criminals."

The description is not of a person-to-person conflict but it is an aggression against the collective representation of Faina's social affiliation, private entrepreneurs, the group with which she strongly identifies. And the aggression comes from another collective representation: society, landlords, tax authorities. The same description applies to her last job where she was fired by "the communist representatives."

Faina's story includes also the ideal of nonaggression. She had no problem with being a female manager because it was before "the women's movement started to make a fuss about being a woman." Instead of self-assertion and aggressiveness, she emphasizes humility and the repression of the self that has been a part of her socializing process. It meant, for example, that one never complained about anything:

> "I have been brought up to refrain from making a number of myself. Like when I lived in that house I owned, I always said "Come to 'our' place." I never made a fuss about myself . . . I have never complained about anything to anybody."

The only thing about which Faina was bitter was the bombing of her home during the war. Some further expressions of aggression she articulated regarded "niggers," whom she refused to see on television, and young doctors at the health center "who did not know much of anything."

## C. LIFE AS A HURDLE RACE

This way of life was usually formed in connection with sociohistorical changes that affected the development of the respondents in various ways. In this way of life category, events of social history most clearly made an impact on individual history, starting from early childhood during the Civil War.

Hillevi is a 73-year-old widow with a rural background who used to work in a factory. She lost her father in 1918 in the Civil War. She was the only child. She does not remember her father, and started her story from her mother's point of view:

> "My mother was a widow because her husband died in the war. Her life was very difficult. But then she married again because we needed a place to live."

The stepfather went to Russia where he died in a prison in the 1930s. Hillevi and her mother went after him but they returned to Finland before the Winter War (1939). Their home was in Karelia, which is now Russian territory, and they were evacuated. World War II struck this cohort just when they were setting up their families. The husbands were enrolled and the women were left alone, often with small children. This happened also to Hillevi who was evacuated with her son: "The evacuated people were treated like scum. We were nothing."

We noted before that women often tell their stories through other people, in the plural or in the third person. Here, the interviewee was "one of the evacuated." Her ideal can be seen in her description of her stepfather as kind, and in that there were never any fights in the childhood home.

Conflicts had a negative impact on Hillevi. Six months earlier she had broken off contact with her daughter and her children after a quarrel. She told the interviewer about this very emotional event only at the end of the almost 11-hour-long interview. As a child the daughter had to live with her grandmother when Hillevi was forced to move away to get work. In the quarrel the daughter accused her of abandoning her. In Hillevi's opinion the daughter did not understand the circumstances in which they were living at the time. They had not spoken to each other in the six months after the quarrel. Hillevi's husband had also caused some conflicts with his drinking, but here the repressive coping of this generation was again evident: sweep difficulties under the carpet.

> "When it's done, it's done, it doesn't matter after that. Those things are not worth talking about anymore . . . it's useless to bring them up anymore."

Hillevi's coping with difficulties can be seen as typical of her generation. Theirs was a very different coping ideal from the one we have today of living through emotions and acting out feelings.

In another life history in the category of "life as a hurdle race," a woman told us she and her closest ones were followed by aggressions all through their lives. Her father was the victim of an attempted robbery in his workplace, and later in the Civil War he was assaulted by soldiers. However, her father used violence on the children after drinking. Later on she experienced violence in dance halls and she was assaulted by her landlord. She was also a witness to a suicide attempt in the family, and, "remote-controlled by fate," she married a man who turned out to be a violent drunk.

In some cases she broke all contacts with people who had displayed aggression toward her. This happened, for example, with an employer who had strongly criticized her. She resigned immediately. This is a typical course of action in Finnish working and rural culture: after a confrontation all connections are cut off at once. Her other way of coping with the expressions of aggression from the men around her was a kind of combination of rationalization and double standards. She considered her husband and father were basically good men but illness and alcohol could cause occasional bursts of violence. Men were sometimes aggressive but she thought that it was in their nature and they could not help it.

## IV. A Life without Aggression

A successful integration, accepting one's life as it has been, means that expressions of aggression do not form a purpose of life in old age.

### A. THE SWEET LIFE

In this way of life category there were practically no expressions of aggression in the life histories.

Linda is a 77-year-old retired office manager who was one of eight children in a skilled worker family with upward mobility. The aggressions she encountered were in connection with sociohistorical events: one brother was arrested for joining the Red Guard in the Civil War and she was afraid her friends at school might find out about it; another brother was killed in World War II. She grew up in a happy family with loving parents, fell in love, and got married. After that, most of the story concerned her husband. She was proud to tell us so much about him.

> "There was some trouble in the company [of her husband] and we sold it. He didn't want to argue. He was a cheerful man and very much liked by everybody."

An existence without conflicts as an ideal was evident in many contexts of her story:

> "I never heard swearing or quarreling in my childhood home or in my own home. Now when you hear them swear on streetcars, it's terrible."

The women of this generation, who grew up with their own ideals but later met different attitudes in a changing world, will keep on following the original way of life to which they were socialized. Accepting the new values would mean renouncing the significance of the life lived. Linda, like others in this category, was satisfied with her self image:

> "I am not bitter like so many others. I still laugh very easily."

Linda said she had had a happy life. It is obvious that the picture of the sweet life and a happy old age excludes aggressions and conflicts. This way of life was characterized by factors of upbringing which, according to Lagerspetz, create nonaggressive behavior. These factors are warmth and love; education to an inner control; identification with parents; parents' interest in children; and a mutual interaction between children and parents (Lagerspetz, 1977).

## B. THE ARDUOUS WORKING LIFE

This is a typical way of life among male careerists, represented in this study by two unmarried women from rural areas. Among this generation, work is generally a central factor in giving meaning to life but it is not the main factor, as in this way of life.

Airi is an unmarried, retired head nurse. Her father was a higher civil servant and they had two, sometimes three, maids. The aggressions she encountered happened during the Civil War when the rebels came and watched their house, and during World War II, when her brother was killed. During this war Airi herself advanced into a leading position in her work. The ideal of this way of life—not to show your emotions or aggressions—was best seen when she learned that a part of Karelia was incorporated into Russia:

> "There were many women, nurses and so on, from Karelia who learned that they didn't have a home anymore. When we heard that nobody even flinched. You could only see the tears running down their cheeks. Professor Nordenswan from Sweden

> [who had not lost anything] jumped up and cried that he has to get the first flight back home because next the Russians are heading towards Sweden. And those who had just lost their homes sat there silently. But they sure felt something in their hearts."

In Airi's opinion there is such a great difference between the Finns and the Swedes (to the former's advantage). This way of life is characterized by a lack of aggression and a control over one's feelings. Airi's father was "a friend to everybody." Her life was good and led by the word of God. In her life, there were no aggressions other than those she now felt in connection with her strong religiousness and with a life without sexuality:

> "During the last weeks I have prayed many times, I have prayed to God to take me to the heavenly home . . . the Devil torments all the time, one has to be so careful."

If the formation of one's life is seen as a work of God's hand and providence, it implies that the person should submit to adjust herself to whatever life has to give.

## C. THE DEVOTED SILENCED LIFE

A quiet submission culminated in "the devoted silenced life." Respondents in this way of life described themselves as driftwood, but they finish their stories still somehow satisfied in old age. In this way of life people apply a form of passive adjustment (Tornstam, 1987) where an individual is able to manipulate her needs and lower her aspiration level at the same time as she is able to integrate the life lived and end up quite satisfied in old age.

Denise is a 78-year-old unmarried, retired office employee with an academic education. She grew up as one of two children in a working-class family in a small town. She had a good but distant relationship with her mother, but was closer to her father. She was not punished physically and nobody ever "raised a voice at home." But the whip hung over the door post:

> "We had a strict family; you didn't talk to adults unless you were asked. You could not stand up to them if you were scolded. So you were a little repressed at home . . . But I don't blame my parents. They meant well. The main thing was to learn to be decent. That is unheard of now. I am shocked to hear the children of today scream at their parents."

Self-assertion, which has also been described as sound aggressiveness, was quite opposite to the socialization typical of that generation, especially with women, or in a working-class and agrarian environment. Denise was a teenager when her brother's alcoholism ruined her adolescence but she managed to hide it from everybody. She took care of her father for twenty years after her mother had died. She considered that to be her duty which she did not actually like very much, but there was no choice:

> "We spent the summers in a villa in Turku. My father planted vegetables and I had to weed. It was not fun. But I managed to hide it. He thought I liked it . . . It was not useless, I guess. I learned resignation."

In this case, self-sacrifice and the understanding of other people's needs emerged as the guiding principles of life, and these prevented expressions of aggression (Lagerspetz, 1977). There was also an evident tendency to avoid all conflicts. At the time of the interview, Denise was living in a service home:

> "I get mad when I hear people complain about the food, both sad and mad. But we are all old here and you can't say anything. You just have to swallow your anger."

## V. Discussion

The life histories of elderly women showed relatively few expressions of aggression. When they emerged, the respondents were often the objects of other people's aggression, and that corresponded with the repressed egos of the respondents.

There are several explanations for the lack of expressions of aggression, both psychological and sociocultural. First, according to Erikson (1982), one of the developmental tasks in old age is the integration of the self. By integration he means that one accepts one's life just the way it has turned out. This would imply that strong aggressive expressions among elderly women would be a sign of disintegration and anxiety. This could only be seen in "the bitter life." As was stated in the introduction, in this integration process an individual does not "copy" experiences from the past and later relive the past events; instead, respondents reconstruct their lives from what gives meaning to old age. So even if there had been expressions of situation-related aggression, they were not conveyed to old age if the integration process was successful. According to Erikson, this developmental task is common for both men and women.

A second explanation is offered by the theory of gero-transcendence (Tornstam, 1989). While aggression is based on an engaged ego perspective with an acting self, the theory of gero-transcendence is founded on the assumption that our way of looking at our lives changes with time into a more inner-directed ego perspective. Jung has also written about this kind of change (1930). The aged cross over from a microperspective to a macroperspective when they interpret their lives. This theory of gero-transcendency is also based on a common course of development for both sexes.

A third explanation is connected with cohort differences, and originates in the socialization of this generation. Attitudes like "you are not to complain as long as you have food and shelter" or "I never say anything bad about people" or "I have no quarrel with my neighbors" are very common. This generation should be examined from the unique historical perspective which formed them (see

Inglehart, 1977): they lived in a rural society where the struggle for survival was essential. The life histories deal also with the process of urbanization, the acquisition of material necessities, and new work relations. This cohort has mainly experienced sociohistorical aggressions: in childhood, the Civil War, then, the Great Depression, later, World War II, at the beginning of their new family life. The emphasis of compromise solutions may have become a part of the coping processes of this generation.

A fourth explanation is tied to the dimension of social class. The majority of the respondents came from rural, working-class environments to the state capital, Helsinki. Their entrance into working life often happened through a period as a maid in upper middle-class families. They learned obedience and submission in functioning on other people's terms, and that did not leave much room for expressions of aggression. If one reads the life histories without knowing the background of the respondents, it is the social affiliation—the class perspective—which first becomes manifest.

A fifth explanation, which is more applicable to the women of this generation, touches upon the concept of locus of control. When many women interpret their lives as predestined or directed by God, it is understandable that they strive to adapt themselves to it, rather than rebel against these superior powers.

A sixth explanation is partly an expansion of the locus of control concept, but above all, gender based. We can separate the life histories with a female and a male self. The male subject is determined, makes independent decisions, takes responsibility for his life, and men's stories have only few contradictions and side tracks. The narrating self in women's stories is more contradictory and less integrated, it is anecdotal. Women describe other people's lives and their relations to these significant others; they perceive events with "other people's eyes" and often use "we" instead of "I." Achievements are not as manifest as in men's biographies, which can sometimes resemble *curricula vitae*. Women more often use the passive tense than do men; this use by women reflects them more as objects—objects for men's feelings—than subjects of their own lives (cf. Bertaux-Wiame, 1981; Fahlgren, 1987; Vilkko, 1987).

A seventh explanation is also tied to gender and connects with the fact that women in general express less aggression than men. Women are brought up to control expressions of violence (Lagerspetz, 1977). We have already suggested that women have a better understanding of, and identification with, other people during the life course, and this prevents expressions of aggression (Kaufman, 1970). Lagerspetz suggests that empathy not only decreases aggressiveness but, like unselfish behavior in general, increases alternative behavior strategies such as helpfulness (Lagerspetz, 1977). The type of self-assertion by which a person pushes his own interests with a firm conviction, a type which can be seen as a positive form of aggression, is rare among this generation of women. They pursue their interests most when it is obvious that those interests also offer a favorable outcome for their closest ones.

An eighth explanation is based on the situation of women in old age. It is a fact that among single elderly women, the majority are widows or divorced. It is reasonable to assume that this circumstance forms a new social barrier which makes it socially unacceptable to express overt aggressions about the deceased: *De mortuis nihil nisi bene.*

To sum up, we can distinguish different types of explanations for the lack of expressions of aggression in the life stories of aged women. Some of these explanations are based on the generation we studied and, of these, some are gender related. Certain explanations are sociocultural and they deal with the conditions under which people have lived. Some explanations are psychological and they deal with the adjustment of individuals and the reinterpretations of aggressive events during the life span. Among the sociocultural explanations we can make a distinction between factors tied to the life lived and factors tied to old age per se.

## References

Bertaux-Wiame, I. (1981). The life-history approach to the study of internal migration. *In* D. Bertaux (Eds.), *Biography and Society. The Life History Approach in Social Sciences.* London: Sage.

Björnberg, U., Bäck-Wiklund, M., Lindfors, H., & Nilsson, A. (1982). *Livsformer i en region. En jämförande analys av familje- och samhällsliv i 1970-talets Sverige.* Kungsälv: Liber.

Bruner, J. (1990). *Acts of Meaning.* London: Harvard University Press.

Bruun, K. (1972). *Alkoholi: Käyttö, vaikutukset ja kontrolli.* Helsinki: Tammi.

Erikson, E. H. (1982). *The Life Cycle Completed.* New York: Norton.

Fahlgren, M. (1987). *Det underordnade jaget. En studie om kvinnliga självbiografier.* Stockholm: Bokförlaget Jungfrun.

Gergen, M. M. (1988). Narrative structures in social explanation. *In* C. Antaki (Ed.), *Analyzing Everyday Explanation. A Casebook of Methods.* London: Sage.

Glaser, B., & Strauss, A. (1967). *The Discovery of Grounded Theory.* Chicago: Aldine.

Haavio-Mannila, E., Jallinoja, R., & Strandell, H. (1984). *Perhe, työ ja tunteet. Ristiriitoja ja ratkaisuja.* Juva: WSOY.

Inglehart, R. (1977). *The Silent Revolution. Changing Values and Political Styles among Western Publices.* Princeton, New Jersey: Princeton University Press.

Jung, C. G. (1930). Die lebenswende, Lecture. Ges. Werke 8, Olten 1982. In Danish in F. Alt (1984). Jung. Texter og tanker. Copenhagen: Borgens Forlag.

Kaufman, H. (1970). *Aggression and Altruism.* New York: Holt, Rinehart & Winston.

Kohli, M. (1981). Biography: account, text, method. *In* D. Bertaux (Ed.), *Biography and Society. The Life History Approach in Social Sciences.* London: Sage.

Kohli, M. (1986). Social organization and subjective construction of the life course. *In* Q. B. Sörensen, F. E. Weinevi, & L. R. Sherrod (Eds.), *Human Development and the Life-Course. Multidisciplinary Perspectives.* New Jersey: Lawrence Erlbaum.

Kvale, S. (1977). Dialectics and research on remembering. *In* N. Datan & H. W. Reese (Eds.), *Life-Span Developmental Psychology—Dialectical Perspectives on Experimental Research.* New York: Academic Press.

Lagerspetz, K. (1977). *Aggressio ja sen tutkimus.* Helsinki: Tammi.

Roos, J. P. (1985a). *Eläntapaa etsimässä. Tutkijaliiton julkaisusarja 34.* Jyväskylä: Gummrus OY.

Roos, J. P. (1985b). Life stories of social changes: Four generations in Finland. *International Journal of Oral History, 3*, 179–190.

Roos, J. P. (1987). *Suomalainen elämä. Hämeenlinna: Karisto OY.*

Roos, J. P. (1988). Elämäntavasta elämäkertaan. *Tutkijaliiton julaisusarja* 52. Jyväskylä: Gummerus OY.

Rubinstein, R. L. (1988). Stories told: In-depth interviewing and the structure of its insights. *In* G. Rowles & S. Reinharz (Eds.), *Qualitative Gerontology*. New York: Springer.

Ruth, J.-E. (1991). Reliabilitets - och validitets - frågan i kvantitativ respektive kralita-tiv forskningstradition. *Gerontologia, 4*, 277–290.

Ruth, J.-E., Öberg, P., Fromholt, P., Sigurdadottir, S., Tornstam, L., & Waerness, K. (1989). Livsformer och livshtoria hos äldre. *Gerontologia, 2*, 142–154.

Saarenheimo, M. (1989). Persoonallisuuden integraatio näkökulmana ikääntyneidenmielenterveyteen. Elämäkertatutkimus 75-vuotiaista kotona asuvista helsinkiläisistä. Licentiatavhandling i tillämpad psykologi. Helsinfors universitet.

Saarenheimo, M. (1991). Vuorovaikutuksellinen muisteleminen vanhuudessa. Tarkennettu tutkimussuunnitelma. Suomen Akatemia.

Strauss, A., & Corbin, J. (1990). *Basics of Qualitative Research. Grounded Theory and Techniques.* Newberry Park: Sage.

Tornstam, L. (1987). Ageing and self-perception: A systems theoretical model. *In* L. Levi (Ed.), *Society, Stress and Disease. Vol. 5, Old Age*. Oxford: Oxford University Press.

Tornstam, L. (1989). Gero-transcendence: A reformulation of the disengagement theory. *Aging, 1*, 55–63.

Vilkko, A. (1987). Tarina tarinasta - erään naisomaelämäkertaaineiston tarkastelua. Sosiaalipolitiikan pro gradututkielma. Helsingin yliopisto.

Öberg, P. & Ruth, J.-E. (in press). Hyvä vanhuus - kaikesta huolimatta. *In* J.-E. Ruth & A. Uutela (Eds.), *Muuttuva vanhuus.*

# III

# CULTURAL DIFFERENCES IN REGARD TO FEMALE AGGRESSION

14

# Matrifocality and Female Aggression in Margariteño Society

H. B. Kimberley Cook

I. INTRODUCTION
II. ETHNOGRAPHIC BACKGROUND
III. THE FORMS AND CONTEXTS OF FEMALE AGGRESSION
A. Fighting
B. Social Control
IV. FEMALE SEX-ROLE BEHAVIOR AND AGGRESSION
V. MATRIFOCALITY AND FEMALE AGGRESSION
VI. CONCLUSIONS
REFERENCES

## I. Introduction

This chapter* examines the nature of female aggression in a native population on the island of Margarita, Venezuela. From both intrasocietal and cross-cultural perspectives, Margariteño women are extremely aggressive. In this chapter, I describe culturally patterned forms of female aggression and the contexts in which they occur. Native Margariteños regard the aggressive conduct of women in their society as part of normal female sex role behavior. This study explains female aggression in Margarita by describing historical circumstances and cultural features that have affected a tradition of matrifocality in native communities on the island. I suggest that matrifocality is the central variable underlying culturally institutionalized patterns of female aggression in Margariteño society.

*Material in this paper is reprinted by permission of the author from Cook, H. B. K., in press, *Small town, big hell: An ethnographic study of aggression in a Margariteño community*. Fundación La Salle de Ciencias Naturales, Instituto Caribe de Antropología y Sociología, Caracas, Venezuela.

## II. Ethnographic Background

Margarita Island is located approximately twenty miles off the coast of eastern Venezuela in the state of Nueva Esparta.[1] Native Margariteños are mestizos of mixed Indian, African, and Spanish ancestry who traditionally were known as a peaceful, hard-working people (McCorkle, 1965; Alexander, 1961). In past decades, a rising population along with periodic shortages of employment opportunities on the island resulted in many Margariteño men migrating to other parts of the country for extended periods of time, leaving a high percentage of females on the island who stayed behind to maintain themselves and their families (Alexander, 1961).

Since the opening of a free port in 1975, the island has undergone intense modernization and change. It supports a large, socially and economically heterogeneous population that includes native Margariteños, Venezuelans, and foreigners; the latter are drawn to the island's resort areas by a prosperous tourist industry.

The changes brought about in the past few decades have diminished the island's peaceful ambience (Urbano, 1981) and blurred the distinction between native Margariteños and outsiders. While native Margariteños have traditionally participated in a variety of occupations, through the process of acculturation, many have become more economically stratified and urbanized.

This research focuses on a socioeconomically marginal population of native Margariteños who have traditionally made a living from subsistence fishing.[2] My findings are based on a 9-month ethnographic study of native Margariteño aggression that I conducted in a community on the island from September 1987 through May 1988.[3] I shall refer to this community as San Fernando.

The native Margariteños of San Fernando are connected to other similar communities on the island through flexible sociocentric networks that are based primarily on family ties. In marginal communities, these networks provide informal social security through cooperation, but simultaneously generate a considerable amount of interpersonal tension and conflict (see Cook, in press). In San Fernando, aggression occurs on a regular basis, but rarely results in serious injury or violence.[4] Most aggression is expressed verbally, passively, indirectly, or

[1]For background information on the island's history and people see Subero (1986); Navárez (1986); McCorkle (1965); and Orona (1968).

[2]See Mata Marín *et al.* (1975) and Mata Marín (1976), for a listing and description of marginal, native Margariteño communities.

[3]Fieldwork for this project was funded by a grant from the Organization of American States (FO4519). My findings in this study are also based upon previous ethnographic research that I have conducted on the island since 1979. While in Venezuela, I received institutional support from the Fundación la Salle de Ciencias Naturales, Instituto Caribe de Antropología y Sociología.

[4]While conducting research in 1987–1988, most crime still occurred in commercial areas of the island by outsiders during vacation seasons. See Republica de Venezuela, Estado Nueva Esparta (1987).

involves some harmless shoving or short-lived fistfighting. It is usually confined to same-sex participants, and occurs in a variety of contexts that include witchcraft, fighting, social control, socialization, and ritual events and activities (see Cook, in press).

## III. The Forms and Contexts of Female Aggression

Female aggression in native Margariteño society sharply contrasts with the intrasocietal tradition of peacefulness as well as with cross-cultural research that characterizes women as the less aggressive sex (D'Andrade, 1974; Brown, 1991). In his 1965 ethnography of the native Margariteños of Bella Vista, McCorkle states,

> Margaritan women, unlike their men, often engage in loud disputes and are willing to fight for an immediate objective; consequently the water vehicles are accompanied by policemen and the jails are likely to be full of women during acute water shortages. In June of 1952 the geographer Alexander saw the women of Fajardo tear the clothing off a policeman in the course of a general fight over water (McCorkle, 1965, p. 67).

My fieldwork in San Fernando confirms McCorkle's characterization of native Margariteño women as extremely aggressive. Based upon 42 cases of conflict that I recorded over a 9-month period, I found that women exhibit more verbal aggression than men. Quarrels between women occur out in the open, in the streets, and are often viewed as a form of public amusement. Upon several occasions I observed women engaged in ferocious verbal fights among themselves, accompanied by fist waving, insults, and the hurling of pebbles at the feet of their opponents.

Eighteen of the 42 cases of conflict that I observed involved the use of physical aggression. Of the eighteen cases, 8 (44%) involved the use of physical aggression by women. Male physical aggression is confined largely to fistfights, which arise spontaneously and usually stop after the first punch is thrown.[5] In contrast, the use of physical aggression by women is more serious. Based upon documented self-reports, I found that women are more violent than men in the expression of aggression.

While controversy exists concerning sex differences in the use of some types of aggressive behavior, cross-cultural and interdisciplinary studies strongly suggest that males show greater amounts of physical aggression and violence

[5]Native Margariteño men do not learn to fistfight and are rather inept at it. Fistfighting among men is short-lived. The use of weapons such as guns or knives is strictly prohibited in native Margariteño culture (McCorkle, 1965; Cook, in press).

than females (Parke & Slaby, 1983; White, 1983; Brown, 1991). The use of physical aggression by native Margariteño women sharply contrasts with these findings. The form of aggression that women use is shaped by the specific contexts listed above. In this section I will describe the use of verbal and physical aggression as it occurs in the contexts of fighting and social control.

## A. FIGHTING

In San Fernando, women often engage in fighting. Fighting among women is conspicuous. It usually takes place in open areas such as the middle of the street and involves the use of verbal and physical aggression. While women use aggression against men in some contexts (see B. Social Control), they do not fistfight with men. All of my informants agree that they have never heard of a case where a man has used physical aggression against a woman. This was explained to me by an older woman:

> Women don't usually fight with men because men are too strong, but some native Margariteño women are strong enough to fight with men. Take Celia, for example. Celia is a very strong woman. She can physically defend herself against men. I could as well when I was younger. But Celia is very strong.

Fighting between women occurs for various reasons but often involves disputes over authority. In one case a verbal screaming match broke out between a senior woman and her niece in which the niece was sharply criticized for taking up with a man of whom the senior woman disapproved. On another occasion I was verbally assaulted by a woman in her sixties for criticizing the way in which a local church service had been conducted. Although my opinion was shared by the majority of people who attended the service, I was singled out and given a 20-minute tongue-lashing for having expressed an opinion contrary to hers. This same woman came back the next day and ferociously restated that her beliefs were not to be contradicted.

Older, more experienced women in the community exercise unquestioned authority and their juniors are expected to abide by their wishes. This point was made clear to me one evening when I was walking up the street to visit a friend and her family. I had gone halfway to her house when a 60-year-old woman stepped out in the street several houses in front of me and started yelling, "And where do you think you are going? You have no business leaving your house at night!" I started to explain that I was only walking a short distance to visit a friend, but was cut off in mid-sentence by the woman who grabbed my arm and forced me into a chair in front of her neighbor's house. She continued: "You are not allowed to leave your house at night. I have lived in this town my whole life and I can go where I choose. But, you are new here and you will not leave your house at night again!"

The most common theme underlying fights between women has to do with paternity issues. One incident occurred five months into my fieldwork and was initiated by a genealogical survey that I was conducting. Genealogical ties are complex in San Fernando, and I always cross-checked my information with numerous informants. One afternoon while I was sitting with a group of people at a *ranchería*, I commented that I was confused by information that a woman, Anita, had given me concerning her relatives. Another woman, Maria, told me that Anita's father was only a stepfather, and that Anita's children had not been fathered by one man, as I had been told, but rather by numerous men. That afternoon a screaming match broke out between Anita and Maria.

Fights involving paternity issues are vicious and occasionally erupt into physical aggression. Another case involved a 35-year-old informant and two women from a neighboring town. The story went as follows:

> Three months after I had given birth to my youngest son, Juan, I got in a fistfight with two women from the town of X. It was two of them against me. The fight broke out because they said that the father of my son was not my husband; they called him illegitimate. We had a real fistfight and the *patrulla* (state police) came. I didn't have to go to jail because I had my baby with me. It was dangerous because I had a fistfight only two months after I was pregnant.

Although women occasionally use verbal and physical aggression in fights among themselves, their use of aggression in the context of social control is far more serious and striking. According to self-reports, it often involves the use of violence.

## B. SOCIAL CONTROL

In native Margariteño society, women use aggression as a means of social control, specifically to control male deviance. Women are extremely efficient at this and often state: "*Yo se parar el macho*" (I know how to stop male misconduct/machismo). In San Fernando, male machismo or misconduct consists of rowdy drunkenness, occasional fistfighting, or disrespectful behavior. Drunkenness and fistfighting are sometimes overlooked, but disrespectful behavior, especially when it is directed towards a woman, is considered serious and women do not tolerate it.

The concept of *parar el macho* was explained to me by an older townswoman in the following way:

> We [women] do not put up with the *fastidioso* [annoying] behavior of men. We know how to *parar el macho*. We tell men to get lost when they get to be too much. If a man bothers me, I slap him in the face or I hit him over the head with a bottle. Once my women friends and I threw a guy on the ground because he was being disrespectful.

I asked one of my female informants how it is that women can *parar el macho*, considering the obvious fact that men are larger and stronger than women. She answered:

> Yes, men are stronger. My husband is a fisherman. He is very strong. When we were moving to our new house, I used to watch him carry large heavy things. I thought to myself, he is as strong as a dinosaur! But if he ever did anything to me, if he ever laid a hand on me, I could defend myself because he has to go to sleep sometime. If he ever disrespected me, I would wait until he slept and throw boiling oil on him.

The concept of *parar el macho* is accepted by men as well and is considered to be part of female behavior. As one 22-year-old informant stated,

> When I first got married, I used to talk disrespectfully to my wife. We were both living in my mother's house at the time. One day my mother took a board and hit me across the mouth. Blood came out of my lip. I cried and said, "Mama, why did you hit me?" She answered, "So that you learn respect for your wife." She was right, I needed to learn respect for my wife.

Stopping macho behavior often involves prevention, a warning. This was demonstrated to me when I was invited to accompany a group of fisherman to a neighboring island one morning. When I returned home in the afternoon, I told my informants in San Fernando that I had had a wonderful day, and that I was treated very nicely. One of the senior women broke out laughing and said,

> I made sure that you were treated well. You are a guest in this community. You are not some tourist looking to have an adventure. I know those fishermen that you went with today. They are family. They are also *sin vergüenzas* [trouble makers]. They are very mischievous and get into trouble a lot. Before you left this morning, I told them they had better be on their best behavior. I told them that you are one of our family and that if even the slightest little thing happened, that I would come after them. I told them that you are an *infierno* [hellish]. I said to them, do you see that knapsack that she carries? She is no one to mess with! She carries a gun in there and she isn't afraid to use it. This woman is no one to mess with! When I told them this, they started to smile, but they got the point. They knew that they had better behave themselves.

Women will sometimes prevent incidents of male misconduct by physically removing men from potentially explosive situations. In one case, a young crew member of a fishing boat spoke badly about his captain to other workers. When the captain found out, he became furious and insisted that the young man repeat his insulting remarks in public. When the young man tried to leave, the captain went after him yelling, "Come back here. You are not leaving." As the young man attempted to back off from the situation, the captain pursued him through the street. As a crowd grew, the captain took off his shirt, threw it on the ground, and yelled, "If you are a man, you will come and fight!" The captain drew close to the young man and hit him on the arm. This was not a well-delivered punch, but rather a slap. In response, the young man became angry and started to exchange verbal insults about the captain's mother. At this point, two townswomen pushed through the crowd to the center of the conflict. Although at first he resisted, one woman took the captain by the upper arm and led him home. At the same time, the second woman took the young man and led him down the street in the opposite direction. In San Fernando men's disruptive behavior is tolerated up to a point, after which the women become enraged and resort to the use of physical aggression to *parar el macho*.

Another example occurred one afternoon in San Fernando while I was walking through town with a stack of notebooks collecting genealogical information. I returned to the house where I was residing and found four men who were visiting from a distant town. As I approached the house, I leaned over the wall to rest. The men had never visited our town before and were unaware that I was part of the community. One of the men rose, taking his *cédula* (identification) out of his pocket. He put it up against my face, on my nose and said, "Here lady, are you looking for this?" In order to avoid trouble, I walked away and sat two houses down, across the street. As I walked away, the man made an insulting gesture with his hand at me. At this point the senior woman stood up, walked over to the man, grabbed him by the shoulders and shoved him against the wall and said,

> This woman is one of us. She is a *señora* and lives in this house. I do not put up with a lack of respect in my house. If you continue to behave like this, I am going to stuff all of you in your car, and you can go home!

After a while, I crossed the street and returned to my house. This time, the man greeted me with a respectful, "Buenas tardes, Señora" (Good afternoon, Madame). That evening my friend and her husband sat around and discussed the incident. The husband laughed loudly and proudly exclaimed: "Yes, my wife knows how to *parar el macho*."

Our disrespectful guest had received rather gentle treatment in comparison to the numerous reports I was given of women using violence to control men in other situations. I did not observe these cases first hand, and it is possible that the intensity of the violence reported has been exaggerated. Several informants who observed them agree that they occurred as they were reported to me. The following is one of the cases reported to me by a senior woman in San Fernando.

> When I was a young woman, I worked for a rich man who was the owner of commercial fishing boats. At the time, I was with a man named Juan. We were not married but he was my man at that time. One time, he slapped me on the top of the head. He was very disrespectful and used to smart-mouth me. I was young, and the owner of the commercial fishing boats said to me, "You don't have to take that from him. The next time he does that to you, take this stick and give him a good blow." So the next time he did it, I warned him. Then I went and got a pole and hit him real hard across the forearm. I broke it and it was bleeding. He cried. I had really injured him.

## IV. Female Sex-Role Behavior and Aggression

Cross-cultural and interdisciplinary studies suggest that when incidents of female aggression occur, they are often redefined as something else, ignored, or are interpreted as "abnormal" and "manly" (Kerns, 1989; Schuster & Hartz-Karp, 1986; Benedek & Farley, 1982). Regardless of the context, Margariteño women express aggression with a socially recognized authority that goes largely unquestioned. The use of verbal and physical aggression by women is not considered abnormal. A woman's physical strength and ability to defend herself is a source of pride and is central in the self-concept of women.

As part of my initiation into female society, I was told that I had better learn how to be *guapa* (physically strong). When I asked one of my main informants, a woman in her sixties, about female aggression she said,

> Women in Margarita are '*guapa*'. When we fight, we punch and tear each other's hair. A long time ago, I had a fight with a woman. I chased her all around the *ranchería*. When I caught her, I grabbed her by the hair and pushed her face into the mud. She was screaming, but I wouldn't let go. I was stronger and I laughed. She didn't talk to me for years afterwards, but later we became friends again.

Another woman suggested that in order to defend oneself, it is important to learn how to fight effectively. She said, "Kim, if you really want to hurt another woman, you punch her in the breast. If you want to hurt a man, you strike him in the testicles. But with a woman, you hit her in the breast because it really hurts."

Female aggression is an integral theme in the native system of aggression that men recognize. Several of the men in the community told me that if I wanted to learn to be a woman in their society that I would have to learn to be tough. One fisherman took it upon himself to help me out with this. He said, "You shouldn't slap with your hand, you should make a fist and hit with your knuckles. Even if you are smaller, that doesn't leave you at a disadvantage, it means that you can get on the inside and punch better." Another fisherman said that I should be careful not to let another woman grab my hair, or trip me by the ankle.

## V. Matrifocality and Female Aggression

The central variable underlying female aggression in Margariteño culture is matrifocality.[6] In Margarita, matrifocality is caused by low male salience. I used the

[6]The term "matrifocality" has been used to describe varying degrees of female involvement and importance in cultural systems cross-culturally. For information on the topic of matrifocality, see (Gonzalez, 1970; Kerns, 1989). For a more thorough discussion of matrifocality in Margariteño society see (Cook, in press).

term *low male salience* to refer to a general pattern in native Margariteño society that is characterized by male absence, unavailability, and low male reliability. This general pattern is produced by male out-migration, polygyny, and male transience. Although low male salience has been produced by various conditions, it is probably rooted in historical patterns of outmigration:

> Following the War of Independence (c. 1852), islanders began to move in increasing numbers from Margarita into eastern Venezuela. The basic reason for the movement now was rising population and deteriorating natural resources. The numbers involved in this movement are not known but there was a continuous flow of people from Margarita to the mainland—a flow that increased during periods of drought on the island. The migrants were mainly men and while many of them planned to return following a period of employment many others remained on the mainland. A preponderance of women, because of the emigration of men seeking work, is an old circumstance on Margarita. It was first noticed, to my knowledge, in 1852. In 1873, there were 1,000 women to each 941 men. By 1941, the figures were 1000 women to 900 men (Alexander, 1961, pp. 555–556).

The nature of fishing activities has also required men to be absent from their communities. In his 1968 ethnography of the Margariteño community of Punta de Piedras, Orona states:

> With respect to the work organization of fishermen, the men work in groups on the *rancherías*. They maintain close communication with the house but they are for the most part away from it. They come home on the weekends, the interims between *temporadas* [seasons], or when someone has died in town . . . If the men work on a *ranchería* that is located on Margarita near the town, then they come home at night. But the general pattern is to maintain the *ranchería* on Cubagua and come to Margarita to fish only because of inclement weather. Because of the partial absence of the man, the house is managed entirely by the woman (Orona, 1968, p. 94).

The second variable producing low male salience is polygyny. Polygyny is a common marriage pattern in Margarita, with men maintaining two separate households (McCorkle, 1965). Values of moral authority dictate that these households must be located either in separate towns or in distant locations. This results in some men being alternately absent from each household for extended periods of time.

The third variable affecting low male salience is male transience. In San Fernando and other marginal communities on the island, marital unions are unstable, and transience is expected of men; nonetheless, male transience generates a considerable amount of hostility. Most women complain bitterly that men simply are irresponsible, having affairs with women and then leaving them alone to care for and support the children that these men fathered. This is simply considered to be the nature of men. My female informants believe that while women do not need to have more than one man, men by nature are compelled to engage in frequent sexual unions with other women. One female informant explained it as follows: "Its men's nature to have different women. That's the way men are. Women are different. What is important to us is our children. A woman does not have to run around like a man does. Her place is in the home with her children. Men are different."

In native Margariteño society, low male salience has left women as the stable, reliable figures, ultimately responsible for the survival of themselves and their families. Their importance is reflected in the central roles they assume in social and economic matters. While Margariteño social structure is based upon bilateral kinship, many of my informants also trace descent matrilineally through ascending kin for three or four generations. In Margarita, the presence of matrilines, which are reported for other Caribbean societies (see Kerns, 1989), are a result of the socioeconomic importance of women.

Women also hold a prominent position in native Margariteño society as mothers. The bond between a woman and her children is the strongest and longest lasting type of social relationship in native Margariteño society. Women frequently say that their children are their wealth. One woman explained this as follows:

> Men come and go, but a woman's children are her wealth. I don't care what my husband does. Tonight he is out at a dance with other women, but I don't care. I am going to stay home with my two year-old son, because he is the one who will take care of me when I am old. He will always come back and take care of me.

The central social roles that women play in Margariteño society do not afford them high status (see Cook, in press), although they do derive considerable informal power from their social position and their importance in social relations. It is this informal power that, in part, underlies their ability to use various types of aggressive behavior in different contexts, specifically the context of social control.

Low male salience has also resulted in many women in native communities assuming partial or full economic responsibility for their families. In Margariteño society, cultural ideals concerning the sexual division of labor confine women to domestic activities as mothers in and around the household. A standard belief in native Margariteño society is that "the woman's place is in *la casa* (the home), and the man's is in *la calle* (the street, or public sphere)." In contrast to these ideal standards, low male salience has meant that women have traditionally had to participate in work activities that are arduous and take them away from the household setting (See Orona, 1968).

In socially and economically marginal communities many female work tasks involve tough, physical labor. In the last few years most fishermen in the community have acquired gas stoves for cooking. Previously, however, they cooked with wood, which was traditionally the woman's job to collect. I have accompanied women on firewood-gathering outings. The job is physically strenuous. If the wood is being collected in the *monte* (wilderness), it is necessary to hike out through cactus-infested underbrush in searing heat. If wood is scarce in the *monte*, it is necessary to paddle by canoe (and there is usually a good head wind), to mangrove swamps in search of branches that are dry enough to burn. Once there, the next task is to hack down suitable branches at the stump and collect kindling. This task is made particularly difficult in the *monte* by the unrelenting presence of small flies that gather around one's face and the threat of other stinging insects. When gathering wood in the *monte*, women must transport it home by carrying it on top of their heads. Some of my lighter loads have weighed as much as 20 lbs. Bringing it back in a canoe is considerably harder, since it weighs down the craft and makes paddling nearly impossible. Unlike carrying wood on one's head, where it is possible to stop and rest, in a canoe resting means getting blown back by wind and currents. Resting is not an option. Once home, the wood has to be chopped with an axe and stacked in the kitchen.

Another activity that women have performed until recently is carrying water from a tank or spigot in the center of town to their houses. Water is transported in large plastic buckets, which, when full, weigh roughly 15 or 20 lbs. Several trips (about fifteen) per woman are necessary in order to fill the water drums at home. Women carry the water by balancing it on their heads. Personally, I found the most difficult and precarious part of this activity to be the act of lifting some twenty pounds of water from the ground straight up to a vertical position over my shoulders and high enough to rest on top of my head (the way my friends gracefully did it). During my last field season, I thought I had acquired a reasonable amount of proficiency at this until a male observer, who had been comfortably seated in the shade at a distance, said: "I saw you carrying the water with the other women. You don't do it right yet. You are always soaked after the first load."

The economic contributions of women have been of vital importance to family and community survival in marginal communities. Women have frequently had to participate in extra jobs outside of the community, in addition to their traditional tasks in and around the home. For example, many of my female informants make an economic contribution by selling food and clothing to tourists, and by working at various jobs in the city of Porlamar.

The nature of women's economic activities affects the socialization of children and their perceptions of female aggression. Women's responsibilities leave them little time to put up with their children's disruptive behavior, and in frustration, women often resort to the immediate use of physical aggression as a disciplinary technique (Brown, 1973). Children are slapped, spanked with boards, hit, and occasionally thrown out of the way. Through socialization, women provide their children with an aggressive female role model which is legitimized by the important contributions that women make to their family's survival.

From an early age, female children learn the concept of *guapa* and acquire physical strength and skills by helping their mothers carry out daily tasks. The association between physical strength, assertiveness, and womanliness is often reinforced in the minds of female children through the criticism they receive while performing tasks such as carrying water. In one example I heard a mother yell at her 9-year old daughter: "Maria, you will never be a woman. Look, you are already 9-years old and you can not even lift the water on top of your head without spilling it. Your dress is soaked!"

The important socioeconomic role that women play also affects the socialization of males and male acceptance of female aggression in later life. Native Margariteño women do not put up with disrespectful behavior from men and this attitude is passed on to their sons through socialization, as in the case of the 22-year-old mentioned previously who was reprimanded for disrespecting his wife.

## VI. Conclusions

The case of female aggression in Margarita contrasts with cross-cultural and interdisciplinary studies that generally characterize women as the less aggressive sex. Female aggression in Margarita could be viewed as atypical, an aberration of normative patterns of female behavior. I suggest that there are several reasons for believing otherwise. First, the independent variables affecting cultural patterns of female aggression in Margarita are commonly found elsewhere in the world. Male outmigration, polygyny, and transience, all produce low male salience, which is sometimes associated with matrifocality and is reported for other Caribbean societies (Otterbein, 1967; González, 1970). Second, in societies with culturally-patterned male sex role models that place an emphasis on *machismo* or aggressive male behavior, incidents of female aggression, especially when directed toward men, may not be reported. For example, while native Margariteño women have been noted for their extreme aggression, the U.S. Army Handbook for Venezuela reports,

> Another interesting phenomenon is the extremely low incidence of crime among Venezuelan women. Although women account for about 25% of all crime worldwide, in Venezuela they account for less than 3% (American University, Foreign Area Studies, 1977 p. 244).

Third, numerous studies on sex differences in aggression focus on variables affecting the socialization of aggression in children (Lambert, 1979; Whiting & Whiting, 1975; Parke & Slaby, 1983). While there is evidence supporting the stability or continuity of aggressive behavior in males, some investigators argue that females exhibit less stability over time (Parke & Slaby, 1983). This has been disputed by other investigators (Parke & Slaby, 1983). Thus, the aggressive behavior of female children may not reflect that of adult females. More research on the study of adult female aggression is needed. Fourth, incidents of female aggression are rarely described in the ethnographic literature. I suggest that the reason why these data are not given more weight in comparative studies on aggression is because male aggression is often visually more spectacular, and, as mentioned above, potentially more disruptive and dangerous than female behavior. It thus tends to attract more attention from observers in the community and ethnographers.

The case of Margarita indicates that women should be considered as potentially important actors in the expression and control of aggression in human populations.

## References


Alexander, C. S. (1961). Margarita Island, exporter of people. *Journal of Inter-American Studies, 3(4)*, 549–557.

American University, Foreign Area Studies (1977). *Area handbook for Venezuela*. Washington, D.C.: U.S. Government Printing Office.

Benedek, E. P., & Farley, G. A. (1982). Women and violence. *In* M. T. Notman & C. C. Nadelson (Eds.), *The Woman Patient: Volume 3: Aggression, Adaptations, and Psychotherapy*. New York: Plenum.

Brown, D. E. (1991). *Human Universals*. New York: McGraw-Hill.

Brown, J. K. (1973). The subsistence activities of women and the socialization of children. *Ethos 1(4)*, 413–423.

Cook, H. B. K. (in press). *Small town, big hell: An ethnographic study of aggression in a Margariteño community*. Fundación La Salle de Ciencias Naturales, Instituto Caribe de Antropología y Sociología, Caracas, Venezuela.

D'Andrade, R. G. (1974). Sex differences and cultural institutions. *In* R. Levine (Ed.), *Culture and Personality: Contemporary Readings*. Chicago: Aldine.

González, N. (1970). Towards a definition of matrifocality. *In* N. E. Whitten, Jr., & J. F. Szwed (Eds.), *Afro-American Anthropology*. New York: Free Press.

Kerns, V. (1989). *Women and the Ancestors: Black Carib Kinship and Ritual*. Urbana and Chicago: University of Illinois Press.

Lambert, W. W., & Tan, A. L. (1979). Expressive styles and strategies in the aggressive actions of children of six cultures. *Ethos, 7*, 19–36.

Mata Marín, E. (1976). Algunas características de la marginalidad en siete comunidades costeras del Distrito Díaz-Estado Nueva Esparta. Trabajo presentado por Erlinda Mata Marín, como requisito parcial para ascender a la categoría de Profesor Asistente, Universidad de Oriente, Núcleo de Nueva Esparta, Departamento de Socio-Humanidades [Venezuela].

Mata Marín, E., & Brito de Guerra, L. (1975). *Resultados de una encuestra*. Universidad de Oriente, Núcleo de Nueva Esparta, Departamento. Socio-Humanidades, Guatamare, Nueva Esparta, Venezuela.

McCorkle, T. (1965). *Fajardo's People: Cultural adjustment in Venezuela; and the little community in Latin American and North American contexts*. University of California at Los Angeles, Latin American Center. Caracas: Editorial Sucre.

Navárez, H. J. (1986). *Memoria historica de la peninsula de Macanao*. Porlamar, Margarita, [Venezuela]: Artes Graficas, BEMA.

Orona, A. R. (1968). The social organization of the Margariteño fishermen, Venezuela. Ph.D. dissertation, University of California, Los Angeles.

Otterbein, K. F. (1967). Carribbean family organization: A comparative analysis. *American Anthropologist, 67,* 66–79.
Parke, R. D., & Slaby, R. G. (1983). The development of aggression. *In* P. H. Mussen (Ed.), *Handbook of Child Psychology (4th Ed.), Vol. 4.* New York: Wiley.
Republica de Venezuela, Estado Nueva Esparta (1987). Memoria y cuenta 1987: Que el ciudadano, Dr. Vicente Mata Estaba, Director de Civil y Politica presenta a la asamblea legislativa en sus sesiones ordinarias de febrero de 1988.
Schuster, I., & Hartz-Karp, J. (1986). Kinder, keuche, kibbutz: Women's aggression and status quo maintenance in a small scale community. *Anthropological Quarterly, 59(4),* 191–204.
Subero, J. M. (1986). *Historia Popular de Margarita.* Porlamar, Margarita, [Venezuela]: Artes Graficas, BEMA.
Urbano, Taylor S. H. (1981). Evolucíon socio-histórica del delito en el Estsado Nueva Esparta. Trabajo presentado por Henry Urbano Taylor S., como requisito parcial para optar a la categoriá de Profesor Asistente, Universidad de Oriente, Núcleo de Nueva Esparta, Departamento de Socio-Humanidades, 1981 [Venezuela].
White, J. W. (1983). Sex and gender issues in aggression research. *In* R. G. Grees & E. I. Donnerstein (Eds.), *Aggression: Theoretical and Empirical Reviews, (Vol. 2): Issues in Research.* New York: Academic Press.
Whiting, B. B., & Whiting, J. W. M. (1975). *Children of Six Cultures: A Psychocultural Analysis.* Cambridge, Massachusetts: Harvard University Press.

# 15

# Interfemale Aggression and Resource Scarcity in a Cross-Cultural Perspective

Ilsa M. Glazer

I. INTRODUCTION
II. SOCIAL FORMATIONS, RESOURCE CONTROL, AND GENDER
III. AGGRESSION AND GENDER
IV. AIM OF THE STUDY
V. ONE-ON-ONE AGGRESSION IN PREMODERN AND MODERN ZAMBIA
VI. INTERGROUP AGGRESSION BETWEEN SOCIAL CLASSES IN MODERN ZAMBIA
VII. ONE-ON-ONE AGGRESSION IN TRADITIONAL CHINA
VIII. INTERGROUP AGGRESSION IN REVOLUTIONARY CHINA
IX. ZAMBIA AND CHINA COMPARED
X. CONCLUSION: CROSS-CULTURAL PERSPECTIVES
REFERENCES

## I. Introduction

Women have long been stereotyped as the peaceful, nurturant sex in contrast to man, the hunter. As a critic of gender stereotyping in aggression studies, the author has elsewhere shown that females are as responsive as males to social forces promoting aggression, and that styles of female aggression are specific to culture and socioeconomic class (Schuster, 1983a, on Zambia; Schuster & Hartz-Karp, 1986, on the Israeli kibbutz).

Stereotypes change in response to changing fashions. The analyses cited above were responses to sociobiological writings, whose implicit agenda was to deny equal opportunity for women in the workplace by showing that given a choice, women prefer mothering and homecraft over jobs (Tiger & Shepher, 1975). The analysis of Zambia utilized an ecological paradigm, viewing aggression as the product of competition for scarce resources within a given social structure. The argument was that both genders respond with aggression to conditions of resource scarcity. Resource scarcity is only one among many analytic paradigms; the Israeli kibbutz study derived interfemale aggression from the nature and structure of work roles.

This chapter reexamines the "peaceful female" stereotype. It suggests that women tend to have the most peaceful, cooperative relationships with each other when they control resources and their distribution, and the least cooperative, most aggressive relations when men are in control. The more subordinate women are to men and the more dependent they are on patriarchal social structures, the more injury they inflict on each other. Male control of formal political power, of economic resources, and of female sexuality heightens interfemale aggression. Female access to legitimate leadership roles, control of economic resources important to the society, and control of their own sexuality reduces interfemale aggression.

## II. Social Formations, Resource Control, and Gender

In today's global village, men control the world's resources and their distribution. Societies differ only in the extent to which *some* women have access to *some* local resources. Interfemale aggression must be understood in the context of women's universally limited access to resources relative to men. Furthermore, colonization on a global scale has incorporated virtually all premodern societies. Today's states reflect this process. In considering peaceful relations among women in independent, self-sufficient small-scale societies of the past, it should be understood that the conditions under which such social formations thrived no longer exist. Today, women are dependent on men in both the domestic and public domains even if, as rural peasants or urban workers, they participate in production. Therefore, in order to gain the broadest perspective on reduced interfemale aggression, premodern social formations of the past are included in the present analysis.

## III. Aggression and Gender

Aggression is a category coded in the Human Relations Area Files (HRAF), a major resource for ethnographies of premodern societies. Female aggression rarely appears, because HRAF tends to equate aggression with physical violence. Brown and Schuster (1986) suggest that while men are more frequently violent than women, the genders are equally verbally aggressive and equally prone to utilize symbolic and other covert forms of aggression. Envy and spite know no gender; violence tends to. Men are more aggressive than women because they are more violent.

## IV. Aim of the Study

This study examines the impact of social change on the interfemale aggression in Zambia and China and compares other societies with similar social structures. It shows the relation between interfemale aggression and male control of resources. The study distinguishes between one-on-one and intergroup aggression, reflecting conditions in social structures. One-on-one refers to two individuals in conflict over the same resource. Intergroup refers to conflict organized at the level of social classes, age, or other distinctive social categories in which competition for resources is a conflict between social groups.

## V. One-on-One Aggression in Premodern and Modern Zambia

Premodern Zambian society consisted of independent kingdoms, small chiefdoms, and acephalous egalitarian societies. They all had sparse populations, simple subsistence horticulture economies, and ample farmland. In the absence of significant storable surpluses, societies lacked substantial differences in wealth and lifestyle. The domestic domain was the focus of most daily social life, the size of a household a major criterion of wealth. Most societies were marked by economic and ritual interdependence of the genders in a complex web of brother/sister and husband/wife relationships. Brother/sister ties were important because most societies were matrilineal. Matrilineality holds important consequences for the intensity of interfemale aggression.

Matrilineality was a system of inheritance and descent centered on the female line. Women had farming rights in the lands of their matrilineages, and their children belonged to their group. Their closest lifelong ties were with their brothers rather than with husbands. In these societies, celibacy was considered unnatural; a woman had the right to sexual intercourse so as not to "waste" her fertility. Divorce was easy and frequent. A woman and her brother had authority over her children. The system therefore *fragmented* male power, for men did not control their own sons, nor was their control over women's sexuality an issue of momentous concern. In contrast, patrilineal societies become obsessed with controlling female sexuality to ensure paternity. In Zambia's matrilineal societies, male concern over the *size* of the lineage, and therefore its power, meant that men wanted to see their sisters pregnant. They were dependent for political strength on women to whom they had no sexual access. The issue of *specific* paternity was of lesser significance than the fact of their sister's fertility.

In these precolonial Zambian societies, interfemale aggression seems to have been rare. The only consistent mention of aggression among women, such as the use of magic to keep a man's love exclusive and to injure rivals, was between co-wives or a wife and her husband's lover, a competition for exclusive sexual access to the man (Colson, 1958; Richards, 1940). A synonym for co-wife in some Zambian languages is "envy," and it was believed that the jealous co-wife could use magic to make her rival's children sick. It is unlikely that other manifestations of interfemale aggression were widespread and unrecorded, since ethnographies are extremely detailed. Rather, it is more likely that aggression was reduced by socioeconomic structures which maximized women's freedom. Matrilineality reduced the intensity of interfemale aggression, that is, the possibility of causing genuine injury to a co-wife, because a dissatisfied wife had the option of returning to the land of her own matrilineage together with her children, and subsequently having children by other men. Yet another important check on the intensity of interfemale aggression was the possibility of a woman with a strong, charismatic personality becoming a religious and political leader. Zambian history is rich in instances of such women (Schuster, 1983b; Poewe, 1981; Smith & Dale, 1920).

With Britain's imposition of colonial rule, the previous interdependency of the genders changed. Women became dependent on men. Men became a resource worth competing for, particularly in the urban class-based society. Interfemale one-on-one aggression became a conspicuous feature of the urban landscape. Africans were the lowest socioeconomic class. Men's positions were determined by occupation and income, women's by their relation to men. The trend begun during the colonial period continued and intensified following independence in 1964. An African ruling elite and a small middle class emerged as the result of the state educational and training policies. Some women benefitted, becoming elites and subelites in their own right, earning wages higher than those of most men. Others joined the informal economic sector, earning wages equal to most urban men's and higher than rural men's. Urban marriages continued to be unstable (though necessary for the status enhancement of elites and subelites), at the same time as it increased the standard of living for proletarians, and remained essential for physical survival for the masses of unemployed urban women (Schuster, 1979, 1987).

The increased dependency of women on men was not matched by increased male responsibility toward women. Traditional husband/father obligations were minimal and were profoundly unsettled by migration and urbanization. There was no incentive for men to support women, and most tended to be unreliable supporters at best. A mother could no longer be certain of her son's aid in her old age; a sister was unsure of her brother's support; a wife could not count on her husband. In this social context, one-on-one interfemale aggression over the scarce resource of male support became *normative*. Various social categories of women competed. Women sharing the same household inevitably came into conflict, whatever their relationship or reason for living together. Sexual rivals, whether over a fleeting encounter at a bar or a long-term relationship, continued to be at least as aggressive as co-wives were traditionally. But the stakes and the style changed. Aggression was exaggerated by dependency.

## VI. Intergroup Aggression between Social Classes in Modern Zambia

Paralleling the increased incidence of one-on-one aggression was the appearance of conspicuous intergroup aggression between women of different social classes. Detailed in Schuster (1983a), intergroup aggression will be briefly summarized here.

Women of the political elite became the *de facto* allies of the poorer classes against the emerging group of subelites. The aggression was expressed in speeches, scapegoating, and interference in the lifestyle and newly-won benefits granted to the women. Interfemale class conflicts derived from increasing dependence on men. Competition for men was related to class position. Subelites competed for men with both elites and poor. Whereas elite women were limited in potential marriage partners to elite men, subelites could marry "up" hypergynously, marry men of their own social category, or marry successful businessmen of a category just below their own. Elites and poor targeted different population pools of men and hence did not compete with each other.

## VII. One-on-One Aggression in Traditional China

Since about 1000 B.C., Chinese social structure excluded the possibility of links among women and the development of group identity. Women lacked access to economic, political, and ritual roles. Physical mobility was restricted by footbinding, which began about A.D. 960 and waned in the 1920s. Women were valued for their household labor, sex, and reproduction. They were totally dependent on men from birth. Aggression was therefore largely confined to one-on-one confrontations within the household.

The ideal household was a patrilocal, patrilineal, patriarchal, multigenerational extended family living under one roof, contributing their incomes to a common purse. Wealthy households were larger and more complex than poor households. The more complex the household composition, the more targets for interfemale aggression. The social system pitted females against each other, virtually guaranteeing rivalry. The birth of a daughter was a sad event; rearing her was, and still is, considered a luxury. Costly to feed, she must be married off at great expense just when her labor power begins to be of value. Female infanticide continues to be practiced. Traditionally, mothers sold daughters into slavery, prostitution, or gave them up for adoption. In 1910, 70% of Taiwanese daughters were given up for adoption (Wolf, 1972).

In order to save money, parents who gave up daughters for adoption adopted female infants to replace them. For the same cost of rearing a girl, the adopted daughter could later be married to their son, saving the cost of a wedding. Mothers and adopted daughters conflicted, for it was in the mother's interest to get the maximum work out of her adopted daughter at the least possible cost. Adopted daughters could be sold if need be. Adopted daughters and natural born sisters were "natural enemies." Higher in status, natural daughters commanded the labor power and obedience of adopted daughters.

Mothers-in-law had rights to the labor of daughters-in-law and to their obedience. Since widows were not permitted to remarry, and since daughters-in-law could be sold or pawned (Baker, 1979), mothers-in-law and daughters-in-law were also "natural enemies." It was likewise with sisters-in-law, as the older sister-in-law was deprived of her husband's earnings so that a younger son of the household could be married (Wolf, 1972). The new bride, anxious to please her mother-in-law, was more compliant than the older sister-in-law. In addition, the sisters-in-law competed for jointly held family property for their own sons. Wealthy households of royalty, gentry, and merchants included one or more concubine, and sometimes second wives. These women were "natural enemies" (Croll, 1978a).

Within the stratified household, the form of interfemale aggression was a function of age and status. Beatings of younger women by older women were common. Mothers beat daughters-in-law, daughters, and adopted daughters. Slaves were safe targets for women who vented on them the aggression they dared not express in other relationships (Wolf, 1972). Women in weak positions expressed their aggression in violent temper tantrums, by withdrawing labor, or by complaining to women from other households met in the course of performing household chores such as drawing water at the village pump or washing clothes at the riverside. Gossip was the resort of the powerless to manipulate public opinion and so to contain abuse (Wolf, 1974; Baker, 1979). Possibilities of mutually useful, if fragile, alliances existed between these women of different village households. These are, however, beyond the scope of this paper.

Although divisiveness was inherent in the social structure, it is important to recognize that women's vulnerability did not preclude all possibility of cooperation. The social structure could not function without cooperation among women.

## VIII. Intergroup Aggression in Revolutionary China

Social upheaval generated conflict between age groups and social classes in the years immediately following the Maoist revolution. In its concept of gender equality, and its recognition that freedom requires an economic base to sustain it, the Marriage Law of 1950 was among the world's most progressive. The law aimed at destroying the authority of the multigenerational extended family. It abolished child betrothal, arranged marriages, concubinage, polygyny, interference in widow remarriage, allowed women to sue for divorce, distributed land equally to men and women, and gave women formal rights in shared household property (Johnson, 1980; Yang, 1959; Wolf, 1985).

Organizational support for implementing the reforms was provided by the Democratic Women's League, which was subdivided into women's associations in villages and urban neighborhoods. In 1950 the League had 30 million members (Yang, 1959). Cadres of trained, uniformed professional young urban women assisted study groups and organized mass meetings and exhibitions publicizing family problems. These intellectual cadres became a political elite. The technique used to gain acceptance of the reforms was to raise women's consciousness, make them articulate their experiences of oppression, translate their individual experiences into collective analysis, evolve a collective identity, and redefine their position within the family, village, and factory. Their interests as women were held to differ from that of the men in their social class (Croll, 1978a).

Elite cadres found allies among the socially vulnerable: adopted daughters-in-law, child brides, junior wives, concubines, slaves, prostitutes, factory workers, midwives, and sorcerers (Croll, 1978b; Yang, 1959; Wolf, 1974). The alliance was achieved with difficulty (Wolf, 1974), requiring special techniques for holding meetings and exhibitions (Yang, 1959). In theory, the problem for vulnerable women was alleged to be the difficulty of transforming the old Confucian social order. In practice, the source of the problem was older women and women of wealthy households, the traditional power holders over young and poor women (Johnson, 1980; Croll, 1978b; Yang, 1959). Young women rebelled against older women. They sued their families in court when blocked from love marriages; they sued for divorce and for property settlements. In the early 1950s, domestic disharmony and labor-capital struggles ranked as the most frequent items of litigation in cities (Yang, 1959).

These acts of rebellion were taken as aggression by older women; love marriage humiliated the mother, who traditionally would have worked with the marriage broker to handle negotiations. In the elimination of this function, the mother's prestige and self-esteem were threatened in a world of limited options; mothers-in-law suffered likewise in no longer assuming compliance in brides. Women suing for divorce threatened the authority of mothers-in-law and deprived them of labor. The threatened women fought back. Wealthy women boycotted women's meetings, implying that women who attended were morally suspect. Older women attempted to bar young women from the meetings, and beat them on their return home (Yang, 1959; Johnson, 1980).

The backlash by older women and their male allies, husbands and fathers, local court judges, village cadres, and urban workers, grew. By 1955, with a national economy gearing itself to the development of heavy industry which excluded women from production, the rebellion was redefined as selfish and counter to broad socialist duties, and family harmony was reemphasized. Young women committed suicide in alarming numbers (Johnson, 1980; Yang, 1959). In Chinese belief, the ghost of a suicide brings tragedy to those responsible (Wolf, 1972). Suicide was thus an act of aggression. Thirty years after these events, Chinese society has in fact been largely transformed. Chinese girls go to school and women work outside the home. "Good daughter-in-law, kind mother-in-law" campaigns continue, indicating that much of the dynamic described here remains, though perhaps lessened in intensity. An indirect indication is Wolf's (1985) finding that where women farmers predominate, women are most generous in evaluating women's intelligence; where men continue to dominate, women continue questioning women's intelligence. The implication is that increased economic independence increases self-respect and respect for others, increasing cooperation.

## IX. Zambia and China Compared

Premodern Zambia and China offer stark contrasts in the freedom of choice accorded to women and their independence from male authoritarian control. The intensity of interfemale aggression reflects these contrasts. Premodern Zambia maximized women's independence of movement, sexuality, economy, and leadership. Interfemale aggression was weak. In prerevolutionary China, women's existence was predicated on male whim. Interfemale aggression was found in all household relationships. Despite enormous differences between the two states, the experience of postcolonial Zambia and postrevolutionary China offer striking parallels in the rise of group aggression and in its intensity. Changes in intergroup aggression are linked to changes in women's dependency on men.

## X. Conclusion: Cross-Cultural Perspectives

The ethnographic literature suggests that matrilineality and matrilocality are the key to peaceful interfemale relations. When generations of related women and girls lived together all their lives and formed cooperative work groups, as among Brazil's Munducucu and the United States' Native American Hopi and Zuni, interfemale aggression was insignificant (Murphy & Murphy, 1974; Benedict, 1934). However, in societies past and present, most of the world's women have been, and continue to be, embedded in patriarchal extended family households, vulnerable and dependent for survival on men as fathers, husbands, and sons. The Chinese type of interfemale aggression is widely documented in such households throughout the world, including Africa outside the matrilineal belt, and the Eurasian land mass. Details of cooperation and conflict among women and the impact of state modernization policies vary. But the underlying dynamic is the same: interfemale aggression is heightened when men control women's options.

## References


Baker, H. D. (1979). *Chinese Family and Kinship*. New York: Columbia University Press.

Benedict, R. (1934). *Patterns of Culture*. New York: Mentor.

Brown, P., & Schuster, I. (1986). Introduction: Culture and aggression. *Anthropological Quarterly, 59(4),* 155–159.

Colson, E. (1958). *Marriage and Family among the Plateau Tonga*. Manchester: Manchester University Press.

Croll, E. (1978a). *Feminism and Socialism in China*. London: Routledge & Kegan Paul.

Croll, E. (1978b). Rural China: segregation to solidarity. *In* P. Caplan & J. M. Bujra (Eds.), *Women United, Women Divided*. London: Tavistock.

Johnson, K. A. (1980). Women in the People's Republic of China. *In* S. Chipp & J. Green (Eds.), *Asian Women in Transition*. University Park: Pennsylvania State University Press.

Murphy, Y., and Murphy, R. (1974). *Women of the Forest*. New York: Columbia University Press.

Poewe, K. (1981). *Matrilineal Ideology: Male–Female Dynamics in Luapula, Zambia*. London: Academic Press.

Richards, A. I. (1940). *Bemba Marriage and Present Economic Conditions*. Rhodes-Livingstone Papers No. 40.

Schuster, I. M. G. (1979). *The New Women of Luska*. Palo Alto: Mayfield.

Schuster, I. M. G. (1983a). Women's aggression: an African case study. *Aggressive Behavior, 9(4),* 319–331.

Schuster, I. M. G. (1983b). Constraints and opportunities in political participation: the case of Zambian women. *Geneva Africa, 21(2),* 7–37.

Schuster, I. M. G. (1987). Kinship, life cycle and education in Lusaka. *Journal of Comparative Family Studies, 18(3),* 363–388.

Schuster, I., & Hartz-Karp, J. (1986). Kinder, kueche, kibbutz: female aggression and status quo maintenance in a small scale community. *Anthropological Quarterly, 59(4),* 191–199.

Smith, E., & Dale, A. M. (1920). *The Ila-Speaking Peoples of Northern Rhodesia. V. 2*. New Hyde Park: University Books (1968 Ed.).

Tiger, L., and Shepher, J. (1975). *Women in the Kibbutz*. New York: Harcourt Brace Jovanovich.

Wolf, M. (1972). *Women and the Family in Rural Taiwan*. Stanford: Stanford University Press.

Wolf, M. (1974). Chinese women: old skills in a new context. *In* M. Z. Rosaldo and L. Lamphere (Eds.), *Women, Society, and Culture*. Stanford: Stanford University Press.

Wolf, M. (1985). *Revolution Postponed: Women in Contemporary China*. Stanford: Stanford University Press.

Yang, C. K. (1959). *The Chinese Family in the Communist Revolution. Chinese Communist Society: the Family and the Village*. Cambridge: MIT Press (1965 Ed.).

16

# "Women Are Women and Men Are Men": How Bellonese Women Get Even

Rolf Kuschel

I. INTRODUCTION
II. A BRIEF HISTORY OF BELLONA
III. THE SOCIAL POSITION OF WOMEN ON BELLONA
IV. BELLONESE WOMEN'S ACTION POTENTIALS
A. Homicide
B. Hiring Assassins
C. Hair Pulling
D. Displacement of Aggression
E. Suicide
F. Verbal Aggression
G. Mocking Songs
H. Nonverbal Expression of Aggression
V. CONCLUSION
REFERENCES

## I. Introduction

This chapter deals with different manifestations of female aggression on the Polynesian Outlier Bellona, in the Solomon Islands. Although Bellona is a small island of only 17 square kilometers and its population before the introduction of Christianity in 1938 probably never exceeded 500–600 individuals at a time, the islanders lived in a world of strife and social unrest. It is this pre-Christian Bellona, with its 600-year history of violent blood feuds, with which I am concerned.

When studying the behavior of people in other societies, whether industrial or nonindustrial, one is always faced with the problem of the culture-boundedness of meaning. People in other cultures do not necessarily use the same categories as we do, and concepts and behavior can be embedded in a social context different from our own. A lack of perceptual and cognitive awareness may easily result in category mistakes. What could be more devastating than categorizing a man's minor beatings of his wife as part of a battered wife syndrome when it appears in a society where "women expect this kind of treatment and many of them measure their husband's concern in terms of the frequency of minor beating they sustain" as among the Yanomamö people described by Chagnon (1977, p. 83)? To reveal, penetrate, and understand their view of the world is one of the main cores of social anthropology, as Monberg (1978, 1990) has argued so cogently. This, however, is and will probably always be an ideal, since "anthropology operates according to norms and values that do not inhere in primitive society" (Wilson, 1970, p. xvii–xviii). Even when we come fairly close to seeing the world as the people under study do in a few limited areas, the anthropologist's problems are not dissolved. He also has to translate the local intelligibility into his scientific colleagues' conception of intelligibility. Such a translation process is hardly ever "noiseless," it is vulnerable to distortion and may often require what Winch (1970, p. 99) called "a considerable realignment of our categories."

When, here, we talk about Bellonese women and men, one should bear in mind that on Bellona, as in many other cultures, there existed variations in people's behavior more differentiated than can be portrayed in a short chapter such as this. Some women, for example, have a venomous tongue and use a racy vocabulary whereas others guard their tongues. The same goes for men: some are vindictive, others more peaceful. Some strictly obey the rules of abstention from sexual relations when occupying the role as an acting priest-chief, whereas others go so far from these rules as to rape their mother's sister while occupying the same religious role. Keeping these precautions in mind we will now proceed to describe and analyze the range of possibilities which Bellonese women had at their disposal to express hostile behavior. Before entering the domain of female aggression, we must give a short description of the Bellonese society.

## II. A Brief History of Bellona

What makes Bellona an interesting site for study is not only its small size and population, but also its long isolation. Before Christianity's introduction, contacts with the outside world were scarce, both in terms of interaction with other South Pacific islanders, and with Europeans and Americans (Kuschel, 1988c).

Bellona is a patrilineal society consisting, in 1938, of a total population of 440 people divided into 2 clans, 2 subclans, and 21 lineages, with a patrilocal residence pattern. The basic productive unit was the household, which functioned as an independent social and economic unit. It consisted of a married couple and their children, including adopted children.

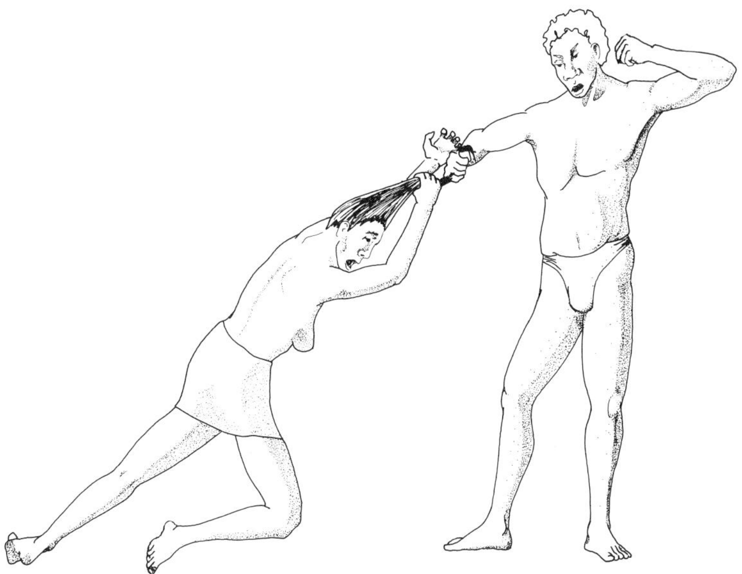

**Figure 1** Treatment of an obstinate wife (drawing by Perry Dockins).

The Bellonese society has been in a state of constant strife and controversy. Areas of conflict were numerous, covering: claims to land; setting up borderlines; rights of access to crops; fruit trees and timber for building canoes; envy; deceitful behavior; spreading of rumors; denigrating insults; taunt songs; jealousy; troubles between spouses; and rivalries and spiteful malice between co-wives, to name a few.

The conflict management techniques resorted to by men consisted of verbal aggression; threats; destruction of others' property; and physical violence (Fig. 1), often resulting in homicides which could develop into feuds. The development of marital and other conflicts has been dealt with elsewhere (Kuschel, 1988a,b; see also Monberg, 1991).

## III. The Social Position of Women on Bellona

Bellona was an unmistakably masculine society. The adage, "Women are women" is heard often and reflects the unquestionable verity, stressed even more strongly in the expression, "[A man] didn't regard his wife as being a person, [she was] just a woman," that a profound status inequality exists between men and women, that there are two kinds of human beings, males and females.

It was generally accepted that women should respond quickly and unquestioningly to the demands of men, especially their husbands. Though physically strong and hardworking, women were said to have acquired little knowledge of significance, be very emotional, and lack psychological strength compared to men. Thus, only men could perform rituals to the gods. Should a woman transgress this taboo, it was believed that the members of the heavenly abodes would feel nauseated and humiliated and punish her and her family (see Monberg, 1991). The weakness of women was also given as the rationale why men should not kill a person of the opposite sex; although this rule was not totally observed, as Kuschel (1988a) records six such homicides, these seem to be exceptionally impulsive and unplanned.

Women's inferiority meant they could not own land, and in the practice of avoidance behavior, it was *their* duty to keep out of a man's, and especially a brother's, way. Thus, all religious, economic, and social decisions were reached by men who had more status and power than women. According to Elbert (1964) men acceded superiority of women only in composing traditional *tangi* songs in which they "praise a husband's prowess in fishing, planting, and warfare."

There was a clearly defined division of labor between sexes. The man built and maintained the hut, hollowed out canoes, felled trees, planted gardens, fished, and participated in the fightings. On the other hand, the woman burned felled trees and underbrush, weeded gardens, collected and transported firewood, prepared food, plaited baskets and mats, sewed pandanus leaves together for roof thatching, and took care of the children as well as putting up most of the effort to keep the settlement clean. Nevertheless, the men did not regard these important subsistence activities as work comparable to their own, usually brushing them aside with a remark that, "this is women's work!" The disparity also existed at the social and economic level, where only men controlled family wealth and had sovereignty in all major decisions.

The Bellonese showed a clear preference for male children. From early childhood the girls experienced the status disparity between sexes. They were told their brothers had more privileges, and whenever their brothers wanted something in their sisters control, they must hand it over. This status difference was especially conspicuous in the distribution of food. An illustrating example is the old custom that when the meat of a shark was distributed, the men received the best parts, whereas the women had to be content with the shark's head. According to oral tradition (Kuschel, 1975, p. 72), this part was unattractive, because when a culture hero had named the "fish" in the ocean, he urinated on its head. Men and their sons were served food first. Only after they had taken the edge off their appetite could others partake in the meal. While men were served inside the hut, women usually ate outside the hut or inside the kitchen hut, which was their exclusive domain.

In a few instances marriage enhanced the position of a woman. Whereas before marriage she had had to obey her father and brothers, she now had to comply with her husband's wishes. After a hard day's work in the gardens, the wife carried the heavy burdens of garden products or firewood on her back, perhaps with a toddler on top, while the husband walked in front, carrying only his weapons. On arrival at the settlement the woman had to prepare the food well or invite a sound kicking or beating from her husband, possibly with the butt-end of an adze.

In sexual matters the husband had the lead, deciding when and where to engage in sexual activities. A wife hardly ever took the initiative but if she rejected her husband's advances, she laid herself open to thrashing. Jealousy could put a severe strain on married life. Marital fidelity was an ideal, but every so often the rule was transgressed. Depending on the husband's temperament, he would scold or divorce his wife. In a few such cases, such as that of Tekata'angaba, the wife was beaten to death. During an argument with her husband, Ta'akihenua, about her negligent preparation of food, he got angry and struck her. When she fell down in agony, her husband saw love-scratches under her armpits. Ta'akihenua pulled out his stone adze and smashed its butt-end against the neck of Tekata'angaba, who died (Kuschel, 1988b, p. 55).

Though marriage could be harsh it also gave the woman a certain protection, not only socially and economically but also sexually. Though other men would make advances toward her, she could never be forced into a sexual relation she objected to, because a violent lecher would fear her husband's wrath. The importance of such protection can be seen in an incident which took place as late as 1938. A man's advances to an unmarried woman had been repeatedly rejected. One day he appeared at her settlement with his axe dangling over his shoulder, demanding a favor from her (Fig. 2). Being alone and scared she agreed but managed to cheat him by suggesting he walk ahead of her in the bush. She managed to escape and took refuge with another family. Only after she got married did she dare to travel alone on the island again. Conversely, in all the collected cases of rape the victims were unmarried and of low-status families who could not protect them efficiently. When one such woman refused a man's advances, he spied on her and when he found her alone in the forest collecting nuts, repeatedly smashed his adze at her head until she gave in (Kuschel, 1988b, p. 186).

In a marriage a husband had certain rights to correct his wife's behavior. He could scold or denigrate her, or give her a hard blow on the back with his fist, a cudgel, or the blunt side of an axe. Only if he struck her mouth with his fist, tore apart her earlobe, lacerated her forehead, burned her body with hot stones, was responsible for her suicide or killed her, would her agnates, especially her brothers, interfere (Kuschel, 1988b, p. 747). They could scold the offender, destroy some of his material valuables, or even threaten to kill him.

From the short description above, Bellonese society can be included in the long list of wife-beating societies. Wife beating seems to have been a very frequent phenomenon on the island. But again, great variations among the families

**Figure 2** An effective argument: the blow of an axe (drawing by Perry Dockins).

existed. Some men were notorious for battering their wives. In a crosscultural study of family violence, Levinson discovered two main causes leading to wife beating, namely, "that wife beating is more likely to occur and more likely to be frequent in societies in which men control the family wealth and adults often solve conflicts by resorting to physical violence" (1989, pp. 89–90). The present study clearly supports Levinson's central conclusion.

## IV. Bellonese Women's Action Potentials

Until now we have looked upon women's position in the Bellonese society as well as men's hostile behavior. But which modes of aggressive behavior did women use among themselves and toward their male offenders?

Although many anthropological, psychological and sociological studies on aggression define the key term "aggression" in such a way that it contains both physical and verbal aggression (van der Dennen, 1980), the main research interest focuses upon physical aggression. Reasons for this imbalance probably stem from the fact that verbal aggression is so common that scientists can hardly see the woods for the trees. Verbal aggression does not leave any behavior traces; words are believed to be harmless. A thorough understanding of women's conflict strategies, however, can be obtained only by unraveling all the different ways women have at their disposal of being aggressive, that is, their physical, verbal, and nonverbal expressions.

## A. HOMICIDE

Bellonese women applied less physical violence than men. Whereas men fairly frequently used homicide as the ultimate conflict resolution, committing 195 murders or attempted murders according to oral traditions in the last 600 years, women hardly ever resorted to killing. In the same period, only one case is recorded in which a woman killed with premeditated malice. After long-standing jealousy, the murderess killed her co-wife with a heavy stick while both were collecting sea shells (Kuschel, 1988b, p. 120). In one other situation a young woman attempted murder when caught by a young boy in the act of helping herself to some food in another man's garden. Scared of being revealed she tried to silence him by smashing his head with stones; the boy survived and, because he came from a low-status family, no retaliation was taken against the woman (Kuschel, 1988b, p. 314).

At the social level of explanation we find that Bellonese women were scared of using killing as a mode of conflict resolution because of the imminent danger of becoming victims of a vengeance killing. However, this interpretation does not exclude the possibility that there might exist a more profound explanation at the sociobiological level.

During attacks on their husbands, women would sometimes courageously intervene in the battle and defend the head of the family. Mostly, though, the women had to retreat due to the attacker's tangible threat to kill them by a club or axe (Kuschel, 1988b, pp. 225, 307, 374). Only in one instance did a wife manage to save her husband's life. She rolled a stone from the top of a hillock down upon an attacker who had tried to sneak up in the dark of the night. Due to her alertness she saved her family's lives and killed the attacker (Kuschel, 1988b, p. 99).

## B. HIRING ASSASSINS

In situations of utter despair a woman had an alternative strategy for sending her enemy to the heavenly abodes. She could persuade her kinsmen or affines to render aid, as was done by a woman whose husband was killed by her own brothers. She went to her husband's agnatic kin and persuaded them to revenge her husband's death (Kuschel, 1988b, p. 81). If help from agnatic kin was impossible, women could in extreme situations ask for help from the hereafter. This was done by a mother whose two sons had been killed by her own brother. In deep grief the mother prayed to a powerful ancestor to revenge the slaughter of her sons. According to oral tradition, the mother's request was heard (Kuschel, 1988b, p. 39). Women could also use rhetorical talents to persuade their sons to avenge an earlier humiliation committed toward their family.

### C. HAIR PULLING

An effective and humiliating form of physical assault consisted of hair pulling. The attacker grabbed the other person's hair and hanked it back and forth, trying to pull her antagonist to the ground. Once the opponent was grounded the victor raked her long fingernails down the loser's face, neck, or chest. Such a treatment was felt as a serious humiliation and could only be used by a woman toward another woman. A woman was only allowed to touch a man's hair as an aftermath to a happy lovers' meeting.

### D. DISPLACEMENT OF AGGRESSION

If the object of one's aggression could not be located or if he was physically too strong, a woman could launch a physical assault against other persons or objects. This is what psychologists have called displacement of aggression. It is an ancient behavior on Bellona which can still be observed. It was used by women and elder children. In a study of patterns of aggression on Bellona, Prætorius (1970) found that several of her female informants after disputes with their spouses had turned their aggression toward their young children. The same pattern of displacement was found among siblings. Elder children, when reproached or hit by their parents, turned around and struck their younger siblings. But as stressed by Prætorius, this action pattern seems to be structured, because the person receiving the final beating usually is one who is liked by the original object of one's aggression. As reported elsewhere (Kuschel, 1988a), a woman grabbed a thick stick after a dispute with her husband, and hit her husband's favorite son, 7- or 8-years-old, so hard on his head that blood ran down his face.

### E. SUICIDE

In situations where a woman saw no other options of retorting to a serious wrongdoing, she could use suicide as a means of achieving revenge. This is not restricted to Bellona. As Counts (1980) observed, "It appears that suicide is a mode of social interaction that is adopted by women of many cultures because they lack an effective, more direct means of affecting the behavior of others." The almost "classical" suicide on Bellona is that committed by the woman Kingima'a. She had left her husband to participate in a large feast held by her father. After five days she returned to her settlement, loaded with presents of food for her husband. Kingima'a walked into the settlement where her husband was pulling weeds. He did not greet her with a word. Finally Kingima'a gently touched his head but his whole body stiffened. Humiliated, Kingima'a went off into the bush, climbed to the top of a hibiscus tree, untied her loincloth, tied it around her neck, and jumped down. Her dangling body was not discovered until a few days later. After the sad news had spread, Kingima'a's agnatic kinsmen planned to kill her husband. But since in his behavior he showed great sorrow they desisted.

Unless suicide was committed by a person known to be mentally ill, it was regarded as part of a social interaction between members of Bellonese society. As opposed to the traditional European way of looking at suicide solely from its antecedents, on Bellona one has to look at its consequences as well. For example, a husband who was the cause of his wife's suicide was made responsible for the deed by the victim's agnatic kin. Unless he in his behavior expressed great remorse and sent expiation gifts to appease the deceased's kin, they would plan a raid against him.

Whereas in Western Samoa "it is frequently conflict between parents and children which precedes adolescent suicide" (White, 1985, p. 6), on Bellona suicide appeared only among adults. Marital conflicts were the most frequently recorded reasons for women to take their own lives voluntarily. Two ways of achieving the goal could be used. One could take a canoe out to sea; due to the long distance between Bellona and the nearest island, only miracles could save a single female paddler's life. Alternatively, one could climb a tree, tie a loincloth around one's neck, and jump down. Women irresolute in their decision hid in the bush for some days, counting on being spotted.

The threat of committing or attempting suicide was a very forceful cry of despair which society did not ignore. Kinsmen, affines, and friends would immediately visit the calpable party and try to smooth out the discrepancies between the involved people.

## F. VERBAL AGGRESSION

The main expression of female aggression was in the use of ill words. It seems as if angered women used swear words more frequently than men, and could go on for hours shouting abuses, invectives, and scurrilous words at their opponents, even a long time after they had left. "Tonguing" was not a private affair. The offenses were often yelled out in a loud and shrieking voice, frequently to the great amusement of bystanders.

Complaints about the bad behavior of their own children would usually be expressed by an enumerating of their bad traits, such as being lazy, stupid, careless, feckless, reckless, and so on. Verbal aggression toward children or adolescents other than one's own would sometimes include the use of denigrating nicknames, followed by more kin-related accusations. A considerable list of earlier offenses committed by his or her family would be enumerated. Theft, incest, greed, and consumption of tabooed food were the things usually mentioned.

A husband who had sufficiently aggressed his wife could be subject to the same kind of verbose accusations, developing into more personal complaints about his lack of skills in fishing and gardening. In extreme cases the wife would not abstain from putting curses on him. Verbal expressions would often have a scatological or sexual content, such as, "I defecate in your mouth," "Piss in your mouth!," "Eat your flatus!," or even worse, "Copulate with your mother!," "Copulate with your sister!" The latter curse was especially injurious due to the existing brother–sister avoidance taboo.

An extension of verbal aggression existed in which the enraged woman mentioned her tormentor's name in the defecation area in order to let his ancestors or deities be repelled by having such a worshipper. Since a woman could not address members of the heavenly abode directly, she spoke in a nondirect way. The typical formula was: "This is the life principle of X who cursed me. I brought along a stick [symbolizing the culprit] to the defecation area so that he might be neglected and die." The woman would then thrust the stick into a heap of excreta.

Depending on the man's personality he would accept more or less of her humiliations. But even for a man of gentle disposition the time came when he would no longer stand being chided and he could either leave the place of accusations or silence his wife by beating her mercilessly with a stick, club, or the blunt side of his axe. In one case, after a woman for hours on end had caustically accused her husband of laziness, weakness, and womanishness, he finally felt so ashamed that he collected his belongings, left the island in a canoe, and was never seen again. Who said words could not kill a man? Grønbech (1931), who wrote about the ancient Scandinavians' conception of honor, said, "But blood need not be shed to endanger life. Honour might ooze out as fatally from the wound made by a blow from a stick, or by a sharp word, or even by a scornful neglect. And the medicine is in all cases the same" (p. 71).

The worst thing a woman could do was to humiliate and ridicule her husband in public, or participate in joining other people laughing at him in an embarrassing situation. One day, while a man husked coconuts, he accidentally farted while thrusting a coconut onto the husking stick. Everybody laughed and eventually his wife laughed, too. The man felt so humiliated by his wife's behavior, that he jumped up and let himself fall down upon the pointed husking stick. It punctured his buttocks and he died from internal bleeding.

In order to understand such a vehement reaction we have to remember that in Bellonese society shame and honor are closely related. Shame is nearly always a reaction to being humiliated or dishonored, and "a reduction of honor," says Johansen (1962), "is a reduction of the quality of life." A man without honor is not a man, therefore he has to act. However, a woman had to guard her tongue when airing hostile feelings toward an adult male other than her husband. A stranger's tolerance for caustic remarks and accusations from a woman would be much smaller than that of an overbearing husband. If a woman could not curb her passions, a raid might be planned against her husband, sons, or agnatic kin.

## G. MOCKING SONGS

The history of humankind is full of examples of men using their fantasy to circumvent dangerous situations. When topics could not be approached directly there was always an astute way in which to express oneself. When, on Bellona, it was too dangerous to aim a complaint straight at a certain person, the message could be conveyed by way of little songs. The composer would be known only to a few people, but the words circulated expeditiously around the island, because men and women sang the song without knowing against whom it was aimed. An unmarried woman who had become pregnant and whose lover was joking about it, composed the following little song: "You make fun of [my] pregnancy. Drink the foetal water." The last part of this epigrammatic song is a severe curse. A man whose name was connected with unclean things like the excreta of women giving birth would be stigmatized in the eyes of his fellow men and even the gods were said to feel nauseated and thus suspend their protection (Monberg, 1974).

## H. NONVERBAL EXPRESSION OF AGGRESSION

In order to understand the total complex of aggressive expressions one has to include the area of nonverbal behavior. This may demand great toil and effort, because some of these expressions may be embedded in a cultural web which a foreign eye will have difficulties noticing. However, when trying to penetrate other cultures, one has to be aware of the context in which the behavior occurs, the same behavior indicating different things in different social contexts.

Unfortunately, females' nonverbal expressions of aggression have not been studied thoroughly on Bellona Island. We do know that if a woman isolated herself from other people and repeatedly poked her nose with a small piece of wood, she was in a state of high tension. Other people usually tried to avoid her in order to not invite a bawling-out. A more sophisticated way of showing hostility appears in the foxy way in which a woman nonverbally behaved toward her own sister. Her husband and his sister-in-law had gone to the coast to collect marsh crabs. They did not return to the settlement in the evening, but spent the night near the beach. The next morning when the sisters prepared a fire for the catch, the wife in stern concentration fanned the smoke into her rival's face, almost suffocating her.

## V. Conclusion

Women did not control the economic resources on the island. They were precluded from direct interaction with the religious world and were constrained from overtly challenging the dominant power of males. Nevertheless, the Bellonese women had developed a great variety of hostile expressions. But in comparison with men's action potentials, asymmetry emerges. Where men's main activities concentrated on physical threats and assaults, women primarily expressed their hostility in a verbal mode. In extreme situations a wronged married woman could, as a cry of despair, commit suicide, a subtle strategy to counter her tormentor.

When Christianity was introduce to the island in 1938 the Bellonese continued their traditional way of life for many years. Though women's social status today has increased compared with the time before 1938, there is still a long way to go before social equality is reached. In 1977 a representative of the Women's Committee arrived on Bellona from Honiara, the capital of the Solomon Islands. She gave a lengthy talk on the topic "Women are Human Beings" and focused especially on the following items: "Women need to be treated and respected as human beings; women are not working slaves; women are not sex objects; women are not punching bags; women are not baby machines." Everybody on the island listened politely and in great silence, but afterward hardly anyone asked questions. After the lecturer had left the island, the Bellonese women felt disoriented and the men shrugged their shoulders saying, "Women are women and men are men!"

## References

Chagnon, N. A. (1977). *Yanomamö. The Fierce People.* New York: Holt, Rinehart and Winston.

Counts, D. A. (1980). Fighting back is not the way: suicide and the women of Kaliai. *American Ethnologist, 7,* 332–351.

Elbert, S. H. (1964). Abstract from the VII. Intern. Congress of Anthropological and Ethnological Sciences. Moscow, August 3–10.

Grønbech, V. (1931). *The Culture of the Teutons. Vol. I.* London: Humphrey Milton, Oxford University Press.

Johansen, J. Prytz (1962). *Maori og Zuni.* København: Gyldendals Forlag.

Kuschel, R. (1975). *Animal Stories from Bellona Island (Mungiki). Language and Culture of Rennell and Bellona Islands, Vol. IV.* Copenhagen: The National Museum of Denmark.

Kuschel, R. (1988a). *Vengeance is Their Reply: Blood Feuds and Homicides on Bellona Island. Part 1: Conditions Underlying Generations of Bloodshed. Language and Culture of Rennell and Bellona Islands, Vol. VII:Part 1.* København: Dansk psykologisk Forlag.

Kuschel, R. (1988b). *Vengeance is Their Reply: Blood Feuds and Homicides on Bellona Island: Part 2: Oral Traditions. Language and Culture of Rennell and Bellona Islands, Vol. VII:Part 2.* København: Dansk psykologisk Forlag.

Kuschel, R. (1988c). A Historical Note on the Early Contacts between Bellona and Rennell Islands and the Outside World. *Journal of Pacific History, 23(2),* 191–200.

Levinson, D. (1989). *Family Violence in Cross-Cultural Perspective.* London: Sage Publications.

Monberg, T. (1974). Poetry as coded messages: The Kananga of Bellona Island. *Journal of the Polynesian Society, 83,* 427–442.

Monberg, T. (1978). A Proposal for an Anthropological and Ethnological Conference on Problems Concerning Human Rights and Epistemology in the Social Sciences. *Uomo, Vol. II(2),* 165–171.

Monberg, T. (1991). *Bellona Island Beliefs and Rituals.* Honolulu: University of Hawaii Press.

Prætorius, U. (1970). Aggressionsmønstre og deres socialisation på Bellona, et polynesisk ø-samfund. Copenhagen, University of Copenhagen, Master's thesis.

van der Dennen, J. M. G. (1980). *Problems in the Concepts and Definitions of Aggression, Violence, and Some Related Terms.* Polemologisch Instituut, Groningen, PI/14.

White, G. M. (1985). Suicide and Culture: Island Views. *In* F. X. Hezel, D. H. Rubinstein, & G. M. White (Eds.), *Culture, Youth and Suicide in the Pacific: Papers from an East-West Center Conference.* Working Paper Series Pacific Islands Studies Program, University of Hawaii at Manoa.

Wilson, B. R. (Ed.) (1970). *Rationality.* Oxford: Basil Blackwell.

Winch, P. (1970). Understanding a Primitive Society. *In* B. R. Wilson (Ed.), *Rationality.* Oxford: Basil Blackwell.

17

# *Female Aggression among the Zapotec of Oaxaca, Mexico*

Douglas P. Fry

I. INTRODUCTION
II. DEFENSE OF THE COMMUNITY
III. POLITICAL VIOLENCE
IV. AGGRESSION DURING THE REVOLUTION
V. INTERPERSONAL HOMICIDES
VI. PHYSICAL AGGRESSION
VII. APPEAL TO AUTHORITIES
VIII. PHYSICAL PUNISHMENT OF CHILDREN
IX. VERBAL AGGRESSION
X. INDIRECT AGGRESSION: GOSSIP AND WITCHCRAFT
XI. CHILDREN'S AGGRESSION
XII. DISCUSSION
REFERENCES

## I. Introduction

In this chapter, I focus on physical and verbal, direct and indirect aggression of Zapotec women. I compare female aggression with male aggression in an attempt to provide a balanced overview of aggressive behavior in Zapotec culture. The data suggest that Zapotec women make greater use of indirect aggression and are less reliant on direct, physical aggression than men. Many aspects of Zapotec women's aggression are typical of female aggression in other cultures.

The Zapotec are the largest indigenous group in the Mexican state of Oaxaca, numbering over 300,000, and they inhabit the central Valley of Oaxaca, the Isthmus of Tehuantepec, and parts of the mountainous (*Sierra*) regions of the state (Fry, in press). In all regions, the Zapotec are primarily town-dwelling peasant farmers. A typical Zapotec community has a Catholic church, a central plaza, local governmental buildings, a primary school, perhaps a health clinic, and probably several small dry goods stores. The majority of Zapotec practice subsistence and cash agriculture with some animal husbandry, the primary subsistence crops being maize, beans, and squash (Fry, in press).

The Zapotec world view includes a cast of supernaturals: witches, male and female devils, images of Christ, and animal guardians. Illness may be attributed to improper religious conduct, soul loss, envy, anger, the evil eye, fright sickness, and witchcraft (Kearney, 1972; O'Nell, 1975).

In this chapter, I draw upon the anthropological literature on the Zapotec as well as my own ethnographic and ethological research in two Valley of Oaxaca communities, San Andrés and La Paz.[1] I wish to emphasize that considerable variation exists in custom and behavior among the Zapotec people. For example, regarding levels of aggression, some Zapotec communities are very peaceful while others are more violent. Historical, social structural, and psychocultural variables probably interrelate in accounting for this pronounced variability in violence (Fry, 1986, 1988).

## II. Defense of the Community

Defending the community is a male concern (Dennis, 1987, p. 35). Periodically, *tumultos*, or brawls, may erupt over contested tracts of land ". . . when crowds of men are massed along the border (during a land survey, for instance); insults begin to be exchanged, rocks are thrown and soon a small battle rages" (Dennis, 1973, p. 421). Some intercommunity land disputes, with alternating periods of peace and violence, have lasted for centuries (Dennis, 1973; 1987).

On occasion, Zapotec men also have protected their community from bandits and cattle rustlers. In one altercation early in this century, the men of San Andrés fought off a band of cattle rustlers. Informants report that upon a prearranged signal (the ringing of the Church bell), the townspeople, armed mostly with clubs and *machetes*, attacked the better-armed thieves, killing most of the 10- to 20-member bandit gang, but suffering high casualties in the process.

## III. Political Violence

Some Zapotec communities, but by no means all, have histories of factionalism and/or political bossism which contribute to violence. Ugalde (1973) discusses how the Valley Zapotec community, Díaz Ordaz, was divided into two political factions in the 1920s and 1930s. "In 1935 the fight reached a climax with the killing

[1]San Andrés and La Paz are pseudonyms, used to protect the privacy of individuals in these communities. The data reported in this chapter were collected in 1981–1983, 1986, and 1991.

of several leaders of each group; afterward the *cacique* [political boss] went into exile" (Ugalde, 1973, pp. 128–129). Kearney (1972, p. 3) reports that the Sierra Zapotec town of Ixtepeji was under the control of a series of political strong-men through the 1800s who ruled "with severity."

## IV. Aggression during the Revolution

Some Zapotec communities, such as San Andrés and La Paz, were relatively unaffected by the Mexican Revolution (1910–1920), in comparison to others, such as Ixtepeji in the *Sierra*, which became enmeshed in the struggle. Tamayo (1956, quoted in Kearney, 1972, p. 32) writes: "Eight hundred Ixtepejanos were captured and the town burned. The victorious troops with an absurd rage and cruelty then burned down several other towns."

Standing as an anomaly to Zapotec women's nonparticipation in territorial and political violence are the deeds of Angela Jimenez, daughter of an Isthmus Zapotec mother, and a Spanish father. In 1911, when she was 15, the Mexican federal troops, *federales*, searched the Jimenez home for rebels. An officer attempted to rape Jimenez' sister. Grabbing the officer's gun, the sister reportedly killed him and then committed suicide (Salas, 1990, p. 71). "With this incident vividly imprinted in her mind, Jimenez joined her father in the Sierra Madre, vowing to become a soldier who killed *federales*. Jimenez disguised herself as a man and started calling herself 'Angel'" (Salas, 1990, p. 71). She served as a flag bearer, explosives expert, spy, and soldier during the revolution. Twice captured by *federales*, she escaped execution on both occasions by changing from her male disguise into female garb and passing by the sentries.

In summary, it is Zapotec men, not women, who protect their community from outside threats, such as during *tumultos*, and who may also participate in violent political quarrels within their community. The women tend not to take part in political aggression, but we see an occasional exception such as Angela Jimenez.

## V. Interpersonal Homicides

When I asked two Zapotec women from La Paz whether a quarrel is more dangerous between men or between women, both answered, "Between men." I asked them why. One responded, "Because men are the ones that kill" (fieldnotes, January, 1991).

Taylor (1986) examined the archival records of two Catholic parishes in the Valley Zapotec region and found evidence of 107 homicides for the years 1700–1870. Information on the sex of assailants was usually missing, but 97 (91%) of the victims were males. Kappel (1978) investigated homicides in one Valley

Zapotec community by searching the civil death register for crimes and then interviewing persons familiar with the cases. For the 100-year-period 1870–1970, both the victims and assailant could be identified with certainty in 55 of 81 homicides. All 55 killers were men, and 48 (87%) of the victims were men (Kappel 1978).

Notable is the rarity of female killers among the Zapotec. Parsons (1936, p. 395), however, recounts the gossip that a Valley woman from Mitla may have arranged for her son-in-law to kill her brother in a feud over land inheritance. Whether or not this woman was behind her brother's death (and Parsons reports that this is an open question), the fact that some people believed that she was responsible is noteworthy in this examination of female aggression, as is the assumption that she had the actual murder committed by a male accomplice.

Several reasons for Zapotec homicides can be cited. Jealousy and disputes over women are a recurring theme (Fry, 1986, 1988; Kappel, 1978; Parsons, 1936, p. 442; Ugalde, 1973, p. 129; also cf. O'Nell, 1975). I found most recent homicides in San Andrés to be over women (Fry, 1986). Zapotec homicides may also result from quarrels over land or water rights (Fry, 1986, 1988; Selby, 1974, p. 64), avenging the death of a family member (Fry, 1986; Kappel, 1978; Ugalde, 1973, p. 129), drunken altercations (Kappel, 1978; Kearney, 1972, p. 104; O'Nell, 1981; Parsons, 1936, p. 403), or some combination of such factors, including, at times, political feuds as mentioned above (cf. Parsons, 1936, p. 160; Ugalde, 1973). Regarding cases with female victims, Selby (1974, pp. 64–66) reports that a man killed a woman neighbor out of fear of her witchcraft, and O'Nell (1975) reports an alleged murder of a wife by her husband for reasons unknown.

In summary, the most frequent pattern of Zapotec interpersonal homicide occurs when a male kills another male, frequently due to jealousy over a woman, although other factors also contribute to homicides. Zapotec women are rarely if ever homicidal, although Kappel (1978) and Selby (1974, p. 54) mention that they may occasionally practice infanticide by neglecting an unwanted infant.

## VI. Physical Aggression

Burbank (1987) points out that when discussing whether males are *more* or *less* aggressive than females, we should specify whether more or less refers to frequency or intensity. For the Zapotec, women are *less* physically aggressive than men in *both* senses. Chinas's (1973, pp. 100–101) observation for the Isthmus Zapotec is relevant: "Violence is an expected male behavior pattern, especially dangerous when the man is intoxicated. Anger is an emotion which is always thought to be perilously close to the surface in the male personality, an emotion which can suddenly flare into violent acts. Women too are capable of anger, but a woman's anger is seen as less apt to result in violence and less threatening to community solidarity, since it is most often confined to the private domain."

My own observations in San Andrés and La Paz also indicate that women's physical aggression is both less intense and less frequent than men's aggression (also cf. Sumner, 1978). Especially in San Andrés, I witnessed men punching, kicking, and forcefully grappling with each other on various occasions (Fry, 1986, 1988, 1990). By contrast, I observed only two physical exchanges between adult women. The following passage describes one instance of female fighting which occurred at a San Andrés wedding celebration, and also mentions differences in intensity compared to male fighting:

> Two women started having a fight. They screamed at each other, pushed and pulled at the other's arms and bodies, and tried to slap. Slaps were usually blocked. At one point, one woman put her arm around the neck of the other woman in that familiar San Andrés hold. One woman seemed to be more defensive than the other . . . The more aggressive orange bloused women was about 45 years old, as was her opponent.
>
> . . . It took three women to drag "Orange Blouse" away from the other woman into the shaded area, and this took a couple of minutes of struggling. After about five minutes, "Orange Blouse" emerged from the shaded area, and headed right for the other woman to continue the fight. Again they wrestled, again they were separated. The women slapped and pushed, and pulled each other's arms. [Earlier, when two men] . . . had been fighting, they beat and punched each other as well as wrestled. At one point, one of the two women pushed the other in the breasts, hard—one hand for each breast. . . . [Two men,] each about 25 years, emerged from the house, exchanging a few punches, beats, and words. They separated on their own—maybe 30 seconds was all they fought. The dancing started up and one man, Eusebio, asked "Orange Blouse" to dance. She danced, then attacked her opponent, then danced some more. Her opponent . . . between fights simply talked with other women by the door to the house" (fieldnotes, April, 1982; cf. Fry, 1986, pp. 337–343).

The second fight between women which I personally observed took place on an extremely crowded bus on a hot and dusty afternoon as people were returning from the market *plaza*.

> Two women "slapped each other in the face and on the head while verbalizing the whole time in Zapotec. After maybe three slaps each, the smaller one (from San Andrés) tried to prevent the other one (larger/taller/older from San Juan) from slapping her by holding her arms at the wrists. She then moved away . . ." (fieldnotes, October, 1981).

Parsons (1936, p. 160) describes the only incident of physical fighting among Zapotec women I found in the literature.

> "One day two market women, sisters, got into a fight—or rather, one woman, envious of the amount her sister was selling, assaulted her. She clutched at her hair and shook her so hard that her money fell out of the front of her dress. As she stooped to pick it up the aggressor threw a stone at her."

Sumner (1978) mentions that Zapotec women fight over men. When I queried as to why women fight, a San Andrés woman responded: "If the husband talks with another woman, the woman is jealous." I asked her if a woman would hit her rival. "Yes," she replied. A man from San Andrés explained that men fight over women and also women fight over men, "but with their hands only. Yes, the women fight, they slap each other!" [He laughs] (fieldnotes, January, 1991).

Burbank (1987) found that cross-culturally, women were more likely to use a weapon against a man than against a woman and concludes it is likely that "women perceive that their male targets are bigger, stronger, and more capable of aggressive retaliation . . ." (p. 91). An event I was told about is in line with this interpretation. "The [frequently beaten] wife was always returning to her parents house which is across the road from Roberto's house. One time the 'bad man' came over and threatened to kill his mother-in-law. She went and got her own rifle and he ran away from the house" (fieldnotes, August, 1986).

Regarding physical altercations between spouses, on three occasions I witnessed husbands beating their wives with sticks (Fry, 1986). On several other occasions, men struck or threatened to strike women. I never saw a wife physically attacking her husband, but one woman from San Andrés relates how she hit her husband of some 27 years with a stick to wake him up. She said that she was mad at him because he drank *mescal* the night before, came home late, and was still asleep in the morning when there was work to be done. I asked her, in general, who hits other people more—men, women, or is there no difference? She responded that the men hit more, and her husband agreed. Later when I asked her which sex was more rowdy or mischievous, she responded that the men were (again her husband agreed), and she added, "the men come home from drinking and give the wives a hit even though they are asleep!" (fieldnotes, January, 1991).

Sumner (1978, p. 6) observes for a Valley town that "women do not often attack men physically, while men do occasionally beat their wives." A 65-year-old San Andrés man told me: "The men hit the women more, because the women get out of line. And later, they obey the men. But when I get very mad . . . well, the men, when they get very mad, they grab a stick and they hit them, but only two or three blows"[2] (fieldnotes, January, 1991). Also relevant to this discussion of the relative intensity and frequency of physical aggression is O'Nell and O'Nell's (1977) research on Zapotec dreaming. Their findings show that Zapotec men dream about physical aggression more than the women.

Thus Zapotec women do on occasion physically attack other persons of either sex (cf. Parsons, 1936, p. 160). In comparison to male aggression, however,

[2]The verbatim quotation in Spanish reads: "Los hombres pegan más a las mujeres. Porque las mujeres están poco en orden, sí, están poco en orden a los hombres. Y luego obedece hombres. Pero yo cuando ya, ya cuando yo se enojo mucho . . . pues, los hombres, cuando ya se enojan mucho, agarran una bara y los pegan, pero dos o tres barazos, y allí no más."

such events occur relatively infrequently and tend not to inflict the same degree of pain or injury as male attacks. The men punch, kick, and grapple, while the women slap, push, and pull. While informants view female physical aggression as most typically resulting from jealousy over a male, such fighting (as well as verbal aggression, malicious gossip, and witchcraft, to be discussed shortly) may have other causes such as feuding over inheritance, envy of others, revenge, or self-defense.

## VII. Appeal to Authorities

One recourse for a beaten wife, rather than fighting back, is to file a complaint with the community authorities. In one instance, a young San Andrés husband had hit his wife on the head hard enough to cause an obvious, swollen lump. The woman's parents accompanied her to court and in large part spoke on her behalf. The husband explained he was very intoxicated and that he was sorry he had hit her so hard. The authorities lectured and fined the young husband. An interesting question is whether women utilize the local authorities more often than men.

## VIII. Physical Punishment of Children

Both Zapotec men and women have been observed physically punishing children, sometimes severely (cf. Fry, 1986; Kearney, 1972, p. 62, 73; Parsons, 1936, p. 87), although some parents avoid using physical punishments (cf. Fry, 1986). Mild physical corrections, for example a slap or a rap with the knuckles, were always delivered by women in La Paz and usually (79% of the time) administered by women in San Andrés. More severe beatings with sticks were never observed in La Paz, but were administered by women in San Andrés in seven out of the eleven episodes personally witnessed (Fry, 1986). In San Andrés, one woman picked up her son by the ears; another mother lobbed a grapefruit-sized rock at her daughter (Fry, 1986). The observation that women, more often than men, punish children may simply reflect the women's more frequent association with the children, although administering discipline also may be perceived as a female duty.

## IX. Verbal Aggression

In both incidences of physical aggression witnessed between Zapotec women, verbal attacks were part and parcel of the exchanges. Women may on occasion scold their husbands, adult sons, and daughters, and they may also argue with other persons of either sex. Selby (1974, pp. 64–66) notes a case of a woman threatening her neighbor with illness through witchcraft. It is difficult to conclude whether women verbally argue and insult more or less than men. Two La Paz informants told me that women and men insult others to about the same degree. In any case, it is commonly held that quarrels and arguments among men are more dangerous due to their greater likelihood of escalating to violence (cf. Chinas, 1973; Kearney, 1972).

## X. Indirect Aggression: Gossip and Witchcraft

With consistency, fieldworkers have emphasized how the Zapotec perceive their social world as rife with hostility (Chinas, 1973; Kappel, 1978; Kearney, 1972; Parsons, 1936; Selby, 1974; Sumner, 1978). Of the *Sierra* Ixtepejanos, Kearney (1972, p. 44) writes, "the individual is essentially alone in a hostile world in which nothing is secure," and among the Isthmus Zapotec, Chinas observes, "the universe is perceived as filled with threats and dangers." They fear, for instance, illness, ghosts, being alone, envy, anger, thieves, burglars, bats, and witches (Chinas, 1973, p. 80).

Björkqvist, Lagerspetz, and Kaukiainen (1992) and Lagerspetz, Björkqvist, and Peltonen (1988) present evidence that Finnish school girls use indirect forms of aggression, such as gossip and manipulation of social relationships, more often than their male counterparts. With indirect aggression, the identity of the aggressor may never become known to the victim, and physical strength is not a prerequisite for an effective attack. Two types of indirect aggression familiar to the Zapotec are malicious gossip and witchcraft, and these forms of aggression are sometimes interrelated. Zapotec women appear to employ these kinds of indirect aggression more regularly than men.

One of Sumner's (1978) informants explained that when people engage in malicious gossip, "all sorts of heavy things float to the surface, things which should remain at the bottom, should not be stirred up . . . it's like a can of lard, if you tip it over, it will spread, slowly, but it will spread and spread." Although men certainly gossip, my impression is that Zapotec women do so to a greater degree. In reference to land disputes, Dennis (1987, p. 23) notes a concern about women saying too much: "Women are sometimes said to be unable to keep such secrets." Recently I asked several people from La Paz and San Andrés what they thought regarding gossip by men and women. A man I questioned said that it depended on one's personality, but three women emphatically nominated their own sex as gossiping more than men. One woman from La Paz explained, "The women gossip more. And that's why they don't go out. When a woman comes by, soon the whole town knows!" (fieldnotes, January, 1991). Supporting the Zapotec image of women as gossipers is their belief in the "supernatural evil gossiper," the *wana bieha*. "The *wana bieha* is more evil hearted than the witch and more so than the person who picks fights, or lies, or is abnormal. Her awesome malignity derives from the fact she is a talebearer about sexual infidelities. She has supernatural powers to ensure that her gossip is always believed . . ." (Selby, 1974, pp. 79–80). The *wana bieha* is a woman's role. Her evil gossip about sexual relations creates conflict and undermines social relationships; this can be a very potent form of indirect aggression.

The Zapotec also believe that witches can cause misfortune, illness, and death (e.g., Parsons, 1936, p. 118, 138). While witches can be of either sex (Selby, 1974), in the Isthmus "women are thought to be witches more often than are men . . ." (Chinas, 1973, p. 84). In agreement with this observation, in La Paz informants expressed concern over two witches in their town, both of whom were women. I have no information on the sexes of witches in San Andrés, but for a nearby town, Sumner (1978) speaks of witches using only female pronouns (also cf. Parsons, 1936, pp. 131–141). At least tentatively it would seem that women are more often perceived as practicing this form of indirect aggression than are men. It is interesting that while nearly everyone fears witchcraft, hardly anyone views themself as a witch, although others may (Selby, 1974).

## XI. Children's Aggression

One question on a 50-item questionnaire administered to men in San Andrés and La Paz asked: Who fights more, boys, girls, or do they both fight the same? Girls were perceived to fight either the same as or less than boys by all but 1 respondent out of 45. In San Andrés, 50% (14) said boys and girls fight equally and 50% (14) thought boys fight more. In La Paz, 65% (11) answered that boys and girls fight equally, 29% (5) said boys fight more, and 6% (1) thought girls fight more.

In an ethological study of children's aggression, I observed 3- to 8-year-old children, 24 from San Andrés and 24 from La Paz, using focal individual sampling procedures (cf. Fry, 1986, 1988). For overall rates and durations of play and serious aggression, these Zapotec children do not exhibit significant sex differences. However, interesting patterns are apparent in the gender composition of the dyads. Recently I used binomial tests to evaluate the null hypotheses that (1) boys initiate play and serious aggression equally toward female and male partners, and (2) girls also initiate play and serious aggression equally toward partners of either sex (Fry, 1990). Results presented in Table 1 show that both girls and boys tend to choose same-sexed play partners significantly more often than opposite-sexed play partners. The least frequent of the four pairings was for a male to choose a female play partner.

**Table 1**
**Partner Choice for Play Aggression: Sex Composition of Dyads**

| Number of episodes | | | | | |
|---|---|---|---|---|---|
| Sex of initiator | | Sex of recipient | | $z$ | 2-tailed $p$ |
| Male | 373 (51.3%) | Male | 266 (36.6%) | 8.23 | $p < .00001$ |
| | | Female | 107 (14.7%) | | |
| Female | 353 (48.6%) | Male | 122 (16.8%) | 5.80 | $p < .00001$ |
| | | Female | 231 (31.8%) | | |

Regarding serious aggression, girls initiated with other girls 93% of the time, significantly more often than with boys (Table 2). However, it was not significantly more likely for boys to initiate serious aggression with boys (54%), as opposed to girls (46%).

## XII. Discussion

Cross-culturally, women are less likely than men to commit homicide (Daly and Wilson, 1988, pp. 137–161 and references therein), and this generality applies to the Zapotec. In comparison to the men, Zapotec women are less often physically aggressive, and their attacks, which usually consist of slapping, pulling, and pushing their opponent, are less severe and usually noninjurious. Sex differences are less apparent regarding verbal aggression, although additional information is needed on this topic.

The distinction proposed by Björkqvist, Lagerspetz, and Kaukiainen (1992) and Lagerspetz, Björkqvist, and Peltonen (1988) between direct and indirect aggression is applicable to the Zapotec. Zapotec women are perceived as using indirect forms of aggression (gossip and witchcraft) more often than the physically more aggressive men. The *wana bieha* is a woman. In the Zapotec belief system, a woman can draw on supernatural forces to attack rivals and seek revenge, as in the explanation for a young man's illness: "After the young man had left his first wife, for a younger woman, he was walking along one night when he was beckoned to by somebody he took to be his former wife. He followed the women . . . [a supernatural spirit], who led him off to a ravine and left him. Then he fell ill" (Parsons 1936, p. 139).

**Table 2**
**Partner Choice for Serious Aggression: Sex Composition of Dyads**

| Number of episodes | | | | | |
|---|---|---|---|---|---|
| Sex of initiator | | Sex of recipient | | $z$ | 2-tailed $p$ |
| Male | 50 (62.6%) | Male | 27 (33.8%) | .57 | $p = .28$ |
| | | Female | 23 (28.8%) | | |
| Female | 30 (37.5%) | Male | 2 (2.5%) | 4.74 | $p < .00001$ |
| | | Female | 28 (35.0%) | | |

Burbank (1987) found that women attack other women in 91% of 137 societies where information was reported on female aggression, but that they attacked men in only 54% of these societies. Other women appear to be the targets of Zapotec women's physical attacks more often than men, although Zapotec women attack opponents of either sex, physically, verbally, and indirectly. It seems likely that women in Zapotec culture fear the consequences of physically attacking men who are stronger and perceived as more capable of violence; women are well aware that men beat their wives and are "the ones who kill." The data on aggressive initiations among children in San Andrés and La Paz show a similar pattern wherein girls hardly ever aggressively attacked boys—only 7% of the time. It would be interesting to assess the degree to which the different sexes are the targets of Zapotec women's and girls' *indirect* aggression.

Schuster (1983) argues that much female–female aggression in Zambia is over men, who represent important resources to women. Burbank's (1987, p. 93) findings support the interpretation that much female aggression cross-culturally "is largely a form of female competition, often over matters of direct relevance to life and livelihood." Given the division of labor in Zapotec society, women and men fill complementary economic roles within marriage. In terms of economic well-being, a man is a valuable resource to his wife. Informants in San Andrés maintain that the reason women physically fight is over men. Thus Schuster's (1983) and Burbank's (1987) conclusions regarding competition may be relevant to at least some altercations among Zapotec women. However, the fact that Zapotec men fight over women more regularly and more severely, sometimes killing rivals, than women fight over men is in accordance with the evolutionary principles of sexual selection for male–male competition and parental investment theory (cf. Symons, 1979). In any case, it is clear that Zapotec women do act aggressively, although their ferocity and aggressive tactics differ from those used by males.

## Acknowledgments

I would like to thank Kathy M. Fry for assisting with the field research in many ways. I am also indebted to Hal Serrie, Margarita Lezcano, and Jim Welch for offering suggestions for improving this chapter. The analysis and writing of the chapter were facilitated by Faculty Development Grants from the Dean of Faculty, Lloyd Chapin, at Eckerd College, and I am grateful for this support.

## References

Björkqvist, K., Lagerspetz, M. J., & Kaukiainen, A. (1992). Do girls manipulate and boys fight? Developmental trends in regard to direct and indirect aggression. *Aggressive Behavior, 18.*

Burbank, V. (1987). Female aggression in cross-cultural perspective. *Behavior Science Research, 21,* 70–100.

Chinas, B. L. (1973). *The Isthmus Zapotecs.* New York: Holt, Rinehart, and Winston.

Dennis, P. A. (1973). The Oaxacan village president as political middleman. *Ethnology, 12,* 419–427.

Dennis, P. A. (1987). *Intervillage Conflict in Oaxaca.* New Brunswick, New Jersey: Rutgers University Press.

Daly, M., & Wilson, M. (1988). *Homicide.* New York: Aldine.

Fry, D. P. (1986). An ethological study of aggression and aggression socialization among Zapotec children of Oaxaca, Mexico. Ph.D. dissertation, Indiana University. Ann Arbor, Michigan: University Microfilms.

Fry, D. P. (1988). Intercommunity differences in aggression among Zapotec children. *Child Development, 59,* 1008–1019.

Fry, D. P. (1990). Play aggression among Zapotec children: Implications for the practice hypothesis. *Aggressive Behavior, 16,* 321–340.

Fry, D. P. (in press). The Zapotec. *In The Encyclopedia of World Cultures.* (Robert Van Kemper and Fernando Barbachano, eds.) New Haven, Connecticut: Human Relations Area Files Press.

Kappel, W. (1978). The biological face of antiviolence. Paper presented at the Meeting of the International Society for Research on Aggression, Washington, D.C., September.

Kearney, M. (1972). *The Winds of Ixtepeji: World View and Society in a Zapotec Town.* New York: Holt, Rinehart, & Winston.

Lagerspetz, K., Björkqvist, K., & Peltonen, T. (1988). Is indirect aggression typical of females? Gender differences in aggressiveness in 11- to 12-year-old children. *Aggressive Behavior, 14,* 403–414.

O'Nell, C. W. (1975). An investigation of reported "fright" as a factor in the etiology of *susto*, "magical fright." *Ethos, 3,* 41–63.

O'Nell, C. W. (1981). Hostility management and the control of aggression in a Zapotec community. *Aggressive Behavior, 7,* 351–366.

O'Nell, C. W., & O'Nell, N. D. (1977). A cross-cultural comparison of aggression in dreams: Zapotecs and Americans. *International Journal of Social Psychiatry, 23,* 35–41.

Parsons, E. C. (1936). *Mitla: Town of the Souls, and Other Zapotec-Speaking Pueblos of Oaxaca, Mexico.* Chicago: University of Chicago Press.

Salas, E. (1990). *Soldaderas in the Mexican Military: Myth and History.* Austin: University of Texas Press.

Schuster, I. (1983). Women's aggression: An African case study. *Aggressive Behavior, 9,* 319–331.

Selby, H. A. (1974). *Zapotec Deviance.* Austin: University of Texas Press.

Sumner, M. L. (1978). The social face of antiviolence. Paper presented at the Meeting of the International Society for Research on Aggression, Washington, D.C., September.

Symons, D. (1979). *The Evolution of Human Sexuality.* New York: Oxford University Press.

Tamayo, Carlos (1956). *Oaxaca en la Revolución.* Mexico.

Taylor, W. B. (1986). Homicidio en el distrito de Tlacolula, Oaxaca, 1700–1880: Un examen preliminar de las actas de defunción. *In* M. de los Angeles Romero Frizzi (Ed.), *Lecturas Históricas del Estado de Oaxaca, Volumen II, Epoca Colonial.* Mexico City: Instituto Nacional de Antropología e Historía.

Ugalde, A. (1973). Contemporary Mexico: From hacienda to PRI, political leadership in a Zapotec village. *In* R. Kern (Ed.), *The Caciques.* Albuquerque: University of New Mexico Press.

18

# *Lady Macbeth as a Problem for Shakespeare*

Pekka Niemelä

I. MACBETH WAS A VIKING
II. THE WITCHES WERE NORDIC NORNS
III. A GUESS THAT LADY MACBETH IS A VIKING WOMAN
IV. IS THE GUESS FOUL OR FAIR?
REFERENCES

Shakespeare creates a powerful woman, Lady Macbeth, but at the same time makes her a nonwoman. He has Lady Macbeth say,

> "Come, you spirits that tend on mortal thoughts, unsex me here; And fill me, from the crown to the toe, top-full Of direst cruelty. Make thick my blood, Stop up th'access and passage to remorse, That no compunctious visitings of nature Shake my fell purpose nor keep peace between Th' effect and it. Come to my woman's breasts, And take my milk for gall, you murd'ring ministers, Wherever in your sightless substances You wait on the mature's mischief. Come, thick night, And pall thee in the dunnest smoke of hell, That my keen knife see not the wound it makes, Nor heaven peep through the blanket of the dark To cry 'Hold, hold.' (Shakespeare, 1962, Act I, Scene V, ll. 40–54)

Shakespeare could not create a female being who would be as aggressive and powerful as Lady Macbeth was, and female as well. He needed to unsex her. There have been many attempts to understand Shakespeare's relation to Lady Macbeth (e.g., Freud, 1957; Blum, 1986). None of the earlier attempts to understand Lady Macbeth, however, has taken into consideration her possible cultural background. She was, perhaps, a Viking woman.

## I. Macbeth Was a Viking

The plot is set in Scotland about A.D. 1000, a fact which is often forgotten both by theater directors and actors. The theater sets, decorations, and costuming of the play are most often set in the renaissance style, only 100 years before Shakespeare's own time, whereas the time difference is almost 600 years. And, by the time of Macbeth, Scotland was more than half pagan, and both culturally and politically almost dominated by the Nordic Viking culture.

But how much did Shakespeare know about this Nordic tradition, and how did he get the information? As far as we know he read the story of Macbeth in Raphael Holinshed's Chronicles (Hoslay, 1968, p. 17), first published in 1587, only a few years before he wrote the play. Shakespeare's plot follows what Holinshed writes.

We may ask how reliable is Holinshed, and what were his sources? It is obvious that his work is a compilation of various handwritten manuscripts from monasteries and some official legal documents. The problem is that while his material from England is fairly reliable, that is not the case concerning the material from Scotland, especially since Holinshed wrote his Chronicles from an English viewpoint.

Let us go back to Macbeth's real cultural background: the fierce competitive combination of Scottish and Viking traditions. By the time of Macbeth, there was not only one king in Scotland, as it might have appeared from Holinshed's English viewpoint. The country was actually divided among several kings, their kingdoms often changing more than once during one generation. Holinshed does not write about this, and Shakespeare does not know about it. The best way to obtain information about conditions in Scotland at that time are the Nordic sagas: Sturlasson's "Heimskringla" (1906), and especially the "Orkneyinga Saga," the History of the Earls of Orkney (1982, Chapter 10, pp. 35–36), this latter saga preceding "Heimskringla" by at least 100 years. Notice that the distance in time between Holinshed and the historical events of Macbeth was 500 years while the "Orkneyinga Saga" was virtually written at the time the events of Macbeth took place.

What we learn from the "Orkneyinga Saga" are facts about the political and martial turbulence in the area around the year 1000. Macbeth is mentioned, and the descriptions of the main political events match Holinshed's account, but the richness of historical information, especially concerning culture and social structure is superior. In the Orkneyinga Saga we find, in addition to Macbeth, also Malcolm and Duncan, as well as many other similarities of the story.

## II. The Witches Were Nordic Norns

Shakespeare starts his play Macbeth in the following way:

> An open place. Thunder and lightning. Enter three Witches.
>
> 1 Witch. When shall we three meet again? In thunder, lightning, or in rain?
>
> 2 Witch. When the hurlyburly's done, When the battle's lost and won.

3 Witch. That will be ere the set of sun.
1 Witch. Where the place?
2 Witch. Upon the heath.
3 Witch. There to meet with Macbeth.
1 Witch. I come, Graymalkin.
2 Witch. Paddock calls.
3 Witch. Anon!
All. Fair is foul, and foul is fair:
    Hover through the fog and filthy air.
(Witches vanish.) (Shakespeare, 1962, Act I, Scene I, ll. 1–12)

The setting is somber, mystical, and frightening, and would have been felt so especially at the time of Shakespeare and his contemporaries. The principles of electricity, thunder, and lightning were unknown, and witch-hunts were a matter of only yesterday.

From the very beginning the audience knows that unnatural forces are going to play an important part in the destiny of the persons depicted in the play. The skilled playwright pushes the audience's imagination backward to a mythical time with principles completely different to ours: "Foul is fair, and fair is foul."

The fact that Shakespeare followed Holinshed's story and that Holinshed writes about what is described in the Orkneyinga Saga, gives us a hint about the witches in the play: They were the Norns, the three Weird Sisters spinning the yarn of fate for mortals (Sturluson, 1907). Not only Macbeth, but numerous Nordic characters in the Sagas were led to their fate through the intervention of the Three Norns. The principle was that you could not escape your destiny once it was set.

As for the Three Weird Sisters, they appear in Holinshed thus:

> "It fortuned, as Macbeth and Banquo journeyed toward Forres, where the King then lay, they went sporting by the way together without other company save only themselves, passing through the woods and fields, when suddenly, in the midst of a laund, there met them three women in strange and wild apparel, resembling creatures of elder world; whom when they attentively beheld, wondering much at the sight, the first of them spoke and said, "All hail, Macbeth, Thane of Glamis!" The second of them said, "Hail, Macbeth, Thane of Cawdor!" But the third said, "All hail, Macbeth, that hereafter shalt be King of Scotland!" (Hoslay, 1968, p. 17).

This conversation, almost word for word, is used by Shakespeare in the play. But Holinshed continues:

> ". . . . But afterwards the common opinion was that these women were either the Weird Sisters, that is (as ye would say), the goddesses of destiny, or else some nymphs or fairies endued with knowledge of prophesy by their necromantical science, because everything came to pass as they had spoken." (Hoslay, 1968, p. 17–18).

From here on the plot in the play follows Holinshed to the end, except for some minor changes in the characters.

## III. A Guess That Lady Macbeth Is a Viking Woman

There is, however, one important character Shakespeare elaborated beyond Holinshed: Lady Macbeth. She is only mentioned once in the chronicle:

> ". . . The words of the three Weird Sisters also greatly encouraged him hereunto (the murder plan); but specially his wife lay sore upon him to attempt the thing, as she that was very ambitious, burning in unquenchable desire to bear the name of a queen. . . ." (Hoslay, 1968, p. 28).

So, what about her? Is it not enough to accept her as a character created by the foremost playwright in the world? Obviously not, since scores of sharp brains in the fields of history, literature, psychiatry, psychoanalysis, and other fields of scholarly learning have tried to explain the wickedness of the lady. But after all, was she really all bad?

Going back to Lady Macbeth, and women's situation in her Viking culture, we find ample evidence of exceptionally powerful female characters, making decisions on war and peace, life and death, most often within the clan or kindred system. We have to remember that legal authority was nonexistent, so social and kinship alliances were the only insurance against threats from outside. Thus, the relations to kin became crucially important, and consequently women's status was high, in a system where the men could be away on their raids for years.

True, there is no mention of Lady Macbeth in the old Viking sagas. But in the Orkneyinga Saga there are, at the time of Macbeth, several female characters who equal Lady Macbeth in power and cruelty. For instance, there is Frakokk (Orkneyinga Saga, 1982, p. 50–92), wife of Ljot the Renegade of Sutherland, who goes to Orkney with her nephew Earl Harald after her husband's death. There she helps her sister make a poisoned shirt which inadvertently kills Earl Harald. She is driven away by Earl Paul and goes to live on her estate in Sutherland. Then, she gathers forces in the Hebrides and sails to Orkney and is finally burned to death in her house by Svein Asleifarson.

Lady Macbeth fits well into the company of high-status Viking women, who did their utmost for power and kin, and who were not considered, in their own culture, any less the woman for it.

## IV. Is the Guess Foul or Fair?

The idea that Lady Macbeth really was a Viking woman is only a guess. There are no data in the old Nordic sagas about Lady Macbeth. This is just one more explanation for Lady Macbeth's evil and cruelty. Evil and horrible can also describe the three witches. The witches and Lady Macbeth strengthen in the drama the idea of an evil, dangerous woman. Would Shakespeare have some personal gain in describing such female cruelty?

We may question why Shakespeare begins his drama with the three Weird Sisters, an illusion and hallucination of destiny set in a mythical age. At the time Shakespeare wrote his drama, there was much interest in the mystical and in witches. The reigning monarch was, at the time the drama was written, James I. It is well known that James was very interested in the occult. He had participated in witch trials in Scotland, and even published a book on witchcraft and demonology.

Furthermore, the drama was written some years after the death of Queen Elizabeth I, who executed Mary Stuart. James I was the son of Mary Stuart. Perhaps Shakespeare wanted to depict Queen Elizabeth as Lady Macbeth, and thus gain the acceptance and favor of James I. In that case, Lady Macbeth is to Shakespeare less of a problem but more of a benefit, as Lady Macbeth used her husband and the witches.

## References


Blum, H. P. (1986). Psychoanalytical Studies and Macbeth. *In* (A. S. Eissler, ed.) *The Psychoanalytic Study of the Child, Volume 41*, pp. 585–599. New Haven: Yale University Press.

Freud, S. (1957). Some character-types met with in Psycho-analytic work. *In The Standard Edition of the Complete Psychological Works of Sigmund Freud, Volume XIV*. London: Hogarth Press.

Hoslay, R. (Ed.) (1968). *Shakespeare's Holinshed. The Source of Shakespeare's Histories & Tragedies. Holinshed's Chronicles Selected, Edited and Annotated by Richard Hoslay*. New York: Capricorn Books.

*Orkneyinga Saga*. (1982). *The History of the Earls of Orkney*. Translated by H. Palsson and Paul Edwards. Bungay: Penguin Books.

Shakespeare, W. (1962). *In* (K. Muir, ed.) *Macbeth*. London & Cambridge, Massachusetts: Methuen & Harvard University Press.

Sturluson, Snorre. (1906). *The Heimskringla I–III*. S. Laing (Ed.). London: Norroena Society.

# IV

# FEMALE AGGRESSION AND ITS SOCIAL SETTINGS

19

# Sex and Violence on Acali: Six Females and Five Males Isolated on a Raft on the Atlantic and the Caribbean for 101 Days

Santiago Genovés

I. INTRODUCTION: DISSATISFACTION AND AGGRESSION, SEX AND VIOLENCE
II. THE RAFT LABORATORY
III. SEX
IV. SEX AND FRICTION, CONFLICT AND VIOLENCE
V. SEX AND VIOLENCE ON ACALI: THE HYPOTHESIS
VI. SEX AND VIOLENCE ON ACALI: THE EVIDENCE
VII. DISCUSSION AND DISCUSSIONS OF SEX AND VIOLENCE ON ACALI
REFERENCES

## I. Introduction: Dissatisfaction and Aggression, Sex and Violence

Armed conflict is the major cause of death today. Pretexts—rational or not—of *differences*, in religious, political, economic, folkloric, linguistic, or other cultural systems, lead larger or smaller groups to battle for dominance, to kill or die, as well as to inflict and suffer mental and physical pain. The two World Wars, the Spanish Civil War, the Korean War, the Vietnam War, the Gulf War, and around 350 more horrific wars since 1946 constitute a reality that cannot be hidden.

On the interpersonal level, too, the major cause of friction, aggression and aggressiveness, and violence is the quest for power, leadership, and position. Even though we may not like the fact, there are human factors that clearly explain why this is so, and which can be viewed objectively. For there are two basic ways in which we come to know ourselves: (1) through introspection which can be slow and difficult; (2) from the image of ourselves and our actions as reflected by others. Theoretically, and possibly practically, the more people see us, the more complete this image and our self-knowledge.

Hence the search for success; for position and power in politics and industry, for "Hollywood," for cultural distinction in its varied forms. We are human beings, and as such want to constantly achieve greater things; that is how we left the sea, how we reached America or the moon, how we invented the hand axe or the wheel, developed jet propulsion and electronics, how we split the atom. Our great achievements stem from dissatisfaction; so do, internally or externally, our great struggles.

Dissatisfaction leads us to try for and reach unknown horizons where, because they are new to us, our accustomed patterns of social interchange and communication are no longer valid. In the process of establishing new ones, conflict and friction inevitably appear. Perhaps one day, when science has faced the objective fact of this inevitability, we shall establish relations as we, subjectively, feel they ought to exist.

For, what we must deal with are sex and violence. In 1939, Dollard *et al.* offered, as the conclusion of their research, the idea that *inhibition leads to frustration, which leads to aggression.* Regarding Darwin's conception of evolution, while this idea still works as the theoretical basis underlying studies of aggression, we add to or subtract from it in accordance with our own conclusions. Freud compared sex to the way leadership, position, and power at all levels lead to friction, conflict, and death, calling it "the motor that makes the world turn." Unamuno thought that motor was envy. For my part, I believe it is *envy of the other person's sexuality.*

It is clear that the enormous accumulation of experimental data, my own as well as others', acquires true validity only when set within a general integrated theoretical, scientific, *and* philosophical framework. A full understanding of a building can never be reached by the mere description and appraisal, however diligent and detailed, of the bricks.

We are born and die in a solitude inherent to our nature, and make relationships, activities, undertakings, institutions, and societies to escape this. That is, throughout our lives, *communication inhibits the (normal and inevitable) evolution of human solitude.* What we learn of normality and variability from scientific observation must thus be combined with the irreproducable and scientifically immeasurable solitude of each individual's behavior and biology. It is, therefore, a question of recognizing and combining external and internal appraisal when studying human behavior in general, and sex, friction, and conflict in particular, if we are to avoid the mistake of using the word "scientific" because of *methodology* for work neither logically reasoned nor profound.

## II. The Raft Laboratory

I have already published 19 articles concerning so-called "raft experiments" taking part in both the Ra I and Ra II expeditions as well as the one which is the subject of this chapter. In addition to these, I have researched the violent conflicts in the Basque (Genovés 1980b; 1980c; 1981). These support at the group level the conclusions of the raft experiments at the individual level: that the *inhibition-frustration-aggression* link is valid when explaining the sources of social conflict.

The raft *Acali*, "the house on the water" in Nahuatl, measures only 12 × 7 meters. On this escape-proof laboratory, 11 volunteers, 6 females and 5 males, spent 101 days on the Atlantic Ocean and the Caribbean Sea, away from the conventions, publicity, and manifold other factors that usually repress human behavior. The volunteers answered questions about their behavior during that time: of 10,068 answers, 858 concern "sex and violence."

Convention is undoubtedly a useful element in the social world in which we all live and develop. However, it is taboos, myths, and prejudices as socioeconomic, cultural, and professional conventions (of good manners, of respect for hierarchy and order, of consideration for age or sex) which make us constantly conceal, disguise, divert, and falsify our true, natural actions, reactions, or thoughts. We do not agree, we are not unaware of the unjust, misplaced, extemporary nature of what we may have heard or seen, and still less have we been unaffected by it. But we do not express ourselves, we keep silent.

Now, in moments of real stress, of real crisis, our true temperaments, personalities, and motivations with regard to sex and violence emerge. Hence, the importance of experiments with rafts; a flimsy, vulnerable rudimentary vessel isolated on the high seas is a laboratory of human behavior in a state of frequent crisis and almost constant stress. On Acali, the volunteers came close to, or reached, a certain normality, as conventional, religious, and consumer attitudes, preconceptions, and pressures gradually disappeared.

## III. Sex

From man's inherent solitude, the sexual act brings him closest to brotherhood. Biologically and culturally it enables us to transcend time, perpetuating ourselves in offspring, while desire motivates creative achievement. The nakedness and proximity necessary for the sexual act of love, of giving, banishes inhibition; and when there is giving without inhibition, where there is *unity*, there is no violence.

Since 1948, a series of valuable studies of this sexual behavior have appeared, notably Kinsey, Pomeroy, and Martin (1948); Kinsey *et al.* (1953); Oraison (1966); Masters and Johnson (1966, 1970); Rocheblave (1968); Amoroso (1971); Serrano (1971); Woolfolk (1971); Zwang (1972); Zubin and Money (1974); Asayama (1975); Hite (1976); and Offit (1978). These studies are extremely important, but limited to statistical analysis, and while Offit (1978) alone among them approaches the problematics of sexual behavior, not even this report sheds light on the topic of sex and violence.

So we must go through a second group of literature where such light on the problematics of sex mythology, behavior, and processes can be found. This endless list includes Shakespeare, Freud, Foucault, Sade, García Lorca, de Beauvoir, Bataille, Levy-Strauss, and Lacan, and offers more insights than the previous list of researchers, in a general perspective and framework. This giving in unity is the opposite of violence, hence has an important place in the study of sex, aggression, and violence; if *only* giving, or *only* receiving is found in the sex act, there is disunity, imbalance, and violence.

## IV. Sex and Friction, Conflict and Violence

The belief that one is receiving less, in quantity or quality, than one is giving, and the need to always receive more, are sources of friction, conflict, and violence particularly characteristic of the consumeristic world. Leaving aside sadistic or masochistic practices, men generally want to give themselves without inhibition in the sexual act; so do women—the generalization of women's *biological* receptiveness to a behavioral expectation is quite wrong.

It is clear that in a world dominated by men, the sexual behavior—or the behavior preceding sex—of males is exaggerated, while that of the female is repressed. The male aggression, *machismo* (which is exclusive to the Latin countries which gave it the name only in certain forms of its external expression) is nearly always simply the male's expression of his conscious sexual biological inferiority. Owing to their sexual-biological makeup, women are absolutely always open to sexual intercourse, always capable of sexual reception. The male is not: fatigue, alcohol, tobacco, age, and any of the variants of psychological fixation affect his ability to "perform," in addition to the biological fact that he is not capable of maintaining an infinite series of erections.

Furthermore, it is clear that in the intimate field of sexual behavior, as direct results of conventional attitudes, considerable inhibitions exist. These in turn lead to conflict and aggression. When these conventional attitudes disappear, so do inhibitions and this resultant aggression.

## V. Sex and Violence on Acali: The Hypothesis

The majority of specialist advisors to the Acali experiment, myself included, expected sexual relations and behaviors on the raft to cause friction, conflict, and violence, and to interfere with other interpersonal relations.

## VI. Sex and Violence on Acali: The Evidence

Neither hypothesis was supported by the observations drawn from an integration of the 858 answers given by the volunteers [details of methodology can be found in Genovés (1980), statistical procedures in Genovés (1977, pp. 45–86)]. Rather, just as on Acali conventional attitudes disappeared for men and women alike (there was no "after you, sir," no "I'd like to, but have an important meeting to attend"), so there was none of the conventional *behavior* which leads to aggression: women did not have skirts under which to "keep their legs together"; men displayed physical strength, but they did not display "machismo." Specifically we found that: (1) on the raft, free of the inhibitions that characterized female sexuality on land, women express a sexual drive or desire much greater than what would be considered normal or expressed in a conventional situation; and (2) when freed of the overwhelming conventional need to show themselves interested in sexual activity, men, in contrast, pursue sexual encounters much less frequently than what is considered (on land) *normal* for them.

Further, the difference, the deviation from the "norm" is much greater for women than for men. The claim can be made, then, that in a male world—with the prevailing patterns of sexual behavior drawn up, laid down, and *enforced* by men—normal sexual thresholds are much closer to the biological reality established (as on the raft) for men than those established for women. The fact that sexual relations existed between any given pair did not result in inhibitions for either sex, within or outside that pair.

This, then, is the real point to emerge from Acali: when there is no inhibition or sexual frustration, there are no aggressions traceable to sexual relations.

## VI. Discussion and Discussions of Sex and Violence on Acali

In addition to confirming in practice the findings of Dollard *et al.* (1939) as regards sex, and giving new bases for the methods and techniques of Masters and

Johnson (1966), our study (see Genovés, 1975a) also supports the conclusions drawn by Prescott (1975). According to Prescott, in 48 of 49 "primitive" societies studied, no violence was found among adults, essentially because of norms of behavior, of presexual or sexual knowledge, and because of the somatosensory freedom among children and youths free of sexual inhibitions with respect to both themselves and adults.

We also carried out studies away from the raft. Of the over 4000 media "clippings" which were analyzed, 3227 (80%) referred to the "sex raft" ("la balsa del sexo," "la radeau du sex," "la zattera del'amore," etc.). We suspect they were imagining constant orgies, constant intercourse, constant inhibition and sexual frustration, semiconstant sexual attacks, semiconstant sexual threats, and semiconstant sexual violence. This was clearly a result of the pressures of convention which the mass media encouraged. However, it was just as clearly and without doubt a projection of the sexual inhibitions, frustrations, and aberrations which those pressures produce onto the raft Acali, where the reality, as we have seen, in no way coincided with media opinions of it.

In general and in particular, our study establishes that the norms of sex behavior, taken as more or less valid conventions with traditional or innovative cultural variants, are in fact *masked* by what "is expected," within a culture, of adult males and females. This leads to a constant state of conscious or unconscious unrest, desubication, and anguish, which in turn leads to conflict, aggression, and violence. The study of sex behavior in the conventional human zoo cannot reflect anything other than the relationship between convention and sex. This is sufficient for matters of sex and violence, but offers little in regard to what, given our biological makeup, could be.

## References


Amoroso, H. (1971). *La condición Sexual de las Francesas*. Grijalbo, México.

Asayama, Sh. I. (1975). Adolescent sex development and adult sex behaviour in Japan. *The Journal of Sex Research, 11*, 2–91.

Dollard, J., Doob, L. W., Miller, N. E., Mowrer, C. H., & Sears, R. R. (1939). *Frustration and Aggression*. New Haven, Connecticut: Yale University Press.

Genovés, S. (1971). Ra I and Ra II, Balsa de Papyrus, atraviesa el Atlántico. (Expedición Antropológica, Experimento Humano). *Tribuna Médica XVII*, 10, 11, & 12, (224–231, 246–257, 278–280) México.

Genovés, S. (1974). Encounter on a raft: The voyage of Acali. *Human Behaviour*, January, 16–23.

Genovés, S. (1975a). *Acali*. Barcelona: Editorial Planeta.

Genovés, S. (1975b). Una nueva concepción de los problemas sexuales. *Ciencia y Desarrollo, CONACYT, 1*, 28–31.

Genovés, S. (1975c). The voyage of the Acali. *Group. News Journal of the Eastern Group Psychotherapy Society*, July 1–5, U.S.A.

Genovés, S. (1976a). El experimento Acali. *Ciencia y Desarrollo, CONACYT, 11, (8)*, 4–7.

Genovés, S. (1976b). Behaviour and violence: Where are we in respect to some basic issues. *Perspectives in Biology and Medicine, 20,* 20–29.

Genovés, S. (1977). Acali, Ra I and Ra II. Some conclusions and hypothesis concerning human friction under isolation and stress, with special reference to intelligence and personality assessment. *Aggressive Behaviour, 3,* 163–171.

Genovés, S. (1980a). *The Acali Experiment.* (Corrected and enlarged edition). New York: Times-Books.

Genovés, S. (1980b). Violencia: Algunos datos obtenidos en el experimento Acali. Simposio, Academia Nacional de Medicina. *Gaceta Médica de México, 116, (5),* 204–208.

Genovés, S. (1980c). Violencia: Consideraciones finales. Simposio. Academia Nacional de Medicina. *Gaceta Médica de México, 116, (5),* 210–212.

Genovés, S. (1981). La violencia en Euzkadi y en sus relaciones con España. (Estudio antropo-psico-sociológico). *Ciencia y Desarrollo, 37,* 137–153.

Genovés, S. (1984). The violence in the Basque Provinces. Relations with the rest of Spain. *Aggressive Behavior, 10, (1),* 27–32.

Hite, S. (1976). *The Hite Report.* New York: Dell.

Kinsey, A. C., Pomeroy, W. B., & Martin, C. E. (1948). *Sexual Behavior in the Human Male.* Philadelphia: W. B. Saunders.

Kinsey, A. C., Pomeroy, W. B., Martin, C. E., & Gebbard, P. N. (1953). *Sexual Behavior in the Human Female.* Philadelphia: W. B. Saunders.

Masters, W. H., & Johnson, V. E. (1966). *Human Sexual Response.* London: J. & A. Churchill.

Masters, W. H., and Johnson, V. E. (1970). *Human Sexual Inadequacy.* J. and A. Churchill. London.

Offit, A. (1978). *The Sexual Self.* New York: Lippincott.

Oraison, M. (1966). *Le Mystère Humain de la Sexualité.* Paris: Seuil.

Prescott, J. W. (1975). Body pleasure and the origins of violence. *The Futurist,* April, 64–74.

Rocheblave, A. M. (1968). *Lo Masculino y lo Feminino en la Sociedad Contemporánea.* Madrid: Ciencia Nueva.

Serrano, V. R. (1971). *La Sexualidad Femenina.* Barcelona: Pulso Editorial.

Woolfolk, W. (1971). *La Pareja Ideal.* Grijalbo, México.

Zubin, J., & Money, (Eds.). (1974). *Contemporary Sexual Behavior.* Baltimore: H. Johns Hopkins University Press.

Zwang, W. (1972). *La Fonction Erotique.* 2 vols. Laffont, Paris.

20

# Sex Differences in Conflict and Aggression in Individual and Group Settings

Jacob M. Rabbie, Charles Goldenbeld,

and Hein F. M. Lodewijkx

I. INTRODUCTION
II. EXPERIMENTAL PROCEDURE
III. SEX DIFFERENCES IN CONFLICT AND AGGRESSION
A. Conflict
B. Aggression
IV. CONCLUSION
REFERENCES

## I. Introduction

In experimental social psychology, sex differences in aggression are almost exclusively studied at an intraindividual, personal, or interpersonal level of analysis. In our research program on conflict and aggression we have argued that these sex differences should also be investigated at the intragroup, intergroup, and societal levels of analysis.

We have been interested in the question of whether groups consisting of males and females react with more aggression in experimental games than single males and females do to the norm violation of another individual or another group. Our research is guided by a Behavioral Interaction Model (BIM) which attempts to integrate a variety of social psychological theories in the area of intra- and intergroup conflict and aggression (Rabbie, 1987, 1989, 1991a,b: in press a,b; Rabbie, Schot, & Visser, 1989; Rabbie & Lodewijkx, 1991a,b).

Consistent with the interactionist position of Lewin (1936), our model assumes all behavior, including the aggressive behavior of males and females, is a function of the external environment and cognitive, emotional, motivational, and normative orientations. These psychological orientations are in part elicited by the environment and in part they are acquired by individuals, and by groups, organizations, and other open social systems in the course of their development.

The main function of these orientations is to reduce the uncertainty in the external environment to such a level that it enables individuals or groups to cope effectively with the environment in an effort to achieve desirable or avoid undesirable outcomes. The environment consists of three components: (1) a physical (task) environment; (2) an internal and an external social environment, that is, the behavior of other people within and external to the social system; and (3) an interdependence structure between the parties with respect to their goals and means which may be loosely or tightly coupled and symmetrical or asymmetrical with regard to the power relations between the actors or parties. In interaction with each other, these psychological orientations produce a meaning structure or interpretive system concerning the environment, which in turn generates various action tendencies in the actor, leading to intentions and goal-directed behavior designed to maximize outcomes (Ajzen & Madden, 1986). Although many types of meaning structures may exist, we have focused our attention on relational and instrumental meaning structures (or global orientations) which emerge from a combination of specific cognitive, emotional, motivational, and normative orientations.

In a *relational* orientation, the aim is to achieve a mutually satisfying relationship with the other as an end in and of itself. In an *instrumental* orientation, the other is used mainly as a means to achieve economic and other tangible outcomes outside the relationship. These basic instrumental and relational orientations, in combination with *cooperative* and *competitive* motives, result in four types of cooperation and competition. The aim of (1) instrumental cooperation or (2) instrumental competition is to maximize economic or other tangible outcomes, by either cooperation or competition, whichever seems the most promising strategy in attaining one's aims at the lowest possible costs; (3) relational cooperation is aimed at developing a mutually satisfying relation with another person or group as an end in and of itself; (4) relational competition or social rivalry is aimed at achieving prestige, status, recognition, or a "positive social identity" in comparison with another individual or group (Tajfel & Turner, 1986). Very similar distinctions can be made for instrumental and relational fairness and altruism (see Rabbie, Schot, & Visser, 1989).

We propose that females tend to have a more relational-moral orientation toward others, while males are likely to have a more instrumental-power orientation toward other people. These sex differences in orientation and behavior may hold not only for humans but for nonhuman animals as well. In his observations of sex differences in chimpanzees, de Waal (1989) has noted that:

> Adult male chimpanzees seem to live in a hierarchical world with replaceable coalition partners and a single permanent goal: power. Adult females, in contrast, live in a horizontal world of social connections (de Waal, 1989, p. 51).

Following this analysis, we will use the terms instrumental and relational for, respectively, a "vertical" instrumental-power orientation and a "horizontal" relational-moral orientation.

It may well be that groups have a different function for males than for females. For the more instrumental males, groups or organizations are perceived as means to gain power, enabling them to achieve goals external to their relationship. For the more relational women, groups and families are primarily viewed as arenas for developing interpersonal and communal relationships with each other that allow individuals to grow and prosper. In this view, males have a more collective, group-centered approach to the social environment, while women view the social world from a more relational, interpersonal perspective. Although males tend to have a stronger instrumental orientation, and score lower on the relational orientation than females, there is still a great deal of overlap between the sexes in this respect (Lodewijkx, 1989).

Our distinction between instrumental and relational orientations is based on a cross-national negotiation study conducted by Kelly *et al.*, (1970). Factor analyses of preexperimental self-ratings on various personality attributes used in this study yielded two independent factors which were closely related to the Evaluation and Potency factors consistently revealed in semantic differential research (cf. Osgood, May, & Miron, 1965). Kelly and Thibaut (1978) referred to these factors as a dynamic-instrumental task (or D) factor and an evaluative-moral (E) factor. They considered the D factor as more characteristic of males and the E factor more typical of women. Other authors have made similar observations but have used different labels such as agency and communion (Bakan, 1966), instrumental competence versus warm-expressive traits (Williams & Best, 1982), masculinity and femininity (Spence & Helmreich, 1978), and instrumental task and socioemotional interdependence (Deutsch, 1982). Although these dimensions have a kind of family resemblance to each other, each reflects a different shade of meaning, and is also measured differently. We prefer *instrumental* and *relational* orientations measured by asking subjects to rate themselves and others on a variety of bipolar adjectives such as aggressive/nonaggressive and friendly/hostile (Carson, 1969), respectively, prior to the introduction of experimental variables.

The main aim of this chapter is to examine whether these instrumental and relational orientations of men and women affect their conflict and aggressive behavior in response to the norm violation of another individual or group, specifically as a result of whether they must act collectively as group members or individualistically as single persons. We have suggested that males, like groups, have a more collective orientation to others in the congruent environment of experimental games. Females, like individuals, appear to have a more self-centered attitude toward the incongruent, impersonal, strategic contexts of experimental games we have used to study sex differences in conflict and aggressive behavior.

## II. Experimental Procedure

Aggression has been defined as behavior intended to inflict harm or injury on other people (Baron, 1977). Experimental laboratory research on aggression has been dominated by the "teacher–learner" paradigm (e.g., Buss, 1963), in which male and female college students take the role of a teacher who must deliver electric shocks or other aversive stimuli, such as irritating noise, to punish the "learner" for apparent errors. To the subjects, the learner appears to be a subject like themselves. In fact, he or she is a confederate of the experimenter who makes standard errors in a learning task. The intensity, duration, and frequency of the noxious stimuli are used as indications of physical aggression.

As we have argued elsewhere, it is debatable whether this paradigm studies aggression at all (Rabbie & Lodewijkx, 1987). It has been shown that subjects consider their shock behavior not as an aggressive act but as altruistic behavior, helping the learner to accomplish his or her learning task (Baron & Eggleston, 1972). Thus, it is not clear whether the "aggression" was intended to harm or hurt the other, a crucial element in Baron's definition. The real purpose of the experiment in the teacher–learner paradigm is carefully concealed from the subjects. Unlike the subjects in our experiments, they are *not* told that they can deliver painful white noise to the other as a way to express disapproval of the other's behavior. Most importantly, the aggressive behavior in the traditional paradigm is not part and parcel of a continuous interactive process between the actors, in which aggression is only one of the responses they can make to settle the conflict among themselves. In this paradigm there is no way to study the history of the conflict and the impact that it may have on the aggressive behavior of individuals and groups over time.

In our research we have used experimental games, such as the Prisoner's Dilemma Game (PDG) or the Power Allocation Game (PAG) (Rabbie & Lodewijkx, 1991a), in an attempt to correct these deficiencies. These games permit the comparison of the conflict and aggressive behavior of individuals and groups with each other. In the course of these games, the programmed party, a single individual or a group, which could be seen on a television screen in front of the subjects, reacted initially very positively and cooperatively to the choices of the naive subjects who acted either as single individuals or as group members. However, near the end of the game, the other party violated important social norms, for example, by breaking a promise or by unfairly giving much more money to themselves than to the subjects. In the PDG research the other party had always made a cooperative choice and promised to make another cooperative choice on the last and critical trial. Contrary to this promise, the opponent made a competitive choice, inflicting a financial loss on those subjects who had made a cooperative choice on that trial. It has been shown that it is not the competitive choice of the other, but the norm violation which arouses angry aggression in individuals and groups (Rabbie & Horwitz, 1982; Rabbie, 1992; Brown, 1986).

In the PAG, the programmed opponents abused their power unfairly to give much more money to themselves than to the subjects. The subjects alone had the voluntary choice to react to the norm violation (or abuse of power) of the opponent by sending painful white noise to them. The intensity, duration, and frequency of the white noise constituted our measure of physical aggression. It should be noted that the programmed party in these experiments was perceived by subjects as a fellow subject. Unknown to the subjects, the behavior of the programmed party was prerecorded on video tape.

## III. Sex Differences in Conflict and Aggression

### A. CONFLICT

One of the most surprising findings in the PDG literature, in contrast to the prevailing sex stereotypes in our society, has been that males make more cooperative C choices while females tend to make more competitive and defensive D choices (Colman, 1982). However, Colman's "sex difference mystery" needs to be qualified. Males are not always more cooperative than females in a PDG. Rather, they tend to follow a more cooperative, instrumental *strategy* than females if the other party can be expected to reciprocate to cooperative initiatives. Thus, they are more likely than females to make a first cooperative choice, and then they will match the choice the other has made on the previous trial in an effort to influence the other's behavior in a more cooperative direction (Rabbie, 1991a). It has been shown that this contingent cooperative tit-for-tat (TFT) strategy is the most effective way to maximize one's outcome by mutual cooperation (Axelrod, 1984). Thus, males follow a more contingent responsive TFT strategy in the PDG than females, their behavior best predicted on the basis of the choices made by the other player, whereas females' game behavior can be best predicted on the basis of their own prior behavior in the game (Lacy, 1978).

Our explanation of this sex difference has been that the impersonal, strategic task environment of the PDG is probably more congruent with the instrumental, agentic orientation of males than with the more relational or communal orientation of females, who have no opportunity to satisfy their relational needs in the anonymous impersonal environment of the PDG. We assume that these impersonal and strategic task environments evoke cognitive, emotional, motivational, and normative orientations which induce people—men and women—at least temporarily, to maximize economic or other tangible outcomes. The more instrumental men realize that the interdependence structure of the PDG is such that it is better to strive for the long-range goal of instrumental mutual cooperation than for mutual competition, provided that the other can be expected to cooperate as well (Pruitt & Kimmel, 1977). As a consequence, males are more sensitive and responsive to the game behavior of the other party than females.

The more relational people, particularly women, are less sensitive to strategic aspects of the PDG, and are therefore less responsive to the behavior of the other. We hypothesized that they would be more sensitive and responsive to possible socioemotional aspects of the PDG situation. Consistent with this, we have found that individual women became more cooperative, and individual males more competitive in a PDG when they had the opportunity actually to see the other player, prior to seeing him or her on the television screen during the experiment (Lodewijkx, 1985). Without that opportunity, individual males were more cooperative than individual females. Presumably, seeing a person "live" before seeing him or her only on a screen elicits relational cooperation in females and relational competition or social rivalry in males.

If individual males tend to follow a more cooperative TFT strategy than females, it is to be expected that they would be more cooperative in their orientations and behavior than individual females when playing against a cooperative opponent. It was found, indeed, that single males, who were urged to maximize only their individual interests, were more cooperative in their behavior and orientations than single females given identical instructions (Lodewijkx, 1989).

In a recent study, it appeared that males, like groups, took a more cooperative, "collective" stance in their orientations and behavior in the PDG, whereas females showed a more competitive-individualistic approach to the game (Rabbie & Lodewijkx, 1991b). This finding is consistent with observations of Wilson (1971) that males and groups (especially groups consisting of males) are likely to follow a more cooperative TFT strategy in the PDG than females and individuals, provided that the other player appears to follow a cooperative strategy as well (Rabbie, Visser, & van Oostrum, 1982).

### B. AGGRESSION

What is the influence of an individual or a group context on the aggressive behavior of men and women? The literature on aggression by individual males and females indicates that differences in aggressive behavior are relatively small as compared with sex differences in influenceability and helping behavior (Eagly, 1987). In addition, these sex differences seem to interact with various situational variables (Frodi, Macaulay, and Thome, 1977; White, 1983; Eagly & Steffen, 1986). With respect to the importance of situational variability, White (1983) has observed that:

> In situations where the aggressive action is justified, empathy is not aroused, anonymity is ensured and anger arousal and provocativeness are of equal intensity, gender differences will be minimal (p. 22).

A more recent meta-analysis by Eagly and Steffen (1986) confirms this conclusion. They find that, on the average, individual men are somewhat more aggressive than individual women but that these sex differences are inconsistent across studies. In laboratory studies especially, it was found that the tendency for men to be more aggressive than women was more pronounced for aggression that produced pain or physical injury than for aggression that produced psychological or social harm. Moreover, these sex differences were larger to the extent that women perceived, more so than men, that enacting a behavior would produce harm to the target, and guilt and anxiety as well as danger to oneself.

Eagly and Steffen (1986) interpret their findings in terms of their social-role theory. They assume that aggression, like other social behaviors, is regulated by social norms that apply to individuals based on the roles they occupy because of their socially identified gender. In their view, the male gender role includes norms which encourage and approve many forms of aggression, while the traditional female gender role places little emphasis on aggressiveness. Moreover, the primacy that this role gives to caring and other relational or communal qualities may favor behaviors incompatible with aggressiveness. They argue that the female gender role's emphasis on caring and concern for others' welfare may increase perceived likelihood of guilt and anxiety about causing other people to suffer. Consistent with this role analysis, we expected that the more instrumental-power-oriented males would react with more physical aggression to a norm violation in a PDG than would the more relational-moral-oriented females.

In his dissertation, Lodewijkx (1989) compared the instrumental and relational orientations and subsequent aggressive behavior of males and females with each other in an individual and a group setting and found, consistent with our hypothesis, small but significant sex differences. Over all conditions combined, males reacted with more angry physical aggression to the norm violation than did females. Interestingly, this sex difference in aggression can be attributed much more to the relational-moral orientation than to the instrumental-power orientation of the subjects. It appeared that the relational-moral orientation inhibited the expression of physical aggression, but more so for women than for men.

Goldenbeld and Rabbie (1991) found more direct evidence for this hypothesis. Women expressed more moral objections to the use of the white noise apparatus than did men. If this variable is included in a covariance analysis, the sex difference in physical aggression disappears completely. This finding suggests that the sex difference in aggression is at least partially mediated by the difference in normative orientation between men and women.

There is other evidence that suggests that females are more sensitive than males to the normative pressures in the internal social environment. In one study (Rabbie, Lodewijkx, & Broese, 1985), individuals acted alone or as members of five-person groups. Aggression measures were obtained for each single individual and each of the members in the five-person group. Subjects were made less identifiable (more anonymous) by placing them in a darkened room. None of the single females responded aggressively to the other party's norm violation, while *all* of the single men did. Apparently, when women are by themselves, under a minimum of social control by fellow subjects or the experimenter, they tend to rely only on their own internal standards of appropriate behavior, leading to little or no aggression. In the group condition, males behaved more aggressively than females. More important, a highly significant interaction effect indicated that females, stimulated by their fellow group members, reacted with a greater intensity of aggression to the norm violation of the programmed opponent in the light (high social control) than in the dark (low social control) condition. Men, on the other hand, did not differ in their aggression in either condition.

Thus, females seem to conform more to an emergent group norm to punish the other for her norm violation, presumably in an effort to maintain friendly and smooth interpersonal relations within the group even to the detriment of the other party (Turner & Killian, 1972; Eagly, 1978). They might have felt relieved to express their aggression when they saw that other group members were doing the same thing, so legitimizing their own aggressiveness.

Recent studies (Goldenbeld, 1992), provide further evidence in support of this "modeling" hypothesis (Bandura, 1983). In a first experiment, females displayed little or no aggression when encouraged by a fellow member (actually a confederate of the experimenter) to abstain from aggression. For females, the accountability to the *external* social environment, that is, the experimenter, had no additional effect on their aggression. The aggression of males was also strongly inhibited by the nonaggressive model but not as much as females. In general, the model had a massive impact on the aggressive or nonaggressive behavior of both males and females. Interestingly, the subjects did not seem to be aware of this massive influence, or at least they did not want to report it in our questionnaire.

In a second experiment, females, but not males, were influenced by the normative statements of a model in the dyad that legitimated aggressive retaliation prior to the actual norm violation of the opponent. It should be noted that both males and females were equally affected by aggressive role models. Presumably, males do not like to be told directly what to do by a fellow male subject but they are as much influenced as females by less obtrusive manipulation, such as aggressive modeling (Bandura, 1983).

Sex differences in aggression were studied in an individual and a group setting in a third experiment (Goldenbeld & Rabbie, 1991). Consistent with the findings of Rabbie, Lodewijkx, and Broese (1985), we found single females expressed less physical aggression than single males, while in the group setting, females reacted as aggressively as males.

An earlier review, based mainly on laboratory studies, concluded that females did not differ from males in physical and indirect forms of aggression (Frodi, Macaulay, & Thome, 1977). A more recent review of Eagly and Steffen (1986), and our own research, indicate that individual males are more physically aggressive than individual females.

With respect to indirect aggression, there is recent evidence that females use more relational forms of aggression than males. In an important field study of 11- to 12-year-old school children, Lagerspetz, Björqvist, and Peltonen (1988) questioned boys and girls about what they would do when they felt angry about another boy and girl in the class. Consistent with their hypothesis, they found that while boys preferred more direct forms of aggression, girls preferred more indirect forms, that is,

> circumventory behavior that exploits social relations among peers in order to harm the person at whom the aggression is directed (Lagerspetz, Björkqvist, & Peltonen, 1988, p. 409).

It is quite likely that these differences in findings between Frodi, Macaulay, and Thome (1977) and the more recent findings we have reported can be attributed more to differences in methods and research settings used to study direct and indirect forms of aggression than to any actual sex differences in aggressive behavior. These divergent findings argue strongly for a multimethod approach in laboratory and field studies that examines conflict and aggression in research settings which are either congruent or incongruent with the relational and instrumental orientations of males and females acting as single individuals or as interacting group members.

## IV. Conclusion

Our research suggests that in anonymous, impersonal game situations, individual males show more physical aggression than individual females. However, at a group level of analysis it appears that the aggressive behavior of females can be enhanced or inhibited by the specific internal normative environments of the groups. Males seem to be less affected in their aggressive behavior than females whether they are acting as individuals or interacting with other group members. These findings lend support to the notions of Deaux and Major (1987) that in order to explain sex differences in type and degree of aggression, we should not only take socialization processes and gender roles into account but also realize that gender-related behaviors are highly flexible and strongly affected by more immediate situational influences.

## Acknowledgments

The research was supported by the Netherlands Organization for the Advancement of Research (NWO). The authors wish to thank Ronald L. Cohen, Bennington College, Bennington, Vermont, for his helpful comments regarding the language and logic of this paper.

## References

Ajzen, I., & Madden, T. J. (1986). Prediction of goal directed behavior: attitudes, intentions and perceived behavioral control. *Journal of Experimental Social Psychology, 22,* 453–474.

Axelrod, R. (1984). *The Evolution of Cooperation.* New York: Basic Books, Inc.

Bakan, D. (1966). *The Duality of Human Existence.* Chicago: Rand McNally.

Bandura, A. (1983). Psychological mechanisms of aggression. *In* R. G. Geen & E. I. Donnerstein (Eds.), *Aggression. Theoretical and Empirical Reviews. Vol. 1.* New York: Academic Press.

Baron, R. A. (1977). *Human Aggression.* New York: Plenum.

Baron, R. A., & Eggleston, R. J. (1972). Performance on the "aggression machine": motivation to help or harm? *Psychonomic Science, 26,* 321–322.

Brown, R. (1986). *Social Psychology.* (2nd edition). New York: Free Press.

Buss, A. H. (1963). Physical aggression in relation to different frustrations. *Journal of Abnormal and Social Psychology, 67,* 1–7.

Carson, R. C. (1969). *Interacting Concepts of Personality.* Chicago: Aldine.

Colman, A. (1982). *Game Theory and Experimental Games. The Study of Strategic Interaction.* Oxford: Pergamon Press.

Deaux, K., & Major, B. (1987). Putting gender into context: An interactive model of gender-related behavior. *Psychological Review, 94,* 369–389.

Deutsch, M. (1982). Interdependence and psychological orientation. *In* V. J. Derlega & J. Grzelak (Eds.), *Cooperating and Helping Behavior.* New York: Academic Press.

Eagly, A. H. (1978). Sex differences in influenceability. *Psychological Bulletin, 85,* 86–116.

Eagly, A. H. (1987). *Sex Differences in Social Behavior: A Social-Role Interpretation.* Hillsdale, New Jersey: Erlbaum.

Eagly, A. H., & Steffen, V. J. (1986). Gender and aggressive behavior: A meta-analytic review of the social psychology literature. *Psychological Bulletin, 100,* 309–330.

Frodi, A., Macaulay, J., & Thome, P. R. (1977). Are women always less aggressive than men? A review of the experimental literature. *Psychological Bulletin, 84,* 634–660.

Goldenbeld, Ch. (1992). Aggression after provocation. (In Dutch). Ph.d. dissertation. University of Utrecht. ISOR.

Goldenbeld, Ch., Rabbie, J. M. (1991). *Effects of modelling and norm setting on aggressive behavior of males and females.* Paper presented at the 6th European Conference of the International Society for Research on Aggression (ISRA), Jerusalem, Israël, 23–28 June, 1991.

Kelly, H. H., & Thibaut, J. W. (1978). *Interpersonal Relations: A Theory of Interdependence.* New York: Wiley, Inter-Science.

Kelly, H. H., Shure, G. H., Deutsch, M., Faucheux, C., Lanzetta, J. T., Moscovici, S., Nottin, Jr., J. M., Rabbie, J. M., & Thibaut, J. W. (1970). A comparative experimental study of negotiation behavior. *Journal of Personality and Social Psychology, 16,* 411–438.

Lacy, W. B. (1978). Assumptions of human nature, and initial expectations and behaviors as mediators of sex-effects in Prisoner's Dilemma Research. *Journal of Conflict Resolution, 22(1),* 269–281.

Lagerspetz, K. M. J., Björkqvist, K. & Peltonen, (1988). Is indirect aggression typical of females? Gender differences in aggressiveness in 11-12 year-old children. *Aggressive Behavior, 14,* 403–414.

Lewin, K. (1936). *Principles of Topological Psychology.* New York: McGraw-Hill.

Lodewijkx, H. F. M. (1985). *Sex differences in instrumental and relational cooperation and competition in relational and instrumental research settings.* (In Dutch). Unpublished manuscript, University of Utrecht.

Lodewijkx, H. F. M. (1989). *Aggression between individuals and groups.* (In Dutch). Dissertation, University of Utrecht, Delft: Eburon.

Osgood, C. E., May, W. H., & Miron, M. S. (1965). *Cross-cultural universals of affective meaning.* Urbana, Illinois: University of Illinois Press.

Pruitt, D. G., & Kimmel, M. J. (1977). Twenty years of experimental gaming: critique, synthesis, and suggestions for the future. *Annual Review of Psychology, 28,* 363–392.

Rabbie, J. M. (1987). Armed conflicts: towards a behavioral interaction model. *In* J. von Wright, K. Helkama, & A. M. Pirtilla-Backman (Eds.), *European Psychologists for Peace.* Proceedings of the Congress in Helsinki, 1986.

Rabbie, J. M. (1989). Group processes as stimulants of aggression. *In* J. Groebel and R. A. Hinde (Eds.), *Aggression and War. Their Biological and Social Bases.* Cambridge: Cambridge University Press.

Rabbie, J. M. (1991a). Instrumental intra-group cooperation. *In* R. A. Hinds and J. Groebel (Eds.), *Cooperation and Prosocial Behaviour.* Cambridge: Cambridge University Press.

Rabbie, J. M. (1991b). A Behavioral Interaction Model: A theoretical frame work for studying terrorism. *Terrorism and Political Violence, 3(4),* 133–162.

Rabbie, J. M. (1992). Effects of intra-group cooperation and intergroup competition on ingroup-outgroup differentiation. *In* A. Harcourt and F. de Waal (Eds.), *Coalitions and Alliances in Humans and Other Animals.* Oxford: Oxford University Press.

Rabbie, J. M. (In press). A Behavioral Interaction Model: Towards an integrative framework for studying intra- and intergroup behavior. *In* K. S. Larsen (Ed.), *Peace Research* (tentative title). Beverly Hills, California: Sage.

Rabbie, J. M., & Horwitz, M. (1982). Conflict and aggression among individuals and groups. *In* Hiebsch, H., Brandstätter, H., & Kelly, H. H. (Eds.), *Social Psychology.* Amsterdam: North-Holland Publishing Company.

Rabbie, J. M., & Lodewijkx, H. F. M. (1987). Individual and group aggression. *Current Research on Peace and Violence, 10,* 91–101.

Rabbie, J. M., & Lodewijkx, H. F. M. (1991a). Aggressive reactions to social injustice by individuals and groups: Towards a Behavioral Interactive Model. *In* R. Vermunt & H. Steensma (Eds.), *Social Justice in Human Relations, Vol. 1.* New York: Plenum.

Rabbie, J. M., and Lodewijkx, H. F. M. (1991b). *Self-centered and group-centered behavior of males and females in symmetric and asymmetric relationships.* Paper presented to the 3rd International Conference on social value orientations in interpersonal and intergroup relations, 8–12 September, University of Leuven, Belgium.

Rabbie, J. M., Visser, L., & van Oostrum, J. (1982). Conflict behavior of individuals, dyads and triads in mixed motive games. *In* H. Brandstätter, J. H. Davis, and G. Stocker-Kreichgauer (Eds.), *Group Decision-Making.* London: Academic Press.

Rabbie, J. M., Lodewijkx, H., & Broeze, M. (1985). *Deindividuation and emergent norms in individual and group aggression.* Paper presented to the European conference "The Social Psychology of Social Problems," Poland, University of Warsaw, 2–6 October.

Rabbie, J. M., Schot, J. C., & Visser, L. (1989). Social identity theory: a conceptual and empirical critique from the perspective of a Behavioral Interaction Model. *European Journal of Social Psychology, 19,* 171–202.

Spence, J. T., & Helmreich, R. L. (1978). *Masculinity and Femininity.* Austin: University of Texas Press.

Tajfel, H., & Turner, J. C. (1986). The social identity theory of intergroup behavior. *In* S. Worchel and W. G. Austin (Eds.), *Psychology of Intergroup relations.* Chicago: Nelson-Hall.

Turner, R. H., & Killian, L. M. (1972). *Collective Behavior* (2nd edition). Englewood Cliffs, New Jersey: Prentice-Hall.

Waal, F. de. (1989). *Peacemaking Among Primates.* Cambridge, Massachusetts: Harvard University Press.

White, J. W. (1983). Sex and gender issues in aggression research. *In* R. G. Geen and E. I. Donnerstein (Eds.), *Aggression, Theoretical and Empirical Reviews. Vol. II.* New York: Academic Press.

Williams, J. E., & Best, D. L. (1982). *Measuring Sex Stereotypes: A Thirty Nation Study.* Beverly Hills, California: Sage.

Wilson, W. (1971). Reciprocation and other techniques for inducing cooperation in the Prisoner's Dilemma Game. *The Journal of Conflict Resolution, 15,* 167–195.

21

# The Other Sex: How Are Women Different? Gender, Dominance, and Intimate Relations in Social Interaction

Bodil Lindfors

I. THE INVISIBLE SEX
II. THE PASSIVE SEX
III. THREE STUDIES ON SOCIAL INTERACTION
A. Study 1
B. Study 2
C. Study 3
IV. DOMINANCE AS AN INTERVENING VARIABLE IN SEX-TYPED BEHAVIOR
V. THE NONVERBAL RESIDUAL
VI. SOCIAL CONTEXT: THE INHERENT LOGIC OF THE RELATIONSHIP
VII. CONCLUSIONS: HOW ARE WOMEN DIFFERENT?
REFERENCES

The understanding of aggression as part of the continuum of communicative behavior has too frequently been limited to the extreme end of the scale: in fact, much more frequent in humans than actual physical violence are verbal and nonverbal forms of aggression. Gender, dominance, and social context have all been shown to be important determinants of interaction. After a brief review of some recurring problems in research on sex differences, three experimental studies are summarized here. As existing models are found to be insufficient to explain the results of these studies, dominance and relational intimacy are suggested as intervening variables in explaining sex-typed behavior.

# I. The Invisible Sex

Traditionally, men have been preferred as subjects in social experimental research, sometimes as a matter of course, sometimes with the rationale that women, due to their hormonal cyclicity and resulting emotional lability, might turn out to be less reliable subjects (Boyatzis, 1977). The results are then blithely extrapolated to encompass humanity in general, thus revealing the underlying conception of man as the norm and woman, at most, as an aberration. In an otherwise encyclopedic article on nonverbal communication in human social interaction, Argyle fails to mention gender as a source of possible difference, except for the statement that "he will behave differently to males and females" (Argyle, 1972, p. 263). Sex, when considered, typically appears as a control variable which is rarely mentioned in the title or key words of the study (cf. Baird, 1976). An even worse practice is found in studies where groups of females were simply dropped from the analysis when they achieved "unsuitable" pretest scores (Festinger, Pepitone, & Newcomb, 1952; Berkowitz, 1956). While such a practice would probably not be used today, and the invisibility of women is slowly changing as a result of criticism from the feminist movement, the basic conception of woman as the Other, the "second sex" (de Beauvoir, 1957) is still prevalent in the scientific community.

# II. The Passive Sex

What, then, is the emerging picture of sex differences in social research? From the early studies in the 1950s (e.g., Strodtbeck & Mann, 1956) to quite recent ones, we find that women talk less than men (Baird, 1976; Frances, 1979; Lockheed & Hall, 1976); interrupt less, especially in cross-sex interaction (Eakins & Eakins, 1978; Zimmerman & West, 1975); make less task-oriented and more socioemotional responses (Anderson & Blanchard, 1982; Aries, 1982); express more agreement and make more back-channel or supportive responses (Baird, 1976; Natale, Entin, & Jaffe, 1979); show more tension and less aggression (Piliavin & Martin, 1978); and that even dominant women will defer to men in group task performance (Megargee, 1969; Klein & Willerman, 1979).

The picture is not as uncomplicated as it may seem at a quick scanning of the literature, however. A perceptual bias is created by the fact that authors often fail to report negative results as important contributions to the bulk of empirical evidence, and that even when reported, negative results are seldom noted among the main findings. Studies which show sex differences are frequently cited in literature, while those in which no differences are found are more easily passed by. For example, studies showing women's greater self-disclosure will be more readily quoted than the almost equal number of studies showing no sex differences (cf. Baird, 1976; Cozby, 1973).

The "male activity–female passivity" dichotomy has a certain satisfying simplicity to it, which may account for its popularity despite research evidence to the contrary; where sex differences are found, they are mostly differences in *type* of activity, such as goal-seeking behavior or forms of aggression (cf. Anderson & Blanchard, 1982; Frodi, Macaulay, & Thome, 1977; Lagerspetz, Björkqvist, & Peltonen, 1988). The persistent notion that men are more active than women in social interaction cannot be explained away as mere perceptual bias, however. Rather than asking which sex is more active, the question should be: in which circumstances, on what measures, will men be found to be more active than women? women more active then men? which men? and which women?

While conducting research on alcohol and social interaction, I often found myself wondering whether our subjects belonged to a different population than those depicted in (mainly American) contemporary research reports. From the literature on alcohol, I had been led to expect that women who have or believe they have consumed alcohol would be prone to react with lowered self-esteem, increased anxiety, and less self-disclosure, while men would typically show the opposite pattern of reaction (cf. Wilson, 1988). Yet our female subjects either did not differ from men (Lindfors & Lindman, 1987) or were more active, talkative, and dominant, less tense, and more self-disclosing than men (Lindfors *et al.*, 1987). One simple way of explaining the discrepancy would be the passage of time; one might expect women to behave differently in the 1980s than they did in the 1960s or even the 1970s. Another explanation would be differences between Finnish and American society; Finns have been considered more reticent than Americans, but sex differences may nevertheless be less pronounced in the Finnish population. However, thinking in terms of populations is probably less fruitful than trying to define the circumstances in which men and women will behave according to the accepted sex stereotype, and, conversely, the circumstances in which their behavior will deviate from the expected.

To that effect, I propose to summarize three of our studies on social interaction. While only one of these studies focuses directly on sex differences, they all contribute some material to the ensuing discussion.

## III. Three Studies on Social Interaction

### A. STUDY 1

The effects of alcohol and preexisting intimacy on verbal and nonverbal interaction were studied in cross-sex dyads. Twenty-four married or cohabiting couples took part in two experimental discussions: in one discussion they were together as a couple; in the other discussions they were in dyads with opposite-sex strangers. Alcohol was served at one of the sessions in a counterbalanced design.

Alcohol was found to increase social activity and dominance. Self-disclosure also increased when alcohol was served, particularly between couples. However, strangers were otherwise more active than couples, talked more, interrupted more, and felt themselves to be less anxious. Women were more active and dominant, less tense, more intimate, and more self-disclosing in their interactions than men. They also laughed more. No other verbal or nonverbal sex differences were found (Lindfors *et al.*, 1987).

## B. STUDY 2

Groups of men and women were selected from the extremes of the high- to low-dominant scale, on the basis of the Cesarec-Marke Personality Scheme and peer ratings, from a population of 531 students. Twelve single-sex groups of three subjects were observed in discussion. One person was then moved from each group to create new groups of one man and two women or one woman and two men. All groups were homogeneous with respect to dominance.

Dominance was more important than sex in determining behavior. High-dominant subjects were rated as more active and dominant, more self-disclosing, engaged and receptive, less tense, and less serious than low-dominant subjects. They also felt less anxious than low-dominant subjects. High-dominant subjects changed posture more and gesticulated more, talked more, interrupted, and were interrupted more. They expressed more agreement but also more disagreement, more conclusive statements, and more task-related questions and answers than low-dominant subjects. High-dominant groups were found to be more democratic, more friendly and more engaged and less tense and less serious than low-dominant groups.

Sex differences were found mainly in nonverbal behavior. Women were rated as less serious; they laughed more, nodded more, and changed their postures less than men. Women also looked more at others, were looked at more, and made more back-channel responses (Table 1). No gender differences as a result of the change from same-sex to mixed-sex group were found, except that men smiled more and were looked at more in mixed-sex groups (Lindfors *et al.*, 1989).

## C. STUDY 3

Groups of high- and low-dominant women were selected among 229 female students by the Cesarec-Marke Personality Scheme and peer ratings, as above. Eighteen dyads of either high-dominant, low-dominant, or mixed (high/low) dominance composition were observed before and after the consumption of alcohol or a control beverage.

Dominant subjects were rated as more active and dominant, more aggressive and less anxious, and more self-disclosing and engaged than nondominant sub-

**Table 1**
**Sex Differences in Small Group Interaction**

| | Females | | Males | | | |
|---|---|---|---|---|---|---|
| | Mean | SD | Mean | SD | F(1,32) | *p* |
| Laughs | 17.39 | 9.75 | 6.67 | 5.54 | 15.52 | < .001 |
| Nods | 28.89 | 30.84 | 8.72 | 11.38 | 6.49 | < .05 |
| Changes posture | 15.67 | 10.90 | 23.06 | 11.18 | 5.77 | < .05 |
| Looks at other | 206.33 | 97.46 | 107.72 | 64.19 | 13.01 | < .01 |
| Looked at by other | 306.56 | 220.33 | 217.67 | 141.72 | 7.38 | < .05 |
| Serious | 4.60 | 1.10 | 5.83 | 0.69 | 29.94 | < .001 |
| Back-channel responses | 127.67 | 20.35 | 17.25 | 11.86 | 4.30 | < .05 |

jects. They talked more, interrupted more, gesticulated more, and their visual dominance ratio (looking while talking/looking while listening) was higher than that of nondominant subjects. While alcohol did not change the behavior of nondominant subjects, dominant subjects began looking at their interlocutor more while speaking and averting their gaze less, becoming even more dominant, less anxious, and less restrained, but also less receptive and less supportive (Lindman *et al.*, 1990).

## IV. Dominance as an Intervening Variable in Sex-Typed Behavior

Henley (1975, 1977) has suggested that observed sex differences in nonverbal behavior may be traced to differences in power. While power and dominance in some instances may be interchangeable, it seems important to distinguish them from *status* (denoting one's relative position in a social hierarchy), as is not always done. To make a further distinction, dominance as a *personality* characteristic involves the desire or predisposition to influence others, while dominance as a *group* characteristic describes the individual's relative position or rank within a group (Ellyson & Dovidio, 1985).

The subjects in Study 2 and 3 above had been selected to represent the extreme ends of the high-low dominance scale both on personality measures and peer ratings of actual behavior. The results in terms of gender and dominance indicate that such differences as have been frequently regarded as male sex-typed behavior (amount of speech, speaking turns, interruptions, task-related behavior, expressive gestures, visual dominance, and observer ratings of aggressivity, dominance, engagement, and low anxiety) should be regarded as expressions of dominant behavior irrespective of gender.

A general weakness in the literature on gender differences in social interaction is that within-gender differences in power and dominance are rarely accounted for (Drass, 1986; Kollock, Blumstein, & Schwartz, 1985). There are, however, several exceptions to this methodological oversight:

1. In group discussions where males and females were similar in dominance and sex-role self-concept, women were more active verbally than men in mixed groups, but conformed to sex roles in terms of interaction style and nonverbal behavior (Aries, 1982).
2. Females have been found to be as consistent as males in using forms of control such as initial eye-gaze dominance, initial speaking order, and speaking time (Lamb, 1981).
3. The more "male-like" (e.g., aggressive, assertive, dominant) a person's gender identity, regardless of actual sex, the more conversational overlaps and interruptions he or she will make (Drass, 1986; Kollock, Blumstein, & Schwartz, 1985; Roger & Schumacher, 1983) and the more actively he or she will participate in verbal interaction (Kelly, Wildman, & Urey, 1982).

Dominance has been regarded as a central aspect of the male sex role (Argyle, 1969; Drass, 1986; Lockheed & Hall, 1976). Certainly, there are gender differences with respect to social influence or status. In most societies, men are more highly evaluated by both sexes, and more desirable traits will be attributed to men (Berger, Rosenholtz, & Zelditch, 1980; Lockheed & Hall, 1976; McKee & Sherrifs, 1957; Martin & Shanahan, 1983). However, there is some evidence that in high-IQ and highly educated populations, sex differences in dominance as a personal and group characteristic will tend to disappear (Aries, 1982; Gleser, Gottschalk, & Watkins, 1959; Terman & Miles, 1936). An interesting parallel can be drawn between Study 1 and the studies by Kennedy and Camden (1981, 1983b) showing that in natural work groups of highly educated, career-oriented men and women, women were actually more verbally active and interrupted more than men.

## V. The Nonverbal Residual

Sex roles may be changing faster on verbal than on nonverbal levels of behavior (Aries, 1982). Like Kennedy and Camden (1983a), we found that of the traditional sex-typed behavioral differences, those that remained were forms of nonverbal and paraverbal behavior. When dominance was controlled for, as in Studies 2 and 3, the only verbal category that differentiated between the sexes was back-channel or minimal response, a mainly supportive behavior somewhere in between the verbal and nonverbal (Duncan & Fiske, 1977). It does not seem to be related to dominant or nondominant behavior styles, as had previously been suggested

(Kollock, Blumstein, & Schwartz, 1985) but rather, like nods and smiles, to the general display of interest and support that is characteristic of women's social interaction (de Boer, 1987; Frances, 1979; Roger & Schumacher, 1983).

The suggestion of Frances (1979), that smiling and laughing may indicate the social insecurity of women, does not seem valid in the present context. It may be important, however, that nods and smiles are much more frequent between strangers than between intimates; being part of the social "safety net" of politeness, they can be discarded in close relationships. When intimacy was varied as part of the design, sex differences in nodding and smiling did not reach significance, although women still were found to laugh more than men (Study 1).

## VI. Social Context: The Inherent Logic of the Relationship

Paradoxically, social context is a relatively neglected area in social experimental research. Studies concerned with actual interaction typically observe unacquainted subjects in highly artificial experimental paradigms. By contrast, most social interactions take place between people who know each other well or even intimately, in situations that are more or less familiar, well defined, and goal directed (cf. Harré, Clarke, & De Carlo, 1985; Lindfors & Lindman, 1987).

One of the criticisms of studying people involved in intimate relationships is that people will have opportunity to create their own personal division of power, so that the observations "will not necessarily apply to more impersonal situations where people rely more on social position for guidance" (Drass, 1986, p. 294). Although the conclusion is probably correct, it would seem to motivate more research on intimate relationships, rather than the opposite.

There are, however, a number of studies that show the importance of social context in terms of personal relationships. Heiss (1962) found that the degree of male dominance decreased as the intimacy of the relationship increased. Among married couples, males and females were equally active, but males in mixed-gender dyads of strangers were found to break the silence twice as often as females (Shaw & Sadler, 1965). In friendship-groups of college students, women talked more than men (Askinas, 1971). Women were also more active than men in small natural workgroups, where people presumably knew each other well (Kennedy & Camden, 1981, 1983a,b). Even when observed in a waiting room situation with strangers, women were found to talk more than men, look more, and use more expressive gestures (Ickes & Barnes, 1977).

Men and women who are being observed in a laboratory setting in the company of strangers might easily revert to more stereotyped sex roles than they would assume in a more natural, social environment. While being in the laboratory with your spouse may provoke some anxiety, it does not seem to induce sex-typed behavior. Overall, we found men more socially inhibited than women, and this effect was mainly produced by reversed sex-role behavior in terms of activity in the couple dyads (Study 1). This result may reflect the situational demands of the experiment as well as the dominance relationships between the spouses. Men have been shown to self-disclose more than women to strangers or distant acquaintances, while women disclose more to intimates (Rosenfeld, 1979; Stokes, Fuehrer, & Childs, 1980). There are reasons to believe that the discrepancy in self-disclosure between spouses might have been more stressful to the men.

On the other hand, Bernstein (1981) argues the definitional importance of distinguishing between dominance *relationships*, involving two or more individuals, and dominance *ranks* assigned to an individual. The distinction also implies nontransitivity. Thus, women may be dominant in their intimate relationships if nowhere else; a woman ranking low in dominance may dominate over a man ranking high in dominance, depending on the inherent logic of the relationship. Conversely, high-dominant women may be submissive to men with lower dominance ratings (Klein & Willerman, 1979; Megargee, 1969).

## VII. Conclusions: How Are Women Different?

According to the "sex roles differentiation" model (Bales & Slater, 1955; Parsons & Bales, 1955), men and women are socialized into sex-typed behavior at an early age. Differences in observed activity levels would be attributed to differences in male and female aggressiveness which could either be innate or the result of early socialization. An alternative explanation would be provided (e.g., Hochschild, 1973; Lockheed & Hall, 1976) by situational sex-role norms.

Since the mid-seventies, the theoretical model most widely used is the "status characteristics/expectation states" model, in which gender is viewed as a diffuse status characteristic which entails expectations for normatively appropriate behavior. Males are thought to be more competent than females and will therefore be given more opportunities to engage in task-oriented activity (Berger, Cohen, & Zelditch, 1972; Martin & Shanahan, 1983).

While the status characteristics model has the advantage of greater flexibility than the sex-roles differentiation model, it still seems to predict that, other status characteristics being equal, men will have an advantage over women in most social situations—especially those pertaining to work. This assumption does not stand up well to empirical evidence. For example, after reviewing earlier research, Anderson and Blanchard (1982) conclude that there do not appear to be any major sex differences in the interaction profiles of men and women. As an explanation for the sex differences found in the studies presented above (Studies 1 and 3), the model is clearly insufficient.

Lockheed & Hall (1976) formulated three generalizations from previous research evidence on sex differences in mixed-sex discussion groups:

1. Men are more active than women; that is, the average man initiates more verbal acts than does the average woman.
2. Men are more influential than women.
3. Men initiate a higher proportion of their acts than women in task-oriented categories of behavior, while women initiate a higher proportion of their acts in social-emotional categories.

While these generalizations may be valid in many instances of social interaction, we need to qualify them as follows:

1. Men are not necessarily more verbally active than women; rather, verbal activity seems to be associated with dominance. Dominance, of course, has often been regarded as a typically male characteristic. However, in highly educated, occupationally high-status populations, differences in dominance will tend to disappear or even be reversed (Kennedy & Camden, 1981).
2. Social context, both in terms of relational intimacy and situational demands, is important in determining the degree of behavioral dominance displayed (cf. Klein & Willerman, 1979). The rule seems to be that social insecurity, for example, being observed in a laboratory group discussion in the company of strangers, will result in more sex-typed behavior than informal settings, familiarity, or intimacy between the interaction partners.
3. Apart from the sex-typed behavior that can be explained by dominance and situational variables, there are genuine differences between masculine and feminine conversational styles which are mainly found in nonverbal and paraverbal dimensions of behavior. These may be regarded as the remnants of gender-specific "cultures" acquired at early stages of social development and subsequently overlaid by adult behavior patterns (de Boer, 1987).

## References

Anderson, L. R, & Blanchard, P. N. (1982). Sex differences in task and socioemotional behavior. *Basic and Applied Social Psychology, 3,* 109–139.

Argyle, M. (1969). *Social Interaction.* London: Tavistock Publications.

Argyle, M. (1972). Nonverbal communication in human social interaction. *In* R. A. Hinde (Ed.), *Nonverbal Communication.* Cambridge: Cambridge University Press.

Aries, E. (1982). Verbal and nonverbal behavior in single-sex and mixed-sex groups: Are traditional roles changing? *Psychological Reports, 51,* 127–134.

Askinas, B. E. (1971). The impact of coeducational living on peer interaction. (Doctoral dissertation, Stanford University, 1971). *Dissertation Abstracts International, 32,* 1634-A.

Baird, J. E., Jr. (1976). Sex differences in group communication: A review of relevant research. *The Quarterly Journal of Speech, 62,* 179–192.

Bales, R. F., & Slater, P. (1955). Role differentiation in small decision making groups. *In* T. Parsons & R. F. Bales (Eds.), *Family, Socialization and Interaction process.* New York: Free Press.

Berger, J., Cohen, B. P., & Zelditch, M., Jr. (1972). Status characteristics and social interaction. *American Sociological Review, 37,* 241–255.

Berger, J., Rosenholtz, S. J., & Zelditch, M. (1980). Status organizing processes. *Annual Review of Sociology, 6,* 479–508.

Berkowitz, L. (1956). Personality and group position. *Sociometry, 19,* 210–222.

Bernstein, I. S. (1981). Dominance: The baby and the bathwater. *The Behavioral and Brain Sciences, 4,* 419–457.

Boyatzis, R. E. (1977). Alcohol and interpersonal aggression. *In* M. M. Gross (Ed.), *Alcohol Intoxication and Withdrawal. Vol. 3 B.* New York: Plenum.

Cozby, P. C. (1973). Self-disclosure: A literature review. *Psychological Bulletin, 79,* 73–91.

de Beauvoir, S. (1957). *The Second Sex.* New York: Alfred A. Knopf.

de Boer, M. (1987). Sex differences in language: Observations of dyadic conversations between members of the same sex. *In* D. Brouner & D. de Haan (Eds.), *Women's Language, Socialization and Self-Image.* Dordrecht, The Netherlands: Fon's Publications.

Drass, K. A. (1986). The effect of gender identity on conversation. *Social Psychology Quarterly, 49,* 294–301.

Duncan, S., & Fiske, D. W. (1977). *Face-to-Face Interaction: Research, Methods and Theory.* New York: Wiley.

Eakins, B. W., & Eakins, R. G. (1978). *Sex Differences in Human Communication.* Boston: Houghton Mifflin.

Ellyson, S. L., & Dovidio, J. F. (1985). Power, dominance and nonverbal behavior: Basic concepts and issues. *In* S. L. Ellyson & J. F. Dovidio (Eds.), *Power, Dominance and Nonverbal Behavior.* New York: Springer-Verlag.

Festinger, L., Pepitone, A., & Newcomb, T. (1952). Some consequences of deindividuation in groups. *Journal of Abnormal and Social Psychology, 47,* 382–389.

Frances, S. J. (1979). Sex differences in nonverbal behavior. *Sex Roles, 5,* 519–535.

Frodi, A., Macaulay, J., & Thome, P. R. (1977). Are women always less aggressive than men? *Psychological Bulletin, 84,* 634–660.

Gleser, G. C., Gottschalk, L. A., & Watkins, J. (1959). The relationship of sex and intelligence to choice of words: A normative study of verbal behavior. *Journal of Clinical Psychology, 15,* 182–191.

Harré, R., Clarke, D., & De Carlo, N. (1985). *Motives and Mechanisms: An Introduction to the Psychology of Action.* London: Methuen.

Heiss, J. S. (1962). Degree of intimacy and male–female interaction. *Sociometry, 25,* 197–208.

Henley, N. M. (1975). Power, sex, and nonverbal communication. *In* B. Thorne & N. Henley (Eds.), *Language and Sex: Difference and Dominance.* Rowley, Massachusetts: Newbury House.

Henley, N. M. (1977). *Body Politics: Power, Sex and Nonverbal Communication.* Englewood Cliffs, New Jersey: Prentice-Hall.

Hochschild, A. R. (1973). A review of sex role research. *American Journal of Sociology, 78,* 1011–1029.

Ickes, W., & Barnes, R. D. (1977). The role of sex in unstructured dyadic interactions. *Journal of Personality and Social Psychology, 35,* 315–330.

Kelly, J. A., Wildman, H. E., & Urey, J. R. (1982). Gender and sex-role differences in group decision-making social interaction. *Journal of Applied Social Psychology, 12,* 112–127.

Kennedy, C. W., & Camden, C. T. (1981). Gender differences in interruption behavior: A dominance perspective. *International Journal of Women's Studies, 4,* 135–142.

Kennedy, C. W., & Camden, C. (1983a). A new look at interruptions. *The Western Journal of Speech Communication, 47,* 45–58.

Kennedy, C. W., & Camden, C. (1983b). Interruptions and nonverbal gender differences. *Journal of Nonverbal Behavior, 8,* 91–108.

Klein, H. M., & Willerman, L. (1979). Psychological masculinity and femininity and typical and maximal dominance expression in women. *Journal of Personality and Social Psychology, 37,* 2059–2070.

Kollock, P., Blumstein, P., & Schwartz, P. (1985). Sex and power in interaction: Conversational privileges and duties. *American Sociological Review, 50,* 34–46.

Lagerspetz, K. M. J., Björkqvist, K., & Peltonen, T. (1988). Is indirect aggression typical of females? Gender differences in aggressiveness in 11- to 12-year-old children. *Aggressive Behavior, 14,* 403–414.

Lamb, T. A. (1981). Nonverbal and paraverbal control in dyads and triads: Sex or power differences? *Social Psychology Quarterly, 44,* 49–53.

Lindfors, B., & Lindman, R. (1987). Alcohol and previous acquaintance: Mood and social interactions in small groups. *Scandinavian Journal of Psychology, 28,* 211–219.

Lindfors, B., Lindman, R., Väänänen, S., & Österman, K. (1987). *Alcohol and intimacy: Qualitative aspects of interaction.* Paper presented at the Fourth European Conference of the International Society for Research on Aggression, Seville, Spain, April 20–24, 1987.

Lindfors, B., Lindman, R., Koivumäki, K., & af Schultén, M. (1989). *Sex and dominance: Mood and socioemotional behavior in small groups.* Paper presented at the Fifth European Conference of the International Society for Research on Aggression, Szombathely, Hungary, June 25–30, 1989.

Lindman, R., Lindfors, B., Möller, M., & Paajanen, S. (1990). *Alcohol and dyadic interactions of high dominant and low dominant women.* Paper presented at the Fifth European Conference on Personality, Rome, Italy, June 12–15.

Lockheed, M., & Hall, K. P. (1976). Conceptualizing sex as a status characteristic: Applications to leadership training strategies. *Journal of Social Issues, 32,* 111–124.

McKee, J. P., & Sherriffs, A. C. (1957). The differential evaluation of males and females. *Journal of Personality, 23,* 356–371.

Martin, P. Y., & Shanahan, K. A. (1983). Transcending the effects of sex composition in small groups. *Social Work with Groups, 6,* 19–32.

Megargee, E. I. (1969). Influence of sex-roles on the manifestation of leadership. *Journal of Applied Psychology, 53,* 377–382.

Natale, M., Entin, E., & Jaffe, J. (1979). Vocal interruptions in dyadic communication as a function of speech and social anxiety. *Journal of Personality and Social Psychology, 37,* 865–878.

Parsons, T., & Bales, R. F. (1955). *Family, Socialization and Interaction Process.* Glencoe, Illinois: Free Press.

Piliavin, J. A., & Martin, R. R. (1978). The effects of the sex composition of groups on style of social interaction. *Sex Roles, 4,* 281–296.

Roger, D. B., & Schumacher, A. (1983). Effects of individual differences on dyadic conversational strategies. *Journal of Personality and Social Psychology, 45,* 700–705.

Rosenfeld, L. B. (1979). Self-disclosure avoidance: why I am afraid to tell you who I am. *Communication Monographs, 46,* 63–74.

Shaw, M. E., & Sadler, D. W. (1965). Interaction patterns in heterosexual dyads varying in degrees of intimacy. *Journal of Social Psychology, 66,* 345–351.

Stokes, J., Fuehrer, A., & Childs, L. (1980). Gender differences in self-disclosure to various target persons. *Journal of Counseling Psychology, 27,* 192–198.

Strodtbeck, F. L., & Mann, R. (1956). Sex role differentiation in jury deliberations. *Sociometry, 19,* 3–11.

Terman, L. M., & Miles, C. (1936). *Sex and personality: Studies in masculinity and femininity*. New York: McGraw-Hill.

Wilson, G. T. (1988). Alcohol and anxiety. *Behavioral Research and Therapy, 26,* 369–381.

Zimmerman, D., & West, L. (1975). Sex-roles, interruptions and silences in conversations. *In* B. Thorne & N. Henley (Eds.), *Language and Sex: Difference and Dominance*. Rowley, Massachusetts: Newbury House.

22

# *Alcohol and Female Disinhibition*

Ralf Lindman

I. INTRODUCTION
II. ANXIETY
III. SEXUALITY
IV. AGGRESSION
V. GENERAL PERSPECTIVE
A. Physiological Models
B. Cognitive Models
REFERENCES

## I. Introduction

Alcohol has a perplexing variety of effects, in the words of Miller (1956), "making some bellicose, others lacrymose, some amorous, and others loquacious." The bewildering array of behaviors attributed to alcohol poses a formidable task indeed for anyone attempting to predict, from a single theoretical framework, the occurrence of any particular event. However, by the simple assumption that many apparently unrelated behaviors are *inhibited* before drinking, it becomes possible to "explain" them in terms of a single action principle, namely *dis*inhibition. What is often neglected is to then demonstrate that alcohol can increase the frequency or intensity of behaviors known to be normally suppressed by some controlling influence (Carpenter & Armenti, 1972), and that the effects are restricted to those behaviors and not just due to a general activation of all behaviors (Woods & Mansfield, 1983). The present chapter will focus on alcohol effects on behaviors commonly believed to be inhibited in sober women, notably on interpersonal behaviors and expressions of sexual and aggressive impulses.

## II. Anxiety

The notion that alcohol serves as an anxiolytic is firmly rooted in folk wisdom, and it has also constituted by far the most influential theoretical influence guiding psychological alcohol research. Social anxiety, particularly the fear of interpersonal evaluation, has been shown to elicit drinking under experimental conditions, and interpersonal anxiety and stressful social situations are among the most common determinants of alcohol abuse (Wilson, 1988). As many supposedly disinhibited behaviors are thought to be held back by anxiety in sober individuals, it is pertinent first to consider differences between men and women in the ways that alcohol may affect their social anxiety.

Gender-dependent differences in the effects of alcohol on social anxiety and related phenomena have been observed in several studies. Dose-dependent anxiolytic effects to a maximal limit of 1 g/kg were shown by Wilson, Abrams, and Lipscomb (1980) in male subjects who had been asked to favorably impress female students. A similar study by Sher and Walitzer (1986) also found a dose-dependent effect on heart rate. Using the balanced placebo design, Wilson and Abrams (1977) had earlier shown that male subjects who believed that they had consumed alcohol showed less anxiety as assessed by autonomic arousal and behavior observation than those who believed that they were sober, regardless of whether a low alcohol dose had been consumed or not. Similar expectancy effects have been reported for male subjects' self-disclosure during social interaction (Caudill, Wilson, & Abrams, 1987).

While the available evidence thus tends to support an anxiolytic effect in male social drinkers, an entirely different picture emerges from studies with female subjects. Women who had been led to believe that they were intoxicated showed more instead of less social anxiety in several independent studies (Polivy, Schueneman, & Carlson, 1976; Abrams & Wilson, 1979; Sutker *et al.*, 1982), also displaying less self-disclosure than sober peers, irrespective of whether they had drunk alcohol or not (Caudill, Wilson, & Abrams, 1987). The dose–response relationship between increasing blood alcohol levels (BAL) and anxiety reduction observed for men (Wilson, Abrams, & Lipscomb, 1980) could not be shown in female subjects (Wilson *et al.*, 1989). Consistent with these experimental data, surveys indicate that women expect less relaxation and tension reduction from a few drinks than do men (Rohsenow, 1983).

Gender differences can be interpreted in various ways, and drinking experience may be a factor. Levenson, Oyama, and Meek (1987) found that alcohol reduced physiological measures of stress equally in both men and women when the extent of their drinking experience was allowed for. Feelings of shame and guilt may be associated with drinking among women to a greater extent than they are among men. Intoxicated women, but not men, report lowered self-esteem (Konovsky & Wilsnack, 1982). Studies on nonverbal communication have shown avoidance of eye contact by intoxicated female students interacting with sober peers consistent with embarrassment or shame (Lindman, 1980). In a partial replication, gaze avoidance disappeared when the situation was made less embarrassing to the subjects by having them interact with intoxicated instead of sober peers (Lindman, 1983).

Women's responses to alcohol also depend on personality differences and situational factors. Dyadic interactions of female students who were classified as either assertive/dominant or timid/withdrawn by peer estimates and personality measures were observed before and after the consumption of alcohol or a placebo beverage by Lindman *et al.*, (1990). Significantly increased verbal and nonverbal activity was observed in the high-dominant women at mean BALs of 0.57 g/liter, while the interactions of the low-dominant subjects were not perceptibly changed. However, self-reports indicated that subjects of both categories *felt* significantly more sociable, talkative, and elated after drinking, and that the low-dominant women also *felt* less embarrassed, suggesting that alcohol-induced "disinhibition" may exist as a state of mind without necessarily being manifest in behavior. Whether or not disinhibited behaviors will actually be displayed may be determined by individual factors, such as personal goals acquired through social learning, or even by hormonal background as shown in aggressively predisposed men (Lindman, Järvinen, & Vidjeskog, 1987). The influences of these factors are currently being studied in female subjects.

The extent to which alcohol will increase self-disclosure has also been shown to depend on situational factors such as the personal relationship between interaction partners. Lindfors *et al.*, (1987) found significantly increased self-disclosure in intoxicated male and female subjects given a dose of 0.75 g/kg, an increase that was more pronounced when the subjects interacted with their spouse or cohabiting partner than when they interacted with a stranger of the opposite sex.

## III. Sexuality

A link between alcohol and sexuality was proposed by Abraham (1926) who was also among the first to consider gender differences. Assuming that libidinal energy was freed when repression was lifted by alcohol, he suggested that men might be more attracted to drinking than women because of the subjectively experienced sexual vitality associated with it, an effect he thought might be less attractive to women because of their culturally derived fear that drinking would detract from their femininity. Mechanistic and social learning concepts were thus combined in this early theory, but subsequent experimental research soon became dominated by direct-cause models. Until recently the importance of learned and situational factors was stressed mainly by anthropological and sociological theorists (e.g., MacAndrew & Edgerton, 1969). Examples of the direct-cause approach are the "chemical trigger" hypothesis (Rada, 1975) and the idea that alcohol anesthetizes higher neural control centers to "release" sexual impulses (Harger, 1959). Since ethanol is distributed throughout the brain, however, there is no obvious reason to assume that specific neural control centers should be especially susceptible to its actions (Woods & Mansfield, 1983). The existence of cultures where drinking is negatively or not at all related to sexual behaviors also poses a problem for direct-cause models, as do some of the gender differences in response to alcohol.

The development of penile and vaginal plethysmography resolved many of the methodological problems encountered in experimental research. Penile tumescence and genital vasoconstriction data now provide generally accepted measures which can be used alongside subjective estimates of sexual arousal (Abel & Blanchard, 1976; Farkas & Rosen, 1976; Geer, Morokoff, & Greenwood, 1974).

Experimental studies have generally found declines in physiological response to erotic stimuli in women as well as in men, at least at elevated blood alcohol levels, but subjective data present a more complicated picture. Farkas and Rosen (1976) found a slight increase in penile tumescence at a BAL of 0.25 g/liter but marked declines at higher levels when male university students were shown erotic films. In another study with male subjects, with doses ranging as high as 1.8 ml/kg, Rubin and Henson (1976) found a similar reduction in sexual arousal during erotic film viewing as BALs increased. Physiological data were, however, not well correlated with the subjects' self-reports about how alcohol usually affected their sexual behavior.

Reduced sexual excitement was found in female subjects as well when genital vasoconstriction during exposure to erotic films was measured (Wilson & Lawson, 1976a). Self-reports, however, indicated enhanced sexual arousal at higher levels of intoxication even when the physiological reactions showed the opposite. Why subjective sexual arousal was consistent with physiological measures in men but not in women is an intriguing question. Given that alcohol apparently affected physiological response to erotic films similarly in men and women, we may assume that cognitive rather than pharmacological factors were responsible for the gender difference.

The effects of alcohol on orgasmic-ejaculatory response have been studied. Malatesta *et al.* (1979) found that male social drinkers needed increasing time to ejaculate via masturbation as BALs increased over a range of 0.03–0.09 g/liter. Decreased sexual arousal, pleasure, and orgasmic intensity were also reported at increasing BALs, some subjects failing to reach orgasm altogether at the highest dose. For women in an analogous study (Malatesta *et al.*, 1982), similar depressant effects of alcohol were found. As intoxication increased, however, these women also reported correspondingly increased subjective sexual arousal and orgasmic pleasure, as did the female subjects observed by Wilson and Lawson (1976a).

Whether sexual response was affected more by pharmacological or cognitive factors was studied by systematically varying subjects' expectancies about alcohol dosage in experiments with men (Wilson & Lawson, 1976b) and women (Wilson & Lawson, 1978). Although penile tumescence was not induced in the male subjects who were exposed to erotic materials at low levels of intoxication, those who believed that they had drunk alcoholic beverages, regardless of whether or not the drinks they had consumed had actually contained alcohol, reported greater subjective arousal and showed significantly greater erectile response on direct physiological measures. When the subjects were women, however, the experiment (Wilson & Lawson, 1978) yielded somewhat different results. Expectancy manipulation did not affect physiological indices of sexual arousal, although actual alcohol did produce a decrease in genital vasoconstriction. Paradoxically, however, the more intoxicated the women said they felt (including many in the placebo condition who were among those reporting intoxication) the higher the intensity of the sexual arousal they said that they experienced.

Sexual pleasures associated with drinking thus appear to be determined by beliefs and expectancies, in women even more markedly so than in men. The cognitive factors are apparently strong enough to override the pharmacological actions of ethanol which at the physiological level are mainly depressant. From a clinical perspective, therefore, the consequence is that any reinforcing enhancement of sexual arousal experienced through drinking seems to be more psychologically than pharmacologically determined (Lang & Frank, 1990).

## IV. Aggression

It has been suggested that alcohol may facilitate aggression directly through pharmacological action, "energizing" or "triggering" aggressive behaviors through brain biochemistry (Mark & Ervin, 1970) or "releasing" innate or provoked aggressive impulses ordinarily under the control of higher brain centers by anesthetizing those centers (Chafetz & Demone, 1962). An alternative theoretical position favors a social learning interpretation of the drinking-aggression relation, arguing that cultural norms regarding the behaviors to be exhibited by inebriates are learned and may be specific to one's personal characteristics, such as gender and race, and vary with physical setting or social situation (Lang, 1983).

There is little experimental evidence to suggest increased physical aggression in women after drinking. In real life, however, the most likely social setting to elicit alcohol-related female aggression is the family. One study of family violence in the United States reported that a number of women with drinking problems were at least moderately violent toward their husbands when they were drinking (Frieze & Knoble, 1980). Since violence in these cases was directed against the husband only, and the husband tended to be more violent than the wife, Frieze and Schafer (1984) concluded that the violence displayed by the woman was not so much a result of her own drinking as a reaction to the alcohol-induced violence of the husband.

In a recent study (Lindman *et al.*, 1993), males arrested for spouse abuse were interviewed with their spouses and compared to control subjects with respect to biochemical and questionnaire data. At the time of arrest, the offenders' mean intoxication level was high (35.9 m*M*), but not significantly higher than that of nonviolent pub patrons, and they did not differ from controls with respect to serum testosterone, cortisol, or glucose. It is thus unlikely that blood alcohol level or acute hormonal changes were specifically associated with violence. However, the responses to the Straus Conflict Tactics Scale (Straus, 1979) indicated that offenders and their spouses engaged in verbal aggression nearly twice as often as control families (46% vs 26%) when attempting to resolve family conflicts, thus presumably providing some of the cues necessary to provoke physical aggression. At the time when the abuse incidents occurred, all men were intoxicated as were most of their wives: 74% as reported by the men, 63% as reported by the wives. The women who were most drunk tended to suffer more injuries than those who were less intoxicated (von der Pahlen & Öst, 1991).

## V. General Perspective

### A. PHYSIOLOGICAL MODELS

The notion that disinhibition would result from the removal of negative or inhibitory cortical influences has been criticized by Woods and Mansfield (1983) on the grounds that ethanol is rapidly distributed throughout all of the brain, which makes it unlikely that it would have preferential access to the cortex. These authors suggest the reticular activation system (RAS) might be more susceptible to depressant drugs due to the cumulative effects on many individual synapses. If ethanol were to selectively influence the RAS, cortical functions in general and behaviors related to arousal in particular might also be affected. Ethanol has been shown to have a biphasic effect on electroencephalographic arousal, increasing activation at lower doses and decreasing arousal at higher doses (Kalant, 1975; Murphree, 1973; Pohorecky, 1977). Ethanol also elicits an increase in blood level of cortisol (Noble, 1973), an arousal-inducing stress hormone. In physiological terms, many enhanced behaviors at low alcohol doses could thus be understood in terms of a nonspecific arousal increase which is reversed at higher dose levels.

### B. COGNITIVE MODELS

Steele and his colleagues (Steele & Josephs, 1988; Steele & Southwick, 1985) interpret many of alcohol's effects on social behaviors and emotions as stemming from a general impairment of perception and thought. They have outlined three types of socially significant alcohol effects: drunken excess (transforming social behaviors so that they become more extreme); drunken self-inflation (rendering the future rosy); and drunken relief (from stress, depression, and anxiety). All three are essentially interpreted as the results of cognitive impairment, in the sense that alcohol is thought to restrict the range of cues, internal as well as external, that we can perceive in a situation, and is also assumed to impair our ability to process and extract meaning from the cues and information we do perceive (Steele & Josephs, 1990).

Since social learning involves sex-role socialization, men and women may experience quite different types of inhibition conflict associated with drinking, and may consequently be "disinhibited" in different ways. Banaji and Steele (1989) have proposed that alcohol may disinhibit conflicts arising from self-evaluation. Extending their reasoning, one might speculate that gender-dependent differences in the ways that alcohol affects subjective sexual arousal may arise because of differences in inhibition conflict. Assuming that inhibition conflict is generally stronger in women than in men, for instance through norms acquired through social learning, the alcohol-induced disinhibition of self-evaluative conflict might result in greater changes in women than in men. More intense sexual pleasure could then be experienced by women after drinking, not so much because excitatory cues would become stronger (in fact they would probably become physiologically weaker), but because self-evaluation would be impaired and guilt feelings would be more difficult to access. Men, having fewer guilt feelings anyway, would experience correspondingly weaker self-evaluative conflict when sober, and alcohol-induced disinhibition might not generate enough cognitive impact to override the physiologically depressant actions of alcohol.

In the case of aggression, perceiving and thinking may be restricted so as to leave one still able to respond to salient, immediate cues, but less able to respond to peripheral cues and embedded meanings such that, when the salient cues elicit violence and the peripheral ones inhibit it, alcohol intoxication releases violence. By similar reasoning, exaggerated prosocial behavior may be induced by alcohol, not because alcohol would necessarily transform anyone, male or female, into a warm and helpful being, but because an intoxicated person of either sex may in effect be controlled exclusively by immediate cues that elicit helpfulness and generosity. Sexual risk taking and excessive tipping might serve as other examples of atypical behaviors where the inebriate is led by immediate cues to act in ways which may seem hard to comprehend by his or her sober self.

The cognitive impairment model would explain *how* alcohol might have certain effects, but does not explain *when* they will occur. Steele and Josephs (1990) propose that drunken excess would occur in situations that, *if a person were sober*, would involve a response provoked by strong, salient cues being inhibited by other strong cues that require further processing for comprehension. Lacking access to the contingencies of their actions, two persons may drift into escalatory aggression by mutually responding to immediate provocative cues, as elegantly demonstrated in Zeichner and Pihl's (1979) "eye-for-an-eye" experiment analogue. Unable to comprehend the provocative nature of their verbal aggression, intoxicated women may thus more or less unwittingly set themselves up for spouse abuse.

## References

Abel, G. G., & Blanchard, E. B. (1976). The measurement and generation of sexual arousal in male sexual deviates. *In* M. Hersen, R. Eisler, & P. M. Miller (Eds.), *Progress in Behavior Modification*. New York: Academic Press.

Abraham, K. (1926). The psychological relations between sexuality and alcoholism. *International Journal of Psychoanalysis, 7,* 2–10.

Abrams, D. B., & Wilson, G. T. (1979). Effects of alcohol on social anxiety in women: Cognitive versus physiological processes. *Journal of Abnormal Psychology, 88,* 161–163.

Banaji, M. R., & Steele, C. M. (1989). The social cognition of alcohol use. *Social Cognition, 7,* 137–151.

Carpenter, J. A., & Armenti, N. P. (1972). Some effects of ethanol on human sexual and aggressive behavior. *In* B. Kissin & H. Begleiter (Eds.), *The Biology of Alcoholism, Vol. 2: Physiology and Behavior*, pp. 509–543. New York: Plenum.

Caudill, B., Wilson, G. T., & Abrams, D. B. (1987). Alcohol and self-disclosure: Analyses of interpersonal behavior in male and female social drinkers. *Journal of Studies on Alcohol, 48,* 401–409.

Chafetz, M., & Demone, H. (1962). *Alcoholism and Society*. New York: Oxford University Press.

Farkas, G. M., & Rosen, R. C. (1976). Effect of alcohol on elicited male sexual response. *Journal of Studies on Alcohol, 37,* 265–272.

Frieze, I. H., & Schafer, P. C. (1984). Alcohol use and marital violence: Female and male differences in reactions to alcohol. *In* S. C. Wilsnack & L. J. Beckman (Eds.), *Alcohol Problems in Women*. New York: Guilford Press.

Frieze, I. H., & Knoble, J. (1980). *The effects on alcohol on marital violence*. Paper presented at the Annual Convention of the American Psychological Association, September 1–5, Montreal, Canada.

Geer, J., Morokoff, P., & Greenwood, P. (1974). Sexual arousal in women: The development of a measurement device for vaginal blood volume. *Archives of Sexual Behavior, 3,* 559–564.

Harger, R. (1959). The pharmacology and toxiology of alcohol. *In* AMA Committee on Medicolegal Problems (Ed.), *Chemical Tests for Intoxication: Manual*. Washington, D.C.: American Medical Association.

Kalant, H. (1975). Direct effects of ethanol on the nervous system. *Federation Proceedings, 34,* 1930–1941.

Konovsky, M., & Wilsnack, S. (1982). Social drinking and self-esteem in married couples. *Journal of Studies on Alcohol, 43,* 319–333.

Lang, A. R. (1983). Drinking and disinhibition: Contributions from psychological research. *In* R. Room & G. Collins (Eds.), *Alcohol and Disinhibition: The Nature and Meaning of the Link*. NIAAA Research Monograph 12, Washington, D.C., U.S. Government Printing Office, pp. 48–90.

Lang, A. R., & Frank, D. I. (1990). Drinking and sexual functioning—Acute doses of alcohol and sexual response. *Clinical Practice in Sexuality, 5,* 10–18.

Levenson, R. W., Oyama, O. M., & Meek, P. S. (1987). Greater reinforcement from alcohol for those at risk: Parental risk, personality risk and gender. *Journal of Abnormal Psychology, 96,* 242–253.

Lindfors, B. J., Lindman, R. E., Väänänen, S., & Österman, K. (1987). *Alcohol and intimacy: Qualitative aspects of interaction*. Paper presented at the IV European Conference of the International Society for Research on Aggression, April 20–24, Seville, Spain.

Lindman, R. E. (1980). Alcohol and eye contact. *Scandinavian Journal of Psychology, 21,* 201–205.

Lindman, R. E. (1983). Alcohol and the reduction of human fear. *In* L. Pohorecky & J. Brick (Eds.), *Stress and Alcohol Use*, pp. 249–260. New York: Elsevier-North Holland Biomedical.

Lindman, R. E., Järvinen, P., & Vidjeskog, J. (1987). Verbal interactions of aggressively and nonaggressively predisposed males in a drinking situation. *Aggressive Behavior, 13,* 187–196.

Lindman, R. E., Lindfors, B. J., Möller, M., & Paajanen, S. (1990). *Alcohol and dyadic interactions of high dominant and low dominant women.* Paper presented at the Fifth European Conference on Personality, June 12–15, Roma-Ariccio-Nemi, Italy.

Lindman, R. E., von der Pahlen, B., Öst, B., & Eriksson, C. J. P. (1993). Serum testosterone, cortisol, glucose, and ethanol in males arrested for family violence. *Aggressive Behavior* (in press).

MacAndrew, C., & Edgerton, R. (1969). *Drunken Comportment: A Social Explanation.* Chicago: Aldine.

Malatesta, V. J., Pollack, R. H., Crotty, T. D., & Peacock, L. J. (1982). Acute alcohol intoxication and female orgasmic response. *Journal of Sex Research, 18,* 1–7.

Malatesta, V. J., Pollack, R. H., Wilbanks, W. A., & Adams, H. E. (1979). Alcohol effects on the orgasmic-ejaculatory response in human males. *Journal of Sex Research, 15,* 101–107.

Mark, V., & Ervin, F. (1970). *Violence and the Brain.* New York: Harper & Row.

Miller, N. E. (1956). Effects of drugs on motivation: The value of using a variety of measures. *Annals of the New York Academy of Sciences, 65,* 318–333.

Murphree, H. B. (1973). Electroencephalographic and other evidence for mixed depressant and stimulant actions of alcoholic beverages. *Annals of the New York Academy of Science, 215,* 325–331.

Noble, E. P. (1973). Alcohol and adrenocortical function of animals and man. *In* P. G. Bourne & R. Fox (Eds.), *Alcoholism. Progress in Research and Treatment.* New York: Academic Press.

Pohorecky, L. A. (1977). Biphasic action of ethanol. *Biobehavioral Reviews, 1,* 231–240.

Polivy, J., Schueneman, A. L., & Carlson, K. (1976). Alcohol and tension reduction: Cognitive and physiological effects. *Journal of Abnormal Psychology, 85,* 595–600.

Rada, R. (1975). Alcohol and rape. *Medical Aspects of Human Sexuality, 9,* 48–65.

Rohsenow, D. J. (1983). Drinking habits and expectancies about alcohol's effect on self versus others. *Journal of Consulting and Clinical Psychology, 1,* 752–756.

Rubin, H., & Henson, D. (1976). Effects of alcohol on male sexual response. *Psychopharmacology, 47,* 123–134.

Sher, K. J., & Walitzer, K. S. (1986). Individual differences in the stress-response-dampening effect of alcohol: A dose-response study. *Journal of Abnormal Psychology, 5,* 159–167.

Steele, C. M., & Josephs, R. A. (1988). Drinking your troubles away II: An attention-allocation model of alcohol's effect on psychological stress. *Journal of Abnormal Psychology, 97,* 196–205.

Steele, C. M., & Josephs, R. A. (1990). Alcohol myopia. Its prized and dangerous effects. *American Psychologist, 45,* 921–933.

Steele, C. M., & Southwick, L. (1985). Alcohol and social behavior: 1. The psychology of drunken excess. *Journal of Personality and Social Psychology, 48,* 18–34.

Straus, M. A. (1979). Measuring intrafamily conflict and violence: The conflict tactics (CT) scales. *Journal of Marriage and the Family, 41,* 75–88.

Sutker, P. B., Allain, A. N., Brantley, P. M., & Randall, C. (1982). Acute alcohol intoxication, negative affect and autonomic arousal in women and men. *Addictive behavior, 7,* 17–25.

von der Pahlen, B., & Öst, B. (1991). Alkohol och familjevåld. En multimodal studie av hustrumisshandel. Unpublished Master's thesis, Department of Psychology, Åbo Akademi, Åbo, Finland.

Wilson, G. T. (1988). Alcohol use and abuse: A social learning analysis. *In* C. D. Chaudron & D. A. Wilkinson (Eds.), *Theories of Alcoholism.* Toronto: Addiction Research Foundation.

Wilson, G. T., & Abrams, D. B. (1977). Effects of alcohol on social anxiety and physiological arousal: Cognitive versus pharmacological processes. *Cognitive Therapy and Research, 1,* 195–210.

Wilson, G. T., & Lawson, D. M. (1976a). The effects of alcohol on sexual arousal in women. *Journal of Abnormal Psychology, 85,* 489–497.

Wilson, G. T., & Lawson, D. M. (1976b). Expectancies, alcohol and sexual arousal in male social drinkers. *Journal of Abnormal Psychology, 85,* 587–594.

Wilson, G. T., & Lawson, D. M. (1978). Expectations, alcohol and sexual arousal in women. *Journal of Abnormal Psychology, 87,* 358–367.

Wilson, G. T., Abrams, D. B., & Lipscomb, T. R. (1980). Effects of increasing levels of intoxication and drinking pattern on social anxiety. *Journal of Studies on Alcohol, 41,* 250–264.

Wilson, G. T., Brick, J., Adler, J., Cocco, K., & Breslin, C. (1989). Alcohol and anxiety reduction in female social drinkers. *Journal of Studies on Alcohol, 50,* 226–235.

Woods, S. C., & Mansfield, J. G. (1983). Ethanol and disinhibition: Physiological and behavioral links. *In* R. Room & G. Collins (Eds.), *Alcohol and Disinhibition: The Nature and Meaning of the Link.* NIAAA Research Monograph 12, Washington, D.C., U.S. Government Printing Office, pp. 4–23.

Zeichner, A., & Pihl, R. O. (1979). Effects of alcohol and behavior contingencies on human aggression. *Journal of Abnormal Psychology, 88,* 153–160.

23

# Battling Amazons: Responses to Female Fighters

Gordon W. Russell

I. INTRODUCTION
II. METHOD
A. Experiment 1
B. Experiment 2
III. RESULTS AND DISCUSSION
REFERENCES

## I. Introduction

Throughout history one can trace a sporadic interest in contests featuring female combatants. Harris (1966) briefly notes that Spartan women competed in wrestling matches during the fifth and fourth centuries B.C.; a practice that would better equip them to be mothers of Spartan soldiers. Boxing, however, was not open to women in any of the Greek states (p. 181).

Guttmann (1991) has ably documented early accounts of female fighters in England, France, and America. For example, working class women in nineteenth century France wrestled and boxed in circuses and music halls. London, too, was a center for female boxers in the eighteenth century. However, it should be left to journalist Max Viterbo to capture in words the spirit of the experience for those at ringside. His firsthand account of a 1903 visit to a Rue Montmartre, Paris venue describes the scene and response of the spectators:

> The room was wild with impatience. The stale smell of sweat and foul air assaulted your nostrils. In this overheated room the spectators were flushed. Smoke seized us by the throat and quarrels broke out . . . a lubricious gleam came to the eyes of old gentlemen when two furious women flung themselves at each other like modern bacchantes—hair flying, breasts bared, indecent, foaming at the mouth. Everyone screamed, applauded, stamped his feet (cited in Guttmann, 1991, p. 100).

Across the Atlantic, intermittent attempts have been made to interest paying audiences in the spectacle. Boxing matches have been promoted periodically in New York from the nineteenth century up to the present (Guttmann, 1991; The New York Times, 1989).

While there is a general literature assessing the effects on observers of viewing aggression against women, with few exceptions, the aggressors have been males (e.g., Donnerstein & Linz, 1986; Malamuth & Check, 1981). Thus, for example, Malamuth and Check (1981) had males attend full-length Hollywood movies in which the female leads are physically abused and raped by the protagonist (despite their ordeals, they fall in love with their attackers!). Subjects subsequently scored higher on Burt's (1980) Rape Myth Acceptance (RMA) and Acceptance of Interpersonal Violence (AIV) scales than men assigned to a nonviolent control film condition.

The effects of observing specifically interfemale aggression were examined in an investigation that used short film clips featuring ladies' professional wrestling and mud wrestling (Russell, Horn, & Huddle, 1988). Males exposed to both versions of wrestling action scored higher on a measure of aggression than subjects in a no-film control condition. Viewing the female combatants did not however, produce changes in either the RMA or AIV measures.

Several recent investigations make clear that the effects of viewing fight sequences are not uniform across subjects but rather, are mediated by individual differences, for example, social desirability (Russell & Pigat, 1991), and hypermasculinity (Russell, 1992). For example, males with strong macho tendencies showed increased aggression in response to viewing professional and amateur boxing matches (Russell, 1992). In contrast, subjects scoring low on a measure of hypermasculinity showed no increase in aggression. When hypermasculinity was alternatively operationalized as the subject's choice of an alcoholic rather than a nonalcoholic beverage at the start of the experiment, beer drinkers showed the predicted increase in aggression only to the amateur film; pop drinkers exhibited increased aggression only to the professional bout.[1] Inasmuch as macho men have a history of sexual aggression and hold calloused sex attitudes toward women (Mosher & Anderson, 1986), hypermasculine males would be predicted to be relatively unresponsive to scenes of interfemale aggression.

The response of males generally to scenes of female violence may be reduced for a somewhat different reason, that of its intensity exceeding tolerable limits. For example, Tannenbaum and Goranson (cited in Goranson, 1970) had men watch a particularly savage boxing match in the company of a confederate coviewer. In contrast to control subjects who listened to a taped ending that simply reviewed highlights of the match, others assigned to a *negative outcome* version learned that the defeated boxer sustained a cerebral hemorrhage and later died.

[1]Hypermasculinity scores and choice of beverage were related, $r(107) = .47$, $p < .0005$.

When provided with the opportunity to shock the confederate "learner," subjects in the negative outcome condition administered shocks of significantly *lower* intensity.

The present investigation sought to extend earlier findings within an individual differences paradigm that examined the role of a macho personality in influencing responses to viewing interfemale aggression. Specifically, males viewing women engaged in inappropriate sex-role behavior (cf. Paul & Baenninger, 1991), that is, fighting, the intensity of which exceeds acceptable limits, would be predicted to be less aggressive, more supportive of female victims generally, and less accepting of violence in their own relationships with women. Films were chosen to represent female aggression at two points along an intensity continuum. One film could be described as relatively light-hearted in comparison with the other that featured in graphic detail a bout in which the combatants inflicted substantial damage on one another.

## II. Method

### A. EXPERIMENT 1

#### *1. Subjects*

Subjects were male volunteers ($N$ = 97) recruited from introductory psychology classes at the University of Lethbridge, Alberta, Canada. Their mean age was 20.9 years (SD = 4.3). Subjects earned a 1% research participation bonus in the course.

#### *2. Measures*

The dependent measures were the aggression scale (short form) of the Nowlis (1965) Mood Adjective Check List (MACL) and Burt's (1980) AIV scale. The MACL provides a self-report measure of one's current affective state. Subjects are asked to rate the degree to which each of a set of adjectives describes their present mood state, for example, *aggression:* grouchy, rebellious, angry; *elation:* elated, overjoyed, pleased.

The AIV scale was developed as a means of assessing attitudes endorsing coercion as a legitimate tactic to gain sexual compliance in intimate relationships. Subjects are asked to indicate the extent of their agreement with each of six statements on accompanying seven-point scales anchored by "Strongly Agree" and "Strongly Disagree." A sample item is: "Sometimes the only way a man can get a cold woman turned on is to use force." Subjects were also asked to complete the assault scale of the Buss-Durkee hostility inventory (BD) (Buss & Durkee, 1957).

Subjects additionally read transcripts that summarized the details of two court cases, one in which the accused was found guilty of physically assaulting and injuring a young woman and the other in which a man was convicted of rape. Subjects were asked to recommend a financial award for damages to the plaintiff in the first trial and to set a prison term in the second case.[2]

#### *3. Films*

Subjects watched 14-minute clips from one of the following films:

*White Winter Heat* (1987): an exciting and fast-paced film that highlights top flight skiers on some of the world's most spectacular runs.
*Buxom Boxers* (1987): This clip featured the final bout on a female boxing card in which bikini-clad fighters wore oversized gloves and protective headgear. Midway through the second round they inexplicably lost their tops in the heat of the battle. Throughout the bout the ring announcer offered sexually suggestive remarks intended to amuse those at ringside.
*Battling Amazons* (1987): This film also featured attractive women in a three-round bout in which the fighters wore regulation-sized gloves, were not given headgear and were allowed to kick their opponent. The sexual theme was subdued, for example, their costumes remained intact. However, the aggression was brutal with one of the fighters being knocked unconscious by a kick to the head. Both cards were staged in nightclub settings for the benefit of enthusiastic male audiences.

#### *4. Procedure*

Two to four subjects and a male confederate were escorted into the lab and seated along a conference table facing a television monitor. Against the background of soft rock music, they were offered a 355-ml can of light (4% alcohol/volume) beer (Bud, Coors, or Labatt's) or a 355-ml can of three brands of caffeine-free pop (Orange Crush, Root Beer, or 7-Up). Using a partial blind procedure, subjects were at this point randomly assigned to one of the three film conditions. To further enhance the simulated nightclub atmosphere, the confederate expressed enthusiasm (i.e., "All right!") as the film began. All measures were completed at the conclusion of the film.

### B. EXPERIMENT 2

#### *1. Subjects*

The subjects ($N$ = 61) were female volunteers recruited under the same conditions as the males in Experiment 1. The mean age was 21.8 years (SD = 7.0). However, no attempt was made to simulate a nightclub atmosphere nor were they offered a beverage. Otherwise, the same procedures were followed.

[2]I wish to thank Dolf Zillmann for making the assault and rape transcripts available.

### 2. *Measures*

In addition to the MACL, subjects completed the Hostility toward Men scale (Check, Elias, & Barton, 1988) and the Faith in People scale (Rosenberg, 1957), alternatively interpreted as a measure of misanthropy. The women also read the same court transcripts and made recommendations for a financial award to the plaintiff and prison sentence for men convicted of physical assault and rape, respectively.

## III. Results and Discussion

The MACL aggression scores were analyzed in a 3 (films) × 2 (beverage) ANOVA using an unweighted means analysis. The main effects of beverage were significant with pop drinkers scoring higher than beer drinkers across levels of the film variable, $F(1,92) = 5.515$, $p = .021$. However, neither the film main effect, $F(2,92) = 1.99$, (ns), nor the interaction term, $F < 1$, was significant. Keeping in mind that no attempt was made to simulate a nightclub atmosphere, the results for females are superimposed on the results for males in Figure 1. A one-way analysis of variance of MACL aggression scores in Experiment 2 yielded significant main effects across the film conditions $F(2,60) = 14.24$, $p = .0001$. Protected $t$-tests were applied to these and all subsequent comparisons. Whereas levels of aggression did not differ between females assigned to the *Buxom Boxers* and *Battling Amazons* films, both films produced more aggression than did the control film.

As seen in Figure 1, the aggression of women increased dramatically in response to scenes of females fighting. By contrast, that of males remained unaffected by the content of *either* version of female mayhem. While a wealth of empirical studies have confirmed the general prediction that males exposed to intermale and male-to-female aggression exhibit increased aggression (e.g., Geen, 1983; Goranson, 1970; Donnerstein & Linz, 1986), the present findings suggest the possibility that males watching females locked in combat may represent a special circumstance in which viewer aggression is not increased.

One explanation may lie with the sexual and humorous themes that pervaded both fight clips. Baron (1976) has established that the induction of responses that are incompatible with aggressive behavior, for example, sexual arousal and humor, effectively reduces aggression. One can safely assume that the female subjects in Experiment 2 found the boxers to be neither sexually titillating nor were they amused. For the males, the sight of scantily clad women was sexually arousing (cf. Baron, 1974, 1976; Guttmann, 1991, pp. 258–265), while the guffaws that greeted the films (especially, *Buxom Boxers*) gave evidence that many males were highly amused. Thus, while viewer aggression in the general case typically increases in response to scenes of violence, the aggression of subjects experiencing *mild* sexual arousal and/or amusement is mitigated in such circumstances.

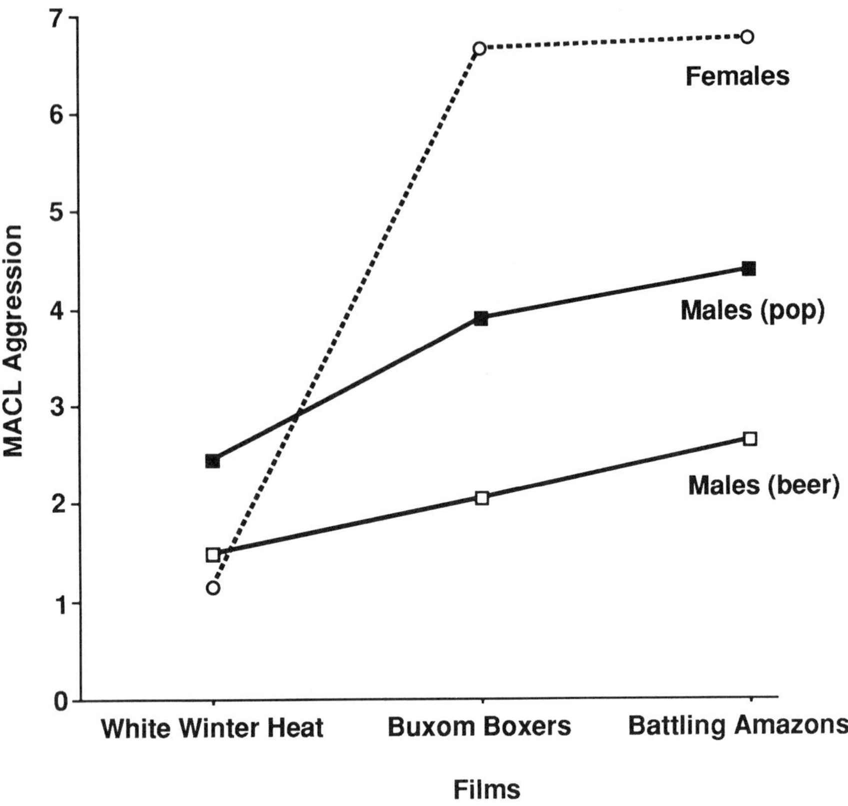


**Figure 1** MACL aggression as a function of films and beverage choice.

In the earlier Russell *et al.* (1988) experiment, males watched either a ladies' professional wrestling match or actresses grappling topless in a makeshift mud pit. Subjects judged both films to be equally degrading for the actresses and women in general. The resulting increase in viewer aggression was consistent with research showing that exposure to displeasing and disturbing erotica results in increased retaliatory aggression (Zillmann, Bryant, Comisky, & Medoff, 1981). The boxing films in the present experiments, if they were displeasing and disturbing, were likely so only for females and those choosing pop. The fact of a strong relationship between the choice of pop and religiosity (Russell, 1992) suggests that those males in particular may have been angered and acutely troubled by the sight of women violating the standards for female conduct promulgated in the teachings of their faith.[3]

[3] $r(107) = -.32, p < .005$.

The results of the individual differences analysis of aggression revealed that across levels of the film variable, pop drinkers were more aggressive than beer drinkers. The choice of beer over pop has recently been shown to be strongly related to hypermasculine tendencies (Russell, 1992), a personality syndrome in which alcohol plays a prominent role as does an attitude of sexual callousness toward females (Mosher & Anderson, 1986; Mosher & Sirkin, 1984). What is suggested is that macho beer drinkers trivialize and are relatively unresponsive to the plight of females generally, a suggestion borne out by their recommendations of lower awards for the female plaintiff in the assault scenario, $F(1,92) = 5.43$, $p = .022$. Rather, it was the pop drinkers who reacted aggressively to all three films—this, despite findings that beer drinkers scored substantially higher on the

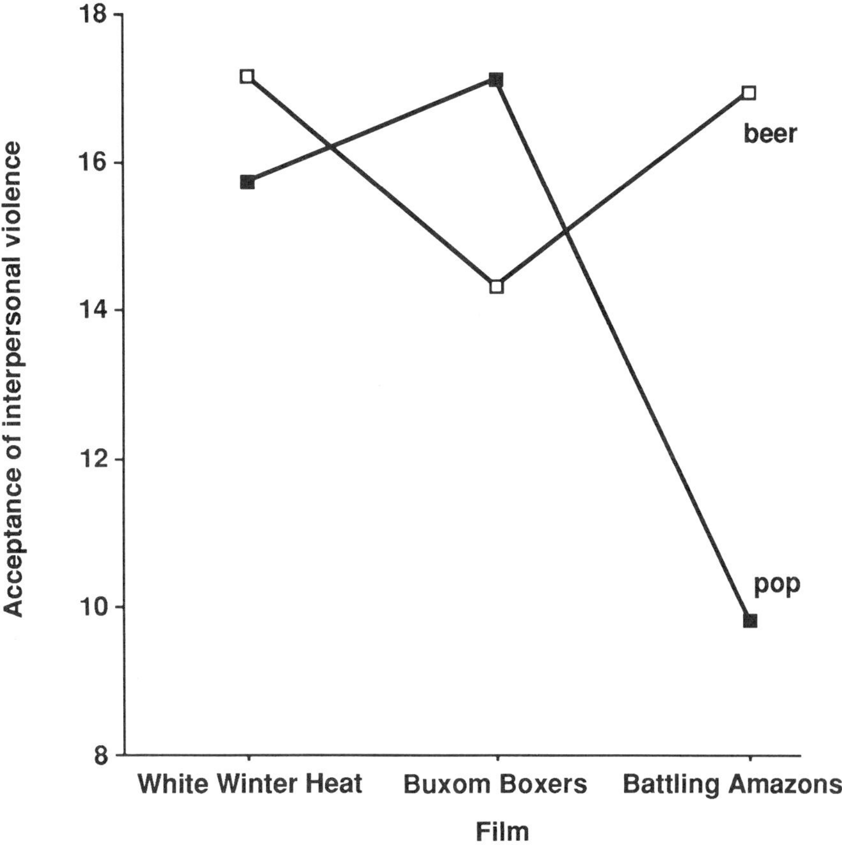


**Figure 2** AIV responses as a function of films and beverage choice.

**Table 1**
**MACL Responses to Type of Film and Beverage Choices**

| | Males | Females |
|---|---|---|
| Aggression | | |
| Films | ns[a] | Ski < Buxom & Amazon[b] |
| Beverage | pop > beer | |
| Elation | | |
| Films | Ski > Buxom & Amazon | Ski > Buxom & Amazon |
| Beverage | ns | |
| Surgency | | |
| Films | Ski > Buxom & Amazon | ns |
| Beverage | pop < beer | |
| Anxiety | | |
| Films | ns | ns |
| Beverage | pop > beer | |
| Social affection | | |
| Films | Ski & Buxom > Amazon | ns |
| Beverage | ns | |
| Skepticism | | |
| Films | Ski < Buxom & Amazon | ns |
| Beverage | ns | |

[a]ns, Nonsignificant.
[b]Ski, Buxom, and Amazon represent the films *White Winter Heat, Buxom Boxers,* and *Battling Amazons*, respectively.

BD trait measure of assaultiveness, both in the present, $F(1,92) = 19.82$, $p < .0001$, and in an earlier investigation (Russell, 1992).

The prediction that exposure to interfemale aggression would effect a basic change in men's attitudes received conditional support. The interaction presented in Figure 2 reveals a major attitudinal shift, one that is confined solely to men choosing pop while watching the *Battling Amazons* film, $F(2,91) = 4.75$, $p = .011$. Pop drinkers were far less accepting of violence in their relations with women than men in any of the remaining conditions after viewing the more brutal of the two fight clips. The MACL results presented in Table 1 provide a further hint of the factors that underlay the improvement in attitudes.

In addition to higher aggression, pop drinkers also experienced higher anxiety and less surgency than their beer-drinking coviewers. One might speculate that they were more troubled by their initiation to the spectacle of women brutalizing each other in violation of social and, possibly, religious standards for female behavior.

Female subjects did not differ across the film conditions in either the amounts they awarded the plaintiff or in their sentencing recommendations for the rapist, F's < 1. Whereas Hostility Toward Men scores did not differ across levels of the film variable, F < 1, Faith in People scores were somewhat lower for subjects viewing the boxing films, $F(2,58) = 3.122$, $p = .0516$. The effects of the fight clips on women can be summarized as instigating an angry, dispirited reaction, one possibly giving rise to a misanthropic outlook. Seemingly, men were not the target of their hostility; rather, their anger was more diffuse and directed toward those who would stage female boxing matches or, equally likely, toward the task requirements of the experiment itself.

## References


Baron, R. A. (1974). The aggression-inhibiting influence of heightened arousal. *Journal of Personality and Social Psychology, 30,* 318–322.

Baron, R. A. (1976). The reduction of human aggression: A field study of the influence of incompatible reactions. *Journal of Applied Social Psychology, 6,* 260–274.

Burt, M. R. (1980). Cultural myths and supports for rape. *Journal of Personality and Social Psychology, 38,* 217–230.

Buss, A. H., & Durkee, A. (1957). An inventory for assessing different kinds of hostility. *Journal of Consulting Psychology, 21,* 343–349.

Check, J. V. P., Elias, B., & Barton, S. A. (1988). Hostility toward men in female victims of male sexual aggression. *In* G. W. Russell (Ed.), *Violence in Intimate Relationships* (pp. 149–162). Great Neck, New York: PMA Publishing Corp.

Donnerstein, E., & Linz, D. (1986). Mass media sexual violence and male viewers. *American Behavioral Scientist, 29,* 601–618.

Geen, R. G. (1983). Aggression and television violence. *In* R. G. Geen & E. I. Donnerstein (Eds.), *Aggression: Theoretical and Empirical Reviews* (Vol. 2, pp. 103–125). New York: Academic Press.

Goranson, R. E. (1970). Media violence and aggressive behavior: A review of experimental research. *In* L. Berkowitz (Ed.), *Advances in Experimental Social Psychology* (Vol. 5, pp. 1–31). New York: Academic Press.

Guttmann, A. (1991). *Women's Sports: A History.* New York: Columbia University Press.

Harris, H. A. (1966). *Greek Athletes and Athletics.* Bloomington, Indiana: Indiana University Press.

Malamuth, N. M., & Check, J. V. P. (1981). The effects of mass media exposure on acceptance of violence against women: A field experiment. *Journal of Research in Personality, 15,* 436–446.

Mosher, D. L., & Anderson, R. D. (1986). Macho personality, sexual aggression, and reactions to guided imagery of realistic rape. *Journal of Research in Personality, 20,* 77–94.

Mosher, D. L., & Sirkin, M. (1984). Measuring a macho personality constellation. *Journal of Research in Personality, 18,* 150–163.

New York Times, The. (1989). "In This Corner Wearing Heels and a Tiara. . . ." Issue 11, 1:1, January 18.

Nowlis, V. (1965). Research with the Mood Adjective Check List. *In* S. S. Tompkins & C. Izard (Eds.), *Affect, Cognition, and Personality* (pp. 352–389). New York: Springer.

Paul, L., & Baenninger, M. (1991). Aggression by women: Mores, myths, & methods. *In* R. Baenninger (Ed.), *Targets of Violence and Aggression* (pp. 401–441). North Holland: Elsevier.

Rosenberg, M. (1957). *Occupation and Values.* Glencoe, Illinois: The Free Press.

Russell, G. W. (1992). Response of the macho male to viewing a combatant sport. (*Submitted*).

Russell, G. W., & Pigat, L. (1991). Effects of modelled censure/support of media violence and need for approval on aggression. *Current Psychology: Research and Reviews* **10,** 121–128.

Russell, G. W., Horn, V. E., & Huddle, M. J. (1988). Male responses to female aggression. *Social Behavior and Personality, 16,* 47–53.

Zillmann, D., Bryant, J., Comisky, P. W., & Medoff, N. J. (1981). Excitation and hedonic valence in the effect of erotica on motivated intermale aggression. *European Journal of Social Psychology, 11,* 233-252.

# V

# THE AMBIVALENCE OF MOTHERHOOD

24

# *The Great Mother*

Johannes Myyrä

I. INTRODUCTION
II. MOTHERHOOD AND FEMININITY
III. THE PRIMORDIAL UNITY
IV. THE GREAT MOTHER
A. The Good Mother
B. The Terrible Mother
V. THE SLAYING OF THE MOTHER
VI. THE SPLITTING OF THE MOTHER ARCHETYPE: CONTEMPORARY CULTURE AND THE PSYCHOANALYSIS OF PATRIARCHY
A. The Splitting and Repressing of the Archetype
B. Why Accept the Splitting of the Archetype?
C. The Splitting of the Archetype and Its Effects on Women: Clinical Example 1
D. The Splitting of the Archetype and Its Effects on Men: Clinical Example 2
VII. CONCLUDING COMMENTS: ACCEPTING AND REJECTING THE SPLITTING OF THE ARCHETYPE
REFERENCES

## I. Introduction

This chapter is based on psychoanalytical investigations of the Jungian archetype of the Great Mother. It sets in their historical contexts contemporary realizations of this archetype, and looks at the relationship between these and recent "feminist" analyses, particularly those of Julia Kristeva (1983) of the role of women in western culture. It suggests that the contemporary culture, which splits off the terrible aspects of the mother archetype, leads to patriarchal definitions of femininity, oppression of women's rights, and destruction of nature in our society. It attempts to demonstrate the applicability of this archetype to contemporary psychoanalysis and the whole culture by the use of clinical examples.

## II. Motherhood and Femininity

We develop our first communicative, semiotic signs in contact with the mother's body and our bodies will always contain memories and traces of her care. This first relationship is characterized by what is called the primary narcissism; it is this relationship, and not the mother herself, which is idealized in the image of mother. We formulate an imaginary concept of *maternality* to express the essence of *motherhood*. In the same way we confound *femininity* (an ideological concept defined mostly by men in order to subordinate females) and *womanliness* (the existential fact of being a woman).

Carl Jung (1938, 1954) states that our image of woman is more determined by our archetypal heritage than by our actual experiences with a real mother. According to Jung, these inherited archetypes are predispositions, common to all human beings, to certain mental images, and they influence, in this case, both our personal attitudes toward women and the definition of a woman's position in the whole culture. Jungian psychoanalysts have investigated the Mother archetype and its development through the history of humankind. Neumann (1954, 1955) has arranged the changes of the archetype according to a line of development, which seems to be valid both for the individual and the whole human race. The image of mother has, as Neumann shows, varied a great deal in different cultures and at different times.

In "Stabat Mater" Julia Kristeva points out that "we live in a civilization where the consecrated (religious or secular) representation of femininity is absorbed by motherhood" (Kristeva 1983, p. 295). Our patriarchal culture needs to place women in a position of otherness congruent with the imagined and enforced subordinating position of femininity. The only exclusively female attribute enabling a definition of the essence of femininity is motherhood. The contemporary picture of maternality is greatly influenced by the image of the Virgin Mary, Mother of God, who bears the attributes that western civilization favors in a mother.

## III. The Primordial Unity

In a Jungian analysis of life, the first "archetypal" situation is symbolized by the uroboros, the snake biting itself and so forming an eternal self-feeding circle. At the beginning of life the individual is merged with the divine without any knowledge of his own existence, a helpless newborn in Mother Nature's arms, totally dependent on her good or bad will.

Where do we come from? According to our experience, the only answer is: from a woman, from her womb. Originally, we cannot know the father's role in the begetting. This place of the origin is later symbolized by, for example, the ocean, the lake, the earth, the cave, the house, and the city with its walls; the greater thing containing, sheltering, and feeding the smaller. This is the female side of the uroboros archetype: the great and good mother.

The individual experiences himself only sporadically during the uroboric state. He is like an island in an ocean, always ready to sink back into its depths. This state is recalled as a hiding place in later life, giving shelter and pleasure when needed during difficult periods. The desire to merge with a containing and sheltering womb that makes us regress to this intrauterine state is seen in the use of drugs or alcohol or even mysticism to attain unconsciousness. It is our fight against this original regressive tendency, this *uroboric incest*, which makes us human beings. At this stage this "incest" has no sexual connotation, expressing only our longing for a life which is unconscious and free from responsibility. Psychotherapists record meeting this mental state in the common reverie with their silent patients.

## IV. The Great Mother

The individual becomes more and more separated from the symbiotic relationship with the uroboric world, where there are no differences between mother and father, himself, and his surroundings, and is born, separated from the common mother–child body, as an *individual* in a world full of pleasures, painful experiences, and fears. So the period dominated by the great mother begins. This archetype consists of two opposite figures: the loving and nurturing *Good Mother*, and the *Terrible Mother*. The Good Mother is the goddess of plentiful existence, the life-giving earth, and beautiful and nourishing nature full of wonders and grace. The Terrible Mother is the goddess of death, pestilence, hunger, and floods. She lives, for example, in the figures of the power of instincts and in the image of the beautiful seductive "femme fatale" who leads the individual into destruction and chaos.

### A. THE GOOD MOTHER

#### *1. The Mother Goddess and Her Divine Child*

This is the first image of the mother–child relationship. Mother is often symbolized by the sea, the lake, the river in which the child swims like a fish. The child is still completely dependent on his mother and there are no conflicts in their relationship. The giving and loving mother nurtures and shelters her child. This is the mother our culture admires and can be found in the figures of the Virgin Mary and of Lemminkäinen's mother in the Kalevala (1985), resuscitating her son.

As these examples imply, the child in this archetypal image must be killed as an offering, and his death followed by resurrection. Thus he is born to be killed and killed to be resuscitated. In this way he follows the life of the vegetation of the earth. He is not scared of death because even death is his mother. But the individual begins to be conscious of himself and the tragic aspects of life: impotency, isolation, temporality, and death. This consciousness renders regression back to the unconscious uroboric bliss more and more difficult.

### *2. The Mother Goddess and Her Son Lover*

In mythology this is the next phase. The son is loved, castrated, killed, and mourned by the mother who gives new birth to him every spring. The loving mother here tends to be changed very easily to the goddess of death. She is characterized as using her son only as a begetting phallus. In myths all "son-lovers" are described as very beautiful creatures who are transformed into flowers, anemones, hyacinths, violets, and narcissuses symbolizing their vegetative life. The phallus is the most important organ of this son's body but its only purpose is to give pleasure to his mother and not himself. Thus he can be castrated after having completed the function she requires. Son-lovers are not yet heroes, have no individuality of their own, and are defined by their mother's desire.

Their mother goddess is often depicted as a virgin, which means she belongs to no particular man, she belongs to all men. She is a temple prostitute, a magnified womb which gives itself to anybody. She is anonymous and veiled in the same way as a bride during the wedding ceremony.

## B. THE TERRIBLE MOTHER

This is the feminine as a negative charm with a compelling power; woman as wild goddess with bloody rituals demanding human offerings, originally always men; Mother Earth drinking blood to become fertile every spring.

Since ancient times blood is the sign of the female. In primitive societies this blood was seen as the origin of the fetus, menstruation blood ceasing during pregnancy. Swedish psychoanalyst Eva Basch-Kåhre (1990) describes how we are all born with the taste of blood in our mouths; during childbirth small blood vessels are torn causing this peculiar sensation which some psychoanalytic patients can recall during their regression. This experience connects the female, the blood, and the fertility with each other. For a man, bleeding means mostly death, while a woman survives many "mysteries" through blood: menstruation, defloration, and childbirth. The image of blood still lives in modern theories as a sign of woman; Basch-Kåhre (1990) invented the *Blood law* as a female equivalent to Lacan's (1953) *Father's law*.

The generative and nourishing, protecting, and warming aspects of the world, of life, nature, and soul have been projected on femininity. But death and destruction, danger and distress, hunger and nakedness belong to the image of the feminine. They characterize the Dark and Terrible Mother. The womb becomes the devouring maw of the grave and of death. The woman who generates a life takes it back into herself, using disease, hunger, hardship, and war. The goddesses of war and hunting express man's experience of life as a woman exacting blood (Neumann, 1955).

The Terrible Mother is the tiger, the vulture, and the coffin and the flesh-eating sarcophagus. She is Tiamat, mother of the Babylonian gods, the open gullet seeking to devour the Sun god, Marduk, her own son. She is Medea, who kills her children in her jealous rage, and Clytaemnestra who murders her husband in the *Orestia* (Graves, 1960). In our fairy tales she becomes a witch who eats children, or a devouring dragon. In contemporary fiction she can still be the blood-sucking vampire, as Adma D'Heurle points out in Chapter 26, this volume. She is the beautiful and distant mother in Tarkovsky's (1973–1974) autobiographical film *The Mirror*, when she washes her hair and is revealed as a monsterlike figure. In more conventional psychoanalytic narratives, she is found in the Kleinian concept of the bad breast (Klein, 1975) or in Alice Miller's descriptions of the bad mother (Miller, 1979).

The Terrible Mother also has another aspect: the seductive femme fatale, attracting men by her beauty and giving them extreme pleasure. Her rites include sexuality and wild orgies, and with her power she literally changes men into animals, she controls men's erections, either turning them impotent or using their phalluses for her own pleasure. At this level female sexuality is experienced as something very dangerous to be controlled and repressed. The irresistible "vamp," destroying a lover's life in a passionate affair is still a common cinematic image, although its classic portrayal is perhaps that of Marlene Dietrich in *Blue Angel*. Some of transvestites' most outrageous figures are testimonies of the fascination and hate that this archetypal image evokes in men.

In myths the hero is mostly a man. This is the consequence of the fact that in our culture the consciousness and its vehicle, language, are considered to be masculine. Even recent theories privilege women with only the nonverbal, semiotic aspect of communication. While the woman is allowed to represent the unconscious side of our being, she becomes "the unknown foreigner" in us, and we are afraid of her voice.

## V. The Slaying of the Mother

The hero's task is to separate the world parents from the eternal sexual intercourse. After this he has to slay his mother in order to become an individual. In the

*Orestia*, the murder of the actual mother is committed by Orestes and accepted by the gods, but more commonly in myths and fairy tales this theme is expressed by fighting with the dragon or some other monster. Often the fight takes place in a cave or a grotto. This underground location symbolizes the devouring aspect of the female.

The slaying of the mother is a necessity. If an individual cannot murder his good mother he remains an infant, looking for new objects for his dependency needs; if the terrible mother is not murdered the individual remains in fear that the feminine will castrate and destroy him and does not find a way to real women and *bodiliness*. According to Jungian psychoanalysis, the individual who is unable to commit this act tends to concentrate on abstract ideas but be unable to build close lasting relationships.

The symbol of the slaying of the mother means that we must free ourselves from the archetypal images instead of projecting them on real women. The only way to do this is to become conscious of both the cultural and personal images that we have of women and to take a critical attitude toward the prevailing notions of femininity.

## VI. The Splitting of the Mother Archetype: Contemporary Culture and the Psychoanalysis of Patriarchy

### A. THE SPLITTING AND REPRESSING OF THE ARCHETYPE

Contemporary patriarchal culture splits the mother figure by repressing the terrible aspect of the female. Only the Good Mother exists in the consciousness, while the unconscious is totally dominated by the Terrible Mother. This leads to oppression of women and to what I have referred to as *femininity* being the only possible position for women in our culture. Women must repress their powerful, phallic aspects in order to be accepted in our society. Feminists are still seen as dangerous and/or foolish women who are unable to accept this feminine female position.

Because of the splitting of the mother archetype in our culture, the Terrible Mother is repressed from the consciousness. The prevailing picture of motherhood is that of a suffering mother, *Mater Dolorosa*; childbirth is considered to be painful labor, as stated in the Bible. Voices that speak of the sexual pleasure of delivery are considered obscene, and remain unheard. Male envy wants to change it into a very dangerous experience that must be protected by medical equipment and a sterile, dull environment.

According to this ideology of femininity, the mother's heart suffers all possible pains even in later life. Women must become mothers who sacrifice themselves in order to feel at least like "good enough mothers." Not a word is allowed to be said about the destructive, aggressive aspects of motherhood. Kristeva (1983) has analyzed the best-known example of this kind of mother, the Mother of God, the Virgin Mary, pointing out how rarely Mary speaks in the Gospels, being instead reduced, as most women even today, to a mere bodiliness. But not much is left, in biblical reference, of her body—only her ears, breasts, and tears. The female sexual organ is effectively changed into an innocent shell, eroticizing hearing, voice, or even understanding.

## B. WHY ACCEPT THE SPLITTING OF THE ARCHETYPE?

Why do women accept this kind of definition of maternality and femininity? The Virgin Mary offers many compensations for lost womanliness. She is the embodiment of the dream of unisexuality: she needs no man to beget her son. She can heal the narcissistic wound caused by the obligation to be only of one sex. She is also beyond death. She does not die but is transported to heaven by her son. Being *Maria Regina*, Queen of Heaven, she compensates for the subordinate position that women have on earth. This grandiose fantasy is balanced by the figure of the Virgin kneeling in front of her son. She is also alone of her sex, excluding all other women from the scene. The immense value of pain and self-sacrificing love is emphasized in her figure. Identification with her gives women protection against their desire for murder and destruction.

Men gain freedom through this image from their paranoid fear of a strong and independent woman and from the female desire that still remains unexpressed. Their unconscious mind is dominated by the Terrible Mother, and everything uncontrollable in women becomes men's enemy, justifying the oppression of women's rights.

Such are the "gains." But the negative consequences are much more severe. For women, the image means that they cannot find their own *desire* and their own voice to express it because the only symbolic function allowed to them is understanding. They are to be an attentive ear for the (*only* one) man's voice. Often they are still condemned to regress to the narcissistic level of relationship dominated by the Mother's (the *other's*) desire. What the other person wants from them is more important than finding their own desire. "Femininity" does not have such characteristics as the demand of one's own rights or assertive aggressiveness, which easily evoke the archetype of the Terrible Mother. Pirkko Niemelä (Ch. 25, this volume) has described how some mothers are unable to set boundaries for their children because they are terrified by this archetype and afraid of being identified with it.

## C. THE SPLITTING OF THE ARCHETYPE AND ITS EFFECTS ON WOMEN: CLINICAL EXAMPLE 1

The following clinical example illustrates how the archetype lives in contemporary women. A 35-year-old female patient whose mother had commited suicide suffered from a long depression. She had great difficulties becoming pregnant. She did not want to be identified with the Terrible Mother living in her memories. After some years of psychoanalysis she became pregnant and had a son. She lost all her own desires and lived only through and for her son. She could not admit her anger at a dependent child and was ready to make all kinds of sacrifices in her personal life. She could not stop breast-feeding even though her baby became allergic to her milk. The analysis helped her to express even her ambivalent feelings, which most often came out in her fear of harming her baby by her nurturing. Her husband felt neglected and began to project the Terrible Mother on her by pointing out that she was a failure as a mother. She accepted her husband's definitions and became very depressed. In the analysis she could eventually see the difference between herself and the archetypal image projected on her, and she gained a lot of self-confidence as a mother.

## D. THE SPLITTING OF THE ARCHETYPE AND ITS EFFECTS ON MEN: CLINICAL EXAMPLE 2

Because of the split archetype, men must go on with their paranoid fantasies about the feminine and about female sexuality. They are forced to project all the unknown in themselves on women who become the very personification of the destructive forces of the unconscious. Women are considered unpredictable, unreliable, exotic, mysterious creatures with a great treasure in their inner space, which men are to be envious of. The consequence of defining woman as the bodiliness and man as the spirit is that men lose contact with their own living bodies and sensations. In turn, this means that they are prone to various somatic illnesses trying to repress all the signs of fatigue and need for rest. They are unable to find a respectful relationship with nature which belongs to women, to Mother Earth.

The following example describes the difficulties a man may face in forming a realistic picture of a mother because of the idealized archetypal projection. A 30-year-old male patient suffered from terrible anxiety attacks which he connected with his birth experiences. He had great feelings of guilt because he felt that he had nearly destroyed his mother's body by his birth. His mother had told him that his head was too big for him to be born. During the analysis he learned that his head had been quite normal but his mother had both physical and psychical difficulties in becoming a mother. His archetypal image of a good mother excluded all the destructive sides of motherhood and he was doomed to depression and afraid of his own aggressive power. He felt very easily that the analyst criticized his mother. He was very afraid of the things that could come up if he remembered something negative about his mother. He had to cling to the idealized image in order to avoid his own feelings of rage caused by the lack of maternal care. Later he remembered how his mother had left him alone for long periods because of her own depressive illness.

## VII. Concluding Comments: Accepting and Rejecting the Splitting of the Archetype

The splitting of the archetype makes real sharing between the sexes impossible as is demonstrated vividly by the recent emergence of the ideology of *differentialism* in some militant feminist groups. According to this ideology, the man and the woman are different in their essence and nothing can bring them close to each other. Human nature in general is a concept without real foundations, a male invention aiming to reduce female specificity to nothing. This ideology states that the woman is the eternal incarnation of the giving maternality, of peace and of nature, attacked by men who are warriors by instinct and ready to rape any woman (Badinter, 1991).

Instead of living according to the archaic archetypal images Jungian analysis suggests we should try to become conscious of their existence in us and in our culture in order to free ourselves from their terrible power. Thus, we should meet each other as human beings without projecting the archetypal images on the opposite sex.

## References

Badinter, E. (1991). La chasse aux sorciers. *Le Nouvel Observateur, 1406,* 50–51.

Basch-Kåhre, E. (1990). *Kvinnliga och manliga mönster.* Stockholm: Natur och Kultur.

Graves, R. (1960). *The greek Myths: 2.* Middlesex: Penguin Books.

Jung, C. G. (1938/1954). Psychological aspects of the mother archetype. *In* Jung, C. G. (1980). *The Archetypes and the Collective Unconscious.* Princeton: Princeton University Press.

Kalevala (1985). *The Kalevala, Epic of the Finnish People.* Helsinki: Otava.

Klein, M. (1975). *The Psychoanalysis of Children.* New York: Delta Books.

Kristeva, J. (1983). *Histoires d'Amour.* Paris: Denoel.

Lacan, J. (1953). Some reflections on the ego. *International Journal of Psychoanalysis, 34.*

Miller, A. (1979). *Das drama des begabten Kindes und die Suche nach dem wahren Selbst.* Frankfurt am Main: Suhrkamp Verlag.

Neumann, E. (1954). *The Origins and History of Consciousness.* Princeton: Princeton University Press.

Neumann, E. (1955). *The Great Mother.* Princeton: Princeton University Press.

Sterberg, J. (1930). *Der blaue Engel (The Blue Angel).* Berlin.

Tarkovsky, A. (1973–74). Serkalo (*The Mirror*). Moscow: Mosfilm.

**25**

# *Vicissitudes of Mother's Hate*

Pirkko Niemelä

I. PROCESSING AMBIVALENCE
A. Ambivalence about Motherhood
B. Emotional Processing of Ambivalent Feelings
II. OBSTACLES TO PROCESSING
A. Ideal Mother Image
B. Denial of Anger
III. EXPRESSIONS OF MOTHER'S HATE
A. The Longitudinal Study of Mothers
B. Hate in Childbirth Pain
C. Hate in Breast-Feeding
D. Wish Not to Have a Child
E. Hate as Worries about the Baby
F. Hate in Mother's Behavior When with the Child
G. Hate in the Split of the Good Child/the Bad Husband
IV. EFFECTS OF MOTHER'S DENIAL OF HATE ON HER CHILD
A. Insecurity
B. Afraid of Anger
C. Much Indirect Anger
D. The Child's Process of Separation-Individuation Hindered
V. DEFENSIVE HINDERING VERSUS EMOTIONAL PROCESSING
REFERENCES

## I. Processing Ambivalence

### A. AMBIVALENCE ABOUT MOTHERHOOD

Motherhood is often a very complicated matter for a woman, at least nowadays, in our western culture. Before motherhood, the woman has created her own life; she works, has her own career and her own projects. When she then has her baby, she has to give up much of her earlier life, and thus she loses some freedom. The changes in her life often make her sad or angry, as it is not easy for her to relinquish the life she has led, even if she wants to become a mother and have a child. She has conflicting emotions about motherhood and is ambivalent, both wanting motherhood and also wanting to retain her earlier life. Her relationships with other people also change. Before parenthood the partners often had plenty of time and attention for each other, and they have spent their free time as they wished. The baby changes all this, as she/he becomes the center of the family and all the attention and concern is given to him/her. The mother often has conflicting feelings about her double role as a mother and as a wife, and she may be afraid of losing her partner. She feels alone, sad, and angry when her partner does not understand her ambivalence about motherhood.

The mother has many kinds of feelings toward her child. During her pregnancy, as she does not yet know her child, she projects onto the child the feelings that she has toward the significant persons in her life. The mother who was emotionally secure as a baby, and who experienced the comfort and warmth of her own mother, experiences her own unborn baby in the same way. She feels a happy child inside her. But the mother who experienced neglect from a mother who left her wet, hungry, crying, and furious, experiences her own baby also as demanding and furious (Lagercranz, 1979).

Not only during her pregnancy, but also with her baby, her toddler, and her growing child, the mother has ambivalent feelings about her child. The child may make her happy and proud, but also angry. She may be annoyed when the baby does not want to suck, and exasperated when the baby does not sleep but cries for hours. She may be irritated by childcare and furious when her toddler refuses to obey. She may feel embittered if she has the main responsibility for childcare while her husband focuses on his work. She feels both love and hate toward her child; often conscious love and unconscious hate.

## B. EMOTIONAL PROCESSING OF AMBIVALENT FEELINGS

According to several researchers of the mother's feelings and psychological processes during pregnancy and after, the amount of ambivalence the mother feels is not critical. What is critical is what she does with her feelings, that is, how she copes with her conflicting feelings about motherhood and about her child (Breen, 1975; Lagercranz, 1979; Raphael-Leff, 1991).

A pregnant woman is often said to cry or be angry for no reason. She herself may accept this, and pay little attention to her own feelings. However, she may also pause and focus on her feelings. She may notice, admit, and accept that she is angry. Her feelings can be understood as information about herself, that is, how she is really experiencing her life situation. She wishes to experience motherhood as happy, and does so, on a conscious level. Anger tells her that she is angry about something, but often she isolates her anger from the content, that is, what she is angry about.

The next step in the emotional processing is to explore what her anger is related to. It may be difficult for her to find the connection, as she has suppressed it. In order to explore the connection, she needs both internal resources, the capacity to process emotional information, and external resources, a relationship so safe that she dares to start exploring her feelings and seeking the links. The links can often be found in two directions: from her earlier experiences and from her present relationships. Through this psychological work she comes to understand the intensity and quality of her own feelings, as well as relate them to something in her past and/or present life situation, for example, to the relationship with her partner. Through the emotional processing the mother learns to know her own feelings and needs better. She can come in contact with parts of herself that she has not accepted earlier. Through a better knowledge of herself, she can also improve her relationships with the people who are significant to her.

In order to support pregnant mothers' processing of their ambivalence about motherhood, small discussion groups were arranged (Niemelä, 1985). The group discussions were focused on the mothers' ambivalent feelings and on processing them. The group members, with the help of group leaders, supported each other to acknowledge, accept, and explore their anger and other feelings.

Twenty-one "group" mothers participating in these discussion groups, and 35 "control" mothers, not participating in the groups, were interviewed individually before and after childbirth. Comparison of the "group" mothers and the "control" mothers showed that there were many significant differences between the two groups, presumably due to the psychological work supported in the discussion groups. The "group" mothers experienced their child's birth and breastfeeding more positively. They also developed a closer relationship with their partners after the child's birth as well as a closer mother–child relationship, than did the "control" mothers.

## II. Obstacles to Processing

### A. IDEAL MOTHER IMAGE

Niemelä (1982, 1985) has studied the image of the ideal mother in several studies, by means of statements that mothers have rated on 7-point scales. A factor analysis revealed the following factors. Factor I includes the statements "an ideal mother is always patient," "never feels annoyed with the child," "never resents childcare," "loves the child from the beginning," and "is always stable in her mood." This factor is called "An Ideal Mother Denies Her Own Feelings."

The second factor includes the statements "an ideal mother is unselfish," "is self-sacrificing," "gives in," "forgets her own needs because of the needs of the child," and "adapts her life to the needs of the child with pleasure." This factor is labeled "An Ideal Mother Forgets Her Own Needs."

Factor III includes the statements "an ideal mother attempts to be a perfect mother," and "gets all her life satisfaction through motherhood." This factor is called "The Perfect Mother."

The mothers also rated themselves as mothers by means of the same statements. The mothers who agreed with the above description of an ideal mother, saw themselves as fulfilling their ideal. The acceptance of the Ideal Mother Image correlated also with an attitude called here "Idealizing Motherhood." This attitude is measured by statements like "a woman should become a mother in order to be a real woman," and "pregnancy and childbirth make a woman a real woman."

Being in contact with one's own feelings, that is, being angry, particularly with the child, does not fit in at all with the above image of an Ideal Mother. Therefore, even if it is generally difficult for a woman to be angry toward another person, it is especially forbidden to be angry toward one's child or to be frustrated about one's maternal role.

### B. DENIAL OF ANGER

As the Ideal Mother Image forbids feelings of anger and hate, it is difficult for many mothers to process their ambivalent feelings. Instead, they cope with their feelings of anger and resentment through denial. Women often use the defense called "reaction formation" when they deny their anger as well as their deeper feelings of hate, a combination of the present resentments, and their own early childhood fury. They wish to see their life, their situation, and also their own feelings as totally positive. They express only happiness and pride about their motherhood and about the child. But where does the hate go?

## III. Expressions of Mother's Hate

### A. THE LONGITUDINAL STUDY OF MOTHERS

In the longitudinal study of mothers (Niemelä, 1982), those who idealize motherhood and accept the Ideal Mother Image are compared with those who do not idealize motherhood and who do not agree with the Ideal Mother Image described above, nor do they rate themselves according to this image.

The mothers came to the study through antenatal centers, where the nurses selected for the study 38 mothers who were "normal": they were 20–30 years old, had no psychiatric history, had a permanent relationship with the child's father, had a normal pregnancy without complications, and were expected to have a normal delivery. All the mothers had a normal delivery, except for one who had a Caesarean section. One month before the expected date of delivery, the mothers were interviewed for the first time, and the data collected later were related to their attitudes about motherhood during their pregnancy. The mothers and their oldest child were interviewed and tested 1 month after the delivery, as well as 1, 2, 3, 4, and 8 years after the birth of the child.

About one-third of the mothers idealized motherhood and accepted the Ideal Mother Image. These attitudes about motherhood were fairly constant, at least during the eight years of study. The mothers who idealized motherhood and accepted the Ideal Mother Image, will be referred to as "idealizing mothers" or "mothers denying anger," or "denying mothers," and they are compared with the rest of the mothers in the study. The group differences reported are significant, at least at the $p < .05$ level.

## B. HATE IN CHILDBIRTH PAIN

The idealizing mothers experienced more pain in their delivery than did other mothers, both according to their own estimations 1 month after the delivery and according to the midwives' estimations immediately after the child's birth. They asked for more pain-relieving medicine during the delivery, and they were also given more.

How should the above data be interpreted? Within Klein's (Klein, 1988) frame of reference, the data might be understood in such a way that even if the mother, on a conscious level, welcomes her baby and feels only love toward it, she projects her unconscious hate and hating thoughts about the child onto the fetus. Accordingly, the fetus becomes a persecutor, and the mother is afraid that the baby might harm her in the delivery. Therefore, the mother may experience her delivery as more painful than other mothers do.

It is further possible that the mother is defending herself against the enemy inside her. Her whole body is in continuous readiness to fight back, as are the muscles in the walls of her uterus. The hardened and rigid muscles make it more difficult for her to give birth. It should be emphasized here that at the same time as the mother fights her baby, she has a conscious wish to deliver a healthy baby, and to love her child.

## C. HATE IN BREAST-FEEDING

The mothers denying anger enjoyed breast-feeding less than other mothers did, and they also breast-fed for a shorter time. This is unexpected in the Finnish breast-feeding climate, as the importance of breast-feeding is emphasized by the mother/baby center nurses, and is often seen as a sign of good mothering. If the mother unconsciously experiences her child as a dangerous enemy, it is understandable that she would hardly want to give the child her milk and would not enjoy breast-feeding. She may also feel guilty about her hate and, therefore, in addition, may experience herself and her breast as so evil that she is afraid to give the child her bad milk.

### D. WISH NOT TO HAVE A CHILD

There was a tendency, not quite statistically significant, for these mothers to take a longer time to conceive and become pregnant. Even if they wanted to become mothers on a conscious level, somehow their bodies resisted the pregnancy. Further, most of these mothers had only one child, while most other mothers in the study had two children. Moreover, these mothers claimed during their pregnancy, to a greater extent than other mothers, that they found it difficult to imagine having a living being inside them. Perhaps, while they wish to become mothers, they do not have a strong desire to have a child.

Even if these mothers emphasize that they want to be mothers, and resent nothing about motherhood and the baby, it seems that their bodies resist motherhood. The body does not want to conceive, the delivery is more painful, and further, the breasts do not want to feed the baby. It is as if the anger and hate that cannot be processed through the conscious mind are expressed through the body.

### E. HATE AS WORRIES ABOUT THE BABY

When the child was 1 month old, the mothers rated their agreement with statements about childcare. The mothers who denied their anger agreed more than other mothers that "I am afraid that something might happen to the baby now that she/he is completely in my care," "I go often and check the baby when she/he is sleeping," and "I worry whether the child gets enough love." Even if most new mothers nowadays are somewhat insecure about baby care, the other mothers agreed less with these statements. The behavior depicted in the statements can be understood as unconscious anger, as there is the expectation and the fear that some harm might befall the baby. The mother may be unconsciously afraid that her own unconscious bad thoughts might harm the baby.

### F. HATE IN MOTHER'S BEHAVIOR WHEN WITH THE CHILD

By means of systematic observations in situations when the mother and the child were present at the same time, the mothers denying their anger were observed to be more permissive and overprotective with the child than were other mothers. These mothers also acted more on the child's conditions, and "helped" the child unnecessarily.

With a growing child, part of the upbringing consists of setting limits for him/her. Mothers denying anger cannot use their aggression in a positive way, as energy needed for setting limits. Instead of telling the child what they want, they are overly permissive. It is also possible that if the mother projects her own anger onto the child and, consequently, sees the child as an aggressive and dangerous enemy, she, through her permissiveness, attempts to placate the child. This is also a way to control the child.

According to the observations, these mothers also controlled their children more than other mothers in that they continuously followed them with their eyes. These mothers, further, were rated as less accepting of anger and aggression in their children than other mothers. The mothers first projected their own anger onto their children, and then controlled the anger in their children. This psychological mechanism, called *projective identification*, has been described by, Klein (1937) and Sandler (1987). When a mother projects the part of her own personality that contains her anger, the part not accepted by herself, onto the child, and controls this part in her child, she can no longer see the child as the child really is, as himself or herself, but sees the child as her own projection. Nor can the mother see herself as she really is, but sees herself as totally loving and good.

The mothers denying anger were also observed to reward the child's clinging contact. These mothers had more difficulties in letting the child go. Perhaps they needed to convince themselves that they were good mothers, whom the child would not want to leave. When the children were 4 years old and started going to the playground by themselves, these mothers reported that they did not know what to do and that they missed their child when she/he was away from home. These mothers thus appear to be more dependent upon their child's company than other mothers in the study. These mothers also agreed with the statement that the child grows up too quickly.

## G. HATE IN THE SPLIT OF THE GOOD CHILD/ THE BAD HUSBAND

After the child's birth, the partner relationship of the denying mothers deteriorated more than that of the other mothers in the study. Even considering that the beginning of parenthood is often a strain for a couple, the partner relationship deteriorated more in the case of the mothers denying anger. Most clearly, this change was seen in terms of lack of sexual interest.

One way for a mother to disguise her anger toward her child from herself is to displace her anger into the partner relationship. The mother sees everything about motherhood as positive but sees her partner as negative. The mother projects the good into her motherhood and the bad into her marital relationship. Thus, she can see herself as totally good as a mother and her husband as bad. This kind of archaic psychological mechanism is called a *split*, and has been described, for example, by Kernberg (1975).

# IV. Effects of Mother's Denial of Hate on Her Child

## A. INSECURITY

At the age of 2 or 3 years, the children of the denying mothers were observed in a testing situation to be more restless, timid, and clinging than the other children. They also concentrated poorly, lacked initiative, were more passive, and needed more encouragement. Their feelings of basic security seemed to be lower than that of other children in the study. They obviously felt less secure with their mothers, who emphasized the happiness of motherhood and denied the anger.

The child, however, experiences the mother's anger, even if the mother, on a verbal level, emphasizes her love. It is all the more threatening for the child when the mother is not aware of her anger and has no conscious control of it, but expresses it covertly.

## B. AFRAID OF ANGER

The children were tested at the age of 3 years with a projective family test. By means of a mother doll, a father doll, and a child doll, the children were shown several family situations, and their responses were recorded and interpreted. The children of the mothers denying anger were more upset by the situations where a mother doll or a father doll showed anger.

When the mother, in her interaction with the child, is aware of her anger and is able to express it in some unthreatening way, and further, when she also accepts the child's frustration and anger, then the child also experiences that anger can be expressed and accepted. When the mother is able to contain the child's contradictory feelings about her, the child can identify with the mother's containing function. Then, neither the child's own anger, nor the mother's or any other person's anger is threatening. Bick (1968) describes how the formation of a "psychological skin" occurs during the early interaction between the mother and her child. Then the child can start to bear her/his own anger when together with her/his mother. When the mother cannot accept her own anger, nor accept or contain that of her child, the latter cannot develop an adequate protection for anger. The child is upset both with his/her own anger, and with the mother's and the father's anger.

## C. MUCH INDIRECT ANGER

At the age of 2 years, the children of the mothers who deny their anger were, according to the observations, generally more negative toward the tester and the testing situation than the other children in the study. Also, at the age of 3, they were less cooperative in the testing situation. However, at the age of 4 they were as agreeable as the other children in the study. Perhaps they were still indirectly aggressive, but they had learned to conceal it. The fact that they still had more anger was expressed through the projective test, CAT (Children's Apperception Test), where the children told stories about animals in different family situations. According to the interpretations of the children's stories, there was more anger in the stories of the children of the mothers denying their anger. However, the anger was expressed in a very indirect way; the child did not identify with the animals which were angry, but expressed anger, for example, through indirect revenge.

### D. THE CHILD'S PROCESS OF SEPARATION-INDIVIDUATION HINDERED

Several observations about the children of the denying mothers reported above could be interpreted as indications of difficulties in the child's separation from the mother and his/her individuation (Mahler, Pine, & Bergman, 1975). For example, the child's clinging behavior with the tester, and the fact that the child feels insecure with the tester, separated from the mother, indicate difficulties in the separation process. In addition, many observations about the behavior of the denying mothers in interaction with their children predict difficulties in the child's separation from the mother; for instance, the fact that the mothers enforce dependency by rewarding the child's clinging contact does not facilitate the child's separation.

One necessity for the child's separation is that the child can be in contact with her/his own anger. The separation from the mother is possible only through adequate amounts of frustration and anger (Kohut, 1971). In interactions bringing about a child's separation, the child demands from the mother something that the mother does not want to give, while the mother does not fulfill the child's demands. This makes the child want to separate and become more independent from the mother. But when the mother does not let herself become irritated or deny the child anything, the child is less motivated to separate. The child's individuation is also hindered by denial of anger and irritation between the mother and her child. The mother who cannot accept and admit her own anger cannot accept anger in her child either. The mother wants to have a child who is always nice and satisfied, never angry and frustrated. The child soon learns this, and attempts to be as the mother wants. This prevents the child from becoming a separate individual.

## V. Defensive Hindering versus Emotional Processing

In conclusion, when the mother cannot accept and process her anger, but denies it, the anger does not vanish; it is channeled by means of archaic defense mechanisms. The above data are understood through the mechanisms of denial, projection, projective identification, and splitting. These archaic defenses hinder the individual from perceiving the external reality. They distort the perceptions about oneself and about others. The mother cannot see her child as the child really is; she cannot perceive her child's real feelings and needs, and she is unable to see her child as a different, intact being, separate from herself. Nor can the child, in the interaction with her/his mother, develop the ability to see other people as they are.

The mother's perception of her partner is also distorted, and so the relationship between the partners suffers. Moreover, the mother sees herself distortedly. She denies some aspect of herself, and falsifies and deforms other parts. She cannot see herself as a total person as she has projected aspects of her own personality onto other people, and introjected other aspects that are not true of herself.

As she has distorted herself, she cannot process her emotions in a way that would lead to new, creative solutions. In order to free herself from this negative development, the mother has to be able to realize that both aspects, the loving mother and the hating mother, are parts of herself. Only then will she be able to feel the wholeness within herself again.

## References

Bick, E. (1968). The experience of the skin in early object relation. *International Journal of Psychoanalysis, 48,* 484–486.

Breen, D. (1975). *The Birth of a First Child.* London: Tavistock Publications.

Kernberg, O. (1975). *Borderline Conditions and Pathological Narcissism.* New York: Jason Aronson, Inc.

Klein, M. (1988). Love, guilt and reparation. *In* M. Klein, *Love, Guilt and Reparation, and Other Works 1921–1945.* London: Virago Press, Ltd.

Kohut, H. (1971). *The Analysis of the Self. The Monograph Series of the Psychoanalytic Study of the Child. Monograph no 4.* New York: International Universities Press, Inc.

Lagercranz, E. (1979). *Förstföderskan och hennes barn.* Stockholm: Wahlströ m och Widstrand.

Mahler, M. S., Pine, F., & Bergman, A. (1975). *The Psychological Birth of the Human Infant.* New York: Basic Books.

Niemelä, P. (1982). Idealizing motherhood and later reality. *In* H.-J. Prill and M. Stauber (Eds.), *Advances in Psychosomatic Obstetrics and Gynecology* (pp. 348–353). Berlin: Springer-Verlag.

Niemelä, P. (1985). *Vauva on tulossa - elämä muuttuu.* Helsinki: Otava.

Raphael-Leff, J. (1991). *Psychological Processes of Childbearing.* London: Chapman and Hall.

Sandler, J. (1987). The concept of projective identification. *In* J. Sandler (Ed.), *Projection, Identification and Projective Identification* (pp. 13–26). London: H. Karnac (Books), Ltd.

26

# *Vampire and Child Savior Motifs in the Tales of Isak Dinesen*

Adma d'Heurle

I. INTRODUCTION
II. THE VAMPIRE IN HISTORY, MYTHOLOGY, AND LITERATURE
III. PALLEGRINA LEONI, THE EMBODIMENT OF AN ARCHETYPE
IV. IMAGES OF THE CHILD SAVIOR
REFERENCES

## I. Introduction

A master of the art of story telling, Isak Dinesen[1] has put forth, in her public statements and in her art, an ardent defense of the story as a literary genre. Cardinal Salviati of "The Cardinal's First Tale" speaks in her voice when he says "Mistake me not . . . the literature of which we are speaking—the literature of individuals, if we may call it so,—is a noble art, a great, ernest and ambitious human product. But it is a human product. The divine art is the story" (Dinesen, 1975). The world of Dinesen's stories is exotic and removed as it is concrete and palpable and the characters move in her well-drawn and clearly proscribed universe as actors on a stage. Unlike the internal perspective that is demanded of the psychological novel and other genres of the literature of individuals, the approach to her stories needs to remain external. The characters can be looked at from a distant perspective and viewed as patterns on a psychic landscape. In Johannesson's words (1961):

[1]All excerpts from "The Dreaming Child" from *Winter's Tales* by Isak Dinesen © 1942 are reprinted by permission of Random House, Inc. All excerpts from "Echoes" from *Last Tales* by Isak Dinesen © 1957 by Atlantic Monthly, Inc., are reprinted by permission of Random House.

> "The characters are types, never individuals, . . . They are larger than life, and their behavior is artificial and stylized . . . They act as if they were on the stage, plucking quotations out of the air in order to define their roles which are often re-enactments of classical or mythical roles . . . The events are never unique or isolated, but have already been fitted into an orderly pattern in which they stand out very clearly within a meaningful relationship: they have become ritual and myth." (1961, p. 26)

This mythic quality is systematically cultivated by Dinesen and is underscored through her numerous biblical, literary, and mythological references. Psychological analysis in terms of background and personality dynamics has little relevance to her "larger than life" characters, for they are not so much persons as they are symbols or archetypes in Northrop Frye's terms:

> The symbol . . . is the communicable unit, to which I give the name archetype; that is, a typical or recurring image . . . which helps to unify and integrate our literary experience (1973, p. 99).

For Frye these symbols or archetypes are not proto-images of the collective unconscious in the sense of Jung, but literary motifs, conventions, or associative clusters. Their ability to integrate literary experience and their communicable power stems from the fact that they are representations of common elements in human experience (Frye, 1973).

> This emphasis on impersonal content has been developed by Jung and his school, where the communicability of archetypes is accounted for by a theory of a collective unconscious—an unnecessary hypothesis in literary criticism, so far as I can judge (pp. 111–112).

Dinesen's tales, like most forms of popular literature, abound in archetypal representations. For in the final analysis it is, as Andrew Loewinger (1977, p. 474) suggests in his review of Dinesen's posthumous tales, the purpose of the storyteller's art to make myth real through retelling.

In this chapter we shall focus on two archetypes that Dinesen draws with unusual clarity—the vampire and the child savior. Reverberations of these two motifs may be picked up in a number of the tales, but they appear most clearly in "Echoes" and "The Dreaming Child."

## II. The Vampire in History, Mythology, and Literature

The first archetype, that of the vampire, has haunted the human imagination since antiquity. The vampire is not an abstract demon from Dante's hell but a living or rather resuscitated being that haunts the world of the living. The female vampire, the counterpart of the male evil magician, has been known to many cultures and goes by different names. In India the embodiment of the vampire is Kali who is usually presented in painting and sculpture with skulls around her neck or dancing on a corpse. The Aztecs knew her as did the Vikings, and to the ancient Hebrews she was known as Lillith. The poet Robert Bly (1978, p. 31) has described this ubiquitous mythical image eloquently. "No Kali energy at all," he wrote, "appears in the Virgin Mary, an image of woman which is entirely post-Eve." Her image was not unknown to the Greeks:

> For this Mother the Greek matriarchies always used the mask of Medusa. Living snakes rose from her head, to suggest the fantastic concentration of Great Mother energy she contained; . . . and it was said that if a man looked into her eyes he turned to stone . . . In other words, the concentration of Great Mother energy was so great that it stopped the developing masculine consciousness in its tract . . . The job of this Mother is to end the intensification of mental life . . . to end ecstasy and spiritual growth. (Bly, p. 41)

In his history of witchcraft in the Middle Ages, Michelet (1939) points out that the female vampire or witch came to prominence as companion to the lady of the court whose ability to maintain power over men depended on her "being alone and without rivals." The vampire's task was to "rouse her [the chatelaine] to abuse this divinity of hers and to make mock of this herd of besotted and submissive males . . . as they are all so impotent to please her she chooses a lover more impotent still, a little lad to lavish her caresses upon" (p. 123). Michelet supports his thesis with anecdotal accounts of vain caprices and sordid cruelties that were directed toward impotent and hopeless young victims:

> It is, in a sense, the very thing often cast up against the Sorceresses, that "they ate children." At any rate, it is drinking their life blood. With all her tender ways and motherly affectations, the fair lady whose caresses are so soft is a vampire to drain the blood of her weakling victim, —nothing more nor less. (p. 123)

The validity of Michelet's reconstruction of the historical development of the role of the female vampire is, of course, open to question. However, the fact remains that an amazing degree of consistency can be found in the description of this archetype as it appears in history, in mythology, and in literature. In a recent article Ulanov (1977) summarizes the most universally salient characteristics of the witch or female vampire as she appears in myths and folktales. Here she relates the vampire's demand for blood to the insatiable hunger which extends to the spiritual realm: "Witches have consuming hunger for the human soul" (p. 6). Other characteristics of this dark archetypal figure that Ulanov stresses are her physical and psychological remoteness from the human community and her frenzied passion for power which mixes with her sexuality and bewitches her victims. The close association of eroticism with the demonic power and cannibalistic tendencies of vampires has often been noted. In his treatment of the imagery of cannibalism, Frye (1973, p. 149) underscores this particular association:

> The demonic erotic relation becomes a fierce destructive passion that works against loyalty or frustrates the one who possesses it. It is generally symbolized by a harlot, witch, siren, or other tantalyzing female.

Ulanov finds the psychological meaning of the vampire characteristics to lie in their collective representation of a reversal of what is generally perceived as the natural flow of human energies or the proper order of behavior. Whereas a good mother gives nurturance to the young who require care, the vampire uses the young for her selfish ends, and where a human being is expected to respect the sacredness of another's God-given soul, the vampire usurps the souls of her victims (Ulanov, 1977, p. 7). This reversal is symbolized by the vampire's physical and psychological isolation from the human community. Alien to human sensibility as the vampire may be, myth and popular literature have kept her archetypal image alive in the human imagination. A faithful representation of it is found in Dinesen's (1975) story "Echoes."

## III. Pallegrina Leoni, the Embodiment of an Archetype

With bold strokes the opening passages of the tale introduce the heroine, leaving no doubt of her identity as a female vampire. Pallegrina Leoni, the singer, was thought to have died in a fire which destroyed the theater where she sang twelve years previously. In the course of her wanderings the resurrected heroine comes to the remote mountain village where the story is set. She arrives in the evening burdened with few belongings and no memories. She had escaped from a lover whose passion for her threatened to "hold her fast in a definite, continued existence" and intends to travel further not toward any goal ahead but like "someone running before the wind" (Dinesen, 1975, p. 153). In the closing scene Pallegrina Leoni becomes aware that she had the mark of Cain on her forehead, but to the reader, the mark of Cain is visible from the beginning of the tale (p. 189). The strange traveler who describes herself as having been an angel once, and is now a messenger sent out on a long journey is hungry as she arrives to the town. She was a baker's daughter but the feeling of hunger is not foreign to her:

> "As a child she had often been hungry; through the faint ache in her stomach she once more became the light-footed ferocious wench who had sniffed in smells of food in the evening air, lonely with the loneliness of very young beings, and in a strange way safe." (p. 154)

Pallegrina Leoni's first encounter in the new town is with old Niccolo, her male counterpart, who lives anonymously in the realm of darkness. "Niccolo's face was not wrinkled but hardened like a big old yellow bone" (p. 154). The old man stood up stiff and straight, the image of a dead sailor with a weight tied to his feet. This encounter reveals more of the woman's vampire nature and foreshadows the central plot. It did not take Pallegrina long to identify the old man as a stranger to the human community, a traveler before the wind in whose bearing was a "namelessness akin to her own" (p. 155). Pallegrina sucked his story out of him and pulled slowly as if with rusty chains, deep memories from his childhood—long buried memories of his mother singing for her children, of stolen apples, a sister's broken nose and of his having eaten of the flesh of his dead companion. Of herself, Pallegrina said little and that only in ambiguous and obscure terms. Void of genuine mutuality, the exchange between the old man and his rare guest failed to provide a remedy for their loneliness. When they came together in a sexual embrace it was the incestuous relation of a mother and her child:

> "he raised one arm and dropped it heavily acrossed her breast. His big head followed it; he bored it down into the freshness of her hair and the softness of her bosom beneath it—indeed, for a minute, like a babe seeking and pressing towards his mother's nipple." (p. 163)

Niccolo, the man Pallegrina brought back to life, only to make him lay as a babe at her breast, before she abandons him to his loneliness, is one of three men who appear in the heroine's life before the main plot unfolds. The other two men who are briefly mentioned are her captive and devoted friend the Jew Marcus Cocozza, always in the wings and ever ready to provide her with all she needs, and Lincoln Forsner, the lover she had fled from whose image ran fleetingly through her mind as she lay beside Niccolo. Pallegrina's relation to the three men foreshadows her seductive, engulfing, and destructive love for the child Emanuele, her main victim.

It is significant that the conscious awareness that accompanies Pallegrina's image of her abandoned lover is one of a sense of pity for human beings that sucks the marrow from her bones (p. 163). This pity surfaces again in Pallegrina's love for her young pupil when it comes to full bloom, bringing her immeasurable but temporary happiness.

> "Her love for her pupil had in it both adoration, triumph and infinite tenderness. All obsessed by her longing to give, she behaved to the child who was to receive like a lioness to her cub. She could not keep her hands from his thick hair, but pulled it and twisted it round her fingers; she folded his head in her arms and pressed it to her breast. Pellegrina had never yearned to have children of her own, but had, long ago, jested with Marcus Cocozza about the idea of the mighty singing bird surrounded by a nestful of young squallers with open beaks." (p. 175)

The cry in her heart "must pity of human beings forever be sucking the marrow out of my bones" is heard again at the moment of her final defeat when she comes to realize that Emanuele, whom she calls "my child, dear Brother and Lover," had escaped from her deathly embrace (p. 189).

As the central plot evolves, dramatic tension is maintained, in part, by glimpses of the possibility for more beneficent outcomes of the actions of the heroine who is driven by her pity for humankind. A different course, for example, could be envisioned when she identified the town as a place "where one may stay on," and when hearing Emanuele's voice for the first time she was "filled with immense joy and was floating in light. After a long time she cried in her heart: 'O Sweet, Sweetness of Life! Welcome back!'" (p. 167).

At the climax of the story, Pallegrina names two forgotten kinds of happiness that "came back to her and grew upon her day by day: The first of the two was this; that hard work had once more come into her existence . . . The second happiness . . . was her love for her pupil" (p. 174–175). By this point, the course of the story's action is determined and it is clear to the reader, if not to the heroine herself, that the work and love that brought her happiness and "rendered her and her pupil ageless" are themselves the cause of her fall. It is here that the demonic as the reversal of the natural order of things becomes most clear. The work that could have served another, and augmented her own virtue and wisdom, was directed to satisfy her insatiable hunger for power. It is significant that one of her most blatant claims for limitless power—for divinity—is made in the context of her satisfaction with her ability to overcome difficulties and perfect her work:

> "The very difficulties she met were inspiring to her, and she laughed to herself as she recalled old sayings of Marcus Cocozza; 'sorrow is turned into joy before her. Her heart is as firm as stone, aye, like the nether millstone. Out of her nostrils goeth fire, and a flame goeth out of her mouth.' She did not, though, meet with many difficulties, her instrument gave itself into her hands unrestrainedly." The pupil was her instrument and she "felt her fingers to be one with its strings." (p. 173, 174)

When he sang, she

> "felt her own lungs drawing breath in his body and his tongue in her mouth. A little later she made him talk and made his eyes meet hers, and she sensed, as she had often done before, the power of her beauty and her mind over a young male being, her heart cried in triumph. 'I have got my talons in him. He will not escape me.'" (p. 172)

Pellegrina's love, like her work, allowed no room for the beloved to exist as other. It was a cloying, devouring love that obliterated the identity of the beloved child, brother, and lover.

Biblical imagery and direct biblical references which are widely used in Dinesen's work are used particularly frequently throughout this story. The name of the child Emanuele brings directly to mind the prophecy of Isiah and its evocation in the Gospel of St. Matthew:

> "Behold a virgin shall be with child, and shall bring forth a son, and they shall call his name Emmanuel, which being interpreted is, God with us." (1:23)

The references are accentuated in the second half of the story, making quite evident the analogy with the temptations of Christ. Pallegrina's description of the fame and power that awaits her pupil and her offers of precious gifts are identical to the lures with which the Devil sought to tempt Jesus.

After the blood ritual, Emanuele perceives the danger to his soul. He asks about the mysterious provider whom nobody had seen and rejects the gifts with a definitive "I want nothing from him" (p. 182). Emanuele then leaves Pallegrina's house where he had been happy and "heard his own beautiful voice coming to him from somewhere else, he knew not where" (p. 183). He was gone for three days before Pallegrina began her search for him. The image of the driven woman pursuing the child here and yon, with her hair loosened and floating after her, calling after him with her husky voice is unmistakably the image of the hungry vampire (pp. 183–184). The pursued child eventually stops and tells her before he hurls the stone why he could not go back to her: "You are a witch. You are a vampire. You are wanting to drink my blood . . . Once . . . I thought that I should die if I were to leave you. Now I know that I should die if I went back to you" (pp. 185–186).

## IV. Images of the Child Savior

The association of Emanuele with the Christ image is quite explicit in this struggle with the demon who would usurp his soul. It is reinforced throughout with numerous references to his uniqueness among men; "a being without blemish," someone who is spoken of "with solemnity," "a chosen vessel," and a bearer of a "faith in which he had grown up: that in all his world he was the Chosen and Elect" (p. 177). These designations and the unusual circumstances of his infancy and miraculous survival are some of the main attributes of the child savior archetype. This archetype Dinesen also projects quite clearly in "The Dreaming Child." In "Echoes" the archetypal image is perhaps a little less distinct, reflected as it is in two of the characters. The young foster sister Isabella is Emanuele's counterpart and an active agent in the battle against evil. Her awareness of the danger to Emanuele preceeds his own awakening to the threat that his teacher's devotion presents to him. Isabella made her decision to become a nun so she "may pray all day" for her brother before his own rejection of Pallegrina's gifts and his open resistance to her. In her innocence, the child Isabella understands that Pallegrina herself is also in need of her prayers. When the child first appears in the story, she is standing in church after the others have left "troubled by the idea that the fine unknown lady might be dead" (p. 167). As she takes leave of the same fine lady many months later, she tells her that she intends to pray for her also:

> "I thought by myself . . . that after you had seen and known all the glory of the world you had come up here to our town to find your soul again and to save it. Therefore,

I resolved that in Greccio when I pray for Emanuele, I shall pray for your soul too." (p. 180)

When Emanuele's image appears to Pallegrina Leoni reflected in the water of the trough where she had come to wash the blood from her forehead, it was the last time that she would see his face.

It would, she knew, be the last time, for on parting from him she must again give up remembering . . . She thought at last: "Oh, my child, dear Brother and Lover. Be not unhappy, and fear not. It is all over between you and me. I can do you no good and I shall do you no harm. I have been too bold venturing to play with human hands on an Aeolian harp. I beg pardon from the north wind and the south wind, from the east and west wind." (p. 189)

There was no cleansing power in the water of the trough and no redemption in Pallegrina's moment of recognition of her plea to the winds. The image of the child that she had called Brother and Lover she knew she would never see again, for she recognized that she had to continue her wanderings, with that gnawing pity for humankind in her bones, and that she must again give up remembering. This brief moment of recognition is simply what Johannesson describes as the arrival of the characters in Dinesen's stories to an appointed end. Unlike the recognition of self, reality, illusion, error, mistaken expectation, and defeat that Conrad's characters, for example, experience, this moment of arrival at new awareness for Dinesen's heroine is void of personal insight. It is simply the ordinance of fate (Johannesson, 1961, p. 25). Pallegrina's admission of her boldness in "playing with human hands on an Aeolian harp" and of her defeat, is coupled with her acceptance of her role in God's "terrifyingly fanciful" plan. "The Lord," she had told Niccolo, "likes a jest, and that a *da capo* which means: taking the same thing over again is a favorite jest of his" (Dinesen, 1975, p. 160). Shortly before she undertook to train Emanuele's voice, which she identified as her own, she reflected upon the Phoenix:

It is an old story. But God likes a *da capo*. Years ago this boy was still a baby. He may well have been born at the hour of the Opera fire in Milan. Was, then, that fire in reality kindled by my own hand? And was the flaming death of the old Phoenix and the radiant birth of the young bird but one and the same thing? (p. 170)

At the end of the story, Pallegrina is resigned to her fate as vampire, a woman with no memory and no roots in a human community. She is ready to resume her circular wanderings with no goal in view driven before the wind. But the child Emanuele is saved from her web. He is alive with the promise of future possibility, triumphantly out of the vampire's prison and her arid world of determined repetitiveness. He has kept alive the promise of singing in his own voice and the hope of giving his town its own priest-saint.

The similarity between Emanuele and the hero of "The Dreaming Child," Jens, puts into relief the outline of the archetypal image of the child savior. For

Jens, as for Emanuele, there was no question of his being the "favorite of fortune." The world's attitude, as well as his own apprehension, confirmed his uniqueness. The circumstances of his birth and his infancy were also out of the ordinary. Many of the references to him in the story (Dinesen, 1970) suggest his Christ-like image although he is also compared with Joseph the dreamer, and with the Greek god of love. To the mother who waited for him, Jen's coming was, in its way, miraculous:

> How very different, Emilie said to herself, would the case have proved had she been expecting a child in the orthodox way of women. There was indeed something neat and proper about settling the affairs of nature according to your own mind. (p. 167)

Jens is described as a royal presence who commanded respect and inspired awe (p. 170, 171, 178). Jacob, his adoptive father, found it difficult to protect him, and his mother came to realize that "however generous she would be to him, he would always be the giver" (p. 173, 175). The child's radiance is emphasized through the repeated use of light imagery, suggesting the radiance of Christ at his baptism by John the Baptist (p. 168, 169). This divinity was also as a god of love:

> Except for his size, Jens had no resemblance to the classic portraits of Cupid; all the same it was evident, that, unknowingly, the shipowner and his wife had taken into them an amorino. He carried wings into the house, and was in league with the sweet and merciless powers of nature, and his relation to each individual member of the household became a kind of aerial love affair. (pp. 171–172)

The resurrected world of spring into which Emilie and Jacob walked shortly after Jens's death attests to his being in league with the powers of nature.

The cumulative effect of the association of Jens with Christ is such that it appears natural that Emilie would quote the scripture when speaking of him without herself being aware that she was doing so:

> "He told me many things which none of you heard. I saw that we could not find another such as he, that there was none so wise." She did not know that she was quoting the Scripture, any more than the old shipowner had been aware of doing so when he ordained Jens to be buried in the field of his fathers and the cave that was therein - this was a small trick peculiar to the magic of the dead child. (p. 186)

In his life Jens's spell was such that "people were made to see themselves with the eyes of the dreamer, and were impelled to live up to an ideal" (p. 172). Through his power the residents of the mansion were transformed; the old disgruntled housekeeper became a "benevolent guardian of human welfare" and the coachman rode proudly "combining within his own person the vigour of the two bay horses." In his death, as in his short life, the child had the power to transform the lives of those who were close to him. His sacrificial death meant the birth of a new truth and a new life for Emilie and Jacob. Emilie, who had been closest to him, was quite changed by his death. She was the descendent of a long line of traders who were "unswerving servants of facts," and herself was marked by a "rigidity of mind" which contrasted with the suppleness of her body. She had been unable to understand her husband's tendency to believe what people told him:

> "I cannot see . . . how one can well wish to believe or not to believe. I wish to find out the truth. Once a thing is not true," she added, "it matters little to me whatever else it may be." (pp. 163–164)

Jens's death released Emilie from her bondage to reality and brought her the gift of belief. She found, as she put it, "a grace in the world" and new powers of the imagination. She was able to look back and remember and mourn for Charlie, the man she had loved, and to understand the world in a new way:

> "It is difficult," she said, "to explain what it feels like to understand things. I have never been good at finding words . . . But it has seemed to me ever since March, since the Spring began, that I have known well why things happened, why, for instance, they all flowered . . . The generosity of the world; Papa's and your kindness too! As we walked in the woods today I thought that now I have got back my sight, and my sense of smell, from when I was a little girl." (p. 187).

In essence, Jens's death and Emanuele's deliverance were similar in their import. The two child saviors brought into the world a new power of possibility and hope. Jens saved his world from the bondage of reality and thus effected a new outlook on the future and a new relationship to the memory of the past. Emanuele broke the chain of compulsion and mechanical repetitiveness, and in his way made possible the survival of memory and the birth of a new future.

## References

Bly, Robert (1973). *Sleepers Join Hands* (p. 41). Harper and Row.

Bly, Robert (1978). On the great mother and the new father. *East–West Journal*, •, 31.

Dinesen, Isak (1970). The Dreaming Child. *In* I. Dinesen, *Winter Tales* (pp. 163–164, 167–173, 175, 178, 186–187). New York: Vintage Books.

Dinesen, Isak (1975). The Cardinal's First Tale. *In* I. Dinesen, *Last Tales* (p. 24). New York: Vintage Books.

Dinesen, Isak (1975). Echoes. *In* I. Dinesen, *Last Tales* (pp. 153–155, 160, 163, 167, 170, 172–175, 177, 180, 182–186, 189). New York: Vintage Books.

Frye, Northrop (1973). *Anatomy of Criticism* (pp. 99, 111–112, 118, 149). Princeton, New Jersey: Princeton University Press.

Gospel of St. Matthew, The. 1:23.

Johannesson, Eric O. (1961). *The World of Isak Dinesen* (pp. 25–26). Seattle, Washington: University of Washington Press.

Loewinger, Andrew (1977). The storyteller's laughter. *The Nation*, •, 474.

Michelet, Jules (1939). *Satanism and Witchcraft* (pp. 123–124). New York: The Citadel Press.

Ulanov, Ann Belford (1977). The witch archetype. *Quadrant, 10(1)*, 6–7.

# FEMALE AGGRESSION IN SUBHUMAN SPECIES

27

# *Female Aggression among the Great Apes: A Psychoanalytic Perspective*

Reijo Holmström

I. INTRODUCTION
II. THE OBJECTS OF THE STUDY
III. RESEARCH APPROACH AND METHODOLOGY
IV. THE NATURE OF AGGRESSION IN THE GREAT APES
A. Power Struggles among Females
B. The Occurrence of Aggression in a Sexual Context
C. Aggression in the Mother–Child Relationship
D. The Oedipal Constellation in the Female
V. ORALITY IN THE FEMALE
VI. FROM POLYGAMY TO MONOGAMY
VII. SUMMARY
REFERENCES

## I. Introduction

This chapter deals with the forms taken by aggression in our nearest relatives, the great anthropoid apes. Underlying the discussion are the ethological descriptions of these apes which have appeared during the last several decades. The author himself is not by profession an ethologist, much less a fieldworker; as an enthusiastic amateur biologist, however, he has applied the findings of ethological observation concerning the great apes to human psychoanalytic developmental theory.

## II. The Objects of the Study

Our nearest animal relatives are the African great apes, the chimpanzee and the gorilla. The human chromosomes and those of the great apes, for instance, are astonishingly similar (Lagerspetz, 1989). When the intensive study of these apes on the basis of new ethological observation techniques began in the 1960s, the chimpanzee turned out to be the easiest to approach; the gorilla presented more difficulties.

The mountain gorilla (*Gorilla gorilla beringei*), the rarest of the three gorilla subspecies, is now in danger of extinction. There are a total of some 400 individuals remaining, living in the volcanic tropical rain forest area of Central Africa. The old male, the silverback, is the leader of a harem consisting of a number of females, together with juveniles and young males, the blackbacks. The gorilla, despite its awe-inspiring appearance and great size, is a pure herbivore. Its only natural enemy is another silverback, which aims to either carry off the other's females or capture part of its territory. As a selective herbivore, the gorilla needs an extensive territory. The leading male has an exclusive right to mate with all the mature females. Socially mature young males leave their original group and wander off to establish groups of their own. Mature young females either change groups or stay with that of the mother. There is severe competition between the silverbacks over those young females which have not yet settled down permanently in a particular group. Sometimes the conflict is settled by means of threats; often, however, the situation leads to violent combat, forming a sharp contrast to the otherwise peaceful behavior of the gorilla.

The chimpanzee (*Pan troglodytes*) has spread over a broad area in the Central African tropical rain forest. The chimpanzee communities observed by Jane Goodall for over thirty years live in Tanzania, close to the eastern shore of Lake Tanganyika. The chimpanzee is omnivorous; it has a particular preference for food rich in protein. In obtaining such food, there is a clear division of labor between the sexes: the males form small hunting parties to hunt small game, while the females have specialized in "fishing" termites out of their nests with a long grass stem. The chimpanzees live in large "fusion–fission" communities, consisting of several dozen individuals. The males stay more or less together in their own adult groups, characterized by a precise hierarchical structure and by a power struggle for the position of leading male. The looser groups of females also have a clear pecking order. In general, a young male has a higher status in the hierarchy than the females have.

The chimpanzees show three kinds of mating behavior. The first of these is typically promiscuous: adult males mate with a female in estrus, taking turns according to their status in the hierarchy. In the second alternative, a powerful alpha male may reserve a female for his own use during her estral peak, thus ensuring the reproduction of his own genes. The third form, that of consortship, resembles the human pair bond: the male stays together with a selected female over a longer period of time and takes her to an outlying area of the territory, in order to avoid competition with other males. This allows a lower status male to ensure access to a female in estrus; he runs the risk, however, of attack by the males of the adjacent territory. The estrus of the chimpanzee female, with its highly visible swollen and reddened genital area, lasts about ten days; its peak coincides with ovulation. The menstrual cycle is approximately 36 days (Goodall, 1986, p. 445).

## III. Research Approach and Methodology

The paleontologist Louis Leakey, whose special field was human prehistory in Africa, in selecting researchers for ethological field work among the great apes, farsightedly chose enthusiastic young women for this job. It was on Leakey's initiative that the National Geographic Society undertook the financing of Dian Fossey's (1983) gorilla research in Ruanda and Jane Goodall's (1986) work with the chimpanzees in Tanzania.

Characteristic of this approach to ethological field research is the most delicate and subtle observation, avoiding all violence; the fieldworker spends months patiently becoming accustomed to field conditions and adapting to the living conditions of the animals being observed. These two young women, Fossey and Goodall, were capable of such a feat. A similar attitude is demanded of the mother, who must adapt herself to the "wild" sensitivity and helplessness of the newborn infant. In recent years these two aspects have again become the focus of scientific attention, in research concerning the early formation of object relations in the infant (Stern, 1985) and the social relationships of the great apes (Goodall, 1986). Both areas of research yield valuable information on the early development of the human species.

## IV. The Nature of Aggression in the Great Apes

In the great apes, as in large mammals in general, the life styles of the male and the female diverge after sexual maturation. In the male, skill in combat increases the individual's evolutionary potential. In the chimpanzee, this struggle culminates in the competition for alpha status and for optimal access to the females. Thus, larger size and physical strength confer on the male an evolutionary advantage, serving his ability to compete with other males over territory and to defend the females.

Sexuality is an old phenomenon in nature. Depending on the species, the sexes invest varying amounts of energy in successful reproduction. In this respect there are differences between different groups of animals, as shown, for example, by comparisons of classes of birds and mammals (Liberg & von Schantz, 1985). In mammals, motherhood is a visible and central aspect; it cannot be concealed or transferred to another individual, as sometimes happens in birds. Fatherhood, on the other hand, is a clearly defined phenomenon in monogamic bird species, while in mammals, including human beings and the great apes, it is a more complex affair and less easy to determine.

In mammals, the female has to invest more time and energy than the male in caring for the offspring: the long gestation period, the risky delivery and extended lactation, often followed by a further period of several years of caring for the child's basic needs. This is essential in species in which the infant is exceptionally undeveloped, as in primates, compared, for example, to bovine or cervine species.

In the early stages, the gorilla or chimpanzee female has to protect and defend her offspring from the intrusive approach of other members of the group. Initially the infant is carried in the ventral position under the female's stomach, and later on her back. The mother's sufficient aggressiveness and ability to defend her offspring are a condition for the latter's survival and at the same time the key to success in the internal social hierarchy of the group (Goodall, 1986, p. 356).

Territorial changes are also a strain on the female's defenses because of struggles over territorial boundaries, the moving of the female from one territory to another, or the conquest of the territory by a new male. In these conflicts the female is sometimes forced to allow the killing of her offspring, if her own male or males are unable to protect the territory. In the long run, this makes biological sense; the new territorial divisions are usually advantageous as a growing environment for the next generation. If, on the other hand, the male or males are still capable of defending their territory, the female may take part in the combat even at risk of being seriously wounded (Fossey, 1988, pp. 70, 89; Goodall, 1986, p. 511). For these species, possession of a sufficiently extensive territory is a condition of survival.

## A. POWER STRUGGLES AMONG FEMALES

Even *within* the territory, the female may have to defend her offspring. There is a status hierarchy among the females, determined to a great extent on the basis of the female's assertiveness. The offspring of the leading females seem to be more successful, and to act aggressively and domineeringly in turn in their own juvenile groups. In these fights, the mother, if necessary, helps her offspring. When full-grown, the latter may in turn come to the defense of the mother if necessary.

The power struggle among the females within the territory may also take indirect forms. In the gorilla harem, the dominant female, aided by her adult daughter, cannibalistically fed on the offspring of a lower-status female; this occurred secretly at night, to evade intervention from the leading male of the harem (Fossey, 1988, p. 77).

A similar series of events in the chimpanzee community, though far more destructive, is described by Goodall (1977, 1986, p. 451). During the four years 1974–1977, one of the leading females, together with her full-grown daughter, carried off from the females of the group and cannibalized a total of eleven young,[1] that is, almost all the offspring born during that period. The aggressive behavior which occurred in these abductions was weaker than that in the combats among males, and was even accompanied by attempts at consolation. When the abduction had been successful and feeding on the victim had begun, the victorious female might consolingly touch the deprived mother sitting next to her (Goodall, 1986, p. 351).

The leading female of the Kasakela chimpanzees, Flo, was sexually active but also assertive. During her long reign the community was a strong one. By 1967, however, Flo was already old, and was forced to abdicate in favor of Circe, a strong female who had come from outside the group. Circe, however, died (of unknown causes) in 1968, after which two atypical females, Gigi and Passion, seized power (Goodall, 1986, p. 438). The definite leader, Gigi, was an exceptionally masculine female, large-sized and sterile. She was more comfortable in male groups, and took an eager part in the "civil war" of 1974–1977, in which a daughter group that had split off in 1972 was destroyed.

At the same time, Passion, who was number two in the female hierarchy, concentrated on the destruction of the young offspring of lower-status females; this had negative consequences for the strength and survival of the group. We can only speculate whether the fate of the Kasakela group might have been different if the female who rose to power after Flo had been one who made more constructive use of her aggressiveness. The considerable decline in the size of the group's territory observed in the following years reflects the importance of the leading female or females in maintaining the group's capacity for survival.

The killing of offspring by males differs from that by females in that the males are not concerned primarily with feeding on the victims. Their main preoccupation is with the defense of the territory or the abduction of a female. The infant usually dies in the struggle, but cannibalism does not necessarily take place (Fossey, 1988, p. 70; Goodall, 1986, p. 522).

The cannibalism practiced by the females seems socially appropriate, in that when it occurs within the territory and in the presence of the possible father, no sign is left of the occurrence. If the destruction of a competitor's offspring is to succeed without the consequences which might be expected on the part of the males, it must take place in secret. In cases where the chimpanzee female defending her offspring called for help, the males sometimes arrived in time to prevent bloodshed (Goodall, 1977, p. 270).

[1]In her most recent work, Goodall (1991) has reduced the number of victims to six.

## B. THE OCCURRENCE OF AGGRESSION IN A SEXUAL CONTEXT

In the life cycle of the great apes, reproduction and the struggle for power both occupy a central position; it is to some extent arbitrary to keep them apart. In some situations, however, the link between the two is particularly clear.

One interesting form of aggression in females, which is directly linked with the sexual act, is refusal of incest; this has been observed both in gorillas (Fossey, 1988, p. 74) and in chimpanzees (Goodall, 1986, p. 466). This incest taboo is especially clear between mothers and sons; traces of a prohibition on sibling incest occur, at least in chimpanzees. Inhibition of father–daughter incest evidently does not yet occur in the great apes.

Sexual relations between mother and son occupy a special position in these apes. Full-grown males very rarely attempt such relations. If, however, this should occur, the female will protest extremely strongly and will attempt to escape from the situation. Of the hundreds of successful matings observed, only a few involved a mother and an adult son (Goodall, 1986, p. 467). This refusal on the part of the female is quite categorical, even when the male involved has a high status—including the alpha male of the group.

The ethological descriptions indicate that the decisive role in this absence of mother–son incest is played by the aggressive and unconditional refusal of the female. Previously (Holmström, 1991) I have discussed the matter from the point of view of the male. Over the years, through her various senses, the female develops a clear image of her offspring. Familiarity, for example a familiar odor, overcomes sexual attraction, even during estrus. The core of the taboo on mother–son incest is thus very old in origin, and its categorical nature is maintained precisely by the females. This is one example of the way in which the maintaining of norms is the responsibility of the females in particular.

Why is it the mother who is more uncompromising in an incest situation? Presumably, although the duration of familiarity is equally long for both, its character is fundamentally different. The mother has become familiar with her offspring already within her body, has given birth, and has lactated and reared it from infancy to adolescence. For the mother, the offspring has been part of herself, of her own body. For the young male, on the other hand, the mother has always been basically the same, part of the outside world.

At an evolutionary level considerably more primitive than the great apes, the baboons have been found to make use of sexuality in the struggle for power (Kummer, 1957). In the gorillas and chimpanzees, the way in which an ally is made use of is more complex. A suitable ally among the chimpanzees may be the mother, a sibling, or a high-status male. In a triadic situation, an alliance between two of the parties is usually enough to resolve the conflict with the defeat of the third. In the status hierarchy, each member of the group has a precisely defined place, and the moves needed to resolve a power conflict need not be particularly dramatic. The emotional link no longer occurs as a gesture of sexual offer, as in the baboons, but takes subtler forms.

In the chimpanzee community, the female in estrus has a high status, almost as high as the alpha male, for the duration of her estrus. A young, sexually mature female who is free of the care of offspring is highly valued among both gorillas and chimpanzees. Such a female can move freely at the territorial boundaries between groups and can move from one group to another before she finally settles down in one group. The competition over such a female between the males of different groups is considerable (Fossey, 1988, p. 68; Goodall, 1986, p. 514). An anovulatory female who is accompanied by a young infant will not receive the same considerate treatment (Goodall, 1986, p. 495).

## C. AGGRESSION IN THE MOTHER–CHILD RELATIONSHIP

In the beginning, contact and communication between the mother and the newborn infant chimpanzee takes oral forms. The infant bites at the mother's arms and hands; the latter responds by lifting the infant toward her stomach and chest. The infant's rooting and climbing reflexes help it to find the breast and begin sucking. The infant's biting instinct is directed to anything in the environment, and in return triggers such behaviors as biting, touching of the face and mouth, and hugging and playing, in highly complex order (Plooij, 1979).

The care of the infant requires experience and assertive decisiveness on the part of the female. Experienced gorilla and chimpanzee mothers possess the necessary skills. The immature aggressiveness and inadequate care offered by an inexperienced mother can be dangerous to the infant. The new mother with her first child may treat the latter with the same roughness that she is used to in playing with playmates of the same age (Fossey, 1988, p. 75). The bond between the mother and daughter is closer and more durable than that with male offspring. The daughter is given the opportunity to learn from the mother the basic skills needed in caring for offspring. The mother, together with a full-grown daughter are also able to protect an infant from the various dangers threatening it (Fossey, 1988, p. 76; Goodall, 1986, p. 376).

## D. THE OEDIPAL CONSTELLATION IN THE FEMALE

In human psychosexual development, the transition from a dyadic to a triadic relationship is a central event, which, in the psychoanalytic literature, is termed the Oedipus complex (Freud, 1905). In the case of the great apes, since they do not have the nuclear family, we cannot speak of an Oedipus complex; the term "Oedipal constellation" has therefore been used. From the daughter's point of view, the Oedipus complex in the female has a briefer history than in the male; a close mother–son relationship goes back millions of years further in history than a similarly distinct father–daughter tradition. The closeness and stability of the father–daughter relationship is correspondingly less. This is seen in human beings too, in that father–daughter incest is more common than incest between mother and son (Meiselman, 1978; Sherkov, 1989).

The gorillas have a clearly defined harem system, ruled by the silverback, who in general mates with all the adult females, including his own mature daughters. Fossey (1988, p. 75) describes a group in which two silverbacks, father and son (Beethoven and Icarus) share the leadership and defense of the harem. The two leading females, Effie and Marchessa, in turn produced most of the offspring in the group. Both females had a dominant genetic trait which was overtly inherited by the offspring: in Effie, strabismus, and in Marchessa, syndactyly. Their offspring were thus easily recognized. During the years 1960–1982 Effie had one son, Icarus, and five daughters; during the same period, Marchessa had one daughter, Pantsy, and two sons, in addition to one infant which disappeared immediately after birth. A little later, Pantsy, now full-grown, had a son called Banjo, who disappeared at six months. At the same time ape bones were found in the feces of Effie and her daughter Puck. After losing the son fathered by her own father, Pantsy turned her attention to her half-brother Icarus. At first the old male Beethoven interrupted their erotic play and himself copulated with his daughter, but later he accepted the union between Pantsy and Icarus, which produced two offspring. At this time Beethoven was already about 47 years old and seriously disabled from numerous fights, so that he needed the help of his son Icarus in defending the group.

In the power struggle between the two leading females, Effie and Marchessa, the former was victorious, due in part to the help of her son Icarus and her daughter Puck. The victims were the aging Beethoven, who lost the exclusive right of sexual access to the harem, and the competing female Marchessa, who lost two of her offspring and died in 1981. The victory was symbolized by the violence done to Marchessa's dead body by Icarus. The father–daughter inbreeding, which had already shown its genetic drawbacks, was now replaced by a sister–half-brother relationship, in which the genetic pool was larger.

In the chimpanzee community, the prevailing promiscuity means that there is no clearly identifiable father. Thus, father–daughter incest is a common occurrence. In the great apes, father–daughter incest—the incestuous aspect of the female Oedipus complex—is more common than mother–son incest, around which an inhibiting taboo has evolved.

There is an intense struggle for advantageous social status, as close as possible to the leading male. In this struggle, the cannibalistic feeding on the competitor's offspring is an effective weapon, made use of among both gorillas and chimpanzees. The consequence of such an act may be the losing competitor's move to another group.

## V. Orality in the Female

The easier regression toward orality, which is typical of the female in humans, is historically old. The greater orality of women's dreams (Holmström Hanses, & Uotila, 1990), and the wicked child-eating witch of folktales (Landtman, 1917), have their phylogenetic equivalents. This aspect is stressed in Kleinian child-analytic theory (Klein, 1961). The common occurrence of anorexia and bulimia in women also supports this point of view.

The female's orality, and her more flexible tendency toward regression, play an advantageous role in the successful development of the mother–child relationship. The mother's ability to adapt herself to the infant's helpless condition, and to initiate a process of interaction within which the latter can begin to acquire the skills it will need, is of the utmost importance in terms of the child's future development (Winnicott, 1971). The essential tradition is transmitted by means of nonverbal, analogic-iconic communication (Bateson, 1972), directly from the mother's subconscious to that of the child, through the primary process (Matte-Blanco, 1988). Crucial conditions for this process of interaction include amodal perception and affective attunement (Stern, 1985). The basic tradition is as if it were literally absorbed with the mother's milk (Spitz, 1965). It is through the mother that the community adapts and integrates the newcomer into its tradition, as Erikson (1950) was one of the first to point out.

## VI. From Polygamy to Monogamy

Temporary pairing occurs in the chimpanzees as one of the three most common forms of sexuality (Goodall, 1986, p. 450), but it is not the prevailing form of reproduction. Promiscuity is most common among the chimpanzees, but consortship may be a competing form, and increasing in incidence (Goodall, 1986, p. 485).

One factor in the evolution of monogamy may be the loss of a visible estrus and its replacement by continuous sexual availability. There is no longer a particular recognizable time at which fertility is certain; in order to ensure the reproduction of his own genes, the male therefore has to enter into a permanent pair-bond. This development of concealed ovulation is considered to be particularly advantageous to the female. The risks attached to gestation and childbirth have always been considerable, and have further increased since the adoption of an upright position. With the increase in intelligence and in the capacity for logical thinking, the female's ability to predict her time of ovulation has played a crucial role (Burley, 1979); a woman who has been able to recognize her ovulatory period has been able to avoid sexual intercourse at the critical time, has had fewer pregnancies, fewer offspring, and her genes have been eliminated in the process of natural selection. The loss of conscious awareness of estrus may help to explain the prevalent difficulty in understanding female sexuality (Makari, 1991). The earlier distinct period of estrus and explicit sexuality have largely been transferred to the subconscious, and sexuality has taken on an enigmatic veil of mystery.

The evolutionary tradition of the pair-bond has been relatively brief compared, for example, to the history of the mother–daughter relationship or the group relations of adult males. The importance of the pair-bond and especially of the female in the transmission of tradition, for example, the incest taboo, the care of the offspring, eating customs, and the use of tools, is especially great for species in which the offspring remain dependent for many years, life is relatively long, and, as in the case of the great apes, the members are able to learn and have a good memory. The importance of the early maternal relationship in the creation and continuation of the cultural experience has been discussed in similar terms by Winnicott (1971, pp. 96–103).

## VII. Summary

This chapter deals with the early history of female aggression from a psychoanalytic point of view and in the light of recent ethological research concerning the great apes.

Typical of these apes is a difference in size between the sexes. Direct physical aggression is easier for the males both in comparison to females and in comparison to other physical efforts. There is a division of labor between the sexes with regard to the use of aggression; in the male, the main areas in which aggression is used are the struggle for power within the group and the defense of the territory against external enemies.

Because of her smaller body size, the female has to resort to indirect aggression and to other forms of aggressive behavior than those used by the male. Similar findings have been obtained in human research (Lagerspetz, Björkqvist, & Peltonen, 1988). The female makes use of aggression in the following situations and forms:

1. As direct aggression, in the power struggle among females, in competing for herbivore food and for advantages for their offspring.
2. As indirect aggression, in the power struggle among females, by cannibalistically feeding on the competitor's offspring.

3. As indirect aggression in sexual contexts, directed against the male; by competition for food, refusal of cooperation or sexual access, and feeding on the male's offspring.
4. As indirect aggression through the offspring, by rearing the young, transmitting important models of behavior from one generation to the next. The female prevents and restrains certain kinds of action in the offspring, permitting and favoring others.

This multiplicity of forms taken by female aggression plays a significant role in the carrying forward of the chain of generations. The female plays a crucial role in the early care of the offspring, from carrying it in her own body through face-to-face lactation and a long period of close care through early childhood. The central role of the female during these formative years means that even her relatively mild and indirect aggression takes on significance as either a constructive or a destructive force.

## References

Bateson, G. (1972). *Steps to Ecology of Mind.* New York: Random House.

Burley, N. (1979). The evolution of concealed ovulation. *The American Naturalist 114,* 835–858.

Erikson, E. H. (1950). *Childhood and Society.* New York: Norton.

Fossey, D. (1983). *Gorillas in the Mist.* Boston: Houghton Mifflin. (1988 paperback ed., London: Penguin Books).

Freud, S. (1905). *Three Essays on the Theory of Sexuality.* Standard Edition 7. London: Hogarth Press.

Goodall, J. (1977). Infant killing and cannibalism in free-living chimpanzees. *Folia Primatologica 28,* 259–282.

Goodall, J (1986). *The Chimpanzees of Gombe. Patterns of Behavior.* Cambridge: Belknap Press of Harvard University Press.

Goodall, J. (1991). *Through a Window. 30 Years with the Chimpanzees of Gombe.* Boston: Houghton Mifflin.

Holmström, R. (1991). On the phylogeny of the oedipus complex. Psychoanalytic aspects of the ethology of anthropoid apes. *Psychoanalysis and Contemporary Thought 14,* 271–316.

Holmström, R. Hanses, O., & Uotila, H. (1990). The sleep, dreams and sleep rituals of healthy subjects. *Nordisk Psykiatrisk Tidskrift 44,* 353–363.

Klein, M. (1961). *Narrative of a Child Analysis.* London: Hogarth Press.

Kummer, H. (1957). *Soziales verhalten einer mantelpavian-gruppe.* Bern: Hans Huber.

Lagerspetz, K. (1989). Biologinen ihmiskäsitys (The biological concept of man). *In* M. Kamppinen, P. Laihonen, & T. Vuorisalo, *Kulttuurieläin. Ihmistutkimuksen biologiaa.* (*In The Cultural Animal. Essays on the Biology of Culture.* Only in Finnish). Helsinki: Otava.

Lagerspetz, K. M. J., Björkqvist, K., & Peltonen, T. (1988). Is indirect aggression typical of females? *Aggressive Behavior 14,* 403–414.

Landtman, G. (1917). *Ur sagans barndom. Berättelser av vildfolket i Nya Guinea.* (*Of Childhood of Fairy Tales. Stories of Wild People in New Guinea*). Helsingfors: Holger Schildt.

Liberg, O., von Schantz, T. (1985). Sex-biased philopatry and dispersal in birds and mammals: the oedipus hypothesis. *American Naturalist 126,* 129–135.

Lorenz, K. (1963). *Das sogenante Böse. Zur Naturgeschicte der Aggression.* Wien: Borotha-Schoeler.
Makari, G. J. (1991). German philosophy, Freud and the riddle of the woman. *Journal of American Psychoanalytic Association, 39,* 183–213.
Matte-Blanco, I. (1988). *Thinking, Feeling and Being.* London: Routledge.
Meiselman, K. C. (1978). *Incest. A Psychological Study of Causes and Effects with Treatment Recommendations.* San Francisco: Jossey-Bass.
Plooij, F. (1979). How wild chimpanzee babies trigger the onset of mother–infant play—and what the mother makes of it. *In* M. Bullowa (Ed.), *Before Speech. The beginning of Interpersonal Communication.* Cambridge: Cambridge University Press.
Sherkov, S. P. (1989). Evaluation and diagnosis of sexual abuse of little girls. *Journal of American Psychoanalytic Association, 37,* 347–369.
Spitz, R. A. (1965). *The First Year of Life.* New York: International Universities Press.
Stern, D. N. (1985). *The Interpersonal World of the Infant. A View from Psychoanalysis and Developmental Psychology.* New York: Basic Books.
Winnicott, D. W. (1971). *Playing & Reality.* London: Tavistock Publications.

28

# *Aggression in Canine Females*

John Paul Scott

I. INTRODUCTION
II. AGGRESSION IN CANINE FEMALES
A. Overall Plan
B. Importance of Social Relationships
C. Male–Male Relationships
D. Female–Female Relationships
E. Male–Female Relationships
F. Relationships between Mothers and Offspring
III. THE EXPRESSION OF AGONISTIC BEHAVIOR IN RELATIONSHIPS BETWEEN PUPPIES AND HUMANS
A. The Use of Punishment in Rearing Puppies
B. Establishment of Dominance without Punishment or Conflict
C. The Expression of Playful Aggressiveness in Response to Handling
IV. APPLICATIONS TO HUMAN AFFAIRS
REFERENCES

## I. Introduction

Until Lagerspetz's (1961) research, studies on genetic variation in agonistic behavior in house mice, beginning with my original paper (Scott, 1942), had been confined to preexisting differences among inbred strains that had been produced by deliberate random breeding between brothers and sisters. Lagerspetz first used the basic experimental technique of selective breeding and obtained positive results with selecting male albino mice for low and high degrees of fighting behavior expressed toward a male intruder that had been placed in an isolated male's cage. The success of this technique led such later workers as Ebert (1983) to do further selection experiments. Ebert selected for low and high frequencies of agonistic behavior in wild female house mice and obtained similar changes in behavior.

Lagerspetz and Lagerspetz (1983) followed up the earlier study with a Mendelian cross-breeding experiment whose results yielded heritability estimates of .42 to .65. Inheritance did not follow any simple Mendelian pattern, as the range of the $F_1$ covered the entire range of the two parent strains, and the $F_2$ was no more variable than the $F_1$. This result is consistent with the hypothesis that most genetic variation in complex traits is produced by gene combinations rather than simple additive effects of single genes (Scott, 1989).

Meanwhile, Scott and Fuller (1965) were conducting a long-time study on genetics and the social behavior of dogs, using five different dog breeds. Rather than conducting a selection experiment as Lagerspetz did, they made use of breed differences that had been previously produced by selection in the hands of dog breeders. Two of the five breeds, beagles and cocker spaniels, had been selected for nonaggressiveness, a trait that would be useful in the kinds of hunting activity for which these breeds were used. They very seldom got into fights when we reared puppies of either breed together. A third breed, the wire-haired fox terrier, which had been selected as an attack dog in hunting foxes, had the reputation of being highly aggressive, and we found that puppies of this breed readily got into fights with each other even at a very early age. In some cases, fox terrier puppies made group attacks on single litter mates and severely injured them, even at the early age of seven weeks. Little is known about the antecedence of the African basenji except that it was kept by Pygmy tribes in central Africa and used for hunts in which the game was driven into nets. Those that we reared together were highly aggressive as both puppies and as adults. A fifth breed, the Shetland sheep dog, appeared to be intermediate with respect to the expression of aggressiveness.

In my early research I, like any male of my generation, had assumed that only males would fight, or at least that fighting was unimportant in the female sex. Consequently, I had concentrated my research on male mice. But when Fuller and I set up a new program on the genetics of social behavior in dogs at the Jackson Laboratory, we included studies of the development of genetic differences not only among different breeds of dogs but also between males and females. The results were one of the most interesting findings regarding the differences between male and female aggression that had been so far discovered, and I shall summarize these here.

I should add that the cultures of western Europe, including those of the European settlers of North and South America, have in the past strongly emphasized male precedence and male superiority. Women in these cultures have had to struggle for opportunities and recognition in intellectual activities.

Again, like most males of my generation, I had as a young person absorbed this bias, and it was only after I began to appreciate the importance of culture, and after I had met many women who were my mental equals or superiors, that I began to discard it.

At the same time, anyone who is interested in the effects of genetics on behavior should remember that sex is inherited, that is, it is determined in the vast majority of children by a chromosomal composition of XX in a female child versus XY in a male. Since this difference involves a whole chromosome carrying many genes, it should result in larger differences than any single gene.

The result is a complex interaction between culture and genetic variation. To me, the most satisfactory statement of this interaction (no simple statement can be entirely accurate or truthful), is that females and males share the same genes, but some of these genes and gene combinations are expressed differently in the two sexes. With this in mind, I set up the program of research on genetics and social behavior in dogs in such a fashion that we attempted to treat male and female puppies alike in every way. One of the things that we tested and observed was agonistic behavior, mainly between the developing puppies but also between the mothers and their offspring and, to a limited extent, between human handlers and their dog subjects.

## II. Aggression in Canine Females

### A. OVERALL PLAN

In setting up our experiment I tried to design a rearing system that would keep the puppies in as good health as possible and give them as ideal an environment as we could within the confines of a laboratory. At the same time I tried to minimize variation in environmental factors as much as possible and, within the system, to test puppies of known genetic backgrounds in a variety of situations that were appropriate to their ages as they developed from birth to 1 year of age. Among these tests was one that measured differences in the development of aggressiveness. We soon discovered that the most reliable method of eliciting aggressive behavior between puppies was to give two puppies one fresh beef bone. We therefore designed a test situation in which every combination of puppies in a litter was tested with a single bone for a period of ten minutes. The observers recorded all behaviors that were elicited. The test was repeated every 2 weeks from 5 to 15 weeks and given again at 1 year of age.

### B. IMPORTANCE OF SOCIAL RELATIONSHIPS

In this and other experiments we discovered that the most important variable affecting the expression or nonexpression of aggression was the nature of the social relationship in which it took place. As we repeated our test, at 2-week intervals, we were able to observe the development or nondevelopment of dominance relationships between each pair of litter mates. As it turned out, it was changes in the development of these dominance relationships that gave us the clearest picture of genetic differences involving agonistic behavior.

These relationships involved three possible combinations: male–male, male–female, and female–female. Agonistic behavior in each of these relationships was expressed in clearly different fashions.

## C. MALE–MALE RELATIONSHIPS

In all three relationships the puppies tended to develop a dominance order in which one puppy of the pair habitually seized the bone and kept it. The degree of dominance varied according to the breed; the more aggressive breeds such as the basenjis and wire-haired fox terriers stood near the top. Other breeds might develop relationships in which the first puppy to get the bone took it and kept it, or some might look as if they were taking turns in an irregular fashion, but in no breed, even the most peaceful, were there relationships in which two puppies actually shared the same bone. In their struggles to possess the bone, if there was no clear decision at first, the male puppies of the more aggressive breeds sooner or later got into what appeared to be real fights, quite different from the milder struggles in which one puppy attempted to pull the bone away from the other. In such fighting each puppy attempted to seize the other by the back of the neck and force it to the ground. The puppy that was able to do this became dominant, while the loser left the bone in the other's possession and so became subordinate. Once this dominance–subordination relationship was established, it tended to become permanent. In such initial fights, all of which took place before 15 weeks of age, no real damage was done. The puppies attacked the least vulnerable portion of the opponent's body, the neck region which is not only protected by a longer mane of hair but where the skin is loose and quite tough. Since the first teeth of a puppy are quite small, and the second set does not appear till later, the teeth did not inflict serious damage. Once dominance was established, aggressive behavior was reduced to threats on the part of the dominant puppy and avoidance by the subordinate one. Some relationships appeared to be more consistent than others, and we defined complete dominance as the ability of one of the competing pups to possess the bone in nine out of ten minutes of the test, or to repossess it at will.

## D. FEMALE–FEMALE RELATIONSHIPS

In these combinations, actual fighting of the sort described above was extremely rare. Nevertheless, females often established dominance relationships by threats and vocalizations rather than actual fights. Thus, a smaller yappy female might completely dominate a larger passive one.

## E. MALE–FEMALE RELATIONSHIPS

The only clear-cut breed differences that we observed appeared in this relationship. In both wire-haired terriers and basenjis, males developed clear-cut dominance over females, but no such differences appeared in beagles, cocker spaniels, and Shetland sheep dogs. The explanation was, of course, that males are somewhat larger and are on the average 15% heavier than females. In any actual fight the male would tend to win. While the female in such a combination might never initiate a fight, the male often would do so. We concluded that males and females were different in their tendency to express overt fighting, and also that when they fought, the difference in size gave an advantage to the male. In the two most aggressive breeds, males became dominant over females in almost 100% of the combinations, but in the less aggressive breeds, in which overt fighting was less likely to be expressed, females became dominant as often as males. In short, we discovered a sex difference in the expression of overt fighting, males attempting to control a conflict over food by actual force, whereas females tended to do this by threats and vocalizations. This does not mean that females cannot fight, because they can and do fight in response to attacks by either other females or males.

## F. RELATIONSHIPS BETWEEN MOTHERS AND OFFSPRING

Of the dozens of mothers that were carefully observed as they reared their litters, we saw only one case in which a mother had actually injured a puppy, a cocker spaniel mother who had obviously bitten her young puppies around the head and neck. Since this was so uncommon, we assumed that it was a case of pathological behavior. Certainly it was very rare, and we had ample opportunity to observe mother–young interactions, as every litter that went through our "school for dogs" was observed every working day for a ten-minute period through the age of 10 weeks for a total of 60 observations covering 10 hours of time. If there were any cases of violent behavior by the mother, we had ample opportunity to observe them.

What we did see was the one situation in which mothers and young came into a conflict over food. Canine mothers wean their young at approximately 7 weeks of age and the process may go on for a week or two. Some mothers continue to give milk for longer periods and we observed a few that were actually nursing their young at 10 weeks when they were finally separated. But for most mothers, the milk flow decreases greatly at around 7 weeks, and it must be uncomfortable for them if the pups continue to suckle. Furthermore, the young puppies by then have developed sharp, needlelike teeth and we frequently saw scratches on the breast that indicate that puppies had accidentally bitten their mothers. The actual process of weaning takes place as follows. Puppies do not wean themselves, and we would see a puppy at the weaning age approaching its mother confidently and attempting to nurse from one of her nipples, even though the mother might be standing up rather than lying down in the usual nursing position. The mother would reply with a ferocious growl and rush at the puppy with teeth bared and mouth open. The puppy usually rolled over on its back, yapping as if in pain. However the mother had not touched it with her teeth. Negative training was accomplished entirely through threats and vocalization rather than actual pain or injury.

Thus, the canine mothers can control their infants by threats and vocalizations when a conflict arises. Actual conflicts seldom occurred, and we never saw a case of a mother actually attacking her offspring in the process of weaning. Nevertheless, mothers normally become dominant over their puppies, whether a male or female. A mother will maintain this dominance over her adult offspring, and on the few occasions where we saw a male offspring attempting to mate with his mother in estrus, she repulsed him. Thus, a mother can establish dominance over a male offspring by nonviolent methods.

## III. The Expression of Agonistic Behavior in Relationships between Puppies and Humans

Insofar as it is permitted, a puppy reared as a pet will transfer its behavior that is normally given to other dogs to human beings, and it will also develop the dominance–subordination relationships that are typical of relationships between dogs. Similarly, dog owners often attempt to transfer to dogs the kind of training, especially of the social sort, that they might express toward their own children as a parent.

### A. THE USE OF PUNISHMENT IN REARING PUPPIES

Dog owners frequently use punishment to control undesirable behavior in their pets. The usual result is to establish a dominance–subordination relationship, with the human occupying the dominant role. This relationship is long lasting and the dog involved seldom, if ever, rebels even after it becomes an adult.

In our experimental program with genetics and social behavior in dogs, however, we decided to never punish the puppies. The environment in which they were reared was such that they could seldom do anything that would be harmful. We did this because punishment is effective as a training method only if it is given differentially for undesirable behavior. If we started punishing the puppies we would have to punish some and not others, and to punish some infrequently and others more often. The result would be a confusing variable whose effects might or might not be produced by genetic differences.

### B. ESTABLISHMENT OF DOMINANCE WITHOUT PUNISHMENT OR CONFLICT

We were surprised to discover that these unpunished puppies nevertheless began to give signs that they were extremely subordinate to human beings. Reviewing our interactions with them, we saw that we had from the day of birth onward picked up these puppies, carried them around to be weighed, tested, or moved about for any other reason. All this began before the development of any agonistic behavior, and we never saw the young puppies resist. They simply lay quiet and relaxed in what we presumed to be the warm comfort of our arms, and we continued this catching and holding behavior even when the dogs became adults. If we ever wanted to control an adult dog for any reason, all we had to do was to walk toward it as if we were going to pick it up, and it would immediately flatten out on the ground in a posture of extreme subordination. The posture of subordination varied among breeds but all became subordinate whether or not they were highly aggressive among themselves. We concluded that we had established dominance by restraint rather than by violence.

In establishing this dominance we never used the vocal threat technique of the dog mothers, but the fact that such techniques will work can be demonstrated easily by any dog owner. Speaking to a pet loudly and severely is usually enough to stop any undesirable behavior. This is most effective if it is used in a low tone of voice similar to the natural growls of a dog. If one wishes, it should be easy to establish dominance over a puppy by using techniques similar to that of the mother, namely a combination of threatening movements and loud vocalizations, especially in the lower register of tones.

## C. THE EXPRESSION OF PLAYFUL AGGRESSIVENESS IN RESPONSE TO HANDLING

We also attempted to measure the development of the dog–human relationship by devising a test in which an experimenter did in a standardized fashion all of the things that dog owners routinely do to a pet or strange dog. This "Handling Test" included standing still, walking toward the puppy, walking away, squatting and holding out the hand, petting the puppy, calling it, and picking it up, all repeated once. We developed four different measures of the ensuing behavior, one of which we called playful aggression. This consisted mainly of playful biting and pawing which, if encouraged, could eventually develop into a more serious kind of conflict.

The test was administered by male and female investigators on alternate weeks. They were all instructed to give the test in exactly the same way, but the puppies nevertheless responded somewhat differently to male and female handlers, showing significantly higher scores toward female handlers in all breeds at 5 and 7 weeks of age (Scott, 1992a). We concluded that the puppies were in some way responding to sex differences, perhaps to physical size, differences in odor, or subtle differences in behavior that were not apparent to the human observer.

We concluded that the puppies could respond differentially to human male and female handlers, but found no evidence that male and female puppies were responding differently from each other. This was similar to results in all of the tests that we administered to the puppies, whether they were problem solving, forced training, emotionality, or general activity. Breed differences, however, were universal in all of the tests, the most pronounced being those of the emotionality and physiological reactions, such as heart rate changes. The only significant differences between the two sexes were in agonistic behavior as expressed among the dogs themselves. We concluded that in the dog species, agonistic behavior is organized somewhat differently in the two sexes, although the basic patterns of behavior such as barking, growling, biting, and the like are quite similar in both sexes.

## IV. Applications to Human Affairs

No species can be used as an exact model for another, as once two species have diverged in evolution, they no longer share the same gene pool, and the processes of evolution continuously make them more and more different. Thus, findings in any species can never be applied directly to another. But it is still legitimate to consider the findings in one species as possible hypotheses to explain the behavior of another.

The domestic dog should be a fertile and unusually legitimate source of such hypotheses, for the following reasons:

1. Dogs were first domesticated at least ten to twelve thousand years ago and have been a part of human social systems ever since (Scott, 1968). This suggests that they must share at least some aspects of human behavior, even though they have definitely not become four-legged humans. Almost all of our domestic animals are highly social in nature, and the fact that the dog became the first domestic animal indicates that its social behavior and organization were initially similar to that of humans, and that it has since become more similar through the processes of selection.
2. In the primary food-getting activity of dogs, either males or females make good hunters. In our laboratory experiments with dogs we found no indications that females were different from males in any problem-solving ability. This suggests the hypothesis that the basic abilities in the human species are likewise shared by both sexes, and that genuine genetic differences between them are few and hard to find, other than those attributable to average physical size and muscular strength.
3. The only important differences that we found between the two sexes in the different dog breeds were those that I have briefly described above, namely, the way in which their agonistic behavior is expressed.

I therefore suggest the hypothesis that humans may share similar tendencies with respect to the expression of agonistic behavior in the two sexes.

In the human species, neither males nor females are anatomically well adapted for physical combat (Scott, 1992b), and it is only with tools or learned techniques, such as boxing or karate, that physical conflicts become injurious or fatal. On the average, human males are physically stronger with respect to muscular activity and are somewhat taller and heavier than females, although there is a great deal of overlap in all respects.

Again, with considerable overlap, there is some evidence that females enjoy superior language ability. At any rate, female human babies begin to talk sooner, again, on the average and not necessarily in particular cases. One might therefore expect a greater tendency to verbal rather than physical expression of agonistic behavior in human females.

I cannot speak for any culture other than my own, but I can state that in both the North American and European varieties of English-speaking culture, physical punishment has long played a major role in child rearing, and that a major disgrace is the extent to which child abuse occurs in the United States. I suggest that this is not only undesirable but unnecessary. Our experiments with the canine puppies show that dominance can be established—where physical control is necessary—by restraint and not through pain, by simply picking the puppies up day after day, starting soon after birth. This is the same sort of behavior that human mothers apply daily with their babies. I therefore suggest the hypothesis that physical restraint rather than violence is the preferred method for controlling a child's behavior. This hypothesis can be tested by any parent.

I also suggest that negative control of undesirable behavior can be established by threats and vocalizations, and that it produces more desirable results than actual physical punishment. If canine mothers can do this, and dogs have a minimal amount of vocal ability compared to the human species, there is no reason why humans could not use similar abilities, augmented by their ability to explain exactly what the vocalizer wants or does not want. If there is any species that has superior vocal ability, it is humans. Vocal control should be the norm.

What we really need is some way in which to put these scientific findings into effect. As all of us know, our scientific papers usually reach very narrow audiences. What we need is scientific knowledge on how to bring about desirable cultural change on a large scale and with a speed that is measured in years rather than centuries. The body of knowledge on the causes of aggression that has been accumulated by investigators such as Lagerspetz and the numerous other workers in this field is now well established, and can be used to control destructive violence, especially that which is directed against children.

## References

Ebert, P. D. (1983). Selection for aggression in a natural population. *In* E. C. Simmel, M. E. Hahn, & J. K. Walters (Eds.), *Aggressive Behavior: Genetic and Neural Approaches* (pp. 103–127). Hillsdale, New Jersey: Erlbaum.

Lagerspetz, K. M. J. (1961). Genetic and social causes of aggressive behavior in mice. *Scandinavian Journal of Psychology, 2,* 167–173.

Lagerspetz, K. M. J., & Lagerspetz, K. Y. H. (1983). Genes and aggression. *In* E. C. Simmel, M. E. Hahn, & J. K. Walters (Eds.), *Aggressive Behavior: Genetic and Neural Approaches* (pp. 89–101). Hillsdale, New Jersey: Erlbaum.

Scott, J. P. (1942). Genetic differences in the social behavior of inbred mice. *Journal of Heredity, 33,* 11–15.

Scott, J. P. (1968). Evolution and domestication of the dog. *Evolutionary biology, 2,* 243–275.

Scott, J. P. (1989). *The Evolution of Social Systems.* New York: Gordon & Breach.

Scott, J. P. (1992a). The phenomenon of attachment in human–nonhuman relationships. *In* H. Davis, & D. Balfour (Eds.), *The Inevitable Bond.* New York: Cambridge University Press.

Scott, J. P. (1992b). Aggression: function and control in social systems. *Aggressive Behavior, 18,* 1–20.

Scott, J. P., & Fuller, J. L. (1965). *Genetics and the Social Behavior of the Dog.* Chicago: Chicago University Press.

29

# *Sex, Drugs, and Defensive Behavior: Implications for Animal Models of Defense*

D. Caroline Blanchard and Robert J. Blanchard

I. SEX DIFFERENCES IN ANTIPREDATOR DEFENSIVE BEHAVIORS
A. The Anxiety/Defense Test Battery
B. Sex Differences in the Anxiety/Defense Test Battery
C. Sex Differences in the Fear/Defense Test Battery
D. Sex Differences in Antipredator Ultrasonic Vocalizations
II. SEX DIFFERENCES: IMPLICATIONS FOR THE BIOLOGICAL BASES OF DEFENSE
III. IMPLICATIONS OF SEX DIFFERENCES FOR ANIMAL MODELS OF DEFENSIVE BEHAVIOR
REFERENCES

In examining conspecific fighting, aggression and defense may be regarded as complementary and interlocking aspects of a behavioral unit or entity, a view conceptualized in Scott's (1958) term "agonistic behavior." This conceptualization is strongly supported by analyses of intraspecific aggressive and defensive behaviors, emphasizing the extent to which behaviors from each category may serve as strategies effective in the context of particular behaviors from the other category (Blanchard & Blanchard, 1977). As an example, in rats the upright defensive posture, or, lying on the back, may be an effective defense because they protect the back, the specific target of offensive bites in this species. Thus, in this conspecific context, the complementary aspects of aggression and defense are clear, although the mechanisms underlying each may be strikingly independent.

However, defensive behavior has a major, and perhaps even more basic, function. Any species that is subject to predation (certainly the vast majority of mammalian species) has an antipredator defense repertoire with behavioral elements that touch virtually every aspect of the lives of these animals, and in which the consequences of an inadequate or inappropriate response may be immediate and fatal. Research on reactions of wild and laboratory rats to predators such as cats or humans has a long history in psychology (e.g., Yerkes, 1913; Stone, 1932; Curti, 1935; Blanchard & Blanchard, 1971). The results of these studies are in agreement with the view that a range of antipredator defenses are innately organized in these animals, that is, occur in adults with minimal or no directly relevant experience, and in accordance with important features of the eliciting stimulus and situation. The mammalian defenses are increasingly recognized as an important focus for study, on both a behavioral and a biological level, leading to the development of research paradigms which will provide greater specificity, control, and analytic precision in the understanding of these evolved neurobehavioral systems (Blanchard, Blanchard, & Hori, 1989). Some of these new paradigms have produced data indicating that gender is an important determinant of defensive behavior, and detailing gender interactions with biological systems controlling defense. The relative utility of antipredator defense and conspecific defense paradigms for description and analysis of such gender differences also provides an important point of comparison for these approaches.

# I. Sex Differences in Antipredator Defensive Behaviors

Our recent work indicating a systematic gender effect on antipredator defensive behavior has been in the context of two sets of tests, a Fear/Defense Test Battery (F/DTB) and an Anxiety/Defense Test Battery (A/DTB), each designed to produce and polarize a number of specific defensive behaviors. The two test batteries are differentiated by a focus: in the F/DTB, the focus is on defensive behaviors seen in the context of a present, discrete, approaching predator; the A/DTB employs situations previously associated with the presence of a predator, or partial predator stimuli, such as the odor of a cat. This division was based on an earlier analysis (Blanchard & Blanchard, 1989), indicating that different defensive behaviors are elicited in these two situations, and also that the defensive behaviors responding to anticipated, as opposed to actual, threat provide a closer analogy to both the situational and behavioral aspects of anxiety. In our laboratory, these test batteries are used primarily in conjunction with administration of anxiolytic or anxiogenic drugs, and the drug profiles thus constructed have proved to be consonant with this hypothesis.

## A. THE ANXIETY/DEFENSE TEST BATTERY

The Anxiety/Defense Test Battery consists of 3 tests, each of which has been subject to some degree of evolution and refinement over time. Two of these (Blanchard, Blanchard, & Weiss, 1990) involve situations in which a cat is presented (providing a dangerous situation) and then removed, and in the third, a partial threat stimulus (the odor of a cat) is presented (Blanchard *et al.*, 1990).

The first two of these situations, involving cat presentation, elicit proxemic avoidance of the cat area, with or without freezing, and interference with nondefensive behaviors. Measures of eating (preferred foods) and drinking (following a single, mild deprivation period) are taken to evaluate this interference. However, the central element of defensive behavior to potential threat is the "risk assessment" pattern, a set of long-duration behaviors which involve orientation to dangerous places, followed by approach and investigation of these (Blanchard, Blanchard, & Rodgers, 1991). While orientation is a virtually inevitable accompaniment of reactivity to a localizable potential threat, the approach/contact/investigative components are strongly inhibited by freezing and proxemic avoidance of stimuli with a high threat potential, and occur much later. These are primary reactions, however, in the cat-odor test. Thus, these three situations are varied, in order to obtain relatively independent measures of each behavioral tendency.

The tests of the A/DTB have now been run in 10 separate studies. These drug tests typically involve a vehicle control group exposed to the threat stimulus, 2–3 drug groups, treated identically, except that they are administered varying doses of the drug to be tested, and a vehicle control group not exposed to the threat stimulus. Comparisons of the two vehicle-injected groups, exposed or not exposed to the cat/cat odor, provide evidence of the elicitation of defensive behaviors in each individual study, and indicate that the vehicle-injected, threat-exposed group against which the drug groups are tested is, in fact, defensive. Male and female subjects (typically 8 each) comprise each group.

A particular advantage of this system, in terms of analysis of sex differences, is that these studies can indicate not only that there are male–female differences in behavior, but also the direction of the difference. This might not be important if defensive behavior were a unitary system providing only one measure, the magnitude of which could be interpreted unequivocally. However, the defense patterns are complex, and the measures of these situations show changes—albeit systematic changes—in both directions. Thus, from an analytic standpoint, it is very important that the behavioral control afforded by comparison of the two vehicle-injected groups can provide an indication of how increased defensiveness changes individual behaviors in this particular test situation, such that gender differences can be evaluated against this background.

## B. SEX DIFFERENCES IN THE ANXIETY/DEFENSE TEST BATTERY

Figure 1 presents an overview of the effects of cat or cat-odor presentation on the measures of the three A/DTB tests, for a set of 5, directly comparable studies. This figure is abridged from Blanchard, Shepherd, Carobrez, & Blanchard,

| | Number of studies | Threat effects | Sex differences | Female-threat parallels |
|---|---|---|---|---|
| **PROXEMIC/AVOIDANCE TEST** | | | | |
| Location near cat Area | 5 | ↓ ↓ ↓ ↓ ↓ | ♀↓ - - ♀↑ SxT | mixed |
| Mid-Chamber location | 5 | ↓ - - - - | ♀↓ ↓ - - - | Y |
| Location far from cat Area | 5 | ↑ ↑ ↑ - - | ♀↑ - - - - | Y |
| Transits | 5 | ↓ ↓ ↓ ↓ - | ♀↓ ↓ - - - | Y |
| Crouch | 5 | ↑ ↑ ↑ - - | ♀↑ - - - SxE | Y |
| Rear | 5 | ↓ ↓ ↓ - - | ♀↓ - - - - | Y |
| Locomote | 5 | ↓ ↓ ↓ - - | ♀↓ - - - - | Y |
| Lie | 5 | - - - - - | ♀↓ ↓ - - - | - |
| Groom | 5 | ↓ - - - - | ♀↓ - - - SxT | Y |
| **EAT/DRINK TEST** | | | | |
| Eat frequency | 5 | ↓ ↓ ↓ ↓ ↓ | ♀↓ ↓ - - - | Y |
| Drink frequency | 5 | ↓ ↓ ↓ - - | ♀↓ ↓ - - - | Y |
| **CAT ODOR TEST** | | | | |
| Flat back app. dur. | 3 | ↑ ↑ ↑ | ♀↑ - - | Y |
| Contact duration | 3 | ↓ ↓ - | - - - | - |

**Figure 1.** Reliable effects of cat or cat odor (threat stimulus) exposure and gender differences in comparable studies using the Anxiety/Defense Test Battery.

(1991), presenting only measures taken in the post-cat period. The results of these comparisons indicate excellent consistency in threat stimulus exposure effects across these studies. Reliable threat stimulus exposure effects were obtained in one or more studies, for 12 of the 13 post-cat measures of the 3 tests, and, where differences were obtained, the direction of difference for subjects exposed to the threat stimulus in comparison to nonexposed controls was completely consistent. Gender differences were also obtained in one or more studies for 12 of these measures. For 10 of the 11 measures, where reliable differences were found for *both* sex and cat-exposure effects, obtained gender effects consistently indicated that females showed higher levels of the behavioral changes characteristic of exposed animals. In addition, the sex interactions with time or threat stimulus exposure noted for some studies are consonant with this interpretation.

While this figure indicates that, overall, female differences were less common than cat or cat-odor exposure effects, it should be noted that these females were randomly selected, and doubtless comprised animals at varying stages of the estrous cycle. If estrous phase is involved in gender effects on defensiveness, as it appears to be in reactivity to some anxiolytic drugs (Fernandez-Guasti & Picazo, 1990), these findings may suggest an even more robust gender effect at specific estrous phases, as well as an important effect of estrous phase-related hormones on these measures.

## C. SEX DIFFERENCES IN THE FEAR/ DEFENSE TEST BATTERY

In apparent contrast to the A/DTB, studies using the F/DTB have not provided any significant sex differences (Blanchard, Shepherd, Carobrez, & Blanchard, 1991). We initially interpreted this as indicating that sex differences do not occur in defensive responding to present, approaching, or contacting threat stimuli, noting also that the specific behaviors elicited and measured in these situations are very different indeed from those of the A/DTB: flight, freezing, startle, defensive threat (sonic) vocalization, and jump attack with biting.

However, the early F/DTB studies (Blanchard, Flannelly, & Blanchard, 1986) focused on wild-trapped wild rats, animals showing great defensiveness to the approaching and contacting threat source (the human experimenter). Both male and female wild rats appeared to be near-maximally defensive, producing a possible ceiling effect which made measurement of increased female defensiveness very difficult. A more recent F/DTB study (Blanchard, Weatherspoon, Shepherd, Rodgers, & Blanchard, 1991) used rats bred in the University of Hawaii breeding facility from wild-trapped stock. Since only about 50% of wild-trapped females breed in captivity, some degree of self-selection for breeding, associated with levels of stress occasioned by captive conditions and proximity to humans, is predictable, as are possible effects of early experience with human handling in the process of cage cleaning and other animal caretaking duties. The result is that while these animals continue to show clear defensive reactions to human approach and handling they are less defensive than the wild-trapped rats, and thus provide a greater opportunity for increases, as well as decreases, in defensiveness to be evaluated.

In two drug series reported in Blanchard, Weatherspoon, Shepherd, Rodgers, and Blanchard (1991), gender differences continued to fail to achieve a reliable level of statistical significance. Sex effects, however, *approached* significance ($.10 > p > .05$) on five of the dozen or so measures in one study, and on three measures of the other study. Two of these, flight duration and reactions to dorsal contact, were the same for both studies. The near differences thus obtained were in the direction of enhanced defensiveness for females. While this pattern of findings does not provide convincing evidence of gender difference in the F/DTB, it does at least re-open the question of the generality of enhanced female defensiveness, clearly demonstrated in the A/DTB, but not even suggested, prior to this study, in the F/DTB.

## D. SEX DIFFERENCES IN ANTIPREDATOR ULTRASONIC VOCALIZATIONS

An additional, and perhaps more complex, antipredator defensive behavior has also been the subject of recent work in this laboratory. Ultrasonic vocalizations occur in both infant and adult rats, under a variety of circumstances, such as maternal separation/cooling in infants (Panksepp, 1982; Winslow & Insel, 1991), intraspecific agonistic encounters (Sales & Pye, 1974), during and after copulation (Barfield & Thomas, 1986), and in situations associated with pain (Van der Poel *et al.*, 1989). Ultrasonic vocalizations (18–26 kHz) also occur when rats are exposed to a cat. However, these antipredator ultrasounds, like many other defensive behaviors, are also tightly controlled by additional features of the situation (Blanchard, Blanchard, Agullana, & Weiss, 1991). Thus, individual rats exposed to a cat in an open area show no ultrasounds, but group-housed rats in a burrow system affording concealment from the cat make ultrasounds at a high level during the presence of the cat and for about 30 minutes afterward, a time period when they are located almost exclusively within the burrow system. However, female rats individually run in a novel apparatus affording concealment make no ultrasounds either to the cat or when replaced in the apparatus 24 hours later.

When one-male, one-female groups were housed in similar burrow systems, with a cat placed in the apparatus just after one member of each pair had been removed, females showed reliably more frequent vocalizations and longer total vocalization durations during the cat period (Blanchard, Agullana, Magee, Weiss, & Blanchard, in press). Since location in the burrows appeared to be a major correlate of vocalization, it might be noted that subjects of both sex spent almost all of the test period in the burrows, and no reliable differences in burrow location were obtained. In a second study from the same series, sonographic analyses of ultrasonic cries for males and females indicated that females made reliably more individual ultrasonic pulses, and had a reliably shorter mean pulse duration.

Pulse form also demonstrated gender differences. Ultrasonic vocalizations were recorded by a Racal store 4DS instrumentation recorder connected to an Ultrasound Advice SM2 microphone and a SP2 preamplifier, and analyzed using a Kay DSP1 5500 digital sonograph. These sonographic analyses indicated a variety of different pulse forms in the 18–28-kHz range, which were sorted into six categories based on the type of frequency modulation which occurred over the length of the individual pulse. For males, the most common pulse form (about 70%) was negatively accelerated descending, with a gradual frequency-down modulation over the first third to half of the pulse to a relatively stable baseline. This pulse form was reliably less common (about 25%) for females, which tended to show more linearly descending and U-shaped pulses. Female base frequencies (kHz) were reliably higher than those of males. Pulse-train parameters were also analyzed, based on log survival analyses of interpulse intervals for individual animals to obtain pulse intervals differentiating pulse trains from pulses within a train. While males and females did not differ reliably in either the mean duration of intertrain intervals, or average pulse-train duration, females showed reliably shorter durations of interpulse intervals within trains, and a higher average number of pulses per pulse train. Thus, while these pulse-train and pulse-parameter differences cannot be related to a clear defense intensity dimension (no such dimension being available, at present), it is clear that, with reference to antipredator ultrasonic vocalization, as with the variety of defensive behaviors measured in the A/DTB, female response shows clear and reliable differences from that of males.

## II. Sex Differences: Implications for the Biological Bases of Defense

One important rationale for interest in gender differences in animal models of defensiveness is that rates of defense-linked psychopathologies, such as depression and anxiety, are substantially higher in women than in men (Robins *et al.*, 1984; Silverman, 1968). These differences appear even when the effects of factors such as differential diagnostic biases for men and women and differential experience with aversive life events are discounted (Amenson & Lewinsohn, 1981). The findings outlined above, of high-magnitude sex differences in defense for male and female rats, clearly support the possibility that gender-linked biological factors are involved in the higher rates of relevant clinical psychopathology for women, and further suggest the value of examining gender interactions with drug effects on these behaviors.

This examination is considerably complicated by the complexity of the defense system, and the various interactions of defense-related behaviors as measured in the A/DTB. Since females often show different baselines than males, sex × drug interactions can reflect a floor or ceiling effect for one gender only. In addition, when no baseline effects are apparent, sex × drug interactions may represent a truly differential effect of that drug on one or the other sex. A number of sex × drug interactions have been obtained for the various compounds run in the A/DTB, many of which are described in Blanchard, Shepherd, Carobrez, and Blanchard (1991). Particularly consistent interactions have been obtained for serotonergic compounds, suggesting that females are more sensitive to compounds selective for 5-$HT_{1A}$ and 5-$HT_2$ receptor subtypes, as well as to imipramine, while male response to compounds selective for 5-$HT_3$ receptors may be greater. These findings are generally congruent with recent work indicating the involvement of serotonin systems in other behaviors showing gender differences (Kennett *et al.*, 1986; Heinsbroek *et al.* 1988), or of direct gender differences in the functioning of regional 5-HT systems (Haleem, Kennett, & Curzon, 1990).

While sex × drug interactions have also been obtained in A/DTB studies involving benzodiazepines (generally indicating heightened male responsiveness) and ethanol, these were generally less powerful than those found with the serotonin systems. The NMDA antagonist, MK-801, however, produced A/DTB results suggesting an anxiolytic profile for both males and females, but with females showing additional and puzzling effects. In home-cage tests not involving threat, females, but not males, showed dose-dependent effects on locomotion and crouching, along with a loss of balance at the highest dose, effects which tended to mask their A/DTB profiles.

These findings suggest that gender interactions with drug effects may either involve differential effects of these drugs on defensiveness for males and females, or may reflect gender-related effects not related to defensiveness per se, which interact with defense measures. In either case, the issue is not only a matter of understanding these relationships on a basic science level. Since women constitute a majority of the potential client population for anxiolytic and antidepressant drugs, any such substantial gender-, or sex hormone-linked difference has significant implications for the development, testing, and therapeutic use of these compounds. These considerations reflect something of the complexity of the defense systems and their neurobiological correlates, and point out the necessity for detailed, analytically efficient animal models of defensive behavior, in which responsiveness to gender may be an additional criterion of relevance.

# III. Implications of Sex Differences for Animal Models of Defensive Behavior

The above patterns of sex and sex × drug interactions are complex, but very apparent, in antipredator defensive behaviors. In this context, it is interesting to speculate about the difficulties that might be encountered in demonstrating such gender effects on defensive behavior and their biological bases, in conspecific defense.

Conspecific defense necessarily involves either a male, or a female (or, for the sake of completeness, a gender-manipulated) attacker. Female rats attacked by males, and male rats attacked by females, are confronted with an opponent affording stimuli which elicit a host of social, sexual, and agonistic behaviors.

Same-sex dyads have some of these same disadvantages, plus the obvious problem that females show different attack patterns and much lower levels of attack than do males. In mixed-sex pairs, the simple fact of sexual size dimorphism for rats means that either size or age must necessarily differ for female–male as opposed to male–male dyads. With reference to the latter point, it might be noted that a standard cat threat stimulus is also relatively larger for female rats. However, given the initial cat–rat weight differential, this is clearly less important. Also, an odor has no easily dimensioned "size" with reference to a particular subject, and cat odor produces much the same pattern of gender differences in defensiveness as do the other tests of the A/DTB. Thus, while an elaborate system of systematic manipulations and controls might reduce some of the problems in interpretation of differences in defensiveness for males and females in conspecific encounters, it is clear that gender differences in defense tests involving threatening conspecifics could be analyzed only very gradually and with a great deal of uncertainty.

This is not to say that conspecific defense paradigms have no value. They obviously reflect an evolved neurobehavioral system of great importance to rats, as to other mammals. The point, however, is analytic precision and simplicity. Given the host of relationships embedded in conspecific encounters, and the variety of behavioral systems elicited by conspecifics, a threatening conspecific presents complexities which are counterproductive to analysis of the defense systems. These defense systems are sufficiently complex, alone, that they tax the analytic capabilities of any existing research laboratory. We suggest antipredator models as one particularly productive approach to minimalization of confounding or extraneous factors in the analysis of defensive behavior.

Finally, a sampling of the literature suggests that approximately 85% of animal tests of anxiolytic drug effects involve male subjects only. The clinical literature also is heavily weighted toward the use of male subjects, and subject gender is so lightly regarded that a recent sampling of abstracts from this literature indicates that the vast majority of these do not even mention subject gender. While it is premature to conclude that females show a more conservative defense pattern across mammalian species, the parallels between enhanced female antipredator defense in rodents and the higher levels of defense-related psychopathologies in women strongly suggest the importance of focused attention on gender differences in the defense systems and their neurobiological bases.

## Acknowledgments

The research reported in this chapter was supported by National Institutes of Health Grants AA06220 and MH42803, and by Research Careers in Minority Institutions (RCMI) Grants RR03061 and RR01825.

## References


Amenson, C. S., & Lewinsohn, P. M. (1981). An investigation into the observed sex difference in prevalence of unipolar depression. *Journal of Abnormal Psychology, 90,* 1–13.

Barfield, R. J., & Thomas, D. A. (1986). The role of ultrasonic vocalizations in the regulation of reproduction in rats. *Annals of the New York Academy of Science, 474,* 33–43.

Blanchard, R. J., and Blanchard, D. C. (1971). Defensive reactions in the albino rat. *Learning and Motivation, 21,* 351–362.

Blanchard, R. J., & Blanchard, D. C. (1977). Aggressive behavior in the rat. *Behavioral Biology, 21,* 197–224.

Blanchard, R. J., & Blanchard, D. C. (1989). Anti-predator defensive behaviors in a visible burrow system. *Journal of Comparative Psychology, 103,* 70–82.

Blanchard, R. J., Flannelly, K. J., and Blanchard, D. C. (1986). Defensive behaviors of laboratory and wild *Rattus norvegicus. Journal of Comparative Psychology, 100,* 101–107.

Blanchard, R. J., Blanchard, D. C., & Hori, K. (1989). Ethoexperimental approaches to the study of defensive behavior. *In* R. J. Blanchard, P. F., Brain, D. C. Blanchard, and S. Parmigiani (Eds.), *Ethoexperimental Approaches to the Study of Behavior* pp. 114–136. Dordrecht: Kluwer Academic Publishers.

Blanchard, R. J., Blanchard, D. C., and Weiss, S. M. (1990). Ethanol effects in an Anxiety/Defense Test Battery. *Alcohol, 7,* 375–381.

Blanchard, R. J., Blanchard, D. C., Weiss, S. M., & Mayer, S. (1990). Effects of ethanol and diazepam on reactivity to predatory odors. *Pharmacology, Biochemistry, and Behavior, 35,* 775–780.

Blanchard, D. C., Blanchard, R. J., and Rodgers, R. J. (1991). Risk assessment and animal models of anxiety. *In* B. Olivier, J. Mos, & J. L. Slangen (Eds.), *Animal Models in Psychopharmacology* pp. 117–134. Basel: Birkhauser Verlag AG.

Blanchard, R. J., Agullana, R. L., Magee, L., Weiss, S., and Blanchard, D. C. (in press). Sex effects on the incidence and sonographic characteristics of antipredator ultrasonic cries in the laboratory rat (*R. norvegicus*). *Journal of Comparative Psychology.*

Blanchard, R. J., Blanchard, D. C., Agullana, R., and Weiss, S. M. (1991). 22kHz alarm cries in the laboratory rat. *Physiology and Behavior, 50,* 967–972.

Blanchard, D. C., Shepherd, J. K., Carobrez, A. P., and Blanchard, R. J. (1991). Sex effects in defensive behavior: Baseline differences and drug interactions. *Neuroscience and Biobehavioral Reviews, 15,* 461–468.

Blanchard, D. C., Weatherspoon, A., Shepherd, J. K., Rodgers, R. J., and Blanchard, R. J. (1991). "Paradoxical" effects of morphine on anti-predator defense reactions in wild and laboratory (*R. norvegicus*) rats. *Pharmacology, Biochemistry, and Behavior, 40,* 819–828.

Curti, M. W. (1935). Native fear responses of white rats in the presence of cats. *Psychological Monographs, 46,* 78–98.

Fernandez-Guasti, A., and Picazo, O. (1990). The actions of diazepam and serotonergic anxiolytics vary according to the gender and the estrus cycle phase. *Pharmacology, Biochemistry, and Behavior, 37,* 77–81.

Haleem, D. J., Kennett, G. A., & Curzon, G. (1990). Hippocampal 5-hydroxytryptamine synthesis is greater in females rat than in males and more decreased by the 5-HT$^{1a}$ agonist 8-OH-DPAT. *Journal of Neural Transmission, 79,* 93–101.

Heinsbroek, R. P. W., Feenstra, M. G. P., Boon, P., Van Haaren, F., & van de Poll, N. E. (1988). Sex differences in passive avoidance depend on the integrity of the central serotonergic system. *Pharmacology, Biochemistry, and Behavior, 31,* 499–503.

Kennet, G. A., Chaouloff, F., Marcou, M., & Curzon, G. (1986). Female rats are more vulnerable than males in an animal model of depression: the possible role of serotonin. *Brain Research, 382,* 416–421.

Panksepp J. (1982). Toward a general psychobiological theory of emotions. *Behavioral Brain Science, 5,* 407–467.

Robins, L. N., Helzer, J. E., Weissman, M. M. Orvaschel, H., Gruenberg, E., Burke, J. D., & Regier, D. A. (1984). Lifetime prevalence of specific psychiatric disorders in three cities. *Archives of General Psychiatry, 41,* 949–958.

Sales, G. D., & Pye, S. (1974). *Ultrasonic Communication by Animals.* New York: Wiley.

Scott, J. P. (1958). *Aggression.* Chicago: University of Chicago Press.

Silverman, C. (1968). *The Epidemiology of Depression.* Baltimore, Maryland: Johns Hopkins University Press.

Stone, C. P. (1932). Wildness and savageness in rats of different strains. *In* K. S. Lashley (Ed.), *Studies in the Dynamics of Behavior.* Chicago: University of Chicago Press.

Van der Poel, A. M., Noach, E. J. K., & Miczek, K. A. (1989). Temporal patterning of ultrasonic distress calls in the adult rat: Effects of morphine and benzodiazepines. *Psychopharmacology (Berlin) 97,* 147–148.

Yerkes, R. M. (1913). The heredity of savageness and wildness in rats. *Journal of Animal Behavior, 3,* 286–296.

Winslow, J. T., and Insel, T. R. (1991). Endogenous opioids: do they modulate the rat pup's response to social isolation? *Behavioral Neuroscience, 105,* 253–263.

30

# Aggression and Aggressiveness in Female Golden Hamsters: The Attack Priming Effect as Tour Guide to the Central Mechanisms of Aggression

Michael Potegal

*Lately it occurs to me,*
*What a long strange trip it's been.*
— The Grateful Dead, "Truckin"

I. FIRST STEPS
II. PHENOMENA THAT MAY BE EXPLICABLE IN TERMS OF AGGRESSIVE AROUSAL: THE PROMISED LAND
III. IN SEARCH OF THE NEURAL FLYWHEEL
IV. YOU CAN'T GET THERE FROM HERE: CIRCUMPERAMBULATIONS, DIGRESSIONS, AND DEAD ENDS
V. STUDIES OF AGGRESSIVE AROUSAL IN HAMSTERS AND RATS: ON THE YELLOW BRICK ROAD
VI. NOTES TOWARD A THEORETICAL MODEL OF AGGRESSIVE AROUSAL: TRAVELER'S TALES
VII. GENERAL APPROACH TO INVESTIGATING THE NEURAL MECHANISMS OF AGGRESSION USING THE PRIMING EFFECT: ROYAL ROAD OR PRIMROSE PATH?
VIII. THE EVIDENCE FOR NEUROANATOMICAL LOCALIZATION AND, MAYBE, MECHANISM OF AGGRESSIVE AROUSAL: THE FIRST MILESTONES
IX. THE FUNCTIONAL SIGNIFICANCE OF THE CMA LOCALIZATION: THE NEXT LANDMARK
X. ANNOTATING THE ITINERARY
XI. THE ROAD AHEAD
XII. THE HUMAN CONDITION: ANGER (CONSCIOUS AND UNCONSCIOUS), AGGRESSIVE AROUSAL, AND VIOLENT BEHAVIOR
XIII. THE MEDIAL AMYGDALA, TEMPORAL LOBE EPILEPSY, AND ANGER
XIV. FIGURE AND GROUND REVERSAL IN THE ANALYSIS OF AGGRESSION: LOOKING AHEAD TO LOOKING BACK
XV. A CONFLUENCE OF PILGRIMS
REFERENCES

## I. First Steps

Having obtained my Bachelors degree in physics rather than psychology and having taken exactly two courses in psychology as an undergraduate, I arrived in the MIT graduate program in psychology with a great but poorly defined interest in the general phenomenon of "emotion." Once there, my interest in aggression as a research challenge was awakened by reading the accounts of Lorenz, Leyhausen, and other ethologists. This was 1964, and I also encountered the then recent rediscovery of shock-induced fighting by Ulrich and his colleagues (Ulrich & Azrin, 1962). It seemed that a variety of fascinating phenomena might be analyzed with a number of experimental techniques. Besides having a natural interest in the subject, doubtless with deep psychodynamic roots, I was also moved to pursue research on aggression for the very practical reason that the reading in this area appeared more manageable than the literature on "emotionality" (a code word for fearfulness) which was, even then, voluminous.

During this period I became acquainted with the proposition that the orderly sequence of acts comprising many "instinctual" behaviors was the consequence of the successive presentation of, and the animal's reaction to, a naturally ordered series of stimuli (e.g., a bird builds a nest whereupon the stimuli from the nest elicit the next step in parental behavior). In the extension of this argument to agonistic interactions, presumably, display by one combatant induces counterdisplay in its antagonist in an escalating counterpoint. This description of events emphasizes that view that each behavioral act is under the control of the immediately available stimuli; it minimizes the role of internal, motivational factors. This proposition stands in contrast to a more ethological view that instinctual behavior consists of a sequence of internally organized acts with successively higher thresholds so that as the "mood" of the organism intensifies it becomes more likely to perform acts later in the sequence.

On the stimulus control hypothesis, the organization of instinctual behaviors might not be different in principle from the operant "chaining" of behavior, as when students in a conditioning laboratory "shape" a rat to carry a miniature replica of their school flag up, across, and down a series of ladders for a food reward. Indeed, Ulrich and colleagues used operant conditioning procedures to condition fighting in rats; when a water-deprived "experimental" rat struck a "control" animal, a buzzer was activated signaling the availability of water. However, when two such trained and water-deprived "experimental" rats were placed in the operant chamber they "would often grapple with each other and continue to fight and did not respond immediately to the buzzer by drinking" (Ulrich *et al.*, 1963, pp. 467–468). Reading between the lines, one can almost hear the writers' bewildered disappointment in the failure of this standard discriminative stimulus procedure to control behavior.

Aggression, once provoked, reorganizes subsequent behavior. Here enters the notion of aggression as a motivational system. I first encountered Kirsti Lagerspetz's account of the evidence for the motivational aspects of aggression in her 1969 summary chapter "Aggression and aggressiveness in laboratory mice." (The present chapter is similarly titled as an homage, imitation being the sincerest form of flattery). I still have the autographed copy of her original monograph (Lagerspetz, 1964). She made several important points in that monograph, some had already occurred to me but others had not. Aggression shows all the classical defining characteristics of a motivated behavior: for example, the same stimulus, presented on different occasions, may or may not elicit aggression depending upon the internal state of the organism. Aggression is goal directed in the sense that the organism may alter its strategies during repeated attempts at attacking a given target. For example, resident rats will dig under and turn over an anesthetized intruder presented in the supine position in order to deliver a bite to its dorsal surface, the usual target site for offensive attacks (Blanchard, Blanchard, Takahashi, & Kelley, 1975). In the case of offensive (intraspecific) aggression in rodents, at least, correlational studies suggest a close relationship among different experimental measures, for example, threat versus attack frequency and latency (e.g., Brain & Poole, 1974). The same conclusions have been drawn from cluster (dendrogram), factor, and transition frequency analyses of the relationship among various acts and postures classified as offensive aggression (e.g., Simon, Gray, & Gandelman, 1983). These results suggest that offensive aggression consists of a small set of highly correlated social behaviors which reflect the operation of a more-or-less unitary motivational mechanism (cf. Adams, 1979).

The most important motivational feature of aggression for the present purposes is its persistence over time, for example, in the form of protracted fights between antagonists who refuse to give up. In such cases, the stimuli from the antagonist may act to maintain or even increase aggressive motivation. However, aggressive behavior can persist even after the provoking stimulus has been withdrawn (e.g., Heiligenberg, 1974). In humans, persistence of aggressive motivation over a delay imposed between the provocation and the opportunity to attack is the stuff of folklore; it has also been demonstrated experimentally (e.g., Konecni, 1975; Buvinic & Berkowitz, 1976). Using the attack priming paradigm described below, I have found that allowing a female golden hamster a single attack upon a conspecific increases the attacker's aggressiveness for at least half an hour (Potegal & Popken, 1985; Potegal, 1991). In the absence of external stimulation such persistence must clearly be mediated by internal processes. For the want of a better term I have called these process(es) "aggressive arousal."

It is true that we can be misled by our language(s); because we have an adjective "X" which describes some category of behavior does not mean X exists as a behavioral entity. In English, for example, the word "aggressive" is used to describe both human hostility and assertiveness, personality characteristics that are, in fact, not closely associated (e.g., Margalit & Mauger, 1984). We must remain sensitive to the dangers of the reification of abstract words. Nonetheless, because I, like Kirsti, felt (and still feel) that aggressive behavior is more than pieces and patches, I have been interested in exploring the behavioral and neural organizing principles for this class of behaviors.

## II. Phenomena That May Be Explicable in Terms of Aggressive Arousal: The Promised Land

Much ethological field work has been devoted to observations of the species-typical displays that often precede overt fighting. Among bird species, for example, certain combinations of head, wing, and body posture predict attack by blue tits (Stokes, 1962) while different calls signal different attack probabilities in blackbirds (Dabelsteen & Pedersen, 1990). Encounters between red stags, in which the winner may be predicted by its relatively greater rate of roaring before combat is joined, is a classic case (Clutton-Brock & Albon, 1979). Laboratory examples include the much-studied agonistic postures of the rat in which lateral threat posture typically precedes a full aggressive posture which precedes a bite-and-kick attack (e.g., Lehman & Adams, 1977). The probability of fighting and/or winning can be predicted by gill erection, body, and/or eye color in various species of fish (e.g., Evans, 1985; Stacey & Chiszar, 1975; Martin & Hengstebeck, 1981). Initial agonistic postures predict contest winners in both chickens (Foreman & Allee, 1959) and jungle fowl (Wilson, 1974).

One prediction arising from game theoretic analyses of animal conflicts is that such autonomic and behavioral signals would be more adaptive as bluff concealing actual intent than as veridical advertisement of aggressive arousal since it is less risky to scare off a rival by looking and acting fierce than to reveal information on the true readiness to fight (e.g., Turner & Huntingford, 1986). This bluff hypothesis has been disconfirmed in a number of cases including those cited above. Although attack cannot generally be predicted with a probability of 1.0, these behavioral and autonomic stigmata do indicate an increased probability of aggression. Thus, in keeping with the earlier ethological interpretation, threat displays can be expressive, reflecting underlying motivation. Lehman and Adams (1977) refer to low and high "intensity" postures of offense in the rat, the term intensity implying motivational state. Other factors may affect the displays' expressive nature, of course, particularly in higher species where "deceptions" of various kinds may occur (for a more detailed discussion of the interaction between the expressive aspect of display and its communication/negotiation function, see Hinde, 1985). Nonetheless, when a sequence of displays preceed attack, the hypothesis that these may indicate increasing degrees of aggressive arousal remains viable until proven otherwise.

When it comes to actual fighting, the distribution of agonistic encounter durations in many species tends to be bimodal or J-shaped with many brief encounters and a smaller number of prolonged fights (e.g., Tooker & Miller, 1980). The occurrence of the longer fights could be accounted for by the simultaneous increase in the aggressive arousal of both combatants. Increased levels of aggressive arousal may produce a "commitment" to aggression (Bronstein, 1981) because this arousal renders the combatants less sensitive to painful and/or other distracting stimuli.

Aggressive arousal may be involved in another phenomenon associated with intraspecific fighting. Field reports indicate that significant, maladaptive reductions in antipredator vigilance occur during these conflicts. Human observers find that they can move closer then usual to the animals without eliciting flight during these events (e.g., Rand, 1942). In a field study of voles (Colvin, 1973) and a laboratory study of marmosets (Lipp, 1978) observers even report instances in which they were able to easily capture animals engaged in an agonistic encounter, presumably because the animals' attention was focused on their antagonist and not on the human "predator." At least one instance of real, lethal predation upon an animal engaged in high-intensity conspecific threat has been reported in blackbirds (Dabelsteen & Pedersen, 1990). These anecdotal accounts of the narrowing of attention during combat need to be verified by systematic studies. This phenomenon could be quantified by using a salient stimulus to distract subjects from their contact with an intruder during the various stages of an encounter. As example, the response to a preferred food item, a touch on the flank, or a mildly noxious air puff to the face could be compared before, during, or after an overt attack.

Finally, there are field observations of the "redirection" of attack, so named by Bastock, Morris, and Moynihan (1953), in which an animal involved in an aggressive interaction subsequently seeks out and attacks another individual which was uninvolved in the original encounter. The victims of these attacks are often animals with which the aggressor has had amicable relations. Redirection has most often been reported in colonies of monkey, where a subordinate attacked by a dominant will seek out a still lower ranking animal (e.g., Kawamura, 1967). Among mice, females, which are ordinarily not subjected to aggression by males, may be the target of redirected attack (e.g., Eisenberg, 1962; Simmel & Walker, 1970). The phenomenon of redirection, too, has been recreated in the laboratory. Alberts and Galef (1973) noted that presenting an anesthetized intruder to one of a pair of peacefully cohabiting resident rats elicited aggression which was redirected to the companion animal. Obviously, in order for attack to be redirected, there must be an aggressive arousal which persists throughout the delay between the original provocation and the search for a suitable target.

The analysis of aggressive arousal may provide a theoretical background for linking (1) the displays preceding attack; (2) the duration, intensity, and outcome of the actual fighting; (3) the narrowing of attention during the encounter; and (4) the redirection of aggression following the encounter. An earlier paper, which describes at length the evidence for aggression as a positive reinforcer, also suggests that carrying out an attack is rewarding especially or only when aggressive arousal is high (Potegal, 1979). In short, there are a diversity of important phenomena in aggressive behavior which may be explained in terms of common mechanisms of internal mediation.

## III. In Search of the Neural Flywheel

Early investigations sometimes found that different experimental measures of motivation had different time courses or responded differently to one or another treatment. This led to the criticism that hypothesizing theoretical motivational states such as anger is useless, at best. However, a unitary motivational signal, originating from a particular neural circuit, might be differently transformed as it is transmitted to different locations throughout the nervous system, so that locomotor, frequency, and choice measures of motivation might differ even though they were all influenced by the same signal. The unity of behavior, as exemplified by goal directedness, must be offset by a flexibility that allows the organism to adapt to local conditions.

The behavioral evidence for the persistence of aggressive arousal inspired my search for the responsible circuitry in the CNS and for a model of its operation. At one time I amused myself with the metaphor of a neural flywheel, the brain's equivalent of a mechanical device which, once set spinning, continues to drive the machinery due to its great moment of inertia. More contemporary, and possibly more appropriate metaphors might be the decay of excitation in an electronic circuit or the "relaxation" of a physical system to a state of lower energy. A glimpse of the road ahead was afforded by early brain stimulation studies which reported that autonomic and behavioral signs of aggression persisted more frequently and for longer periods following stimulation of the amygdala than following stimulation of the hypothalamus or the central gray (e.g., Hilton & Zbrozyna, 1963).

## IV. You Can't Get There from Here: Circumperambulations, Digressions, and Dead Ends

Like certain Old World explorers, I set out confidently in the wrong direction to find the countries of my imagination. I first attempted to study intraspecific aggression in singly housed rats; the colony model for eliciting aggression in this species (Blanchard & Blanchard, 1980; Lore, Nikoletseas, & Farina, 1980) was then not even a rumor. Only a few of these isolated animals would attack a conspecific intruder. An incidental observation of one these rats catching a fly led to a study of the "satiation" of muricide (Potegal, Marotta, & Gimino, 1975), to the conjecture that digging might be a displacement activity which could substitute for predatory killing (Potegal *et al.*, 1979), and to the conclusion that muricide was an inappropriate model for the investigation of aggressive arousal.

I subsequently chose female hamsters as the main subject of my studies of intraspecific aggression because a high proportion of them are aggressive when singly housed but, like other female rodents, their bites on conspecifics are partially inhibited so they inflict little or no tissue damage (cf. Blanchard *et al.*, 1980). I thought to use hypothalamic stimulation as a probe for central state, reasoning that less stimulation current and/or time would be required to elicit attack in an animal when its aggressive arousal was high than when it was low. This still strikes me as a reasonable idea but eliciting aggression in hamsters by hypothalamic stimulation proved to be easier thought than done. To get more information from each implanted animal I turned to movable electrodes. Beginning each electrode descent with the tip dorsal to the hypothalamus led to the discovery that septal stimulation inhibited aggression (Potegal, Blau, & Glusman, 1981). This observation led, in turn, to a series of studies of septal/GABAergic function in aggression that were interesting in themselves but proved to be a long detour on the path to understanding aggressive arousal.

## V. Studies of Aggressive Arousal in Hamsters and Rats: On the Yellow Brick Road

I returned to the study of aggressive arousal in 1979 using a behavioral approach which derived from an effect first reported by Lagerspetz (1964). She had found that having just had a brief fight with a conspecific would reduce a mouse's latency to enter a compartment where it would find another animal to attack. In my laboratory this became the attack priming effect: "Priming" a female hamster by allowing it a single attack on an intruder placed into its home cage decreases the latency and increases the probability of attack on a second, "probe" intruder (Potegal & tenBrink, 1984). The intruders in these experiments are treated with methotrimeprazine, a long-acting analgesic/sedative which reduces the variability in their behavior, eliminating wild flight in particular, and protects them against the stress of being attacked. Since the hamsters do not appear to discriminate one drug-treated intruder from another, the change in latency from priming to probe trial must be internally mediated, that is, it must involve a change in aggressive arousal. By interpolating delays of various durations between priming and probe trials I established that this arousal lasts at least 30 minutes (Potegal, 1990). Attack priming is specific to aggression in that primed animals show no changes in eating or in locomotion in a running wheel (Potegal & tenBrink, 1984). The effect has been replicated in male rats (Potegal, 1991).

Mounting an attack on a conspecific involves detecting, tracking, and biting the other animal. To determine if the priming effect might depend on this particular combination of acts per se, hamsters were trained to pursue a hamster-sized block of wood moving back and forth through their cage in order to obtain the sunflower seeds which had been taped to it. The animals quickly learned to follow the block and remove the seeds; they also often spent some time gnawing on the block. Each hamster was then given, in ABBA or BAAB order, two priming/probe trial pairs and two woodblock/probe trial pairs (i.e., in the latter case exposure to and pursuit of the woodblock was followed by an intruder presentation). A repeated measures ANOVA of the priming, probe, and post-woodblock attack latency data, skew corrected by log transformation, showed significant differences among the three conditions. Post hoc Scheffé tests showed that the difference came entirely from the reduction in attack latency produced by priming. That is, probe attack latencies following a priming attack were significantly shorter than the latencies on priming trials or on trials following a woodblock presentation. These results indicate that the priming effect is not dependent upon the sensorimotor acts of pursuit and biting.

## VI. Notes toward a Theoretical Model of Aggressive Arousal: Travelers' Tales

At least two theoretically separable processes may account for the priming effect. One possibility is that exposure to and exploration of the first intruder increases aggressive arousal to the point at which an attack is elicited. When the second intruder is presented, arousal is already high and an attack occurs more quickly. Note that under this interpretation the attack on the first intruder is merely a "marker" of the change of state. That is, the first attack signals that a change of state is occurring but does not itself play a causal role in reducing subsequent attack latency. The alternative possibility is that it is the occurrence of the first attack itself which somehow shortens the subject's latency to perform the second attack.

A substantial body of evidence shows that rodent aggression is strongly controlled by olfactory/vomeronasal stimuli (e.g., Murphy, 1976). In male mice, preputial gland pheromone has been identified as the crucial stimulus eliciting aggression (Ingersoll *et al.*, 1986). The importance of these stimuli for priming in hamsters was first suggested by the observation that the effect is more consistent and pronounced if time in contact with the intruder is used as the dependent measure instead of the more usual measure of elapsed time since introduction of the intruder (Potegal, 1990). During contact the subject explores the intruder's anogenital region, ear, corner of mouth, eye, and flank, all of which bear specialized glands. Experiments carried out following this discovery showed that allowing subjects to investigate an anesthetized intruder systematically reduced subsequent attack latency; the longer the durations of contact, the shorter the subsequent attack latencies. The latencies reach an asymptotic level with 60 seconds of contact which reduces them almost to the level obtained by attack priming. This finding is consistent with reports that exposing wild rats to an anesthetized intruder elicits aggression redirected to a cohabiting conspecific (Alberts & Galef, 1973).

The second theoretical possibility, that performing the first attack changes the animal's state, preparing it to attack more rapidly when a second target appears, implies that the priming effect is an instance of a positive feedback process. Positive feedback processes have been claimed to contribute to episodes of extreme violence in humans (Baenninger, 1974; Zimbardo, 1969). This hypothesis remains speculative. It is clear from the woodblock experiment cited above that pursuit and biting of an object per se are insufficient to produce a reduction in attack latency. The fact that attack latency shortens systematically with increasing exposure to an anesthetized intruder argues against a step change. On the other hand, even the maximally effective 1-minute exposure to the anesthetized intruder does not completely reduce attack latencies to the level achieved by attack priming. I conjecture that a priming time course study using interpolated delays under a minute might reveal a short-lived increase in aggressive arousal which is coupled to the overt commission of an attack.

If overall levels of aggressive arousal fluctuated over days, one would expect a positive correlation between the attack latencies on the priming and probe trial on a given day. In three studies carried out several years apart I repeatedly found no correlation between priming attack latency and the following probe attack latency (Potegal & tenBrink, 1984; Potegal & Popken, 1985; Potegal, 1990). At the same time, of course, probe latencies were generally shorter than priming latencies. It occurred to me that these two disparate facts might be reconciled in a stochastic model in which the probability of attack shifted from a low value on the priming trial to a higher one on the probe trial. To understand the relationship between latency and probability, imagine the simplest case in which the probability of attack remains constant from minute to minute within a trial. If the attack probability during a 10-minute priming trial is 0.4/minute, for example, calculation of conditional probability leads to an expected latency of the first attack within that trial of 2 minutes (assuming that a trial with a failure to attack is assigned a latency of 10 minutes). If the attack probability on the following probe trial increases to 0.65/minute, the expected latency of first attack becomes 1 minute. Note, however, that the latency on a given probe trial cannot be predicted from the latency on the priming trial which preceded it. A graphical way to convert latencies to probabilities is the log survivorship plot (see Bressers, *et al.*, 1991 for a recent explanation of survivor analysis). A group of hamsters were each given 10 or more priming/probe trial pairs with a minimum 48-hour interpair interval. When the log survivorship functions of the appropriately normalized priming and probe trials were plotted separately and compared, it became apparent that attack probability does not remain constant over the trial but increases steadily: the longer the contact duration, the greater the probability of the attack (Potegal & Coombes, in preparation). This finding is entirely in keeping with the results using the anesthetized intruder. These data are still being analyzed; at this time the difference between between the priming and probe trials appears to involve a parameter shift such that attack probability increases more rapidly on the probe trial.

## VII. General Approach to Investigating the Neural Mechanisms of Aggression Using the Priming Effect: Royal Road or Primrose Path?

Correlating aggressive behavior with endogenous markers of neural activity is not a new idea. However, many earlier studies correlated neurochemical variables with aggressiveness in the absence of a detailed characterization of the behavior (e.g., the neurochemistry of isolated rodents has been compared to that of group-housed ones, the latter being generally less aggressive, but isolated and group-housed animals also differ along many other dimensions). In other studies animals have been lumped into fighting or nonfighting groups without an effort being made to correlate the neurochemical characteristics of a given animal with its behavior. Payne, Andrews, and Wilson (1984), for example, allowed hamsters to fight for 10 minutes, after which they were sacrificed for measurements of serotonin metabolism. Because the significance of a 10-minute fighting period for each individual animal had not been established beforehand, it remained unclear if the neurochemical data related to the actual duration of fighting, the relative pain and stress experienced during the fight, the fatigue resulting from the fight, the subsequent probability of fighting or fleeing, or simply the metabolic requirements of 10 minutes of vigorous activity.

Attack priming is a rapid and inexpensive paradigm with a number of important advantages for exploring the neural bases of aggression. Data can be easily obtained about the aggressive characteristics of individual animals which can then be correlated with measures of neural function. Attack primed animals can be compared with equally aggressive nonprimed animals. If animals which have been previously tested on a number of priming/probe trial pairs are sacrificed after a priming trial, endogenous measures of neural function can be correlated with both attack latency on the priming trial (i.e., behavior immediately preceding the measurement of neural function) and mean attack latency on past probe trials (i.e., probable future behavior).

## VIII. The Evidence for Neuroanatomical Localization and, Maybe, Mechanism of Aggressive Arousal: The First Milestones

A great deal of recent work has shown that the proto-oncogene *c-fos* is one of a number of "early intermediate" genes whose protein products are expressed in neurons within 30 minutes of activation (depolarization and calcium release); the expression of the *c-fos* protein persists for an hour or two thereafter. A recent review of the process can be found in Sheng and Greenberg (1990). In brief, once the protein has been synthesized on cytoplasmic ribosomes by *c-fos* mRNA, it migrates back to the nucleus, combines as a dimer with another nuclear protein such as *c-jun*, and binds to the DNA AP-1 site. Here, it regulates the expression of other genes. Immunocytochemical mapping of the *c-fos* protein in the nuclei of activated cells has proven to be a valuable technique for localization of function in the CNS.

In my hands this technique has recently yielded evidence that the corticomedial amygdala (CMA) is a potential locus for mediating aggressive arousal. The number of activated neurons in and around the medial nucleus of the amygdala is higher in attack primed hamsters then in unperturbed animals of matched baseline aggressiveness (Potegal, Ferris, & Skaredoff, 1991). This effect was neuroanatomically specific in that no such increases were found elsewhere, including the lateral, basolateral, or central amygdaloid nuclei or a number of other limbic and hypothalamic structures. The effect was also behaviorally specific in several ways: There were no significant differences in the general activity of primed and control animals in the hour that elapsed between the final observation and sacrifice. Furthermore, there was no correlation between CMA *c-fos* expression and the motor activity that followed the priming trial (note that motor activity has often been used as a measure of general arousal). *c-fos* expression was also unrelated to any specific behaviors which occurred in this period.

Further evidence for behavioral specificity comes from a yoked control group of hamsters, each of which had matched for baseline aggressiveness with an animal in the priming group. After pretraining on the woodblock pursuit task described above, the yoked controls were allowed to pursue, make contact with, and gnaw on the block for a period of time equal to the duration of a priming trial of the matched animal in the priming group. CMA *c-fos* expression also turned out to be greater in primed animals than in these yoked controls. Thus, the greater *c-fos* expression in attack primed animals was not simply due to the localization, pursuit, and biting of a salient object but appears to be specifically related to aggressive behavior.

Within the primed group, the aspect of aggressive behavior most clearly associated with the number of CMA cells expressing *c-fos* was the mean priming latency over all trials. Longer contact durations correlated with higher nuclear counts ($r = .7$, $p < .02$). When similar experiments were carried out with male rats, the same relationship between CMA *c-fos* expression and mean latency was obtained ($r = .73$). In both species, the correlation between mean contact duration and *c-fos* expression was greatest for the lateral aspect of the CMA (e.g., Winans' area $C_1$ in the hamsters): $r = .73$, $p < .02$; $r = .85$, $p < .05$ for hamsters and rats, respectively.

The CMA is the major site of olfactory and vomeronasal input to the amygdala (e.g., Scalia & Winans, 1975). That *c-fos* expression increased with longer exposure to the intruder might be expected from the nature of the input; more prolonged contact with the intruder implies a more prolonged stimulation of the cells receiving the input. In another experiment, a 1-minute exposure to an anesthetized intruder increased *c-fos* expression in the posterior part of the CMA to levels found in primed animals. This suggests that exposure to the olfactory and vomeronasal cues from an intruder is sufficient to activate CMA neurons, even when an attack is not carried out. These latter findings are consistent with the importance of contact in producing the priming effect and with the observation that contact with an anesthetized intruder is sufficient to reduce subsequent attack latency almost to the primed level. However, *c-fos* expression was more associated with the *mean* contact duration on all trials than with the particular duration of contact on the trial that just preceded sacrifice. This difference was particularly clear for the lateral CMA *c-fos* nuclei in the rats: the correlation coefficient for mean contact duration was $r = .85$, for contact duration preceding sacrifice $r = .30$. One possible interpretation of this finding is that *c-fos* expression reflects the general level of sensory-neural CMA activation required to release attack rather than the particular acute history of CMA stimulation. It is even possible that CMA activation relates directly to the attack probabilities which have been determined by survivor analysis.

## IX. The Functional Significance of the CMA Localization: The Next Landmark

The functional significance of the CMA localization was evaluated by bilateral radio frequency lesions of the area. To examine the effect of passing an electrode through the tissue lying dorsal to the CMA, electrode track puncture wounds were made in one control group. A cortical lesion was made in a second group to control for the effects of destroying a volume of brain tissue. CMA lesions significantly increased the latency and reduced the number of attacks relative to the control groups. This finding is consistent with earlier lesion studies in hamsters (e.g., Shipley & Kolb, 1977; Takahashi & Gladstone, 1988), rats (e.g., Miczek, Brykzynski, & Grossman, 1974; Koolhaas, Schuurman, & Wiepkema, 1980), and mice (Kemble, 1981). Histological examination revealed that CMA lesions were distributed along the rostro-caudal length of the amygdala. Correlation analysis showed that the more rostral the lesion, the longer the mean elapsed time to the first bite on either trial. This relationship between lesion site and behavioral effect was confounded by the fact that the more anterior lesions were larger. However, the correlation between lesion volume and attack latency was nonsignificant and a partial correlation between lesion site and attack latency which removed the effect of lesion size remained significant.

CMA lesion and control animals were also given two consecutive 10-minute trails in a running wheel. There were no significant differences among the groups in latency to enter the wheel and no correlation within the CMA group between entry latency and lesion site or size. There were also no differences between groups in the number of revolutions they turned in the wheel. However, all animals in both control groups and 10 of the 11 CMA animals increased the number of turns in the second trial. This produced a highly significant locomotor practice effect. A lack of interaction indicated that this practice effect occurred equally strongly in all groups. These findings indicate that CMA lesions do not increase general timidity, do not produce a general locomotor impairment, and do not affect hamster's ability to increase their behavior through experience. The elimination of these alternative explanations strengthens the hypotheses that CMA *c-fos* expression marks a process coupled to aggressive arousal and that the CMA is part of the neural circuitry mediating aggressive arousal.

Clearly the CMA exercises a relatively specific control over intraspecific aggression in rodents. The contributions of anterior and posterior parts of the CMA remain to be resolved. It may be that, although proportionately greater *c-fos* expression occurs in the posterior CMA during priming, the neurons controlling attack are located more anteriorly. Alternatively, it remains possible that the posterior CMA neurons are those which control attack and that the anterior electrolytic lesions destroyed caudally directed afferents to and/or rostrally directed projection fibers from these neurons. These possibilities need to be investigated with axon sparing ibotenic acid lesions placed at different sites within the CMA.

## X. Annotating the Itinerary

Two comments on these observations, one technical the other theoretical, need be made. *c-fos* expression has attained a certain notoriety as a neuroanatomically diffuse response which can be elicited by the most trivial of stimuli. In part this reputation stems from its association with generalized seizure activity, this being the experimental circumstance in which its expression in the CNS was discovered (Morgan *et al.*, 1987). That *c-fos* expression was so selectively restricted in the current studies may well relate to the facts that animals were tested in their home cage in their home room, that having attacked intruders in their cages on a number of prior occasions they were well habituated to the test situation, and that they had experienced no counter attacks on these occasions.

The second comment is that, as noted above, I have long felt that the temporal persistence of aggressive motivation is a fact whose theoretical importance needs to be emphasized and whose mechanism(s) should be explained. Because of this conviction much of my research effort has been devoted to elucidating the time course of the priming effect. These studies have shown that engaging in an aggressive encounter sets in motion a sequence of internal events. The priming effect is robust at 30 minutes following an initial attack but is less before and after this point. This observation may be of particular interest in view of the well-established delay of about 30 minutes between neuronal stimulation and the appearance of *c-fos* protein. There is a small irony in that the experimental technique which has finally yielded strong evidence for the localization of at least one mechanism underlying attack priming happens to reflect a genomic modulation of neural events; of necessity, such modulation involves processes which are protracted in time. At least one part of the neural flywheel has been identified.

## XI. The Road Ahead

A number of studies have suggested that movement of the opponent can release aggression in rodents. Lagerspetz and Portin's (1968) comparison of attacks by mice upon moving and nonmoving inanimate targets showed that movement is a major feature of the stimuli eliciting attack in this species. Flight by a subordinate animal elicits chase and attack by a dominant in colonies of rats in the wild (Calhoun, 1962) and guinea pigs in the laboratory (Grant & MacKintosh, 1963). Several studies using anesthetized or freshly killed targets have shown that movements of conspecifics are important in initiating or facilitating offensive attack in mice (Cairns & Scholz, 1973; Mettälä-Portin, 1966) and rats (Alberts & Galef, 1973; Blanchard, Fukanaga, Blanchard, & Kelley, 1975).

In hamsters, too, flight by one animal can elicit chase by another (Grant & MacKintosh, 1963; Grant, MacKintosh, & Lerwill, 1969). It has been found that enucleation does not reduce hamster aggression (Murphy, 1976), suggesting that visual movement is not necessary for attack. It may be sufficient, however. Does visual movement contribute directly to CMA activation as might be expected if this area sets the global tone of aggressive arousal? From our current knowledge of neuroanatomy this seems unlikely since input from higher levels of the visual system is thought to be directed to the lateral and basolateral nuclei only (e.g., Turner & Herkenham, 1991). However, it should be noted that neurons of the medial amygdala in the monkey are responsive to visual stimuli (e.g., Brothers, Ring, & Kling, 1990). Clearly, the medial amygdala in higher species has access to visual information; the pathways by which this information reaches it are unknown.

The findings described above highlight the importance of the medial amygdala in the control of aggression in hamsters and rats, two species of rodent. Because olfactory and vomeronasal input has such a major control over aggression in rodents, the question must be raised whether this area of the brain retains an important role in the aggressive behavior of microsmatic species where olfactory/vomeronasal stimuli are of lesser importance. The functions of the CMA in aggression should be examined across a wider range of species. This would, of course, require the development of species-appropriate, ethologically valid behavioral paradigms. It would be particularly important to examine the role of the CMA in primate species. In this context it is important to note that not only are medial amygdala neurons in monkeys responsive to visual stimuli, they are attuned to facial expression (e.g., Brothers, Ring, & Kling, 1990), suggesting that they play a role in mediating social interactions in this species.

## XII. The Human Condition: Anger (Conscious and Unconscious), Aggressive Arousal, and Violent Behavior

Anger is an emotional experience which is both commonplace and compelling. Some academic psychologists have argued that anger is the result of a generalized arousal experienced in the presence of aggression-eliciting cues; if the same generalized arousal is experienced in the presence of flight-producing cues it will be experienced as fear (for review see Zillmann, 1979). This hypothesis and its many variants originate from Schacter and Singer's findings that subjects injected with epinephrine, a drug which produces autonomic activation, will experience either mirth or anger as they are cued to do so by a happy or angry individual in their environment (for review see Schacter, 1964). This may indeed be true of artificial situations (e.g., where physiological arousal is induced by drug injection or vigorous physical exercise) or ambiguous ones which have elements of real danger. If someone sticks a gun in your face you may feel angry, frightened, or both. However, increasing general arousal by noise, heat, or exercise fail to increase self-reports of anger and/or objective measures of aggressive responding (for review see Rule & Nesdale, 1976; Blanchard, 1984). Most research in the area has found that particular provocations, usually involving insult and/or frustration, are necessary to elicit anger and overt aggression. General arousal, environmental cues, and cognitive alterations in the subjects' understanding of the situation and the motivation of their provoker can modulate the anger and aggression. Such results have led to a distinction between generalized arousal and aggressive arousal among humans, the latter of which is subjectively experienced as anger (e.g., Rule & Nesdale, 1976). It is indeed a long road from intraspecific biting attack by rodents to our subjective feelings. If the *c-fos* data reported above have any relevance to our emotional behavior, however, they may represent the first steps toward identifying the neural substrate of felt anger.

These speculations also bear on the notion of "unconscious anger." Since anger is a felt emotion, the idea of "unconscious anger" would appear to be an oxymoron. Now, however, it could be visualized as a pattern of activity brewing in the amygdala that does not rise to consciousness. Happily, tests of such hypotheses may be within the technological reach of brain imaging techniques like PET scanning.

It has often been pointed out that anger and aggression are dissociable: among adults most anger does not result in damage or often even in physical expression (e.g., Averill, 1982). Conversely, horrendously destructive and violent acts can be committed without feelings of anger in the perpetrators. However, among cases of homicide in urban areas of the western world in which any motive at all could be established, the motive for 30–50% of murders has been described as an "immediately preceding physical or verbal conflict: a quarrel, fight, rage, brawl, altercation" often within the family or between lovers (Curtis, 1974, pp. 70–71). In the real world anger leads to violence often enough to be a major social issue.

## XIII. The Medial Amygdala, Temporal Lobe Epilepsy, and Anger

There are individuals whose attacks of rage, destructive and terrifying to family members, are brought on with little or no provocation and are not responsive to medication. Some of these individuals experience an aura or prodrome which warn them that a rage attack is imminent, much like the olfactory/epigastric auras that signal more typical temporal lobe seizures. In other cases the rage comes on suddenly and without warning. A few of these individuals have been implanted with chronic, in-dwelling depth electrodes to determine if subcortical seizure foci might be the cause of their problem. Neurologists and neurosurgeons who have dealt with these patients have been impressed by the association between the attacks and seizure activity recorded from the amygdala (e.g., Mark & Ervin, 1970; Smith, 1980; Ferguson, Rayport, & Corrie, 1986). Geschwind, Bear, and their colleagues have claimed that increased hostility is part of a temporal lobe epilepsy syndrome (e.g., Bear *et al.*, 1982). The significance of these rage attacks has been downplayed by investigators who argue that although they appear very forceful and may result in damage to household objects they generally do not result in serious injury to other people. But isn't this the way with most ordinary anger? A more serious criticism has been raised by psychologists whose large-scale surveys have failed to show increased aggressive behavior in temporal lobe epileptics (for review see Whitman, King, & Cohen, 1986). While this is not the place to review the controversy in detail, it is noteworthy that in a few cases where both surface and depth recordings were made simultaneously, the depth electrodes sometimes picked up activity that the surface ones did not (Smith, 1980). Hence, seizures can be occult and the seizure activity in individuals with rages could be missed by the scalp EEGs that are routinely used to diagnose temporal lobe epilepsy. Given the rodent CMA data described above, it is particularly noteworthy that in three patients who were carefully studied, rage was associated with seizures of the more medial aspect of the amygdala (Smith, 1980).

The phenomenon of rage attacks with little or no provocation is not unknown to the parents of two- and three-year-olds whose tantrums can similarly explode without warning. It is sometimes the case that only one child in the family will have severe temper problems. The fact that the other children do not have tantrums at that age indicates that there are no particular familial reasons for the tantrums. When, as is often the case, there is no reason to believe that the particular child has been abused, a neurological explanation for the tantrums of the terrible twos is at least as plausible as the usual psychodynamic ones. I am suggesting the possibility that twos may be terrible for some children because they are going through a transient developmental stage when their amygdala is particularly susceptible to disturbance.

## XIV. Figure and Ground Reversal in the Analysis of Aggression: Looking Ahead to Looking Back

Attack priming has been developed as a behavioral paradigm to create an aggressive arousal as "pure" as possible using a "natural" stimulus situation. This was done in order to investigate the neural basis of aggression uncontaminated by the drugs, footshocks, brain lesions, or brain stimulation which are often used to elicit it in the laboratory. Having putatively identified a locus of activity associated with "pure" aggression, we can now ask: Is there a correlation between the effect of a given experimental manipulation (e.g., tail pinch, footshock) on attack probability and its effect on CMA activation? Suppose there is a correlation across a range of manipulations and that other lines of evidence confirm this region as exerting a supraordinate control over aggressiveness. Theoretical figure and ground may then reverse, to use a favorite perceptual metaphor of Hans-Lukas Teuber, one of my teachers at MIT. CMA activation replaces intraspecific aggression as the major focus. We then ask: What are the other behavioral concomitants of CMA activation? Does it facilitate the agonistic display preceding attack? Is it involved in the narrowing of attention and in the other behavioral phenomena associated with fighting? If the CMA is activated and there is no opportunity to attack, do displacement behaviors increase?

Put another way, the long-term theoretical significance of these findings lies in their potential for restructuring our thinking about the organization of aggression. There are precedents for the restructuring of psychological thinking by physiological revelation. Following the observation that distinctly different brain states are associated with REM and nonREM sleep, we now talk about REM sleep instead of dreaming sleep, knowing that REM is associated with a particular physiological state and that dreams are one, possibly epiphenomenal, manifestation of that state. Another example is the classification of behaviors as regulatory or nonregulatory, following from the elucidation of homeostasis as it was developed in physiology. A recent example is the re-emergence of the "Hebbian synapse" as the theoretical basis of learning following the discovery of the importance of heterosynaptic facilitation in the phenomenon of long-term potentiation. Suppose it turns out that the state of the medial amygdala, or the circuitry of which it is a part, determines one's state of "anger" whether or not one is conscious of the affect. I suggest that a classification based upon CMA activation and its concomitants may replace behavioral typologies of aggression. Instead of offense we may eventually talk about CMA-type aggression versus, for example, basolateral amygdala-type aggression which may be more fear/defense related. Alternatively, defensive aggression might turn out to be a function of *simultaneous* CMA and basolateral activation.

## XV. A Confluence of Pilgrims

Kirsti Lagerspetz was one of the original founders of the International Society for Research on Aggression (ISRA). The very existence of ISRA represents an implicit consensus among students of animal and human behavior, social and experimental psychologists, and members of other academic disciplines that there is something common to the diverse set of behaviors we call "aggressive." Is it possible that what we "aggressologists" have in common is a concern with the various manifestations of amygdaloid activity?

## References

Adams, D. (1979). Brain mechanisms for offense, defense, and submission. *Behavioral and Brain Sciences, 2,* 201–241.

Alberts, J. R., & Galef, B. G., Jr. (1973). Olfactory cues and movement: Stimuli mediating intraspecific aggression in the wild Norway rat. *Journal of Comparative and Physiological Psychology, 85,* 233–242.

Averill, J. (1982). *Anger and Aggression.* New York: Springer-Verlag.

Baenninger, R. (1974). Some consequences of aggressive behavior: A selective review of the literature on other animals. *Aggressive Behavior, 1,* 17–38.

Bastock, M., Morris, D., & Moynihan, M. (1953). Some comments on conflict and thwarting in animals. *Behaviour, 6,* 66–84.

Bear, D., Levin, K., Blumer, D., Chetham, D., & Reider, J. (1982). Interictal behavior in hospitalized temporal lobe epileptics: relationship to idiopathic psychiatric syndromes. *Journal of Neurology, Neurosurgery, and Psychiatry, 45,* 481–488.

Blanchard, D. C. (1984). Applicability of animal models to human aggression *In* K. J. Flannelly, R. J. Blanchard, and D. C. Blanchard (Eds.), *Biological Perspectives on Aggression.* New York: Alan Liss.

Blanchard, R. J., & Blanchard, D. C. (1980). The colony model: Experience counts. *Behavioral and Neural Biology, 30,* 109.

Blanchard, R. J., Blanchard, D. C., Takahashi, T., & Kelley, M. J. (1975). Attack and defensive behavior in the albino rat. *Animal Behaviour, 25,* 622–634.

Blanchard, R. J., Fukanaga, K., Blanchard, D. C., & Kelley, M. J. (1975). Conspecific aggression in the laboratory rat. *Journal of Comparative and Physiological Psychology, 89,* 1204–1209.

Blanchard, R. J., Kleinschmidt, C. F., Fukanaga-Stinson, C., & Blanchard, D. C. (1980). Defensive attack behavior in male and female rats. *Animal Learning and Behavior, 8,* 177–183.

Brain, P. F., & Poole A. E. (1974). Some studies on the use of "standard opponents" in intermale aggression testing in TT albino mice. *Behaviour, 50,* 100–110.

Bressers, M., Meelis, E., Haccou, P., & Kruk, M. (1991). When did it really start or stop: the impact of censored observations on the analysis of duration. *Behavioral Processes, 23,* 1–20.

Bronstein, P. (1981). Commitments to aggression and nest sites in male *Betta splendens. Journal of Comparative and Physiological Psychology, 95,* 436–449.

Brothers, L., Ring, B., & Kling, A. (1990). Response of neurons in the macaque amygdala to complex social stimuli. *Behavioral Brain Research, 41,* 199–213.

Buvinic, M. L., & Berkowitz, L. (1976). Delayed effects of practiced vs unpracticed responses after observation of movie violence. *Journal of Experimental and Social Psychology, 12,* 283–293.

Cairns, R. B., & Scholz, S. D. (1973). Fighting in mice: Dyadic escalation and what is learned. *Journal of Comparative and Physiological Psychology, 85,* 540–550.

Calhoun, J. B. (1962). The ecology and sociology of the Norway rat. U.S. Department of HEW, PHS Publication No. 1008. Washington, D.C., U.S. Government Printing Office.

Clutton-Brock, T. H., & Albon, S. D. (1979). The roaring of red deer and the evolution of honest advertisement. *Behaviour, 68,* 145–170.

Colvin, D. V. (1973). Agonistic behavior in males of five species of voles *Microtus. Animal Behaviour, 21,* 471–480.

Curtis, L. (1974). *Criminal Violence.* Lexington, Massachusetts: D.C. Heath and Co.

Dabelsteen, T., & Pedersen, S. B. (1990). Song and information about aggressive responses of blackbirds, *Turdus merula,* evidence from interactive playback experiments with territory owners. *Animal Behaviour, 40,* 1158–1168.

Eisenberg, J. F. (1962). Studies on the behavior of *Peromsycus maniculatus gambelli* and *Peromyscus californicus parasiticus. Behaviour, 19,* 177–207.

Evans, C. S. (1985). Display vigor and subsequent fight performance in the Siamese fighting fish, *Betta splendens. Behavioural Processes, 11,* 113–121.

Ferguson, S. M., Rayport, M., and Corrie, W. S. (1986). Brain correlates of aggressive behavior in temporal lobe epilepsy. *In* B. K. Doane and K. E. Livingston (Eds.), *The Limbic System: Functional Organization and Clinical Disorders.* New York: Raven Press.

Foreman, D., & Allee, W. C. (1959). A correlation between posture stance and outcome in paired contests of domestic hens. *Animal Behaviour, 7,* 180–188.

Grant, E. C., & MacKintosh, J. H. (1963). A comparison of the social postures of some common laboratory rodents. *Behaviour, 21,* 246–259.

Grant, E. C., MacKintosh, J. H., & Lerwill, C. J. (1969). The effect of a visual stimulus on the agonistic behaviour of the golden hamster *Behaviour,* 73–77.

Heiligenberg, W. (1974). Processes governing behavioral states of readiness. *In* D. S. Lehrman, J. S. Rosenblatt, R. A. Hinde, & F. Shaw (Eds.), *Advances in the Study of Behavior, Vol V.* New York: Academic Press.

Hilton, S. M., & Zbrozyna, A. W. (1963). Amygdaloid region for defence reactions and its efferent pathway to the brainstem. *Journal of Physiology, 165,* 160–173.

Hinde, R. A. (1985). Was "The Expression of the Emotions" a misleading phrase? *Animal Behaviour, 33,* 985–992.

Ingersoll, D. W., Morley, K., Benvenga, M., & Hands, C. (1986). An accessory sex gland aggression-promoting chemosignal in male mice. *Behavioral Neuroscience, 100,* 777–782.

Kawamura, S. (1967). Aggression as studied in troops of Japanese monkeys. *In* C. Clemente & D. Lindsley (Eds.), *Aggression and Defense. Brain Function.* Berkeley: University of California Press.

Kemble, E. (1981). Some behavioral effects of amygdaloid lesions in Northern grasshopper mice. *In* Y. Ben-ari (Ed.), *The Amygdaloid Complex,* IRSERM symposium No. 20. Amsterdam: Elsevier/North Holland Press.

Konecni, V. J. (1975). Annoyance, type and duration of post annoyance activity and aggression: The "cathartic effect." *Journal of Experimental Psychology, 104,* 76–102.

Koolhaas, J. M, Schuurman, T., & Wiepkema, P. R. (1980). The organisation of intraspecific agonistic behaviour in the rat. *Progress in Neurobiology, 15,* 247–268.

Lagerspetz, K. (1964). Studies on the aggressive behaviour of mice. *Annales Academiee Scientiarum Fennicee* Sarja-Ser. B nide-Tom. 131 Helsinki: Suomalainen Tiedakatemia.

Lagerspetz, K. (1969). Aggression and aggressiveness in laboratory mice. *In* S. Garattini & E. B. Sigg (Eds.), *Aggressive Behavior.* New York: Wiley.

Lagerspetz, K., & Portin, R. (1968). Simulation of cues eliciting aggressive responses in mice at two age levels. *Journal of Genetic Psychology, 113,* 53–63.

Lehman, M., & Adams, D. B. (1977). A statistical and motivational analysis of the social behaviors of the male laboratory rat. *Behaviour, 61,* 238–275.

Lipp, H. P. (1978). Aggression and flight behavior of the marmoset monkey *Callithrix jacchus:* an ethogram for brain stimulation studies. *Brain, Evolution and Behavior, 15,* 241–259.

Lore, R., Nikoletseas, M., & Flannelly, K. (1980). Aggression in rats: Does the colony-intruder model require a colony? *Behavioral Biology, 28,* 243–245.

Margalit, B. A., & Mauger, P. A. (1984). Cross-cultural demonstration of orthogonality of assertiveness and aggressiveness—Comparison between Israel and the United States. *Journal of Personality and Social Psychology, 46,* 1414–1421.

Mark, V. H., & Ervin, F. R. (1970). *Violence and the Brain.* New York: Harper & Row.

Martin, F. D., & Hengstebeck, M. F. (1981). Eye colour and aggression in juvenile guppies, *Poecilia reticulata Peters. Animal Behaviour, 29,* 325–331.

Mettälä-Portin, R. (1966). Further analysis of target movement as a stimulus for fighting in mice. *Rep. psychol. Instit. University of Turku, 22,* 1–10.

Miczek, K. A., Brykzynski, T., & Grossman, S. P. (1974). Differential effects of lesions in the amygdala, periamygdaloid cortex and stria terminalis on aggressive behaviors in the rat. *Journal of Comparative and Physiological Psychology, 87,* 760–771.

Morgan, J. I., Cohen, D. R., Hempstead, J. L., & Curran, T. (1987). Mapping patterns of *c-fos* expression in the central nervous system after seizure. *Science, 237,* 192–197.

Murphy, M. (1976). Olfactory stimulation and olfactory bulb removal: Effects on territorial aggression in male Syrian golden hamsters. *Brain Research, 113,* 95–110.

Payne, A. P., Andrews, M. J., & Wilson, C. A. (1984). Housing, fighting, and biogenic amines in the midbrain and hypothalamus of the golden hamster. *In* K. Miczek, M. Kruk, & B. Olivier (Eds.), *Ethopharmacological Aggression Research.* New York: Alan Liss.

Potegal, M. (1979). The reinforcing value of several types of aggressive behavior: A review. *Aggressive Behavior, 5,* 353–373.

Potegal, M. (1990). Attack independent components of aggressive arousal in female hamsters. *Eastern Psychological Association, Proceedings and Abstracts, 61,* 10.

Potegal, M. (1991). Time course of aggressive arousal in female hamsters and male rats. *Eastern Psychological Association, Proceedings and Abstracts, 62,* 11.

Potegal, M., & Popken, J. (1985). The time course of attack priming effects in female golden hamsters. *Behavioral Processes, 11,* 199–208.

Potegal, M., & tenBrink, L. (1984). Behavior of attack-primed and attack-satiated female golden hamster (*Mesocricetus auratus*). *Journal of Comparative Psychology, 98,* 66–75.

Potegal, M., Marotta, R., & Gimino, F. (1975). Factors in the waning of muricide in the rat: 1. Analysis of intra-and intersession decrement. *Aggressive Behavior, 1,* 277–290.

Potegal, M., Gimino, F., Marotta, R., & Glusman, M. (1979). Factors in the waning of muricide in the rat. II. Digging Behavior. *Aggressive Behavior, 5,* 283–290.

Potegal, M., Blau, A., Black, M., & Glusman, M. (1980). A technique for the study of intraspecific aggression in the golden hamster under conditions of reduced target variability. *Psychological Record, 30,* 191–200.

Potegal, M., Blau, A., & Glusman, M. (1981). Inhibition of intraspecific aggression in male hamsters by septal stimulation. *Physiological Psychology, 9,* 213–218.

Potegal, M., Ferris, C., & Skaredoff, L. (1991). The corticomedial amygdala and hamster agonistic behavior. *Society for Neuroscience Abstracts, 17,* 877.

Potegal, M., & Coombes, K. Attack priming in hamsters, mesocricetus auratus: Attack latency and probability as a function of the duration of contact with a conspecific intruder. (In preparation).

Rand, A. L. (1942). Results of the Archbold expeditions. *Bulletin of the American Museum of Natural History,* No 44, U,517–524.

Rule, B. G., & Nesdale, A. R. (1976). Emotional arousal and aggressive behavior. *Psychological Bulletin, 83,* 851–863.

Scalia, F., & Winans, S. (1975). The differential projections of the olfactory bulb and accessory olfactory bulb in mammals. *Journal of Comparative Neurology, 161,* 31–56.

Schacter, S. (1964). The interaction of cognitive and physiological determinants of emotional state. *In* L. Berkowitz (Ed.), *Advances in Experimental Social Psychology, Vol 1.* New York: Academic Press.

Sheng, M., & Greenberg, M. E. (1990). The regulation and function of *c-fos* and other intermediate early genes in the nervous system. *Neuron, 4,* 477–485.

Shipley, J. E., & Kolb, B. (1977). Neural correlates of species-typical behavior in the Syrian golden hamster. *Journal of Comparative and Physiological Psychology, 91,* 1056–1073.

Simmel, E. C., & Walker, D. A. (1970). Social priming for agonistic behavior in a "docile" mouse strain. *American Zoologist, 10,* 486–487.

Simon, N. G. Gray, J. L., & Gandelman, R. (1983). An empirically derived scoring system for intermale aggression in mice. *Aggressive Behavior 9,* 157–166.

Smith, J. S. (1980). Episodic rage. *In* M. Girgis & L. G. Kiloh (Eds.), *Limbic Epilepsy and the Dyscontrol Syndrome*. Amsterdam: Elsevier/North Holland Biomedical Press.

Stacey, P. B., & Chiszar, D. (1975). Changes in the darkness of four body features of bluegill sunfish (*Lepromis macrochirus Rafinesque*) during aggressive encounters. *Behavioral Biology, 14,* 41–49.

Stokes, A. W. (1962). Agonistic behaviour among blue tits at a winter feeding station *Behaviour, 19,* 118–137.

Takahashi, L. K., & Gladstone, C. D. (1988). Medial amygdaloid lesions and the regulation of sociosexual behavioral patterns across the estrous cycle in female golden hamsters. *Behavioral Neuroscience, 102,* 268–275.

Tooker, C. P., & Miller, R. J. (1980). The ontogeny of agonistic behaviour in the blue gourami, *Tricogaster trichopterus* (Pisces, Anabantoidei). *Animal Behaviour, 28,* 973–988.

Turner, B., & Herkenham, M. (1991). Thalamoamygdaloid projections in the rat: A test of the amygdala's role in sensory processing. *Journal of Comparative Neurology, 313,* 295–325.

Turner, G. F., & Huntingford, F. A. (1986). A problem for game theory analysis: assessment and intention in male mouthbrooder contests. *Animal Behaviour, 34,* 961–970.

Ulrich, R. E., and Azrin, N. H. (1962). Reflexive fighting in response to aversive stimulation. *Journal of the Experimental Analysis of Behavior, 5,* 511–520.

Ulrich, R., Johnston, M., Richardson, J., and Wolff, P. (1963). The operant conditioning of fighting behavior in rats. *Psychological Record, 13,* 465–470.

Whitman, S., King, L. N., & Cohen, R. L. (1986). Epilepsy and violence: A scientific and social analysis. *In* S. Whitman & B. P. Hermann (Eds.), *Psychopathology in Epilepsy*. New York: Oxford University Press.

Wilson, R. (1974). Agonistic postures and latency to the first interaction during initial pair encounters in the red jungle fowl *Gallus gallus*. *Animal Behaviour, 22,* 75–82.

Zillmann, D. (1979). *Hostility and Aggression*. Hillsdale, New Jersey: Erlbaum.

Zimbardo, P. G. (1969). the human choice: Individuation, reason, and order vs deindividuation, impulse and chaos. *In* W. J. Arnold & D. Levine (Eds.), *Nebraska Symposium on Motivation*. Lincoln, Nebraska: University of Nebraska Press.

31

# Aggressive Female Mice and Learning-Sensitive Open-Field Parameters

Béatrice Kvist

I. INTRODUCTION
II. GENERAL METHODS
A. Subjects
B. Housing
C. Apparatus
D. Procedure
III. EXPERIMENT I
A. Results
IV. EXPERIMENT II
A. Results
V. DISCUSSION
REFERENCES

## I. Introduction

An important contribution to the research on aggression was made by Lagerspetz (1961) who initiated a selective breeding experiment on aggressiveness and nonaggressiveness in the late 1950s. Lagerspetz developed the two now well-known mouse strains of high (Turku Aggressive or TA) and low (Turku Nonaggressive or TNA) levels of aggressiveness, respectively. The fifty-second generation is presently at hand. Because of the low levels of aggressiveness in the females the selection has been based only on the aggressiveness scores of the males, but sister–brother matings have been avoided (Lagerspetz, 1964). Although female mice are not usually spontaneously aggressive it is possible to evoke aggressive responses equal to those of males in females of the TA strain by subjecting them to a combined neonatal and adult androgen treatment (Lagerspetz & Lagerspetz, 1975). Further evidence of a correlation between male and female aggressiveness in these strains was provided by Sandnabba (1988), who provoked aggressive responses in the TA female mice during the gestation and lactation periods.

Positive correlations between aggressiveness and revolving drum motor activity as well as between aggressiveness and open-field (OF) ambulation were found by Lagerspetz (1964) in male mice of the $S_3$ generation of the TA strain. She also discovered "a tendency to positive interdependence, rather moderate in degree" (p. 89) between aggressiveness and maze learning in the parental and $S_1$ generations. Kvist (1989) subjected male mice of the $S_{45}$ generations of both strains to learning experiments and found that TA males acquired the technique of maze running faster than TNA mice. The indication of differences in male mice in the OF parameter (OFP) ambulation and in maze learning between the TA and TNA strains makes it seem reasonable to presume that there may also be female strain differences in these variables. It seems furthermore consistent to suggest on the basis of earlier findings (Kvist, 1983) that strain differences in females are reflected as differences in quantitatively and/or qualitatively learning-sensitive OFP. Open-field ambulation as quantitatively learning-sensitive (Lagerspetz, Kvist, & Lagerspetz, 1980), and OF thigmotaxis as qualitatively learning-sensitive OFP (Kvist & Selander, 1991) as well as rearing (not yet investigated in conjunction with maze learning) are at present parameters in the focus of interest. Namely, Tachibana (1985) computed a principal-component analysis, indicating that ambulation, rearing, and penetration into the inner area (thigmotactic behavior), interpreted as "bodily activity measures," had high loadings (between .84 and .95) on the first principal component. Furthermore, van Abeelen (1977) stated that locomotor activity and rearing are under monogenic control and causally related. These facts lend support for the thought that the three OFP might be interrelated. Consequently, the purpose of the study is threefold: first, to compare the maze-learning ability of females of the TA and TNA strains; second, to study female strain OFP differences; and third, to investigate OFP patterns in conjunction with maze-running of the TA and TNA female mice. The following hypotheses were addressed:

1. Aggressive female mice learn the maze more quickly than nonaggressive females.
2. Aggressive females ambulate more, are more thigmotactic, and rear more than the nonaggressive mice.
3. Aggressive females exhibit more changes in learning-sensitive OFP in conjunction with maze running than nonaggressive female mice.

## II. General Methods

### A. SUBJECTS

Female mice of the fifty-second generation of the two selectively bred lines for high TA (Turku aggressive) and low TNA (Turku nonaggressive) respectively, levels of aggressiveness (Lagerspetz, 1964) were used. The selections were derived from an outbred Swiss albino stock which was known to have a good capacity for breeding. All generations were bred in the laboratory at the Department of Psychology at Åbo Akademi University. The maintained unselected Swiss albino strain, called the normal strain (N), served as a control group. N was initially brought from Malmö, Sweden to Turku, Finland. All animals were weaned at four weeks of age. The characteristics of and differences between the female mice of the strains in question are indicated in Table 1.

### B. HOUSING

From the beginning of the experiments the mice were housed individually in wire-topped laboratory polycarbonate cages measuring 13.5 × 23.5 × 13 cm. The animals were maintained in a noiseless breeding room with artificial lighting (lit from 7:00 A.M.. to 7:00 P.M. daily) and a room temperature of approximately 22°C. Standard laboratory animal food pellets and tap water were available ad lib except during maze learning when the food supply was restricted to one meal ad lib per day and 3 g per night.

### C. APPARATUS

For measuring *open-field activity* two types of OF were used: a circular and a square one with exactly the same area (1274 cm$^2$). The *circular* OF has been described in detail by Lagerspetz (1964). It consisted of a circular, flat, white, wooden arena (diameter 40 cm) with a 20-cm-high wall of flat, white iron plate. The field was marked by thin black lines into three concentric circles which were divided by lines radiating from the center. The lines subdivided the floor into a total of 19 partitions to aid the marking of the track of the animal on a similarity divided map. The *square* OF consisted of a flat, white, wooden arena measuring 35.7 × 35.7 cm. It was surrounded by a 23-cm-high, flat, white, veneer wall. The square arena was divided into 25 squares to aid the marking of the track of an animal on a similarly divided map.

For the purpose of measuring *thigmotactic behavior* when recorded in the circular OF, 7 center partitions indicated inner circle and 12 partitions indicated outer circle ambulation; when measured in the square OF, 9 center partitions indicated inner square and 16 partitions indicated outer square ambulation. Center or wall starting point for the animal could be used.

**Table 1**
**Characteristics of Female Mice**

| Source | TA $n$ | TA Mean | TA (SE) | N $n$ | N Mean | N (SE) | TNA $n$ | TNA Mean | TNA (SE) | Relations between strains | $t$-values |
|---|---|---|---|---|---|---|---|---|---|---|---|
| Number | 10 | | | 9 | | | 9 | | | | |
| Selection | 52 | | | Unselected | | | 52 | | | | |
| Age (months) | | | | | | | | | | | |
| When experiment starts | | 11 | | | 11 | | | 11 | | | |
| At the weighing | | 12 | | | 12 | | | 12 | | | |
| When experiment ends | | 12.5 | | | 12.5 | | | 12.5 | | | |
| Weight (g) | | 27.5 | (0.5) | | 27.5 | (0.4) | | 26.0 | (0.6) | TA > TNA[e] | 1.88 |
| Aggression scores[a] | | 5.6 | (0.4) | | normally distributed | | | 2.2 | (0.5) | TA > TNA[f] | 5.31 |
| Estrous cycle (days)[b] | | 3.5 | (0.3) | | 3.9 | (0.4) | | 4.9 | (0.5) | TA < TNA[e] | 2.50 |
| Defecation (boluses)[c] | | 17.1 | (1.3) | | 18.9 | (1.6) | | 15.3 | (2.5) | | |
| Urination (spots)[c] | | 1.8 | (0.3) | | 5.1 | (0.7) | | 6.2 | (1.5) | TA < N[f] TA < TNA[g] | 4.38; 2.93 |
| Latency to move[d] | | 1.9 | (0.9) | | 10.9 | (1.3) | | 15.7 | (2.3) | TA < N[f] TA < TNA[f] | 5.68; 5.76 |

[a] TA assessed on the basis of their brothers' ($n = 30$) aggression scores; TNA assessed on the basis of their brothers' ($n = 38$) aggression scores (Lagerspetz, 1964).

[b] Assessed on the observed opening of the vaginal introitus (Bronson, Dagg, & Snell, 1966).

[c] Calculated during five hours from 10:00 A.M. to 3:00 P.M. in an aluminum cage (21 × 21 × 12 cm).

[d] Time taken in seconds to move from the starting unit to another field unit.

[e] $p < .05$.

[f] $p < .001$.

[g] $p < .01$.

In *maze learning*, a linear eleven-point maze (157 × 22 × 18 cm) made of galvanized iron plating and with detachable partitions was used (Kvist, 1985). The partitions were rearranged from the primary to the secondary learning period.

### D. PROCEDURE

*Open-field ambulation* testing was performed in a noiseless experimental room under artificial lighting conditions in a room temperature of 22°C; the testing commenced at 5:00 P.M. The ambulation in the OF was registered on a map (see Apparatus). The track of the animal was marked in a manner suggested by Broadhurst (1960), that is, by recording how many times an animal moved from one floor unit to another. Each move thus indicated an ambulation score and the total sum of the scores over a 2-minute period was recorded. The arena of the OF was cleaned with a wet paper towel between successive recordings. The OF ambulation of each mouse was recorded immediately before and approximately 25 minutes after maze learning.

In order to test *maze learning*, the animals ran the maze once a day. Standard laboratory animal food pellets were available ad lib in the goal box where the animal stayed for 5 minutes after which it was allowed access to an unlimited food supply contained in a glass jar for 20 minutes. Running times from the start box to the entrance of the goal box and error scores (number of entrances to blind alleys) were recorded. The maze was cleaned by brushing off the surface with a brush between each test run.

*Thigmotactic ratio* is a measure of the thigmotactic tendencies, or wall-seeking, exhibited by the mouse. The measure is derived by dividing the number of inner partitions entered by the total number of partitions entered. Hence, the greater the ratio, the more prone the mouse is to staying far from the wall and ambulating in the inner part of the field (Valle & Bols, 1976).

*Rearing* was recorded by counting the number of times the animal rose on its hind legs.

## III. Experiment I

This experiment determined the aggressive, nonaggressive, and normal females' base lines of the three OFP ambulation, thigmotaxis, and rearing. A reliability check of recordings in a circular and a square OF, respectively, was also undertaken. Further, the purpose of the present experiment was to discover learning differences between TA and TNA females, as well as to investigate their patterns of the OFP ambulation, thigmotaxis, and rearing in conjunction with maze running. The OF tests were undertaken using center starting point in a circular field.

**Table 2**
**Correlations Between Base line Open-Field Parameters Displayed by Female Mice during 14 Days in Two Differently Shaped Fields**

| Parameters | TA Mean ($n$ = 10) | TA SE | N Mean ($n$ = 9) | N SE | TNA Mean ($n$ = 9) | TNA SE | Relations between strains | $t$-values | Shape of field |
|---|---|---|---|---|---|---|---|---|---|
| Ambulation[a] | 1.14 | (.19) | .68 | (.15) | .38 | (.09) | TA > N[c] TA > TNA[b] | 1.87; 3.44 | Square |
| $r_S$ | | *.90*[b] | | *.98*[b] | | *.72*[c] | | | |
| | 1.29 | (.22) | .78 | (.16) | .43 | (.07) | TA > N[c] TA > TNA[d] | 1.82; 2.71 | Circular |
| Thigmotaxis | .17 | (.04) | .39 | (.23) | .38 | (.09) | TA < TNA[c] | 2.07 | Square |
| $r_S$ | | *.77*[c] | | *.77*[c] | | *.72*[c] | | | |
| | .17 | (.04) | .31 | (.08) | .43 | (.11) | TA < TNA[c] | 2.37 | Circular |
| Rearing | 2.34 | (.78) | .56 | (.38) | .65 | (.19) | TA > N[c] TA > TNA[c] | 1.97; 1.99 | Square |
| $r_S$ | | *.60*[c] | | *.58*[c] | | | | | |
| | 2.11 | (.75) | .56 | (.39) | .06 | (.11) | TA > N[c] TA > TNA[c] | 1.76; 2.47 | Circular |

[a]The average total ambulation scores divided by 19 circular and 25 square open-field units, respectively.
[b]$p < .001$.
[c]$p < .05$.
[d]$p < .01$.

### A. RESULTS

The base line results are presented in Table 2, which indicates that TA females ambulated in both types of field more than TNA females (Figure 2). Aggressive females kept closer to the wall (Figure 3) and reared more than TNA and N females (Figure 4), both in the circular as well as in the square field. The reliability between the two OFP was high and significant with one exception. Namely, TNA mice hardly exhibited any rearing behavior at all (Table 2).

The results of the maze running are presented in Figure 1 and in Table 3. All animals progressed during the period of maze running but aggressive females ran the maze faster and committed less errors than the nonaggressive mice.

The results of the ambulation are indicated in Figure 2. The maze learning did not produce a quantitative change in the ambulatory behavior of the female mice. Since the curves from before to after training did not differ, ambulation was calculated on the average scores of the two daily recordings. Aggressive females were found to ambulate more than TNA [1.19 (.20) and 0.34 (0.08), $t(17) = 3.65$, $p < .001$] and N subjects [0.64 (0.13), $t(17) = 2.16$, $p < .025$]. The results with regard to thigmotactic behavior are shown in Figure 3. Data are presented in Table 4. Although TA mice entered more inner partitions after every learning session, they exhibited more wall-seeking behavior throughout the learning period than the TNA mice. In all strains the thigmotactic behavior changed in conjunction with maze running.

The results pertaining to rearing are presented in Figure 4. The effect of maze running on rearing was clearly visible in the TA but hardly notable in the TNA females. The strain differences in this regard are presented in Table 5.

## IV. Experiment II

Was the effect of maze running on the qualitative OFP thigmotaxis and rearing seen in Experiment I factual or was it an effect of the location of the OF starting point? In order to answer this question Experiment II replicated the procedure from Experiment I with a wall instead of a center starting point in a circular OF. The detachable partitions of the maze were rearranged and the animals acquired a new maze path to the goal box.

### A. RESULTS

The results of the maze running are depicted in Figure 1. Transfer from the primary to the secondary training period was obvious (Table 3); the mice started on the first day of training of the latter period from a significantly lower level both in terms of running times and errors scores as compared to the results of the former period. TA females, again, ran the maze faster and committed less errors than

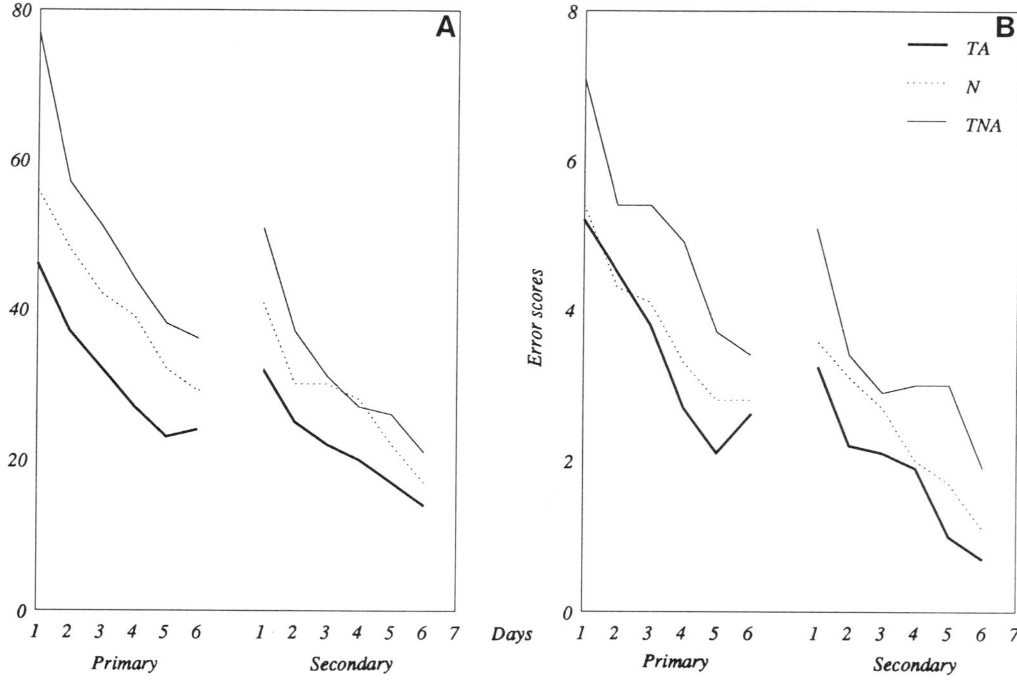


**Figure 1.** **A.** Maze learning running times for the primary and the secondary maze-running periods. When calculated on daily individual running times in both periods TA female mice ran the maze faster than both N ($p <$ .05–.005) and TNA mice ($p <$ .001–.0005) during all the days of experimentation. **B.** Maze learning error scores. TA mice committed less errors than did TNA subjects from day 3 to 5 ($p <$ .05–.005) during the primary training period. During the secondary period of maze running it can be observed that TA mice made less errors than their TNA counterparts on days 1, 2, 4, 5, and 6 ($p <$ .05–.0005) (see Table 3).

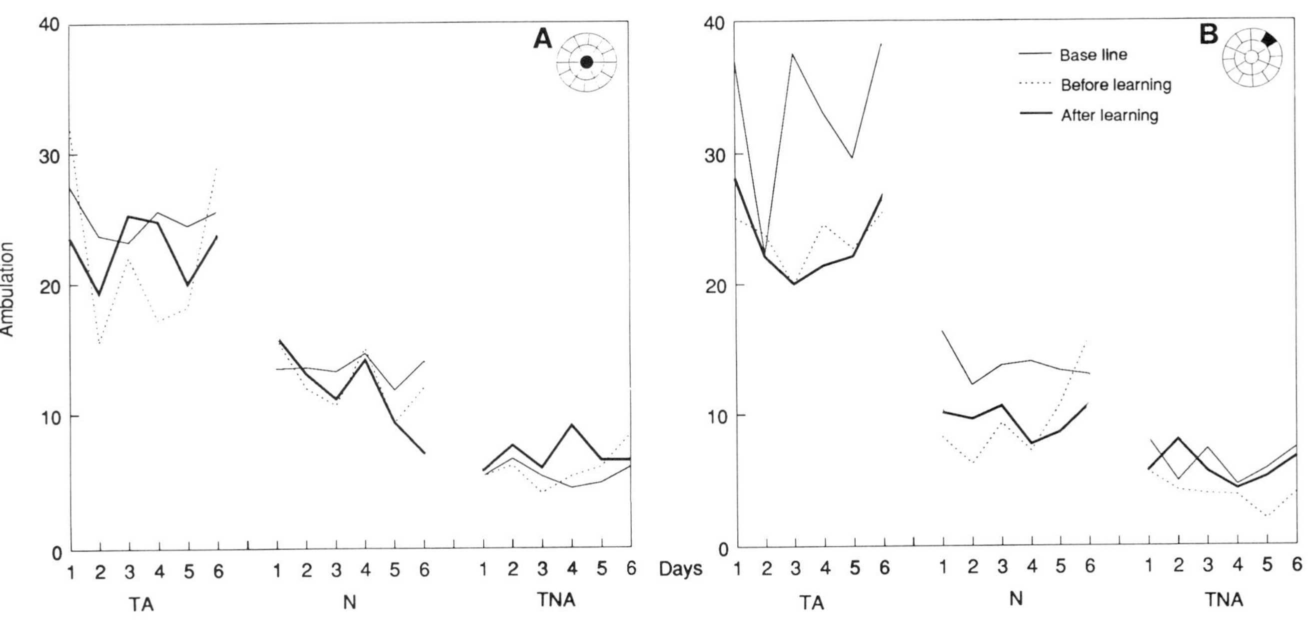


**Figure 2.** Ambulation curves displayed by TA, N, and TNA females. **A.** Center-starting, and **B.** wall-starting ambulation. Significant differences between the base lines of the three strains were found in both A and B (ANOVA, $F(2,15) = 413.96$, and 80.94, respectively, $p < .001$). The base line of the TA females was significantly higher with wall-starting points ($t(10) = 3.061$, $p < .01$). In TA females the learning-related ambulation differed with wall-starting from the base line ($t(10) = 3.50$, $p < .01$).

**Table 3**
**Differences in Learning Displayed by TA, N, and TNA Females**

| Learning measures | Strain | Day 1 Mean | Day 1 SE | Day 6 Mean | Day 6 SE | *t*-values | Order of maze running |
|---|---|---|---|---|---|---|---|
| Running times | | | | | | | |
| Day 1 compared to day 6 | TA | 45.5 | 3.0 | 24.2 | 1.1 | 6.66[a] | Primary |
| | N | 56.0 | 3.4 | 29.1 | 2.6 | 6.41[a] | |
| | TNA | 77.0 | 8.8 | 35.6 | 3.6 | 4.36[a] | |
| | TA | 32.0 | 2.2 | 13.5 | 0.7 | 7.71[a] | Secondary |
| | N | 41.1 | 2.7 | 17.2 | 1.7 | 7.71[a] | |
| | TNA | 51.1 | 4.8 | 20.6 | 1.6 | 6.10[a] | |
| Error scores | | | | | | | |
| Day 1 compared to day 6 | TA | 5.2 | 0.8 | 2.6 | 0.6 | 2.68[b] | Primary |
| | N | 5.4 | 0.5 | 2.8 | 0.3 | 4.41[a] | |
| | TNA | 7.1 | 0.9 | 3.4 | 0.7 | 3.27[b] | |
| | TA | 3.3 | 0.3 | 0.7 | 0.3 | 6.84[a] | Secondary |
| | N | 3.6 | 0.3 | 1.1 | 0.4 | 5.10[a] | |
| | TNA | 5.1 | 0.5 | 1.9 | 0.4 | 5.00[a] | |

[a] $p < .001$.
[b] $p < .01$.

the TNA mice. All animals ran the maze faster and received less error scores on the last day as compared to the first day of maze running (Table 3).

In the aggressive females in contrast to the TNA animals, the thigmotactic behavior appeared to be learning sensitive, even with a wall starting point (Figure 3, Table 4). In the TA females, rearing also seemed to be most learning sensitive (Figure 4, Table 5). Rearing always correlated significantly for aggressive females with ambulation ($r_s = .68–.83, p < .025–.005$) independent of maze learning and field characteristics, that is, OF shape and starting point.

## V. Discussion

The selective breeding experiment on aggression initiated by Lagerspetz more than thirty years ago has effectively changed the biological and behavioral profile of the aggressive and nonaggressive mice as compared to each other and to the maintained normal control stock (Lagerspetz, 1961, 1964; Lagerspetz & Lagerspetz, 1971, 1975). When mapping the characteristics of the female mice, effective strain differences were already observed. For example, the aggressive females had shorter estrous cycles than those of the nonaggressive females. The estrous cycles have traditionally been considered to influence female OF behavior (e.g.,

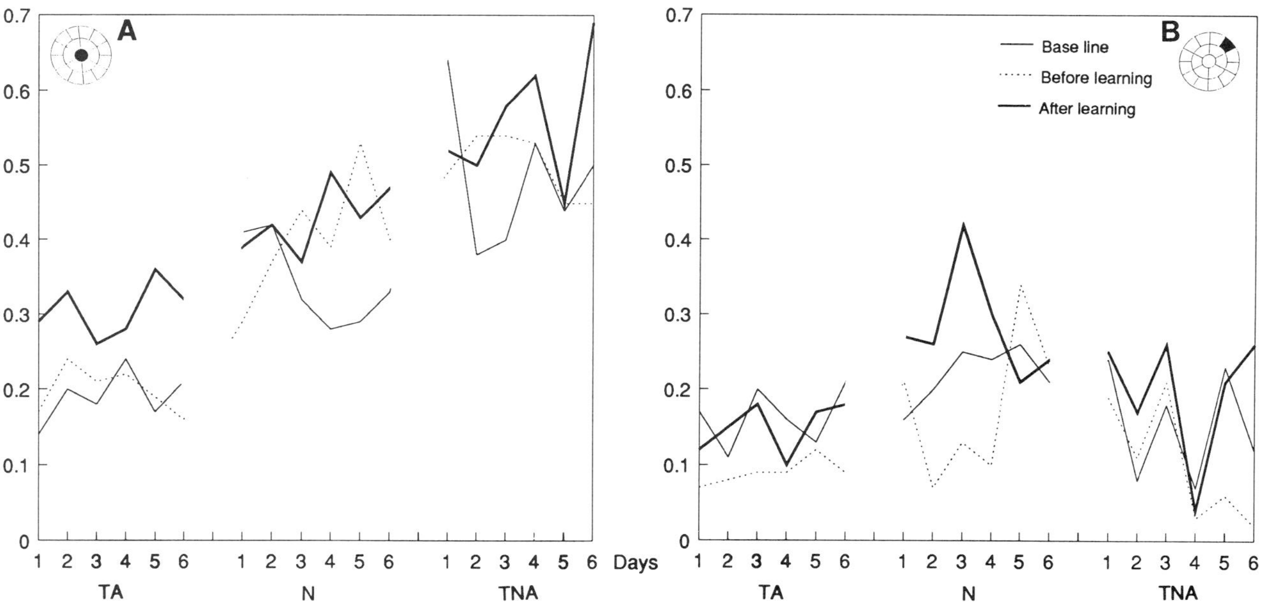


**Figure 3.** Thigmotactic behavior displayed by the females of the three strains. **A.** Recording in the circular OF with a center starting point; **B.** shows curves with a wall starting point. Statistical results are given in Table 4.

**Table 4**
**Differences in Thigmotactic Behavior Exhibited by TA, N, and TNA Female Mice**

| Thigmotactic behavior | F | Experimental days | *t* | Strains | Starting point |
|---|---|---|---|---|---|
| Between strains | | | | | |
| Base line | 14.97[a] | 1 to 6 | | TA–N–TNA | Center |
| After learning | 28.90[a] | 1 to 6 | | | |
| After learning | 6.00[b] | 1 to 6 | | TA–N–TNA | Wall |
| Between strains | | | | | |
| Base line | | | 4.59[c] | TA < N[d] | Center |
| | | | 5.17[c] | TA < TNA | |
| After learning | | | 5.48[c] | TA < N | |
| | | | 8.02[c] | TA < TNA | |
| | | | 3.97[a] | N < TNA | |
| After learning | | | 4.08[a] | TA < N | Wall |
| Within strain | | | | | |
| Between base line, before and after learning | 23.79[a] | 1 to 6 | | TA | Center |
| | 11.45[a] | 3 to 6 | | N | |
| | 9.93[a] | 2 to 6 | | TNA | |
| Between base line, before and after learning | 10.16[a] | 1 to 6 | | TA | Wall |
| | 9.27[a] | 1 to 4 | | N | |
| Between lines | | | | | |
| Base line–after learning | | | 5.92[c] | TA | Center |
| Before–after learning | | | 5.96[c] | TA | |
| Base line–before learning | | | 4.16[a] | N | |
| Base line–after learning | | | 5.00[a] | N | |
| Base line–before learning | | | 2.97[b] | TNA | |
| Base line–after learning | | | 3.99[b] | TNA | |
| Base line–before learning | | | 4.47[c] | TA | Wall |
| Before–after learning | | | 3.88[a] | TA | |
| Before–after learning | | | 3.84[a] | N | |

[a] $p < .01$.
[b] $p < .05$.
[c] $p < .001$.
[d] <, Mouse enters less inner partitions.

Munn, 1950). However, the effect of the estrous cycles in mice has not been indicated to be large enough to compromise the validity as regards the OFP in question when applying the results across the sexes (Kvist & Selander, 1992).

In congruence with previous results of maze learning of the TA and TNA *male* mice (Lagerspetz, 1964; Kvist, 1989) the aggressive females learned the maze paths faster than the nonaggressive ones, a fact which confirmed the first hypothesis. Furthermore, the aggressive females were found to be more active in forms of ambulation and rearing as well as more thigmotactic than nonaggressive mice,

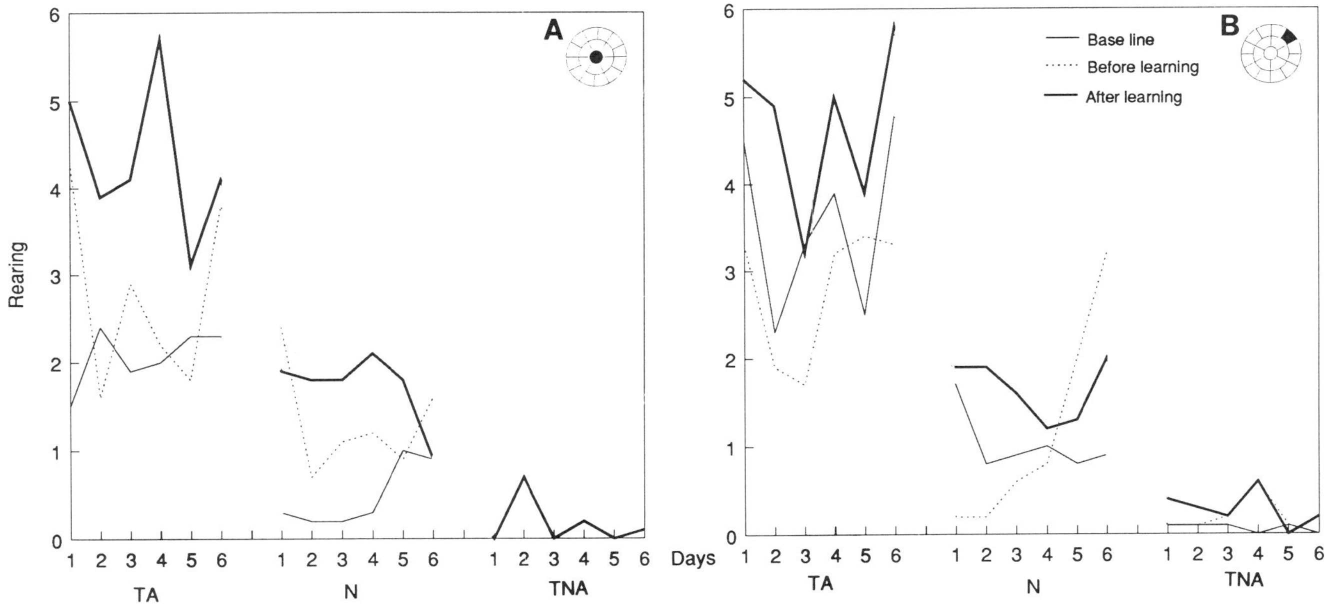


**Figure 4.** Rearing behavior displayed by TA, N, and TNA females. **A.** Curves measured in the circular OF with a center starting point; **B.** wall starting point. Differences between the strains are presented in Table 5.

**Table 5**
**Differences in Rearing Displayed by TA, N, and TNA Females**

| Rearing behavior | F | Experimental days | $t$ | Strains | Starting point |
|---|---|---|---|---|---|
| Between strains | | | | | |
| Base line | 49.99[a] | 1 to 6 | | TA–N | Center |
| After learning | 40.58[a] | 1 to 6 | | TA–N | |
| Between strains | | | | | |
| Base line | | | 7.07[c] | TA > N | Center |
| Between strains | | | | | |
| After learning | | | 6.37[c] | TA > TNA | Center |
| Within strain | | | | | |
| Between base line, before and after learning | 11.10[a] | 1 to 6 | | TA | Center |
| | 9.23[a] | 1 to 6 | | N | |
| Between base line, before and after learning | 6.19[b] | 1 to 6 | | TA | Wall |
| Between lines | | | | | |
| Base line–after learning | | | 5.68[c] | TA | Center |
| Before–after learning | | | 2.66[b] | TA | |
| Base line–after learning | | | 5.00[c] | N | |
| Base line–after learning | | | 1.96[b] | TA | Wall |
| Before–after learning | | | 3.73[a] | TA | Wall |

[a] $p < .01$.
[b] $p < .05$.
[c] $p < .001$.

which sustained the second hypothesis. The normal mice always had intermediate frequencies for all behaviors recorded.

There are many positive correlative relationships encouraging the thought that aggressive females—being better maze learners and the most active—are brighter than nonaggressive ones. Positive correlations between aggressiveness and the maze-learning ability, aggressiveness, and ambulation as well as between aggressiveness and motor activity have been found (Lagerspetz, 1964; Lagerspetz & Lagerspetz, 1974) and, further, between maze learning and motor activity (Tuttle & Dykshorn, 1929; Rundquist, 1933). In addition, the TA females have been found to score higher on maternal behavior than TNA mice (Lagerspetz & Wuorinen, 1965), and a positive relationship between maternal behavior and maze-learning ability has been indicated (see Munn, 1950). Though the explanation that aggressive females are brighter than nonaggressive ones sounds plausible, it is obviously an oversimplification to cover the facts. Male TA mice have been found to be superior only in maze learning involving active motor responses, but not in passive avoidance conditioning, demanding the acquisition of still-standing (Kvist, 1989). Complex factors other than the inclination to be active, are involved in maze learning, for example, the capacity to become aroused by separate stimuli. This character has been indicated to differ between TA and TNA mice (Lagerspetz, Tirri, & Lagerspetz, 1968). On the other hand, differences in thigmotactic tendencies, observed in the present study, may also play a role in maze learning (Fredricson, 1953; Waters, 1937).

The results of the present study pointed out that the females of all three strains displayed a great transfer from the primary to the secondary maze running session, which probably influenced the learning sensitivity of the OFP during the secondary learning period. With regard to the OFP ambulation, a long-term effect of maze learning was observed in aggressive females in the form of an increased base line ambulation before the secondary learning period. Daily effects of learning were most evidently exhibited by aggressive females in the OFP thigmotaxis and in rearing, the learning sensitivity of which was confirmed by the present results. The nonaggressive females, with their greater latency to move, appeared with regard to thigmotaxis to be more influenced by the location of the field starting point than by learning, although their only rearing responses were noticed after maze running. These results lent support to the third hypothesis.

In conclusion, aggressive female mice were better maze learners, ambulated more, were more thigmotactic, and reared more than nonaggressive female mice. Aggressive females seemed to be more influenced by maze running than by field characteristics when compared to the nonaggressive females. The aggressive females displayed qualitative but not quantitative OFP changes in conjunction with maze learning.

## Acknowledgment

The author is obliged to R. K. Selander for recording the animals.

## References

Broadhurst, P. L. (1960). Experiments in psychogenetics. Applications of biometrical genetics to inheritance of behaviour. *In* H. J. Eysenck (Ed.), *Experiments in Personality* (pp. 3–102). London: Routledge & Kegan Paul.

Bronson, F. H., Dagg, C. P., & Snell, G. D. (1966). Reproduction. *In* E. L. Green (Ed.), *Biology of the Laboratory Mouse* (pp. 187–204). New York: McGraw-Hill Book Company.

Fredericson, E. (1953). The wall-seeking tendency in three inbred mouse strains (*Mus musculus*). *Journal of Genetic Psychology, 82,* 143–146.

Kvist, B. (1983). Open field activity after learning in mice. *Scandinavian Journal of Psychology, 24,* 313–324.

Kvist, B. (1985). *Open field activity after learning in mice.* Reports from the Department of Psychology at Åbo Akademi. Monograph Supplement, 2, 1–128.

Kvist, B. (1989). Learning in mice selectivity bred for high and low aggressiveness. *Psychological Reports, 64,* 127–130.

Kvist, S. B. M., & Selander, R. K. (1991). A qualitative aspect of learning-sensitive open field ambulation in mice. *Scandinavian Journal of Psychology, 32* (in press).

Kvist, S. B. M., & Selander, R. K. (1992). Maze-running and thigmotaxis in mice: applicability of models across the sexes. *Scandinavian Journal of Psychology, 33* (in press).

Lagerspetz, K. M. J. (1961). Genetic and social causes of aggressive behaviour of mice. *Scandinavian Journal of Psychology, 2,* 167–173.

Lagerspetz, K. M. J. (1964). Studies on the aggressive behaviour of mice. *Annales Academiae Scientarium Fennicae, Ser. B, 131, 3,* 1–131.

Lagerspetz, K. M. J., & Lagerspetz, K. Y. H. (1971). Changes in the aggressiveness of mice resulting from selective breeding, learning and social isolation. *Scandinavian Journal of Psychology, 12,* 241–248.

Lagerspetz, K. M. J., & Lagerspetz, K. Y. H. (1974). Genetic determination of aggressive behaviour. *In* J. H. F. van Abeelen (Ed.), *The Genetics of Behaviour* (pp. 321–346). Amsterdam: North Holland Publishing Company.

Lagerspetz, K. M. J., & Lagerspetz, K. Y. H. (1975). The expression of the genes of aggressiveness in mice: The effect of androgen on aggression and sexual behavior in females. *Aggressive Behavior, 1,* 291–296.

Lagerspetz, K. M. J., & Wuorinen, K. (1965). A cross-fostering experiment with mice selectively bred for aggressiveness and non-aggressiveness. Reports from the Institute of Psychology, University of Turku, 17, 1–6.

Lagerspetz, K. Y. H., Kvist, B., and Lagerspetz, K. M. J. (1980). Several types of learning increase open field activity in mice. *Scandinavian Journal of Psychology, 21,* 215–222.

Lagerspetz, K. Y. H., Tirri, R., and Lagerspetz, K. M. J. (1980). Neurochemical and endocrinological studies of mice selectively bred for aggressiveness. *Scandinavian Journal of Psychology, 9,* 157–160.

Munn, N. L. (1950). *Handbook of Psychological Research on the Rat.* Boston: Houghton Mufflin Co.

Rundquist, E. A. (1933). Inheritance of spontaneous activity in rats. *Journal of Comparative Psychology, 16,* 415–438.

Sandnabba, N. K. (1988). Maternal aggression as a correlated character in selection for aggressiveness in male mice. *International Journal of Neuroscience, 41,* 351.

Streng, J. (1974). Exploration and learning behavior in mice selectively bred for high and low levels of activity. *Behavior Genetics, 4,* 191–204.

Tachibana, T. (1985). Mapping of open-field behavior in rats and integration of various independent study results. *Physiology and Behavior, 34,* 83–87.

Tuttle, W. W., & Dykshorn, S. (1929). A comparison of spontaneous activity of the albino rat with the ability to learn, with special reference to the effect of castration and ovariectomy on these processes. *Physiological Zoölogy, 2,* 157–167.

Valle, F. P., and Bols, R. J. (1976). Age factors in sex differences in open-field activity in rats. *Animal Learning & Behavior, 4,* 457–460.

Abeelen, van, J. H. F. (1977). Rearing responses and locomotor activity in mice: Single-locus control. *Behaviorial Biology, 19,* 401–404.

Waters, R. H. (1937). The wall-seeking tendency and the maze learning in the white rat. *The Journal of Psychology, 4,* 23–26.

32

# Aggressive Behavior in Female Mice as a Correlated Characteristic in Selection for Aggressiveness in Male Mice

N. Kenneth Sandnabba

I. INTRODUCTION
II. SELECTION FOR AGGRESSION IN MICE
III. MATERNAL AGGRESSION
A. Methods
B. Results
IV. PREDATORY AGGRESSION
A. Methods
B. Results
V. THE EFFECT OF ANDROGENS AND LEARNING ON AGGRESSION IN FEMALES
A. Methods
B. Results
VI. PREFERENCES OF FEMALE MICE FOR MALE ODORS
A. Methods
B. Results
VII. CONCLUSION
REFERENCES

## I. Introduction

In animal research, aggression is a behavioral disposition which usually appears as sexually dimorphic. This assumption is probably partly a function of the traditional approach of research in this field. Until recently the subjects selected for study in aggression research have been male mammals, and many researchers have concluded that in most species, females are less aggressive than males. Indeed, when two adult female rodents meet in a neutral testing area, they are unlikely to fight, whereas adult males are likely to do so. Consequently, it is not surprising that the majority of all research on mouse aggression has involved studies of aggression among males. However, research on mice as well as on other mammals has also shown that aggression is influenced by numerous environmental and physiological factors and this has led researchers to question whether aggression is a unitary behavioral trait. An alternative conceptualization of aggression suggested by Moyer (1976) is that it describes behaviors that are basically similar in appearance but which are actually discrete traits, each independently controlled by its own genetic and neural mechanisms. Among the six different forms of aggression suggested by him, maternal and predatory aggression are also identified as separate from intermale aggression.

The present chapter deals with a comparison between the aggressive expressions of females from two lines of mice selectively bred for intermale aggression. Studies on maternal and predatory aggression form part of this research. The effects of a combination of androgen treatment and learning on the aggressive behavior of females are also examined. Finally, the preferences of females for male odors of more and less aggressive individuals is investigated.

## II. Selection for Aggression in Mice

It has been recognized for several decades that genetic factors contribute to the variation in intermale mouse aggression. Differences between various inbred mouse strains have been demonstrated in the disposition for this kind of aggressive behavior (Scott, 1966; Hahn & Haber, 1982). Response to selection for high and for low aggression has also been demonstrated. The first selective breeding program for aggression in mice, based on the aggressiveness of males, was started in 1959 by Kirsti Lagerspetz and has continued to the present (Lagerspetz, 1961, 1964; Lagerspetz & Lagerspetz, 1971, 1983; Sandnabba, 1986a, 1990). The present work forms a part of the ongoing series of selective breeding studies that have established a high-aggressive (Turku Aggressive, TA) and a low-aggressive (Turku Nonaggressive, TNA) strain from an outbred Swiss albino foundation stock. The parental strain, designated the Normal strain, has been kept as a control line and has been bred without regard to the behavior of the males in the aggression tests. In each generation, male aggressiveness in the selected lines has been assessed by means of standard dyadic tests at approximately three months of age. At the end of the 7-minute test period the behavior of the mouse is rated on a 7-point scale for aggressive behavior developed by Lagerspetz (1964). In the first ten generations, the males were selected on the basis of their mean scores on at least seven test trials conducted on different days. The reliability of the aggression scores was found to be rather high (Lagerspetz, 1964). Thus, in later generations, the selection has been made on the basis of two test trials. As the females of the foundation stock used did not show differences in aggressive behavior when tested in a corresponding way, they were selected for breeding on the basis of their brothers' aggressiveness. Brother–sister mating has been avoided. Significant line differences in aggressiveness were obtained among the male descendants as early as in the second generation (Lagerspetz 1961, 1964).

A comparable selective breeding for more and less aggressive lines of mice was later carried out by van Oortmerssen and Bakker (1981), and by Cairns and his co-workers (1983). Ebert and Hyde (1976) based their selection on females from wild mouse populations. It has generally been reported that the females of the male selected lines have not exhibited differing behavior in terms of aggressiveness (Lagerspetz, 1964; Lagerspetz & Lagerspetz, 1983; van Oortmerssen & Bakker, 1981). In the different lines established by female selection, the males have not demonstrated corresponding differences (Ebert & Hyde, 1976). Does this mean that the aggressiveness of males and females is genetically independent and mediated by different physiological mechanisms?

## III. Maternal Aggression

Numerous observations of both natural environment and the laboratory testify to the fact that during gestation, parturition, and lactation, animals of a variety of species, including the mouse, will exhibit intense aggressive behavior toward an intruder (Gandelman, 1972; Broida & Svare, 1982; Ogawa & Makino, 1984; Roubertoux & Carlier, 1988). This behavior is usually referred to as maternal aggression (Moyer, 1976). Aggressive behavior in female mice is mainly confined to late pregnancy and early midlactation (Noirot, Goyens, & Buhot, 1975, Svare & Gandelman, 1973). The function of maternal aggression is to protect newborn offspring from potential predators until such time as the young are able to defend themselves (Broida & Svare, 1982). The behavior may also serve an important dispersal function and is therefore thought to play an instrumental role in mammalian population regulation (Rowley & Christian, 1977). It can be concluded from the aforementioned studies that the elicitation of maternal aggression is influenced by the sex, age, reproductive status, and the individual's degree of familiarity with the opponent. Male intruders are attacked more fiercely than any type of female opponent and unfamiliar animals are attacked more viciously than familiar animals. Previous studies have demonstrated consistent patterns of strain differences in maternal aggression (St. John & Corning, 1973) as well as differences correlated with selective breeding for interfemale aggression (Hyde & Sawyer, 1979) and intermale aggression (Hood & Cairns, 1988). The objective of the present experiment was to examine whether maternal aggression is a correlated characteristic of intermale aggression in the high-aggressive TA and low-aggressive TNA strains.

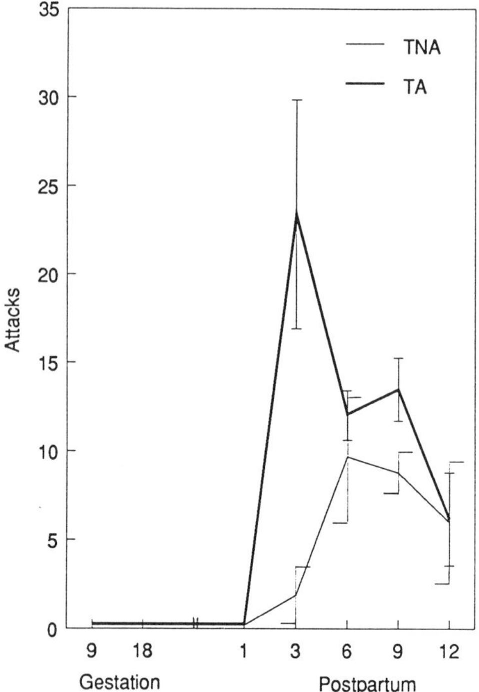


**Figure 1.** Mean frequency of attack on intruders by pregnant and postpartum females of the $S_{47}$ generation of selective breeding for high (TA) and low (TNA) levels of male aggressiveness.

## A. METHODS

A total of 70 TA and 70 TNA nulliparous females of the forty-seventh generation of selection were used. All females were socially reared in same-sex groups from weaning until they were used in the experiment. Males from the same generation of selection were used for mating with the subjects. After mating, all females were housed individually. The subjects were randomly assigned to be tested for aggression only once. A 7-minute aggression test was administered on day 9 and day 18 during the gestation period, and on day 1, 3, 6, 9, and 12 postpartum. For the aggression tests an unfamiliar intruder was put into the home cage of the female.

## B. RESULTS

During the gestation period and on the first day after parturition, the tested females did not show any signs of aggression as can be seen in Figure 1. Differences between the strains in their frequency of attacks were registered for the females tested on the subsequent postpartum days. These differences reached significant levels on day 3 [$t(18) = 3.14$, $p < 0.005$] and day 9 [$t(18) = 2.41$, $p < 0.025$]. For the TA and TNA females tested on day 12 no differences in the frequency of attacks on the intruders were observed.

In accordance to the findings of Hood and Cairns (1988), these results demonstrate that maternal aggression is a correlate of intermale aggression, as the separations of strains is quite good and in the expected directions. The lack of aggressive responses on the first day after parturition was expected, since it has been reported that female mice become completely docile for a period of approximately 48 hours after giving birth (Svare, 1989). This is the time when female mice typically mate again. Thus, the fact that they do not attack a male is biologically significant. The present findings are congruent with those of a number of studies on mice demonstrating that maternal aggression declines substantially by the second week of lactation (Svare *et al.*, 1981; Hood & Cairns, 1988). The second peak in aggression that was observed on the 9th day after parturition is reminiscent of a similar aggressive peak within this time period reported earlier for rats (Erskine, Barfield, & Goldman, 1978; Flannelly, Flannelly, & Lore, 1986) and hamsters (Wise & Ferrante, 1982). The present results also suggest that the physiological mechanisms controlling postpartum- and gestation-induced aggression are different, since both the TA and TNA females failed to show aggression during gestation.

# IV. Predatory Aggression

Evidence regarding relationships between intermale fighting and predatory behavior have yielded inconsistent results. In some cases a positive relationship has appeared (Thomas, 1969), while in others no covariation has been found (Brain & Al-Maliki, 1978; Lynds, 1980). A study by Ebert (1983) indicated an absence of a relationship also between interfemale aggression and predatory aggression in two lines selectively bred for interfemale aggression. However, predatory aggression seems to be related to the intermale aggression in the high-aggressive TA and low-aggressive TNA males (Sandnabba, in preparation). Since the experiment described earlier demonstrated that maternal aggression is a correlate of intermale aggression in these lines, the present experiment was conducted in order to determine whether females of the TA, TNA, and N strains also show differences with regard to predatory attack.

## A. METHODS

Ten females from each of the three lines served as subjects. The TA and TNA females were of the fifty-second generation of selection for intermale aggression.

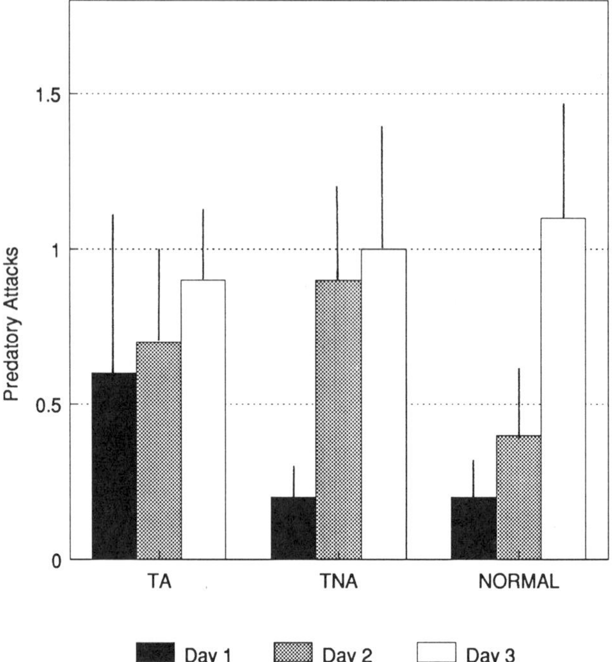


**Figure 2.** Mean frequency of attack on crickets by females from the parental (Normal) strain and females of the $S_{52}$ generation of selective breeding for high (TA) and low (TNA) levels of male aggressiveness.

The females were tested for 3 consecutive days, were slightly food but not water deprived prior to testing, and they had had no exposure to crickets prior to testing. Testing consisted of dropping a live cricket into the home cage. Cricket- or locust-killing behavior has been used as a model of predatory aggression in mice (Brain & Al-Maliki, 1978; Lynds, 1980).

## B. RESULTS

From Figure 2 it can be seen that the females, independent of strain, committed approximately the same number of attacks on the crickets (nonsignificant strain differences). It can also be seen that the number of attacks increased with experience.

The results of this study indicate the absence of a relationship between intermale aggression and predatory aggression in females. The results support the conclusions drawn by other researchers who have compared the predatory aggression of female and male mice (Butler, 1973; Brain & Al-Maliki, 1978; Ebert,

1983). It cannot, however, be ruled out that a correlation exists between maternal and predatory aggression, since the females in this experiment were not studied during gestation and lactation. The low rate of cricket killing performed by the females is, on the other hand, congruent with the low aggressiveness of the females under normal conditions reported earlier (Lagerspetz, 1964; Lagerspetz & Lagerspetz, 1983). The females of the TA and TNA strains have also been found not to differ from one another in dominant behavior with regard to food (Lagerspetz, 1964).

## V. The Effect of Androgens and Learning on Aggression in Females

Early androgenization has an organizational effect that stimulates the development of testosterone-sensitive neural circuits that facilates intermale aggression (Edwards, 1969; Gandelman, Rosenthal, & Howard; 1980). Neonatal administration of androgens has been found to increase the aggressiveness of female mice, especially after additional androgen injections in adulthood (Bronson & Desjardins, 1970; Barkley & Goldman, 1977). In an earlier study (Lagerspetz & Lagerspetz, 1975) it was shown that some of the difference in aggressiveness between TA and TNA mice is due to genotype and hormone interaction, and that neonatal and adult androgen injections activate the genetically determined mechanisms which influence aggression in females of the TA, but not the TNA, strain.

Early experience and learning have frequently been shown to affect the development and expression of aggressive behavior. Male mice defeated in aggressive encounters with conspecifics show a decrease in aggressive behavior, while success in fights causes increased aggressiveness (Scott, 1958; Lagerspetz, 1964; Lagerspetz & Sandnabba, 1982). The purpose of the experiment described below was to investigate whether also the aggressiveness of androgenized TA females is affected by learning.

### A. METHODS

A total of 44 TA females of the twenty-seventh generation of selection were injected with testosterone immediately after birth and when fully grown. They were then divided into three groups. The females of group A were trained in order to enhance their aggressiveness, that is, they were encouraged to attack a docile male opponent. The females of group N were trained toward decreased aggressiveness by attacking highly aggressive males. The females of group C served as controls and were isolated. The aggressiveness of the females was assessed by means of the standard dyadic aggression test (Lagerspetz, 1964; Sandnabba, 1986a). The females were given aggression scores on a 7-point scale,

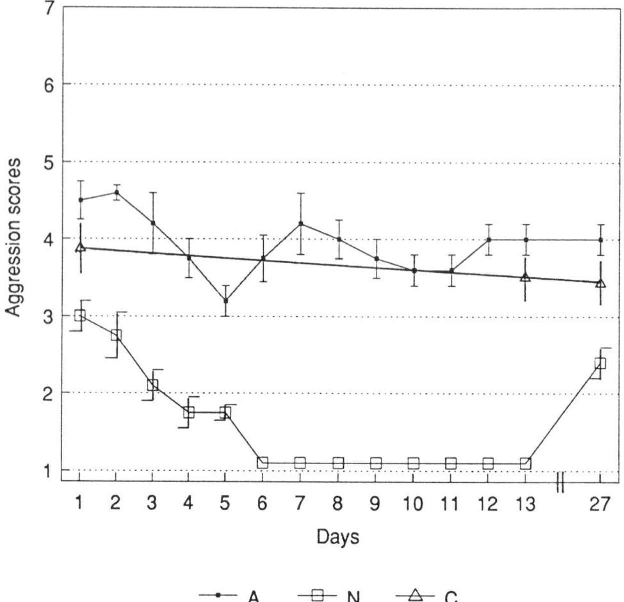


**Figure 3.** Mean level of aggressiveness of androgenized TA females trained toward enhanced aggressiveness (A), trained toward decreased aggressiveness (N), or isolated (C).

where 7 represents the highest degree of aggression (i.e., the opponent is attacked most of the time and starts to bleed), and 1, the lowest (i.e., no signs of aggression).

B. RESULTS

From Figure 3 it can be seen that females of group N were totally nonaggressive after six days of training [$t(10) = 3.62$, $p < 0.005$, when day 1 and day 6 are compared]. On day 13, when the training was completed, all groups differed significantly from each other in terms of aggressiveness [$f(2,41) = 8.43$, $p < 0.001$]. The females of group N were significantly less aggressive than both the females of group A [$t(20) = 4.62$, $p < 0.001$] and those of group C [$t(31) = 3.51$, $p < 0.001$].

The results showed that the aggressiveness of the androgenized TA females could be affected by experience in the same way as the aggressiveness of males. In accordance with earlier reports on male aggressiveness (Lagerspetz, 1964), the training toward nonaggressive behavior was more successful than the training to enhance aggressiveness. Howard and his co-workers (1981) found that isolation intensifies the aggression-enhancing effects of androgenization in females. This was not observed in the isolated females of the control group but it is interesting to observe that the females trained toward nonaggressiveness showed increased aggression after only two weeks of isolation. Also, males trained toward nonaggressiveness have been found to get back their original potential for aggressive behavior in about 2 weeks (Lagerspetz, 1964; Sandnabba, 1986a).

## VI. Preferences of Female Mice for Male Odors

Several investigators have shown that female mice are capable of selecting mates on the basis of certain odor cues indicative of genetic quality (Yamazaki *et al.*, 1979; Lenington & Egid, 1985; Novotny *et al.*, 1990). Female mice have also been found to show a preference for male odors of high-ranking and aggressive individuals (Scott & Pfaff, 1970; Jones & Nowell, 1974; Sandnabba, 1985, 1986b). An interesting question that these observations give rise to is whether female mice always, independent of their own genotype, prefer the odors of highly aggressive males.

### A. METHODS

Fourteen females of both the TA and TNA strains served as subjects. They were of the forty-third generation of selection for intermale aggression. The preferences for male odors was examined in a manner described earlier by this author (Sandnabba, 1985; 1986a,b). An open field was covered with soiled sawdust from a highly aggressive TA male, soiled sawdust from a nonaggressive TNA male, and clean sawdust.

### B. RESULTS

Figure 4 illustrates that there exists a significant difference between the preference of choices of the TA and TNA females [$f(1,78) = 12.19, p < 0.01$]. The TA females preferred the areas soiled by nonaggressive TNA males as compared to both the TA-soiled areas [$t(13) = 2.38, p < 0.05$] and the clean areas [$t(13) = 2.21, p < 0.05$]. The TNA females, on the other hand, preferred the odors from the areas soiled by highly aggressive TA males [$t(13) = 2.46, p < 0.05$] and the clean areas [$t(13) = 2.45, p < 0.05$].

The present results show that female mice seem to prefer the strange odor of a male of an alien strain to the odors of a male of their own strain. However, when the choice is between males of unknown strains, females prefer the odors of the more aggressive male (Sandnabba, 1985). This would also counteract inbreeding and lead to a more varied gene pool.

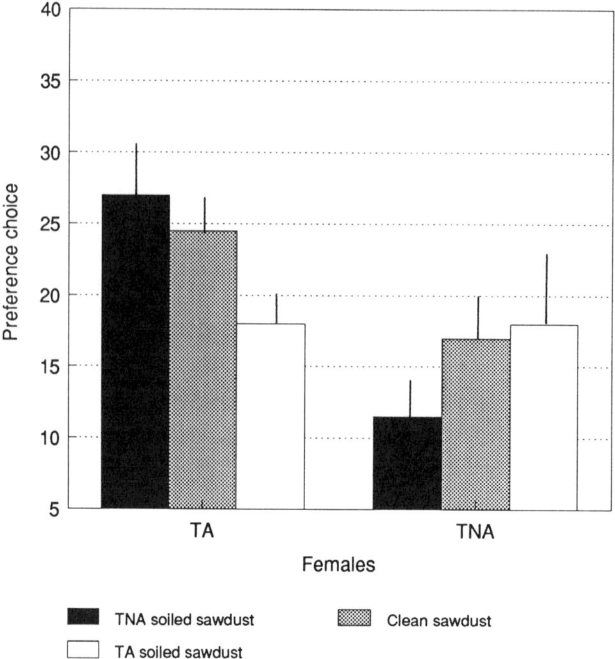


**Figure 4.** Mean preferences of TA and TNA females ($S_{43}$) for areas of an open field covered with sawdust soiled by TA and TNA males, and with clean sawdust.

# VII. Conclusion

Aggressive and maternal behavior are important categories for the survival of most species of mammals. Intermale and maternal aggression seem to be correlates of each other, and it is thought that common genes are involved in the regulation of these behaviors. Furthermore, it is possible to evoke typically male aggression through androgenization in females showing more postpartum aggression. The absence of attacks by females tested under the standard conditions used for males is in accordance with the low rates of predatory attacking in the lines studied. These findings obviously contradict Moyer's (1976) assertion that several distinct types of aggression exist, each with its own neural and genetic substrates. A network of olfactory communication for individual recognition seems also to provide scope for selective mating based on genetically determined aggressiveness.

Aggressive dispositions determined by heredity might appear as sexually dimorphic but they are obviously shared by both sexes and dimorphic only in threshold, frequency, or forms of manifestation. Aggressive behavior may not itself be sexually differentiated, but may emerge as the by-product of some other dimorphic pattern, for example, the secretion of testosterone.

## References


Barkley, M. S., & Goldman, B. D. (1977). Testosterone-induced aggression in adult female mice. *Hormones and Behavior, 9,* 76–84.

Brain, P. F., & Al-Maliki, S. (1978). A comparison of "intermale fighting" in "standard opponent" tests and attack directed towards locusts by "TO" strain mice: Effects of simple experimental manipulations. *Animal Behaviour, 26,* 723–737.

Broida, J., & Svare, B. (1982). Postpartum aggression in C57BL/6J and DBA/2J mice: experiential and environmental influences. *Behavioural and Neural Biology, 3,* 76–83.

Bronson, F. H., & Desjardins, C. (1970). Neonatal androgen administration and adult aggressiveness in female mice. *General and Comparative Endocrinology, 15,* 320–325.

Butler, K. (1973). Predatory behavior in laboratory mice: Strain and sex comparison. *Journal of Comparative Psychology, 85,* 243–249.

Cairns, R. B., MacCombie, D. J., & Hood, K. E. (1983). A developmental-genetic analysis of aggressive behavior in mice: I. Behavioural outcomes. *Journal of Comparative Psychology, 97,* 69–89.

Ebert, P. D. (1983). Selection for aggression in a natural population. *In* E. C. Simmel and M. Hahn (Eds.), *Aggressive Behavior: Genetic and Neural Approaches*, (pp. 103–127. Hillsdale, New Jersey: Erlbaum.

Ebert, P. D., & Hyde, J. S. (1976). Selection for agonistic behavior in wild female *Mus musculus. Behavior Genetics, 6,* 291–304.

Edwards D. A. (1969). Early androgen stimulation and aggressive behavior in male and female mice. *Physiology and Behavior, 4,* 333–338.

Erskine, M. S., Barfield, R. J., & Goldman, D. B. (1978). Intra-specific fighting during late pregnancy and lactation in rats and effects of litter removal. *Behavioral Biology, 23,* 206–218.

Flannelly, K. J., Flannelly, L, & Lore, R. (1986). Postpartum aggression against intruding male conspecifics in Sprague-Dawley rats. *Behavioural Processes, 13,* 279–286.

Gandelman, R. (1972). Mice: Postpartum aggression elicited by the presence of an intruder. *Hormones and Behavior, 3,* 23–28.

Gandelman, R., Rosenthal, C., & Howard, S. M. (1980). Exposure of female mouse fetuses of various ages to testosterone and the later activation of intraspecific fighting. *Physiology and Behavior, 25,* 333–335.

Hahn, M. E., & Haber, S. B. (1982). Individual recognition by natural concentration of olfactory cues in mice. *Psychonomic Science, 12,* 183–184.

Hood K. E., & Cairns, R. B. (1988). A developmental-genetic analysis of aggressive behavior in mice. II. Cross-sex inheritance. *Behavior Genetics, 18,* 605–619.

Howard, S. M., Gandelman, R., & Rosenthal, C. (1981). Isolation potentiates the aggression-activating property of testosterone in female mice. *Physiology and Behavior, 26,* 971–972.

Hyde, J. S., & Sawyer, T. F. (1979). Correlated response in selection for aggressiveness in female mice. II. Maternal aggression. *Behavior Genetics, 9,* 571–577.

Jones, R. B., & Nowell, N. W. (1974). A comparison of the aversive and female attractant properties of urine from dominant and sub-ordinate male mice. *Animal Learning and Behavior, 2,* 141–144.

Lagerspetz, K. M. J. (1961). Genetic and social causes of aggressive behaviour in mice. *Scandinavian Journal of Psychology, 2,* 167–173.

Lagerspetz, K. M. J. (1964). Studies on the aggressive behaviour of mice. *Annales Academiae Scientarum Fennicae,* Series B, 131, 3.

Lagerspetz, K. M. J. (1971). Learning and suppression of aggressiveness in animal experiments: A reinterpretation. *Reports from the Institute of Psychology*, University of Turku, 35.

Lagerspetz, K. M. J., & Lagerspetz, K. Y. H. (1971). Changes in the aggressiveness of mice resulting from selective breeding, learning and social isolation. *Scandinavian Journal of Psychology, 12,* 241–248.

Lagerspetz, K. M. J., & Lagerspetz, K. Y. H. (1975). The expression of the genes on aggressiveness in mice: The effect of androgen on aggression and sexual behaviour in females. *Aggressive Behavior, 1,* 291–296.

Lagerspetz, K. M. J., & Lagerspetz, K. Y. H. (1983). Genes and aggression. *In* E. C. Simmel & M. Hahn (Eds.), *Aggressive Behaviour: Genetic and Neural Approach* (pp. 89–101). Hillsdale, New Jersey: Erlbaum.

Lagerspetz, K. M. J., & Sandnabba, K. (1982). The decline of aggressiveness in male mice during group caging as determined by punishment delivered by the cage mates. *Aggressive Behavior, 8,* 319–334.

Lenington, S., & Egid, K. (1985). Female discrimination of male odors correlated with male genotype at the T-locus is a response to T-locus or H-locus variability. *Behavior Genetics, 15,* 53–67.

Lynds, P. G. (1980). Intermale fighting and predatory behavior in house mice: An analysis of behavioral content. *Aggressive Behavior, 6,* 139–147.

Moyer, K. E. (1976). *The Psychobiology of Aggression.* New York: Harper & Row.

Noirot, E., Goyens, J., & Buhot, M. C. (1975). Aggressive behavior of pregnant mice toward males. *Hormones and Behavior, 6,* 9–17.

Novotny, M., Jemiolo, B., & Harvey, S. (1990). Chemistry of rodent pheromones: molecular insights into chemical signalling in mammals. *In* D. W. Macdonald, D. Müller-Schwarze, & S. E. Natyncruk (Eds.), *Chemical Signals in Vertebrates* (Vol. 5). Oxford: Oxford University Press.

Ogawa, S., & Makino, J. (1981). Maternal aggression of inbred strains of mice: *Effects of reproductive states. Japanese Journal of Psychology, 52,* 78–84.

Ogawa, S., & Malcino, J. (1984). Aggressive behavior in inbred strains of mice during pregnancy. *Behavioral and Neural Biology, 40,* 195–204.

Roubertoux, P. L., & Carlier, M. (1988). Differences between CBA/H and NZB mice on intermale aggression. II. Maternal effects. *Behavior Genetics, 18,* 175–184.

Rowley, M. H., & Christian, J. J. (1977). Competition between lactating *Peromyscus leucopus* and juvenile *Microtus pennsylvanicus. Behavioural Biology, 20,* 70–80.

St. John, R. S., & Corning, P. A. (1973). Maternal aggression in mice. *Behavioral Biology, 9,* 635–639.

Sandnabba, N. K. (1985). Differences in the capacity of male odours to affect investigatory behaviour and different urinary marking patterns in two strains of mice, selectively bred for high and low aggressiveness. *Behavioral Processes, 11,* 257–267.

Sandnabba, N. K. (1986a). Heredity, fighting experience and odour cues: Factors determining the aggressive interaction in mice. *Reports from the Department of Psychology at Åbo Akademi,* Monograph Supplement, 3.

Sandnabba, N. K. (1986b). Effects of selective breeding for high and low aggressiveness and of fighting experience on odor discrimination in mice. *Aggressive Behavior, 12,* 359–366.

Sandnabba, N. K. (1990). Differences between aggressive and non-aggressive mice in odour signals and marking behaviour. *In* D. W. Macdonald, D. Muller-Schwarze, & S. E. Natynczuk (Eds.), *Chemical Signals in Vertebrates* (Vol. 5.). Oxford: Oxford University Press.

Sandnabba, N. K. (in preparation). Predatory aggression in lines of mice selectively bred for intermale aggression.)

Scott, J. P. (1958). *Aggression.* Chicago: University of Chicago Press.

Scott, J. P. (1966). Behaviour of mice and rats: A review. *American Zoologist 6,* 687–701.

Scott, J. W., & Pfaff, D. W. (1970). Behavioral and electrophysiological responses of female mice to male urine odors. *Physiology and Behavior, 5,* 407–411.

Svare, G. (1989). Recent advances in the study of female aggressive behavior in mice. *In* S. Parmigiani, D. Mainardi, & P. Brain (Eds.), *House Mouse Aggression: A Model for Understanding the Evolution of Social Behavior.* London: Gordon & Breach.

Svare, B., Betteridge, C., Katz, D., & Samuels, O. (1981). Some situational and experiential determinants of maternal aggression in mice. *Physiology and Behavior, 26,* 253–258.

Svare, G., & Gandelman, R. (1973). Postpartum aggression in mice. Experiential and environmental factors. *Hormones and Behavior, 4,* 323–334.

Thomas, K. (1969). Predatory behavior in two inbred strains of laboratory mice. *Psychonomic Science, 15,* 13–14.

van Oortmerssen, G. A., & Bakker, T. M. C. (1981). Artificial selection for short and long attack latencies in wild *Mus musculus domesticus. Behavior Genetics, 11,* 115–126.

Wise, D. A., & Ferrante, F. (1982). Effect of conspecific sex on aggression during pregnancy and lactation in golden hamsters. *Aggressive Behavior, 8,* 243–251.

Yamazaki, K., Yamaguchi, Andrews, P. W., Peake, V., Boyse, F. A., & Thomas, L. (1979). Recognition among mice: evidence from the use of a Y-maze differentially scented by congenic mice of different major histocompatibility types. *Journal of Experimental Medicine, 150,* 755–760.

33

# Biological Correlates of Attack on Lactating Intruders by Female Mice: A Topical Review

Marc Haug, Frank J. Johnson, and Paul F. Brain

I. STIMULUS CONDITION FOR AGGRESSION
II. ROLE OF GENOTYPE
III. ROLE OF HORMONES
A. Effects of Hormonal Manipulation of the Female
B. Effects of Hormonal Manipulation of the Male
IV. ROLE OF CENTRAL NEUROTRANSMITTER
V. BIOLOGICAL FUNCTIONS OF AGGRESSION
VI. FINAL COMMENTS
REFERENCES

Attempts to understand the role of biological factors in controlling the probability of attack, best involve investigations on as many situations as possible given the diverse nature of aggression (Brain, 1991).

Since Beeman's (1947) study of the androgenic control of intermale fighting in mice, the male rodent has been almost exclusively used by the behavioral research community as the "reference model" for any studies pertaining to aggression. It is generally assumed that males of most species are the more aggressive sex, with females only rarely entering into fights. Recent attempts, however, have countered assumptions about male dominance and superiority over females in all competitive situations. It is now recognized that the female of the species may become very aggressive and even attack and defeat male conspecifics, even when she is not in a maternal state. One perhaps most intriguing example of a behavioral situation in mice where females appear more aggressive than males is the attack that is exhibited toward lactating intruder conspecifics. This account consequently focuses on some of the biological factors which reduce or increase the probability of seeing this particular form of "aggression."

# I. Stimulus Condition for Aggression

The relationship between pheromones and aggressive behavior has been widely studied in a variety of vertebrate animals. Several studies have looked at the olfactory transmission of information about social status in rats (Krames, 1970), gerbils (Thiessen, Friend, & Lindzey, 1968), hamsters (Johnson, 1973), and mice (Reynolds, 1971; Kimelman & Lubow, 1974), while others have suggested that the relationship between fighting and olfaction is far more complex (see e.g., Edwards, Thompson, & Burge, 1972), involving specific odors acting synergistically with other sensory modalities such as, for example, tactile stimuli.

Data on the attack directed toward lactating intruders both indirectly and directly support the view that olfactory cues are involved in releasing such behavior. First, it has been demonstrated that resident mice attack lactating intruders to a much greater extent than they do cycling virgin animals (Haug, 1972, 1973a). It has been subsequently shown that the mouse's stage of lactation affects the degree to which she is attacked, with the end of the second week postpartum being the most effective in stimulating such responses (Haug, 1973a). Haug (1973b) also showed that residential female mice attacked adult virgin cycling intruders more intensively if the latter had previously lived in the home cage of a lactating mouse still nursing her pups. As female mice rendered anosmic by surgical ablation of their olfactory bulbs or by intranasal $ZnSO_4$ infusion exhibited no attack responses during their encounters with lactating mice, two possible sources of aggression-promoting stimuli from maternal origin were postulated. As the ventral surface of a lactating mouse intruder is sometimes the target of bites from adult female or castrated male residents, maternal milk has been suggested to be one such source. However, reducing milk production by suppressing endogenous prolactin has inconclusive effects on attack (Figure 1). Attention consequently rapidly focused on the alternative of the involvement of maternal urinary factors. Their involvement was convincingly established as resident females attack lactating intruders to a much greater extent than cycling virgin animals, except when the latter are rubbed with urine from mice that have been lactating for two weeks (Haug, 1973b). However, urine from females suckling their pups for one or three weeks are much less potent in this respect, suggesting that these body fluids differ in the *amounts* or *qualities* of contained "pheromone."

# II. Role of Genotype

Ample evidence implicates genotype on aggression in mice (e.g., see reviews by Maxson, Ginsburg, & Trahner, 1979; Selmanoff & Ginsburg, 1981; Hahn & Haber, 1982). Genes are generally implicated by selection studies (Ebert & Hyde,

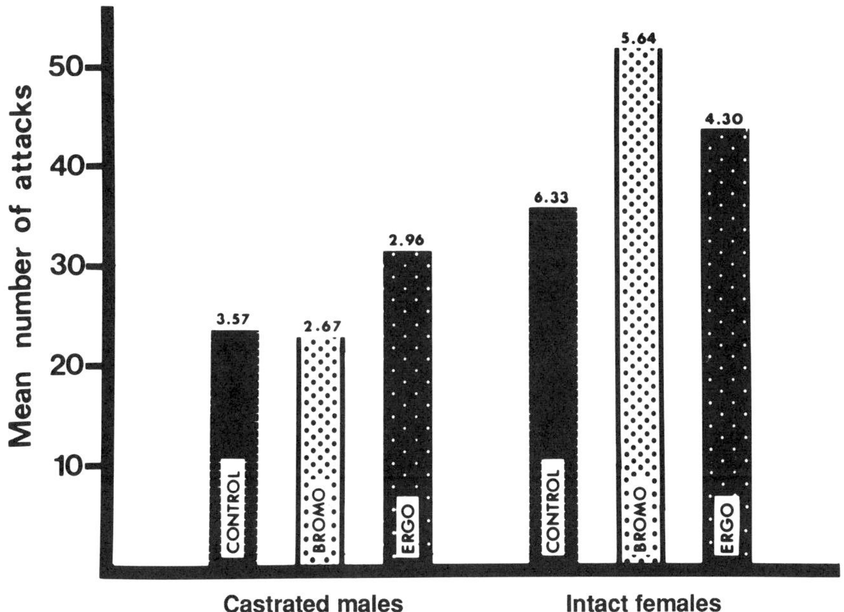


**Figure 1.** Attack (Mean values with standard deviations given as figures on columns) by intact females or castrated males on ergo-treated lactating intruders. Lactating females were administered with pituitary prolactin inhibitors, ergocornine hydrogen maleate (ERGO), or 2-bromo-α-ergocryptine (BROMO) before being introduced in the home cages of triads of adult intact (sham-operated) female or castrated male Swiss strain mice for aggression testing. Treatments were 5 mg/kg and were administered subcutaneously once a day from postpartum day 11 to day 15, when the behavioral testing was performed. A control group (CONTROL) was given an equal volume (0.1 ml) of the oil vehicle. Tests for aggression were as described elsewhere (c.f. Haug *et al.*, 1986b). In both sexes, the aggressive behavior toward the ergo-treated females was indistinguishable from that exhibited toward the oil controls.

1976; Lagerspetz & Lagerspetz, 1968, 1971, 1974) despite some notable failures (see e.g., van Oortmerssen and Bakker, 1981), or crossbreeding investigations (Eleftheriou, Bailey, & Denenberg, 1974).

Different strains of laboratory mice show differing potentials for attack on lactating intruders. For example, Swiss (Haug & Mandel, 1978a) or CFW (Whalen & Johnson, 1988) females show marked responses whereas "TO" strain albinos show little attack on lactating female intruders. In the same way, differences have been found between C57BL/6, C3H/He, BALB/c and DBA/2 strains of mice (Haug & Mandel, 1978a,b). In this test situation, the C57 animals were the most aggressive, whereas mice of the BALB/c or DBA/2 strains showed very few attacks on intruder females. The response does not occur in the C3H/He strain. As data from surveys of inbred strains are unlikely to throw light on the genetic

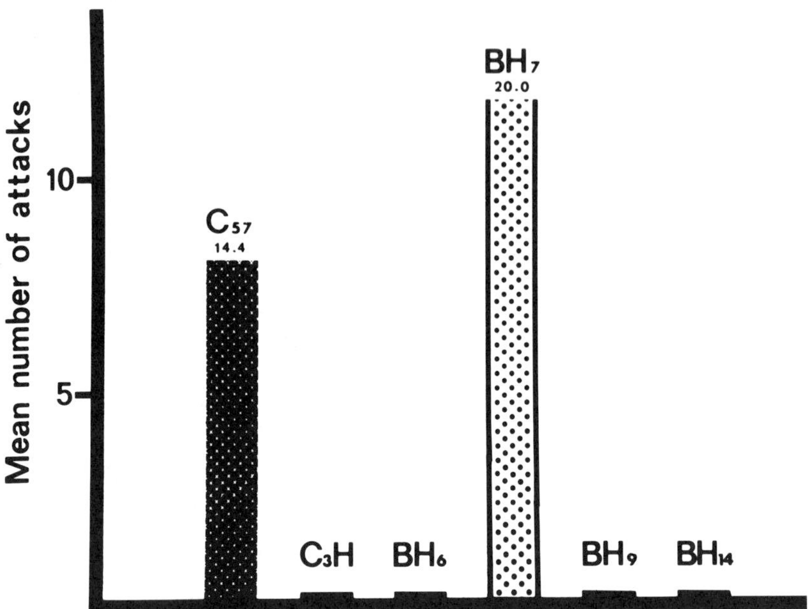


**Figure 2.** Attack (mean values with standard deviations given as figures on columns) by C57 and C3H female mice and by some of their recombinant inbred strains (RIs) on lactating intruders. The methodology used for the production and the development of the RIs consists essentially of establishing closely inbred colonies, originating a pair of $F_2$ segregants from the C57BL/6 × C3H/He parental cross, each of which is initially mated at random. Such a system of mating produces a series of lines (the first of them being here the BH6, BH7, BH9, and BH14 lines) which are homozygous like their parents for either one or the other of the two allelic forms segregating in the parents. Results suggest that the observed difference between the aggression performance between the C57BL/6 and the C3H/He inbred lines obeys a relatively simple genetic determinism. Three RIs of the four studied behaved as did the dominant C3H/He inbred parental line, while the behavior of the remaining line was similar to that of the recessive C57BL/6 parent.

architecture underlining behavioral traits, additional crossbreeding studies were performed. Thus, the aggressive C57BL/6 and the nonaggressive C3H/He inbred strains were first reciprocally crossed to produce $F_1$ hybrids which were tested in adulthood for attack on lactating females. The results were consistent with a directional dominance for low aggression in this situation (Haug *et al.*, 1987). Inbreeding was then practiced to produce a set of recombinant inbred (RI) strains derived from an initial cross between the C57BL/6 and C3H/He mouse strains (respectively, BH1 to BH11). As mentioned by Hewitt and Broadhurst (1983), the particular attractions of RI strains are that (1) extreme tester lines may be chosen from the RI set that are differentiated at the same loci for which there is variation among the testee strains; and (2) a provisional assumption of equality of gene frequencies may be justifiably adopted and the genotypes may be replicated as desired. To date, a series of experiments performed with some of the available genotypes (especially the BH6, BH7, BH9, BH14, and the progenitor inbred strains C57BL/6 and C3H/He) unequivocally show that the RI strain females (cf. Figure 2) behave toward lactating females in a symmetrical manner: some are intensively aggressive (cf. the C57 parental strain) while others fail to show attack (cf. the C3H parental strain).

# III. Role of Hormones

A wide variety of hormonal factors can be implicated in various types of aggression in a range of species. These actions are not, however, simple and are generally guided by the sophistication of the technological "tools" available to the investigator. One may, for example, attempt to correlate the translocation of the hormone into cell nuclei within precise neural regions with the consequent behavioral changes. It is also possible to try to explain the actions of these steroids by some simple but representative manipulations including gonadectomy and gonadectomy combined with sex steroid application. The latter strategy has been used for the study of the attack response on lactating intruders.

## A. EFFECTS OF HORMONAL MANIPULATION OF THE FEMALE

Attack on lactating intruders by Swiss strain females remains stable in its incidence and intensity for at least one month after either prepubertal (day 15) or postpubertal (day 50) ovariectomy (Haug, 1978c; Haug, Mandel, & Brain, 1980a). This result confirms that this behavior is relatively independent of estrogens (see also Debold & Miczek, 1981, for similar statement for social conflict in rats). In contrast, Brain, Haug, and Kamis, (1982) reported an increase in aggression toward lactating intruders in TO strain mice following gonadectomy. The differing genotype and the long period of isolation used in this study may have rendered these ovariectomized females more reactive to the stimulus novelty of lactating intruders.

Implanting ovariectomized adult female residents with testosterone (T), but not with estradiol (E2) (Haug & Brain, 1979, 1983a), or administering neonatally masculinized females with the T precursor dehydroepiandrosterone (DHA) (Haug *et al.*, 1991) reduces their attack on lactating female intruders. As suggested by Johnson and Whalen (1989) the effect of hormonal treatment probably decreases the sensitivity of the resident females to aggression-eliciting urinary cues from the lactating females.

## B. EFFECTS OF HORMONAL MANIPULATION OF THE MALE

In its homotypical expression, attack on lactating female intruders is a characteristic of intact female residents of some strains. Indeed, intact adult males of those same strains very rarely exhibit this response. Interestingly, however, adult resident males only display substantial aggression toward lactating intruders when they are castrated (either prepubertally or postpubertally) (Haug & Brain, 1978d; Haug *et al.*, 1986a,b), and in both isolated and grouped conditions (Haug & Brain, 1983a; Johnson & Whalen, 1989). Male attack is quite similar in appearance and intensity to that seen when intact or ovariectomized females confront lactating females. This heterotypical aggression in males appears unique in the annals of male murine aggression where testicular androgens are frequently cited as being necessary for the normal display of male aggressive behavior (Gandelman, 1980). In the present situation, castration *increases* the probability of aggression occurring.

The fact that a male can behave aggressively in a femalelike fashion can be counterbalanced by hormonal therapy. Both T and E2 reduce attack by castrated male residents (either isolated or group housed) on lactating female intruders (Haug & Brain, 1979; Haug et al. 1986b; Whalen & Johnson, 1987; Johnson & Whalen, 1988, 1989). The effectiveness of both T and E2 in suppressing attacks toward the lactating females suggests that T normally exerts its action after aromatization to E2. Support for this hypothesis has been provided by a study showing that dihydrotestosterone (DHT), a nonaromatizable metabolite of T, despite being administered in hyperphysiological doses (cf T and E2), did not change aggressive responses in test animals (Haug & Brain, 1983a).

There is substantial support from studies employing synthetic estrogens, antiandrogens, antiestrogens, and aromatase inhibitors (which prevent the conversion of T to E2) that aromatization of androgens to estrogens may be implicated in the actions of sex steroids on a variety of behaviors (e.g., intermale aggression, male reproductive behavior, and feeding) in a range of laboratory rodents (Brain & Haug, 1990). Although the studies do not point to an immutable relationship between the motivations for such activities and conversion of T to E2, they do caution against the view that hormones always act in the form in which they are administered.

As in females (cf previous section), DHA strongly reduces the attacks by male castrates on lactating intruders (Haug *et al.*, 1983b; Schlegel *et al.*, 1985). This is of particular interest as DHA has been termed a "neurosteroid" (Baulieu & Robel, 1990) on the basis of its accumulation in rodent brain by *in-situ* mechanisms independent of the peripheral steroidogenic organs (Corpéchot *et al.*, 1981). As males treated with a behaviorally effective dose of DHA showed a more than tenfold increase in levels of DHA in the brain, and a slight, but significant increase of T, the question arises whether DHA has an aggression-suppressive effect per se or is effective after transformation to active metabolites. Indeed, DHA is converted into T (and T into E2) after injection of large amounts of the neurosteroid to rodents (Parker & Mahesh, 1977). Treatment of male castrates with the steroid 3-β-methyl-androst-5-ene-17-one ($CH_3$-DHA), a synthetic derivative of DHA which cannot be metabolized into sex steroids and is not demonstrably estrogenic (Pashko *et al.*, 1984) or androgenic (Haug *et al.*, 1989), reinforces, however, the hypothesis that the behavioral effects of DHA are unrelated to its conversion to metabolites (Young *et al.*, 1991). Ongoing experiments are being carried out to determine whether DHA has an aggression-reducing effect by decreasing the brain level of pregnenolone-sulphate (Δ5-PS), a potent gamma amino butyric acid (GABA)-A receptor antagonist (Majewska & Schwartz, 1987; Majewska *et al.*, 1986; Mienville & Vicini, 1989).

## IV. Role of Central Neurotransmitter

Relationships between central neurotransmitters and aggressive behavior has been sought in a wide variety of vertebrate animals. A number of thorough reviews are available for the interested reader (e.g., Pradhan, 1975; Mandel, Mack, & Kempf, 1979; Mandel *et al.*, 1981). The intention of this chapter is rather to provide a critical discussion focusing on correlations between attack on lactating females with central GABA and serotonin (5-HT).

GABA has been strongly implicated in the modulation of different forms of aggression in rodents. One hypothesis is that aggressive behavior has to be "disinhibited" and that GABA does this by its association with inhibitory fibers (Mandel, Mack, & Kempf, 1979). Indeed, treatment of female Swiss strain mice with sodium valproate (a competitive inhibitor of GABA-transaminase which increases GABA) markedly suppresses their attack on lactating female intruders (Haug *et al.*, 1980b). In contrast, castrated males, as well as showing an increased propensity for attack on lactating females, had higher GABA levels in several neural areas (namely the hypothalamus, olfactory bulbs, and amygdala) than did sham-operated counterparts (Haug *et al.*, 1984). Both female and male Swiss strain mice (Brain & Haug, 1992) whether gonadectomized or sham-operated as adults, show markedly reduced attack after administration of muscimol (a potent GABA agonist) or nipecotic acid amide ($NCS_3$, an inhibitor of GABA uptake). An examination of the relationship between attack on lactating intruders, castration, and brain GABA levels in C57, C3H, and CBA strain male mice (which show different propensities for such behavior) also demonstrated increased GABA in the above already mentioned brain structures which could be correlated with increased aggression (Haug *et al.*, 1987). Finally, an attempt was made to assess the effects of genotype of resident and intruder mice on the attack on a lactating intruder paradigm (Haug *et al.*, 1987). Female C57, C3H, and their reciprocal hybrids (B6HeF1 and HeB6F1) were used as residents, and lactating C57 or C3H were used as intruders. C57 residents showed more attack in this situation than mice of any other genotype, but the genotype of the intruder did not alter the response (see also Haug & Mandel, 1978a,b). Additionally, an attempt was made to correlate these differences in behavior with regional variations in GABA, both by looking at differences between strains and between aggressive and nonaggressive animals of the same genotype. Although some variations in GABA were found here, no evidence was provided for a simple inverse relationship between this neurotransmitter and any neural region and the propensity for attacking lactating female intruders. It is, of course, possible that other aspects of GABAergic functioning such as turnover (Trolin, 1982; Wuttke & Mansky, 1981) or receptor interactions (Richelson & El-Fakahany, 1982; Ticku, 1979), rather than steady-state levels of neurotransmitter, will be implicated in variations in the observed attack differences between females of C57 and C3H strain and their reciprocal hybrids.

There is an extensive literature attempting to specify the role played by serotonergic systems in mediating various forms of aggressive behavior (see e.g., Daruna & Kent, 1976; Pucilowski & Kostowski, 1983; Valzelli, 1982; Miczek & Donat, 1989; Kshama *et al.*, 1990). As expected, the procedures involve the raising or lowering of brain 5-HT, by lesioning the 5-HT-bearing cells of the raphe nuclei or by chemical manipulation of serotonin synthesis or catabolism, and observing the effects upon elicited aggression. Other experiments have attempted to correlate aggressive behavior with changes in 5-HT turnover and to compare these changes with those of other neurotransmitters. To date, attempts to clarify the role played by this neurotransmitter in the attack by female mice on lactating intruders have involved the use of 8-OH-DPAT (a 5-HT agonist) and fluoxetine (an inhibitor of 5-HT re-uptake). No firm conclusions can be drawn at this time, but this attack response tends to be reduced via the actions of these serotoninmimetic drugs (Haug, Wallian, & Brain, 1990).

It is, however, hardly remarkable that no single 5-HT effect has been identified that can consistently be shown to modulate the various forms of aggressive behavior. As suggested earlier, "aggressive behavior" (if such a generalization is justified), is like any other complex behavior, mediated by interacting neural systems, with multiple neurotransmitter systems involvement. It is also likely that when GABA or 5-HT systems are manipulated, other neurotransmitter systems are altered as biological mechanisms redress physiological imbalances. So, although GABA and 5-HT do influence the expression of aggression on lactating females, it appears that such effects are not exclusive, specific, or highly predictable.

# V. Biological Functions of Aggression

The precise utility of this form of aggression is difficult to specify. Indeed, one should note that this type of attack is not seen in all laboratory strains of mouse (Haug & Mandel, 1978a). Brain (1984) has speculated that such responses of residents to lactating intruders partially segregate the latter animals at a time when they have developed maternal aggressiveness in defense of their young. The ecological relevance of the femalelike aggression seen in male castrates must also be questioned as those testosterone-free animals are more than likely quite rare in natural environments. In this regard, Johnson (1989) has speculated that

> studying the aggressive behavior of male castrates is likely no more ecologically relevant than studying the aggressive behavior of testosterone-treated female mice; androgenized female mice are probably just as rare in natural environments. Nonetheless, both male castrates and testosterone-treated females provide unique insights into the nature of the interaction between testicular hormones, the brain and aggressive behavior.

He furthermore stated that

> the ecological relevance of form of aggression is perhaps best evidenced by the fact that lactating female attack is *not* displayed by gonadally-intact males nor castrated and testosterone or estrogen-treated males. Thus, although gonadally-intact male mice may possess the potential for the display of aggressive behavior toward a lactating female, this behavior appears to be under tonic inhibitory control by testicular hormones. Therefore, this inhibition of lactating female attack may be ecologically relevant in that it would be reproductively disadvantageous for a male to attack a female that has recently given birth to pups which he might have fathered.

# VI. Final Comments

In spite of the problems surrounding interpretation of this particular form of behavior, its study does serve to emphasize the futility of expecting to find *a* physiology of aggression. Different forms of fighting behavior seem very likely to be controlled by different biological, situational, and experiential factors, as well as serving different purposes. Detailed investigations on as many different forms of attack behavior, using especially the sadly neglected female of the species, seem highly desirable.

# References

Baulieu, E. E., & Robel, P. (1990).Neurosteroids: a new brain function? *Journal of Steroid Biochemistry and Molecular Biology, 37,* 395–403.

Beeman, E. A. (1947). The effect of male hormone on aggressive behavior in mice. *Physiological Zoology, 20,* 373–405.

Brain, P. F. (1984). Adaptive aspects of hormonal correlates of attack and defense in laboratory mice: a study in ethobiology. *Recent Progress in Brain Research, 53,* 391–413.

Brain, P. F. (1991). *Mindless Violence? The Nature and Biology of Aggression.* Swansea, U.K.: University College of Swansea Press.

Brain, P. F., & Haug, M. (1990). Preliminary investigations on the effects of pituitary-adrenocortical hormones on different forms of aggression in laboratory mice. *In* L. Lara Tapia (Ed.), *Para Conocer al Hombre.* Universidad Nacional Autonoma de Mexico, Mexico, D.F.

Brain, P. F., & Haug, M. (1992). Hormonal and neurochemical correlates of various forms of animal aggression. *Psychoneuroendocrinology* (in press).

Brain, P. F., Haug, M., & Kamis, A. B. (1982). Hormones and different tests for aggression with particular reference to the effects of testosterone metabolites. *In* J. Balthazard, E. Prove, & R. Gilles (Eds.), *Hormones and Behaviour in Higher Vertebrates.* Berlin: Springer-Verlag.

Corpéchot, C., Robel, P., Axelson, M., Sjövall, J., & Baulieu, E. E. (1981). Characterization and measurement of dehydroepiandrosterone sulfate in rat brain. *Proceedings of the National Academy of Sciences U.S.A., 78,* 4704–4707.

Daruna, J. H., & Kent, E. W. (1976). Comparison of regional serotonin levels and turnover in the brain of naturally high and low aggressive rats. *Brain Research, 101,* 489–501.

Debold, J. F., & Miczek, K. A. (1981). Sexual dimorphism in the hormonal control of aggressive behavior in rats. *Pharmacology, Biochemistry & Behavior, 14,* 89–93.

Ebert, P. D., & Hyde, J. S. (1976). Selection for agonistic behavior in wild female *Mus musculus. Behavior Genetics, 6,* 291–304.

Edwards, D. A., Thompson, M. L., & Burge, K. G. (1972). Olfactory bulb removal vs peripherally induced anosmia: differential effects on the aggressive behavior of male mice. *Behavioural Biology, 7,* 823–828.

Eleftheriou, B. E., Bailey, D. W., & Denenberg, V. H. (1974). Genetic analysis of fighting behavior in mice. *Physiology and Behavior, 13,* 773–777.

Gandelman, R. (1980). Gonadal hormones and the induction of intraspecific fighting in mice. *Neuroscience & Biobehavioral Reviews, 4,* 133–140.

Hahn, M. E., & Haber, S. B. (1982). The inheritance of agonistic behavior in male mice: a diallel analysis. *Aggressive Behavior, 8,* 19–38.

Haug, M. (1972). Phénomènes d'agression liés à l'introduction d'une femelle étrangère vierge ou allaitante au sein d'un groupe de souris femelles. *Comptes Rendus de l'Académie des Sciences, 275,* 2729–2732.

Haug, M. (1973a). Mise en évidence d'une odeur liée à l'allaitement et stimulant l'agressivité d'un groupe de souris femelles. *Comptes Rendus de l'Académie des Sciences, 276,* 3460–3467.

Haug, M. (1973b). L'urine d'une femelle allaitante contient une phéromone stimulant l'agressivité de petits groupes de souris femelles. *Comptes Rendus de l'Académie des Sciences, 277,* 2053–2056.

Haug, M. (1978c). Aggression by resident female mice towards lactating and non-lactating intruders: effect of ovariectomy. *IRCS Medical Science, 6,* 106.

Haug, M., & Brain, P. F. (1978d). Attack directed by groups of castrated male mice towards lactating or non-lactating intruders: a urine-dependent phenomenon? *Physiology and Behavior, 21,* 549–552.

Haug, M., & Brain, P. F. (1979). Effects of treatments with testosterone and oestradiol on the attack directed by groups of gonadectomized male and female mice towards lactating intruders. *Physiology and Behavior, 23,* 397–400.

Haug, M., & Brain, P. F. (1983a). The effects of differential housing, castration and steroidal hormones on attack directed by resident mice towards lactating intruders. *Physiology & Behavior, 30,* 557–560.

Haug, M., & Mandel, P. (1978a). Strain differences in aggressive behaviour of female mice against lactating and non-lactating individuals. *Neuroscience Letters, 7,* 235–238.

Haug, M., & Mandel, P. (1978b). Sex differences in aggressive behaviour in various strains of mice. *Aggressive Behavior, 4,* 353–364.

Haug, M., Mandel, P., & Brain, P. F. (1980a). Studies on the biological correlates of attack by group-housed mice on lactating intruders. *In* P. F. Brain & D. Benton (Eds.), *The Biology of Aggression.* The Netherlands: Sijthoff & Noordhoff, Alphen aan den Rijn.

Haug, M., Kim, L., Simler, S., & Mandel, P. (1980b). Studies on the involvement of GABA in the aggression directed by groups of intact or gonadectomized male and female mice towards lactating intruders. *Pharmacology, Biochemistry & Behavior, 12,* 189–193.

Haug, M., Spetz, J. F., Schlegel, M. L., & Robel, P. (1983b). La déhydroépiandrostérone inhibe le comportement agressif des mâles castrés. *Comptes Rendus de l'Académie des Sciences, 296,* 975–977.

Haug, M., Simler, S., Ciesielski, L., Mandel, P., & Moutier, R. (1984). Influence of castration and brain GABA levels in three strains of mice on aggression towards lactating intruders. *Physiology & Behavior, 32,* 767–770.

Haug, M., Brain, P. F., & Kamis, A. B. (1986a). A brief review comparing the effects of sex steroids on two forms of aggression in laboratory mice. *Neuroscience & Biobehavioral Reviews, 10,* 463–468.

Haug, M., Spetz, J. F., Ouss-Schlegel, M. L., Benton, D., and Brain, P. F. (1986b). Effects of gender, gonadectomy and social status on attack directed towards female intruders by resident mice. *Physiology & Behavior, 37,* 533–537.

Haug, M., Ouss-Schlegel, M. L., Spetz, J. F., Benton, D., & Brain, P. F. (1987). An attempt to correlate attack on lactating females and brain GABA levels in C57 and C3H strains and their reciprocal hybrids. *Biogenic Amines, 4,* 83–94.

Haug, M., Ouss-Schlegel, M. L., Spetz, J. F., Brain, P. F., Simon, V., Baulieu, E. E., & Robel, P. (1989). Suppressive effects of dehydroepianodrosterone and 3-β-methylandrost-5-en-17-one on attack towards lactating female intruders by castrated male mice. *Physiology & Behavior, 46,* 955–959.

Haug, M., Wallian, L., & Brain, P. F. (1990). Effects of 8-OH-DPAT and fluoxetine on activity and attack by female mice towards lactating intruders. *General Pharmacology, 21,* 845–849.

Haug, M., Young, J., Robel, P., & Baulieu E. E. (1991). L'inhibition par la déhydroépiandrostérone des résponses agressives de souris femelles castrées vis-à-vis d'intruses allaitantes est potentialisée par l'androgénisation néonatale. *Comptes Rendus de l'Académie des Sciences, 312,* 511–516.

Hewitt, J. K., & Broadhurst, P. L. (1983). Genetic architecture and the evolution of aggressive behavior. *In* E. C. Simmel, M. E. Hahn, & J. K. Walters (Eds.), *Aggressive Behavior: Genetic and Neural Approaches.* Hillsdale, New Jersey; London: LEA Publishers.

Johnson, F. (1989). The development and expression of hormone-independent and hormone-dependent aggressive behavior in male mice: hormone/stimulus interactions. Unpublished Ph.D. dissertation, Department of Psychology, University of California, Riverside.

Johnson, F., & Whalen, R. E. (1988). Testicular hormones reduce individual differences in the aggressive behavior of male mice: a theory of hormone action. *Neuroscience & Biobehavioral Reviews, 12,* 93–99.

Johnson, F., & Whalen, R. E. (1989). Aggression in mice: rapid-onset attack of lactating female mice following termination of hyperphysiological testosterone treatment. *Physiology & Behavior, 46,* 413–416.

Johns, R. P. (1973). Scent marking in mammals. *Animal Behavior, 21,* 521–535.

Kimelman, B. R., & Lubow, R. E. (1974). The inhibitory effect of preexposed olfactory cues on intermale aggression in mice. *Physiology & Behavior, 12,* 919–922.

Krames, L. (1970). Responses of female rats to the individual body odors of male rats. *Psychonomic Science, 20,* 274–275.

Kshama, D., Hrishikeshavan, H. J., Shanbhogue, R., & Munonyedi, U.S. (1990). Modulation of baseline behavior in rats by putative serotonergic agents in three ethoexperimental paradigms. *Behavioral & Neural Biology, 54,* 234–253.

Lagerspetz, K. M. J., & Lagerspetz, K. Y. H. (1968). Neurochemical and endocrinological studies of mice selectively bred for aggressiveness. *Scandinavian Journal of Psychology, 9,* 157–160.

Lagerspetz, K. M. J., & Lagerspetz, K. Y. H. (1971). Changes in the level of aggressiveness of mice as the results of isolation, learning and selective breeding. *Scandinavian Journal of Psychology, 12,* 241–248.

Lagerspetz, K. M. J., & Lagerspetz, K. Y. H. (1974). Genetic determination of aggressive behavior. *In* J. H. F. van Abeelen (Ed.), *Behavioural Genetics.* Amsterdam: North Holland.

Majewska, M. D., & Schwartz, R. D. (1987). Pregnenolone sulfate: an endogenous antagonist of the γ-aminobutyric acid receptor complex in brain. *Brain Research, 404,* 355–360.

Majewska, M. D., Harrison, N. L., Schwartz, R. D., Barker, J. L., & Paul, S. M. (1986). Steroid hormone metabolites are barbiturate-like modulators of the GABA receptor. *Science, 232,* 1004–1007.

Mandel, P., Mack, G., & Kempf, E. (1979). Molecular basis of some models of aggressive behavior. *In* M. Sandler (Ed.), Psychopharmacology of Aggression. New York: Raven Press.

Mandel, P., Kempf, E., Mack, G., Haug, M., & Puglisi-Allegra, S. (1981). Neurochemistry of experimental aggression. *In* I. Valzelli & I. Morgese (Eds.), *Aggression and Violence: A Psychobiological and Clinical Approach.* Edizioni Centro Culturale E Congressi Saint Vincent.

Maxson, S. G., Ginsburg, B. E., & Trahner, A. (1979). Interaction of Y-chromosomal and autosomal gene(s) in the development of intermale aggression in mice. *Behavior Genetics, 9,* 219–226.

Miczek, K. A., & Donat, P. (1989). Brain 5-HT system and inhibition of aggressive behaviour. *In* P. Bevan, A. R. Cools, & T. Archer (Eds.), *Behavioural Pharmacology of 5-HT.* Hillsdale, New Jersey; Hove and London: LEA Publishers.

Mienville, J. M., & Vicini, S. (1989). Pregnenolone sulfate antagonizes GABA-A receptor-mediated currents via a reduction of chanel opening frequency. *Brain Research, 489,* 190–194.

Parker, C. R., & Mahesh, V. B. (1977). Dehydroepianodrosterone (DHA) induced precocious ovulation: correlative changes in blood steroids, gonadotropins and cytosol estradiol receptors of anterior pituitary gland and hypothalamus. *Journal of Steroid Biochemistry, 8,* 173–177.

Pashko, L. L., Ravito, R. J., Williams, J. R., Sobel, E. L., & Schwartz, A. G. (1984). Dehydroepiandrosterone (DHEA) and 3-β-methylandrost-5-en-17-one: inhibitors of 7-12-dimethylbenz-(a)anthracene(DMBA)-promoted skin papilloma formation in mice. *Carcinogenesis, 5,* 463–466.

Pradhan, S. N. (1975). Aggression and central neurotransmitters. *In* C. C. Pfeiffer & J. R. Smythies (Eds.), *International Review of Neurobiology*, Vol. 18. New York: Academic Press.

Pucilowski, O., & Kostowski, W. (1983). Aggressive behaviour and the central serotonergic systems. *Behavioral Brain Research, 9,* 33–48.

Reynolds, E. (1971). Urination as a social response in mice. *Nature, 234,* 481–483.

Richelson, E., & El-Fakahany, E. (1982). Changes in the sensitivity of receptors for neurotransmitters and the actions of some psychotherapeutic drugs. *Mayo Clinical Proceedings, 57,* 576–580.

Schlegel, M. L., Spetz, J. F., Robel, P., & Haug, M. (1985). Studies on the effects of DHA and its metabolites on aggression towards lactating females in mice. *Physiology & Behavior, 34,* 867–870.

Selmanoff, M. K., & Ginsburg, B. E. (1981). Genetic variability in aggression and endocrine function in inbred strains of mice. *In* P. F. Brain & D. Benton (Eds.), *Multidisciplinary Approaches to Aggression Research.* New York: Elsevier/North-Holland Biomedical Press.

Thiessen, D. D., Friend, H. C., & Lindzey, G. (1968). Androgen control of territorial marking by Mongolian gerbil. *Science, 160,* 432–434.

Ticku, M. K. (1979). Differences in gamma-aminobutyric acid receptor sensitivity in inbred strains of mice. *Journal of Neurochemistry, 33,* 1135–1138.

Trolin, G. (1982). GABA turnover in mouse brain: agreement between the rate of GABA accumulation after aminooxyacetic acid and the rate of disappearance after 3-mercaptopropionic acid. *Journal of Neural Transmission, 54,* 265–275.

Valzelli, L. (1982). Serotonergic inhibitory control of experimental aggression. *Pharmacological Research Communications, 14,* 1–13.

van Oortmerssen, G. A., & Bakker, T. C. M. (1981). Artificial selection for short and long attack latencies in wild *Mus musculus domesticus. Behavior Genetics, 11,* 115–126.

Whalen, R. E., & Johnson, F. (1987). Individual differences in the attack behavior of female mice: a function of attack stimulus and hormonal state. *Hormones & Behavior, 21,* 223–233.

Whalen, R. E., & Johnson, F. (1988). Aggression in adult female mice: chronic testosterone treatment induces attack against olfactory bulbectomized male and lactating female mice. *Physiology & Behavior, 43,* 17–20.

Wuttke, W., & Mansky, T. (1981). Gonadal steroids and brain monoamines: how do they interact? *In* W. Wuttke & R. Horowski (Eds.), *Gonadal Steroids and Brain Function.* Berlin: Springer-Verlag.

Young, J., Corpéchot, C., Haug, M., Gobaille, S., Baulieu, E. E., and Robel, P. (1991). Suppressive effects of dehydroepiandrosterone and 3β-methylandrost-5-en-17-one on attack towards lactating female intruders by castrated male mice. II. Brain neurosteroids. *Biochemical and Biophysical Research Communications, 174,* 892–897.

34

# *Female Aggression in Mice: Developmental, Genetic, and Contextual Factors*

Kathryn E. Hood

I. INTRODUCTION
II. GENETIC AND SEX-RELATED DIFFERENCES IN CONTEXTS FOR AGGRESSIVE BEHAVIOR
III. DEVELOPMENTAL AND SEX-RELATED DIFFERENCES IN AGGRESSIVE BEHAVIOR
IV. CONTEXTUAL FACTORS IN THE STUDY OF FEMALE AGGRESSION
V. CONCLUSION
REFERENCES

## I. Introduction

By an auspicious coincidence, my graduate advisor, Luci Paul, presented me with a copy of the remarkable "Studies on the Aggressive Behaviour of Mice" by Kirsti Lagerspetz (1964) just months before I met Robert Cairns, who had independently established a similar set of studies. During my postdoctoral work in his laboratory, we confirmed the Lagerspetz finding of rapid effects of selective breeding on male aggressive behavior, and also the finding that repeated test experience can eliminate line differences in male aggressive behavior. In addition, we confirmed that female mice did not fight (Cairns, MacCombie, & Hood, 1983; Cairns, Gariepy, & Hood, 1990; Lagerspetz, 1969; Lagerspetz & Lagerspetz, 1971). In subsequent studies, we confirmed the Lagerspetz findings that group rearing reduces line differences in males, and that isolation rearing especially enhances aggressiveness by high-aggressive line males (Hood & Cairns, 1989; Lagerspetz & Lagerspetz, 1971).

Female aggressive behavior presented an apparent discrepancy. One explanation for the absence of female aggressive behavior might be that selective breeding effects are sex limited, with effects occurring only in males. However, the ambiguous and mixed findings in the literature suggested other possibilities (see Hood & Cairns, 1988, for discussion). Having discovered in my dissertation research that female rats will vigorously attack a female conspecific when tested in the home cage after group housing (Hood, 1984), I applied the same method to study females from Cairns's NC (North Carolina) lines of mice. Some of the findings from these investigations will be presented here, to extend the comparative developmental perspective on inherited and contextual factors in aggressive behavior.

## II. Genetic and Sex-Related Differences in Contexts for Aggressive Behavior

In the NC selectively bred lines of mice, which were derived from an outbred albino foundation strain (ICR), the aggressive behavior of males has been the criterion for selective breeding. In each generation to the present (25th generation), isolation-reared males from the high-aggressive line were chosen for breeding if they attacked most rapidly and repeatedly during a 10-minute dyadic test with a same-age same-sex conspecific in a neutral arena at age 45 days ($\pm$ 3 days). Males from the low-aggressive line were chosen if they never attacked. Sisters of chosen males were mated with other males from their line. The result of this process was the creation of behaviorally distinct lines of males within a few generations (Cairns, MacCombie, & Hood, 1983), as in Lagerspetz (1964) and Lagerspetz and Lagerspetz (1971). Just as in that work, foundation-strain ICR females tested at day 45 in the dyadic test never attacked (also see van Oortmerssen & Bakker, 1981). In the 5th generation also, females reared in isolation showed no attacks in dyadic tests in a neutral arena at maturity, age 200 days (Hood & Cairns, 1988).

However, when female mice were housed in groups and tested at maturity in the home cage with same-age, same-sex intruders, aggressive behavior was robust and vigorous. Moreover, females from the line of high-aggressive males were more likely to attack the females from the line of low-aggressive males. Even more pronounced line differences were found in studies of postpartum aggression, with parturient females showing higher levels of attacks than males (Hood & Cairns, 1988). These results offer convergent support for the results of Lagerspetz and Lagerspetz (1975). In that work, females from both of the Turku lines were treated with male hormones. Androgen-treated females from the line of high-aggressive males attacked, while androgen-treated females from the line of low-aggressive males failed to attack. Taken together, these outcomes support the conclusion that the inheritance of differences in aggressiveness is not linked with the Y chromosome, but rather with autosomal or pseudoautosomal elements common to females and males. It is the influence of these autosomal elements that becomes evident when females are tested in a context that is appropriate for inter-female aggression. (See Table 1 for a summary of these results.).

In the 11th generation, a parallel mouse colony was established at Pennsylvania State University from the NC lines. In general, the line difference in mature females has been found in every generation tested since that time. Studies of later generations of females from these lines are included in Table 1, and are discussed below.

The behavioral criterion used in these studies is relatively conservative. Selection for breeding is based only on the occurrence of full attacks. In all studies, of females as well as males, an attack is coded only when an animal forcefully pounces upon a conspecific, with biting and wrestling. Other aggressive behaviors, such as bites, feints (lateral display), and lunges (striking with the forepaws) are not included in these scores. The form of female aggressive behavior is exactly like male aggressive behavior, in our observations. However, the contextual and developmental parameters that permit female aggressive behavior to occur differ from those that favor male aggressive behavior.

## III. Developmental and Sex-Related Differences in Aggressive Behavior

Developmental factors have been of primary concern in these investigations, and a developmental analysis was required to detect the line difference in female aggressiveness. In previous work, we proposed that the selective breeding effects in males may be produced by neoteny, a delay in the ontogenetic onset of male aggressiveness. This developmental change over generations of selection was seen as the mediating factor that changed aggressive behaviors (Cairns, MacCombie, & Hood, 1983; Cairns, Gariepy, & Hood, 1990). Had tests of females been implemented at only one time in development, at age 45 days, the phenomenon of female inheritance of male-selected aggressive behavior would have been missed entirely.

Life span developmental patterns of aggressive behavior in each sex were assessed in the 6th generation of selective breeding. To compare the sexes, experimental conditions were used that permit the expression of female aggressive behavior, namely, group rearing and home cage intruder tests. In longitudinal tests at ages 30, 45, 90, 210, and 270 days, male line differentiation appeared at puberty, age 45 days, the criterion age of selection for breeding. Female line differentiation did not emerge until after age 90 days, at mid maturity (Hood, 1988; Hood & Cairns, 1988). In particular, females in the high-aggressive line showed more attacks, but not decreased latency, at midlife, age 270 days, than at young adulthood, age 90 days. Females from the low-aggressive and the control lines did not change, because they rarely attack at any age (Hood, 1988).

One ironic feature of this developmental-genetic analysis was that when females and males were considered together, there were significant line differences

**Table 1**
**Female and Male Aggressive Behavior over 15 Generations of Selective Breeding in Mice: Effects of Rearing Conditions, Test Conditions, and Age**

| Test condition and age | Generation | Sex and rearing | Line | Attack frequency | Attack latency (seconds) |
|---|---|---|---|---|---|
| 10-Minute dyadic test; 45 days | $S_0$[a] | Male; isolation | I | 16.1 | 207 |
| | | | NC | 22.3 | 174 |
| | | Female; isolation | I | 0 | 600[f] |
| | | | NC | 0 | 600[f] |
| 10-Minute dyadic test; 200 days | $S_5$[b] | Male; isolation | High | 28.4 | 80 |
| | | | Low | 13.4 | 374 |
| | | Female; isolation | High | 0 | 600 |
| | | | Low | 0 | 600 |
| 10-Minute intruder test; 45 days | $S_6$[b] | Male; longitudinal heterogeneous group | High | 10.78 | 305 |
| | | | Low | 5.44 | 380 |
| | | Female; longitudinal heterogeneous group | High | 2.44 | 490 |
| | | | Low | 0 | 600 |
| 10-Minute intruder test; 270 days | $S_6$[b,c] | Male; longitudinal heterogeneous group | High | 9.00 | 170 |
| | | | Low | 0.33 | 520 |
| | | Female; longitudinal heterogeneous group | High | 9.44 | 325 |
| | | | Low | 0.66 | 540 |
| 10-Minute intruder test; 90 days | $S_6$[d] | Female; naive homogeneous group | High | 0.27 | 592 |
| | | | Low | 0 | 600[f] |
| | | Female; naive heterogeneous group | High | 0.40 | 550 |
| | | | Low | 0.30 | 554 |
| | | Female; longitudinal heterogeneous group | High | 2.73 | 458 |
| | | | Low | 1.67 | 530 |
| 10-Minute intruder test; 270 days | $S_6$[d] | Female; naive homogeneous group | High | 1.70 | 540 |
| | | | Low | 0 | 600[f] |
| | | Female; naive heterogeneous group | High | 0.91 | 494 |
| | | | Low | 0 | 600[f] |
| | | Female; longitudinal heterogeneous group | High | 7.92 | 308 |
| | | | Low | 0.50 | 550 |
| 3-Minute dyadic test | $S_8$[b,e] | Male; isolation | High | 7.61 | 81 |
| | | | Low | 0 | 180[f] |
| 3-Minute postpartum test | | Female; isolation | High | 15.40 | 15 |
| | | | Low | 0.20 | 170 |
| 10-Minute dyadic test; 200 days | $S_{15}$[d] | Female; isolation; trial 1 | High | 1.25 | 550 |
| | | | Low | 0 | 600[f] |
| | | Female; isolation; trial 2 | High | 1.30 | 410 |
| | | | Low | 0 | 600[f] |

*Continues*

**Table 1 Continued**

| Test condition and age | Generation | Sex and rearing | Line | Attack frequency | Attack latency (seconds) |
|---|---|---|---|---|---|
| 10-Minute intruder test; 200 days | $S_{15}$[d] | Female; homogeneous group;trial 1 | High | 1.84 | 510 |
| | | | Low | 0 | 600[f] |
| | | Female; homogeneous group;trial 2 | High | 1.48 | 485 |
| | | | Low | 1.68 | 560 |

*Note:* Control line values are not shown. In general, they are intermediate between the two selectively bred lines.
[a]From Cairns, MacCombie, & Hood, 1983.
[b]From Hood & Cairns, 1988.
[c]This developmental effect was replicated in the $S_8$ generation. (See Hood & Cairns, 1988): No line difference at age 30 days, but significant line difference at age 130 days.
[d]From Hood, 1988. The line-by-age interaction is significant.
[e]Postpartum females are more aggressive than any other group, by both measures.
[f]Maximum latency score.

in attack latency at every age except day 45, the age at which male behavior is assessed for selective breeding (Hood & Cairns, 1988). This was ironic because in previous work, we had found that for males, line differences are most pronounced at that age (Cairns, MacCombie, & Hood, 1983). When both females and males were contrasted, sex differences in attack frequency were significant at age 45 days, and not at other ages (Hood & Cairns, 1988; Table 1). These outcomes underscore the importance of considering sex-related differences in ontogenetic timing for understanding aggressive behavior.

To test the finding that female aggressiveness increases at midlife in a developmental pattern unlike the male pattern of increased aggressiveness at puberty, additional studies were implemented with the subsequent generations. To establish the differential expression of aggressive behavior over the life span in females and males was the central concern. In particular, further studies were designed to separate the effects of maturation and the effects of repeated test experience, which are confounded in the longitudinal design. In the 5th generation, groups of naive females were tested at age 90 days, and independent groups were tested at age 270 days, for comparison with the longitudinal groups. The results were as expected, with high-aggressive line females, older females, and previously tested females showing enhanced aggressive behavior (Hood, 1988). In 15th generation females, robust line differences were found in 200-day-old females, although the effect of repeated daily trials was to eliminate line effects in attack frequency (but not latency), as several low-aggressive line females became avidly aggressive after the first trial (Hood, 1988). In the 15th generation, isolation housing did not reduce attacks in high-aggressive line females, compared

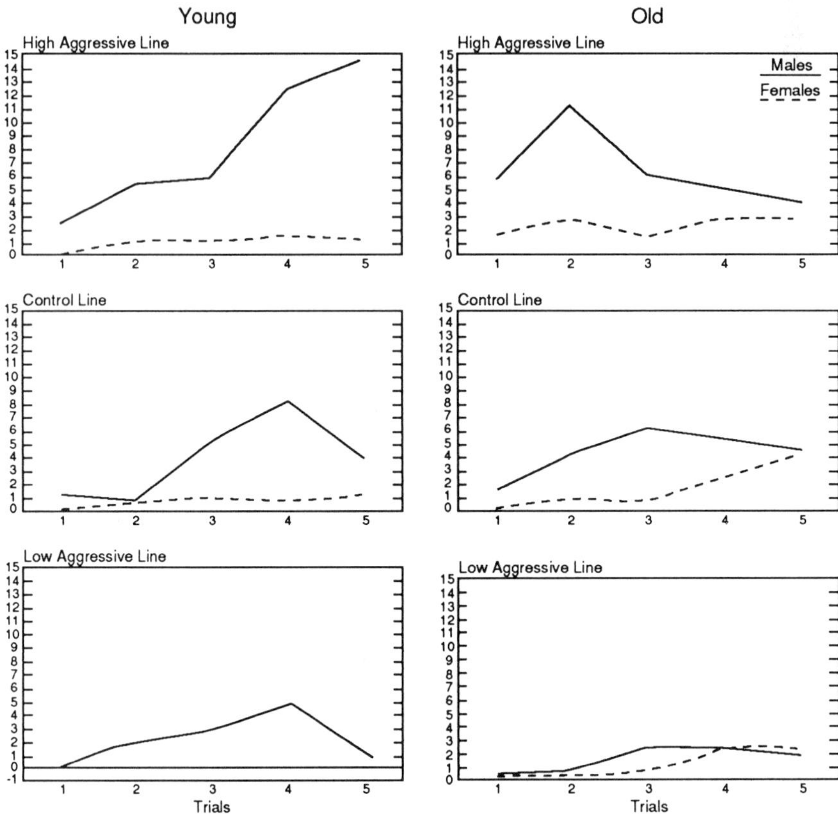


**Figure 1.** Attack frequency in 16th generation mice from lines selectively bred for differential aggressive behavior of males at age 45 days. The "young" animals were tested in a longitudinal design at 23, 30, 37, 44, and 51 days of age. The "old" animals were tested for the first time at age 200 days, and again at 207, 214, 221, and 228 days.

to group-reared females (Hood, 1988; see Table 1). This offers a contrast to the results from earlier generations, in which group rearing was important for the expression of female aggressiveness. One (untested) possibility is that the continued effects of selection pressure have been to shift the phenotypic range of reaction to such an extent that the social context effect is less apparent. Alternatively, the use of different-strain test partners in this work may account for the aggressive behavior of isolated females.

The most recent life span research (Hood, in preparation) confirms the earlier findings, using 16th generation females and males. Two independent sets of animals were reared in small groups and tested in 5 intruder trials, which were given at 1-week intervals. One set of animals was tested early in life, beginning at age 23 days. The other set was tested at maturity, beginning at age 200 days.

The results (Figure 1) show a sharp increase in attack frequency by pubertal males. (Puberty occurs at about trial 4, in that figure, for young animals.) Female aggressive behavior increases over trials in the "Old" group until female attack frequency equals male frequency. Latency scores show parallel patterns. In analyses of variance, sex differences depend on age, but age by itself is not a significant factor.

## IV. Contextual Factors in the Study of Female Aggression

The results of our studies of female aggressiveness in selectively bred lines provide support for a reinterpretation of sex-related factors and sex differences in social behavior. The pattern of sex differences is best conceived not as differences in quantity of a unitary trait of aggressiveness, but rather as differences in the ecological contexts that support aggressive interactions, for each sex. In these studies, two conditions of testing, group rearing and maternal aggression tests, can be thought of as analogues to occasions for female aggressiveness in the natural setting for the species. The use of a "standard" test—one which is in fact appropriate only for males—had previously obscured the cross-sex similarity in the inheritance of aggressive behavior. Once appropriate conditions for aggressiveness were established, in the external social context (Hood & Cairns, 1988), or in the internal hormonal milieu (Lagerspetz & Lagerspetz, 1975), then the lawful relationships between female and male behavior emerged. Future plans for ecological studies of aggressive behavior in this laboratory include establishing natural settings for long-term habitation by females and males, with particular attention to patterns of dispersal (e.g., van Oortmerssen & Busser, 1989).

## V. Conclusion

The application of these comparative findings to an understanding of human aggressive and assertive behavior involves complex issues of interpretation, both in interpretation of behavior (e.g., Cairns & Cairns, 1984) and interpretation of context (Hood, 1991, 1992; Mansfield, Hood, & Henderson, 1989). This is especially true for humans because:

> In every study of human gender differences, biological sex is completely confounded with social and psychological sex . . . Sex is a simple variable in that it is easy to measure; however, as an explanatory referent, it is inherently complex and difficult to interpret. Until these levels of interactions have been studied, including social and experiential factors, any speculation about biological causes of gender differences . . . is premature. (Hood *et al.*, 1987)

## References


Cairns, R. B., & Cairns, B. D. (1984). Predicting aggressive patterns in girls and boys: A developmental study. *Aggressive Behavior, 10,* 229–242.

Cairns, R. B., MacCombie, D. J., & Hood, K. E. (1983). A developmental-genetic analysis of aggressive behavior in Mice: I. Behavioral outcomes. *Journal of Comparative Psychology, 97,* 69–89.

Cairns, R. B., Gariepy, J-L., & Hood, K. E. (1990). Development, microevolution, and social behavior. *Psychological Review, 97,* 49–65.

Hood, K. E. (1984). Aggression among female rats during the estrus cycle. *In* K. J. Flannelly, R. J. Blanchard, & D. C. Blanchard (Eds.), *Biological Perspectives on Aggression.* New York: Allan Liss.

Hood, K. E., (1988). Female aggression in albino ICR mice: Development, social experience, and the effects of selective breeding (*Mus musculus*). *International Journal of Comparative Psychology, 2,* 27–41.

Hood, K. E. (1991). Premenstrual syndrome. *In* R. Lerner, A. Petersen, & J. Brooks-Gunn (Eds.), *The Encyclopedia of Adolescence* (pp. 803–832). New York: Garland.

Hood, K. E. (1992). Contextual determinants of menstrual cycle effects in observations of social interaction. *In* A. Dan & L. Lewis (Eds.), *Menstrual Health in Women's Lives.* Chicago: University of Illinois Press.

Hood, K. E. (in preparation). Aggressive behavior over the life span in female and male selectively bred mice.

Hood, K. E., & Cairns, R. B. (1988). A developmental-genetic analysis of aggressive behavior in mice: II. Cross-sex inheritance. *Behavior Genetics, 18,* 605–619.

Hood, K. E., & Cairns, R. B. (1989). A developmental-genetic analysis of aggressive behavior in mice: IV. Genotype-environment interaction. *Aggressive Behavior, 15,* 361–380.

Hood, K. E., Draper, P., Crockett, L. J., & Petersen, A. C. (1987). The ontogeny and phylogeny of sex differences in development: A biopsychosocial synthesis. *In* D. B. Carter (Ed.), *Current Conceptions of Sex Roles and Sex Typing: Theory and Research* (pp. 49–78). New York: Praeger.

Lagerspetz, K. M. J. (1964). Studies on the aggressive behavior of mice. *Annales Academiae Scientific Fennicae*, Sarja-Series B, 131, 1–131.

Lagerspetz, K. M. J. (1969). Aggression and aggressiveness in laboratory mice. *In* S. Garattini & E. B. Sigg (Eds.), *Aggressive Behavior.* Amsterdam: Exerpta Medica.

Lagerspetz, K. M. J., & Lagerspetz, K. Y. H. (1971). Changes in the aggressiveness of mice resulting from selective breeding, learning, and social isolation. *Scandinavian Journal of Psychology, 12,* 241–248.

Lagerspetz, K. M. J., & Lagerspetz, K. Y. H. (1975). The expression of the genes of aggressiveness in mice: The effect of androgen on aggression and sexual behavior in females. *Aggressive Behavior, 1,* 291–295.

Mansfield, P. K., Hood, K. E., & Henderson, J. (1989). Women and their husbands: Moods and arousal fluctuations across the menstrual cycle and days of the week. *Psychosomatic Medicine, 51,* 66–80.

van Oortmerssen, G. A., & Bakker, T. C. M. (1981). Artificial selection for short and long attack latencies in wild *Mus musculus domesticus. Behavior Genetics, 11,* 115–126.

van Oortmerssen, G. A., & Busser, J. (1989). Studies in wild house mice 3: Disruptive selection on aggression as a possible force in evolution. *In* R. F. Brain, D. Mainardi, & S. Parmigiani (Eds.), *House Mouse Aggression.* New York: Harwood.

# Index

Acali, sex and violence on
discussions, 213–214
dissatisfaction and aggression, sex and violence, 209–210
raft laboratory, 211
sex, 211–212
sex and friction, conflict and violence, 212
sex and violence
evidence, 213
hypothesis, 213
Acceptance of interpersonal violence (AIV), 252, 253
Action potentials of Bellonese women, 178–184
displacement of aggression, 180
hair pulling, 180
hiring assassins, 179–180
homicide, 179
nonverbal expression of aggression, 183–184
songs, mocking, 183
suicide, 180–181
verbal aggression, 181–183
Adolescence, sex differences in aggressive styles during, 55–58
Adolescents, aggressive-hostile behavior in
context and questions, 107–108
remarks, 111
results, 111
Adult aggression and testosterone, 41–43
aggressive behavior, 41–42
changing status, 42–43
questionnaire measures, 41
Adulthood, kinds of covered aggression during, 60–62
rational aggression, 61,62
social manipulation, 61, 62
Advertising, sex roles in, 72–73
Age, and influence of toys and play, 66–67
Aged women, aggression in life stories of
discussion, 143–145
history research and way of life, 133–134
life stories, collection and analysis, 134–136
life without aggression, 140–143
arduous working life, 141–142
silenced life, 142–143
sweet life, 140–141
society and family as sources of aggression, 136–139
bitter life, 136–138
life as hurdle race, 139–140
life as trapping pit, 138–139
Aggression
as antecedent of type A behavior, 127
as concomitant of type A behavior, 126–127
as subcomponent of type A behavior, 123–126
Aggression, analysis of, figure-ground reversal, 345–346
Aggression and alcohol, 245–246

Aggression and gender, crosscultural perspective, 164
*Aggression Approval Scale* (AGGAPS), 79, 86
  discussion, 84–85
  results, 80–84
Aggression, biological functions of, 389
Aggression in canine females, 309–312
  female–female relationships, 310
  male–female relationships, 310–311
  male–male relationships, 310
  mothers and offspring, relationship between, 311–312
  overall plan, 309
  social relationships, importance, 309–310
Aggression, definition, 3
Aggression, female, study of
  conclusions, 13
  definition and form, 4–5
  ethnocentrism, danger of, 6
  male aggression versus female aggression, 8–13
    female–female encounters, 12–13
    female–male encounters, 11–12
    physical aggression, 9–11
  male perspective, 5–6
  methodological and cultural change, 7–8
  methodology, problem of, 6–7
  perspective, emerging, 8
  phenomenon of, 3–4
Aggression in great apes, nature of, 297–303
  indirect aggression in, 304–305
  in mother–child relationship, 301
  oedipal constellation in, 301–303
  power struggle among females, 298–299
  sexual context, occurrence of aggression in, 300–301
Aggression in life stories of aged women, *see* Aged women
Aggression on mice, selection for, 368–369
Aggression, sex differences in, 222–225
Aggression, stimulus condition for, 382
Aggressive arousal in hamsters and rats, 335–336
  anger and violent behavior, 343–344
  neuroanatomical localization and mechanism of, evidence for, 339–340
  phenomena explicable in terms of, 332–334
  theoretical model of, 336–338
Aggressive behavior of female and male mice over 15 generations of selective breeding in mice, 398–399
Aggressive strategies, developmental theory of, 58–60
Aggressive–hostile behavior in adolescents
  context and questions, 107–108
  remarks, 111
  results, 111
Aggressive–hostile life orientations, 110
Alcohol and female disinhibition
  aggression, 245–246
  alcohol, effects of, 241
  anxiety, 241–243
  general perspective, 246–247
    cognitive models, 246–247
    physiological models, 246
  sexuality, 243–245
Alcohol and increased social activity and dominance, 231, 232
Ambivalence
  about motherhood, 273–274
  processing, 273–275
Androgens, *see also* Hormones
Androgens, effect of, and learning on aggression in females, 373–375
  methods, 373–374
  results, 374–375
Anger
  aggressive arousal and violent behavior, 343–344
  indirect, effects of, 280–281
  mother's denial of, 276
Animal models of defense, implications
  gender differences, implications for biological bases of defense, 323–324
  implications of gender differences for animal models of defensive behavior, 324–325
  sex differences in antipredator defensive behaviors, 318–323
    antipredator ultrasonic vocalizations, sex differences in, 322–323
    anxiety/defense battery test, 318–319
      sex differences in, 319–321
    fear/defense test battery, sex differences in, 321–322
Animal to human aggression, complex relation of, 23–24
Animals, male versus female aggression, 21–23
  competitive fighting among rats, 22
  defense, 22–23
  predation, 22
  types of aggressive behavior in animals, 21

*see also* Rodents, aggressive female
Antipredator defensive behaviors, sex differences in, 318–323
Antipredator ultrasonic vocalizations, sex differences in, 322–323
anxiety/defense battery test, 318–319
sex differences in, 319–321
fear/defense test battery, sex differences in, 321–322
Anxiety, and alcohol, 241–243
Anxiety/defense battery test (A/DTB), 318–319, 321, 322, 323, 324, 325
sex differences in, 319–321
Anxious-retaliatory life orientation in social relations, 110
Apes, great, psychoanalytic study of female aggression among
nature of aggression in, 297–303
in mother-child relationship, 301
oedipal constellation in, 301–303
power struggle among females, 298–299
sexual context, occurrence of aggression in, 300–301
orality in female, 303
polygamy to monogamy, 303–304
research approach and methodology, 297
study, objects of, 295–297
summary, 304–305
Archetype of Great Mother, splitting, contemporary culture and psychoanalysis of patriarchy, 268–271
acceptance of, 269
effect on men, 270–271
effect on women, 270
splitting and repressing, 268–269
Assassins, hiring of by Bellonese women, 179–180
Assertive-independent life orientations, 110
Atherosclerosis, 123
Attack on lactating intruders by female mice, biological correlates of
biological functions of aggression, 389
central neurotransmitter, role of, 387–388
comments, 389
genotype, role of, 382–385
hormones, role of, 385–387
effects of hormonal manipulation of female, 385
effects of hormonal manipulation of male, 386–387
stimulus condition for aggression, 382
Attitudes, prior, influence of on toys and play, 67–68
Authorities, appeal to, as Zapotec female aggression, 193

Baby, mother's expressions of hate for as worries about, 278
*Battling Amazons*, film, 254, 255, 256, 257, 258
Behavior of mother with child, expressions of hate in, 278–279
*Behavior Rating Scale*, 80
Beliefs about aggression for boys and girls, *see* Normative beliefs
Bellona, island of, 173–174
history, 173, 174–175
social position of women, 175–178
Bellonese women, aggression of
action potentials of women, 178–184
displacement of aggression, 180
hair pulling, 180
hiring assassins, 179–180
homicide, 179
nonverbal expression of aggression, 183–184
songs, mocking, 183
suicide, 180–181
verbal aggression, 181–183
Bellona, island of, 173–174
conclusions, 184
history of Bellona, 173, 174–175
social position of women, 175–178
Bible, as used by Isak Dinesen, 288–289
Biology and aggression, myth of
animals, male versus female aggression, 21–23
conclusions, 24–25
institutional versus individual behavior, 19–20
politically usefulness of myth, 18–19
myth, 18
refuting myth, 19
relation of human to animal aggression, 23–24
Seville Statement on Violence, 17–18
Bitter life, 136–138
Blood, as sign of female, 266–267
*Body Politics: Power, Sex and Nonverbal Communication*, 20
Boxers, female, literature on, 251, 252
Boy's preferences for war toys, 70

Boys and girls in Finland, quantitative differences in aggressiveness, 100–102
Boys, evidence supporting harmless effects in and risk effects in girls, 125–127
Boys and girls, beliefs about aggression of, *see* Normative beliefs
Breast-feeding, expressions of hate in, 277–278
Buss-Durkee (BD) hostility inventory, 253
*Buxom Boxers*, film, 254, 255, 256, 257

Canine females, aggression in
  aggression in, 309–312
    female–female relationships, 310
    male–female relationships, 310–311
    male–male relationships, 310
    mothers and offspring, relationship between, 311–312
    overall plan, 309
    social relationships, importance, 309–310
  applications to human affairs, 314–315
  dog breeds, studies, 307–309
  expression of agonistic behavior in relationships between puppies and humans, 312–314
    establishment of dominance without punishment or conflict, 312–313
    expression of playful aggressiveness in response to handling, 313–314
    use of punishment in rearing puppies, 312
Central neurotransmitter, role of in attack, 387–388
CHD, *see* Coronary-prone aggression
Child savior and vampire motifs in tales of Isak Dinesen
  child savior, images of, 289–292
  Isak Dinesen, 283–284
  Pallegrina Leoni, embodiment of archetype, 286–289
  vampire in history, mythology and literature, 284–286
Child's process of separation-individuation hindered, 281
Childbirth pain, expressions of hate in, 277
Children, Zapotec
  aggression of, 195–196
  physical punishment of, 193
Children's play, perception of aggression in, 65–68
  observer characteristics that influence perceptions of toys and play, 66–68
    age, 66–67
    prior attitudes, 67–68
    sex, 67
    video games, 68
  toy preference, 69
Chimpanzee, aggression in female, 296–297, *see also* Apes, great
China
  revolutionary, intergroup aggression in, 168–170
  traditional, one-on-one aggression in, 167–168
  Zambia, compared, 170
Chivalry, norm of, 11
Choynowski's Comprehensive Inventory of Aggression, 111
Christ image, as used by Isak Dinesen, 289–292
CMA, *see* Cortico-medial amygdala
Cognitive modeling, 15
Cognitive models, of alcohol and female disinhibition, 246–247
Cognitive script theory, 15
Community, Zapotec, female defense of, 188
Competitive fighting among rats, 22
Conflict, sex differences in, 221–222
Consequences of sex differentiated play, 69–71
  boy's preferences for war toys, 70
    toy gun play, 70
  methodological note, 70–71
  rough and tumble play, 69–70
Coronary heart disease (CHD), 123–124, *see also* Coronary-prone aggression, gender differences
Coronary-prone aggression, gender differences
  collection of present data, 124–125
  conclusions, 127
  coronary heart disease (CHD), 123–124
  evidence supporting harmless effects in boys and risk effects in girls, 125–127
    aggression as antecedent of type A behavior, 127
    aggression as concomitant of type A behavior, 126–127
    aggression as subcomponent of type A behavior, 123–126
Cortico-medial amygdala (CMA), 339–340, 341, 342–343
  localization, functional significance, 340–341

Covered aggression during adulthood, kinds of, 60–62
Crosscultural perspective of interfemale aggression, *see* Interfemale aggression and Resource scarcity in crosscultural perspective

de Beauvoir, Simone, 5
Defense, in animals, 22–23
Defense vs. attack, 4
Defensive hindering versus emotional processing, 281–282
Denial of mother's hate, effects of on child, 280–282
  afraid of, 280
  child's process of separation-individuation hindered, 281
  insecurity, 280
  much indirect anger, 280–281
Developmental theory of aggressive strategies, 58–60
Developmental and sex-related differences in aggressive behavior, 394–401
Dinesen, Isak, 283–284, *see also* Vampire and child savior motifs in tales of
Direct versus indirect aggressive strategies, 11–12, 51–63, 108, 113–114, 196–197, 225, 304–305
Disinhibition of female, and alcohol
  aggression, 245–246
  alcohol, effects of, 241
  anxiety, 241–243
  general perspective, 246–247
    cognitive models, 246–247
    physiological models, 246
  sexuality, 243–245
Displaced aggression, 4, 52
Displacement of aggression, by Bellonese women, 180
Dogs, *see* Canine females
Domestic violence, definition, 5
Dominance, 232, 233
  as intervening variable in sex-typed behavior, 233–234
  without punishment or conflict, establishment of, 312–313

*Echoes*, 284, 289
Elderly women, *see* Aged women
Emotional processing, 274–275
  versus defensive hindering, 281–282
Ethnocentrism, danger of in study of female aggression, 6
Ethnographic background of Margariteño women, 150–151
European rabbit, female aggression in, 33

Faith in people scores, 259
Family and society as sources of aggression, 136–139
  bitter life, 136–138
  life as hurdle race, 139–140
  life as trapping pit, 138–139
Fear/defense test battery (F/DTB), sex differences in, 321–322
Female aggression and matrifocality of Margariteño women, 155–160
Female aggression, contextual factors in study of, 401
Female aggression of Margariteño women, forms and contexts of, 151–155
  fighting, 152–153
  social control, 153–155
Female aggressive behavior, discontinuity in, 116–118
Female great apes, power struggle among, 298–299
Female sex role behavior and aggression in Margariteño women, 155
Female–female encounters of aggression, 12–13
Female–male encounters of aggression, 8, 11–12
Femininity and motherhood, 264
Femme fatale, and image of the Terrible Mother, 267
Fighters, female, responses to
  literature, 251–253
  method, 253–255
  results and discussion, 255–259
Fighting, and Margariteño women, 152–153
Figure/ground reversal in analysis of aggression, 345–346
Finnish girls, changes in patterns of aggressiveness of
  changes in early 1990s, 102–104
  discussion, 104–105
  quantitative differences between girls and boys, 100–102
  research, 99–100

Games and activities, and gender differences in violence, 93–94
Gender-dependent differences in effects of alcohol on social anxiety, 242, *see also* Alcohol and female disinhibition
Gender differences in aggression, 113–115, *see also* Girls, aggressively-inclined
  patterns of adjustment, 116–118
  stability of aggression, gender differences in, 113–115
Gender differences in animal models, implications for biological bases of defense, 323–324
  implications of for animal models of defensive behavior, 324–325
Gender differences in violence, *see also* Sex differences
  conclusions, 96
  evidence on, 89–90
  findings, 91–96
    games and activities, 93–94
    parental behaviors, 91–93
    stability of aggression, 95–96
    television watching, 94–95
  studies, two, 90–92
    measures, 91
Gender, differences of
  conclusions, 236–237
  dominance as intervening variable in sex-typed behavior, 233–234
  invisible sex, 230
  nonverbal residual, 234–235
  passive sex, 230–231
  social context, inherent logic of relationship, 235–236
  studies on social interaction, 231–233
    study 1, 231–232
    study 2, 232
    study 3, 232–233
Gender, social formations and resource control, 164
Genetic and sex-related differences in contexts for aggressive behavior, 396–397
Genotype, role of in attack by female mice, 382–385
Gerbil, Mongolian, female aggression in, 33
Girl's aggressiveness in Finland in early 1990s, changes in, 102–104
Girls and boys in Finland, quantitative differences in aggression of, 100–102, *see also* Finnish girls
Girls and boys, beliefs about aggression of, *see* Normative beliefs
Girls, aggressively inclined, path to adulthood for
  conclusions, 119–120
  discontinuity in female aggressive behavior, 119
  gender differences in aggression, 113–115
  patterns of adjustment, gender differences in, 116–118
  stability of aggression, gender differences, 115–116
Girls, evidence supporting risk effects in and harmless effects in boys, 125–127
Golden hamster, female, aggression and aggressiveness in
  aggressive arousal in hamsters and rats, 335–336
  aggressive arousal, phenomena explicable in terms of, 332–334
  aggressive arousals, theoretical model of, 336–338
  analysis of aggression, figure-ground reversal, 345–346
  anger, aggressive arousal and violent behavior, 343–344
  circumperambulations, digressions and dead ends, 334–335
  CMA localization, functional significance, 340–341
  confluence of pilgrims, 346
  first steps, 330–332
  itinerary, annotating, 341–342
  medial amygdala, temporal lobe epilepsy and anger, 344–345
  neural flywheel, search of, 334
  neural mechanisms of aggression using priming effect, general approach, 338–339
  neuroanatomical localization and mechanism of aggressive arousal, evidence for, 339–340
  road ahead, 342–343
Golden hamster, female aggression in, 32–33
Good Mother, 265–266
  mother goddess and her divine child, 265–266
  mother goddess and her son/lover, 266
Good child/bad husband, split of, expressions of hate in, 279

Gorilla, mountain, aggression in female, 296, 297, *see also* Apes, great
Gossip (indirect aggression), 55–56, 59
Gossip and witchcraft, as indirect female Zapotec aggression, 194–195
Gossip, during adolescence, 56, 59
Great Mother, the, 265–267
conclusions, 271
Good Mother, 265–266
Terrible Mother, 266–267
motherhood and femininity, 264
primordial unity, 264–265
psychoanalytical investigations, 263
slaying of the mother, 267–268
splitting of archetype, contemporary culture and psychoanalysis of patriarchy, 268–271
acceptance of splitting, 269
effect on men, 270–271
effect on women, 270
splitting and repressing, 268–269
Group interaction, small, sex differences in, 233
Gun, toy, boy's preferences for, 70

Hair pulling, by Bellonese women, 180
Hamster, golden, female aggression in, 32–33, *see also* Golden hamsters
Handling, playful aggressiveness in response to, expression, 313–314
Harem system among gorillas, 302
Hate of mother's, vicissitudes of
defensive hindering versus emotional processing, 281–282
effects of mother's denial of hate on child, 280–282
afraid of, 280
child's process of separation-individuation hindered, 281
insecurity, 280
much indirect anger, 280–281
expressions of, 276–279
hate
as worries about baby, 278
in breast-feeding, 277–278
in childbirth pain, 277
in mother's behavior with child, 278–279
in split of good child/bad husband, 279
longitudinal study of mothers, 276–277
wish to not have child, 278
obstacles to processing, 275–276
denial of anger, 276
ideal mother image, 275–276
processing ambivalence, 273–275
ambivalence about motherhood, 273–274
emotional processing, 274–275
*Heimskringla*, 202, 203
Holinshed's Chronicles, and Macbeth, 202, 203
Homicide, by Bellonese women, 179
Hormonal manipulation
of female, effect of, 385
of male, effect of, 386–387
Hormones and human aggression
conclusion, 45–46
discussion, 43–45
influences of testosterone, organizing, 38–40
male aggression, 37–38
puberty, 40–41
testosterone and adult aggression, 41–43
aggressive behavior, 41–42
changing status, 42–43
questionnaire measures, 41
Hormones, role of in attack by female mice, 385–387
Hostility towards men scale, 255, 259
Housing, of female mice, 352
Human-to-animal aggression, complex relation of, 23–24
Hurdle race, life as, 139–140

Impunitive-normative life orientations, 109–110
Indirect aggression, 108, 113–114, 196–197, 225
Indirect aggression, definition, 8
Indirect aggression, among great apes, 304–305
Indirect aggression, gossip and witchcraft, 194–195
Indirect versus direct aggression, research tool for, 54–55
Indirect versus direct aggressive strategies, 11–12, 51–63
conceptions and misconceptions, 51–53
conclusions, 62–63
covered aggression during adolescence, kinds of, 60–62
lack of investigation, 53–54
research tool for indirect versus direct aggression, 54–55

sex differences in aggressive styles during adolescence, 55–58
strategies, aggressive, developmental theory of, 58–60
Inhibition-frustration-aggression link, 211
Insecurity in child, as effect of denial of mother's hate, 280
Institutional aggression, definition, 4
Institutional versus individual behavior, 19–20
Instrumental aggression, 4
Instrumental orientation, definition, 218, 219
Interfemale aggression, 8, 12–13
Interfemale aggression and resource scarcity in crosscultural perspective
aggression and gender, 164
conclusion, 170
intergroup aggression between social classes in premodern and modern Zambia, 166
intergroup aggression in revolutionary China, 168–170
one-on-one aggression in premodern and modern Zambia, 165–166
one-on-one aggression in traditional China, 167–168
social formations, resource control, and gender, 164
stereotypes, 163–164
study, aim of, 165
Zambia and China compared, 170
Intergroup aggression
between social classes in premodern and modern Zambia, 166
in revolutionary China, 168–170
Intermale fighting in animals, 21–22
International Society for Research on Aggression (ISRA), xxiii, 17, 346
Interpersonal homicides, 189–190
Investigation of indirect aggression, lack of, 53–54
Invisible sex, woman as, 230
ISRA, *see* International Society for Research on Aggression

James I, King, 205

Kicking, during adolescence, 56, 57

Lady Macbeth, problem of, 201–205
as Viking woman, 204–204

*Macbeth*, play, and problem of Lady Macbeth, 201–205
*Machismo*, definition, 212
Male aggression versus female aggression, 8–13
female–female encounters, 12–13
female–male encounters, 11–12
physical aggression, 9–11
and testosterone, 37–38
Male odors, preference of female mice for, 375–376
methods, 375
results, 375
Male perspective on female aggression, 5–6
Male power, 20
Margariteño society, matrifocality and female aggression in
conclusions, 160–161
ethnographic background, 150–151
female sex role behavior and aggression, 155
forms and contexts of female aggression, 151–155
fighting, 152–153
social control, 153–155
Margariteño women, 149
matrifocality and female aggression, 155–160
*Maria Regina*, Queen of Heaven, 269
*Mater Dolorosa*, 268
Maternal aggression, 369–371
definition, 5
methods, 370
results, 370–371
Matrifocality and female aggression, 155–160
Maze learning, for female mice, 355
Medea, as Terrible Mother, 267
Medial amygdala, temporal lobe epilepsy and anger, 344–345
Methodological and cultural change on female aggression, recent studies, 7–8
methodology, problem of, 6–7
sex differences with respect to aggression, 7–8
Mexico, *see* Zapotec of Oaxaca
Mice, female, aggressive behavior as correlated characteristic in selection for aggressiveness in male mice

androgens, effect of, and learning on aggression in females, 373–375
methods, 373–374
results, 374–375
conclusions, 376–377
maternal aggression, 369–371
methods, 370
results, 370–371
predatory aggression, 371–373
methods, 371–372
results, 372–373
preference of female mice for male odors, 375–376
methods, 375
results, 375
research, 367–368
selection for aggression on mice, 368–369
Mice, aggressive female, and learning-sensitive open-field parameters
characteristics of, 354
discussion, 360–365
experiment I, 355–357
results, 357
experiment II, 357–360
results, 357–360
general methods, 352–355
apparatus, 352–355
housing, 352
procedure, 355
subjects, 352
research, 351–352
Mice, female aggression in
conclusion, 401
contextual factors in study of female aggression, 401
developmental and sex-related differences in aggressive behavior, 394–401
genetic and sex-related differences in contexts for aggressive behavior, 396–397
studies, 395–396
Mice, female, biological correlates of attack on lactating intruders, *see* Attack on lactating intruders by female mice
Mongolian gerbil, female aggression in, 33
Monogamy to polygamy in great apes, 303–304
Mood Adjective Check List (MACL), 253
response to type of film and beverage choices, 258
results and discussion, 255
Mother image, ideal, 275–276
Mother, slaying of the, 267–268
Mother-child relationship, aggression in great apes, 301
Motherhood
ambivalence of, *see* Great Mother
and femininity, 264
Mothers, longitudinal study of, 276–277
Motivational state, definition, 4
Mouse, female aggression in, 28–31
associated with nonreceptivity, 29
associated with postpartum period, 30
aggression associated with pregnancy, 29
aggression directed to lactating females, 31
other forms of attack, 31
prenatal hormones and interfemale aggression, 28–29
spontaneous interfemale aggression, 29

Neural flywheel, in search of, 334
Neural mechanisms of aggression using priming effect, general approach, 338–339
Neuroanatomical localization and mechanism of aggressive arousal, evidence for, 339–340
Neurotransmitter, central, role of in attack, 387–388
Nonverbal expression of aggression, by Bellonese women, 183–184
Nonverbal level of behavior, 234–235
Nordic sagas, and *Macbeth*, 202
Normative beliefs about aggression for boys and girls, differing
discussion, 84–85
methods, 79–80
measures, 79–80
procedure, 90
subjects, 79
results, 80–84
studies, 77–79
summary, 86
Norns, Nordic, *Macbeth* witches as, 202–203

Oaxaca, Mexico, Zapotec female aggression, *see* Zapotec of Oaxaca
Oedipal constellation in, 301–303

One-on-one aggression
in premodern and modern Zambia, 165–166
in traditional China, 167–168
Open-field activity, measuring, for female mice, 353
Open-field ambulation testing, for female mice, 355
Operationalizations of aggression, 6, 7
Orality in female great apes, 303
*Orestia*, and image of Terrible Mother, 267
Origins of sex differences in play, 71–73
biological bases, 71
sociological factors, 72–73
sex roles in advertising and packaging, 72–73
*Orkenyinga Saga*, 202, 203

Packaging, sex roles in, 72–73
Parental behaviors, and gender differences in violence, 91–93
punishment, 91–93
socialization, 93
Pallegrina Leoni, embodiment of archetype, 286–289
*Parar el macho,* concept of, 153–155
Passive sex, woman as, 230–231
Peer nomination technique, 54
*Peer-nominated Index of Aggression*, 80
Physical aggression, of Zapotec women, 190–193
Physical aggression, 4, 9–11, 53–60
*Physical Aggression,* 10–item scale of, 80
Physiological models of alcohol and female disinhibition, 246
Playful aggressiveness in response to handling, expression, 313–314
Political usefulness of myth of male aggression, 18–19
myth, 18
refuting myth, 19
Political violence, of Zapotec women, 188–189
Polygamy to monogamy in great apes, 303–304
Power Allocation Game (PAG), 220, 221
Predation, in animals, 22
Predatory aggression, 371–373
methods, 371–372
results, 372–373
Primordial unity, 264–265
Prisoner's Dilemma Game (PDG), 220, 221
Processing
emotional, 274–275
obstacles, 275–276
Psychoanalytical investigations, 263
Puberty, aggressiveness of human males at, 40–41
Punishment in rearing puppies, use of, 312
Puppies and humans, expression of agonistic behavior in relationships between, 312–314

Quantitative differences in aggression between girls and boys in Finland, 100–102
Queen Elizabeth I, 205
Questionnaire for the Description of Social Relations of Adolescents, 109

Raft laboratory, on Acali, 211
Rape Myth Acceptance (RMA), 252
Rat
female aggressiveness in types of, 22
male, aggressive behavior in, 21
Rat, female aggression in, 31–32
aggression associated with postpartum period, 32
aggression associated with pregnancy, 32
prenatal hormones and interfemale aggression, 31
spontaneous female aggression, 31
Rational aggression, 61,62
Rearing, by female mice, 355, 363, 364
Redirection of attack, 333
Relational orientation, definition, 218, 219
Repressed aggression, 4, 52
Resource control, social formations and gender, 164
Revolution, Zapotec female aggression during, 189
Rodent, aggressive female
conclusions, 33
species, 28–33
European rabbit, 33
golden hamster, 32–33
Mongolian gerbil, 33
mouse, 28–31
rat, 31–32

studies, 27–28
Rough and tumble play, 7, 9, 69–70

Saint Matthew, gospel of, 288–289
Self-image of girls
and difference aggression measures, correlations between, 104
differences between high or low in terms of self-image, 105
Seville Statement on Violence, 17–18, 19
Sex and friction, conflict and violence, on Acali, 212
Sex and violence on Acali
discussions on, 213–214
and dissatisfaction and aggression, 209–210
evidence, 213
hypothesis, 213
Sex differences, *see also* Gender differences
Sex differences in aggressive play and toy preference
children's play, perception of aggression in, 65–68
consequences of sex differentiated play, 69–71
boy's preferences for war toys, 70
methodological note, 70–71
rough and tumble play, 69–70
origins of sex differences in play, 71–73
biological bases, 71
sociological factors, 72–73
summary, 74
toy preference, 68–69
Sex differences in aggressive styles during adolescence, 55–58
Sex differences in antipredator defensive behaviors, 318–323
Sex differences in conflict and aggression in individual and group settings, 221–225
aggression, 222–225
conclusion, 225–226
conflict, 221–222
experimental procedure, 220–221
study, 217–220
Sex, influence of on toys and play, 67
Sex roles in advertising and packaging, 72–73
Sex-related and developmental differences in aggressive behavior, 394–401
Sex-related and genetic differences in contexts for aggressive behavior, 396–397
Sexual context, occurrence of aggression of female great apes in, 300–301
sexuality, in great apes, 297–298
Sexuality, alcohol effects on, 243–245
Shakespeare, William, and play of *Macbeth*, 201–205
Sibling rivalry, definition, 5
Silenced life, as life without aggression, 142–143
Social context, inherent logic of relationship, 235–236
Social control, and Margariteño women, 153–155
Social formations, resource control, and gender, 164
Social manipulation, 61, 62
Social position of women, 175–178
Social interaction of women and men, studies on, 231–233
study 1, 231–232
study 2, 232
study 3, 232–233
Society and family as sources of aggression, 136–139
bitter life, 136–138
life as hurdle race, 139–140
life as trapping pit, 138–139
Songs, mocking, by Bellonese women, 183
Spartan women, 251
*Stabat Mater*, 264
Stability of aggression, 95–96
gender differences, 115–116
Strategies, aggressive, developmental theory of, 58–60
Suicide, of Bellonese women, 180–181
Sweet life, as life without aggression, 140–141

"Teacher-learner" paradigm, 7, 220
Television watching, and gender differences in violence, 94–95
Terrible Mother, 266–267
Testosterone
and adult aggression, 41–43
aggressive behavior, 41–42
changing status, 42–43
organizing influences of, 38–40
questionnaire measures, 41
*The Dreaming Child*, 284, 290–291

*The Cardinals First Tale*, 283,
Thigmotactic behavior of female mice, measuring, 353
  differences in, 360–362
  ratio, 355
Tiamat, as Terrible Mother, 267
Tit-for-tat (TFT) strategy, 221–222
Toy gun play, boy's preferences for, 70
Toy preference, sex differences in, 68–69
Trapping pit, life as, 138–139

Ultrasonic vocalizations, antipredator, sex differences in, 322–323

Vampire and child savior motifs in tales of Isak Dinesen
  child savior, images of, 289–292
  Isak Dinesen, 283–284
  Pallegrina Leoni, embodiment of archetype, 286–289
  vampire in history, mythology and literature, 284–286
Vampire in history, mythology and literature, 284–286
Verbal abuse, during adolescence, 56, 58
Verbal aggression, 4, 10
  during adolescence, 51–62
  of Bellonese women, 181–183
  of Zapotec women, 193–194
Video games, influence of, 68
Viking
  Lady Macbeth as, 204
  Macbeth as, 201–202
Violence and sex on Acali, 309–313
Violence, gender differences in
  conclusions, 96
  evidence on, 89–90
  findings, 91–96
    games and activities, 93–94
    parental behaviors, 91–93
    stability of aggression, 95–96
    television watching, 94–95
  studies, two, 90–92
    measures, 91
Violence of Zapotec women, political, 188–189
Violent behavior, anger and aggressive arousal, 343–344
Virgin Mary, 269

War toys, boy's preferences for, 70
*White Winter Heat*, film, 254, 256, 257
Wish to not have child, 278
Witchcraft
  and gossip, as indirect female Zapotec aggression, 194–195
  in the Middle Ages, 285
Working life, arduous, as life without aggression, 141–142

Zambia, premodern and modern
  China, compared, 170
  intergroup aggression between social classes in, 166
  one-on-one aggression in, 165–166
Zapotec culture, 187–188
Zapotec of Oaxaca, Mexico, female aggression among
  authorities, appeal to, 193
  children, physical punishment of, 193
  children's aggression, 195–196
  culture, 187–188
  defense of community, 188
  discussion, 196–197
  indirect aggression, gossip and witchcraft, 194–195
  interpersonal homicides, 189–190
  physical aggression, 190–193
  political violence, 188–189
  revolution, aggression during, 189
  verbal aggression, 193–194

ISBN 0-12-102590-X